JOURNAL FOR THE STUDY OF THE NEW TESTAMENT
SUPPLEMENT SERIES

20

Volume II

Executive Editor, Supplement Series
David Hill

Publishing Editor
David E Orton

JSOT Press
Sheffield

Luke
A New Paradigm

Volume II

Part II (cont.). Commentary: Luke 9.51–24.53

Michael D. Goulder

Journal for the Study of the New Testament
Supplement Series 20

Copyright © 1989 Sheffield Academic Press

Published by JSOT Press
JSOT Press is an imprint of
Sheffield Academic Press Ltd
The University of Sheffield
343 Fulwood Road
Sheffield S10 3BP
England

Printed in Great Britain
by Billing & Sons Ltd
Worcester

British Library Cataloguing in Publication Data

Goulder, M.D. (Michael Douglas)
    Luke.
    1. Bible. N.T. Luke - Critical studies
    I. Title   II. Series
    226'.406

    ISSN 0143-5108
    ISBN 1-85075-101-3

CONTENTS

Volume I

Volume II

SECTION 5—THE FIRST HALF OF THE JOURNEY
(9.51-13.21: Mt. 9.36-25.13; Mk 10.1)

The First Half of the Journey

The Galilean Ministry, as it is described in Mark, is now (virtually) complete; but this leaves Luke with the problem of the considerable remainder of Galilean material in Matthew. For Luke has undertaken to write everything in order: but his method of taking first one of his sources and then the other, in blocks, seems bound now to involve him in a contradiction. Hitherto he has resolved this by an ingenious use of 'equivalences', exploiting the occasional summaries as short statements in one Gospel of what was described in full in the other. Nor is he without such a summary now, for Mark writes, 'And rising from there he comes to the borders of Judaea beyond the Jordan, and again crowds accompany him, and again, as he was used, he taught them' (10.1). 'There' had been Capernaum (Mk 9.33), so Luke has authority for a journey from Galilee, teaching as Jesus goes. The problem arises from the fact that much of the Matthaean Galilee matter has been covered already in the Marcan section just finished (Lk. 8.1-9.50). But all the numerous Matthaean expansions of Mark are still ahead: so what has become of Luke's promise of order?

Luke has kept his word, if we will allow him a distinction with which we are also familiar. In writing a biography it is a different matter to keep the *events* in sequence from keeping the *sayings* in sequence; no responsible author will think that he can juggle the facts to his convenience—at least no author as firmly Greek as Luke was—but who can be sure of the dating of this remark or that? Sixty years of form-critical assertion have induced a widespread scepticism on even the former point, but we should not yield to it. Luke says he is writing in order, and furthermore his practice shows that on a credible interpretation he has virtually done so. But his use of the block method could be combined with the attempt to write in order only because one of his two sources was extremely short of narrative.

For notoriously Matthew contains hardly any non-Marcan narrative after the Centurion's son. So Luke has carefully dovetailed his two sources down to this point, and thereafter has breathed more freely. He has already taken liberties with Matthew 11, the Lord's sayings to and about the Baptist. He now has a great many more units of Matthaean teaching to include; and for the first half of the Journey he simply goes back to the point he has reached, Mt. 9.35, and takes them in order.

The violence done to the principle of order is thus minimal. As the Matthaean expansions are almost all *verbal* expansions, it may be felt to be unimportant whether the words were said in this part of the Galilean mission or that. The only incident of note which Matthew may seem to have added is the possessed man who was blind and dumb (12.22-45); and here Luke has felt justified in making an exception to his usual rule of giving Mark preference in all narrative matter. We can see that Matthew is basically expanding the Beelzebul controversy of Mk 3.22-30, perhaps with the aid of traits from the dumb possessed boy of Mk 9.14-29; and at least the link with Mk 3 must have seemed obvious to Luke. But there is no miracle in Mark: the scribes simply come down from Jerusalem and declare that Jesus is casting out demons through Beelzebul. There seems therefore to be a double reason for giving Matthew the preference this time. It is Mark here who is not describing an event but merely a conversation, while Matthew is able to give the occasion of the conversation; and furthermore Matthew has a much fuller and more satisfying account of it. So for once Luke has omitted a pericope in its Marcan sequence (Mk 3.22-30)—camouflaging the omission by making a break from Mark at Mk 3.19, and then resuming with Mk 4.1ff./3.31-35. He can then include the incident with most of its Matthaean comment in his sequence from Matthew at Lk. 11.14-26. So Luke can feel that he has kept to his καθεξῆς principle throughout, and been pretty intelligent about it too.

Luke's solution is thus far satisfactory, but it has its price, which strikes every reader: 'though Jesus is always travelling to Jerusalem, he never makes any real progress on this journey' (K.L. Schmidt, p. 269). The particular reason for that is given in the comments on 9.43b-50. Luke is taking the long Matthaean sequence of additions at a moment where Mark has intimated that Jesus has set off from the north for Jerusalem: so he is already leaving Galilee (Mark), but he cannot actually leave while there is Galilean matter to cover from Matthew. It is for this reason that Jesus is still on the border between (διὰ μέσον) Samaria and Galilee at 17.11, to the dismay of so many commentators. But there is no call for anxiety, or for desperate exegetical expedients: as we shall see, Luke is still treating a text from Matthew 17.

Three additional points may be noted here, one of which will require fuller exposition later on. First, I have spoken of Luke's need to include all the Galilean matter from Matthew before Jesus reaches Peraea and Judaea. But of course exactly the same problem will arise from the 'block policy' with the Judaean/Jerusalem additions in Matthew, as with the Galilean ones. If Luke means (as he does) to take Mark as his guide over the Judaean and Jerusalem narratives, then he will find himself in trouble if he is not careful: for with his present policy he will have Jesus risen from the dead at Mark 16, and a whole stack of important Matthaean additions from Mt. 19–25 still to come. This clearly will not do, and Luke has the prudence to see that it will not do: so he does not sign off the Journey when he has reached the end of the Galilean additions in Matthew, but carries on with the other major additions from Mt. 19–25. Thus we shall find much of the Matthew 23 material in Lk. 11.37–52, and numerous excerpts and echoes from Mt. 24–25 in Lk. 12–13. The justification for moving this matter from the Jerusalem context of Mt. 23–25 to the Galilee context of Lk. 11–13 is a combination of *de verbis non curat ordo*, as above, and *force majeure*. The context in which Matthew set the teaching is not so important—and Luke may be aware that some of these additions are actually Matthew's rather than Jesus'. But in any case Luke cannot have them in an appendix in Lk. 25–27. We may feel, Why did he not insert them where Matthew did as he goes through Mark? The commentator can only note that he does not do so; and suppose that the familiar block policy was his major guide.

A second point will occur to any reader of the Lucan Journey narrative. Most commentaries describe Lk. 9.51–18.14 as Q+L(S) material: but the mixture is not constant. In 9.51–13.21 the proportion of Q and L is far higher than it is in 13.22–18.14. In the earlier section there are 1076 words in common with Matthew out of 3302, one word in three; in the later section the figures are respectively 449 and 2861, one word in six. This disparity coincides with two other features. First, by 13.21 Luke has reached Matthew's Thief, Servant parable and Return from the Marriage (Mt. 24.42–25.13; Lk. 12.35-48); and there is no major use of any further matter from Matthew 25 to the end of the Journey. Secondly, Luke seems to sign-post the half-way mark in the Journey here. We hear much about journeying in 9.51–10.1, and 17.11 is a signal that we are still moving towards Jerusalem; but otherwise mention of Jerusalem is concentrated at 13.22, and more dramatically 13.33f. It looks therefore as if we have three reasons for supposing that Luke divided his Journey narrative in half: he has reached Matthew 25 by Lk. 13.21; thereafter there is much less Matthaean matter than there has been before; and there are actual geographical indicators. First there is the warning of 13.22, 'And he was travelling through towns and villages, teaching and making his journey to Jerusalem', just as 17.11 is a warning that the end is not far ahead. Then comes the theological significance of the whole expedition at 13.33, 'It cannot be that a prophet perish outside Jerusalem'; and the lament over the city, apparently so out of place, seventy miles away—'Jerusalem, Jerusalem. . . ' It seems plain that Luke, who has so far worked with units of not more than four chapters (1.5–4.30), and an average of two and a half, is content with two four-chapter units for his Journey (9.51–13.21; 13.22–18.14).

A third novel feature is also sensed by the reader as he passes 9.51. Hitherto the units into which the text divided have been discrete, varying from about twenty verses in the opening chapters to about seven verses in Lk. 8–9. With the Journey we breathe a freer air. The pericopes may still be limited in length, though now often at the upper end of the range (and once, in ch. 15, we have a single pericope of thirty-two verses). But, to a greater extent than hitherto, they seem to be linked together into *topics*. The topic of Mission, for example, seems to link the whole of 9.51–10.24. 9.51-62 presents the tough calling of a missionary; 10.1-16 gives instructions on mission; 10.17-24 gives thanks for the success of the Seventy-Two. There are three pericopae, divided by familiar Lucan signals, but the mission theme runs through. Similarly we have a series of Controversy scenes in 11.14-54: 11.14-26 the Beelzebul controversy, 11.27-36 the Sign controversy, 11.37-54 the washing controversy. I see this grouping of pericopae into *threes* as pervasive and significant, and this is to be seen in the numbering which I have used: I have signed the coming pericopae (36)(a), (b), (c) and so on. The justification for such grouping is offered in the discussion of each section below; the significance is to be seen in the building up of a Lucan catechesis (cf. pp. 170ff.). The Lucan church is now setting its face towards the Lord's Passion, Resurrection and Ascension in the spring: now is the time for all, and especially any new disciples (9.56-62), to lay to heart what it means to set out with him on the Way.

For sources, there is virtual unanimity among scholars that we have to do with Q and L/S; the discussion is mainly on the extent of Luke's redaction. There are more complex forms of the Q + L view. Streeter's Proto-Luke still appeals to Marshall and others; and George Ogg (*NTS*, 1971) proposed a view that Luke had two independent accounts of Jesus' Journey (9.51-10.42 and 17.11-19.44). The Q/L hypothesis suffers under the disadvantage that it can offer no real explanation of anything; for the hypothesis can simply be varied at will. I am offering to explain our text on the basis of a document we have, Matthew, and habits of exposition which we have been able to infer from watching Luke at work on an agreed text, Mark. I shall claim that Luke's own activity is wider than is often thought on the L hypothesis; there is no need to foreclose on Luke's possession of *any* non-Marcan, non-Matthaean traditions till we have examined the data.

The extent of the Journey narrative is variously understood, 19.27 being a favourite terminus (e.g. Schürmann), or 19.10 (Marshall). Such discussions arise however from a misunderstanding of the reason for the Journey section, which have been set out above. The end of the Journey is not clearly marked because it is not very significant. Most of the 9.51-18.14 section is thought of by Luke as in Galilee—at least till 17.19, probably 18.8. The tale then gears smoothly into Mark at 18.15 and carries on without an intermission. Our best guide to Luke's intentions are his changes of source.

The introduction of so large a block of non-Marcan material, much of it novel, has provoked much discussion of the intention of the author. It has been thought (Schneider) that the ideas of 'travelling' and 'the way', which are so stressed by Luke, indicate both an emphasis on Jesus' way to the cross (and heaven), and also on his disciples' call to share that way. It is hard not to think that something of this is intended. There is much emphasis, especially in the opening verses, on the challenge of discipleship, which is a recurrent theme (12.4-12; 14.25-35). For a liturgical interpretation of the Gospel, such a catechetical section would be very apt: hitherto the story has been concerned mainly with Jesus' actions—now comes his instruction to his new disciples on the way that will lead to his crucifixion and exaltation, and to their baptism at Eastertide. Bo Reicke (*SE* I, 1959), notes the alternation of address to the disciples and the crowds/Pharisees, and interprets this as instruction to the Apostles on church leadership and controversy; but much of the matter concerns the rank-and-file Christian, and the controversial and general material is taken over from the Matthaean source.

A general intention of this kind seems to accord better with the varied contents of the Journey chapters than particular theological themes which have been proposed. Conzelmann (pp. 60-65) makes it plain why he makes his own proposal: if the Journey is not really based on a journey tradition at all, then it is a Lucan construction, and must have some theological purpose. But this is a fallacy. Luke is writing an account of what happened in order, and I have given reasons for thinking that his policy with his sources forced the Journey upon him at this point. Conzelmann sees a Christological key in the 13.31-33 logion, lying as it does between the passion prophecies in 9 and 18. Colin McCown (*JBL*, 1938) saw a mirror of the Church's experience of mission and persecution; Eduard Lohse (*TZ*, 1954) similarly takes this as the beginning of the Gentile Mission, a second great step in the history of salvation. W. Grundmann (*ZNW*, 1959) lays the emphasis on Jesus as wanderer and guest; Michi Miyoshi, *Der Anfang des Reiseberichts*, on the continuity of rejection and mission with Nazareth and the Mission of the Twelve. I should not wish to criticize these and other attempts to isolate important themes over the chapters.

McCown, C.C., 'The Geography of Luke's Central Section', *JBL* 57 (1938), pp. 51-66.

Grundmann, W., 'Fragen der Komposition des lukanischen Reiseberichts', *ZNW* 50 (1959), pp. 252-70.

Lohse, E., 'Missionarisches Handeln Jesu nach dem Evangelium des Lukas', *TZ* 10 (1954), pp. 1-13.

Reicke, B., 'Instruction and Discussion in the Travel Narrative', *Studia Evangelica* I (Berlin, 1959), pp. 206-16.

Ogg, G., 'The Central Section of the Gospel according to St Luke', *NTS* 18 (1971), pp. 39-53.

Miyoshi, M., *Der Anfang des Reiseberichts, Lk. 9.51-10.24* (Rome, 1974).

Sellin, G., 'Komposition, Quellen und Funktion des lukanischen Reiseberichts (Lk. ix.51-xix.28)', *NT* 20 (1978), pp. 100-35.

36. *Mission*, 9.51-10.24

a. *The Rejection at Samaria*, 9.51-62

Luke had provided substitutes for the incidents of Matthew 9 in his seventh chapter; and we have taken the long Marcan sequence in Lk. 8.1-9.50 as the equivalent of Mt. 9.35, 'And Jesus went about all the cities and the villages, teaching in their synagogues and preaching the gospel of the kingdom, and healing every sickness and every disease' (cf. on 8.1-3). The next item in Matthew is the Mission

Discourse (Mt. 10.5-42), prefaced by 'The harvest is great. . . ' (9.36-38), and the naming of the Twelve (which Luke has had already). The opening words of the Mission Discourse in Matthew are, 'Go not on a road of Gentiles and enter not into a town of Samaritans (εἰς πόλιν Σαμαριτῶν μὴ εἰσέλθητε)'. The Twelve are warned that any town or village (ἢ κώμην) that they enter, whose inhabitants do not receive them or hear their words (μὴ δέξηται ὑμᾶς μηδὲ ἀκούσῃ τοὺς λόγους ὑμῶν) will face a worse fate than Sodom and Gomorrah (10.5, 11, 14f.).

Luke has put two and two together. Mark told him (10.1) that Jesus had gone to Judaea via Transjordan, and there must have been some reason for this, especially as (so far as we know) it was quite common for Galilaeans to go through Samaria to Jerusalem (Josephus, *Ant.* 20.118/*B.J.* 232; *Vita* 269). The reason is suggested by Mt. 10.5; there will have been a preliminary incident in which Jesus sent the disciples ahead into one of the Samaritan villages (as he *sent* Peter and John to *prepare* Passover for him, 22.8), and they will have been refused. This would then account for both the exclusion of Samaria at Mt. 10.5 and the turn eastwards. The latter (as I have just explained) is very convenient for Luke, but he has not made it up; it was in Mk 10.1. He shows us that this reasoning was in his mind by keeping close to the Matthaean phrasing, εἰσῆλθον εἰς κώμην Σαμαριτῶν (v. 52). We should have expected τῶν Σαμαριτῶν as at Acts 8.25 or τῆς Σαμαρείας (Acts 8.5). He tells us that the villagers did not receive the party (οὐκ ἐδέξαντο αὐτόν), and that James and John suggested calling down fire from heaven to destroy them. No doubt, as every commentator from Marcion on has noted, Elijah is in mind; but Elijah said, 'Fire shall descend from heaven and *devour* (καταφάγεται) you. . . ' The suggestion comes originally from Matthew's Sodom: cf. Lk. 17.29, 'In the day that Lot went out of Sodom, fire and brimstone rained from heaven and destroyed them all'. If Jesus gave a preliminary version of his coming instructions before the Samaritan excursion, then James' and John's remark would be quite understandable, if wrong-headed.

Mark has set Luke's mind on Elijah for some time (9.8, 19, 30, 33 name Elijah, quite apart from echoes from the marvellous feeding, etc.). Jesus' setting off on the journey that will take him across the Jordan, and ultimately to heaven, suggests the parallel now with the prophet's last journey, which took him across the Jordan and to his being taken up (ἀναλαμβανόμενον, ἀνελήμφθη, 4 Kgdms 2.10f.) to heaven. So just as Luke spoke of the Passion in 9.31 as Jesus' ἔξοδος, so now he describes it as his ἀνάλημψις; and the impressive opening, 'And it came to pass when the days of his ἀνάλημψις were fulfilled...' underscores the significance of the move being made, and its function as the start of a new phase of the ministry. The same verb συμπληροῦσθαι is used at Acts 2.1 for an equally significant new beginning, 'And when the day of Pentecost was fulfilled...' We have a slightly different sense here, 'the days of (sc. leading up to) his taking up'; as in 17.26 where 'the days of the Son of Man' are occupied in idle eating and drinking, etc., and are the days leading up to the Parousia.

The 4 Kgdms 2 background, which is thus in Luke's mind, draws in the story immediately preceding, in 4 Kgdms 1, so similar to the Sodom and Gomorrah incident; for there on two occasions (and nearly on a third), Elijah was about to be arrested, and called for fire to come down from heaven and consume a captain and his fifty. So here James and John say, 'Lord, shall we bespeak fire to come down from heaven and destroy them?'; many MSS, Western, Caesarean, Alexandrian and others, have appended the gloss, 'as also Elijah did', and the tradition goes back to Marcion. But why did Luke think that the rash proponents of such an idea should be James and John? The suggestion arises partly, no doubt, from the previous incident, where John proposed a similarly harsh and defensive notion with the exorcist (9.49); and partly from the surname which Jesus had given the sons of Zebedee, 'the Sons of Thunder' (Mk 3.17), which might seem to imply their predilection for lightning retribution. But Luke's untypical phrasing, 'the disciples James and John', probably suggests also the influence of Mt. 10.1f., 'And calling his twelve *disciples* he gave them authority... first Simon who is called Peter and Andrew his brother, and *James* the son of Zebedee *and John* his brother...' Bespeaking fire from heaven calls for more authority than turning away an odd exorcist: there are the two brothers in the text Luke is taking in hand, with the surnaming of Peter to recall their own surname, and the fact of the Lord's giving them authority.

For the rest Luke has drawn on his familiarity with the LXX, though he has not always given the LXX phrases their LXX meaning. στηρίζειν τὸ πρόσωπον has a hostile sense there, e.g. Ezek. 6.2, 13.17, to set one's face against; while here it signifies only determination—we may suspect the side-influence of Isa. 50.7, ἔθηκα τὸ πρόσωπόν μου ὡς στερεὰν πέτραν. Similarly τὸ πρόσωπον αὐτοῦ ἦν πορευόμενον in v. 53 seems like an echo of 2 Kgdms 17.11 τὸ πρόσωπόν σου πορευόμενον, where the meaning is 'your personal presence going among them'. It is a mistake to speak of Luke misunderstanding the LXX (Dalman, *Worte* 30f.) or to seek Hebrew originals (Marshall): Luke is trying to write a pastiche of septuagintal prose for the present portentous move, and he has succeeded very well.

9.57-60. The thought of Elijah's last journey with his disciple Elisha recalls an earlier saying which Luke has held over from Matthew 8. At 3 Kgdms 19.19 Elijah had called Elisha, who said, 'I will kiss my father and (then) I will follow after you'; and at Mt. 8.19-22 one of Jesus' aspiring disciples had said similarly, 'Lord, permit me first to go and bury my father'. Luke accordingly draws in the whole Matthaean scene, in slightly amended form. Matthew's first postulant had been a scribe, which Luke suppresses; but 'I will follow you wherever you go' is the same, and so is Jesus' reply, 'The foxes have holes, and the birds of heaven nests, but the Son of Man has not where to lay his head'. With the second man Luke transfers the initiative to Jesus, as seems more suitable, 'Follow me' being advanced from Mt. 8.22. The exchange about the man's father and the dead burying their dead is left virtually unaltered; but Luke has unwisely expanded the conclusion, 'But go you and announce the kingdom of God'. This is glossed from Mt. 10.7, 'As you go preach, saying, The kingdom of heaven has arrived'; but the reader is then left wondering how the man can at the same time follow Jesus and also go and preach. We have a characteristic minor Lucan muddle, as indeed we also did in vv. 52f., where Jesus sends his disciples ahead to prepare for him, and is then there himself (§9). With sympathy we may be able to imagine some reconciliation, but the evangelist makes us work.

9.61f. Elisha had been ploughing when he was called, and this suggests an expansion to Luke. Still another says, 'I will follow you, Lord'—'I will follow you' from Matthew's first man again, 'Lord' from his second (probably omitted in v. 59). He continues, 'but first permit me' (from Mt. 8.21 once more) 'to say farewell to those at my home'—extending the previous saying, and perhaps clarifying it. Elisha only wished to kiss his father farewell, but Elijah seems to give him a dusty answer; and none more keen than Luke to stress that the claims of Christ override those of family (14.26f.; 18.29f.). Jesus replies, 'No one who puts his hand to the plough and looks back is fit for the kingdom of God'. The plough is taken from Elisha, the looking back from Sodom, where Lot's wife looked back (ἐπέβλεψεν εἰς τὰ ὀπίσω, Gen. 19.26) and became a pillar of salt.

Despite the minor muddle, the section is highly artistic. The spare sayings from Matthew 8 slot noiselessly into the situation of Jesus' having nowhere in Samaria to lay his head, while simultaneously the Elijah theme, inherited from Mark, is elaborated with the sayings on farewell to father and family. Luke has made the most of this happy combination by introducing the Ascension theology, which is to form so important a part of Luke 24/Acts 1, the fire from heaven and the plough image—all three being powerful imaginative developments. Michi Miyoshi (p. 60) suggests that the increase of the exchanges in vv. 57-62 from two to three is itself an echo of the three conversations between Elijah and Elisha in 4 Kgdms 2. But Luke's brilliance in so interweaving his traditions should not distract us from the practical effect which is among his primary aims. In 1–9.50 Luke has set before his reader-listener the outline of Jesus' deeds. Now, in the space before the Passion, he means to set out what it means to be a disciple; and the first lesson of discipleship is that it is no bed of roses. The Christian has a hard calling. Following Jesus means having no bed for the night; it means the neglect of what are conventionally important family duties; it means putting the proclamation of the gospel before one's home affairs. The would-be disciple in the Lucan church, preparing now for his baptism at Easter, needs to lay to heart from the beginning the high calling to which he aspires, and its cost. His evangelist has not let him down.

Bultmann (pp. 25f.) tends to the view that as a Lucan construction, the Journey implies that vv. 51-56 was a Lucan construction too; though some tradition is possible. So Fitzmyer. But more normally an L tradition is disentangled from the heavy Lucan 'editing'. Thus Miyoshi (pp. 6-15) isolates as pre-Lucan traditions the rejection in Samaria, the sending of the disciples, and the rebuke to James and John. But he himself asks (p. 11) whether 9.52 could be a reminiscence of the command to avoid Samaria in Mt. 10.5. It seems that a serious consideration of this suggestion would move him towards identifying the pre-Lucan tradition with Q/Matthew. This origin will also account for the counter-Lucan tendency of the unit, since

Luke is elsewhere markedly pro-Samaritan (10.33ff.; 17.16; Acts 8): he had a tradition to accommodate here which was hostile to Samaritans, and it was in our form of the Q text he was next to handle, Mt. 10.5. The sending of the disciples can also be inferred from the same text, with the resultant confusion, since the dynamic of the story requires Jesus' own presence and comment. For Miyoshi's stylistic criteria fallacies, cf. pp. 15ff., and below. Schweizer points to the sequence of introductory καί's as evidence of a pre-Lucan source, but this is weak: they are part of Luke's septuagintal style.

For vv. 57-60 Luke is very close to Matthew: Schulz (pp. 434f.) and Polag are content to claim only ἐν τῇ ὁδῷ, εἶπεν and τις from the Lucan variants as Q, but both the latter are favourites of Luke himself. It is not usually observed that logia with pairs of animal images in them are a preserve of Matthew and Luke-Q alone: foxes and birds here, sheep and wolves (Mt. 7.15M), dogs and swine (7.6M), fish and snake (7.10Q), sheep/lambs and wolves (10.16Q), serpents and doves (10.16M), oxen and fatlings (22.4M), gnat and camel (23.24M), hen and chickens (23.37Q), sheep and goats (25.32M). With so many in a single tradition, they are likely to stem from Matthew's own imagination.

There is a variety of opinion over vv. 61f. F. Hahn (*Hoheitstitel*, p. 83) and Martin Hengel (*Nachfolge*, pp. 3f.) ascribe the verses to Q, despite the difficulty of explaining why Matthew should have omitted them. Manson (p. 72) takes them to come from L; but this causes the difficulty of an independent source having a third saying that fits so closely to the Elijah theme of the second. But the closeness to Luke's other phrasing is so marked that many opt for Lucan redaction: Dibelius, *Formgeschichte*, p. 159 n. 1; Schweizer; Schulz, p. 435; Lührmann, p. 58, and in detail Miyoshi, pp. 41-43.

9.51   ἐγένετο-δὲ-ἐν-τῷ...καὶ αὐτός*, ἡμέρα, στηρίζειν, τοῦ + inf.*, πορεύεσθαι, Ἰερουσαλημ*. Hapax: ἀνάλημψις (cf. Acts 1.2, 11, 22).

9.52   ἄγγελος (human), πρὸ-προσώπου*, πορεύεσθαι, (Σαμαριτής), ἑτοιμάζειν. If the harder ὡς is read with p⁴⁵p⁷⁵ א*B, N-A²⁶, there is a parallel at Acts 20.24.

9.53   δέχεσθαι, ἤν + part., πορεύεσθαι, Ἰερουσαλημ*.

9.54   ἰδόντες-δέ, εἶπαν, εἰπεῖν. Hapax: ἀναλίσκειν. θέλειν + subj. 18.41Mk; 22.9Mk. ἀναλῶσαι + πῦρ Ezek. ×3.

9.55   στραφείς*. The additional words, 'You know not of what spirit you are. . . ' are read by the Diglot, and are as old as Marcion, and perhaps John's Gospel (Jn 12.47 is one of a number of texts in John 12 close to Lk. 9–10; cf. my article in *NTS* [1983]). The style is quite Lucan: οὐκ οἶδα. . .ἐστέ, cf. 13.25, 27; ποῖος 7/5/8+3, πνεῦμα an evil spirit 7.21R; 8.2R, εἶναι + gen. = belong to a supernatural power, Acts 27.23; ψυχαί 21.9R, ×8 Acts; 19.10 is close but not identical, so Lucan authorship could be more likely than scribal assimilation. Scribes could have omitted to save James and John. Cf. J.M. Ross (*ET* [1972]), Marshall, Metzger (pp. 148f.).

9.56 πορεύεσθαι, ἕτερος*.

9.57 πορεύεσθαι, (εἶπεν)-πρός*, τις.

9.58 εἶπεν, (οὐκ-ἔχω + noun. clause), (ποῦ), (κλίνειν). Hapaxes: (φώλεος), (κατασκήνωσις).

9.59 (εἶπεν)-δὲ-πρός*, (ἕτερος*), εἶπεν, (ἐπιτρέπειν). ἀπελθόντι is an improvement on Matthew's ἀπελθεῖν καί (8.21).

9.60 εἶπεν-δέ*, (ἑαυτοῦ). Hapax: διαγγέλλειν (Acts 21.26). Of the additional words at the end of the verse, σὺ δὲ ἀπελθών take up ἀπελθόντι, v. 59. 'Proclaiming the kingdom of God' (with a variety of verbs) is Lucan (4.43R; 8.1R; 16.16QD; Acts 20.25; 28.23, 31); διαγγέλλειν here is suggested by ἀγγέλους in v. 52.

9.61 εἶπεν-δὲ*, καὶ = also, ἕτερος*, ἐπιτρέπειν, εἰς-τὸν-οἶκον + gen. ἀποτάσσεσθαι and εὔθετός recur together in 14.33ff., and are part of Luke's message of detachment from family (18.29). Cf. David Seccombe, pp. 97-134.

9.62 εἶπεν-δὲ-πρός*, gnomic οὐδείς, ἐπιβάλλειν-τὴν-χεῖρα. Hapax: ἄροτρον (3 Kgdms 19.19—cf. also ἀκολουθήσω σοι). βλέπων εἰς τὰ ὀπίσω is noticeably closer to Gen. 19.17, 26 than to Mk 13.15f., whence Miyoshi derives it (pp. 52f.). It thus joins the fire from heaven in v. 54 as a double Lucan development of the Sodom theme in Mt. 10.15; and is referred to again at Lk. 17.32. εὔθετός: cf. on v. 61.

Hengel, M., *The Charismatic Leader and His Followers* (ET, *Nachfolge und Charisma*, BZNW 34, Berlin, 1968).
Jervell, J., 'The Lost Sheep of the House of Israel', in *Luke and the People of God* (Minneapolis, 1972), pp. 113-32.
Ross, J.M., 'The Rejected Words in Luke 9.54-56', *ET* 84 (1972), pp. 85-88.
Metzger, B.M., *The Early Versions of the New Testament* (Oxford, 1977), p. 42.
Kuhn, H.-W., 'Nachfolge nach Ostern', in *Fs* Bornkamm (Tübingen, 1980), pp. 107-115.
Seccombe, D.P., *Possessions and the Poor in Luke—Acts* (SNTU 6; Linz, 1982).
Goulder, M.D., 'From Ministry to Passion in John and Luke', *NTS* 29 (1983), pp. 561-68.

b. *The Mission Discourse* 10.1-16

Luke's equivalence of Mt. 9.35 ('And Jesus went round all the towns and villages teaching. . . and healing every disease and every illness') with Mk 4.1–9.40 is not without its problems; for included in the

Marcan sequence was the Mission of the Twelve (Mk 6.7-13/Lk.9.1-6), and here, as soon as he moves over to Matthew, is the Mission of the Twelve again, in a fuller and more moving form. He has resolved the difficulty with his customary ingenuity.

There were two speeches in Mt. 9.36-10.42. The first was short (9.37-38), and was addressed to 'his disciples'; the second was long (10.5b-42), and was spoken to 'the twelve' (10.5a), 'his twelve disciples' (11.1). It was natural to understand the Twelve as a *selection* from a larger number, 'his disciples' of 9.37, because Mt. 10.1 speaks of Jesus 'calling his twelve disciples', which suggests calling from a larger number; and this was implied in Mk 3.13 and said in Lk. 6.13, 'he called his disciples, and *choosing from them* twelve...' So Matthew seems to speak of two addresses on Mission: one to the Twelve (10.5-42), which Luke has already described in its Marcan version at 9.1-6; and one to the larger number of Jesus' disciples, which opened, 'The harvest truly is plenteous...' It is the latter which Luke is about to take now. He specifies the larger number of disciples, he opens the Discourse with the two sentences from Mt. 9.37-38, and he expands this with additional material from the Mission Discourses in Mark 6 and (especially) Matthew 10, as well as from Matthew 11.

10.1. Matthew had prefaced his harvest-and-labourers logia with 9.36, 'And seeing the crowds, he had pity on them, for they were harassed and torn as sheep not having a shepherd'. The last words take Luke's mind to the book of Numbers, where Joshua was appointed Moses' deputy, lest the Israelites be 'as sheep who have no shepherd' (Num. 27.17). Joshua received the Spirit at that time, as it had come earlier to the Seventy elders, Moses' deputies, and to Eldad and Medad in Numbers 11; and it is the earlier story which is more to the point here, for Jesus had need of many assistants for the harvest of souls. So Luke accepts the suggestion that the larger group of disciples was seventy-two in number. Although they are sent to evangelize Galilean Jews, Luke does not miss the overtone of the number seventy-two: for there is in his time one mission of the Twelve to the twelve tribes of Israel, and a second mission of a larger number sent to the seventy-two nations of the world (Gen. 10, LXX). He includes in the present passage instructions such as the testifying with dust, which will be fulfilled in the Gentile mission in Acts. Luke will amplify Matthew's Dinner parable similarly with a second

mission: the first in the streets and lanes of the town, the second in
the highways and hedges without. Without this second symbolism of
the seventy-two, he would hardly have included it.

10.1f. Luke, like other men, has difficulty making up his mind, and
this lands him once more in a minor muddle (§9). He has just
described Jesus' sending of messengers 'before his face' to secure
lodging for him (9.52), and the Samaritans' refusal to 'receive' him;
so he prefaces the present discourse with 'he sent them in twos before
his face to every town and place where he himself would come',
knowing that it will also contain instructions on not being received.
But actually the text in Mt. 9.37f. is already about the harvest of
souls, not beds for the night; and Mt. 10.7ff. even more clearly so.
The sending in pairs echoes Mk 6.7 (though Luke has the same often
elsewhere), and the 'place' (for 'village') is influenced by Mk 6.11. He
then sets off on his Discourse with the opening logia from Matthew
9, 'The harvest truly is plenteous. . . ' These are not in fact very
suitable words with which to open a discourse sending disciples on
mission; prayer is suited to a situation when *other* people are to be
sent on mission, as in the Matthaean context. We should have
expected, 'The harvest truly is plenteous but the labourers are few;
go you therefore. . . ', not 'pray you therefore. . . ' But Luke is faithful
to his source.

10.3. Fortunately the source gives out at this point (Mt. 9.38), and
Luke is at liberty to improvise such things as Jesus would be likely to
have said, as he did on other similar occasions. He supplies the
missing 'Go' himself, and adds Mt. 10.16a, 'Lo, I send you as (sheep)
in the midst of wolves'. Two things may perhaps have influenced him
to substitute 'lambs' for 'sheep'. One is his general preference for the
colourful over the general (§4.8): eggs and scorpions for Matthaean
bread and stones, ravens for Matthaean birds. But there is likely to
be also a particular reason here, for Luke is probably thinking, rather
nicely, 'If the apostles were as sheep among wolves, surely the lesser
disciples were as lambs'. Again, however we may note that the logion
is much more at home in the Matthaean than in the Lucan context.
Luke needs the 'Lo, I send you. . . ' to get the Seventy-two off their
knees and out into the act; but the suggestion of 'wolves' is quite
inapposite. In Matthew the verse served as an introduction to a
prophecy of persecution, trial, betrayal and martyrdom—sheep
among wolves indeed. The worst that is foretold for the Seventy-two
is that they will enter a city and it will not receive them.

10.4. Both the earlier evangelists had included instructions to the Twelve to travel light; and Mark had followed the sending (6.7) directly with the forbidding of bread, pack, money (brass) and a second coat (6.8)—only a stick and sandals were permitted. Matthew has a similar list a little further into the Discourse (10.9f.). He puts the money first, amending Mark to the forbidding of *earnings* (κτήσησθε), and of gold and silver as well as brass. He drops the bread, but forbids pack and second coat. He interprets Mark's permission of sandals as the forbidding of the stronger 'shoes' (ὑποδήματα); and he also (surprisingly) forbids the stick (see on 9.3). Luke follows Mark in placing such instructions immediately after the sending, and also with μὴ...μηδὲ ...μηδὲ...; but he follows Matthew in putting the money first, and in forbidding ὑποδήματα. However he abbreviates the whole business. He cuts out Matthew's earning, as Paul did indeed earn his livelihood, and his gold and silver, which give a false idea of a Christian's standard of living: 'do not carry a purse' is Lucan, and sufficient. The taking of a second coat is also unnecessary for so brief an expedition; and, despite his agreement with Matthew over the stick at 9.3, he omits this too— perhaps mindful of the Marcan permission, perhaps of the realities of travel. A further contributory factor is the image of Elisha, which has not gone away with the change of chapter-number. Gehazi was sent with the prophet's staff (βακτηρίαν) to heal the Shunammite's son (4 Kgdms 4.29): 'Take my staff in your hand and come. For if you find a man you shall not bless him, and if a man bless you you shall not answer him; and you shall lay my staff on the lad's face'. Luke's v. 4b, 'and salute no one on the road' has taken ἀσπάσασθε from Mt. 10.12, but the sense from 4 Kgdms: as at 9.59-62, the preaching of the kingdom is too urgent to allow for conventions.

10.5f. Mark moved on logically from rules on travel to rules on arrival: 'Wherever you enter a house, stay (μένετε) there till you depart thence' (6.10)—the 'thence' being from that *town*, presumably. The more prudent and experienced Matthew amplifies, 'Whatever town or village you enter, enquire who in it is worthy; and stay (μείνατε) there till you depart. As you go into the house, salute it: and if the house be worthy let your peace go upon it, and if it be not worthy, let your peace return to you' (10.11-13). Such cautious enquiries seemed invidious to Luke, who (as we shall see) accepted the Pauline principle of eating what was set before him without asking questions (v. 8); but there is nothing amiss with bidding 'Peace' to one's hosts—the Lord himself did the same on Easter night (24.36; cf. 2.14). So he short-circuits the Matthaean procedure with 'Whatever *house* you enter, first say, Peace to this household'—we may notice that for the building he uses Matthew's (and Mark's) οἰκία, and for the occupants his own preferred οἶκος; and that he uses the Biblical *shālôm*/εἰρήνη as at 24.36. He continues, 'And if a son of peace be there, your peace shall rest upon him; otherwise it will return upon you'. Luke, like many a good Protestant since, feels ill at ease with the notion of blessing houses, etc.: peace to him belongs to people (1.79; 2.29; 7.50; 8.48, etc.) and can only be spoken to Jerusalem as a figure for its inhabitants (19.42). So he transfers the peace from the house to its owner, should he be a 'son of peace'. He likes the Semitic metaphor: sons of light (16.8), sons of this world (16.8; 20.34R), sons of the Most High (6.36QD), sons of God (20.36R), sons of the resurrection (20.36R). His futures are an improvement on Matthew's subjunctives, and he has a more dynamic view of the blessing—ἐπαναπαήσεται ἐπί for Matthew's weak 'go', and 'returns upon' the sender for Matthew's weak 'to'. Here we have once more the influence of Numbers and 4 Kgdms: 'the Spirit rested (ἐπανεπαύσατο ἐπί) on them' (Num. 11.25, the Seventy, v. 26, Eldad and Medad); 'the spirit of Elijah has rested on Elisha' (ἐπαναπέπαυται ἐπί)' (4 Kgdms 2.15).

10.7f. Rules on staying belong logically after rules on arrival, so Luke has taken the 'Stay. . .' section separately, improving again on Matthew. For once the latter's alteration to Mark had landed him in dubious sense: 'Whatever town or village you enter, enquire who in it is worthy; and stay there till you depart'—the 'there' means the *house*, as in Mk 6.10, but reads like the 'town or village'. Luke's 'Stay in the very house. . . Go not from house to house' is a clearer and ampler form of the old Marcan, 'Wherever you enter a house stay there till you depart thence', with Mark's οἰκία and μένετε (cf. 9.4). The positiveness may owe something to Luke's own experience, as at Philippi where he and Paul stayed their time with Lydia (Acts 16.15); and perhaps also again to the memory of Elisha, who regularly spent his time at Shunem in the prophet's chamber provided by the 'great woman' (4 Kgdms 4.8-10).

In Palestine, diet was no problem, for any host could be expected to provide kosher food; so no provision for food rules had been necessary either in the old Marcan tradition, or for the Matthaean community, which salutes the Gentile mission from a distance. But there could be no such expectation for those who carried the gospel to the nations, and tender consciences must be exercised. Paul had discussed the issue in 1 Cor. 9-10. First the missionary had the right, given by the Lord, to be fed by his converts—'Who ever campaigns and pays his own wages? Who plants a vineyard and does not eat its fruit?...' (9.7) Second, one need ask no questions—'Eat (ἐσθίετε) anything sold in the market, without raising questions on ground of conscience. For "the earth is the Lord's and the fullness thereof"... eat whatever is set before you (πᾶν τὸ παρατιθέμενον ὑμῖν ἐσθίετε)' (10.25ff.). The same point seems to Luke to be implied by Matthew's 'For the labourer is worthy of his food (τροφῆς)' (10.10b). So he combines his authorities: 'Stay in the very house', (Mark) 'eating and drinking what they provide'; (Paul) 'for the labourer is worthy of his hire (μισθοῦ)' (Mt. 10.10). 'And whatever town you enter', (Mt. 10.11) 'and they receive you' (cf. Mt. 10.14) 'ἐσθίετε τὰ παρατιθέμενα ὑμῖν' (1 Cor. 10.27). Eating-and-drinking is Lucan, as is τὰ with a prepositional phrase (see below). Luke prefers μισθός to τροφή, as labourers were paid in money, not in kind (μίσθιοι, 15.17, 19; cf. μισθώσασθαι, Mt. 20.1, 7); and a missionary must depend on his hosts for cash (to travel, etc.) as well as for food (Gal. 6.6). But combinations of this kind are always risky, and Luke ends with the slightly unhappy 'whatever town you enter... eat what they set before you': one eats in a house rather than a town, and goes to preach rather than to eat.

Matthew had put the purpose of the mission first, '*Go*... As you go, *preach* saying, The kingdom of heaven has come (ἤγγικεν). *Heal* the sick (ἀσθενοῦντας θεραπεύετε)...' (10.6-8), and the details second—travel, lodging, etc. Luke's revision is systematic: go, travel, lodging, staying—and now the missionary activity. By the same token he reverses the Matthaean sequence preach-heal, for to him the word is grounded in the divine act. The calling of Peter arises from the catch of the fish; the mountain Sermon follows the wonders of 4.31-6.11; 'therefore' links a discourse on the kingdom to the healing of the Bent Woman at 13.18 (cf. 14.1-24; 17.11-21). At 11.20 Luke reproduces the Matthaean logion that the casting out of demons is the sign that the kingdom of God ἔφθασεν ἐφ' ὑμᾶς (11.20QC). So here he has the Lord bid the Seventy-two heal first and preach second, 'The kingdom of God has come'—he adds ἐφ' ὑμᾶς, in virtue of the healings, here also.

10.10f. But what of the all-too-common experience of rejection? Mk 6.11, 'And whatever place does not receive you or hear you. . . '; Mt. 10.14, 'And whoever does not receive you or hear your words. . . ' (since *places* do not hear, and the question is not whether they hear the *missionary* but whether they accept his *words*). Luke writes, 'Whatever town you enter and they do not receive you. . . '; he is adapting to the form of v. 8, 'And whatever town you enter and they receive you. . . ' (cf. Mt. 10.11). Mark's scene is uncomplicated: '. . . go out thence (viz. from 'the place') and shake off the dust (χοῦν) which is beneath your feet for a testimony to them'. Matthew has made things more difficult for himself by bringing the house of the missionary's residence into 10.12f., for he now feels driven to gloss, '. . . go outside that *house or* town and shake off the dust (κονιορτόν) from your feet'. He seems to be involved in two different notions: a house which was 'unworthy' (v. 13) and would not *receive* the missionary, and a town which would not *hear his words*—but in fact these were often the same, since in any place only a minority might hear the gospel, and the crucial test was whether any one family would be sufficiently committed to give him a home. Luke combines his two sources: '. . . go out into its streets' follows Matthew's 'outside that house', rather than Mark's 'out (of the place) (cp. 9.5); his '. . . and say, Even the dust (κονιορτόν) which cleaves to us on our feet from your town we wipe off to you; but know this, that God's kingdom has come', is an expanded oratio recta form of Mark's 'for a testimony to them'. Luke has retained Matthew's κονιορτόν (as at 9.5) and τῆς πόλεως in v. 11 and repeated his ἤγγικεν ἡ βασιλεία (τοῦ θεοῦ). For Luke's oratio recta expansions, cf. §11; for the vocabulary see below. His ἤγγικεν ἡ βασιλεία τοῦ θεοῦ now takes on a more menacing tone: God's Kingdom has drawn near in judgment (cf. v. 12).

10.12. Matthew had closed the rejection topic with a logion which he virtually repeats in 11.24:

Mt. 10.15   ἀμὴν λέγω ὑμῖν, ἀνεκτότερον ἔσται γῇ Σοδόμων καὶ Γομόρρων ἐν ἡμέρᾳ κρίσεως ἢ τῇ πόλει ἐκείνῃ.

Mt. 11.24   πλὴν λέγω ὑμῖν ὅτι γῇ Σοδόμων ἀνεκτότερον ἔσται ἐν ἡμέρᾳ κρίσεως ἢ σοί.

Luke produces a compromise with λέγω ὑμῖν ὅτι Σοδόμοις ἐν τῇ ἡμέρᾳ ἐκείνῃ ἀνεκτότερον ἔσται ἢ τῇ πόλει ἐκείνῃ. We may perhaps detect the influence of πλὴν from Mt. 11.24 in his preceding πλὴν τοῦτο γινώσκετε. Sodom comes next after ὅτι as in the second version also; but as he is speaking of a town (τῇ πόλει ἐκείνῃ) he drops Matthew's favoured 'the land of'—it is the town of Sodom alone in the comparison (= Mt. 11.23). In v. 11 he had spoken of 'the kingdom of God drawing near', and Luke (unlike his predecessors) usually has ἐγγίζειν in the sense of 'near but still not here' (21.8, 20, 28): he has thus just referred to the day of judgment, and supplies 'that day' as at 21.34 for the occasion—he dislikes Matthew's favourite ἐν ἡμέρᾳ κρίσεως (4/0/0+0). The clumsy τῇ ἡμέρᾳ ἐκείνῃ(R)... τῇ πόλει ἐκείνῃ (= Mt.) reveals his secondariness.

10.13ff. Mt. 11.24 had been the climax of Jesus' rebuke to the towns where most of the miracles had been done, for their failure to repent: 'Woe to you, Chorazin, woe to you, Bethsaida; for if the miracles done (γενομέναι) in you had been done (ἐγένοντο) in Tyre and Sidon, they would have repented long since in sackcloth and ashes. But I tell you, it will be more tolerable for Tyre and Sidon on the day of judgment than for you. And you, Capernaum, shall you be exalted to heaven? You shall go down to Hades. For if the miracles done in you had been done (ἐγενήθησαν) in Sodom. . . ' Matthew has a finely balanced strophe/antistrophe, with three lines apiece: the first an address to the town(s), the second 'for if the miracles. . . ', the third, 'But I tell you, it will be more tolerable. . . ' The situation is suitable because Matthew 11 follows the great healings in Capernaum and its environs in Mt. 8-9. It is not at all suitable here, where the mission of the Seventy-two is in southern Galilee, twenty miles from Capernaum which they are nowhere near visiting; and Matthew's parallelism is totally lost, with the suppression of the second Capernaum clause, and the transfer of the first to the introduction (v. 12). Luke allows the context of Mt. 10.15=11.24 to draw in the famous and effective lines on the three cities (Mt. 11.22f.), otherwise with hardly a change. He puts ἐγενήθησαν in the first clause instead of Matthew's second (which he has dropped), perhaps a copying error. He supplies 'sitting' in sackcloth for the better Greek. He puts 'in the judgment' for Matthew's 'on the day of judgment', cf. 11.31, 32QC. He gives ᾅδου an article, as at 16.23. He parallels the passive ὑψωθήσῃ with the passive καταβιβασθήσῃ for Matthew's καταβήσῃ (= Isa. 14.15)—on the p⁴⁵א reading printed by Greeven.

10.16. The remainder of Matthew's great Mission Discourse is concerned with the persecutions which the Twelve must expect (10.17-39), extending to martyrdom. Such perils do not face the Seventy-two immediately and may be kept for a later occasion: Luke is not supposing that Jesus would have said all the same things to the Seventy-two as to the Twelve. However, Matthew does finish his Discourse with some comments on the *receiving* of missionaries, and Luke wisely feels that an adapted version would round off his own wandering address. Mt. 10.40, 'He who receives you receives me, and he who receives me receives him that sent me' was itself an application to the mission situation of Mk 9.37, 'Whoever receives one of such children in my name receives me; and whoever receives me, receives not me but him that sent me'. But, as Matthew himself noted (10.14), what mattered was not just receiving the apostle, but *hearkening* to his words. So Luke opens his summing up, 'He who hearkens to you hearkens to me': Jesus had had a bed in Capernaum, but they had not hearkened to him, and that was the point for the Seventy-two now. Furthermore, both Mark and Matthew had considered the alternative of rejection in their discourses, but Matthew has only acceptance in this conclusion. It seems proper to Luke to give both sides of the penny here also therefore. He has already expressed the antithesis in the redactional 7.29f., 'And all the people hearkening (ἀκούσας) and the toll-collectors justified God. . . but the Pharisees and the lawyers set at naught (ἠθέτησαν) the counsel of God'. So here he provides the same antithesis in the same order: 'He who hearkens (ἀκούων) to you hearkens (ἀκούει) to me, and he who sets you at naught (ἀθετῶν) sets me at naught (ἀθετεῖ)'. The expansion has the disadvantage that it is now difficult to include the promise of 'receiving him that sent me'; and Luke contents himself with the unhappy converse, 'And he who sets me at naught sets at naught him that sent me'. So the Marco-Matthaean rhetoric is preserved, but in a more hostile sense.

The passage has been much discussed, and the balance of critical opinion is heavily against the above exposition, and broadly in favour of a twofold Mission tradition, with one source being Mark, and the Q tradition better preserved in Luke. Matthew has then 'conflated' Q and Mark, and Luke has done something of the same in 9.2-6. In this general sense see Schmid, pp. 257-268; Hoffmann, pp. 237-86; Schulz, pp. 404-19, 360-66, 457-59; Miyoshi, pp. 59-94; Laufen, pp. 201-301. The consensus rests on the fallacies discussed on pp. 11-22. If Q is accepted, then the Lucan form will be bound to seem more original in many points, as Matthew's style is more repetitve than Luke's, and so more easily isolated. But the Q hypothesis has its own difficulties, as will be seen in detail.

10.1 μετὰ-ταῦτα*, ὁ-κύριος = Jesus*, ἕτερος*, ἀνὰ-δύο, πρὸ-προσώπου + gen., πᾶς pleon., πόλις, οὗ, ἤμελλεν*, αὐτός nom. Hapax: ἀναδεικνύναι (Acts 1.24, ἀνάδειξις, Lk. 1.80 = reveal; here = commission cf. BAG *ad voc.* 2) So much of the vocabulary is Lucan (and the link and setting) that the verse is usually allowed to be Lk. R based on Mk 6.7 (Hoffmann, p. 248). The only difficulty is whether we should read Seventy (א ACLW Θ) or Seventy-Two (p⁷⁵BD). Metzger (p. 150) hovers, printing the 'Two' in brackets (cf. his *NTS* [1959] article), while Aland in a note (*ibid.*, p. 151) argues for its inclusion. The point is not very significant, as the symbolism of the Seventy in Numbers 11 can be of Seventy-Two if we include Eldad and Medad (Miyoshi, p. 61), and the Seventy nations of Genesis 10 are Seventy-Two in LXX. The counting of the Genesis 10 nations is not very well testified for either number, though.

10.2 πρός + vb. dicendi*, (δέεσθαι*). For a Q verse the wording is uncomfortably Matthaean. θερισμός 6/1/3QC+0 (Mt. 13.39R), ἐργάτης (= a literal worker) 6/0/3QC+0, the contrast πολύς/ὀλίγος Mt. 7.14QD; 9.37 (= Lk. 10.2); 22.14; 25.21QD, 23QD, Mk -, Lk. 7.47; 12.48; Acts 26.29; μέν. . .δέ 20/6/10+47 (Mt. 3.11R; 13.8R, 23R, 32R, etc.); οὖν 57/5/31+62, often Mt. R; ὅπως 17/1/7 (+ verb. petendi 8.34R); ἐκβάλλειν = *hôtsî*, without hostile meaning, Mt. 9.38 (= Lk. 10.2); 12.20R; 12.35 2QD; 13.52, Mk -, Lk. 10.35, Acts -. δέεσθαι is a hapax in Matthew. Luke's reversal of ἐκβάλῃ/ἐργάτας is a stylistic improvement (Hoffmann, p. 263; Schulz, p. 405).

10.3 (ἐν-μέσῳ). Hapaxes: ἄρνες, (λύκος). ὑπάγειν is not common in Luke (19/15/5+0), but he inserts it editorially at 8.42 (?12.58QD), and retains the imperative at 19.30Mk. Schmid (p. 261) takes Luke for original, but Hoffmann (p. 263) and Schulz (p. 405) think Luke may have inserted the verb and the logion here. Schulz thinks Luke's rare ἄρνες is original, replaced by Matthew's commoner πρόβατα (logic!); Hoffmann that Luke has made the general more precise. Q^Mt again shows Matthaean features: ἰδοὺ ἐγὼ ἀποστέλλω Mt. 11.10R; 23.34; ὡς = as, like 40/20/25 (Mt. 17.2R; 28.3R etc.); sheep and wolves = 7.15, cf. eight other pairs of animals in Mt. (see on 9.58 above). Luke also drops ἐγώ from Mk 14.36 and Mt. 11.10.

10.4 βαστάζειν, βαλλάντιον*, (ὑποδήματα), κατά + acc. Polag prints the whole Lucan verse as Q; but Hoffmann (pp. 264-67) and Schulz (p. 405) note the difficulties, and Laufen (p. 213) puts βαστάζετε βαλλάντιον in brackets. The Matthaean version (10.9-10a) is mostly a redaction of Mark, but βαστάζειν 3/1/5+4 (14.27QD) and βαλλάντιον 0/0/4 (12.33QD) they are reluctant to call non-Lucan. Miyoshi (p. 63) takes 'salute no one...' as pre-Lucan on weak linguistic grounds (κατὰ τὴν ὁδὸν comes ×3 in Acts, and is conceded as Lucan: ἀσπάζεσθαι × 6 Acts); Hoffmann (p. 267) accepts that it may be a Lucan formation.

10.5 εἰρήνη*, οἶκος. Schmid (p.263) argues (correctly) that Matthew's 'town or village' is Mt. R (cf. 9.35): and that his 'enquire who in it is worthy' is equivalent to Luke's 'if a son of peace be there'. He curiously rejects Matthew's ἀσπάσασθε as secondary, although it comes in Lk. 10.4b also; and accepts Luke's 'first say, Peace...' as Luke often avoids oratio recta. But sometimes he also introduces it (9.2ff.; ?10.11QD), and we may compare the frequent soliloquies in Lucan parables (§4.1). He overlooks Luke's fondness for εἰρήνη (though this comes in Mt. 10.13 also), and the change to οἶκος.

10.6 εἰρήνη*, (εἰρήνη*), εἰ-δὲ-μή-γε*, ἐφ'(ὑμᾶς)*. Hapaxes: ἐπαναπαύεσθαι (Num. 11.25f.; 4 Kgdms 2.15), ἀνακάμπτειν. Harnack (p. 58) pointed properly to Luke's fondness for metaphorical υἱός, and Schmid does not answer this by saying (p. 263) that other NT authors like it too. Nor does he note the Numbers/Elisha overtone of ἐπαναπαήσεται, which inclines Polag to take it as Lk. R—Polag prints the last two thirds of the verse almost in the Matthaean form.

10.7 ἔσθειν-καὶ-πίνειν*, τὰ + prep.*. Hapax: μεταβαίνειν (Acts 18.7). αὐτῇ τῇ οἰκίᾳ 'that very house'. Verse 7a is close to Mk 6.10, and Schulz (p. 406) and Polag take v. 7d as Q; but Marshall thinks it may have been Luke's addition for clarification (μεταβαίνειν Acts 18.7). Hengel (*NTS* [1971], p. 36) sees that the food-rule applies to the Gentile mission, but optimistically ascribes this to Jesus. Schmid (p. 264) regards a Lucan substitution of μισθοῦ for τροφῆς as impossible after 7b; but cf. p. 138 above. The 'arcetic' form of the Q saying 'For the labourer...' (predicate-subject-referent-αὐτοῦ) is confined to Matthew and Lk. Q (Mt. 6.34M; 10.10Q; 10.34M; 11.19Q). The Lucan form recurs in 1 Tim. 5.18, which is not an argument for Lucan priority, as the Pastorals may be familiar with L-A.

10.8 πόλις, δέχεσθαι, τὰ + part. παρατίθεσθαι in this sense 11.6; Acts 16.34. Hoffmann (p. 268), Schulz (p. 407) amd Miyoshi (p. 64) see signs of Lucan writing in v. 8b.

10.9 ἐφ'ὑμᾶς*. Hapax: ἀσθενής (Acts 4.9; 5.15f.). Miyoshi (pp. 65ff.) argues for the reversal of the preaching-healing sequence as Lucan, as well as ἐφ' ὑμᾶς and ἀσθενής. Hoffmann (pp. 274ff.) correctly notes the Matthaean nature of Mt. 10.5-8, and concludes falsely that Luke preserves the Q form.

10.10 πόλις, (δέχεσθαι), εἶπον. ἐξελθόντες εἰς τὰς πλατείας αὐτῆς, cf. 14.21 ἔξελθε ταχέως εἰς τὰς πλατείας . . . τῆς πόλεως, also 13.26; Acts 5.15. Hoffmann (pp. 268ff.) attributes the difference from Mt. 10.14b to Lk. R, the oratio recta being a sign of late development (Bultmann), and paralleled at Acts 18.6 with Paul's gesture and word.

10.11 (πόλις), (πούς), πλήν*, γινώσκετε-ὅτι. Hapax: ἀπομάσσεσθαι (cf. ἐκμάσσειν 7.38, 44). Luke has the Seventy-two *wipe* the dust off carefully, whereas at 9.5, cf. Mk 6.11; Mt. 10.14; Acts 13.51 *shaking* off (ἀπο-/ ἐκτινάσσειν) is sufficient. Mark's χοῦς really means heaped up earth (Liddell & Scott), and Luke regularly prefers κονιορτός (9.5; Acts 13.51; 22.23). κολλᾶσθαι 1/0/2+5, but elsewhere of joining people. Schmid (p. 264) correctly sees that Mt. 10.14 is a clarification of Mark, and concludes falsely that Luke is original; Hoffmann (pp. 270ff.) takes vv. 10ff. as 'in general an independent reformulation' of Q, i.e. Lk.R.

10.12 (ἡμέρα), (πόλις). Schmid (p. 267) has no difficulty in pointing to the secondariness of Matthew's house-mission, ἀμήν, ἐν ἡμέρᾳ κρίσεως, καὶ Γομόρρων; and others have added 'the land of' (Miyoshi, pp. 67ff.). It was natural for Schmid to conclude that Luke gave the Q version; but it must seem singular that so few modern exegetes have considered that Matthew might have written the whole logion himself—the rejecting town was already implicitly a successor to Sodom in Mk 6.11; 13.14f.

10.13 (γίνεσθαι ×2), (μετανοεῖν). Hapaxes: (πάλαι), (σάκκος), (σποδός). Schmid (pp. 286f.), Hoffmann (pp. 284f.) and most take Lk. = Q with καθήμενοι alone as Lk. R to make the repentance ritual precise; but then καθήμενοι is the only substantial difference. Note the cliché-pairs, Tyre-and-Sidon, sackcloth and ashes, so common in Matthew; and the religious imagery favoured by the evangelist (*MLM*, pp. 105ff.). Also it is Matthew who especially uses δύναμις to mean a miracle (7/4/2+3—7.22; 11.20R, 21, 23; 13.54Mk, 58Mk; 14.2Mk; Mk 6.2, 5, 14; 9.29; Lk. 10.13QC; 19.37R, Acts 2.22; 8.13; 19.11), and who likes sentences of the form εἰ . . . ἄν (11.21, 23; 12.7R; 23.30; 24.43; Mk -; Lk. 7.39; 10.13QC; 12.39QC; 17.6QD; Acts 18.14).

10.14 (πλήν*). Schmid and Hoffmann (*ibid.*) note correctly ἐν ἡμέρᾳ κρίσεως as a sign of Matthaean writing, but do not consider whether the whole sentence might be written by Matthew, as they correctly say its parallel in 11.23b was. Lk. omits λέγω ὑμῖν, not for no reason (Schmid), but ὑμῖν in. v. 12 meant the disciples, and here would mean the cities.

10.15 N-A²⁶ prints τοῦ before ᾅδου with p⁷⁵BL, and not before οὐρανοῦ, and I have followed; Greeven takes the opposite choices. Luke, as so often (§21) spoils Matthew's beautiful parallelisms, which he thinks to be wordy, finishing on the strong note, 'you shall be brought down to Hades'. Schmid thinks λέγω ὑμῖν (= the disciples) was original in Lk. 10.12, and Matthew's carrying it over (= the cities) involves a tension, cp. σοί, singular, at the end of the verse. But Matthew is just repeating the phrase from v.22a, and means the Capernaumites.

10.16   Schmid (pp. 278f.), consistent to the end, takes the Lucan version as Q, which Mt. has then adapted to Mk 9.37; because 'elsewhere the third evangelist never completes a parallelism'. Similarly Schulz (pp. 457f.). But the argument is circular: Lk. has closer parallels and more of them in 6.20-26 if we are allowed to include them. Hoffmann (pp. 285f.) takes the Mt. form as Q, with Luke making Mt.'s 'receive' more specific with 'hear/set at nought'; so also Miyoshi, pp. 70-73. For the relationship with Jn 12.44ff. cf. my article in *NTS* 29 (1983), p. 562.

Metzger, B.M., 'Seventy or Seventy-Two Disciples?', *NTS* 5 (1958-59), pp. 299-306.
Comber, J.A., 'The Composition and Literary Characteristics of Matt. 11.20-24', *CBQ* 39 (1977), p. 497-504.
Lang, B., 'Grussverbot oder Besuchsverbot? Eine sozialgeschichtliche Deutung von Lukas 10,4b', *BZ* 26 (1982), pp. 75-79.
Harvey, A.E., '"The Workman is Worthy of his Hire": Fortunes of a Proverb in the Early Church', *NT* 24 (1982), pp. 209-221.
Jacobson, A.D., 'The Literary Unit of Q: Lc 10,2-16 as a Test Case', in J. Delobel (ed.) *Logia* (BETL 59; Leuven, 1982)

c. *The Return of the Seventy-Two*, 10.17-24

Mark closed the episode of the Mission of the Twelve (6.7-13) with a note on their joyful return announcing their achievements (6.30) and Jesus' invitation to them to come away (δεῦτε) privately and rest (ἀναπαύσασθε) awhile (6.31); and Luke similarly closes the Mission of the Twelve (9.1-6) with a joyful return and private withdrawal (9.10). Outwardly, Matthew might appear to have omitted these features; but Luke reads him with the understanding that they are implied. For after the rebuke of the cities (Mt. 11.20-24), Jesus thanks his Father that while he has hidden the great mysteries of faith from the wise and understanding, he has revealed them to 'babes' (vv. 25-27)—and who are the babes but the 'little ones'—the missionaries of 10.42? Then he issues an invitation, 'Come (δεῦτε)... and I will give you rest (ἀναπαύσω)... and you shall find rest (ἀνάπαυσιν) for your souls' (11.28-30), which unquestionably echoes Mk 6.31.

Luke has already taken the scene with the Baptist's disciples (Mt. 11.2-19; Lk. 7.18-35), and he has cleverly included the judgment logia on the cities (Mt. 11.20-24) with the earlier Sodom-and-Gomorrah logion (Mt. 10.15) at Lk. 10.12-15. So he has in fact arrived at exactly the point where he sees the return of the missionaries as implied in the Matthaean text (11.25). Such skilful handling clarifies two things which we might otherwise have missed. First we now see an additional reason for his abbreviation of the long Matthaean discourse: he not only prefers his speeches briefer, and finds much of the martyrdom material irrelevant, but he has actually reached the point at Mt. 10.15 where he is able to move on to Mt. 11.20-24. Thus he has placed himself where he needs to be to bring the missionaries back, and wishes to sign the Discourse off as soon as possible. Secondly, we now see a second reason for his taking the Discourse as addressed to a group other than the Twelve; for Matthew apparently describes them as νήπιοι, and that is an expression for immature Christians (1 Cor. 3.1) and hardly suitable for the Church's elect leaders. As the last verses of Matthew's Discourse imply that the Mission included not only apostles but prophets, saints, and even little ones (Mt. 10.41f.), Luke might feel few scruples about omitting 'the Twelve' of Mt. 10.5. He had built his address on Jesus' words to 'his disciples' at Mt. 9.37f., and Mt. 11.25 shows them to have been νήπιοι, beginners at the faith unlike the Twelve.

10.17. Matthew's suggestions can certainly do with clarifying, and Luke prefaces Jesus' thanksgiving for the νήπιοι with a short description of their return. They come back (Lucan ὑπέστρεψαν, cf. 9.10R) with joy (24.52), saying 'κύριε (cf. 10.1 ὁ κύριος), even the demons (often Lk. R) are subject to us in your name'. ὑποτάσσεσθαι is not a normal Lucan word, but is likely to have been drawn in from 1 Cor. 15.24-28: 'Then comes the end, when he *hands over* (παραδιδῷ) the kingdom to God *the Father* (τῷ θεῷ καὶ πατρί), when he has put down all rule and *all authority and power* (πᾶσαν ἐξουσίαν καὶ δύναμιν)... The last *enemy* (ἐχθρός) put down is death. For he has *subjected* (ὑπέταξεν) *all things* under his feet... And when he has *subjected* all to him, *the Son* also shall be *subjected*'. The passage seems already to be in Matthew's mind at 11.25-27 with its rare '*the Son/the Father*' and the *handing over* (παρεδόθη) of *all things*. Luke retains all these at 10.22 and adds *subjected* (vv. 17, 20), '*authority...* over *every power* of the *enemy*' (v. 19). Cf. above p. 141.

10.18 Luke has just been repeating (10.15) Matthew's condemnation of Capernaum, 'Shall you be exalted to heaven? To Hades shall you go down'; and Matthew was already developing Isa. 14.13f., where the king of Babylon says, 'I will ascend into heaven' and is told, 'But now to Hades shall you go down'. But Isaiah actually addresses the king not as a human being, but as a celestial spirit, 'How is the Morning Star, who rises at dawn, fallen from heaven (ἐξέπεσεν ἐκ τοῦ οὐρανοῦ)!' (Isa. 14.12). As the world of the New Testament saw the stars as heavenly spirits (1 Cor. 15.40f., Revelation, *passim*), it is natural for Luke to associate the coming of God's kingdom, with its healings and exorcisms, with the fall from heaven of the supernatural power which has hitherto been frustrating God's grace, and which Paul had seen as subjected to the Son. So he adds Isa. 14.12 to Isa. 14.13, 14, just as he added a third Elisha-type aspiring disciple at 9.61f. to the two already taken over from Matthew. Jesus says, 'I saw Satan fallen (πεσόντα) from heaven (ἐκ τοῦ οὐρανοῦ) like lightning'. The identification of the Morning Star with Satan is unsurprising, since it is Satan's kingdom that is opposed to God's in the evangelical tradition (Mk 3.26; Lk. 11.17-20). It is Luke especially who descries behind the Gospel events the action and overthrow of Satan. Satan enters Judas at 22.3R to inspire the betrayal; Satan asks God for Peter and the apostles to sift them as wheat at Gethsemane (22.31 R?); Satan filled the heart of Ananias to lie to the Holy Spirit (Acts 5.3).

10.19. The overthrow of Satan in heaven is to be seen in the powers given to Jesus' followers on earth; for as the serpent (ὄφις) in Genesis caused the Fall, and was condemned to war against man from the dust (Gen. 3.14f.), so now he shall be trampled on and harmless. The somewhat clumsy form of the sentence ('authority *to* tread. . . and *over*. . . ') is a second echo of a similar clumsiness in Mt. 10.1:

> ἔδωκεν αὐτοῖς ἐξουσίαν πνευμάτων ἀκαθάρτων. . .καὶ θεραπεύειν πᾶσαν νόσον.

We saw Luke introducing it as an MA at 9.1:

> ἔδωκεν αὐτοῖς. . .ἐξουσίαν ἐπὶ πάντα τὰ δαιμόνια καὶ νόσους θεραπεύειν;

and we have it again here with:

> ἔδωκα ὑμῖν τὴν ἐξουσίαν τοῦ πατεῖν . . .
> καὶ ἐπὶ πᾶσαν τὴν δύναμιν τοῦ ἐχθροῦ.

Luke forgot even to mention power over the spirits in his charge at 10.1ff., and goes back now to the Matthaean phrasing. The πατεῖν upon serpents and scorpions is a development of the 'messianic' promise of Ps. 91.13, 'You shall walk upon ἀσπίδα and basilisk, and καταπατήσεις lion and dragon'. The ὄφεις replace asp, basilisk and dragon, from Genesis 3; the scorpion is a pair to the serpent in Deut. 8.15, when Israel went through the desert where was the biting ὄφις καὶ σκόρπιος. Luke introduces scorpions as a pair to serpents again at 11.11f. The phrase ὁ ἐχθρός is unexampled for Satan in the NT apart from here (cf. Mt. 13.39), and is likely to come, along with the rest of the language on the subjection of the powers to Christ, from 1 Cor. 15.24–28 (see on v. 17). The idea of the Christian missionary's invulnerability to snakes is exemplified by Luke alone, in Acts 28.6.

10.20. Luke is an ever-watchful pastor, careful lest the young convert's head be turned by the divine powers so suddenly placed in his hands; he likes to stress the priority of spiritual values, often in a slightly pious way: 'Blessed rather are those who hear the word of God and keep it' (11.28), 'How much more will your Father from heaven give the holy spirit (not Matthew's 'good gifts') to those who ask him!'. So now the Seventy-two are not to rejoice that they have exorcistic authority, but that their names are written in heaven. The image of the book of life is a widespread one (Exod. 32.32; Deut. 9.14; etc.; Phil. 4.3; Heb.12.23; Rev. 3.5); the idea arises from Mt. 11.26=Lk. 10.21d, 'Yea, Father, for so was εὐδοκία before you'—the faith of the 'babes' does not arise from their superior openness, but from God's revelation (ἀπεκάλυψας), and his predestination (εὐδοκία). The formulation with 'your names. . .' is suggested by 'in your name' in v. 17; for the verbal form as congenial to Luke, and not requiring a pre-Lucan source, see below.

10.21f. With so much preamble, Luke is now ready for Jesus' thanksgiving for the 'babes', which he delivers practically word for word from Mt. 11.25–27. With the context of joy (χαρᾶς. . . χαίρετε), he prefaces so profound a prophetic statement with 'In that hour he rejoiced in the Holy Spirit'. The collocation of joy with the Spirit and with prophecy is a Lucan emphasis which we noted in 1.41–44; cf. 1.58, 67; Acts 2.46 and often. Matthew suggests the possibility of man knowing God: 'No one knows (ἐπιγινώσκει) the Father but the Son and he to whom the Son wills to reveal him'. Pauline Christians

thought claims to know God were dangerous (1 Cor. 13.12, 1 Jn. 4.8),
and Luke avoids the suggestion by substituting indirect questions, as
he does elsewhere, 'no one knows (γινώσκει) *who* the Son *is* but the
Father, and *who* the Father *is* but the Son. . .' The logia go well in
the Lucan context as a thanksgiving on the returning missionaries as
the 'babes'; but the force of much of the section is lost when it is
removed from the Matthaean setting. For in Matthew 11 'this
generation' is seen as rejecting the Baptist and Jesus alike; and 'this
generation' meant the Pharisees and Sadducees who had despised
John in Matthew 3, and the Pharisees who had attacked Jesus for
eating and drinking, and being the friend of sinners in Matthew 9. On
the other side, the toll-collectors and sinners of Mt. 11.19 had
accepted both John in Matthew 3 and Jesus in Mt. 4–9. So, as usual,
the context of the Thanksgiving in Q is the context in Matthew: the
'babes' are the sinners who have accepted the gospel, and the 'wise
and understanding' are the Pharisees, etc., who have refused it—both
parts are meaningful. Luke has narrowed the meaning of 'babes' to
his missionaries, and given no meaning to the 'wise', who are not
mentioned as rejecting the message in Lk. 10.17-20, even if he has
implied them in v. 16.

But not only has Matthew provided something very like the Q
context: he has apparently also (at the least) heavily overwritten the
Q logia before Luke saw them—heaven-and-earth (15/1/6), κρύπτειν
(7/0/3+0, 13.35R; 25.18,25QD), ναί (9/1/4, 9.28R; 21.16R), ὁ πατήρ
nominative for vocative, cf. 1.20; 9.27R; 15.22R; 20.30R, 31R,
ἔμπροσθεν (18/2/10+2, 26.70R; 27.11R, 29R), ὁ πατήρ μου (16/0/4,
often R). Note also the cliché pair wise-and-understanding, the
balanced antitheses of 11.25, 26, and the theology of the hiding
(13.35R, 33, 44) and revealing (16.17; 13.11, 16) of the gospel. Those
who defend Q have a Q apparently edited by Matthew.

10.23f. Matthew followed the Thanksgiving with the Comfortable
Words (11.28-30); but Luke has interpreted the 'babes' as the
Seventy-Two, and so general an invitation is not suitable for his
context. He wishes to round off so impressive a prayer with some
words on the same theme of God's revelation to the disciples, rather
than with a new approach to one and all; and there comes to mind
the similar theme from Mt. 13.16f., 'Blessed are your eyes, for they
see, and your ears for they hear. . .' These logia were Matthew's

expansion of the passage in Mark 4 on God's giving to the disciples to know the mystery of the kingdom, so they belong very well with his revealing of 'these things' to the νήπιοι. In Matthew they carry a controversial stress, 'But blessed are your eyes... ears...' in contradistinction to 'those without' who 'seeing do not see and hearing do not hear' (13.13). Luke can drop the ὑμῶν, and write 'Blessed are the eyes which see what you see', doubling the βλέποντες/βλέπουσιν as in Mt. 13.13; and he also drops 'and your ears for they hear', because his Seventy-Two have *seen* the demons made subject to them, and the power of the enemy rendered harmless, but have *heard* very little. However, by fatigue (§19.2) the hearing theme creeps back in the following verse with Matthew's 'and to hear what you hear, and heard not'. Matthew's prophets are very suitable, since Luke has himself referred to Elisha and Isaiah in the pericope; but he has also referred to David's prophecy of treading on snakes, so he substitutes 'kings' for Matthew's 'saints'.

At Mk. 6.31, the δεῦτε ... ἀναπαύσασθε logion was spoken κατ' ἰδίαν to the apostles, and Luke retains the phrase κατ' ἰδίαν in his opening (v. 23).

10.17 ὑποστρέφειν*, καί = also, δαιμόνιον, ὄνομα. The whole verse is usually allowed to be Lk.R: cf. Miyoshi, 96ff., taking ὑποτάσσεται as borrowed forward from v. 20, Schneider, Schweizer.

10.18 εἶπεν-δέ*. The logion is normally attributed to pre-Lucan tradition (Miyoshi, pp. 99ff., etc.); but Hoffmann (pp. 249-54) takes vv. 17-20 as a Lucan construction. The language is perfectly congenial to Luke, as well as the Satan theology: θεωρεῖν 2/7/7+14, lightning 17.24; 24.4; cf. 11.36; 9.29. The pre-Lucan hypothesis faces a dilemma. If the verse was not in Q (Manson, p. 258) was Luke not very fortunate to find another echo of Isaiah 14 to hand? If it was in Q, why did Matthew omit it?—cf. Marshall.

10.19 τοῦ + inf.*, pleon. πᾶς. Hapax: ἀδικεῖν (ἀδικία 0/0/4+2, ἄδικος 1/0/4+1). πατεῖν 21.24R; ἐπάνω 4.39R, 11.44QD. Miyoshi (pp. 101-107) argues to a Palestinian origin from the rabbinic association of serpents and scorpions; but this is congenial to Luke, 11.11f.QD, and Deut. 8.15 could be a text suggested by the Deuteronomic associations of the Journey (cf. 10.25). The link with Ps. 91 is not strong (Grelot, pp. 91f.).

10.20 πλήν*, τοῦτο... ὅτι*, χαίρειν (×2), ὄνομα. Hapax: ἐγγράφειν. With μὴ χαίρετε ὅτι... χαίρετε δὲ ὅτι, cf. 23.28 μὴ κλαίετε ἐπ' ἐμέ, πλὴν ἐφ' ἑαυτὰς κλαίετε, also 12.4f.QC, 12.29ff.QC. πνεύματα without an adj. = evil spirits is unique in Luke, and is likely to be an echo of 1 Cor. 14.32 πνεύματα προφητῶν προφήταις ὑποτάσσεται. A more serious objection to Lucan authorship is ἐν τοῖς οὐρανοῖς, pl., since Luke has a strong preference for the sing. But Paul similarly has (in Rom., 1 & 2 Cor., Gal., Phil., 1 Thess.) sing. × 8, pl. 2 Cor. 5.1 ἐν τοῖς οὐρανοῖς, Phil. 3.20 ἐν οὐρανοῖς, 1 Thess. 1.10 τῶν οὐρανῶν (note ἐν + dat. pl. = *baššāmayîm*); so also Lk. 18.22R; 12.33QD; cf. Acts 2.34; 7.56. The change to ἐν (τοῖς) οὐρανοῖς from Mark at 18.22 shows the phrase is not un-Lucan. Influence from Q=Lk. 12.33 (Schürmann, *TU*, p. 115) is guesswork: Mt. 6.20 (/Lk. 12.33) has θησαυροὺς ἐν οὐρανῷ=Mk 10.21. Hoffmann (pp. 253ff.) takes Luke's motive to be a subtle preparation of his own church for the time when the golden age is over (cf. 22.35ff.).

10.21 ἐν-αὐτῇ-τῇ-ὥρᾳ*, (εἶπεν), (ταῦτα), (γίνεσθαι). Hapaxes: ἀποκρύπτειν (to contrast with ἀποκαλύπτειν, and perhaps influenced by 1 Cor. 2.7-10, ἀποκεκρυμμένην... ἀπεκάλυψεν); (σοφός), (συνετός), (νήπιος). If ἐγένετο εὐδοκία is read, γ. normally precedes the predicate in Luke.

10.22 It is usually conceded that Luke's indirect questions are secondary, cf. 20.7R; 13.25QD, 27QD (Polag, Marshall); so the Lucan version is irrelevant to the great discussion of vv. 21f., which may be passed by.

10.23 στραφεὶς*-πρός, εἶπεν. Schmid (pp. 297f.), Schulz (p. 419), and many take the Lucan setting to be from Q—mainly on the sound ground that they can see how neatly the Mt. version is fitted into its context (Mt. 13.13). It is rarely considered that Matthew might have composed the verses to fit. Schulz allows every actual word of the introduction to be Lucan, even κατ' ἰδίαν. Miyoshi (pp. 132f.) is in two minds whether Luke may not have omitted Q/Mt.'s 'and your ears...' from his stress on revelation as vision.

10.24 Schmid (p. 299) and Schulz (p. 420) can see that δίκαιοι is Matthaean, and therefore take the Lucan 'kings' = Q; but Miyoshi is again cautious. Luke is keen on the Psalms (20.42R; 24.44) which he took to be written by David (20.42, etc.); and the Lucan context has just introduced an echo of Ps. 91. Matthew's ἐπεθύμησαν (hapax) may be influenced by a number of OT texts such as Amos 5.18, οἱ ἐπιθυμοῦντες τὴν ἡμέραν κυρίου;

Luke does not dislike ἐπιθυμεῖν (2/0/4+1), but he uses θέλειν much more often (28+14), and with ἰδεῖν at 8.20R and 23.8R.

Müller, U.B., 'Vision und Botschaft: Erwägungen zur prophetischen Struktur der Verkündigung Jesu', *ZTK* 74 (1977), pp. 416-48.
Grelot, P., 'Etude critique de Luc 10,19', *RSR* 69 (1981), pp. 87-100.
Sabbe, M., 'Can Mt. 11,25-27 and Lc 10,22 Be Called a Johannine Logion?', in J. Delobel (ed.), *Logia*, pp. 363-71.

37. *Jesus' Yoke*, 10.25–11.13

a. *Loving One's Neighbour*, 10.25-37

Matthew follows the Thanksgiving for the Babes with the great invitation, 'Come to me, all who labour... Take my yoke upon you... For my yoke is easy...' (11.28-30). Both the Thanksgiving and the Invitation are Christian versions of Ecclus. 51, which opens ἐξομολογήσομαί σοι κύριε, and continues, 'Draw near to me, you uninstructed... put your neck beneath the yoke... I laboured but a little and found for myself much ἀνάπαυσιν' (vv. 23-27). Jesus ben-Sirah makes no bones about the 'yoke' of wisdom which he is inviting the uninstructed to put on: it is the Torah, 'the book of the covenant of the Most High' (24.23). The yoke is similarly a symbol in many rabbinic writings for the Law (S-B, I, pp. 176f., 608-10, 'the yoke of the kingdom', 'the yoke of the Torah', 'the yoke of the command-ments'); and Billerbeck can say (I, p. 608), 'the expression "to take on oneself the yoke of the kingdom" often means virtually "to recite the Shema"'. However, Matthew is clearly intending to distinguish Jesus' 'yoke' ('my yoke') from the yoke of the Law as understood in Judaism; for he goes on to say that Jesus' burden is light, whereas the scribes and Pharisees bind heavy burdens on men (23.4). In part this distinction is clarified in the following pericopes in Matthew (12.1-14). For Matthew's 'rest for your souls' corresponds to the rabbinic *šbt npšw* (*Cant.R.* 2.2.3, S-B, I, p. 610), and he proceeds to two stories giving Jesus' teaching on sabbath/rest in contradistinction to the Pharisees—the Cornfield and the Withered Hand. Jesus had taken Hosea's line, that mercy (ἔλεος) was more important than sacrifice (12.7); and that a man should be helped even more than a sheep that had fallen (ἐμπέσῃ) into a pit (12.11).

'Yoke' was a common symbol for slavery (1 Tim. 6.1), and Paul had spoken of the law as 'a yoke of slavery' in contrast to Christian freedom (Gal. 5.1). Luke felt the same about the Christian Pharisees of Acts 15.10, 'tempting God to put a yoke on the neck of the disciples, which neither our fathers nor we were able to bear'. So he does not wish to represent the Lord's teaching as a yoke at all. But (as Miyoshi suggests, p. 123) the standard Jewish equivalent of the yoke of the kingdom and the Shema' was to hand. The joining of the two texts Deut. 6.4ff. and 11.13f. was justified by R. Joshua 'so that a man may first take upon him the yoke of the kingdom of heaven and afterward take upon him the yoke of the commandments' (*m.Ber*, 2.2). A bridegroom was exempt from reciting the Shema' on his first night, but Rabban Gamaliel recited it lest he 'cast off from himself the yoke of the kingdom of heaven even for a moment' (2.5). So Luke drops the 'yoke' symbol, and expounds the substance, Jesus' famous dispute with the tempting Pharisee on the Great Commandment, which he brings forward from Mt. 22.34ff./Mk 12.28ff.

10.25-28. The Shema' incident had been recorded by both Luke's predecessors. In Mark a friendly scribe (γραμματεύς) had asked Jesus which was the first commandment of all, and Jesus had replied linking Deut. 6.4f. with Lev. 19.18: the scribe is impressed and Jesus compliments him. Mark opens the Deuteronomy citation with 'Hear, O Israel. . . ', and keeps in the main to the LXX wording, including the repeated preposition ἐξ—'*from* your whole heart. . . '—though he has heart, soul, mind and strength for LXX's heart, soul and power. The friendliness is taken out of the story by Matthew. The Pharisees now gather, and one of them asks the question tempting him (πειράζων αὐτόν): Jesus replies with the same two citations, but Matthew drops the 'Hear, O Israel. . . ' introduction (omitting whatever is unnecessary, as usual), and in part assimilates the text to the Hebrew with the repeated ἐν (*b^e*) for ἐξ—'*with* your whole heart. . . ' for '*from*. . . '— and with the reduction of the notes to three again, heart and soul and mind (for Heb. *m^e'ōd*). The story ends there. The Pharisee is not impressed, and Jesus does not compliment him. After all, he was tempting the Lord, as Israel had been forbidden to do in Deuteronomy 6; by Matthew's day it was clear that friendly scribes had been a flash in the pan—they had usually tempted Jesus (16.1; 19.3; 22.18).

10.25. Luke has taken elements from both these accounts, and from the context in Deuteronomy 6; but he has also been influenced by the Matthew 12 stories in front of him. He takes over Mark's scribe, whom he renders by his customary νομικός. (For the reading νομικός at Mt. 22.35 see below.) His experience of scribes was invariably negative (11.45-54QD, etc.), so he adopts Matthew's 'tempting him', and Matthew's opening, deceitful διδάσκαλε. He uses ἐκπειράζων in piety to Deut. 6.16, 'οὐκ ἐκπειράσεις the Lord your God'. He reformulates the man's question, 'what shall I do to inherit (κληρονομήσω) eternal life (ζωήν)?', replacing the Jewish-theoretical interest with a Lucan, practical one—cf. 10.28 ποίει, 10.37 ποίει. He has the same wording in the mouth of the (Pharisaic) ruler at 18.18, where it is close to Mk 10.17, and the similarity of the two stories has no doubt had its effect.

10.26, 28. In both the earlier forms of the Shema' incident, and also in the Ruler story, it is Jesus who now cites scripture; but in Mt. 12.5 (a Matthaean addition) he asks, 'Or have you not read in the law. . .?' (ἢ οὐκ ἀνέγνωτε ἐν τῷ νόμῳ). So now Jesus asks the scribe similarly, 'What is written *in the law* (ἐν τῷ νόμῳ)? How do you *read* (ἀναγινώσκεις)?'; and this reversal of the position, with Jesus asking the question and the scribe answering, enables Luke to let down the guillotine as at 7.42ff. (§4.6). For there as here it was Jesus asking the question, 'Which of them will love him the more?', and when the inevitable answer is given, down comes the knife with ὁ δὲ εἶπεν αὐτῷ, ὀρθῶς ἔκρινας. Here the decapitation is nearly identical: εἶπεν δὲ αὐτῷ, ὀρθῶς ἀπεκρίθης. The same technique is used even more effectively with the parable following.

10.27. For the citation of Deut. 6.5 Luke wanders between his authorities. Like Matthew he drops 'Hear, O Israel. . .', but continues with his familiar LXX=Mk 'You shall love the Lord your God from (ἐξ) your whole heart'. His preposition then veers three times to Matthew's ἐν = Heb. He has Mark's four 'notes'—heart, soul, mind, strength—but reverses the order of the last two, so bringing διανοίᾳ to the end, as in Matthew. Deuteronomy has three notes in both Hebrew and Greek, as does Matthew. It seems a clear instance of mixed citation from memory.

The passage is a further crux for the standard position, and as so often divides its defenders. One option is to attribute it to L, whether on the basis that Jesus used the same material more than once (Manson, pp. 259f.; Marshall), or because the story is so different from Mk/Mt., as Schmid takes it (pp. 143-47, with echoes of other sources). But these echoes (see above) are persistent, and explanations of the deviant material are now widely taken back to Luke himself. K.L. Schmidt (pp. 281f.) already thought Luke had developed the version on the basis of Mark alone, and is now followed by H. Zimmermann (pp. 245-58) and Schneider. But the MAs seemed to Schmid to forbid this solution, and Schramm (pp. 47f.), Christoph Burchard (p. 43) and Gerhard Sellin (pp. 20-23) add a common non-Marcan source, which to Burchard and Sellin is Q. Schmid (p. 147) feels uncomfortable because the presence of νομικός in the standard texts of Mt. 22.34 would drive him to the conclusion that Luke was known to Matthew, which would destroy his whole book.

In fact, however, the MAs overall tell the other way. (1) νομικός· has been suspected at Mt. 22.34 by a long line of text-critics, including Streeter (p. 320), Hawkins (*OS*, p. 44), Burkitt (*JTS* 26 [OS], p. 283), and Kilpatrick (*JTS* [1950], pp. 56-60); and is now bracketed by N-A[26]. Metzger (p. 59) says, 'its absence from family 1 as well as from widely scattered versional (e syr[s] arm) and patristic (Orig.) witnesses takes on additional significance when. . . Matthew nowhere else uses the word', and thinks scribal introduction from Luke 'not unlikely'. We may further agree with Schmid that the phrase εἷς ἐξ αὐτῶν νομικός is 'remarkably overladen'. (2) There is not the least difficulty in expounding Mt. 22.34-40 as a redaction of Mark, as was done earlier by standard commentators like Allen and McNeile, and now with sophistication by Gundry (pp. 447ff.). (3) Of the nine words that are positive MAs, two groups of three are both characteristic of Matthew and uncharacteristic of Luke, and thus the cause of special difficulty for the standard view. (a) It is a regular feature of Matthew's citations that he may be influenced by the Heb. (or may take advantage of it): 8.17 and 21.5 are famous instances. There is no clear example of Luke's knowledge of the Heb., however. Since (with most editions) it seems proper to read ἐξ. . .ἐν. . .ἐν. . .ἐν. . . at Lk. 10.27, the natural explanation seems to be that Luke began with Mark= LXX, and was then influenced by memories of Matthew's redaction. (b) Mark never uses νόμος at all, and Luke almost always qualifies it ('of Moses', 'of the Lord' etc.). Matthew however likes the absolute use (5.18; 12.5R; 22.36R; 23.23), and uses the phrase ἐν τῷ νόμῳ at 12.5R as well as 22.36. It never recurs in L-A, despite 26 uses of νόμος.

10.25　νομικός*, τις + noun*. καὶ ἰδού 5.12R, 18R; 9.38R etc. ἐκπειράζειν also in citation of Deut. 6.16 at 4.12QC. τί ποιήσας. . .κληρονομήσω 18.18R; cf. Mk 10.17.

10.26　εἶπεν-πρός*, γράφειν. πῶς ἀναγινώσκεις; is difficult. Jeremias (*Theology*, I, p. 187) renders, 'How do you recite?'; but ἀναγινώσκειν means 'read', not recite from memory. Duncan Derrett (p. 224) appeals to *m.Ab.*

Zar. 2.5 for 'How do you expound?', but the words mean 'How do you vocalize?'. Derrett's translation is right, but Luke's Greek is strained, under influence of Mt. 12.5.

10.27 (ἀγαπᾶν), (ὁ-θεός), εἶπεν. Hapax: (ἰσχύς). For rabbinic interpretations of *m^e'ōd^ekā*, the third 'note' of the three in Heb. Shema', cf. Birger Gerhardsson, *NTS* (1968), pp. 167-69. Luke combines Deut. 6.5 and Lev. 19.18 into a single 'commandment' as is implied in his predecessors ('first', 'great').

10.28 εἶπεν-δέ*, ὀρθῶς, ζῆν. ὀρθῶς ἀπεκρίθης echoes Mk 12.34 νουνεχῶς ἀπεκρίθη. 'This do. . . ', cf. Lev. 18.5.

10.30-35. Luke has already told Matthew's two stories of the Cornfield and the Withered Hand (6.1-11). But the topic of the superiority of mercy to sacrifice (Mt. 12.7) is near to Luke's heart; and furthermore the same idea is adumbrated in Mark's form of the Shema' story—'to love one's neighbour as oneself is more than all whole-offerings and sacrifices' (Mk 12.33). So he takes these few hints in his own hands, and fashions them into one of the most memorable of his parables.

The contrast between the man who 'does mercy' and the priest and Levite is latent in Mt. 12.6f., where God prefers mercy to sacrifice, and something greater than the temple is here (cf. 12.5, ἱερεῖς); and the situation of the man who fell (περιέπεσεν, ἐμπεσόντος) among thieves is faintly suggested by Mt. 12.11f., 'What man is there of you who shall have one sheep, and if this fall (ἐμπέσῃ) into a ditch. . . How much more is a man worth than a sheep!' But the crucial feature is supplied by Luke himself. For whereas in all the Marcan and Matthaean parables the hero is a safe member of the upper class—a vineyard-owner, master of a house, estate owner, merchant, flock-owner, king, bridegroom, business-man, etc.—Luke alone has *heroes from the despised classes*, a publican, a beggar, a widow and a Samaritan (§4.7). Luke is sympathetic to *Samaritans*, whose lepers were more appreciative than Jewish lepers, and whose converts to the Gospel were so responsive (Acts 8.6ff.); their refusal of Jesus at 9.52ff. was in exposition of Mt. 10.5 (see above).

The point of the parable is thus a simple contrast, which should not be spoiled by over-interpretation. The man's need is dire. Two representatives of the Temple staff pass by on the other side because they do not have mercy on their neighbour: the man who does have mercy on him is a total outsider, a Samaritan. Luke does not press the point, which he has made perfectly clear. He does not say that they were going up to Jerusalem to sacrifice; indeed, the priest was going down. He does not say they feared defilement, or thought he might be dead: they just did not have mercy on him. He does not say that many priests lived at Jericho: he probably did not know that, and if he did, would also have known that they normally travelled together (cf. Jeremias, *Parables*, pp. 203f.). The mercy-and-not-sacrifice contrast is sufficiently made by the fact that both the heartless passers-by are Temple personnel. Levites are absent from the rest of the synoptic tradition: we may perhaps compare Luke's 'Joseph called Barnabas ( ) a Levite... a great multitude of the priests were obedient to the faith' (Acts 4.36; 6.7).

A parable—or illustration-story, to be precise—requires more plot than the hints in Matthew can provide, and Luke has probably drawn on 2 Chron. 28.1-15. There the Judaean army is defeated by its northern (Israelite) neighbours, and the latter bring home an enormous number of captives; only to be met at Samaria by the prophet Oded declaiming at their impiety. Certain of the leaders then 'rose and helped the captives, and all the naked they covered from the spoil and clothed them and shod them, and they gave them to eat and to anoint themselves and everyone hurt they set upon asses, and took them to Jericho, city of palms, with their brethren, and returned to Samaria' (v. 15 LXX). Although the vocabulary is different in Luke 10 (no γυμνούς, ἐπιχέων ἔλαιον for ἀλείψασθαι, κτῆνος for ὑποζυγίοις), the close general similarity, including the mention of Jericho and Samaria, makes the reference very probable (and widely accepted). The only question is the train of thought. I have suggested elsewhere (*EC*, p. 148) a link through the Elisha sequence, since 2 Chron. 28 is a reformulation of Elisha's call to feed the Syrian captives at Samaria in 2 Kgs 6. But Luke elsewhere draws in slightly random historical echoes—King Toi's embassy for peace in 14, Archelaus in 19—and it may be that the story came to his mind as an instance of Samaritans doing works of mercy to Jews. It is cited in *m.Sot.* 8.1 and Josephus *Ant.* 9.12.2. There is no similar use of a theme from the historical books in the parables of the other Gospels.

The Lucan nature of the parable may similarly be seen from the loving description of the *details* of the incident, so distinctive after the spare contrasts of the other Gospels. Thus only Lucan parables have names in them, Jerusalem, Jericho, Lazarus. Contrast Matthew, 'they took him and cast him out of the vineyard and killed him', with Luke, 'they stripped him and beat him and departed leaving him half dead'. Just as he pictures the violence, so does he paint in the colours of charity: the binding of the wounds, the application of oil and wine, the mounting of the wounded man in his own place on the animal, the inn, the further care on arrival, the payment in advance to the innkeeper, the open-ended undertaking of whatever further expense may be required. Such detailed imagining is not to be found outside Luke (§4.8).

Even more significant is the *positive emotion* underlying the story. The characters of Mark's and Matthew's parables are rather severe; in Matthew's case they may be angry, and the king of 18.27 is sorry for his servant (a unique instance), but only perhaps to highlight the contrasting anger of 18.34 (σπλαγχνισθείς. . .ὀργισθείς). Otherwise their feelings are opaque. But Luke's characters have red blood flowing through their veins. They are not only said to know joy and shame, cunning and anguish; but their behaviour exemplifies such feelings, and the conversations and soliloquies in the parables reveal a whole further spectrum of feelings—complacency, jealousy, humility, irritation, perseverance, etc. In Luke's Father and Two Sons, the father is not only said to be sorry for the prodigal (ἐσπλαγχνίσθη); his every word and action display his warm heart. And so here: the Samaritan was sorry for the man (ἐσπλαγχνίσθη), and his kindly feelings are shown in every detail which follows. It is this positive emotion, the sympathy and joy and responsiveness, this warm heart, which puts the Lucan parables, and especially the Samaritan and the Father and Sons, in a league of their own.

The Good Samaritan is Lucan in other important ways. It is an *illustration (Beispielerzählung)*, like the Rich Fool, or Dives and Lazarus, or the Publican and Pharisee; a type not found outside Luke (§7). It is a *response*-parable, with the practical conclusion an imperative laid squarely on the hearer, 'Go and do thou likewise'. In this it is unlike the Marcan and Matthaean parables of the activity of God, 'The kingdom of God/heaven is like. . .', the indicative parables concerned to teach the significance of Christ's preaching, or the sending and rejection of God's Son, or the imminence of his Return. It is Luke who tells parables that we should always pray and not faint, or beware of covetousness, or count the cost of discipleship. Christological interpretations of the Good Samaritan are pious eisegesis: it is an imperative, hortatory parable, addressed to 'us' (v. 37b, §8).

10.29, 36f. There are two further features of the parable's framing, which are characteristic of Luke. The closing question, 'Which of these three was neighbour...?' required both the exchange of v. 37 and a setting like vv. 25-28 in which the neighbour issue has been raised: it seems probable therefore that vv. 30-35 never existed independently of vv. 25-29, 36f. The final exchange will then be a further instance of a Lucan *guillotine*-question, where the interlocutor is driven to place his own head on the block, and Jesus can gently let down the knife. We had the same at 10.25-28, where it is the scribe who must cite the commandment, and Jesus can say, 'You have answered right. Do this, and you will live'. Even closer is the scene in 7.36-50, where Jesus tells a parable pointed at his Pharisee host, and ends with a question, 'Which of them then will love him the more?' The aristo mumbles the answer, and is duly despatched with, 'You have judged right'. So here, the parable already has the lawyer in his tumbril: 'which of these three...?' elicits from him the reluctant, 'He that did mercy with him', and Luke has his head in the basket with the charitable 'Go and do likewise'.

Much discussion, secondly, has been given to the tension between 'Who is my neighbour?' (sc. who should receive love), and 'Which of the three was neighbour...?' (sc. who gave love). It is too subtle, however, to read theological purpose into this (Sellin, pp. 23-32). It is a straightforward instance of Lucan *muddle* (§9); very similar to the crossing of wires in 7.36-50 between being forgiven the most and loving most, or the contradictory morals adduced from the Unrighteous Steward. Luke's genius is in the telling of stories. He lacks a clear head to satisfy our pedantries.

The parable is normally taken to be Sondergut (L). There has, however, been longstanding recognition that the style is Lucan. V.H. Stanton (*The Gospels as Historical Documents, Part I: The Synoptic Gospels*, p. 300) wrote in 1909, 'The structure of the sentences and the vocabulary in this parable justify us in attributing it, so far as its literary form is concerned, to our evangelist'. Sparks (*JTS* [1943], p. 137) goes further, on sheerly linguistic grounds: 'St Luke is writing the story which he has to tell in his own words... At all events this seems more plausible than the suggestion that he found in L a story already complete, which he then proceeded, not only to septuagintalize, but also to classicize, into exact conformity with his literary style in Acts'. In a long article (*ZNW* [1974], pp. 166-89, [1975] pp. 19-60), Sellin argues for Lucan authorship on a broader base, though he is sceptical of the influence of 2 Chron. 28. Drury (*Parables*, pp. 132-36) sees Luke as the author, contributing the new point that Luke tends to parables 'on the road', cf. Friend, Prodigal. Derrett (*Law*, pp. 208-27) takes the parable to be a midrash on Hos. 6.6 and 2 Chron. 28.15 (etc.); but OT texts cannot take us all the way.

But so treasured a parable is not easily surrendered from being Jesus' own. Even Bo Reicke (*Fs* Stählin), who sees the oil and wine as recalling the sacraments (note the order!), and the Samaritan's return as an echo of the Parousia, denies that it is any forgery of the community: it was Jesus' own intelligent foresight. Jeremias, with his invalid linguistic criteria (see pp. 80-88), has clouded the discussion over the language (*Sprache*, pp. 191ff.): he even attributes ἄνθρωπός τις to 'Trad'. In *Parables* (pp. 202-205) he stresses the lifelike features of the tale, and simply assumes that these go back to Jesus; and this is carried on into modern commentaries like Schneider and Fitzmyer, who pay no attention to the insistently Lucan style of the story (illustration-story, response-parable, sub-culture hero, colourful detail, muddled conclusion, guillotine question, philo-Samaritan sympathies, positive emotions), while citing some of these features themselves! But not only is the language substantially Luke's own: the stylistic features which I have just listed make up the very stuff of the parable. If we took them away, there would be nothing left. Since these features are virtually unparalleled in the other Gospels, the most straightforward view must be to attribute the parable to Luke. But it is not his creation *ex nihilo*: the added (non-Marcan) features in the next Matthaean pericope, Mt. 11.28-12.14, were there to provide the grit for his pearl.

10.29 δικαιοῦν*, ἑαυτόν, εἶπεν-πρός*. πλήσιον anarthrous as predicate recurs at v. 36.

10.30 εἶπεν, ἄνθρωπός-τις*, Ἰερουσαλημ*, καί = also. Hapaxes: περιπίπτειν (Acts 27.31, also of peril), ἐκδύειν (Gen. 37.23 of Joseph, whose situation is similar; often in LXX), ἡμιθανής (*4 Macc.* 4.11). ἄνθρωπός-τις is a favourite and exclusively Lucan opening to a parable: 12.16; 14.16; 15.11; 16.1, 19; 19.12. πληγὰς ἐπιθέντες Acts 16.23, cf. Lk. 12.48. ὑπολαμβάνειν = answer ×22 Job LXX.

10.31 κατά + acc., τις + noun*. Hapax: συγκυρία. ἀντιπαρῆλθεν, double preposition with ἀντι- 0/0/6.

10.32 ὁμοίως*, δὲ-καί*, κατά + acc., τόπος, γίνεσθαι. Hapax: Λευίτης (Acts 4.36). Repeats the substance of v. 31, but with only three words in common: cf. 14.18-20; 19.16-19; contrast Mt. 25.20-23. N-A²⁶ reads [γενόμενος].

10.33 Σαμαρίτης, τις + noun*, κατά + acc. Hapax: ὁδεύειν (συν- ×1 Acts, δι- ×1 +1 Acts).

10.34 ἄγειν. Hapaxes: καταδέειν, τραῦμα (together Sir. 27.21), ἐπιχεῖν (+ oil, Gen. 28.18 and often in LXX—hence oil before wine), κτῆνος (+ ἐπιβιβάσας Acts 23.24), πανδοχεῖον. ἐπιβιβάζειν 19.35R, ἴδιος 18.28R; 6.41QD. ἐπιμελεῖσθαι αὐτοῦ Gen. 44.21 (Joseph). Sellin denies the use of 2 Chron. 28, which is not essential to explaining the story: there is a similar volume of colourful detail in 15.11-32.

10.35 ἐπί + acc. of time, εἶπεν, ἐν-τῷ + inf.*. Hapaxes: πανδοχεύς, προσδαπανᾶν (cf. δαπανᾶν 15.14; Acts 21.24). ἐπὶ τὴν αὔριον Acts 4.5. ἐκβάλλειν = take out, 6.42, etc. Two denaria are Lucan money-levels, §5. ἐν τῷ ἐπανέρχεσθαί με cf. 19.15 ἐν τῷ ἐπανελθεῖν αὐτόν.

10.36 γίνεσθαι. τούτων τῶν τριῶν cf. Acts 1.24 τούτων τῶν δύο. τίς ... δοκεῖ σοι γεγονέναι, cf. 22.24R, τίς αὐτῶν δοκεῖ εἶναι μείζων.

10.37 εἶπεν, (ἔλεος), εἶπεν-δέ*, πορεύεσθαι, ποιεῖν + adv., ὁμοίως*. ποιῆσαι ἔλεος μετά 1.72; cf. 1.58, often in LXX. πορεύου 7.50; 8.48R.

Sparks, H.F.D., 'The Semitisms of St Luke's Gospel', *JTS* (os) 44 (1943), pp. 129-38.

Kilpatrick, G.D., 'Scribes, Lawyers and Lucan Origins', *JTS* (ns) 1 (1950), pp. 56-60.

Gerhardsson, B., 'The Parable of the Sower and its Interpretation', *NTS* 14 (1968), pp. 165-93.

Reicke, B., 'Der barmherzige Samariter', in *Fs* Stählin (1970), pp. 103-109

Derrett, J.D.M., 'The Parable of the Good Samaritan', in *Law in the New Testament* (London, 1970), pp. 208-27.

Burchard, C., 'Das doppelte Liebesgebot in der frühen christlichen Überlieferung', in E. Lohse *et al.* (eds.), *Der Ruf Jesu* (1970), pp. 39-62.

Zimmermann, H., 'Das Gleichnis vom barmherzigen Samariter', in *Fs* Schlier (1970), pp. 58-69.

Sellin, G., 'Lucas als Gleichniserzähler', *ZNW* 65 (1974), pp. 166-89, 66 (1975), pp. 19-60.

b. *Martha and Mary*, 10.38-42

There were two parts to the Commandment which leads to life: the love of our neighbour, which Luke has now expounded so eloquently, and the love of the Lord our God. Luke abbreviated the full Marcan, Deuteronomic form of the commandment, omitting 'Hear (ἄκουε), O Israel, the Lord our God is one Lord. . .'; and he makes use of this now, aided by the suggestion of his basic Matthaean text, 11.28-30, which has the same emphasis on hearing. For the great Invitation was to all who were labouring and weighed down, that they should put aside their burdens and come to Christ and learn from him; for there they would find rest for their souls, where the yoke is easy and the burden light.

Luke composed a *Beispielerzählung*, an illustrative parable, for the second commandment, and he needs a *Beispielerzählung*, an illustrative story, for the first. He has just told the tale of a merciful man, and would like to pair it with the tale of a devout woman; just as he pairs the woman and her lost drachma with the man and his lost sheep, or the penitent whore of 7.36-50 with the penitent toll-collectors and (male) sinners of 7.34f., or Mary with Zechariah. He requires, for full effect, the same basic dynamic of contrast: just as the priest and Levite passed by on the other side, as against the Samaritan who was moved, so now he wants a woman who is labouring and weighed down with her burdens to set against a woman who has come to Jesus and is learning from him the way of the easy yoke.

Luke's familiarity with 1 Corinthians (see ch. 4) enables him to fill in his picture with Pauline colours. 'I want you to be without anxiety (ἀμερίμνους)', the apostle had written, 'The unmarried man cares for the things of the Lord (μεριμνᾷ τὰ τοῦ κυρίου)... but the married man cares for the things of the world (μεριμνᾷ τὰ τοῦ κόσμου)... and is divided (μεμέρισται). And the woman who is unmarried, and the unmarried girl, cares for the things of the Lord (μεριμνᾷ τὰ τοῦ κυρίου), that she may be holy in body and spirit; but the married woman cares (μεριμνᾷ) for the things of the world. I say this for your own advantage, not to lay any restraint on you, but for seemliness and devotion (εὐπάρεδρον) to the Lord without encumbrance (ἀπερισπάστως)' (vv. 32-35). There then is his contrast, provided; and Luke shows elsewhere (14.26QD; 18.29R) how thoroughly he has taken over his master's suspicion of marriage. He pictures Mary as sitting alongside (παρακαθεσθεῖσα) at the Lord's feet, echoing Paul's εὐπάρεδρον τῷ κυρίῳ (Lit. 'a good attendant', 'seated well alongside'). She is hearing (ἤκουεν) his word, and he is spoken of three times as 'the Lord'—'at the feet of the Lord', 'Lord, do you not care?', 'the Lord answered'—echoing 'Hear, O Israel, the Lord...' She has chosen the good μερίς, which will be hers for ever. She is thought of as an unmarried woman, living in her sister's house. Martha is seen as married, or a widow, since she 'receives' Jesus (whether or not we should read in addition 'into her house'). She is cumbered about (περιεσπᾶτο) with a lot of cooking; she is anxious (μεριμνᾷ) and fretted about the things of the world—a big meal, appreciation, resentment at her sister's failure to help. But a few things would have been enough: Jesus' burden is light—or even one, for what matters is learning of him, like Mary, to be holy in body and spirit.

Did Luke have a tradition about the two sisters, or is the tale just an 'ideal scene' (Bultmann, pp. 33, 56f.)? Commentators commonly appeal to John 11f. (12.2, 'Martha was serving'), supposing a lost Lucan-Johannine source to underlie both. But it is impossible to feel any confidence in such argument. Evidence of John's general familiarity with Lucan redaction (Neirynck, *Evangelica*, pp. 335-488) puts the whole lost source in doubt; and there are wide differences in the location (Bethany, Galilee), and no suggestion in Luke that Mary was the sinner of Luke 7. The closeness of the theme to the Invitation in Mt. 11.28ff., and to the Shema', both being passages in Luke's mind, and the closeness of the language to 1 Cor. 7.32-35, including the rare word περισπᾶσθαι, strongly suggest Lucan creativity. We may notice also the parallel to the two brothers in Lk. 12.13, 'Teacher, εἰπὲ τῷ ἀδελφῷ μου to divide the inheritance with me'— the same sibling rivalry, the same appeal to Jesus to give his authority to convention, the same summons to a higher level of the spirit, the same Gospel. Also noticeable is the doubled address, 'Martha, Martha'; we may compare 'Simon, Simon' (22.31), 'Master, master' (8.24R), 'Saul, Saul'. We do not find named characters, with rare exceptions, in the earlier Gospels. Martha and Mary make a happy pair by assonance, like Jerusalem and Jericho in the previous pericope. Perhaps Luke, who was interested in the meaning of Aramaic names (Barnabas, Tabitha), knew that Martha meant 'mistress'; and Mary might seem to him a suitable name for a devout Christian virgin girl. Her place at Jesus' feet seems in line with Luke's thinking also (7.38).

10.38   ἐν-τῷ + inf.*, πορεύεσθαι, αὐτός nom., τις + noun* (x2), ὀνόματι*. ὑποδέχεσθαι 19.6; Acts 17.7, Luke only. N-A[26] prefers the short text (p[45] p[75] B sa) without 'into her house'; εἰς τὸν οἶκον with gen. (Diglot, Greeven, ADW Θ fam. 1, 13, etc.) would be in Luke's style. Martha may have been a widow (Gen. 24.28; 1 Kgs 17.17), or just a married woman (1 Sam. 25.35; 2 Kgs 4.8): unmarried women in charge of a house are a rarity.

10.39 καλούμενος*, καί = also, πούς, ὁ-κύριος = Jesus*. Hapaxes: παρακαθέζεσθαι (καθέζεσθαι 2.46, ×2 Acts ×1 Mt.: Lucan double compound); ὅδε (Acts 21.11).

10.40 ἐφιστάναι*, εἰπεῖν (×2). Hapaxes: περισπᾶσθαι (cf. 1 Cor. 7.35), μέλει (cf. Mk 4.38, οὐ μέλει σοι ὅτι. . .; Acts 18.17), συναντιλαμβάνεσθαι (doubled συν- compounds 2/4/6+10; ἀντιλαμβάνεσθαι 1.54, Acts 20.35 only). Marshall notes 'the recurrence of the same motif' in 1 Cor. 7.35; but the cluster of echoes shows it is not coincidence. διακονία. . .χρεία cf. Acts 6.1-3, where Luke also prefers spiritual to physical service.

10.41 εἶπεν, ὁ-κύριος = Jesus*. Hapax: θορυβάζεσθαι.

10.42 ἐκλέγεσθαι*, ἥτις*, ἀφαιρεῖν*. Hapax: μερίς (Acts 8.21; 16.12 only). The textual crux is notorious. G.D. Fee (Metzger *Fs*, pp. 61-75) seems to offer the best solution, preferring the long text ὀλίγων δέ ἐστιν χρεία ἥ ἑνός. This was known to Origen; and the explanation of it as a conflation in unlikely since testimony to ὀλίγων alone is so weak (38 syr[pal] arm geo). ἑνός alone (p[45]p[75]C*WΘvg Syr[cp]Bas.) is difficult in view of γάρ following. We are left with 'A few (things to eat) are necessary or one (spiritual meal); for Mary. . .', with p[3] ℵ BL fam 1 33 bo. With πολλά/ὀλίγων cf. 12.47f.; 10.2QC; 7.47; 13.22f.QD.

Laland, E., 'Die Martha-Maria-Perikope Lukas 10,38-42', *ST* 13 (1959), pp. 70-85
Baker, A., 'One Thing Necessary', *CBQ* 27 (1965), pp. 127-37
Fee, G.D., ' "One thing is needful"? Luke 10:42', in E.J. Epp and G.D. Fee (eds.), *New Testament Textual Criticism* (*Fs* B. Metzger; Oxford 1981).

c. *Prayer*, 11.1-13

So Jesus' easy yoke consists in part in the commandment to love, and in part in hearing the Lord's word; but there is also a third element. For when in Mt. 11.25 Jesus had prayed, πάτερ . . ., he had bidden his followers, 'Learn of me', and had promised them, 'You shall find (εὑρήσετε) rest for your souls'. Here then is place for the disciples to learn Jesus' fuller form of the πάτερ Prayer from the Sermon on the Mount; to which Luke provides one of his lead-in requests. Not much later Matthew's Sermon provides further teaching on Prayer with 'Ask and you will receive,seek and you will find (εὑρήσετε). . .' (Mt. 7.7); so it is clearly suitable to include that in the present context too. To stress and amplify the teaching of the latter section Luke extrapolates a short illustration-parable of his own, the Friend at Midnight.

11.1-2a. Matthew had set the Lord's Prayer in the course of a general instruction on almsgiving, prayer and fasting, each section opening with a ὅταν clause: ὅταν οὖν ποιῇς ἐλεημοσύνην... καὶ ὅταν προσεύχησθε... ὅταν δὲ νηστεύητε (6.2, 5, 16). Luke takes on the formula, ὅταν προσεύχησθε, which suggests a set-piece instruction, and, as often, supplies a suitable setting, with a question or request to touch it off—cf. 'Teacher, bid my brother...', 'Lord, increase our faithfulness' (§1.4). As the instruction here is to be about prayer, it is suitable that Jesus should be discovered praying—itself a theme Luke is not reluctant to push. But the evangelist is not so sure about special requests on prayer, so he justifies the disciple's remark with, 'as John also taught his disciples'. Lk. 5.33 also referred to John's disciples 'making prayers' (Lk.R), and his understanding of the Baptist's vocation as 'going before' Jesus in so many other ways may have suggested this also.

11.2b-4. Matthew had created the Lord's Prayer himself: partly from Jesus' teaching on prayer in Mark 11, 'When you stand praying, *forgive* if you have anything against anyone, that *your Father who is in heaven* may *forgive you your* trespasses' (cf. Mt. 6.14f.); and principally from Jesus' own prayer in Gethsemane, 'My *Father*,... *thy will be done*', and his words to the disciples, 'Watch and pray that *you enter not into temptation*'. He had amplified this from the Commandments ('the *name* of the Lord... Remember that thou *hallow*...'), the manna story (bread for the day ahead), and other ideas congenial to him; and set out the whole in marked Matthaean language, and in beautiful Matthaean rhythms—three single parallel petitions concerned with God, followed by three double petitions concerned with ourselves. I expounded this proposal in *JTS* (1963), and wish only marginally to amend it.

Luke dislikes Matthew's wordy 'Our Father who art in heaven', which he never has, and which might well seem to him an instance of the πολυλογία against which Mt. 6.7 so wisely warns. At 22.42 he replaces Mark's ἀββᾶ ὁ πατήρ/Matthew's πάτερ μου with plain πάτερ, and has the plain vocative twice again on Jesus' lips in the Passion—'πάτερ, forgive them...', 'πάτερ, into thy hands...'—as well as three times on the Prodigal's (15.12, 18, 21), and at 10.21 = Mt. 11.25, on which he is drawing directly. With figures of 1/0/8, and Luke's further use of plain ἀδελφέ (6.42R) and plain τεκνόν (2.48; 15.31; 16.25, 0/0/3), it may be thought characteristic.

In Exodus God had rained bread on the Israelites τὸ τῆς ἡμέρας εἰς ἡμέραν (16.4), and Matthew had written τὸν ἄρτον ἡμῶν τὸν ἐπιούσιον δὸς ἡμῖν σήμερον: but to Luke the Christian life had a day-by-day character. He adds καθ' ἡμέραν to Mark's taking up the cross at 9.23, and he puts '...δίδου ἡμῖν τὸ καθ' ἡμέραν' here. He has τὸ καθ' ἡμέραν at 19.47R, and (without τό) at Acts 17.11.

Matthew had written ἄφες ἡμῖν τὰ ὀφειλήματα ἡμῶν, and although Luke is familiar with the Semitic sin=debt (7.41ff.; 13.4), his preference is for the straightforward forgiveness of sins (ἄφεσις ἁμαρτιῶν, 1/1/3+5, in many ways the core of his message—24.47); Matthew's debts still shine through in his ὀφείλοντι. Luke changes Matthew's ὡς καὶ ἡμεῖς ἀφήκαμεν to καὶ γὰρ αὐτοὶ ἀφίομεν, to avoid the suggestion of *quid pro quo*: καὶ γάρ is Lucan (2/2/8; 6.32QD, 33QD, 34QD), as is αὐτός nom.; and πᾶς with anarthrous participle recurs at 6.30QD, 40QD.

Thus all the Lucan variations of language can be (and most commonly are) accounted for as Luke's changes. It is not so easy to be confident of motives for omission, in the nature of the case. He leaves out γενηθήτω τὸ θέλημά σου... Elsewhere he uses similar expressions not so much as prayers but rather as bowing before the divine fiat—'not my will but thine be done' (22.42), 'The Lord's will be done' (Acts 21.14). Since the attitude to prayer he wishes to commend is that of one knocking without shame on the gates of heaven despite early disappointments, it is not surprising that he drops this hint of fatalism. He leaves out 'and deliver us from the evil one'; and this has the effect of linking 'And forgive us our sins' to 'and bring us not into temptation', with '(for we forgive our every debtor)' as a parenthesis between. Luke is rather liable to phrases of the form 'this-and-not-that'—'always to pray and not to faint', 'bent and not able to stand', 'silent and not able to speak' (1.20; 12.21; 13.11, 14; 18.1, 16Mk). So he is quite likely to have bracketed sin and temptation together with Matthew's καὶ μή, and left out the last line as overweight.

In this way, he ends with a sparer Prayer than Matthew's. His address is more intimate. He has two balanced petitions concerned with God, looking forward to the authentic Christian hope, the Kingdom, without any 'It is the will of Allah'. He has two quite unbalanced petitions concerned with ourselves: one for our physical needs, the bread for each day ahead; and one for our spiritual needs, the forgiveness and the prevention of our sins. He has avoided Matthew's rhetorical vacuity—but then he has lost the roundedness of his poetic periods, and so the hope of liturgical immortalization. He proceeds, in the rest of the present paragraph, to an expansion of the last two themes: God's provision for the body (ἄρτος), and the soul (πνεῦμα ἅγιον). In the following, Beelzebul pericope, he will speak of the coming of God's kingdom (11.20).

11.5-8. A little further on, Matthew had continued with the topic of prayer, 'Ask and it shall be given you...'; reinforcing our expectations of divine bounty with the comparison of the man (τίς ἐστιν ἐξ ὑμῶν ἄνθρωπος...;) whose son asks him for bread (ἄρτον) and he will give it him (7.7-11). Luke moves to draw the section in; but, as elsewhere (§10), he develops a part of the coming passage into an introductory parable. We have an exact analogue in the development of the Rich Fool, with his barns, and his gathering of his corn, and his care for his soul, and his laying up treasure for himself, out of the following 'Be not anxious for your soul...' discourse. So here he tells a parable beginning τίς ἐξ ὑμῶν...; and concerned with a man who comes asking for three loaves (ἄρτους), and ending, 'He will give him'. The knocking of Mt. 7.7 also suggests that the man is asleep at night, and this Luke duly takes up.

The little story is Lucan in several ways. It is a *response*-parable, told to urge the Christian to action, an imperative parable, unlike the mainly indicative parables of the earlier tradition (§8). It is told, specifically, to encourage Christians to *pray* (αἰτεῖτε), a topic close to Luke's heart. There is only one other parable in the Gospel tradition to the same end, that we 'should always pray and not faint', and that is also in Luke (18.1-8). It is a story about *friends* (φίλοι), like Luke's form of the Lost Sheep (15.6QD), or the Lucan Lost Coin (15.9), or Two Sons (15.29), or Steward (16.9). In fact, so keen is he on the friendship of all concerned that the story is in peril of becoming a *muddle* (§9): for everybody in the tale is called φίλος, with the borrower having a friend, and saying to him, Friend, a friend of mine...- but he will not get his request because he is the sleeper's friend! We may note also, 'Which of you will have a friend... and say to him, Friend...': compare the Lucan hypocrites who say to their brother, Brother (6.42R), or the Lucan son who says to his father, Father (15.12, 18). It is Luke too who can pierce the heart of the *weak excuser* with his οὐ δύναμαι: '*I cannot* rise and give you' echoes the Lucan 'I have married a wife and therefore I cannot come' (14.20QD), and 'I cannot dig' (16.3) (§4.5). Not only is the topic of the parable similar to the Unjust Judge, being perseverance in prayer, but the likeness extends to other features besides. For in both cases God is not compared to an august and honoured figure, like the owners and kings and merchants of Mark and Matthew, but to *a dishonourable figure*—a lazy man full of excuses, in one case, reluctant to get up and enable his friend to fulfil the elementary duties of hospitality; and in the other a corrupt and ungodly judge, who will not give a poor widow her due. There are no other parables like this in the Gospel tradition, but we have a parallel *quanto potius* story in the Unjust Steward, also in Luke; and it is Luke who has other disreputable human heroes to his parables too, like beggars, publicans and Samaritans (§4.7). The phrasing of the two parables is also similar. 'Do not bother me (μή μοι κόπους πάρεχε)', says the sleeper: 'because this widow bothers me (παρέχειν μοι κόπον)', says the judge. 'Though he will not rise and give him because he is his friend, yet because of his shamelessness. . .' (εἰ καί. . .διά γε. . .): 'though I fear not God. . . yet because this widow. . .' (εἰ καί. . .διά γε. . .). παρέχειν and γέ are both Lucan words.

The only point at which the Lucan mode of the parable has been challenged is its *scale*: for Luke has in general a middle-class level for his stories (§5), not so grand as Matthew, but not poor. Here Jeremias, *Parables*, (pp. 157f.) has popularized a romantic background: 'a Palestinian village. . . there are no shops. . . it is generally known who has still got some bread left in the evening. . . a single-roomed peasant's house, in which the whole family slept on a mat'. There is no evidence for any of this! κοίτη is a normal Greek word for a bed, and Luke thought of beds as comfortable middle-class affairs on posts, that you could put a light under (8.16). The man goes to his friend because he has more right to call on a friend at midnight than a shopkeeper. There is no reason for thinking that he is poor, or for that matter Palestinian.

11.9-13. The way is now clear for Matthew's 'Ask and you will receive' passage, which Luke reproduces nearly word for word. He adds the introductory, 'And I say to you', just as he does at 16.9, turning from a parable to its exposition. The stress to Luke falls on the asking and knocking, as he has just emphasized that in the parable. He adds two clumsy clarifications to v. 11, 'Which of you *the father* will the son ask for a fish, and he *for a fish* will give him a snake?'; but then Luke is clumsy with Mark too (§ 19.1). Matthew had the two staples of Palestinian diet in his form of the double logion, bread and fish, as in the feeding of the thousands. He paralleled the flat, round, satisfying loaf with the flat, round, inedible stone, as in 4.3; and the long, thin, slippery, nutritious fish with the long, thin, slippery, lethal snake. Luke has already used up the asking for, and giving of bread in his parable. So he promotes the fish/snake logion to first position, and supplies one of his own for the second. He has already bracketed snakes and scorpions (10.19), so he supplies the scorpion here too, as the second deadly menace, and the similarly shaped and sized egg as its proteinous counterpart.

11.13. Matthew closes the section, 'How much more will your Father in heaven give good things to those who ask him!' Luke nowhere has Matthew's your-Father-in-heaven, but he comes closer here than anywhere else with 'the Father from heaven', another clumsiness, since God is not 'from heaven', and it is difficult to supply 'who (gives gifts)' with Marshall, or to give parallels for ἐξ = ἐν (BDF, p. 437). He also interprets Matthew's 'good things' in a spiritual sense as 'holy Spirit'. His Lord's Prayer began 'Father', and prayed for our daily bread, and a remedy for sin: he closes the section with a parable of God's giving bread, and an assurance of his giving 'holy Spirit', to those who pray.

Much of the Lord's Prayer is close to petitions in contemporary Jewish liturgy, but Matthew's Greek is so rooted in his Semitic thinking that claims of translation from Aramaic (Black, pp. 193ff., 203, Jeremias, *Abba*, p. 160) or Hebrew (Jean Carmignac, pp. 29-52) are unnecessary for his version, and other explanations are available for Luke. If Jesus taught the Prayer, it is hard to explain why Mark omitted it, especially with the context of 11.25 available. It is normal to attribute the present forms to Q, in view of the unique ἐπιούσιος (Ott, pp. 112-23; Jeremias, *ibid.*; Schulz, pp. 84ff., Polag, p. 48), with the Matthaean address and all the extra Matthaean phrases as added by Matthew: the Q version thus was Lucan in form, including Luke's πάτερ, but all the other Lucan differences due to Luke (Schulz). But πάτερ is characteristic of Luke too! Cf. p. 17 for *embarras de richesses*.

The similarities between the Friend and the Unjust Judge have given rise to speculations about their previous history (Wellhausen; Jeremias, pp. 90-94; Ott, pp. 25-29). Schürmann suggested that the Friend was in Q, seeing an echo of Luke's ὅσων χρῄζει in Mt. 6.8 ὧν χρείαν ἔχετε (*Untersuchungen*, p. 119); but the reverse is just as likely. Cf. Catchpole similarly, *JTS* (1983). The general fault here, as with Kenneth Bailey (pp. 119-33), is the failure to notice so many parallel features elsewhere in Luke only.

Polag prints the Matthaean form of Lk. 11.9-13, except for (a) an introductory λέγω ὑμῖν, (b) Matthew's introductory ἤ, which is dropped from 7.9, and (c) Luke's 'the Father from heaven' (so Schulz, pp. 161f.). It is just assumed that Matthew cannot have written his version earlier, including some of his own locutions, which Luke then avoided.

11.1 καὶ-ἐγένετο-ἐν-τῷ-εἶναι-αὐτόν*, τόπος, τις + noun*, ὡς = when*, παύεσθαι, εἶπεν-πρός*, τις, καθώς, καί = also. Schulz, 84, allows the setting to be Luke's creation; cp. Marshall.

11.2 εἶπεν-δέ*, πάτερ*, (ὄνομα). Hapax: (ἁγιάζεσθαι).

11.3 τὸ + prep*, καθ' ἡμέραν. Hapax: (ἐπιούσιος).

11.4 ἁμαρτία, καὶ-γάρ, αὐτός nom., (πειρασμός).

11.5 εἶπεν-πρός*, ἔχειν at the beginning of a parable*, φίλος ×2*, πορεύεσθαι, εἶπεν. Hapax: μεσονύκτιον (Acts 16.25; 20.7), χρᾶν. The τίς ἐξ ὑμῶν opening is taken over from Mt. 7.9, where it also leads to syntactical trouble: the sentence here drifts on to v. 7, and into the subjunctive. Note Luke's colourful specificity (§4.8): midnight, *three* loaves.

11.6 φίλος*, παραγίνεσθαι*, οὐκ-ἔχω + noun clause. ἐπειδή 7.4R, ×3 Acts. παρατιθέναι as in 10.8QD. It is often said that night-time journeys were common to avoid the heat, but the only NT night-time journeys cited are those of the Magi, and of Paul in Acts 23.31, which are untypical.

11.7 εἶπον, παρέχειν*, ἀναστάς. Hapax: κοίτη. κἀκεῖνος 3/2/4+3 (22.12R), ἔσωθεν 11.39f.Q, ἡ θύρα κέκλεισται Acts 21.30; cf. Lk. 13.25. ἤδη = already—the day's business is now done.

11.8 ἀναστάς*, διὰ-τὸ + inf., εἶναι after prep.*, φίλος*, γε*. Hapax: ἀναίδεια. The best meaning is 'because of his (the borrower's) unashamed persistence' (most commentators), rather than Anton Fridrichsen's view that it is the lender's shamelessness which will come to light (cf. Jeremias, p. 158; Bailey, pp. 129-33). ὅσων, cf. ὅς in attraction.

11.9 (ζητεῖν, εὑρίσκειν).

11.10 (ζητεῖν, εὑρίσκειν).

11.11 (μή interrogative).

11.12 (καὶ = also, μή interrogative). Hapax: ᾠόν.

11.13 ὑπάρχειν*, πνεῦμα-ἅγιον.

Goulder, M.D., 'The Composition of the Lord's Prayer', *JTS* (ns) 14 (1963), pp. 32-45.
Jeremias, J., *Abba* (Göttingen, 1966).
Carmignac, J., *Recherches sur le 'Notre Père'* (Paris, 1969)
Berger, K.,'Materialen zu Form und Überlieferungsgeschichte neutestamentlicher Gleichnissen', *NT* 15 (1973), pp. 1-37.
Edmonds, P., 'The Lucan Our Father: A Summary of Luke's Teaching on Prayer?' *ET* 91 (1979), pp. 140-43.
Delebecque, E., 'Sur un hellénisme', *RB* 87 (1980), pp. 590-93
Bandstra, A.J., 'The Original Form of the Lord's Prayer', *Calvin Th.J.* 16 (1981), pp. 15-37.

38. *Controversies*, 11.14-54

a. *Beelzebul*, 11.14-26

Luke has now completed his own version of the topic 'Jesus' Yoke'; the idea came from Mt. 11.28-30, and some of the imagery from the priesthood/mercy-and-sacrifice matter in Mt. 12.5-7, though the greater part of the material was brought from far. But the Cornfield and the Withered Hand in Mt. 12.1-16 (21) have already been covered by Luke in his Marcan section (Lk. 6.1-19), and he moves on now to the next Matthaean pericope, the Beelzebul controversy (12.22-45). This is one of the very few Marcan pieces which Luke has taken in the Matthaean order, and from the Matthaean version: the principal reasons for which he does this are obvious—Matthew's version is so much more full and interesting, for once, and it describes the healing, which Mark does not.

There are, however, some complications. When Matthew was writing his initial section on Jesus' healings (Mt. 8.1-9.34), he included what looks like a kind of brief, anticipatory account in the Dumb Demoniac of 9.32-4; then at 12.22 he describes the healing of a Blind and Dumb Demoniac in a protracted scene (Mt. 12.22-45). The latter moves beyond Mark's controversies over Beelzebul and the blasphemy against the Holy Spirit, to evil speech and the sign of Jonah, before returning to the possession theme with the seven evil spirits.

11.14, 15. All this presents Luke with some problems, and he does his best to simplify the situation. First, he takes it that the two accounts of exorcistic healings, with Pharisees saying that it is the work of Beelzebul, are the same. We noted earlier (p. 407) that in Luke 7 Luke had included forms of all the healings in Matthew 9 other than 9.32-34; and it is typical of the care with which he has tried to do justice to all his material, that he does not just subsume it into the larger Matthew 12 story (i.e. omit it). Mt. 9.32f. read, 'They brought him a dumb man with a demon; and when the demon had been cast out, the dumb spoke and the crowds wondered'. Luke supplies his own form of the opening: 'He was casting out a *demon and it was dumb*'; but he continues, following Matthew, 'and it came to pass *when the demon had* gone *out, the dumb spoke and the crowds wondered*'. In Mt. 9.34 the Pharisees say, 'By the prince of demons he casts out demons', and Luke follows, '*by* Beelzebul *the prince of demons he casts out demons*'. He supplies the name Beelzebul because it is required by the coming Mt. 12.27=Lk. 11.19, 'If I by Beelzebul. . .'; compare also Mt. 12.24.

11.16. Luke resolves on a second simplification, by taking the demand for a sign alongside the Beelzebul comment, the two themes together at the beginning. This looks a sensible move, but in fact Matthew's unit is overweight, and Luke later decides to transfer the sign of Jonah to the next pericope; this is an advantage in giving it a standing of its own, though it leaves the present verse rather isolated. Interestingly, Luke did not look Mt. 12.38 up, but supplies from memory, drawing in fact from the Matthaean redaction of Mk 8.11:

Mt. 12 38   ἀπεκρίθησαν. . . λέγοντες, διδάσκαλε, θέλομεν ἀπὸ σοῦ σημεῖον ἰδεῖν.

Mt. 16.1   πειράζοντες ἐπηρώτησαν αὐτὸν σημεῖον ἐκ τοῦ οὐρανοῦ. . .

Mk 8.11   ζητοῦντες παρ' αὐτοῦ σημεῖον ἀπὸ τοῦ οὐρανοῦ, πειράζοντες αὐτόν

Lk. 11.16   πειράζοντες σημεῖον ἐξ οὐρανοῦ ἐζήτουν παρ' αὐτοῦ

ἐζήτουν παρ' αὐτοῦ comes from Mark; the placing of πειράζοντες and the use of ἐκ from Mt. 16.1.

11.17. The way is now open to resume the main story from Matthew 12. Mt. 12.25: 'But knowing their thoughts he said to them, Every kingdom divided against itself is desolated, and every city or house divided against itself will not stand'. Luke: '*But he knowing their* imaginations *said to them, Every kingdom* divided on *itself is desolated, and* a house on a house falls'. Luke supplies his familiar αὐτός and preferred διαμερισθεῖσα. He uses the LXX διανοήματα which can have a hostile sense (even = idols, Ezek. 14.3f.), just as he uses the similar διανοίᾳ καρδίας in a hostile sense at 1.51; Matthew's ἐνθυμήσεις seemed to neutral. ἐφ'ἑαυτήν slips in from Mk 3.24, cf. Mt. 12.26 ἐφ' ἑαυτόν. He eschews the wordy Semitic parallel kingdom—city/house, omitting the repeated verb as he omitted ἀγαπήσεις at 10.27—though this has the unfortunate effect of obscuring the meaning. He sustitutes οἶκος, which often means a household, for Matthew's οἰκία, and probably intends, 'a household divided against a household falls', This would be realistic, and has its parallel in the five ἐν ἑνὶ οἴκῳ διαμεμερισμένοι at 12.52; and it is confirmed below (cf. on vv. 24ff.).

11.18. Matthew continued (v. 26), 'And if Satan casts out Satan, he is divided on himself: how then will his kingdom stand?' Luke: 'And *if Satan too is divided on himself, how will his kingdom stand?'* — a little shorter and crisper, and with Luke's διεμερίσθη again, and his δὲ καί. But he moves on to still the slight anxiety of having introduced a sidetrack with the sign question at v.16, and adds, 'Because you say (ὅτι λέγετε) that I cast out demons by Beelzebul'. It was an echo of Mk 3.30 that came to his mind then: 'Because they were saying (ὅτι ἔλεγον), He has an unclean spirit'.

11.19f. The next two verses virtually copy out Mt. 12.27f.; 'And if I cast out demons by Beelzebul, by whom do your sons cast them out? Therefore shall they be your judges. But if I by the spirit of God cast out demons, then God's kingdom has come upon you'. Luke's only considerable change is to substitute δακτύλῳ for πνεύματι. C.M. Tuckett has argued that Luke saw the Spirit as anointing Jesus for a ministry of preaching (4.18f.), while the healings were due to δύναμις, and took place 'because God was with him' (Acts 10.38; *Logia*, pp. 349f.). So here Luke prefers not to attribute the exorcism to the spirit of God (a phrase he never uses), but to God's finger, the symbol of his action in Exod. 8.19 and Deut. 9.10. The Spirit is within Jesus, and enables him to perform spiritual wonders, as it does also the Church; God's power/finger were with Jesus and the Seventy-two to the casting out of demons, even if that power is not to be counted on today (10.20). Luke fully concurred with Matthew in seeing Jesus' miracles as transparent signs of God's activity inaugurating his kingdom (18.39; Acts 2.22; 3.6; 4.10; 10.38), and abundant proof of the hard hearts of those refusing them.

11.21f. Matthew now moves on (following Mark) to the parable of the strong man: 'Or how can anyone enter the house of the strong man...?' (12.29f.); and he will return to the image of the house at the end of the pericope, 'When (ὅταν) the unclean spirit... I will return to my house' (vv. 43ff.). Luke intends to bring his paragraph to a close with the latter (vv. 24ff.), but this means an excess of the house image. He has just amended Matthew's kingdom—city/house pair to kingdom—house, and he now amends the strong man to bring him into line with the kingdom image, retaining the house for the seven evil spirits. He opens ὅταν ὁ ἰσχυρός in line with Mt. 12.43 ὅταν τὸ ἀκάθαρτον πνεῦμα; but his strong man has been transposed to a national scale. He is now armed (Lucan perfect part. pass.), and keeps (Lucan φυλάσσειν) his palace (αὐλήν for Matthew's commoner's οἰκίαν—Lucan sandwiched ἑαυτοῦ). The aim of a standing army is normally to keep one's *realm* in peace, but Luke's strong man is concerned only to keep his belongings (Lucan τὰ ὑπάρχοντα αὐτοῦ) in peace (Lucan εἰρήνη), because his Matthaean Vorlage had τὰ σκεύη αὐτοῦ.

11.22. Similarly Matthew's man who enters and binds the strong man in his home is now replaced by one stronger who attacks (Lucan ἐπέρχεσθαι) and conquers him (νικήσῃ) in battle. But whereas the aim of such rebellion is normally to *reign*, Matthew's intruder had in mind merely to despoil the house, and Luke's rebel follows suit; merely interesting himself in the armoury his predecessor had put his trust in (Lucan pluperfect), and the spoils which he can distribute. Luke has thus turned his predecessors' civilian strong man in his home into an instance of a kingdom divided against itself; but the motives for invading a man's home are inapposite for attacking a palace, and reveal Luke's secondariness. The fact that the attack is made on the palace shows that Luke has a rebellion in mind (a kingdom divided)—contrast the *despatch* of an army against a foreign invader in 14.31f.

11.23. A feature of Matthew's discourse is his ability to end a paragraph with an epigram, often of a balanced kind. The following paragraph, on blasphemy, ends, 'By your words you will be justified, and by your words you will be condemned'; and before he goes on to that, he closes the present topic with 'He that is not with me is against me, and he that gathers not with me scatters'. In Matthew this makes the point effectively—the Pharisees who are not 'with'

Jesus are opposing his kingdom and resisting its growth. Luke copies out the verse verbatim, but the *éclat* is gone. The σκορπίζει looks as if it takes up διαδίδωσιν; but then it is Jesus who is the 'stronger' and does the distributing, and it is his adversaries who 'scatter'.

11.24-26. Just as Luke reduced Mark's Harvest Sermon to virtually a single parable, and has regularly limited his use of Matthew's soaring discourses to a single topic, so now. Matthew moved off into blasphemy, evil speaking, Jonah and the Queen of the South (12.31-42), before returning to his subject with the Seven Evil Spirits. Luke has expounded the divided kingdom, and he now seals off the paragraph with the Evil Spirits and their divided house. He copies out the verses almost word for word (see below), and we now see what he meant by 'a house(hold) against a house(hold) falls'. The man has had the unclean spirit driven out, but he cannot maintain his 'house' against a further multiple incursion; so the household is divided, and his last state is worse than the first. Luke leaves out Matthew's concluding, So shall it be for this evil generation': his concern is the spirit in the possessed man, and not its symbolism for the Jewish people.

In the standard view (Schmid, pp. 289-97; Schulz, pp. 203-13, 476-80; Polag, pp. 50-53), Luke has roughly preserved the Q form of the pericope, while Matthew has conflated this with Mark. Thus Polag prints Lk. 11.14-20 as Q with the following changes: (1) v. 14 om. ἐγένετο δέ, (2) om. v. 16, (3) in v. 17 and v. 18 μερισθεῖσα for διαμερισθεῖσα, (4) in v. 17 om. αὐτός, (5) v. 17c read καὶ πᾶσα οἰκία ἐφ'ἑαυτὴν μερισθεῖσα οὐ σταθήσεται, (6) v. 18 om. ὅτι λέγετε... δαιμόνια, (7) v. 19 read Matthew's καὶ εἰ for εἰ δέ. As Matthew has a version so close to Mark at 12.29, and so different a form of the strong man comes in Lk. 11.21f. in the parallel position, Schmid and Polag credit the Lucan version to Q roughly as it stands. For the remainder, Lk. 11.23-26, the wording is very close with Matthew. Schmid understands μὴ εὕρισκον, the omission of σχολάζοντα, and the order of vv. 24d, 26b as Lucan improvements, while μετ' ἐμαυτοῦ and Mt. 12.45e are Matthaean additions. In this way it is possible to credit most of the more obvious characteristic expressions to the evangelists, and to retain a neutral-looking Q. For an exhaustive discussion of the pericope as an instance of Deutero-Markus as the underlying text, cf. A. Fuchs, *Entwicklung*.

There are however, rather numerous difficulties for this overall consensus. Among *the QC expressions*, which have to be credited to Q, a fair number look like the style of Matthew. (1) We may compare:

Lk. 11.14=Mt. 9.33   ἐλάλησεν ὁ κωφὸς καὶ ἐθαύμασαν οἱ ὄχλοι
Mt. 15.31R   ὥστε τὸν ὄχλον θαυμάσαι βλέποντας κωφοὺς λαλοῦντας.

Both combinations, the-dumb-spoke and the-crowd(s)-wondered, are peculiar to these two passages. Matthew favours the plural οἱ ὄχλοι too (33/17) over the singular (B has τοὺς ὄχλους at 15.31); and ἐθαύμασαν οἱ ὄχλοι has its closest parallel at Mt. 7.28R ἐξεπλήσσοντο οἱ ὄχλοι. (2) 11.19: Matthew likes διὰ τοῦτο (10/3/4. often introductory), and has it with a future at 12.31; 21.43R. (3) 11.23: συνάγειν is a favourite Matthaean verb (24/5/6, 26.57R), and in Matthew alone is again contrasted with (δια)σκορπίζειν at 25.24, 26, both QD. (4) Matthew's τότε (90/6/14) comes in Lk. 11.26, and perhaps also at 11.24 (N-A[26] has parenthesis). Twice in a single section (the Seven Spirits) would be a surprising coincidence, and the syntax at Lk. 11.24 seems strained. (5) 11.25 ἐλθὸν εὑρίσκει: cf. Mt. 26.43R ἐλθὼν. . .εὗρεν, 24.46QC ἐλθών. . .εὑρήσει. Matthew likes ἐλθών immediately before the verb (16/5/3, 4.13R; 9.10R; 14.12R; 28.13R). (6) 11.26 παραλαμβάνει: Matthew is partial to παραλαμβάνειν (16/6/6, 27.27R; x6 in 1-2), and has παραλαμβάνει at 4.5QD, 8QD. (7) 11.26 καὶ εἰσελθόντα κατοικεῖ ἐκεῖ: cf. 2.23 ἐλθὼν κατῴκησεν, 4.13 ἐλθὼν κατῴκησεν. Matthew likes ἐκεῖ too 28/11/16+8, and has it as last word in the sentence at 14.23; 15.29R; 19.2R; 21.17R; 27.36R—there is no parallel for this in Mark or Luke, and in Acts only 17.14. For the four-word phrase cf. Mt. 15.29R καὶ ἀναβὰς εἰς τὸ ὄρος ἐκάθητο ἐκεῖ, and 27.36R καὶ καθήμενοι ἐτήρουν αὐτὸν ἐκεῖ. (8) With καὶ γίνεται τὰ ἔσχατα τοῦ ἀνθρώπου ἐκείνου χείρονα τῶν πρώτων cf. Mt. 27.64M/R καὶ ἔσται ἡ ἐσχάτη πλάνη χείρων τῆς πρώτης. Matthew expounds the first/last contrast in 20.1-16. He has ἐκεῖνος as the last word in phrases like τοῦ ἀνθρώπου ἐκείνου 38/7/23, with redactional instances at 3.1; 8.28; 9.22, 31; 13.1; 14.35; 15.22, 28; 21.40.

For the *QD expressions* the greater part are, as I have said, taken to be original in Luke—but then the Lucan QD words contain a number of expressions that are characteristic of Luke. Thus τινες ἐξ αὐτῶν/ἡμῶν/ὑμῶν recurs at Lk. 22.50R; 24.22; Acts 11.20; 15.2, 24; 17.4. φυλάσσειν has figures of 1/1/6+8, with 8.29R and several uses in Acts similar to the present context, with soldiers. τὴν ἑαυτοῦ αὐλήν with the sandwiched ἑαυτοῦ is uncommon in the NT, being found in the synoptics only at Lk. 9.60QC; 13.34QD; 14.26QD, 33QD; Mt. 8.22QC, it could be part of Luke's classicizing. Luke likes εἰρήνη (4/1/13+7, 19.38R), and has ἐν εἰρήνῃ at 2.29 and Acts 16.36. τὰ ὑπάρχοντα αὐτοῦ is well known as a Lucan phrase (2/0/5, 14.33QD). These expressions are all given by Polag, who has taken the responsibility of writing down what Q might have contained; others, like Schmid, can avoid phrases like τὰ ὑπάρχοντα αὐτοῦ, but at the cost of leaving Q undefined. So the weakness with the QD words is not so damaging as with the QC words, where Matthaean authorship looks so plausible. The easiest solution is that Matthew re-wrote the Marcan Beelzebul story twice, once in brief outline at 9.32-34 and once in an expanded form at 12.22-45 (cf. *MLM*, pp. 327, 330-37); and that Luke combined the two into a single manageable unit.

F.G. Downing (*NTS* [1965]) divides the Matthaean version of the pericope into three elements: 12.29, 31a ('A'), where the wording is close to Mark, 33 out of 41 words being the same; 12.24b, 26a, 32b ('B'), where it is related to Mark, 32 out of 82 words being the same; and the rest ('C'), where there is no parallel in Mark. He then argues that Luke has omitted all the A matter; so either he has deliberately omitted every passage where Matthew agrees with Mark (which seems absurd), or he knew a form of Matthew containing only matter differing from, or lacking in, Mark (i.e. Q). The argument is fallacious. 'A' matter consists of only a verse and a half. In Mt. 12.29 23 words out of 27 are indeed identical (or nearly) with Mark; in v. 31a, however, 10 words out of 14 are underlined by Downing, but only five are identical (λέγω ὑμῖν, καί, τοῖς, ἀφεθήσεται). Matthew puts διὰ τοῦτο for ἀμήν, omits ὅτι, puts πᾶσα ἁμαρτία for πάντα τὰ ἁμαρτήματα, and βλασφημία for αἱ βλασφημίαι, drops ὅσα ἐὰν βλασφημήσωσιν and shortens 'the sons of men' to 'men'. So 12.31a is less close to Mark than B matter like v.24b: and Luke has changed 12.29 for a reason—to make an illustration of the *kingdom* divided.

11.14 ἦν + part., δαιμόνιον, καὶ-αὐτὸς-ἦν*, ἐγένετο-δέ*, (δαιμόνιον), (θαυμάζειν)

11.15 τις, εἶπον, (δαιμόνιον ×2)

11.16 ἕτερος*, (ζητεῖν). ἐξ οὐρανοῦ cf. 11.13.

11.17 αὐτός nom., (εἶπον), (ἑαυτόν), διαμερίζειν*, οἶκος ×2. Hapaxes: διανόημα, (ἐρημοῦν).

11.18 δὲ-καί*, (ἑαυτόν), διαμερίζειν*, δαιμόνιον. Acc. + inf. rare in NT; due here to preceding ὅτι (BDF, p. 408).

11.19 (δαιμόνιον), (αὐτός nom.).

11.20 δάκτυλος, (anarthrous θεός), (ἐφ-ὑμᾶς*). It is common to explain Matthew's πνεύματι as a change from Q's δακτύλῳ, in the light of the citation in Mt. 12.18, or as looking forward to 12.43, or as being the same formulation as πνεῦμα θεοῦ 3.16R (cf. list of authorities, Schulz, p. 205). For the fallacy, cf. p. 15. Matthew was indeed rewriting here, but rewriting Mark and with a more free hand; and Luke is rewriting him. Schulz cites authorities for Lucan secondariness also.

11.21 φυλάσσειν*, ἑαυτοῦ sandwiched*, εἰρήνη*, τὰ-ὑπάρχοντα-αὐτοῦ*. Hapax: καθοπλίζεσθαι.

11.22 ἐπέρχεσθαι*. Hapaxes: πανοπλία, νικᾶν, σκῦλον. ἐπάν 11.34QD. Jesus is already ὁ ἰσχυρότερος at 3.16Mk; ἰσχυρότερος αὐτοῦ cf. πονηρότερα ἑαυτοῦ v. 26. αἴρειν 23.18R; 6.29QD, 30QD; 19.21f.QD. πέποιθα ἐπί 18.9. σκῦλα: cf. Isa. 53.12 τῶν ἰσχυρῶν σκῦλα. διαδιδόναι 18.22R; Acts 4.35.

11.23 (μή + part ×2)

11.24 (τόπος), (ζητεῖν), μή + part., (εὑρίσκειν), ὑποστρέφειν*, (οἶκος). Hapaxes: (ἄνυδρος) (ὅθεν)

11.25 (εὑρίσκειν). Luke om. σχολάζοντα, preferring pairs to triples (§24).

11.26 (πορεύεσθαι), (ἕτερος*), (ἑαυτόν), (γίνεσθαι).

Käsemann, E., 'Lukas 11,14-28', *Exegetische Versuche und Besinnungen* (2nd edn; Göttingen, 1960), pp. 242-48.

Légasse, S., '"L'Homme fort" de Luc xi 21-22', *NT* 5 (1962), pp. 5-9.

Lorenzmeier, T., 'Zum Logion Mt 12,28; Lk 11,20', in H.D. Betz and L. Schottroff (eds.), *Neues Testament und christliches Existenz* (*Fs* H. Braun, Tübingen, 1973), pp. 289-304.

George, A., *Etudes sur l'oeuvre de Luc* (SB; Paris, 1978), pp. 128-32.

Fuchs, A., *Die Entwicklung der Beelzebulkontroverse bei den Synoptikern* (SNTU/B5; Linz, 1980).

J.-M. van Cangh, 'Par l'Esprit de Dieu—par le doigt de Dieu (Mt. 12,28 par. Lc 11,20)', in J. Delobel (ed.), *Logia* (1982), pp. 337-42.

Tuckett, C.M., 'Luke 4,16-30, Isaiah and Q', *ibid.*, pp. 343-54.

b. *The Sign of Jonah*, 11.27-36

Commentators often tack 11.27f., the Blessedness of Jesus' Mother, on to the Beelzebul story: its link of thought is remote, but 'while he was speaking' appears to be an association in the evangelist's mind. We should, however, be warned by Luke's ἐγένετο δέ, which has acted as the introduction to a new pericope so often (so in 11.1, 14); and 'while he was speaking' is no more significant here than at 11.37 or 19.11, where new departures are made. Furthermore, after the seven evil spirits in Mt. 12.43-45 follows the visit of Jesus' mother and brothers, which opens, 'While he was still speaking to the crowds' (v. 46, ἔτι αὐτοῦ λαλοῦντος cp. Luke's ἐν τῷ λέγειν αὐτόν). Luke has already taken the Mother-and-Brothers in its Marcan sequence at 8.19-21, and it looks as if he has introduced a substitute version of his own, following the Matthaean order. The climactic line of Matthew's story was 'For whoever does the will of my Father in heaven, he is my brother and sister and mother' (12.50). Luke's final line is similar: 'Blessed rather are those who hear the word of God and keep it'. The contrast between obedience to God and blood relationship as the true blessing is the same, and so is the cool note towards Jesus' mother. With the identical position in Luke and Matthew, following the seven spirits, and the same opening, substitution by Luke seems obvious.

But is it substitution from L, or Luke himself? It would be difficult to find two verses more strongly redolent of the evangelist. It is not just the language: ἐγένετο-δὲ-ἐν-τῷ + inf. + αὐτόν, ταῦτα, ἐπαίρειν, τις + noun, φωνή, κοιλία, αὐτός nom., ἀκούειν-τὸν-λόγον-τοῦ-θεοῦ, φυλάσσειν. There are other more general features which come in Luke's Gospel only. There are voices from the crowd at Lk. 12.13 (εἶπεν δέ τις ἐκ τοῦ ὄχλου αὐτῷ) and 14.15. They are part of a much wider Lucan use of the foil introduction which gives force to Jesus' reply (§ 1.4). The woman here who says, 'Blessed...' is like Elizabeth who says, 'Blessed...' (1.45), and the man in 14.15 who says, 'Blessed...', and those in 23.29 who will say, 'Blessed...'— the only Beatitudes in the Gospels not uttered by Jesus. In 14.15 as here Jesus puts vacuous piety in its place; there with the parable of the Dinner, here with, 'Blessed rather...' The slightly embarrassing, 'Blessed is the womb that bore you, and the breasts which you sucked' echoes the slightly embarrassing 23.29, 'Blessed are the barren, and the wombs that bore not, and the breasts that fed not', often taken as a Lucan equivalent of Mk 13.17. The stress upon hearing the word of God and keeping it has already been seen at 6.47 and 8.15, and runs through both Luke and Acts. Much the easiest view is that Luke read the Mother and Brothers in Mt. 12.46-50, following Beelzebul, and composed a substitute of his own, having used the original at 8.19ff.

The verses present defenders of Q with one of their more uncomfortable dilemmas. If (with Schulz, Polag and most) they are ascribed to L, then we have a remarkable coincidence. Luke not only happened to have, by accident, an incident like Matthew's Mother and Brothers, with (a) the same obedience-rather-than-blood theme, (b) the same cool attitude to Mary, and (c) a similar opening; but he also, by accident, placed it after Beelzebul in the same position as Mt.R. If, on the other hand (with Schürmann, *TU*, pp. 231f.), the verses are ascribed to Q, then we have a different, but equally remarkable coincidence. For now Q had an incident like Mark's Mother and Brothers, with (a) the same obedience-rather-than-blood theme, and (b) the same cool attitude to Mary; and Q also, by accident, placed it after Beelzebul in the same position as Mark. The Lucan nature of the language, mode and thought is an offence to both solutions.

11.29. Luke has held over the Jonah/Queen of the South matter, which seemed overweight and irrelevant to Matthew's Beelzebul topic. He gave the substance of Mt. 12.38, the request for a sign, at 11.16, but the sayings can be treated now—Matthew had made it clear that it was all one occasion with 12.46, 'while he was still speaking τοῖς ὄχλοις'. Luke in fact takes up the Matthaean link in two different verses: we have seen 'It came to pass while he was speaking' at 11.27, and at 11.29 he reintroduces it with 'As τῶν ὄχλων were gathering, he began to say'. As he has a slight preference for the singular, τῶν ὄχλων probably indicates Matthaean influence. Matthew had then opened with Jesus' reply to the Pharisees' request, 'An evil and adulterous generation seeks for a sign, and a sign shall not be given it, except the sign of Jonah the prophet' (12.39). Luke, having left the request behind, phrases as closely as he can: 'This generation is *an evil generation: it seeks a sign, and a sign shall not be given it except the sign of Jonah*'. He uses plain ζητεῖ for ἐπιζητεῖ as in Mk. 8.12 and Lk. 11.16; ends with plain 'Jonah' without 'the prophet' as in Mt. 16.4 (cf. Acts, where 'X the prophet' occurs only twice); and drops μοιχαλίς, which he never uses.

11.30. So far, so good: but a difficulty now opens out. The sign of Jonah in Matthew was Jesus' resurrection (12.40)—Matthew had added the 'except' clause on to Mark's refusal of any sign at all (as at Mt. 19.9). The Ninevites had repented at the preaching of Jonah as one risen from the dead, and would rise at the judgment and condemn this generation; for it failed to respond to the preaching of a greater than Jonah, really risen from the dead. But if one takes 'this generation' to mean Jesus' contemporaries, as seems natural, where is the sense of reproaching them for not repenting at the resurrection of Jesus, who is still speaking to them? The mention of the resurrection throws the whole issue into the future, where it may mean a lot to the Matthaean church, but it deprives the present context of its force. So Luke retains Matthew's sentence-structure, but changes the meaning—a move he makes a fair number of times

(§ 20). Matthew: 'For as Jonah was (ὥσπερ γὰρ ἦν ᾽Ιωνᾶς) in the belly of the whale three days and three nights, so shall the Son of Man be in the heart of the earth three days and three nights'. Luke: '*For* as *Jonah* was (καθὼς γὰρ ἐγένετο ᾽Ιωνᾶς) as sign to the Ninevites, *so shall the Son of Man be* also to this generation'. Lucan καθώς, Luke's preferred γίνεσθαι, Lucan καί = also, betray the editor's touch; but what he has done subtly is to drop the resurrection reference, and to make the comparison between Jonah and Jesus as straightforward preachers of repentance. So the saying becomes relevant to its context, and also to its introduction; for blessed are those who hear the word of the greater than Jonah and keep it. Luke may also, of course, have been glad to be rid of an inaccurate statement that Jesus would be three days and three nights in the tomb.

11.31f. Having dropped the resurrection (Mt. 12.40), and spoken of the preaching to the Ninevites (Mt. 12.41), Luke now moves on the the Matthaean parallel in 12.42, 'The queen of the South. . . ', which he copies out, with the addition of Lucan τῶν ἀνδρῶν (of this generation), and the consequent change from 'it' to 'them'. But, alas, this was too quick; for Mt. 12.42 was parallel to a significant saying in 12.41, 'The men of Nineveh shall rise in judgment with this generation and shall condemn it. . . ' This is too good for Luke to omit, so he tacks it on, despite his having finished with Jonah at 11.30. Fatigue prevents him, this time, from adding 'the men of' to 'this generation'. It may be that the queen of the South caught his eye in that she came to *hear* the wisdom of Solomon, and this gave the echo he wanted with '*hear* the word of God'; but he has spoiled the smoothness of Matthew's progress, and once more redressed the situation a little clumsily (§ 19.1).

11.33. After Mt. 12.46-50, Jesus' Mother and Brothers, comes Mt. 13.1-23, his preaching to the crowds on the Sower. Jesus says to his disciples, 'Blessed are your eyes for they see, and your ears for they hear' (13.16), and those on the good ground are they who hear the word and understand, who bear fruit (13.23)—or, in Luke's own words, 'having heard the word, keep it (κατέχουσιν)'. So Jesus' reply to the woman in 11.28, '*Blessed* rather are those who *hear the word* of God and keep it' is as much a restatement of the next section of Matthew (12.46–13.23) as the woman's own words are in 11.27. Luke has told the Sower already, of course, in its Marcan sequence but he is conscious of its being followed by a saying on Light (Mk 4.21; Lk. 8.16) Mark had continued, 'Does the lamp (λύχνος) come to (ἵνα) be placed (τεθῇ) under the measure (ὑπὸ τὸν μόδιον) or under the bed? Is it not to be placed on the lampstand (ἐπὶ τὴν λυχνίαν). For there is nothing hidden (κρυπτόν) but that it may be revealed. . . ' (4.21f.). Luke's 'No one lights a *lamp* (λύχνον) and *places* it in a cellar (κρυπτήν), nor *under the measure* (ὑπὸ τὸν μόδιον), but *on the lampstand, that* (ἵνα) those entering may see the light' shows contact with Mark with the second 'under' phrase, with the ἵνα and with the tell-tale κρυπτήν, none of which comes in Mt. 5.15. Nonetheless, Matthew's version, 'Nor do they burn *a lamp* and *place* it *under the measure, but on the lampstand,* and it shines for all *those* in the house', has still been influential on the general shape of the sentence, as it was also at Lk. 8.16. Luke adapts the final clause from Matthew here, as he did there, substituting 'those entering' for 'all those in the house': his lamp is in the window, for those entering, for the light symbolizes the preaching of the greater than Jonah, the light to lighten the Gentiles (2.32), for their eyes to see as well as their ears to hear. It is usually thought (Dodd, *Parables*, p. 106) that Luke has added a Hellenistic cellar to a Palestinian one-room house, just as he gave the latter tiles at 5.19 (§ 26).

11.34f. As it stands, Luke's paragraph is short; so he appends a further group of sayings on Light, with the same link-word λύχνος. Mt. 6.22, in a context of laying up treasure in heaven, ran, 'The lamp of the body is the eye. If then your eye is generous (ἁπλοῦς), your whole body will be light'. Luke amends slightly, '*The lamp of the body is your eye.* When *your eye is generous, your whole body* also is *light*': he changes a general, third-person statement ('the body') into a second-person statement ('your eye') in mid-stream, just as he did at 6.20ff. (§ 9.1). καί = also is Lucan, and ὅταν comes in for ἐάν because we may be sometimes generous, sometimes mean. Matthew continued, 'But if your eye is mean (πονηρός), your whole body will be dark. So if the light in you is darkness, how great the darkness!' How memorable are his repetitive Semitic parallelisms! The idiom of the good and bad eye for generosity and meanness (Mt. 20.15) gives him the image of a whole person (house) in light from a single lamp, as in 5.15—or in utter darkness. Poor prosy Luke cannot compete. '*But* when *it is mean, your whole body* also is *dark.* See *then* that *the light in you* is not *darkness.* So if your whole body is light, having no part dark, it will be wholly light, as when the lamp with its ray lightens you'. But not only has Matthew's stark warning on the spiritual consequences of the two treasures become sermonic ('See then'), and vapid ('if it is all light, it is all light'); Luke has also lost his thread of thought. 'Blessed are those who hear the word and keep it' leads on well to the Queen of the South who came to hear Solomon's wisdom, and even to the light on the stand to guide those coming in. But the generous (or single) and bad eyes, and the light and darkness within have lost their force for lack of a context which gives them a clear meaning—the standard nemesis of the too-easy *Stichwort*.

The Marcan form of the no-sign logion at Mk 8.12 is taken to be the earliest by R.A. Edwards, but A Vögtle (pp. 103-36) thinks the Q form in Lk. 11.29 is prior. The Lucan form in vv. 29-32 is generally credited as the Q version: Polag (pp. 52f.) prints the Lucan wording of the sayings apart from: v. 30, ὡς for Lucan καθώς (and Matthaean ὥσπερ—embarras de richesses); om. Lucan καί = also; v. 31 om. Lucan τῶν ἀνδρῶν, αὐτούς for consequent αὐτήν. Schulz (p. 251) thinks the Matthaean form is earlier in v. 29, but there is agreement that the resurrection link with Jonah stems from Matthew (I agree), and that Luke would not have wished to split Matthew's union of the two Jonah verses (less unanimous—Lührmann [pp. 37f.] suggests Luke was closing with Jonah as he had opened with him).

The Matthaean character of the QD words in Matthew—μοιχαλίς (Mt. 16.4R), Jonah 'the prophet', 'three days and three nights', etc.,—can be explained either as Matthew's additions to Q or as Luke's omissions of a Matthaean expansion of Mk 8.12. What is not so easy for the standard position to explain is the Matthaean character of the QC matter in vv. 40-42. Matthew likes the combination οὕτως εἶναι, 13/2/3+1 (1.18R; 13.40R, 49R; 19.10R; 20.16R), often in the future οὕτως ἔσται (12.45; 13.40, 49; 20.26; 24.27, 37, 39), and five times with the sentence form 'As (ὥσπερ). . . so shall be', with an association with the Son of Man (12.40; 13.40; 24.27, 37, 39). The only parallels are QC Lk. 17.24, 26. Anarthrous βασίλισσα νότου follows Matthew's echoing of Semitic constructs, e.g. ἐν οἰκίᾳ Σίμωνος 26.6R, ἡμέρα κρίσεως QD ×4; and Matthew likes ἐγείρεσθαι 28/10/13+1, often in the sense of 'stand up' as here (17.7R, ἐγερθείς ×8), and κρίσις 12/0/ 4+1, and κατακρίνειν 4/2/2+0 (27.3R). He likes ἡ γῆ = the world, 22/4/ 14+10 (6.10R; 16.19R, etc.), and ἦλθον with an infinitive of purpose, 11/4/6 (2.2; 5.17, 17; 8.29Mk; 9.13Mk; 10.34, 34, 35; 12.42QC; 20.28Mk; 28.1R). He is fond of ὧδε, 17/10/16+2 (8.29R; 14.8R; 17.17R; 14.18R), and 12.6 offers a close redactional parallel to the whole clause πλεῖον Σολομῶνος ὧδε with τοῦ ἱεροῦ μεῖζόν ἐστιν ὧδε. More generally Matthew is keen on the Gentile mission, and he has an admiration for Solomon beyond his fellow-evangelists. He likes to pair female with male—birds and lilies, mustard and leaven, toll-collectors and prostitutes, men in the field and women grinding, the sleeping servant and the sleeping virgins—and (unlike the hypothetical Q-form here) always in the order male, female.

The lamp saying in Mt. 5.15 is usually credited to Q (Polag, p. 54; Schulz, pp. 474f.), the Lucan differences being so similar to his changes to Mark at Lk. 8.16: Polag prints οὐ for οὐδέ as the only difference from Matthew. For the eye sayings a middle course is steered, eschewing the two Lucan καίs in 11.34, and the Matthaean οὖν and two ἐάνs, but retaining the fuller, more Semitic form with repeated 'your eye' and ὅλον (Schulz, pp. 468f.). 11.35 is left in the Mt. 6.23b form; 11.36 is sometimes credited to Q (see Polag), without the more Lucan 'not having any part dark', sometimes to Luke (Schulz). The Matthaean nature of 'Q' is less overwhelming here. Matthew has the indefinite plural not only at 5.15 against Mk 4.21, but at 1.23R; 7.16QC; 9.17R (bis); 24.9Mk; and λάμπειν at 17.2R; but the sentence-form and the final clause can be explained simply as the accommodation of Mk 4.21 to the context of Mt. 5.14. Converse general statements like Mt. 6.22f., of the form, If A then B; if non-A then non-B, can be found in Mt. R, e.g. 'For if you forgive men...' (6.14f.). There are also Mt. 16.19 and 18.18, 'And whatsoever you bind...', and 'So whosoever shall break...' (5.19), as well as 10.32f. QC, 'Everyone therefore who confesses...' The phrase ὅλον τὸ σῶμά σου occurs 4/0/1 times, Mt. 5.29R, 30R; 6.22QC, 23QD.

Thus the Q form, as so often, shows strong links with Matthaean style, especially in the Jonah section. Where the Lucan form is alleged to be prior, the reason is usually the Matthaean nature of Matthew's QD words, which can be equally easily explained as Matthew's redaction of his source (?Mark), which has then been changed by Luke.

11.27 ἐγένετο-δέ*, ἐν-τῷ + inf.* + αὐτόν, ταῦτα, ἐπαίρειν, τις + noun*, φωνή, κοιλία*, βαστάζειν (in this sense here only). For the emphatic order τις... γυνή cf. 18.18R; Acts 3.2. ἐπαίρειν φωνήν × 3 Acts.

11.18 αὐτός nom., εἶπεν, ἀκούειν-τὸν-λόγον-τοῦ-θεοῦ*, φυλάσσειν*. Hapax: μενοῦν.

11.29 ἄρχεσθαι-λέγειν, ζητεῖν. Hapax: ἐπαθροίζεσθαι (ἀθροίζεσθαι 24.33 only, συν-×2 Acts only).

11.30 καθώς*, γίνεσθαι, καί = also. καθὼς ἐγένετο... οὕτως ἔσται 17.26QD. τοῖς Νινευίταις cf. Acts 18.8; 28.17 etc. Luke retains Mt.'s real future ἔσται (sc. in the days of the Church), in a weakened sense (sc. in my ministry).

11.31 ἀνήρ*. Hapaxes: (βασίλισσα), (πέρας). With 'the men of this generation', cf. 7.31R (τοὺς ἀνθρώπους).

11.32 (ἀνήρ*), (μετανοεῖν). Hapax: (κήρυγμα). Mt.'s ἄνδρες Νινευίται is an adaptation of Jon. 3.5 οἱ ἄνδρες Νινευΐ, cf. Mt.'s ἄνθρωπος + noun (8/0/1).

11.33 Gnomic οὐδείς, ἅπτειν*. Hapax: κρύπτη. οἱ εἰσπορεύομενοι 8.16R; Acts 3.2; 28.30. The gospel is a light to the Gentiles at 1.78f.; 2.32; Acts 13.47; 26.23.

11.34 καί = also (× 2). Hapax: (ἁπλοῦς). ἐπάν is a reminiscence of 11.22R, for variety from ὅταν.

11.35 Hapax: σκοπεῖν. σκόπει + μή should be followed by subj., cf. βλέπετε μή 21.8; Acts 13.40, but Matthew's ἐστίν has been copied in from fatigue, § 19.2.

11.36 μή + part., τις + noun*, μέρος sing. Hapax: φωτίζειν. ὅλον following the phrase as in 9.25Mk; Acts 21.30. ἀστραπή = rays of light, as in 17.24 (*q.v.*).

Vögtle, A., 'Der Spruch vom Jonaszeichen', in J. Schmid and A. Vögtle (eds.), *Synoptische Studien* (Fs A. Wikenhauser, Munich, 1953), pp. 230-77

Edwards, R.A., *The Sign of Jonah in the Theology of the Evangelists and Q* (SBT 2/18; Naperville, 1971)

Hahn, F., 'Die Worte vom Licht, Lukas 11,33-36', in P. Hoffmann (ed.), *Orientierung an Jesus* (Fs J. Schmid, Freiburg 1973), pp. 107-38.

Schmitt, G., 'Das Zeichen des Jonas', *ZNW* 69 (1978), pp. 123-29.

c. *The Woes Discourse*, 11.37-54

We have been watching Luke work his way through Matthew 10–12, not without some excursuses; and with his completion of the Jonah sayings he has reached the end of Matthew 12, and so come to the continuous Marcan story which he has already handled. The Harvest sermon and the Mother and Brothers (Mt. 12.46–13.23), and the Five Thousand (Mt. 14.13-21) have been taken in Luke 8–9; the Baptist's Death (Mt. 14.1-12) and the Walking on the Water (Mt. 14.22-36) he is omitting (see p. 437). So the pressure of a sequential following of Matthew is lifted, and he can attend to another matter.

It seemed suitable to treat 9.51–10.24 as a single topic, Mission, subdivided into three pericopae: (a) 9.51-62, the Samaritan village and the three aspirants; (b) 10.1-16, the Seventy-Two; and (c) 10.17-24, the Return of the Seventy-Two. Some commentators, as Marshall, have grouped the three units together, and Miyoshi treated them together in a monograph: the mission topic is stressed in 9.52,

60 as well as in the sending and return of the Seventy-Two. Similarly, Marshall and others have seen 10.25-11.13 as a topical unit, and I have argued for this above, again with a triple subdivision. In piety to Matthew I have called the unit 'Jesus' Yoke', but the modern jargon might be 'Christian Spirituality', with (a) 10.25-37 The Commandments—Loving one's Neighbour, (b) 10.38-42 Mary and Martha—Loving the Lord, (c) 11.1-13 Christian Prayer. Again, our present unit is widely recognized as extending from 11.14 to 11.54, and being concerned with Controversies. Once more a threefold subdivision is obvious, and I have justified taking it as (a) 11.14-26 The Beelzebul Controversy, (b) 11.27-36 The Sign Controversy, and now (c) 11.37-54 Woes on the Pharisees and Lawyers. The reason for moving over to a more leisurely, threefold exposition of a topic, in place of the hitherto somewhat staccato succession of Marcan units, is discussed above in ch. 5; but both the *threefoldness* and the persistence of identifiable *topics* seem to be features of the text, and we shall find that they both continue in the matter following.

11.37f. So we may think of Luke as having expounded two controversies from Matthew 12, Beelzebul and the Sign; and of him unrolling his Matthaean scroll in quest of a third, rather than pressing on through Matthew 13. With Matthew 15 he finds what he is looking for: for there it is said that Pharisees and scribes approach Jesus asking why his disciples do not wash their hands when they eat. After a discussion on the oral law, he speaks firmly about defilement coming from within rather than from without. This is just the grist for Luke's mill, and he infers a setting for the occasion in the way we have seen him do with the Catch of Fish, etc. (§13). For the Pharisees could only see (ἰδόντες, Mk 7.2, in the parallel account) that Jesus' disciples did not wash before meals if they were present; so Luke can infer a meal given by such a Pharisee, at which he saw (ἰδών, 38) Jesus himself giving them the lead. Luke in fact tends to think of Jesus being invited to meals by individual Pharisees: we saw him creating such a situation at 7.36ff., and there is another at 14.1ff. Each meal follows the same pattern—a Pharisee's invitation, he takes offence at Jesus, Jesus is rudely or critically treated, he shows up the Pharisee's hypocrisy. On this occasion Luke can infer not only the meal but which meal. For in Mt. 14.23 par. the disciples had left Jesus alone on the land in the evening, and it was the fourth watch (3-6 a.m.) when he had come to them in the boat. When he landed, it was towards dawn therefore, and he was quickly besieged by invalids (εὐθύς, Mk 6.54). It was then (τότε, Mt. 15.1) that the Pharisees spoke to him, so the meal was clearly the morning ἄριστον and not the evening δεῖπνον. Luke says both that the Pharisee asked him to ἀριστήσῃ, and that he did not wash before τοῦ ἀρίστου. The phrasing of the invitation ἐρωτᾷ αὐτὸν ὅπως follows Lk. 7.3QD, and ἠρώτα αὐτόν... εἰσελθών came also in 7.36; the historic present ἐρωτᾷ is usually debited to a source, and we have Matthew's προσέρχονται at 15.1 as a plausible influence.

11.39. The opening section is in fact more closely related to the Mark 7 than to the Matthew 15 version, largely because Mark 7 contains the ἔξωθεν/ἔσωθεν contrast which is taken up so forcibly in Matthew 23, which Luke also means to use. Mark says that the Pharisees do not eat without baptizing themselves (βαπτίσωνται, 7.4), and that they hold to other traditions, baptisms of cups (βαπτισμοὺς ποτηρίων), etc.; and it is from this that Luke describes Jesus as not baptizing himself (ἐβαπτίσθη) before the meal. Mark goes on to speak of Jesus saying that nothing external (τὸ ἔξωθεν) defiles, but evil thoughts from within (ἔσωθεν) do, covetings, wickednesses (πονηρίαι) and the rest (Mk 7.18-23). 'Now do you *Pharisees*', says Jesus in Luke, 'cleanse *the outside* (τὸ ἔξωθεν) of the *cup* (ποτηρίου)... but *inside* (ἔσωθεν) you are full of extortion and *wickedness* (πονηρίας)'. Thus, notes Mark, he declared all foods clean (καθαρίζων πάντα τὰ βρώματα Mk 7.19): 'give alms', says the Lucan Jesus, 'and all is clean to you (πάντα καθαρὰ ὑμῖν)'. Mark's list of defilements ends with folly (ἀφροσύνη)—'all these evils come from within and defile a man' (7.22f.): 'You fools (ἄφρονες)', says the Lucan Jesus, 'did not he who made the outside make the inside also?'. All these references come in the first five verses of the Lucan story, and they include the use of βαπτίζεσθαι in a non-liturgical sense, which is unique in L-A, and πονηρία, which is unique in Luke and comes once in Acts. The slide from the washing of hands to the washing of cups is also in common.

The Marcan teaching on the inside and outside had been taken up by Matthew in Mt. 23.25f., and it is not surprising therefore if Luke glosses Matthew 23 on to Mark 7. Matthew wrote, 'You (scribes and Pharisees) cleanse the outside of the cup and side-dish (παροψίδος), but inside they are full from extortion and rapacity'. Matthew is familiar with Jewish casuistry on the cleansing of vessels (*m. Kel.*

25.1, 7; cf. Neusner *JTS* [1976]), where sometimes the outside surface alone may be cleansed; he points to the hypocrisy of filling them with (ἐξ) the spoils of widows' houses. Luke amends, 'Now do you *Pharisees cleanse the outside of the cup and* dish (πίνακος), *but* your *inside* is *full of extortion and* wickedness'. Matthew's formal Woe is dropped to fit the Mark 7 context, where a straight reproach is more suited. His παροψίς (frowned on by Phrynichus [176] as a low word) is replaced by πίναξ, which perhaps caught Luke's eye at Mt. 14.8, 11. πονηρίας and the inside of the *person* come from Mark. This must appeal to Luke as an improvement, because people, not cups, are full of extortion; but there is a price to pay.

11.40f. Matthew continues, 'You blind Pharisee, first cleanse the inside of the cup that the outside also may be clean'. He is pursuing his transferred use, meaning their rapacity by 'inside the cup'; but Luke has foresworn the inside of the vessels, and cannot follow him. He is therefore reduced to the rather pointless, 'You fools, did not he who made *the outside* make *the inside also*'?, without specifying the inside of what. His ἄφρονες follows Matthew's abusive vocative. But Luke's interest is in the inward life of the person, and he moves on to clarify the muddle with v. 41, 'But as for what is within, give alms, and lo, all things are *clean* to you'. What is the meaning of Matthew's counsel, first to cleanse the inside of the cup? How is a Pharisee in practice to deal with the money he has so dubiously made? He can be like Zacchaeus, who purged his rapacity by giving half his goods to the poor; or like the Rich Ruler, who was to sell all he had and give to the poor; or like the little flock, who are to sell their possessions and give alms (δότε ἐλεημοσύνην, 12.33). So with the Pharisee and his friends: δότε ἐλεημοσύνην. It is the same practical solution to the problem of money which Luke turns up with every time. For the phrasing, πλὴν τὰ ἐνόντα..., cf. 19.27, πλὴν τοὺς ἐχθρούς μου τούτους...

11.42. The verses in Matthew 23 on which Luke has just been drawing are part of a protracted onslaught of the kind which he consistently shows himself to find too long (pp. 38ff.). Matthew had an introduction, seven Woes on the scribes and Pharisees, and a fine peroration. Luke would like to extend his present controversial scene, but he does not want all of Matthew's oratory, and especially the rather fine points about altars and sacrifices, which had no relevance in Greece. So, just as he cut Matthew's eight Beatitudes into two fours, four Beatitudes and four Woes, so here he bisects Matthew's Woes, with three for the Pharisees and three for the scribes, or lawyers, as he prefers to call them. The lawyers are, of course, those who prescribe the law, so he selects for them the parts of Matthew 23 which involve this function. The Pharisees' fault he sees throughout the Gospel as external legalistic religion, and he has no difficulty in instancing that from the same chapter.

The mention of ἐλεημοσύνη draws his eye to the next Woe preceding, Mt. 23.23, 'Woe to you scribes and Pharisees, hypocrites! for you tithe mint and dill and cummin, and have neglected the weightier matters of the law, judgment and ἔλεος and faith'. Dill (*m.Maas.* 4.5) and cummin (*m. Dem.* 2.1) were liable to tithe; mint is doubtful (? 'whatsoever is used for food' *m.Maas.* 1.1). Matthew balances the three *minima legis* with three weightier matters. Having just preempted the requirement of mercy ('give mercy'), Luke reduces the paralleled items to two: 'but *woe to you Pharisees, for you tithe mint and* rue *and* every herb, *and* you pass by *judgment and* the love of God'. For Luke's preference for pairs over Matthew's triples, see §24. Although his knowledge of Jewish practice is, as usual, defective (§26), for rue is specifically exempted from tithe (*m.Shebi.* 9.1), being an evil-smelling herb not used for food, Luke is aware of some Jewish association of mint and rue and herbs in general. For *m.Utz.* 1.2 brackets together 'mint and rue, wild-herbs and garden-herbs' as conveying uncleanness. With 'and every herb', compare 21.29R, 'the fig-tree and all the trees', which also misses the point: not every herb was tithable, and not every tree puts forth leaves in spring. Luke also substitutes 'the love of God' for 'faith' as the context requires an activity rather than a disposition: in the parallel passage in Mark attacking the scribes (12.28-44) the first section declares that to love God with all one's heart is greater than all sacrificial offerings. Luke leaves out Matthew's 'hypocrites': although the Gospel is in general hostile to the Pharisees, he does not wish to be hard on them (13.31), and they are the Church's natural allies, and even some of its members, in Acts. Matthew ended, '(But) this you ought to have done, and not to leave the other undone'. The Law (including tithe-law) remains valid for Jews (16.16), so Luke copies this in (παρεῖναι for ἀφιέναι); but the last thing he expected was that his own congregation would turn up with tithes of mint and rue.

11.43. The memory of the Mark 12 parallel to Matthew 23, with its love of God, draws Luke's mind away from Mt. 23.23 to the question of greetings in the market-place and front seats in the synagogue, the first point of attack in Mk 12.38f. He finds the text in the Matthaean version in front of him at 23.6f., 'they like the chief-place at dinners, and the chief-seats in synagogues, and salutations in market-places'. Luke turns this into a second Woe: 'Woe to you Pharisees, for you love *the chief-seat in synagogues, and salutations in market-places*'. He leaves by the best seats at dinners for ch. 14, and the irrelevant titles, rabbi, etc.; though he will return to the topic of humility (Mt. 23.12) in ch. 14 also.

11.44. This done, he reverts to the passage he has been expounding, Mt. 23.23-26. The following verse takes up a further matter: 'Woe to you, scribes and Pharisees, hypocrites, for you resemble whitewashed graves, which outwardly appear beautiful, but within are full of dead men's bones and all uncleanness' (v. 27). Men think the Pharisees righteous, but within they are full of hypocrisy (v. 28). Matthew is pursuing his outside/inside contrast with the aid of the Jewish practice of whiting graves each year before Passover (*m.Shek.* 1.1). People did not whitewash their tombs in Achaea, so Luke is forced to amend: 'Woe to you, for you are like unseen tombs, and *men* walk upon them and do not know it'. He prefers μνημεῖον to τάφος in any case; but his concern is to retain the point of Matthew's Woe despite the difference of custom. In both Gospels the point is that Pharisees are corrupt at heart, and those who have contact with them may be unaware of their infectious evil. Matthew stressed the rottenness of the Pharisees in themselves, outward piety, inward godlessness: Luke is more concerned with their taint, the effect that contact with them has. He will sum up in a moment: 'Beware of the leaven of the Pharisees, which is hypocrisy' (12.1).

11.45f. So there are three Woes on the Pharisees for their bogus piety: now for their allies, the lawyers. Luke breaks the discourse in half by introducing a characteristic foil objection (§ 1.4), 'Teacher, in saying this you insult us also'—cf. his insertion in the Husbandmen, 'When they heard this they said, God forbid' (21.16R). The main point on lawmaking in Matthew's discourse comes at the beginning (23.4): 'They bind heavy burdens (and hard to bear) and lay them on men's shoulders, but they themselves will not move them with their finger'. This is a different point (δέ) from 23.3, 'they say and do not': Matthew does not reproach the scribes with not tithing herbs, but with not doing the weightier matters. He means that they multiply a Jew's duties to the point where they are intolerable, and will not make the allowances which ordinary living requires. But Luke sees a more sinister feature of the scribal movement than does Matthew the Christian scribe, and the latter's κινεῖν = relax is not enough for him: 'Woe to you lawyers also, for you burden *men* with *burdens* hard to bear, and do *not yourselves* touch the burdens with one of your *fingers*'. He means, 'You know the casuistry that will enable you to escape vexatious duties'. An instance lay before his eyes in the text of Matthew 15/Mark 7, with the Corban ruling: the ordinary Jew had to support his parents, the scribe knew how to get out of it. He stresses the oppressiveness of such rulings with φορτίζετε, drawn in as an echo of πεφορτισμένοι in Mt. 11.28, and δυσβάστακτα (cf. Acts 15.10 οὐδὲ. . .ἰσχύσαμεν βαστάσαι). But the main point is that they do not *touch* (προσψαύετε) such duties with a finger—they evade them. Inconsistency with the tithing comment is forgotten. Suspicion of religious professionals runs deep: as a curate, I was asked by an ingenuous Sunday School teacher, 'Do the vicars keep Lent?'

11.47f. Luke now returns to the climax of Matthew 23, where he left it at the tombs theme. Matthew's final Woe runs (vv. 29ff.), 'Woe to you, scribes and Pharisees, hypocrites! For you build the graves of the prophets and adorn the tombs of the righteous, and you say, If we had lived in the days of our fathers. . .: so that you witness against yourselves that you are sons of those who murdered the prophets'. They recognize that their fathers martyred the prophets, so they are murderers' sons by descent: and true sons you are, says Matthew— like father, like son. The point turns on the double Semitic use of 'son', son by descent and by character. Luke can see Matthew continuing his theme with unabated zeal to the end of the chapter (for he moves here into his peroration), and must take some action to stem the flow if his own discourse is not to lose all balance; so he abbreviates, with disastrous results. *'Woe to you, for you build the tombs of the prophets*, and your *fathers* killed them. So you are witnesses, and consent to the deeds of your fathers, for they killed them and you build'. It is a *non sequitur*: our Victorian Protestant ancestors built the Martyrs' Memorial in St Giles', Oxford, but were far from witnessing and consenting to the Marian fires. This is not the first time that Luke's 'improvements' have landed him in a muddle (§ 19). 'Your fathers' (twice), 'you are witnesses', συνευδοκεῖν and αὐτοί nom. are all testimonies to Luke's hand.

11.49. Matthew now turns to his peroratiom, his διὰ τοῦτο following his succession of οὐαί's as in Isa. 5.24: 'Therefore behold I send to you prophets and wise men and scribes; some of them you will kill and crucify, and some you will flog. . . and persecute'. Matthew is expanding Mk 12.28ff., where Jesus' condemnation of the scribes issues in the prophecy that they will receive the greater judgment. He sees their spiritual failing in the refusal of Jesus' message as continuing in the rejection of the Church's mission, and being punished by the disaster of 70 (22.3-7; 27.25R). The Church's mission is seen from the standpoint of a Christian scribe: it is Jesus ('I') who sends the missionaries, and they are prophets and righteous men (10.41), the righteous men being especially teachers (cf. Acts 13.1, 'prophets and teachers'). Of the teachers a few may be hopefully thought of as σοφούς (*hᵃkhāmîm*, 1 Cor. 1.26); more will be scribes, like Matthew himself (13.52; cf. 7.29R). The mention of prophets, however, causes Luke to make a change. He has just spoken of the killing of the (OT) prophets, so he takes the sending of the prophets to refer to the OT here also. He again prefers a pair to Matthew's triple (§24): (OT) prophets and (NT) apostles. But this entails a change of subject, since it must now be God and not Jesus who does the sending: '*Therefore* also the wisdom of God said, I will *send* among them *prophets and* apostles, and *some of them* they *will kill and persecute* (out)'. Matthew's σοφούς suggests the periphrasis for God, ἡ σοφία τοῦ θεοῦ, keeping the word but changing the meaning (§ 20); Luke used ἡ σοφία absolutely for God at 7.35 ('Wisdom is justified by all her children'; cf. 7.29, 'all the people. . . justified *God*'), and uses 'the angels of God' similarly (12.8; 15.10). God's wisdom is speaking either at creation or in early times, so the future ἀποστελῶ is required in place of Matthew's present with near-future meaning. Luke prefaces ἐκ- to Matthew's διώξετε (Greeven) because he has lived through the Jews' driving of the Church *out of* the synagogue. The only trouble with his broadening of the attack into the OT period is that διὰ τοῦτο has now lost its meaning. The foregoing verses in both Gospels were a reproach to the Jewish leadership for spiritual failure in (supposedly) Jesus' lifetime: Matthew's διὰ τοῦτο makes fine sense, as Jesus prophesies the events of 33-70; but how can God foretell the sending of the *Old Testament* prophets, etc., for the failures of *AD* Judaism? Oh, what a tangled web we weave (§9).

11.50f. Luke's inclusion of the OT prophets was encouraged by
the following verses in Matthew: 'that upon you may come all the
innocent blood shed on the earth from the blood of innocent Abel to
the blood of Zechariah the son of Barachiah, whom you murdered
between the temple and the altar. Amen, I say to you, all these things
shall come on this generation'. Matthew was expounding 23.32, 'Fill
up the measure of your fathers!', with a doctrine of corporate guilt
and punishment. The delation of Jesus and the persecuting of his
Church were the final straw in a history of murder of the innocent
that extended through the OT from Abel in Genesis 4 to Zechariah
in 2 Chronicles 24: the punishment for such a record would fall in 70
(cf. 'and on our children', 27.25). Matthew's style is unmistakable,
the expansion being his own composition; and Luke amends
marginally—'that the *blood* of *all* the prophets that has been *shed*
from the foundation of the world may be required from this
generation; *from the blood of Abel to the blood of Zechariah* who died
between the altar and the House: yes *I say to you*, it will be required
from *this generation*'. 'Blood will be required' is more elegant LXX
Greek than 'blood will come' (Gen. 9.5; 42.22, etc.); Luke thinks of
the prophets as going back to creation (1.70); 'all the prophets' recurs
at 13.28; 24.27; Acts 3.18, 24; 10.43; the perfect participle is an
improvement on Matthew's ἐκχυννόμενον; καταβολὴ κόσμου is the
standard NT expression (×11) for 'creation', and is added to explain
the mention of Abel; 'who was killed' for 'whom you murdered' is
because first-century AD scribes cannot be properly accused of
murdering Zechariah in the eighth-century BC; 'the son of Barachiah'
is dropped because 2 Chron. 24.20 says he was the son of Jehoiada;
the Temple is called οἶκος following Mt. 23.38, for pejorative reasons
as in Acts 7.47; and Luke prefers Greek ναί to Semitic ἀμήν
regularly.

11.52. Luke has not only completed Matthew's last Woe—he has
nearly completed his peroration into the bargain. But he has only
given two Woes on the lawyers, and both balance with the Pharisees
and completeness (Rev. 11.14) require a third. The best candidate is
Mt. 23.13, 'But woe to you, scribes and Pharisees, hypocrites! For
you shut (κλείετε) the kingdom of heaven before men; for you
yourselves enter not, and those entering you do not allow to enter'.
But how do they shut the kingdom? They stop people knowing about
it. Luke: '*Woe to you* lawyers, *for* you have taken away the key

(κλεῖδα) of knowledge: *you* did *not enter* yourselves, and *those entering* you hindered'. John came to give the people knowledge (γνῶσις) of salvation, but the lawyers by their obstruction (5.17ff.; 10.25ff.) have prevented the mass of people receiving this knowledge. They could not actually 'not allow' people in (Mt.), but they could 'hinder' and have. The Woe is quite suited to the lawyers, as the de facto spiritual leaders of Israel; but it makes a sad anticlimax alongside Matthew's magnificent tirade.

11.53f. Matthew 23 left the opposition thunderstruck; but Luke has set up a luncheon-party scene for the occasion (vv. 37f.), and he brings it to a close with some frustrated counter-abuse. The action is based on a slightly earlier moment in Mark 12, when certain Pharisees were sent to trap Jesus in his talk (v. 13, cf. development in Lk. 20.20, 'to hand him over'). But Luke's tell-tale 'the scribes (οἱ γραμματεῖς!) and the Pharisees' show that he has Matthew 23 in front of him. Nor has he forgotten Mt.15. His opening κἀκεῖθεν ἐξελθόντος αὐτοῦ comes from Mt. 15.21 καὶ ἐξελθὼν ἐκεῖθεν; the Pharisaic reaction is probably based on Mt. 15.12 οἱ Φαρισαῖοι ἐσκανδαλίσθησαν; and his ἀποστοματίζειν ... ἐκ τοῦ στόματος αὐτοῦ are probably echoes of Mt. 15.11, 17, εἰς τὸ στόμα...ἐκ τοῦ στόματος.

Although Bultmann (pp. 146ff.) in general accords priority to Matthew, the weight of modern criticism is the other way. Polag (pp. 54-58) prints the text of Luke with the following exceptions: v. 39b nearly = Mt.; v. 41 is a new creation; v. 42 'anice and cummin' for Luke's 'rue and every herb'; v. 43 φιλεῖτε for ἀγαπᾶτε; v. 44 add φαρισαῖοι; om. v. 45; v. 46 = Mt., with opening 'Woe too to you lawyers for'; v. 47 om. τῶν; v. 48 close to Mt.; v. 52b = Mt. Matthew's repetitive style and his artistic structure have been correctly seen to be signs of his handiwork, and the false inference has been drawn that he was adapting Q = mostly Lk. For an account of Matthew 23 as an exposition of Mark 12, 1 Thessalonians 2, etc., cf. my *MLM*, pp. 419-30. For variations of the standard position, see Manson, pp. 94-105, 227-40, 268-70; Ernst Haenchen, *ZTK* (1951), Lührmann, pp. 43-48, Schulz, pp. 94-114; J. Neusner, *NTS* (1976); David Garland, *The Intention of Matthew 23* (1979). On vv. 49-51 see also O. Steck, pp. 29-53, 222-27; J. Suggs, pp. 13-29, 58-61; Hoffmann, pp. 164-71; Schulz, pp. 336-45.

With a limited amount of QC words, the Matthaeanisms are limited. οἱ ἄνθρωποι = men comes twice in the passage, and is a common expression in Matthew (26/5/10, 6.14R, 15R; 9.8R, etc.). Matthew likes ἀπὸ ... ἕως, 8/1/ 1+3, 1.17R (×3); 26.29R; 27.45R; and he is fond of διὰ τοῦτο also, 10/3/

4+1, 13.13R, 52R; 21.43R. 'The scribes (γραμματεῖς) and the Pharisees' in v. 53 looks like a Matthaeanism carried over. But the principal reason for thinking that the Lucan version is secondary throughout is that it seems to represent a series of unhappy alterations of an originally consistent text, well-informed on Judaica, such as we find in Matthew. Thus vv. 39f. has muddled the issue of the outside and inside of the vessel and person, which is clear in Mt.; v. 42 has introduced errors about tithing; at v. 44 Luke lacks the Palestinian custom of whitening tombs; at v. 46 he has a cruder version of the burdens point; at vv. 47f. he has reduced the building of the prophets' tombs to nonsense; at v. 49 his 'Therefore' lacks all logical force. It is the three muddles which make Lucan secondariness so plausible. Polag goes back to Mt. at. 11.48, and makes up a text of his own at 11.41; but he cannot escape διὰ τοῦτο in v. 49—it is there in QC.

11.37 ἐν τῷ + inf.*, ἐρωτᾶν*, Φαρισαῖος sing.*, ἀναπεσεῖν. Hapax: ἀριστᾶν.

11.38 Φαρισαῖος sing.*, θαυμάζειν.

11.39 εἶπεν-δὲ-πρός*, ὁ-κύριος = Jesus, νῦν*. Hapaxes: πίναξ, (γέμειν), (ἁρπαγή), (πονηρία). Resumptive νῦν Acts 3.17, etc.

11.40 (καί = also). Vocative ἄφρων recurs at 12.20: for 'Fools. . . ' followed by a rhetorical question, cf. Mt. 23.17 (μωροί).

11.41 πλήν*, τά = part. Hapax: ἐνεῖναι. ἐλεημοσύνη 3/0/2+8. Marshall takes Luke's form as an interpretation of Q=Mt., cf. Manson, p. 269, Schulz, p. 96; for a criticism of Wellhausen–Black's *dakki* (*o*)/*zakki* hypothesis, cf. *MLM*, p. 426.

11.42 οὐαί + dat.*, (ἔδει*), (ταῦτα), (κἀκεῖνος), (A καί-μή non-A), ὁ-θεός. Hapaxes: (ἡδύοσμον), πήγανον, λάχανον, παριέναι. παρέρχεσθαι 18.37R; παρεῖναι for ἀφιέναι, probably influenced by παρέρχεσθαι.

11.43 οὐαί + dat.*, ἀγαπᾶν, (ἀσπασμός*). Luke dislikes φιλεῖν, 5/1/2+0, but introduces it at 20.46 from reminiscence of Mt. 23.6. Mt. amends Mk to sing. πρωτοκλισίαν at *dinner*, as there was a single place of honour, 'in the bosom of' the host (Jn 13.23); Lk. gives the sing. πρωτοκαθεδρίαν in *synagogue*, following his lead—but in synagogue there was a front *row* of seats for the elders facing the people (*t.Meg.* 4.21).

11.44 Hapax: ἄδηλος. περιπατοῦντες ἐπάνω cf. 10.19 πατεῖν ἐπάνω; 4.39R.

11.45 τις, νομικός*, αὐτός nom., καί = also. ὑβρίζειν 18.32R, Acts 14.5, ὕβρις ×2 Acts. Hist. pres. in dialogue ×8 Lk., × 11 Acts (Neirynck, *MA*, p. 229).

11.46 εἶπεν, οὐαί + dat.*, νομικός*, καί = also, (αὐτός nom.) (δάκτυλος). Hapaxes: φορτίζειν, δυσβάστακτος, προσψαύειν. N-A²⁶ Mt. 23.4 prints καὶ δυσβάστακτα in brackets, with a dissenting note by Metzger himself in the *Commentary* (p. 60). I agree with Metzger in thinking the words an interpolation from Luke 11. Luke likes βαστάζειν, and Acts 15.10 gives a close parallel. Haenchen (pp. 38f.) and Garland (pp. 20f.) are too quick to accuse Matthew of inconsistency: 23.4 is the standard extra-Judaic view of the halakhah as insupportable in everyday life, and none of the detailed charges in what follows accuses the leadership of not keeping the halakhah. 23.3 implies that they are hypocrites, and the hypocrisy consists in missing the weightier matters, e.g. by delating Jesus for crucifixion. For Luke's φορτίζετε φόρτια, cf. 2.8 φυλάσσοντες φυλακάς, and other *etymologische Figuren* listed in Harnack, p. 83; Morgenthaler, *LGZ*, p. 18. For εἰς + gen. cf. 5.3R; 15.15, 26; the phrase gives emphasis (Schulz, p. 107).

11.47 (οἰκοδομεῖν), (οἱ-πατέρες)-ὑμῶν*

11.48 οἱ-πατέρες-ὑμῶν*, αὐτός nom., οἰκοδομεῖν. ἄρα 7/2/6+5, 22.23R; first word as in 11.20; cp. Matthew's ὥστε 15/13/5+8. μάρτυρες εἶναι 24.48, ×4 Acts. συνευδοκεῖν Acts 8.1, 22.20. Manson (p. 101), 'They killed the prophets: you make sure they stay dead', forces the text; Schulz (pp. 109f.), 'they recognize the prophetic word as valid for the past but not for the present', is not said at all. Garland (p. 164) is right: it is a *non sequitur*.

11.49 καί = also, ὁ-θεός, εἶπεν, ἀπόστολος*. ἀποστέλλειν εἰς people, Acts 26.17. N-A²⁶ prints διώξουσιν with p⁷⁵ ℵ BCL Θ etc.; Greeven ἐκδιώξουσιν with ADW fam 13 pl., taking the simple verb as assimilation to Mt. The order 'prophets and apostles' shows the OT prophets are in view (cp. 1 Cor. 12.28, Eph. x3, apostles preceding Christian prophets).

11.50 Hapax: καταβολή. Matthew's ὅπως 17/1/7+14; Luke prefers ἵνα, 41/65/46+15.

11.51 Luke drops τοῦ before αἵματος twice on the LXX model, to save having five τοῦ's in the sentence. ἀπολομένου = 'was killed', Acts 5.37, cf. act. Lk. 19.47; 20.16. The introduction of Matthew's ἀπό makes three ἀπό phrases in a row, which is rather clumsy (§ 19.1). ναὶ λέγω ὑμῖν, 12.5 QD.

11.52 οὐαί + dat.*, νομικός*, αὐτός nom., κωλύειν. Hapax: κλεῖς (Mt. κλείειν).

11.53 περί. Hapaxes: δεινῶς, ἐνέχειν, ἀποστοματίζειν. κἀκεῖθεν ἐξελθόντος αὐτοῦ (p⁷⁵) ℵ BCL etc., N-A²⁶; ADW Θ pl. λέγοντος δὲ αὐτοῦ ταῦτα πρὸς αὐτούς looks like a correction to give better sense.

11.54 τις. ἵνα κατηγορήσωσιν αὐτοῦ Mk 3.1.

Haenchen, E., 'Matthäus 23', *ZTK* 48 (1951), pp. 38-63.
Christ, F., *Jesus Sophia: Die Sophia-Christologie bei den Synoptikern* (Zürich, 1970)
Neusner, J., '"First Cleanse the Inside": The "Halakhic" Background of a Controversy-
   Saying', *NTS* 22 (1976), pp. 486-95.
Garland, D., *The Intention of Matthew 23*(NTSuppl. 52; Leiden, 1979).
Légasse, S., 'L'oracle contre "cette génération"', in J. Delobel (ed.), *Logia*, 237-56.

39. *The Saving of the Soul*, 12.1-40

a. *Fearless Confession*, 12.1-12

The remainder of Matthew 15 comprises the Canaanite Woman,
various healings, and the feeding of the Four Thousand, stories
which Luke omitted in the Marcan sequence for reasons we noted
above (p. 436). With Mt. 16.1, 4 he reaches the demand for a sign,
which he has just expounded (11.16, 29-32); and there is then the
conversation in the boat, which he has not had, and which attracts
his attention for its link with the Woes.

12.1. Jesus says, 'Take heed and beware of (ὁρᾶτε καὶ προσέχετε
ἀπό) the leaven of the Pharisees and Sadducees' (16.6; cf. Mk 8.15,
ὁρᾶτε βλέπετε ἀπό); and again, 'But beware of (προσέχετε δὲ ἀπό)
the leaven of the Pharisees and Sadducees' (16.11). Jesus meant,
Matthew adds, the leaven of their teaching (v. 12). This is just the
sort of connection Luke is pleased to see, so he has Jesus open the
next pericope, '*Beware* for yourselves *of* (προσέχετε ἑαυτοῖς ἀπό) *the
leaven*, which is hypocrisy, *of the Pharisees*'. He drops the Sadducees,
who have little place in his Gospel, and substitutes hypocrisy for
'teaching'. Luke knew there were Pharisees in the Church (Acts
15.5), and he is torn between not wishing to offend them and feeling
them to be wrong-headed. Hence his suppression of Matthew's
insistent ὑποκριταί in the last pericope; but he is in no doubt that
hypocrisy was the word for Pharisaic religion and he means to warn
his congregation on the subject now.

The boat conversation was with the disciples of course (Mt. 16.5),
and Luke has these words spoken 'to his disciples first'; but his own
church contained adherents as well as members, and he likes to
picture Jesus similarly teaching his disciples against a background of
a crowd (6.19f.; 12.54; 16.14, etc.). So he begins here, 'Meanwhile,
the myriads of the crowd being gathered so that they were treading
on one another. . .' Where has this come from? It comes from the
previous story in Matthew, where *the crowd* gathers (15.32, 35) and

is fed, 'and those who ate were four thousand men beside women and children' (v. 38). Luke has again been at work inferring (§13): if there were four thousand men (ἄνδρες) and their wives (γυναικῶν), and goodness knows how many children apiece—why, that takes us well over the ten thousand mark, and if they brought three children each it would be twenty. So that gives us μυριάδες: but how could nearly twenty thousand people get close enough to hear the Lord? Plainly they must have been treading on one another.

12.2f. Hypocrisy is folly, for it is bound to come out. An apt saying comes to mind from Matthew 10, which Luke has left by: 'For there is nothing hidden (κεκαλυμμένον) which shall not be revealed, and secret which shall not be made known' (v. 26). He copies it in with the compound συγκεκαλυμμένον (συν- compounds 21/24/41+47). Unfortunately, Matthew's context is not about hypocrisy coming out, but about preaching the gospel, and continues, 'What I say to you in the dark say in the light, and what you hear in the ear proclaim upon the housetops' (v. 27). Luke responds by one of his boldest moves, retaining the wording but changing the meaning (§20): 'Wherefore whatever you have *said in the dark* shall be *heard in the light, and what you* have spoken *in the ear* in inner rooms shall be *proclaimed upon the housetops*'. The quickness of the tongue deceives the ear: it is a very neat job, marred only by the clarifying addition of 'in the inner rooms', which spoils the beautiful Matthaean balance. Matthew's command to preach publicly what the disciples have heard in private has become a Lucan warning that private hypocrisies will be publicly exposed.

12.4f. Such ingenuity cannot be maintained for long, and Luke now allows the flow of the Matthaean discourse to 'interpret' for him the meaning of hypocrisy. Matthew continued, 'And be not fearful of those who kill the body, but cannot kill the soul; but fear rather him who can destroy both soul and body in Gehenna' (v. 28). Luke can accept that: the worst kind of hypocrisy of all is of those who say they are Christians in private, but will not face persecution. We have moved a bit from the leaven of the Pharisees, but that is bound to happen when ready-made texts are taken from here and there. He writes, 'And I say to you my friends, *be not fearful of those who kill the body*, and after that have nothing further to do. But I will show you whom to fear: *fear him who* after killing has power to cast into *Gehenna*. Yes, I tell you, fear him'. Confession under persecution is a crucial issue for Luke (cf. Schuyler Brown), so he amplifies. 'And I say to you my friends' is in fact required by the new turn the discourse is taking here; Luke had the similar, 'But I say to you who hear' at 6.27QD. The remaining additions merely lend impressive emphasis: for the Lucan nature of their language see below. He is the more willing to allow the Confession theme its head because he read it also in Matthew 16: 'whoever would save his soul. . . ' (v. 25).

12.6f. Matthew went on, 'Are not two sparrows sold for a halfpenny? And one of them will not fall to the ground without your Father'. Luke amends, '*Are not* five *sparrows sold for* two *halfpen*ce? *And not one of them* is forgotten before God'. The point is the cheapness of the birds, so Luke has a handful of them for Matthew's pair; but he keeps the price as close as he can. Luke likes fives (§12): five in a house, five yoke of oxen, five brothers. It is perhaps unfortunate that Matthew should have tried to reassure the confessing Christian with the example of a sparrow that *died*, so he changes this to 'is not forgotten before God', so that martyrdom is not so certain! This chimes in too with Matthew's following, 'But even the hairs of your head are all numbered. So fear not: you are of more value than many sparrows', which he copies in almost as it stands.

12.8f. This brings Matthew to the point: 'So everyone who shall confess me before men, I will also confess him before my Father in heaven: but whoever denies me before men, I will also deny him before my Father in heaven' (vv. 32f.). Luke amends marginally: 'And I tell you, *everyone* who may *confess me before men*, the Son of Man *will also confess him before* the angels of God: *but* he that *denies me* in the presence of *men* shall be *deni*ed in the presence of the angels of God'. He puts πᾶς ὃς ἄν as he does at Acts 3.22R (Deut. 18.19) and 3.23R (Lev. 23.29). He keeps Matthew's ἔμπροσθεν in the first half (18/2/10+2), but slips into his own preferred ἐνώπιον both times in the second (0/0/22+13). He had 'the wisdom of God' as a divine periphrasis at 11.49, and he has 'the angels of God' here, as he will at 15.10, cf. 16.9—he dislikes Matthew's 'Father-in-heaven', and he found the angels in the judgment scene in Mt. 16.27. And here also was the Son of Man: 'For *the Son of Man* shall come in the glory of his Father with his *angels*, and then he shall render to each man according to his work'. Whose angels? Luke thinks, the angels of God, Jesus' Father—who else? He substituted the more numinous 'the Son of Man' for 'me' at 6.22QD, and he will bring it in again from an indirect text at 18.8 and 19.10: this time the Matthew 16 context gives us a clear explanation for both the Son of Man and the angels.

12.10. In his Beelzebul pericope Luke held over Matthew's saying on blasphemy, which he feels (properly) to fit better in the context of Confession. Matthew had altered the force of the blasphemy against the Holy Spirit from Mark, and had expanded: '. . . And whoever says a word against the Son of Man, it will be forgiven him; but whoever says it against the Holy Spirit, it will not be forgiven him, neither in this age nor in that to come' (12.32). He took it that the blasphemy was a Christian's denial of the Holy Spirit he had received at Baptism. He might, before his conversion, have spoken a word of denial (as Peter did), and that would be all right; but not after. Luke warmly concurs, '*And* everyone *who* shall *say a word* at *the Son of Man, it will be forgiven him; but* he who blasphemes at *the Holy Spirit, it will not be forgiven* him'. The πᾶς ὅς he carries over in parallel with the preceding sentence (v. 8), with a participle in the second clause as in v. 9. The future ἐρεῖ arises from the most obvious instances being some way ahead—Peter and Paul. βλασφημήσαντι εἰς is a reminiscence of Mk 3.29, ὃς δ' ἂν βλασφημήσῃ εἰς τὸ πνεῦμα τὸ ἅγιον.

12.11f. The mention of the Holy Spirit recalls a more positive word from a little earlier in the same context. Mt. 10.17-20 had warned that the disciples would be flogged in synagogues, and brought before governors and kings: 'and when they deliver you, do not be anxious how or what you are to speak: for it will be given you in that hour what you are to speak. For it is not you who speak, but the spirit of your Father which speaks in you'. Luke interprets a little: '*And when they* bring *you* in to *synagogues and* rulers and authorities, *do not be anxious how or what you are to* answer or what you are to say: *for the* Holy *Spirit* will teach *you in* that very *hour* what you must say'. Christians were not always 'handed over', but they were always brought into court, Jewish or Gentile. At 20.20R Luke speaks of Pilate, as here, as τῇ ἀρχῇ καὶ ἐξουσίᾳ of the governor. He puts the technical ἀπολογήσησθε for Mt.'s plain 'speak' to suit the law-court situation (21.14R, ×6 Acts). His 'or what you are to say' echoes Mt.'s λαλήσητε in a customary weak tautology; bless and pray for, your enemies and those who hate you

(§22). The Spirit of your Father naturally becomes 'the Holy Spirit' in Luke; ἐν αὐτῇ τῇ ὥρᾳ is a Lucanism; and 'it will be given you' becomes the more specific διδάξει. Luke did well to limit his second Mission Discourse to Mt. 9.37–10.16. The persecution section, Mt. 10.17-33, is a topic on its own, and has been well treated here.

As so often, Matthew's regular style has seduced critics into the Lucan priority fallacy, and especially at 12.32 where his expansion of Mark has led to accusations of conflation. For an account of his exposition of Mk 4.22 and 13.9-11 in 10.26-33, see *MLM*, pp. 349ff. Polag (pp. 58f.) prints Luke 12.2-12 as Q with the following exceptions: v. 2 κεκαλυμμένον; v. 3 om. ἀνθ'ὧν,ὅσα for ὅ, om. ἐν τοῖς ταμείοις; v. 4 om. τοῖς φίλοις μου; v. 6 Mt.'s πεσεῖται ἐπὶ τὴν γῆν ἄνευ for 'is not forgotten before'; v. 7 = Mt., om. οὖν; v. 9 ὅς ἄν + subj. for ἀρνησάμενος, ἔμπροσθεν ×2 for ἐνώπιον; v. 10 ὅς ἐὰν εἴπῃ . . . ὅς δ' ἄν βλασφημήσῃ; v. 11 om. τὰς ἀρχὰς καὶ ἐξουσίας, ἀπολογήσησθε ἢ τί, v. 12 τί εἴπητε.

The difficulty is that the sentence-structure as well as the vocabulary in the QC words is so strongly reminiscent of Matthew. At Mt. 12.11f. Mt. R adds to the Marcan withered hand (a) a *qal wahomer* argument with an animal (sheep), (b) a rhetorical question, οὐχὶ κρατήσει. . . ; , (c) a conclusion, πόσῳ οὖν διαφέρει ἄνθρωπος προβάτου. At 6.25f. Matthew had μὴ μεριμνᾶτε τῇ ψυχῇ/τῷ σώματι, followed by (b) rhetorical question, οὐχὶ ἡ ψυχή. . . ; (a) *qal wahomer* argument with the animals (τὰ πετεινὰ), (c) a conclusion, διαφέρετε αὐτῶν. The Lucan parallel at 12.22f. lacks (b). So here we also have (in QC) μὴ φοβηθῆτε . . . σῶμα, followed by (a) *qal wahomer* argument with the animals (στρουθία), in the form of (b) a rhetorical question, οὐχί. . . ; , with (c) a conclusion πολλῶν σ. διαφέρετε. Even the form 'Do not fear . . . but fear . . . ' recalls Mt. 6.19QD 'Lay not up . . . but lay up. . . ', 5.17M 'Do not think that I came. . . I came', etc. Furthermore, both Lk. 12.8f. and Lk. 12.9 are full converse statements where the second half comes close to repeating the first in negative form. Matthew is especially fond of these: 'For if you forgive men. . . ' (6.14f.R), 'If then your eye is generous. . . ' (6.22f.QD), 'Whoever then breaks one of the least of these commandments. . . ' (5.19M), 'So every good tree. . . ' (7.17QD), 'For broad is the gate. . . ' (7.13f.QD), 'And if the house is worthy. . . ' (10.13QD). With no instance in Mark, and few in Luke (16.10, perhaps 7.47), it seems obvious that such statements are part of Matthew's own clear, rather insistent teaching style.

There are expressions among the QC words which are favourites of Matthew too: Gehenna, 7/3/1, 23.33QD; οὐχί opening a question, 9/0/9, 12.11R; 13.27M; 13.56R; 18.12QD; 20.13M; εἷς ἐξ αὐτῶν 4/0/2, 18.12QD; 22.35R; 27.48R. With 'the hairs of your head are all numbered', cf. Mt.

5.36M 'You cannot make one hair black or white'; and even more, with the sequence 'no sparrow shall fall to the ground without (God): even the hairs...', cf. Mt. 6.26f., 'consider the birds... which of you can add one cubit'—but this is QC. But the most damaging phrase of all is the repeated ἔμπροσθεν τῶν ἀνθρώπων, 6/0/1+0, 5.16M; 6.1M, 2M; 10.32QC, 33QD; 23.14QD. The first five of these all contain the contrast before men/before God, which is also found in Mt. 6.5ff., 16ff. Matthew even also writes ἀρνεῖσθαι ἔμπροσθεν at 26.70R.

The substitution of the Lucan text so widely in the QD words brings the usual *embarras de richesses* difficulties. Luke likes ὑποδεικνύναι, 1/0/3+2, ὑπ. ὑμῖν 1/0/3+1: with 'I will show you whom to fear: fear...', cf. 6.47, 'I will show you to whom he is like: he is like...' (QD). μετὰ ταῦτα is a favourite, 0/0/5+4, 5.27R; 10.1R; as is ἐν αὐτῇ τῇ ὥρᾳ, 0/0/6, 20.19R, 10.21QD; μετὰ τό + inf. recurs at 22.20, Acts 1.3; 7.4; 10.41; 19.13; 19.21; 20.1 (1/2/2+6), and could be paralleled with other prepositions + τὸ + inf. (24/13/71+49); ναὶ λέγω ὑμῖν comes again at 7.26QD; 11.51QD (only); ἔχειν + inf. occurs 1/0/5+6 (Hawkins, p. 40). The paragraph is among the most embarrassing for the Q hypothesis, with the Matthew words so Matthaean, and the Lucan words so Lucan that Polag's Q looks like a conflation of Luke and Matthew—which is precisely what it is. Some of the Lucan phrases can be (and are, by some scholars) avoided, but at the cost of substituting further Matthaean ones. No one can avoid the embarrassment of the QC sentence-forms.

12.1 ἀλληλῶν, ἤρξατο-λέγειν + πρός*, (προσέχετε)- ἑαυτοῖς, ἥτις*. Hapaxes: μυριάς (Acts 19.19; 21.20), ὑπόκρισις. ἐν οἷς Acts 26.12f., cf. ἀνθ' ὧν, v. 3. ἐπισυνάγεσθαι perhaps under the influence of Mt. 23.37, in the verse following the Abel-Zachariah logia ('fairly conclusively', Marshall). ὥστε, cf. Mk 2.2 συνήχθησαν ὥστε ... For ὑπόκρισις as derived from Q/Mt. 23 ὑποκριταί, cf. U. Wilkens, *TDNT* VIII, p. 567. The order of the phrase 'which is hypocrisy' varies: N-A²⁶ follows p⁷⁵ BLe with the harder, earlier position.

12.2 Hapax: συγκαλύπτειν (συν-compound).

12.3 ανθ'ὧν, (εἰπεῖν). Hapax: (σκοτία). ταμ(ι)εῖον 12.24QD.

12.4 φίλος*, μετὰ-ταῦτα*, μὴ + ἔχειν + inf.* Luke omits Mt.'s ψυχή, which he saves till vv. 13-21 for expansion. He likes Jesus to speak affectionately to his followers, 'my friends', 'little flock'.

12.5 ὑποδεικνύναι, τὸ + inf. Hapax: (γέεννα). ναὶ λέγω ὑμῖν introduces an impressive repetition as at 11.51QD. Schulz (pp. 157f.) takes vv. 4f. to be entirely Lucan redaction of Q, in view of the Lucan locutions.

12.6 ἐνώπιον*, ὁ-θεός. Hapaxes: (ἀσσάριον), ἐπιλανθάνεσθαι. The Matthaean version has the closer parallels in Jewish tradition, cf. S-B, I, pp. 582f.

12.7 Hapax: (ἀριθμεῖν).

12.8 (καί = also), ὁ-θεός. The verse is appealed to extensively in the Son of Man debate, the Lucan version being commonly taken as original, and often as dominical—cf. A.J.B. Higgins, pp. 31-33, 80-84. But Bultmann's distinction between Jesus and the Son of Man (pp. 128, 151f.) can hardly be maintained; arguments that the tendency would be towards identifying Jesus and the heavenly judge as 'I' (Schulz, p. 68, and many) are weak. Matthew does the opposite at 16.13R. Luke should be credited with a source, and we have one in Mt. 16.27.

12.9 ἐνώπιον* ×2, ὁ-θεός. ἀπαρνεῖσθαι under influence of Mt. 16.24 (= Mk 8.34); the passive is probably just to avoid repetition.

12.10 βλασφημεῖν εἰς, cf. Acts 6.11. τὸ ἅγιον πνεῦμα is not the most common order in L–A, but cf. Acts 1.8; 2.33, 38; 9.31; 10.45; 15.28. There is no tension with vv. 8f. on the understanding that the distinction is between unbaptized and baptized: Luke shows his embarrassment over Peter's denial (see *ad loc.*). This view (cf. C.K. Barrett, pp. 105-17) is preferable to a distinction between two periods, before and after Jesus' death (Bultmann, p. 138; Tödt, p. 119; Schulz, p. 248); for how then would Paul be forgiven?

12.11 εἰσφέρειν*, εἰπεῖν. The 'rules and authorities' are the Greek courts, replacing Mt.'s sanhedrins. Schulz (p. 442) credits εἰσφέρειν to Q despite 5.18R, 19R; but this is to justify his general view that Matthew is a 'contamination' of Q = Lk with Mark.

12.12 (ἐν)-αὐτῇ-(τῇ-ὥρᾳ)*, δεῖ, εἰπεῖν. τὸ ἅγιον πνεῦμα as in v. 10.

Barrett, C.K., *The Holy Spirit and the Gospel Tradition* (London, 1947).
Lövestam, E., *Spiritus Blasphemia: Eine Studie zu Mk 3,28f par Mt 12,31f* (Lund, 1968).
Boring, M.E., 'The Unforgivable Sin Logion Mark III 28-29/Matt XII 31-32/Luke XII 10: Formal Analysis and History of the Tradition', *NT* 18 (1976), pp. 258-79.
McDermott, J.M., 'Luke xii,8-9: Stone of Scandal', *RB* 84 (1977), pp. 523-37. 'Luc xii, 8-9: pierre angulaire', *RB* 85 (1978), pp. 381-401.
Higgins, A.J.B., *The Son of Man in the Teaching of Jesus* (SNTSM, 39; Cambridge, 1980).
Wrege, H.-T., 'Zur Rolle des Geisteswortes in frühchristlichen Traditionen (Lc 12,10 parr)', in J. Delobel (ed.) *Logia*, pp. 373-77.
Catchpole, D.R., 'The Angelic Son of Man in Lk 12.8', *NT* 24 (1982), pp. 255-65.

b. *The Rich Fool*, 12.13-21

In 12.1-12 Luke was working from the basis of Matthew 16—the leaven of the Pharisees, and the coming of the Son of Man with his

Father's angels to judge those who would not confess their faith. But Mt. 16.24-28 is more specific than this. It is not just that we must take up our cross and follow: there is the especial peril of money. 'For whoever would save his soul shall lose it, and whoever loses his soul for my sake shall find it. For what shall a man be profited if he gain the whole world and lose his soul? Or what shall a man give in exchange for his soul'? (16.25f.). The fourfold threat of the loss of a man's ψυχή, and the spiritual dangers of gain (ever present to our evangelist) suggest an amplification at this point: and Luke produces the parable of the Rich Man, whose profits were so large, who said to his soul, Soul, you have much goods, but God said, This night they require your soul of you.

The theme of the parable is given, then, in Mt. 16.26; but the substance must be found elsewhere, and is taken in fact from Matthew 6, where a similar topic is expounded. 'Do not treasure for yourselves on earth. . . but treasure (θησαυρίζετε) yourselves treasures in heaven. . . Do not be anxious for your soul, what you shall eat (φάγητε) or what you shall drink (πίητε). . . Behold the birds of heaven that they sow not nor reap, nor gather into barns (συνάγουσιν εἰς ἀποθήκας)' (6.19, 26). Luke weaves his story from these celebrated threads. The rich man's lands bore well, and he had not space enough to gather (συνάξω) his corn. So he decided to pull down his barns (ἀποθήκας) and build bigger, and there gather (συνάξω) his produce. He would say to his soul, Relax, eat, drink (φάγε πίε), be merry—but God revealed his folly, for he would die that night. So is everyone who treasures (θησαυρίζων) for himself, and is not rich towards God. As with the 'Ask, seek, knock' logia in Matthew 7, so here. Luke first used the sayings to compose the parable of the Friend at Midnight, and then wrote the passage out. Now he takes the details from Mt. 6.19-26 to write his parable in 12.16-21, and then he gives us the full original in 12.22-34. In both cases he is underlining the Lord's teaching with an illustrative story of his own to the same point and with the same core vocabulary.

Luke always opens his teaching pericope with a few words on the setting (cf. 11.37f.; 12.1), and he likes the device of a foil question/request (§ 1.4) to give the instruction force—'Who is my neighbour?', 'Lord, teach us to pray', etc. We have had someone from the crowd commenting before: 'a woman from the crowd said to him' at 11.27, introducing the Ninevites and the Queen of the South. Now we have almost the same phrase, 'Someone from the crowd said to him': Luke needs something to show an attitude of grasping, and the theme comes to him from 1 Corinthians 6. There Paul rebukes brother (ἀδελφός) for going to judgment (κρίνεται) with brother (v. 6); they will not inherit (κληρονομήσουσιν) the kingdom like that, if they are materialist (πλεονεκταί, vv. 9f.). Luke pictures his man in the crowd saying, 'Teacher, bid my brother (ἀδελφῷ) divide the inheritance (κληρονομίαν) with me'. He can then have Jesus say, 'Man, who made me a judge (κριτήν) or divider over you? Look and keep yourselves from all materialism (πλεονεξίας)'; and the parable of the foolish materialist can follow. 'Look and keep yourselves from (ὁρᾶτε καὶ φυλάσσεσθε ἀπό). . .' is probably an echo of Mt. 16.6 again, ὁρᾶτε καὶ προσέχετε ἀπό the leaven of the Pharisees'. A major Pharisaic fault in Luke's eyes was their graspingness (ἁρπαγῆς, 11.39), their love of money (φιλάργυροι, 16.14).

Other details of the paragraph owe something to the LXX. τίς με κατέστησεν κριτὴν ἢ μεριστὴν ἐφ' ὑμᾶς is formed on the model of τίς σε κατέστησεν ἄρχοντα καὶ δικαστὴν ἐφ'ἡμῶν in Exod. 2.14, a text familiar to Luke and cited word for word at Acts 7.27. The theme and the language of the parable are close to Ecclesiastes. 'There is no *good* for *a man* which he shall *eat* and which he shall *drink* and which he shall show to *his soul, good* in his labour. And I saw this, that it is from the hand of *God*' (2.24). 'To everything there is a time, and a season to every doing under heaven: a time to be born and a time to die. . . a time to *pull down* (καθελεῖν) and a time to *build* (οἰκοδομῆσαι)' (3.1-3). We have already observed Luke's redaction of the Beatitudes with the aid of the following line, 'a time to κλαῦσαι and a time to γελάσαι', he read also of breast-beating and dancing, seeking and losing, loving and hating. 3.13 continues, 'Every *man* who *eats* and *drinks* and sees *good*': the repeated ἀγαθόν may have influenced Luke's repeated ἀγαθά. Ecclesiastes gives the climax of Luke's tale too, though perhaps in a different spirit: 'There is an evil which I saw under the sun, and it is great upon man: *a man* to whom God shall give him *riches* and *possessions* and glory, and he does not lack for *his soul* of all that he shall desire, and *God* will not enable him to *eat* of it, for a stranger shall eat it' (6.1f.). Luke is more pithy, and less attached to the status quo: 'And the things that you have laid up, whose shall they be?' His rich man and Ecclesiastes think much the same: 'There is no good under the sun but to *eat* and to *drink* and to *be merry* (εὐφρανθῆναι)' (8.15).

So the theme of the parable comes in Mt. 16.25f., and its outline in Mt. 6.19-26, and both topic and language show repeated echoes of Ecclesiastes LXX. Has this material been put together then by some pre-Lucan source—even Jesus—or by Luke himself? The evidence of the mode of the parable is heavily in favour of the latter. The Fool is one of the four *illustrative stories* in the Gospel tradition, with the Samaritan, Dives and Lazarus, and the Pharisee and Publican, all in Luke (§ 7). It is not an indicative parable describing the action of God, as is almost invariable in Mark and Matthew, but an *imperative* parable, told to warn the Christian of materialism, as elsewhere Luke warns him to pray and not faint, to go and do likewise, etc. (§8). Whereas in the earlier Gospel tradition rich farmers are images of God (the Husbandmen, the Labourers in the Vineyard, etc.) or of Christ (the Sower, the Tares, etc.), as in the Jewish corpus, it is in Luke alone that the *suspicion of riches* turns such people into horror-figures like Dives (§4.7): indeed the animus against the rich is much more deep-seated generally in Luke than in the other Gospels. Again, whereas in Mark and Matthew judgment is expected with the Parousia, when the sickle is put in, or the reapers are sent out, when the master returns or the bridegroom, in Luke *people just die*, and so go to meet their God, Lazarus and Dives no less than the Fool: Christ's coming in Luke is not so imminent, the times of the Gentiles are not yet fulfilled. We have an exact parallel in Luke for the *prefacing of a new parable* to a piece of similar Matthaean teaching in the Friend at Midnight which prefaces the 'Ask, seek. . . ' sayings. *Soliloquy*, which is a rare occurrence in the earlier tradition (the Husbandmen only), is a common feature in Luke (§4.1). He puts the same τί ποιήσω; in the vineyard owner's mouth, against Mark (20.13R), and three times it comes in the plural in 3.10-14: we have 'What am I to do?. . . This I will do' here, and the closely similar, 'What am I to do?. . . I know what I will do' in Lk. 16.3f. The *opening phrase* ἀνθρώπου τινός is thoroughly Lucan (0/0/8). Lucan too are the *four anarthrous verbs*, 'Relax, eat, drink, be merry'—cf. the poor, the blind, the halt, the lame; good measure, pressed down, shaken together, running over (§23). So too are the 'they' who will require the man's soul, like the *angels* who carry Lazarus' soul to Abraham's bosom (16.22), and who have become the Steward's friends and receive him into eternal habitations. Some of the last details could, of course, have been merely added in by Luke: but others concern the whole mode of the parable—the illustrative story, imperative point, the rich man as a horror figure, the animus against wealth, death rather than parousia, the run-up to 12.22-34, and even the soliloquy. What sort of a parable is left if we take all these elements away?

Jeremias (*PJ*, p. 165) notes that Thomas has both parable (63) and the opening conversation (72), and concludes, a little naively, that they both had a pre-Lucan existence separately: Marshall notes the greater likelihood of Thomas' dependence on Luke. Jeremias' descrying of an eschatological thrust to the parable, despite its apparent appeal to death as the moment of judgment, has also been received sceptically (Schneider). These commentators follow the traditional line of attributing the material to L. The points of correspondence between the Fool and the cares-barns-gathering-eating-drinking-treasuring passage following have then to be explained as a happy accident. Schürmann (*TU*, pp. 119f., 232f.) takes them seriously, and concludes that the paragraph was in Q—Schürmann's ability to notice small 'reminiscences' both ways between Luke and Matthew make his Q enormous; but neither he nor the standard appeal to L take proper account of the deep-rooted Lucan elements analysed above. The attempt to argue a Palestinian background (Jeremias, p. 164; Bailey, pp. 57-73) on the ground that appeal to rabbis was normal, or that brothers sometimes ran a property together (Ps. 133.1!), are thin.

12.13 εἶπεν-δέ*, τις, εἰπεῖν. Hapax: μερίζεσθαι (cf. 15.12 μέρος τῆς οὐσίας; διαμ. 1/1/6+2). διδάσκαλε, standard in Luke from a non-disciple, 3.12R; 7.40, etc. εἰπεῖν = command, 6.46QD.

12.14 εἶπεν, ἄνθρωπε*, ἐφ' ὑμᾶς*. Hapax: μεριστής (cf. 13).

12.15 εἶπεν-δὲ-πρός*, φυλάσσειν*, ἐν-τῷ + inf.*, τις, τὰ ὑπάρχοντα*. Hapax: πλεονεξία (cf. 1 Cor. 6.9). περισσεύειν 9.17R = Mt. τὰ ὑπάρχοντα + dat. 8.3R; Acts 4.32. The phrasing is clumsy, but Marshall's 'The wording is not Lucan' is remarkable.

12.16 εἶπεν-δὲ-παραβολήν* + πρός*, ἄνθρωπός-τις*, πλούσιος*, χώρα. Hapax: εὐφορεῖν. For the opening gen. + τινος cf. 7.2QD.

12.17 ἑαυτόν, τί-ποιήσω;*, οὐκ-ἔχω + noun clause, ποῦ.

12.18 εἶπεν, οἰκοδομεῖν. N-A[26] follows p[75]BL πάντα τὸν σῖτον καὶ τὰ ἀγαθά μου, which would be an instance of Lucan tautology: for ἀποθήκη/ συνάγειν τὸν σῖτον cf. 3.17QC, Mt. 13.30. Greeven reads πάντα τὰ γενήματά μου with D it (syr[s.c]).

12.19 κείμενος*, ἔτος, εὐφραίνεσθαι*. Hapax: ἀναπαύεσθαι. With 'I will say to my soul, Soul', cf. 6.42R, 'say to your brother, Brother', etc.

12.20 εἶπον-δέ*, ὁ-θεός, ἑτοιμάζειν. ἄφρων voc., cf. 11.40QD. ταύτῃ τῇ νυκτί 17.34QD; Acts 27.23.

12.21 ἑαυτόν, A καὶ-μή non-A*, θεός anarthrous. Hapax: θησαυρίζειν (Mt. 6.19). πλουτῶν 1.53.

Dupont, J., 'Die individuelle Eschatologie im Lukasevangelium und in der Apostelgeschichte', in P. Hoffmann, (ed.), *Orientierung* (*Fs* Schmid, 1973), pp. 37-47.
Seng, E.W., 'Der reiche Tor: eine Untersuchung von Lk. xii.16-21 unter besonderer Berücksichtigung form- und motivgeschichtlicher Aspekte', *NT* 20 (1978), pp. 136-55.

c. Detachment before the Son of Man comes, 12.22-40

Modern critics are often influenced by synopses which are governed by the Matthaean parallels, and divide the Lucan teaching into snippets, such as 12.22-34 'on Earthly Cares': but the evangelist himself gives us the units he intends with his customary rubrics. Thus 12.22 opens, 'And he said to his disciples', which at least permits us to think that a new section is beginning (though the division is not very forceful); but the stream of teaching goes on unbroken at 12.35 (and 12.33), and we are surely wiser not to ignore these continuities in the text if we wish to understand his thought. There is however a foil question and a new start at 12.41, and nineteen verses is about the limit that we have come to expect for a pericope, since Mark was left behind (cf. 10.1-16; 11.37-54).

This is important because it enables us to see why Luke moves about his Matthaean Vorlage in the way he does. He is expounding Matthew 16; (a) 'Beware of the leaven of the Pharisees... let him deny himself and take up his cross and follow me' (12.1-12, Fearless Confession); (b) 'Beware of the leaven... For what will it profit a man if he gain the whole world and lose his own soul?' (12.13-21, The Rich Fool); (c) 'What will it profit...? For the Son of Man is coming' (12.22-40, Detachment before the Coming of the Son of Man). We have been able just about to see the Matthew 16 thread under the embroidery from elsewhere in vv. 1-21; it is not lost from view now, but is apparent from the movement of thought at 12.35, with the introduction of the theme, 'the Son of Man comes'.

12.22-25. The Rich Fool has brought Luke's mind to the gathering into barns of Matthew 6, and he now copies out the famous lines, amending and slightly marring them as he goes—for Luke is by no means Matthew's equal in poetic sensitivity (§21). Two particular aversions which he feels, for Matthew's rhetorical questions (Cadbury, pp. 81ff.), and for his triple images (§24), are instantiated more than once. Thus Matthew's opening line goes in nearly as it stands, *'Therefore I say to you, be not anxious for* your *soul, what you shall eat* or what you shall drink, *nor for* your *body, what you shall put on'.* 'Your' is omitted before 'soul' and 'body' in line with the following verse ('the soul. . . the body', cf. 12.4); and Matthew's three verbs eat-drink-put-on are reduced to a Lucan pair eat/put-on. Matthew's *'Is* not *the soul more than food, and the body than raiment?'* loses its rhetorical question form. His 'Behold the birds of heaven *that they sow* not *nor reap* nor gather into *barns, and* your heavenly Father *feeds them. Are you* not *of more value than* them?' is changed more. Luke prefers κατανοήσατε (20.23R, 1/0/4+4), and he replaces Matthew's plain birds with ravens. Ravens are associated with God's providence in the story of Elijah, and they are the object of it in Job 38.41, and especially in Ps. 147, where God clothes (περιβάλλοντι) the heavens, brings forth grass (χόρτος) on the mountains, and gives τροφή to the cattle and the young of the ravens that call upon him (146.9LXX). Also Luke elsewere prefers the colourful to Matthew's plain: eggs and scorpions for bread and stones, lambs for sheep (§4.8). Matthew's three verbs, sow-reap-gather, again become a Lucan pair sow-reap, and to make up for this his barns become a second pair storehouse-nor-barn: Luke added ταμ(ι)εῖον also at 12.3. As usual Matthew's 'your heavenly Father' becomes plain Lucan 'God', and the concluding rhetorical question is again dropped. Matthew was content to end the last two clauses with 'them' (αὐτά/ αὐτῶν), but Luke attempts an improvement by substituting 'the birds' the second time for variety—he has slipped back into Matthew's πετεινά (cf. v. 43). Matthew continues, *'And which of you by being anxious can add to his stature* one *cubit?',* which goes in unaltered, but for the omission of his pleonastic 'one' = 'a' (Mt. 8.19; 9.18; 18.24, cp. Lk. 9.57).

12.26-28. Matthew now moves on to his second stanza; 'And about clothing why are you anxious'; but Luke has misread this, taking it as a sequel to the cubit logion, 'If then you cannot do even the smallest thing, *why are you anxious* about the rest?'. The added οὖν shows the connection he has supposed. ἐλάχιστον = the smallest thing recurs at 16.10 twice and 19.17QD, and is otherwise unknown in the Gospels; ὁ-λοιπός is Lucan (3/2/6+5, 8.10R; 24.9R); and the prosy bathos is all Luke's own (§21). He is better back with Matthew's 'Study *the lilies of the field how* they *grow*; they *toil not, neither do* they *spin: but I say to you* that *not even Solomon in all his glory was arrayed like one of these*'. Luke prefers κατανοήσατε again, and the singular after a neuter plural is better Greek (BDF, p. 73); and he drops the ὅτι (cf. 11.51; 12.8; 17.34; 18.14). Matthew goes on, '*But if God so* clothes *the grass* of the *field, which today is and tomorrow is cast into the oven,* will he not much *more* clothe *you, little-faiths*'? Luke prefers the Septuagintal ἀμφιέζει (×3 Job) to Matthew's ἀμφιέννυσι; he opens 'But if in the field' for emphasis, and puts 'is today and tomorrow is cast' for the chiasmus; and again drops the rhetorical question with a second πόσῳ μᾶλλον.

12.29f. This brings Matthew to his climax, 'Do not be anxious therefore saying, What shall we eat?, or What shall we drink?, or What shall we wear?' Luke's 'And you, seek *not what* you *shall eat* and *what* you *shall drink*, and do not worry' once more reduces Matthew's three to a pair (omitting the clothing, which is the context!); he drops the οὖν, perhaps for this reason, his initial καὶ ὑμεῖς weakly resuming ὑμᾶς from v. 28; and draws in 'seek' from the next verse. His μετεωρίζεσθε is higher class Greek than Matthew's μεριμνᾶν (Polybius, Josephus, cf. BAG); but he may intend a difference of sense, μεριμνᾶν for those who have and fret, like Martha or the Fool, μετεωρίζεσθαι for those who have not and worry. While his poetry is not so bad this time, he has not touched Matthew's sublimity. His predecessor continues, '*For all these things the Gentiles seek*: for *your* heavenly *Father knows that you need* all *these things*'. Luke adds 'the Gentiles of the world' to soften the offence to his own Gentile readers—only worldly Gentiles seek 'these things'. He changes the second 'for' and drops the second 'all', both improvements. Matthew's 'your Father' is retained this time for the doctrine of fatherly providence, but Luke will not have his 'heavenly'.

12.31f. Matthew ends, 'But *seek* first God's *kingdom* and his righteousness, *and* all *these things shall be added to you*'; followed by 'Be not anxious then for tomorrow. . .' The mention of the kingdom brings out Luke's suspicion of Matthew's own worldly proclivities: we have seen the latter before promising the prayerful Christian good gifts (7.11), and Luke rapidly adjusting this to 'Holy Spirit' (11.13). So here the Lucan Christian is not to seek God's kingdom *first* (and 'all these things' second): his is a spiritual religion, with the kingdom only—and no quest for righteousness either, to make poor Paul turn in his grave (ch. 4). The dropping of the 'all' is significant too in lessening the stress on the side-effect benefits of faith. Nor is Luke content with Matthew's final verse, but he develops the spiritual point he is making: 'Fear not, little flock, for your Father has chosen to give you the kingdom'. He wishes to offer a better comfort than the ironic thought that tomorrow's anxieties will keep till tomorrow. In fact the Matthaean stress even on *seeking* the kingdom is too self-regarding for Luke. Jesus covenanted the kingdom to the disciples (22.29), and it was theirs by grace: they were the men of God's εὐδοκία (2.14), and it was εὐδοκία before the Father to reveal it to them (10.21QC). So now there is no need to fear, for 'your Father εὐδόκησεν to give' it to them. The theme of providence through the paragraph, coupled with thought of the disciples as a community, suggests the image of the flock, just as it does at Acts 20.28. With the warm-hearted vocative, 'little flock', cf. 'my friends' (12.4), 'Martha, Martha' (10.41), 'Simon, Simon' (22.31).

12.33f. So there is Matthew's splendid poem: but Luke does not feel quite happy with it. For his church-members were not in any real danger of starvation, but rather of being too comfortable; and his mind goes back accordingly to Mt. 6.19-21, '...but treasure for yourselves (ὑμῖν) treasures in heaven (θησαυροὺς ἐν οὐρανῷ), where neither moth nor rust corrupts, and where thieves do not break through nor steal; for where your treasure is, there will your heart be also'. The last clause he copies in almost as it stands as v. 34 (ὑμῶν for σου, ἔσται last); the former he specifies. The promise of treasure in heaven goes back to the Rich Ruler (θησαυρὸν ἐν οὐρανῷ, Mk 10.21, θησαυρὸν ἐν οὐρανοῖς, Mt. 19.21), and the means thereto were to sell (πώλησον) all (ὅσα ἔχεις, Mk; σου τὰ ὑπάρχοντα Mt.) and give (δός) to the poor. Luke remembers the Matthaean form of the saying and writes, πωλήσατε τὰ ὑπάρχοντα ὑμῶν καὶ δότε ἐλεημοσύνην—as usual he is being realistic, and requires generous alms and not self-beggaring; he put δότε ἐλεημοσύνην at 11.41QD also, and almsgiving is in fact his solution to the money problem (16.9). He also puts Matthew 19's θησαυρὸν ἐν (τοῖς) οὐρανοῖς, as he does in his own version of the Rich Ruler (18.22, τοῖς doubtful), against both Matthew 6 and Mark 10. When considering the money question in 16.1-13, he warns his hearers to make themselves (ποιήσατε ἑαυτοῖς) friends out of the mammon of unrighteousness, so that when it gives out (ἐκλίπῃ) they may have a home in heaven; and so now, he bids them *make themselves* a treasure that does not *give out* (ἀνέκλειπτον) in the same realm. With so many pairs of images, he pairs this one too—treasure that does not give out, purses that do not grown old (βαλλάντιον 0/0/4, 10.4QD, παλαιός ×5 in 5.36-39). He cuts Matthew's triple moth-rust-thief for the last time to thief-moth. He weakens the break-through-and-steal to a feeble Lucan ἐγγίζει, as thieves cannot get *near* the kingdom. Matthew's moths only disfigure (ἀφανίζει) the silks; Luke strengths this to 'ruin' (διαφθείρει).

12.35. So the great passage in Matthew 6 has been given its due. But it was not really Matthew 6 that Luke was striving to expound, not worrying about too little money, and giving away too much: he wanted rather to teach this in the Matthew 16 context, that we should beware of the stuff because judgment may meet us at any time. He gave this message in his own terms with the Fool in the previous pericope; now he puts it in Matthaean terms, with the coming of the Son of Man (v. 40; Mt. 16.27f.). Christ will come at Passover (ch. 5), and the old Passover ritual springs to his mind, 'Thus shall you eat it, *your loins girded* (αἱ ὀσφύες ὑμῶν περιεζωσμέναι)' (Exod. 12.11). Luke takes this metaphorically, of course—Christians are to be ready; and rather than press on with other Exodus metaphors, sandals and staffs, he bethinks himself of a Christian metaphor, the burning lamps. This is again suggested by the next verse in Matthew, the λύχνος of 6.22, amplified from the Bridesmaids of Mt. 25.1-13.

12.36. Matthew's Bridesmaids story is famously unsatisfactory: not only does it give a very confused picture for a marriage, since the bridesmaids should be there to accompany the bride and not to wait at the husband's home; but the unhappy impression is given that the wise girls did well not to share with the foolish, so that the latter were damned. Luke feels that he can have the theme without these scandals, and he drops the parabolic form, and alters much of the detail. He makes Matthew's λαμπάδες, which can mean torches as well as more ordinary lamps (Acts 20.8) into the latter (λύχνοι, as at 11.34-36). He keeps the general marriage situation, with the master (κύριος, Mt. 25.11) returning from the wedding—that is, his own wedding—and the attendants (= the Christians) waiting up for him at night, uncertain when he will come, some of them awake (γρηγοροῦντας, Mt. 25.13), and others not. But whereas Matthew has the bridesmaids as the attendants, which does not correspond to Jewish (or any) custom, Luke replaces them with men, that is the master's staff, who should indeed be ready on such an occasion. Matthew's allegorizing also leads him to place the marriage-feast (γάμοι, v. 10) in the master's home, and Luke changes this to the normal practice, with the feast at the bride's father's house (S-B, I, pp. 500ff.). These improvements however entail a slight reversing of Matthew's roles, for in his parable the master arrives and shuts the door, and then the foolish girls come (ἔρχονται, v. 11) and ask him to open (ἄνοιξον); but in Luke it is the staff who are within, by the dynamic of the story, and it is the master who comes (ἐλθόντος) and knocks, and they open to him (ἀνοίξωσιν). Waiting (προσδέχεσθαι) is Lucan, and knocking rather Lucan; and they open with Lucan alacrity (εὐθέως, §3).

12.37. Other associated phrases from the Matthaean context now leap to mind. In the companion parable of the servant awaiting the return of his master, Matthew wrote, '*Blessed that servant whom* his *master coming shall find* so doing' (24.46); Luke writes this straight out, in the plural for his context, and without the 'his' to give the Christological ὁ κύριος, and with γρηγοροῦντας to end. Luke knew that no human master (17.7ff.) would gird himself (περιζωσάμενος, echoing v. 37), say to his servant (δοῦλον), Come and sit down (παρελθὼν ἀνάπεσε) and serve him (διακόνει); but he also knew that things were not so in the kingdom, but the Lord was among the disciples as ὁ διακονῶν (22.26f.). So he expands the Matthaean blessing: 'Amen, I say to you that he will *gird himself* (περιζώσεται) and sit them *down* (ἀνακλινεῖ), and *come and serve* them (παρελθὼν διακονήσει). Humility is a prized Lucan virtue, especially at the dinner-table (14.7-11). The expansion is suggested by Matthew's following '*Amen I say to you that. . .*' (24.47): but Matthew had the faithful servant set over all his master's possessions, and Luke's Messianic banquet, with Christ serving, seems more meaningful and more spiritual.

12.38-40. Matthew's Servant and his Bridesmaids were both expanded versions of the Marcan Doorkeeper (Mk 13.34-37; cf. *MLM*, pp. 4f., 434-40), who was bidden to watch for the coming of his master—the Church knows not when the master of the house is coming, late, midnight, cockcrow or early. Of these the first half of the night seemed more likely: Passover was over at midnight (*m. Pes.* 10.9), and Matthew's bridegroom came at midnight (25.6). So Luke resumes, 'And if he comes in the second watch (i.e. 'late') or the third ('midnight') and find so, blessed those (servants)'. ἐλθεῖν, εὑρεῖν were in Mk 13.36; ἐλθεῖν, εὑρεῖν οὕτως, μακάριος ἐκεῖνος, were all in Mt. 24.46: we have met Luke's impressive repetitions before (10.11; 11.51; 12.5). A similar point is made in the preceding verses of Matthew (24.43f.): '*But know* that, *that if the householder had known in what* watch *the thief was coming, he would not have* allowed *his house to be broken into.* Therefore *be you also ready, for in an hour when you think not the Son of Man is coming*'. Luke has it nearly word for word: τοῦτο for ἐκεῖνο (cf. τοῦτο γινώσκετε ὅτι, 10.11QD); ὥρᾳ for φυλακῇ in view of ὥρα in the following verse; ἀφῆκεν for εἴασεν (Luke has ἀ. = allow ×6 in the Gospel, ἐ. ×2(3), but 1/7 in Acts); τὸν οἶκον (33+25) for τὴν οἰκίαν (25+12). He also drops Matthew's beloved 'Therefore', opening καί ὑμεῖς as in v. 36.

It is not surprising that Luke, seeking to expound the theme of the Son of Man's coming in Mt. 16.27f., has found the material he is looking for where it is concentrated in Mt. 24.43–25.13; and, as we shall see, the presence of this concentration will continue to draw him away from his serial progression through the First Gospel, as the magnet the steel. But we are probably right to think that Mt. 16 is still the passage open on the table in front of him. His version of the Bridesmaids is allusive, and incorporates material from the middle of the preceding parable, and ends with material from before that on the Thief. The unity of Matthew's thinking, however, has left Lk. 12.35-40 coherent—it is the link with vv. 22-34 which is not so straightforward. And this time the Matthaean text has ensured that the Lucan Christian is taught to expect judgment with the Lord's return, rather than at his own death.

In vv. 22-34 (except v. 32) Luke is close to Matthew, and an origin in Q is generally concluded. The Q version is taken to be close to Matthew. Only the following variations from Matthew are printed by Polag, 60ff: v. 22 omit 'or what you shall drink'; v. 24 'the ravens', 'God', 'how much. . . the birds'; v. 25 om. ἕνα; v. 27 om. 'of the field'; v. 28 ἐν ἀγρῷ and 'how much. . .'; v. 29 καί ὑμεῖς; v. 30 om. 'heavenly' and ἁπάντων; v. 31 om. τοῦ θεοῦ καί δικαιοσύνην; v. 33 ποιήσατε (×2) for θησαυρίζετε, ἔσται last. Even these are in some cases in doubt: Schulz (pp. 149-52) thinks the two 'how much. . . ' clauses are Luke avoiding the unspecific rhetorical question; that the raven has been inserted by him to make a definite counterpart to the definite lilies; and 'the birds' are then his generalizing. Wrege (p. 118) thinks ἕνα has been dropped by Luke as at 20.3R; 21.2R; 22.3R. David Catchpole (*SNTU* [1981-82]) reverses Schulz on the ravens, which were, he claims, the original specific counterpart to the lilies, and dropped by Matthew as unclean: but (it must be replied) Matthew even likens the kingdom to leaven! He also thinks Matthew added πρῶτον to lessen the radicalism of Q/Luke; but Matthew several times uses first/before without such a suggestion (20.16; 21.31; 23.26).

With so much Q material agreed to be in the Matthaean version, there are bound to be expressions in QC which are Matthaean. The opening διά τοῦτο is a favourite of Matthew's, 10/3/4+1, 12.31R; 13.13R; 13.52M; 18.23R; 21.43R; 24.44QD. Matthew likes both τροφή 4/0/1, 3.4R; 10.10QD; 24.45QD, and ἔνδυμα 7/0/1, 3.4R; 7.15M; 22.11M, 12M; 28.3R: we may note his redactional combination of them—'John had τὸ ἔνδυμα . . . ἡ δὲ τροφή. . . ' (3.4). The combination σπείρειν—θερίζειν—συνάγειν εἰς ἀποθήκας recurs (alone in the Gospels) in Matthew's Tares: 'a man σπείραντι . . . did you not ἔσπειρας . . . until the θερισμός, and in time of the θερισμός I will say to the θερισταί . . . but the corn συναγάγετε εἰς τὴν ἀποθήκην μου' (13.24-30). I have commented above (p. 532, on 12.1-12) on the parallel structure of thought between the present passage, with its (a) rhetorical question, οὐχί . . .;, (b) *qal wahomer* argument from the animals (πετεινά), and conclusion μᾶλλον ὑμεῖς διαφέρετε; and Matthew's redaction at 12.11f., with its οὐχί. . .;, its *qal wahomer* with the sheep, and its conclusion 'how much does a man διαφέρει from a sheep'. With the 'interrupting' cubit verse (Catchpole, p. 80), we may compare 5.36M, 'you cannot make one hair black or white', which is also a diversion, as are the numbered hairs of 10.30QC. ὀλιγόπιστοι is a major uncomfortableness: the word is unknown before Matthew, and seems designed to ease Marcan criticism of the apostles' lack of faith at 8.26R; 14.31R; 16.8R; 17.20R. This is its only other occurrence. Matthew is also steadily critical of the worldliness of Gentiles, 5.47QD; 6.7M; 18.17; cf. 10.5M—a tendency not found in the other Gospel traditions. ὁ πατὴρ ὑμων is a favourite expression of Matthew (13/1/3, Hawkins, p. 31), two of the three Lucan uses coming here, the other at 6.36QC (cf. 11.13QC). We have a rather close parallel to οἶδεν γὰρ ὁ πατὴρ ὑμῶν ὁ οὐράνιος ὅτι χρῄζετε τούτων in Mt. 6.8M, οἶδεν γὰρ ὁ πατὴρ ὑμῶν ὧν χρείαν ἔχετε (he has had the 'in heaven' at 6.1, and shortens the phrase in vv. 4, 6, 6). It is Matthew also who elsewhere thinks of the kingdom as something to be sought (ζητεῖτε), for he says it is like a merchant ζητοῦντι fine pearls (13.45M). Finally, if Polag is right to include in Q 'Make not for yourselves treasures. . . ', we have a further beautiful instance of an almost identical converse sentence, so beloved of Matthew: cf. 'For if you forgive men their trespasses, your heavenly Father will also forgive you; but if you do not forgive men, neither will your Father forgive your trespasses' (6.14f.M—other instances p. 532, on 12.8f.).

So, as usual, we find much of Matthew's style appearing in Q: it seems that Lucan redaction is agreed to account for most of the differences this time, and where not ('your Heavenly Father', 'righteousness') we may see Matthaean creativity later pared down by Luke. Catchpole (pp. 77-83) argues from certain weak arguments and connections that the passage cannot come from one hand; but weak arguments and connections are to be found in many writers, and I have given other Matthaean instances of 'interruptions' above.

For vv. 35-40, critics do not have so easy a time. Verses 39f. are nearly identical with Mt. 24.43f., and so from Q; the earlier verses diverge widely, and are credited to Q by Streeter (p. 279), Schürmann (*TU*, p. 124) and others, and to L by Schmid (p. 340), Grundmann, etc. In either case allowance will have to be made for the Lucan parallels noted above (and below), especially with Lk. 17.7-9; so it is really no use just printing our Luke = Q as Polag does. The QC verses carry their usual crop of Matthaean-sounding phrases. οἰκοδεσπότης comes in teaching 7/0/3 times, Mt. 21.33R; 10.25QD, ×4 M; διὰ τοῦτο I have discussed earlier in this section. 'The Son of Man comes' is a phrase Matthew likes, 7/2/3, 16.27R; 16.28R. He rewrites Mk 13.35 γρηγορεῖτε οὖν, οὐκ οἴδατε γὰρ πότε ὁ κύριος τῆς οἰκίας ἔρχεται, at 24.42 γρηγορεῖτε οὖν, ὅτι οὐκ οἴδατε ποίᾳ ἡμέρᾳ ὁ κύριος ὑμῶν ἔρχεται. It is easy to think that v. 43 εἰ ᾔδει ὁ οἰκοδεσπότης ποίᾳ φυλακῇ ὁ κλέπτης ἔρχεται, and v. 44 γίνεσθε ἕτοιμοι, ὅτι ᾗ οὐ δοκεῖτε ὥρᾳ ὁ υἱὸς τοῦ ἀνθρώπου ἔρχεται, are simply Matthew's restatement of the same redaction, using the traditional thief image (1 Thess. 5.2).

12.22 εἶπεν-δὲ-πρός*

12.23 With the neuter πλεῖον, a more important thing, cf. μεῖζον Mt. 12.6R.

12.24 κατανοεῖν*, ὁ-θεός. Hapax: κόραξ. 'Storehouse nor barn'—they are the same, a Lucan duplication (§22). οὔτε 6/4/8+14.

12.25 (προστιθέναι*). Hapax: (πῆχυς). The 'interrupting' parallels at Mt. 5.36 and 10.30, both concerned with hair, suggest that ἡλικία means height, as at Lk. 19.3, and as πῆχυς virtually requires.

12.26 ἐλάχιστον*, περί, ὁ-λοιπός.

12.27 κατανοεῖν*. Hapaxes: (κοπιᾶν), (νήθειν). In Matthew 'the lilies of the field' corresponded to 'the birds of the heaven': Luke drops the second pleonastic genitive to make a pair with his ravens. κρίνον is a symbol for a woman in Cant. 2.1 etc., whence the contrast with Solomon; birds are symbol for a male devil in Mark 4. ὑφαίνει is an improvement on κοπιᾷ, whether by Luke, or (more likely) his Western copyist.

12.28 (ὁ-θεός). Hapaxes: (χόρτος), (κλίβανος), ἀμφιέζειν, (ὀλιγόπιστος).

12.29 ζητεῖν, (φαγεῖν + πιεῖν). Hapax: μετεωρίζεσθαι.

12.30 Hapax: (ἐπιζητεῖν). *'ûmmôṯ ha'ôlām* is a common rabbinic expression of abuse, no doubt all too familiar to Luke from a life of contact with Jewish people.

12.31 πλήν*, (ζητεῖν), (προστιθέναι*). Matthew had the clear contrast, Do not be *anxious* for your needs; *seek* the kingdom first, and God will supply them. Luke's intrusion of ζητεῖτε at v. 29 spoils this: if his churchmen do not even try to make a living, they will surely starve.

12.32 μὴ-φοβοῦ*. Hapax: ποίμνιον (Acts 20.28, 29 only). βασιλεία abs. 22.29, with the same thought. Nom. for voc. 8.54R; 10.21QC; 18.11.

12.33 (τὰ-ὑπάρχοντα*), ἑαυτόν, βαλλάντιον*, μὴ + part., ἐγγίζειν. Hapaxes: παλαιοῦν, ἀνέκλειπτος, διαφθείρειν (see above). W. Pesch (*Biblica* [1960], pp. 356-78) defends Lucan development of Mt.=Q. ἐλεημοσύνη 11.41QD, × 8 Acts.

12.34 (καί = also).

12.35 Hapax: (ὀσφύς) (Exod. 12.22). ἔστω ×5 Acts. The verse is taken as a Lucan composition by A. Weiser (pp. 161-64), Schneider.

12.36 προσδέχεσθαι*, ἑαυτόν, κρούειν. Hapax: ἀναλύειν. ὅμοιοι ἀνθρώποις, cf. 6.48R, 49R ὅμοιός ἐστιν ἀνθρώπῳ. Weiser, 166-171, continues to see Lucan redaction.

12.37 (εὑρίσκειν). παρελθών 17.7; Acts 24.7.

12.38 εὑρίσκειν.

12.39 (γινώσκετε-ὅτι), οἶκος.

12.40 (γίνεσθαι).

Pesch, W., 'Zur Formgeschichte und Exegese von Lk. 12,32', *Biblica* 41 (1960), pp. 25-40.
Meyer, B.F., 'Jesus and the Remnant of Israel', *JBL*4 (1965), pp. 123-30.
Pesch, R., *Die kleine Herde: Zur Theologie der Gemeinde* (Reihe 10, Graz, 1973)
Deterding, P.E., 'Eschatological and Eucharistic Motifs in Luke 12: 35-40', *Concordia Journal* 5 (1979), pp. 85-92.
Catchpole, D.R., 'The Ravens, the Lilies and the Q Hypothesis', *SNTU* 6-7 (1981-82), pp. 77-87.

40. *The Coming Judgment*, 12.41–13.21

a. *Judgment for the Church*, 12.41-53

Luke (the text assures us) has at this point had enough of retailing Matthew 24–25 from memory: he rolls the scroll on to the parable of the Servant (Mt. 24.45-51), and 83 out of 102 words in the two versions are identical. Now that he has reached the congenial topic of the Lord's coming, he develops it in earnest, giving the whole of his triple unit to its exposition. Once more it can be taken conveniently in three pericopae—Judgment for the Church (12.41-53), Judgment for the World (12.54–13.9), and Judgment for the Jews (13.10-21). Each sub-division is opened by the usual Lucan rubric.

12.41. Judgment begins at the household of God, and Matthew's Servant stood for the Christian ('Be ready. . . Who *then* is the faithful servant?'). But Luke wishes to have an introduction for his pericope, and this he draws from the parallel Marcan Doorkeeper, which he has already had in mind with the watches of v. 38. Mark ended the parable ominously, 'What I say to you, I say to all, Watch' (13.37); and Luke turns this into his familiar foil question (§1.4), 'Lord, do you *say* this parable to *us* or also to *all*?' Luke has made Peter the spokesman of the apostles before now (8.45R), and he must seem especially suitable when the parable is about a servant whom the master sets over his household. So Peter becomes the spokesman here too, and the question is answered by the whole following conversation down to 13.21: the preceding parable of the Thief, which tells of the coming of the Son of Man, is spoken to all, for his coming means judgment for the Church (including the Apostless) and for the world and for the Jewish people.

12.42. Of the Church, then, the first to be judged will be the apostles, and the new parable is addressed to Peter and 'us' in the first place. Matthew's parable, with its consistent use of δοῦλος, probably has nothing but the ordinary Christian in mind (cf. the Talents); but Luke, in a series of small changes, transfers the emphasis. First Peter is made to ask the question, and it raises the option of an address to 'us'. Second, in the opening verse (alone), Matthew's faithful 'servant' becomes a steward, οἰκονόμος; and not only is this a word Luke uses elsewhere (16.1ff.), but it is the word which epitomises the apostle's office in 1 Corinthians—'Let a man so account of us, as. . . οἰκονόμους of the mystery of God. Moreover it is required in τοῖς οἰκονόμοις that one be found πιστός' (4.1f.).

Third, whereas in Matthew the master set (κατέστησεν) the servant over his staff (οἰκετεία), thus giving the parable situation, Luke puts the verb in the future (καταστήσει, cf. Mt. 24.47). He thus introduces the suggestion that those who have been faithful apostles *will*, when the Lord comes, be set in authority in heaven (cf. 22.30). Furthermore, this move of thought expands the scale. In Matthew the servant is a major-domo, in charge of a staff of perhaps some dozens. But Luke is now thinking of Peter and the apostles in authority over a Church of some tens of thousands (Acts 21.20), and his mind goes to the story of Joseph in Genesis, who was given charge by Pharaoh of all the land of Egypt. Pharaoh's staff are referred to in Gen. 45.16 as his θεραπεία, and Luke now substitutes this word. Similarly Joseph gave measures of corn (ἐσιτομέτρει) to his family and the Egyptians (Gen. 47.12, 14), and Luke replaces Matthew's plain 'to give them τροφήν' with 'to give measures of corn (τὸ σιτομέτριον)'.

12.43-45. Matthew's parable now follows, almost word for word (see below): Luke, as elsewhere, has started with some bold changes, but drifts back to the text before him, δοῦλος and all (§19.2). Verse 44 is now a straightforward repetition of v. 42 (καταστήσει), with an extension of responsibility. Matthew, slightly illogically, seems to have the same servant both faithful-and-wise in v. 45 and bad in v. 48 ('but if *that* bad servant says'): Luke improves the logic by dropping κακός. Matthew's rather stock description of the servant's misdeeds, beating his fellow-servants, and eating and drinking with the drunkards, is, however, suggestive for Luke's new context. For Paul at Corinth had been up against some false apostles, who thought the kingdom had arrived already (the same context, 1 Cor. 4.8), and who went about hitting people in the face (2 Cor. 11.20), and drinking so much at the agape that they were drunk (μεθύει, 1 Cor. 11.21). So Luke slightly sharpens the language: Matthew's συνδούλους become τοὺς παῖδας καὶ τὰς παιδίσκας, that is Christian men and women; and the apostle no longer merely consorts with drunkards, he eats and drinks and becomes drunk (μεθύσκεσθαι).

12.46. A more important issue, however, arises with Mt. 24.51 = Lk. 12.46b. Matthew, with his firm Jewish upbringing, thought that faithless Christians would go to hell. The allegory spills over into the story, as the returning lord cuts the wicked servant in pieces (διχοτομήσει) and appoints his portion with the hypocrites. Allegations of inconsistency, and proposed Aramaic mistranslations are beside the point (cf. Gundry); in Gehenna being cut in pieces is only the beginning of pangs. But so draconian a doctrine not only revolted Luke's humane feelings; it was also directly contradicted by his mentor Paul in the very passage he has just had in mind. For in 1 Cor. 3.10ff. the apostle treats of the coming fate of the bad apostle. The day, he says (ἡ ἡμέρα, v. 13, Lk. 12.46) will make each apostle's work plain, for the fire will test it. Anyone whose work is burnt up will be punished (ζημιωθήσεται), but he will be saved, yet so as through fire. So Luke makes one change to the Matthaean text, and he adds a gloss. The bad apostle will not be sent, in his view, to hell with the hypocrites; as he has not been πιστός, though (v. 42), faithful, he will have to be punished with the unfaithful (ἄπιστοι, which is substituted for Mt.'s ὑποκριταί). What, then, about διχοτομήσει? Luke retains it, but reinterprets it. For we ourselves might speak, with a slight hyperbole, of one of Wellington's soldiers being cut to pieces on the triangle; and Luke, similarly, takes the word as a colourful expression for such floggings, as were a part of everyday life. It is this interpretation which is then glossed in the two verses following.

12.47. Thus we have an explanation of the floggings in vv. 47f. Matthew had ended, 'There will be weeping and gritting of teeth', with the pains of hell in mind; Luke thinks of the anguished cries and gritted teeth he has witnessed at the whipping of slaves, and he takes Paul's ζημιωθήσεται so. The unfaithful church leader will be saved, but he will be thrashed thoroughly—we can see medieval Purgatory coming round the mountain.

12.48. So justice can be reconciled with mercy. But what of those whose responsibility has been less, but who have been faithless still? The evangelist's kindly heart adduces his familiar doctrine of ignorance (Acts 3.17ff.; 13.27; 17.30; Lk. 23.34, *q.v.*) as a mitigating factor. The apostle should know what he is doing, and deliberate flouting of God's will must bring a severe beating. The ordinary Christian has acted in ignorance, and will receive six of the best.

But could Luke not have some tradition for the last two verses? Indeed he could. Just as he associated the parable of the return from the wedding with the similar Servant and Doorkeeper at vv. 37f., so he associates the Servant now with the similar Talents of Mt. 25.14-30. For there already culpability was the consequence of knowledge:

'You wicked and slothful δοῦλε, you knew...'; and the matter was summed up in a proverb-style conclusion, 'To everyone (παντί) who has, will it be given (δοθήσεται) and he shall abound (περισσευθήσεται); but from him who has not, even what he has shall be taken away from him (ἀπ' αὐτοῦ)' (25.29). Luke models his own adapted conclusion on these words: 'To everyone (παντί) to whom much is given (ἐδόθη) shall much be required of him (ζητηθήσεται παρ' αὐτοῦ), and to him to whom they committed much they will demand more abundantly (περισσότερον)'. The language is quite close, although the meaning is made to fit a new context; but Luke is less skilled at such epigrams than his predecessors—in place of their contrast, he has said the same thing twice, one more tautological repetition (§22). He had a much/little contrast more effectively at 7.47. ζητηθήσεται, 'will be required', is probably still due to the influence of 1 Cor. 4.2, 'It is required (ζητεῖται) in stewards that one be found faithful'. Much of the other language is Lucan (see below).

12.49. The text continues without any break, 'I came to cast fire...', and it cannot be wise to ignore this and presume a break in the sense. Matthew thought that the fate awaiting the faithless was eternal fire prepared for the devil (25.41), and Paul, in the passage Luke has been expounding, sees 'the day' as revealing each man's work with fire (ἐν πυρί, 1 Cor. 3.13ff.). The precise mode of the test is perhaps vague in Paul ('like fire', 'as through fire'), but with time the fire came to be seen as a literal fire on the world. Matthew spoke of stars falling from heaven (24.29), and the image of Lot fleeing from the fires of Sodom was already implied in Mk 13.14, 'let them flee to the mountains', and Mt. 24.40, 'there shall be two in the field'. Luke has a much developed form of the Lot parallel in 17.29-32, and 2 Pet. 3.7 and Revelation 8-9 are categorical. So 12.49 has nothing whatever to do with Pentecost. Luke does not want to give a description of the Last Judgment now, as in Matthew 25; he wants to warn the ordinary Christian as well as the Church's leaders, of the imminence of judgment, and the signs that it is on the way. So he casts his mind back to Matthew 10, where such signs were given: 'Do not think that I came to cast peace on the earth' (v. 34)—not peace, but a sword, said Matthew, as the faith divided families. But judgment, thinks Luke, is fire rather than the sword: '*I came to cast fire on the earth*'. Immediately, though, comes the uncomfortable reflection of the lengthening gap since the Lord's ministry; some reassurance must be given to the hesitant Theophilus that all is well despite the sixty years. Luke knows that Jesus looked forward to the end, but that even he did not know when it would be (Mk 13.32; Mt. 24.36); so he feels justified in adding here, 'how I wish it were already kindled!'

12.50. Mt. 10.34f. was written in the usual Matthaean balanced parallelisms, and Luke has just been attempting the same in vv. 47f.; so he forms a parallel to his opening line, although the subject is drawing him astray from his main objective. If Jesus yearned for the beginning of Judgment, it will have been in part because he wished that his own ordeal was over; and Luke has painted in the colours of his all too human feelings before the cross in 22.41-44. In Mk 10.38 he had spoken of sharing in his Passion as 'being baptized with the baptism that I am baptized with' (τὸ βάπτισμα ὃ ἐγὼ βαπτίζομαι βαπτισθῆναι), so he forms his second colon on the basis of that— 'And I have a *baptism to be baptized with* (βάπτισμα δὲ ἔχω βαπτισθῆναι); and how I am constrained till it is accomplished'. We should note the common order of words, and the assonance ἐγώ/ἔχω with Mark. συνέχειν, ἕως ὅτου + subj., and τελεσθῆναι are all quite Lucan. Although a distraction from the strict topic, the verse is a timely reminder that the new Christian may face such a 'baptism' himself.

12.51. 'Do not think (νομίσητε)', said Matthew, 'that I came to cast peace on the earth: I came not to cast peace but a sword. For I came to divide (διχάσαι)' families. Luke (who still has the scroll open at Matthew 24) approximates: 'Do you think (δοκεῖτε) *that* I came (παρεγενόμην) to give *peace* in *the earth*? No, I say to you, *but* division (διαμερισμόν)'. δοκεῖτε ὅτι...; οὐχί, λέγω ὑμῖν, ἀλλά... recurs in 13.2f., 4.; δοκεῖτε may be carried over from 12.40. παραγίνεσθαι and διαμεριζ- are Lucan. He has substituted fire for Matthew's sword here, but he has not forgotten the image: the sword which Jesus came to bring was spoken of in 2.35 as a ῥομφαία (Ps. 21.21 LXX) which would pierce his mother's soul.

12.52f. Matthew had taken up Mic. 7.6 to describe the divisions that the Gospel would bring: '. . . a man against his father, and a daughter against her mother, and a daughter-in-law against her mother-in-law: and a man's enemies shall be his own household (οἰκιακοί)' (10.35f.). Here is the point that Luke is after; here is the unpleasing sign of the time which a Christian must learn to expect, and experiencing, to know the comfort of its significance. He spells the warning out: 'For there shall be five in one house (οἴκῳ) divided, three against two and two against three'. Luke tends to think in fives—five sparrows, five yoke of oxen, five hundred dinars and fifty (§12)—and with five relations mentioned in Matthew's text, he counts them, and the divisions between them too. Father vs son and the reverse, mother vs daughter and the reverse, mother-in-law vs daughter-in-law and the reverse (v. 53), makes three divisions, so four against one is not on. Luke has been criticized as being prosaic and repetitive, and that he is; but he is speaking of real domestic unhappiness which can tempt a man or woman away from their faith, and defects of style are a risk he is prepared to run.

By common consent, vv. 41-46 are Luke's redaction of Q virtually = Mt. 24.45-51a. Schulz (pp. 271ff.) credits ὑποκριτῶν only to Mt. R; Weiser (pp. 178f., 201f.) accepts this hesitantly, and adds κακός, σύνδουλος; Polag adds the reversing of ποιοῦντα οὕτως and the dropping of ἔρχεσθαι. Per contra, in vv. 49-53 Luke is usually taken to represent Q; cf. Polag, p. 64, where only nine words in 12.51 are printed in the Matthaean form against Luke. Verses 47f. are usually credited to L.

Again, the solid QC block in vv. 42-46, and Luke's visible secondariness over most of the differences, expose the weakness of the Q theory; for so much of the language echoes Matthew elsewhere. The faithful and wise servant—δοῦλος with two adjectives—reminds us of the good and faithful servants and the wicked and slothful servant of the Matthaean Talents. Matthew is the only evangelist who elsewhere has parabolic characters who are φρόνιμος, the Builder (7.24QD) and the Bridesmaids (×4M). Matthew likes τροφή, 4/0/1, 3.4R; 10.10QD. ὃν ἐλθὼν ὁ κύριος αὐτοῦ εὑρήσει looks like Matthew's style. He is fond of ἐλθών in the nominative, 24/13/11, with redactional insertions at 8.14; 9.10; 14.12; 16.13; 27.33; 28.11, 13; and he follows it with εὑρίσκειν again at 12.44QC and 26.43R. He has ὅν followed by aor. part., subject and verb in that order at 13.44M, ὃν εὑρὼν ἄνθρωπος ἔκρυψεν, 13.31QC, 33QC. He particularly likes ὁ κύριος αὐτοῦ/-ῶν, 11/0/2, 10.24QD, 25QD; 15.27R; and from M 18.31, 32, 34; 25.18, 21, 23, 26; and ἀμὴν λέγω ὑμῖν, 31/13/6, with many cases QD, such as 8.10; 10.15. ὁ δοῦλος ἐκεῖνος is another phrase Matthew likes—he has it in the Unmerciful Servant (18.27, 28M), the Wedding-Feast (22.10M) and the Talents (25.19M)—Luke has it ×4 in the present context, Mark not at all. σύνδουλος comes only in Matthew, with four uses in 18.28-33M. Mark has 'that day and hour' at 13.32, with Matthew the same at 24.36 and 'You know not the day nor the hour' at 25.13 on his own as well as here. Nor is it in language only that the parable looks like Matthew. 'My lord delays' shows the same anxiety over the delayed Parousia as 'while the bridegroom delayed' (χρονίζοντος, 25.5M), and 'after a long time' (25.19M). The enthusiasm for punishing the erring Christian is like Matthew too.

The defence of Q is easier in the later section, as Lucanisms like ἀπὸ τοῦ νῦν and διαμερίζεσθαι can be avoided. Some embarrassments remain, like συνέχειν and δοκεῖτε ὅτι;, and most of v. 47 is Lucan (see above and below).

12.41 εἶπεν-δέ*, λέγειν-παραβολὴν-πρός (×2)*, καί = also. The introduction is usually accepted as Lk.R, cf. Weiser, pp. 216-19; but cp. Manson, p. 117; C.F.D. Moule, *Birth*, pp. 146-48.

12.42 εἶπεν, ὁ-κύριος = Jesus*, (τοῦ + inf.*). Hapax: σιτομέτριον. οἰκονόμος and its derivatives come often in 16.1-13. ὁ φρόνιμος for Matthew's καί perhaps because the noun divides the two adjectives, but perhaps a wary echo of 1 Corinthians 4 again, 'we are fools through Christ, but you are φρόνιμοι' (v. 10)—it is the faithful steward who is really the wise one. διδόναι present because the distribution is regular. ἐν καιρῷ is advanced for emphasis. ἄρα, which led on from 24.44 in Matthew, is almost meaningless now.

12.43 (εὑρίσκειν), (ποιεῖν + adv.). Luke has ποιεῖν οὕτως in that order at 2.48, 9.15R; the reverse at 1.25.

12.44 ἀληθῶς-λέγω-ὑμῖν, (τά-ὑπάρχοντα*).

12.45 (εἰπεῖν), (τύπτειν), τε*, (ἐσθίειν/πίνειν*) Hapaxes: (χρονίζειν), μεθύσκεσθαι. ἔρχεσθαι clarifies (Schulz). τοὺς παῖδας καὶ τὰς παιδίσκας, cf. τοὺς δούλους μου καὶ τὰς δούλας μου Acts 2.18 = LXX; but perhaps the change emphasizes their subjection, as συνδούλους does not. For the ecclesiastical allegory, cf. Bo Reicke, *DFZ*, pp. 234-40.

12.46 (ἡμέρα), (προσδοκᾶν*). Hapax: διχοτομεῖν.

12.47 (μή + part., ἑτοιμάζειν, δέρειν. ἐκεῖνος ὁ δοῦλος is carried over from ὁ δοῦλος ἐκεῖνος (v. 45), γνούς from γινώσκετε (v. 39), ἑτοιμάζειν from ἕτοιμοι (v. 40), τοῦ κυρίου αὐτοῦ from v. 43, ποιήσας from v. 43. γνοὺς τό θέλημα (τοῦ θεοῦ), Acts 22.14. πρός = according to.

12.48 μή + part., δέρειν, πολύ* (×3), ζητεῖν. ἄξιον/-α (neuter) + gen. of punishment, 0/0/3+4. πληγαί, 10.30; Acts 16.23, 33 only. παρατίθεσθαι (med.) 23.46; Acts 14.23; 17.3; 20.32 only. περισσότερον 12.4QD. 3rd pl. = God, 6.38QD; 12.20 (Marshall).

12.49 Hapax: ἀνάπτειν (ἅπτειν*). The phrasing is septuagintal. For τί as an exclamation, cf. 2 Kgdms 6.20; for θέλειν εἰ cf. Isa. 9.4. For εἰ as a wish, cf. 19.42 (Leaney). Schulz (p. 258) credits to Lk.R: Schürmann (TU, p. 213), Manson (p. 120), to Q.

12.50 συνέχειν*, ἕως-ὅτου. τελεῖσθαι pass. 18.31R; 22.37R. Helmut Köster (TDNT, VII, p. 885) attributes the verse to Lk.R, as here but most critics suppose Q or L.

12.51 δοκεῖν = think, παραγίνεσθαι*, οὐχί... ἀλλά*, (εἰρήνη*). Hapax: διαμερισμός. δοῦναι seemed more applicable than 'casting peace'; and peace is given on earth, not cast εἰς earth from above. ἀλλ' ἤ = but rather, here only, and 2 Cor. 1.13 in NT: ἀλλά + particle 24.21.

12.52 ἀπὸ-τοῦ-νῦν*, οἶκος, διαμερίζειν*. ἐν ἑνὶ οἴκῳ: Luke again contrasts one with higher numbers with ἐπὶ ἑνὶ ἁμαρτωλῷ, 15.7QD, 10. Matthew uses his preferred κατά, Luke διαμερίζεσθαι ἐπί as at 11.17f. Schulz (pp. 258f.) correctly sees v. 52 as a Lucan expansion of v. 53; but the fifth member of the household is the daughter-in-law, not the mother-in-law! The νῦν means Jesus' lifetime, but Luke's eye is on the time of the Church (cf. G. Klein, ZNW [1964], p. 374).

12.53 διαμερίζειν*. The divisions are in a house, and ἐπί therefore begins by governing the dative. With μήτηρ Luke moves into the accusative, as at 11.17f.: it may be that in this as with οἴκῳ he is following Mic. 7.6, which has the same features. In Micah the aggression is all of the young against the old, but Mk 13.12 ('and the father the child') told Luke that it would be both ways in the Church. Mt. 10.35 needed correcting (Schulz, p. 259).

Betz, O., 'The Dichotomized Servant and the End of Judas Iscariot', Revue de Qumran 5 (1964-66), pp. 43-58.
Braumann, G., 'Leidenskelch und Todestaufe (Mc. 10,38f)', ZNW 56 (1965), pp. 178-83.
Schürmann, H., 'Wie hat Jesus seinen Tod bestanden und verstanden?', in P. Hoffmann (ed.), Orientierung (1973) pp. 325-63.
Bauckham, R., 'Synoptic Parousia Parables and the Apocalypse', NTS 23 (1977), pp. 162-76.
März, C.-P., '"Feuer auf die Erde zu werfen bin ich gekommen..."', in A Cause de l'Evangile (Fs Dupont, 1985), pp. 479-511.

b. The Signs of the Time, 12.54–13.9

The exegesis of the passage turns in part on a textual crux. Mt. 16.2b-3, 'At evening you say...' must stand in some relation to Lk. 12.54-56, 'When you see a cloud...', but the Matthaean verses are missing from ℵ BXΓ fam. 13 syrsin cur copt; Or, being testified in CDLW Θ fam. 1 latt. syrpes har; Theophilus Const.Ap. Eus Chr Euth. N-A[26] prints hesitantly (D grade, Metzger, p. 41), but Greeven accepts them. Older commentators (including myself, *MLM*, p. 381) omitted, partly on the strength of the Egyptian-Syriac MS tradition, partly because πυρράζειν was thought to be Byzantine Greek (Allen, McNeile). But the Western-Caesarean testimony is quite impressive, and recently Gundry has argued that the style is Matthaean. Although he has pressed the argument too hard (maintaining that πυρράζειν is typical because Matthew favours πῦρ; and στυγνάζων has been taken over from Mk 10.22), yet there certainly are genuine Matthaean words (ὀψίας γενομένης 6/5/0, 14.15R; 20.8R, μὲν . . . δέ 20/6/10, 20.23R, οὐρανός 82/18/34, 28.2R, σημεῖον 13/7/11, 24.30R; 26.48R), γάρ. πυρράζειν is not too surprising for Matthew has a certain inclination to verbs in -αζειν, like ἀναβιβάζειν, βιάζεσθαι, σεληνιάζεσθαι. Two further arguments tend in the same direction: (1) it is almost impossible to explain the creation of the verses by copyists' adaptation of Luke 12. There was no need for the insertion; and the wording is totally different. There is no parallel for such a different major intrusion into the Matthaean text. (2) Since Lk. 11.14, Luke has been consistently developing texts from Q/ Matthew—even when he has strayed from the close wording, as at 12.13-21, 47f., there are words near enough to Matthew to evoke claims of a Q *Vorlage*. So we may expect the same here. It is likely then that 16.2b-3 are an integral part of the Matthaean text, and were omitted by an early Egyptian copyist slipping on to 16.4 from familiarity with Mk 8.12.

12.54. Luke has now dealt with the coming judgment as it affects the Church, both its leaders and its ordinary families. So he turns to its demand on the uncommitted, who may also be attending his church in some numbers, and recommences with his usual type of formula: 'And he also said to the crowds'. Although he has moved on in his scroll from Matthew 16 to the similar theme of Matthew 24– 25, he has kept in mind the warning Jesus gave at the beginning of the former chapter on discerning the signs of the times, and it is from here that an appeal can be launched to those who are not yet disciples. Matthew gave two signs on 'the face of the sky': one was the red evening sky portending fine weather, the other the red, lowering morning sky foreshadowing storm (cf. G.A. Smith, *Geography* p. 68, 'Sky drumly all forenoon. . .2.30 Gale blowing'). They are two of his less memorable and felicitous sentences, for the sky is said to

be red in both, and the distinction, which may be plain to a south
Syrian Matthaean congregation, is as uncertain to a Greek as to an
English townsman. Nor is it even made quite clear that when they
say 'Fine weather', they have got it right. So Luke clarifies: 'When
you see a cloud rising in the west, *you say* at once, Rain is coming,
and it happens so'. He takes the rain first because one can see its
coming in the sky most obviously. He replaces the red lowering sky
with a cloud rising in the west, partly because clouds mean rain in
Greece too, and partly because a cloud coming up over the way of the
sea famously foreshadowed rain in 3 Kgdms 18.44. 'At once' is Lucan
promptitude (§3).

12.55. On the other hand, 'and when (you see) the south wind
blowing, you say, It will be hot, and it is'. Luke knew the south wind
as a sure sign of fine weather: it had been his friend in Acts 27.13
(briefly) and Acts 28.13. It 'blew' (ὑποπνεούσης) in the former verse.
Although he was familiar with καύσων in the LXX as a hot desert
wind, he uses the word to mean heat as Matthew does at 20.12 (cf.
Jas 1.11): what is the happy sign of fine weather to the sailor, means a
stifling heat-wave to the Achaean city-dweller.

12.56. Matthew concluded, 'The face of the sky you understand
how to discern, but the signs of the times can you not?', and he went
on to speak of the leaven of the Pharisees (16.6). Luke sharpens the
challenge: 'Hypocrites, you know how to weigh up *the face of* land
and *sky, but* how do you *not* know how to weigh up this *time*'? He
was sympathetic to the Pharisee movement (Acts 23.6, etc), and had
been unwilling to call the Pharisees hypocrites in the last chapter;
but he has no objection to using the word of a heathen who will see
one sign but not another—he had even taken the leaven of the
Pharisees to be hypocrisy at 12.1. He keeps the shape of Matthew's
sentence, but puts οἴδατε for γινώσκετε, and δοκιμάζειν for
διακρίνειν. He adds land to sky because in his version you can *see*
the cloud in the sky all right, but you can only see the south wind
from its effects on the land. Cloud, wind: land, sky, is a chiasmus.

12.57f. Most of the teaching in Matthew is addressed to disciples,
and calls to the public to repent are rare. Luke is a little pressed
therefore for suitable material to further the present topic, and he
draws in the piece on adversary and judge in Mt. 5.25f. Matthew was
in fact discussing something quite different. His context was
concerned with reconciliation: 'Go (ὕπαγε), first be reconciled

(διαλλάγηθι) to your brother (τῷ ἀδελφῷ σου)' (v. 24); and he adds a further illustration on speedy settlement of debts, 'Make terms with your adversary quickly, while you are with him on the road'. Luke takes over the words but alters the meaning with his customary sang-froid (§20): 'For as you go (ὑπάγεις) *with your adversary* to the magistrate, take pains to have been rid (ἀπηλλάχθαι) of him *on the road'.* Jeremias (*Parables* pp. 43f.) is surely right in claiming that the Lucan context gives a different force: we are 'on the road' of life, and shall shortly be standing before God the judge. We must make every effort to be settled with our adversary: perhaps Luke even thinks of Satan here, our accuser (Klostermann, p. 143), for we are not to be reconciled *to* him (διαλλάσσεσθαι + dat.) but *from* him (ἀπαλλάσσεσθαι ἀπό). Luke suggests the allegorical interpretation with his introductory 'And why do you not judge aright even of yourselves?' The road to the judgment seat is linked directly with the recognition of 'this time'.

Matthew describes the consequences of failure to settle with our creditors: 'lest the adversary hand you over to the judge, and the judge to the guard, and you shall be cast into prison'. Luke writes, '*lest* he drag *you* to *the judge, and the judge* shall *hand you over* to the officer, *and* the officer *shall cast* you *into prison'.* Matthew had a Jewish set-up (S-B, I, pp. 289f.) with a judge and a *ḥazzān*, which Luke has adapted into the Roman court with which the followers of St Paul were all too familiar. The presidents were ἄρχοντες in Philippi (Acts 16.19), and Paul and Silas were dragged before them (εἵλκυσαν, but σύρειν is used in Acts 8.3; 17.6). The πράκτωρ (officer) is the constable in charge of the Greek debtor's prison (πρακτορεῖον, Bauer). But Luke's improvements have a way of not lasting. His ravens soon lapsed into being Matthaean birds, and his steward a Matthaean servant: and so here the ἄρχων of v. 58a has become a Matthaean κριτής in v. 58b, and perforce Matthew's παραδιδόναι comes back. With the double repetition of the officials' names—judge, judge; officer, officer—cf. father, son, son, father, etc. in v. 53.

12.59. Matthew's '*Amen I say to you, you shall not come out thence till you pay the last* farthing' goes in almost as it stands, with a mite (21.2) as even smaller than a farthing. Matthew is thinking of the earthly debtors' prison, Luke of the one below.

13.1-9. We can account for the Lucan sequence, then, in the way I have suggested. But it is likely that the inspiration really derives from Matthew 24 still, whence the Servant came (12.41-48). Mt. 24.30 (R) spoke of the sign of the Son of Man that was to appear in heaven, when he should come on the clouds, like the dawn shining from east to west; and we should probably think that it is this which made Luke think of Mt. 16.2f. with its *signs* of the times, and amend them to a *cloud* rising in the *west*. We can find his ὅταν ἴδητε at Mt. 24.33 too. Similarly the image of the judge underlies all Mt. 24.30–25.41, especially the end, though the word does not occur; and it may be that this has suggested Mt. 5.25f. More striking, however, is Mt. 24.32, 'From the fig-tree learn the parable'; for after two introductory comments Luke writes, 'And he told this *parable*, A certain man had a *fig-tree*'.

13.1. The new opening, 'And some were present at that very time. . .' is long enough to raise doubt whether Luke intends a new unit; but 'at that very time' binds 13.1-9 closely to 12.54-59 (as 'In that very hour' tied 10.21f. to what went before); 12.54-59 is too short on its own; and its theme is made plain in the new verses. 13.1 is therefore a standard Lucan foil comment (§ 1.4) to lead up to the sayings following. No doubt the tale of Pilate and the Galilaeans' blood came to Luke in some tradition; the most likely reference that we have in Josephus is to the Samaritans attacked by Pilate while sacrificing in 38 (*Ant.* 18.85-87)—the date would be wrong for Luke as well as the Samaritans, but the level of accuracy would be similar to that in his mention of Theudas' rebellion of 44 in Acts 5.36.

13.2f. Jesus' response to the news is framed with the formula we have just met at 12.51, and which recurs at 13.4f., δοκεῖτε ὅτι. . .; οὐχί, λέγω ὑμῖν, ἀλλά. . . It is not likely to have been shared by Q and L in these three sayings only, as Luke likes δοκεῖν = think and οὐχί, ἀλλά. Much of the language is his (see below), and the stress on repentance is recurrent in Acts (cf. Lk. 24.47); so it is likely that he is drawing in the Pilate story in order to supply an emphasis of his own on repentance for which he had no specific authority in tradition.

13.4f. The same would be true of the Siloam disaster, which was no doubt part of first-century lore (whatever may actually have happened), and which has served Luke as the basis for a second challenge to repent. He has varied the language carefully to avoid repetition—debtors for sinners, men living in Jerusalem for Galilaeans, μετανοήσητε for μετανοῆτε, ὡσαύτως for ὁμοίως. The (Semitic) equivalence of debtors with sinners (Mt. 6.12; 18.24) was suggested by the debt sequence of 12.58f.

13.6-9. The overall theme of repentance as the message of the whole pericope is thus clarified. Weighing up this time meant repenting, and taking pains to be rid of your adversary meant repenting: the unconverted 'crowds' must repent or they will perish. All this then leads up to 'the parable of the fig-tree' hinted in Mt. 24.32—not the little similitude of the leaves in summer, which Luke will take in its Marcan order in 21, but rather Jesus' acted parable of the fig-tree which he withered with a word for its fruitlessness. As it stands in Mark, the tale is a cause of offence to a thinking Greek congregation: Jesus appears irrational in expecting fruit out of season, petulant in withering a valuable and unoffending tree, and nothing but a thaumaturge with his display of naked power. But Luke knows that the force of the story is in its symbolism of the Jewish people, who bear no fruit of good works (Mk 11.15-18; 12.2) and stand under the threat of destruction (12.9, ἀπολέσει); and he determines to re-write the incident as a parable. Jesus saw a fig-tree in Mk 11.13, and came if perhaps he might find something on it, and found nothing, no fruit (v. 14); in Mk 12.1 a man planted a vineyard, and entrusted it to farmers. Luke combines the two: 'A certain man had *a fig-tree planted* in his *vineyard*, and *he came* seeking *fruit on it and found* it *not*'. He also knows from Matthew the fate of unfruitful trees: every one that did not make good fruit was cut down (Mt. 3.10; 7.19), one must make fruit worthy of repentance (Mt. 3.8; Lk. 3.8). Hence, 'And if it *makes fruit* in future, well: otherwise you shall *cut* it *down*'.

But although the outline of the parable is thus given in the tradition, it carries Luke's own trademarks also. It begins '*A certain man...*' (0/0/8): with 'A certain man had a fig-tree', cf. 15.11 'A certain man had two sons', 16.1, 'There was a certain rich man who had a steward'. Luke likes to stress his point by *repeating it in oratio recta*. 'He came seeking fruit on it and found not. And he said... I come seeking fruit on this fig-tree and I find it not; cut it down... otherwise you shall cut it down'; cf. 'he goes after the lost one till he finds it... Rejoice with me, for I have found my sheep which was lost' (15.4, 6), 'lest when he has laid a foundation and cannot complete, all begin to mock saying, This man began to build and could not complete' (14.29f.), §11. We may notice also the *homely* Lucan *scale*, so remote from Matthew's kings and millions (§5): the owner has a single workman, and is concerned about the yield from every corner of his orchard. Nor need we feel too anxious about his *knowledge of agriculture* (§30.2): 'digging round' a fig-tree is likely to mean hoeing with a mattock, cf. Diod. Sic. 5.41.6. Luke is fond of digging (6.48R; 16.3)—at least in imagination—and manure (14.35R). It looks as if he has written his own parabolic version of Mk 11.13f. on the suggestion of Mt. 24.32. To be saved one must repent and make fruit worthy of repentance (Acts 26.20).

Most commentators (e.g. Schulz, Schweizer) take vv. 53-56 to be L matter, with Mt. 16.2f. a copyist's version; but others (Schürmann, *TU*, p. 116; Manson, p. 121; Gundry) assign to Q, with the Lucan form largely original. However, G. Klein (*ZTK* [1964]) thinks the Matthaean version earlier, though for somewhat different reasons than those urged here. Gundry, who treats the passage most fully, takes the Lucan form as original entirely on the characteristic Matthaean vocabulary. But this is the Matthaean Vocabulary Fallacy (pp. 11-15): Matthew may have made his own expansion of the 'sign from heaven' theme in Mk 8.11.

12.57 is usually accepted as a Lucan link (Bultmann, pp. 91, 172; Schulz, p. 421), and the adversary section credited to Q, in the Matthaean form. Polag (p. 66) prints Matthew = Q word for word, omitting only the ἀμήν of Mt. 5.25. But this leads to the usual unobserved trouble. Matthew is fond of (ἀμὴν) λέγω σοι/ὑμῖν οὐ μὴ. . .ἕως ἄν . . . He adjusts Mark to this form at 24.34R, retains it at 16.28, the only Marcan instance, and adds it at 5.18M and 10.23M. He likes ἀποδιδόναι, 18/1/8, 21.41R; 16.27R; 27.58R. With εἰς φυλακὴν βληθήσῃ . . . ἕως ἄν ἀποδῷς τὸν ἔσχατον κοδράντην, compare 18.30 ἔβαλεν αὐτὸν εἰς φυλακὴν ἕως ἀποδῷ τὸ ὀφειλόμενον, v. 34 ἕως οὗ ἀποδῷ πᾶν τὸ ὀφειλόμενον. Matthew likes ἐκεῖθεν too, 12/5/3, often R, and has ἐξελθὼν ἐκεῖθεν at 15.21R. So we may say that thirteen words in a row from εἰς φυλακὴν to ἀποδῷς have a Matthaean ring, more than a quarter of the whole.

13.1-9 is usually taken as L material, though Bultmann (pp. 54f.) regarded vv. 1-5 as a creation of the church, and G. Schwarz (*NT* [1969]) has noted the Lucanness of the introduction. The relationship with Mark 11 is widely noted for the fig-tree parable. Creed and Schneider are reluctant to say which came first, as it was often argued in modernist days that an original parable was misunderstood and turned into a scandalous miracle. But Luke's motive for the opposite move is equally clear, and critics have given no weight to the Lucan mode of the parable set out above. Creed is right in seeing the parable as a challenge to Israel to repent, as this is the theme of the following sections (with increasing despair), and of Acts. The tree, as Luke knew, would never bear fruit, and would be cut down in 70—the same point as Mark 11 was indicating, but more gently pressed.

12.54 καί = also. Hapaxes: ἀνατέλλειν, ὄμβρος. ἔρχεται takes up the 'coming' of the Son of Man in 12.36ff. With 'it happens so', cf. Acts 27.44. Cf. Klein, pp. 386f.

12.55 Hapax: καύσων.

12.56 ὑποκριταί voc., 1st word, 13.15. τὸ πρόσωπον τῆς γῆς 21.35R, Acts 17.26. οἴδατε + inf. 11.13QC, there being no parallel for γινώσκειν + inf. δοκιμάζειν 14.19, perhaps suggested by 1 Cor. 3.13. καιρός sing. 1 Cor. 4.5: 'this time' is the period leading up to the End, cf. the days of Noah, 17.26f. (so Jeremias p. 162; contra Klein).

12.57 δὲ-καί*, ἑαυτόν. ἀφ᾽ ἑαυτῶν 21.30R, with γινώσκετε, developing Mt. 24.32. κρίνειν with καιρός 1 Cor. 4.5; with δίκαιον Acts 4.19. τὸ + adj. 6.45QD; 16.15.

12.58 ὡς = when*. Hapax: ἀπαλλάσσεσθαι (+ ἀπό, Acts 19.12), ἐργασία ×4 Acts.

12.59 καί = even.

13.1 τις, αὐτός-ὁ, περί. Hapax: μιγνύναι. παρεῖναι ×5 Acts. On the historical alternatives see J. Blinzler, *NT* (1958).

13.2 εἶπεν, δοκεῖν = think, ἁμαρτωλός, παρά compar.*, γίνεσθαι, ταῦτα, πάσχειν.

13.3 οὐχί … ἀλλά*, μετανοεῖν, ὁμοίως*. It is unclear whether 'you shall all likewise perish' refers to Judgment Day (= 12.55, 58) or the events of 70 (= 13.9); perhaps Luke was unsure himself.

13.4 πίπτειν-ἐπί, δοκεῖν = think, αὐτός nom., γίνεσθαι, παρά compar.*, Ἱερουσαλήμ*. οἱ-κατοικοῦντες + acc. ×8 Acts. Hapax: ὀφειλέτης.

13.5 οὐχί … ἀλλά*, μετανοεῖν.

13.6 λέγειν παραβολήν, ἡ-παραβολὴ-αὕτη, ἔχειν opening a parable*, τις, φυτεύειν, ζητεῖν, εὑρίσκειν.

13.7 εἶπεν-δὲ-πρός*, ἔτος*, ἀφ᾽οὗ = since, ζητεῖν, εὑρίσκειν, καί = also. Hapaxes: ἱνατί (Acts 4.25; 7.26R), καταργεῖν, ἀμπελουργός. The 'vinedresser' is more specific than Mk's γέωργοι, like the tent-makers, silver-smiths, etc. of Acts. Three years may be a round number (Marshall); but one fears Luke is thinking of the three years of a tree's immaturity (Lev. 19.23).

13.8 καί = also, ἔτος*, ἕως-ὅτου, σκάπτω, περί. Hapax: κόπριον (cf. 14.35 κοπρία). λέγει in parables 19.22QD; 16.7, 29: Neirynck, *MA*, p. 229.

13.9 εἰ-δέ-μή-γε. There is no apodosis to the first clause: BDF p. 454 dignifies this with the word aposiopesis, and thinks it is classical, but it may just be a lapse like 8.13. τὸ μέλλον may also be suggested by Mt. 3.7ff. (τῆς μελλούσης ὀργῆς).

Blinzler, J., 'Die Niedermetzelung von Galiläern durch Pilatus', *NT* 2 (1957), pp. 24-49.

Klein, G., 'Die Prüfung der Zeit (Lukas 12,54-56)', *ZTK* 61 (1964), pp. 373-90.

Schwarz, G., 'Lukas XIII,1-5: Eine Emendation', *NT* 11 (1969), pp. 121-26.

Zeitlin, S., 'Who were the Galilaeans? New Light on Josephus' Activities in Galilee', *JQR* 64 (1973-4), pp. 189-203.

c. *The Bent Woman and the Mustard Seed*, 13.10-21

Mt. 24.32 spoke of the parable of the fig-tree; the Lucan parallel, 21.29, extends this to 'the fig-tree and all the trees', and this is an echo of the present complex, which begins with the fig-tree parable and goes on to the mustard-seed. Luke uses the Matthaean version, where the mustard-seed becomes a tree (Mt. 13.32). This enables him to complete his triple lesson on the coming judgment. He has expounded this first with reference to the Church, both officials and ordinary families (12.41-53); then to the uncommitted, who must repent or perish (12.54–13.9); and now to the Jews. We have seen that the Jewish people is probably already in view from the opening verses of ch. 13, but the theme is now taken up seriously. The parable of the mustard-seed taught that God's kingdom was like a great tree, growing from small beginnings; and that in the end the Gentile peoples, the birds of heaven, would come and nest in its branches. It thus extends the message of Luke's fig-tree parable: with that, Israel will be replaced by the nations.

The Mustard-seed is not weighty enough to be a pericope on its own, even with its (Matthaean) twin piece, the Leaven; so Luke provides an introductory story to make its meaning plain, and links the parabolic climax on with a key 'therefore'—ἔλεγεν οὖν (13.18). Fragmentation into tiny paragraphs in synopses and commentaries distracts attention from the author's plainly signalled links of meaning. He gives us an opening 'rubric' at 13.10, 'And he was teaching. . . ', and another at 13.22. His ἔλεγεν οὖν at v. 18 serves to point the moral: the ruler of the synagogue took offence at Jesus' sabbath healing, and this was a symbol of all the 'rulers' of Israel who opposed him (v. 17); *and so* (Jesus said) the nations would come and inherit the great tree which God had intended for his own people.

Luke needs an introductory story, then, which will symbolise the rejection of Jesus by the Jewish authorities; and he is running short of suitable stories, having used up most of the Marcan stock in 4.31–9.50. Matthew hardly adds to this; but Luke has not forgotten his amplified version of the Withered Hand healing in Mt. 12.9-14, not so long before the Mustard-seed parable in Mt. 13.31f. He has already told the Withered Hand story itself in Luke 6 in its Marcan position, so once more he adopts his policy of substitution (pp. 000f.). He knows that 'Jesus went about all the towns and villages, teaching in their synagogues. . . and healing every disease' (Mt. 9.35); so the man with the dry hand in the synagogue was not an isolated instance. Furthermore, Luke is far from having given examples of *every* disease, and Mt. 8.17 specifically mentions an area not otherwise instantiated, 'He took our ἀσθενείας'. So he feels justified in including a case of ἀσθενεία, *infirmity*, *healed* in a *synagogue* in the course of Jesus' *teaching*.

13.10f. The story is a compound of Lucan phrases and such hints from earlier traditions. 'He was teaching on the sabbath' (sc. day) comes in Lk. 4.31R, and 'a woman having a spirit of infirmity' echoes 'a man having a spirit of a demon' at 4.33. 'Bent and not able to stand up' is one of Luke's 'A and not non-A' phrases, like 'dumb and not able to speak' (1.20) (§ 22). He has thought of a woman-sufferer in substitution for the men of 4.33 and Mt. 12.9, in the same way that the widow of Nain came in for Jairus, and the woman sinner of 7.36ff. with the (male) publicans and sinners of 7.29-35. Eighteen years may have been suggested by the eighteen at Siloam in 13.4, or more likely as three working weeks of years—the ruler says 'There are six days on which one should work', and Israelite slaves served six years (Exod. 21.2; Deut. 15.12); the woman has been three times that in bonds to Satan, like the three years the master waited with his fig-tree.

13.12f. Jesus calls the woman out (cf. 6.8R), and tells her 'You have been released'—the verb, as at 14.5, marks her release from Satan's bondage (cf. 2.29); the perfect its completeness (cf. 5.20). Jesus lays his hands on her as at 4.40R, and she is at once (Lucan παραχρῆμα) made straight; and glorifies God, like Luke's paralytic (5.25), leper (17.15) and blind man (18.43).

13.14f. In Mt. 12.9 'they' asked Jesus if one might heal on sabbath, and Luke, with the healing now done, makes the opposition more pointed: it is a ruler of the synagogue who now speaks, like other Lucan 'rulers' a focus of disaffection, and he cites and applies the sabbath law from Exod. 20.9, '... come and be *heal*ed on them and not on the day of *sabbath*'. With six working days and not sabbath, cf. 'bent and not able to stand up'. The Lord—perhaps as lord of the sabbath—replies, 'Hypocrites!', as at 12.56. Matthew had spoken of a sheep fallen into a pit on sabbath, and Jesus asked, 'Which of you... will not take it and lift it out?'. Luke has described the woman as released (ἀπολέλυσαι), so he applies the same argument to the untying (λύει) of animals: sheep were not tied up on sabbath, but larger animals were, oxen and asses, and released for a drink—or so Luke supposed. His 'Does *not* each *of you on the sabbath*...?' weakly echoes Matthew's sentence-form.

13.16. Matthew adds the conclusion 'How much more then is a man worth than a sheep!', and Luke uses the same argument with his, 'And this daughter of Abraham, whom Satan bound, lo, eighteen years, should she not be released from this chain on the sabbath day?' The image of release suggests the horror of an Israelite woman, a daughter of Abraham, in slavery to alien Satan. Luke had taken an earlier spirit to be the hand of Satan (11.18); the release (λυθῆναι) continues the thought of ἀπολέλυσαι and λύει. With 'lo, eighteen years', compare Lk. 13.7, 'lo, three years'.

13.17. Luke closes his story with the confusion of the critics and the rejoicing of the crowd. The former is derived from Isa. 45.16, '*All those who opposed him* shall be *ashamed* and confounded': the latter is a standard Lucan topic (1.58; 19.37; Acts 3.10; cf. Lk. 7.16).

13.18f. This brings Luke to his real concern, the Mustard Tree. As usual through the Journey, he opts for the Matthaean version, and indeed the Marcan form lacked the key word, δένδρον. Nevertheless, an echo of Mark's parable rings in his mind, with its double question opening, 'How are we to liken the kingdom of God, and in what parable shall we set it?' (4.30). Luke is not averse to vain repetitions (§ 22), and employed a double question to open a parabolic saying at 7.31QD; here he begins, 'To what is *the kingdom of God* like, and *to what* shall I *liken it*?' But thereafter he follows Matthew alone. Mt. 13.31: 'The kingdom of heaven is like a grain of mustard, which a man took and sowed in his field'. Luke: 'It *is like a grain of mustard, which a man took and* put into his garden'. Matthew knows that mustard may be sown as a crop, and must be sown in the open field (*m. Kil.* 3.2; cf. 2.8): Luke is not so strong on Jewish law (§ 26), and thinks a single grain of mustard would go more conveniently in the (herb-)garden. Also 'sowing' is a bit pompous for a single grain, which is merely put (ἔβαλεν) in the garden. Matthew: 'which is less than all the seeds, but when it grows it is bigger than all the vegetables, and becomes a tree'. Luke: 'and it *grew and became a tree*'. Luke is not at all concerned with the smaller-than-all-seeds/ bigger-than-all-vegetables contrast, which is a distraction from the point he is after—that God's kingdom is to become a home for the nations. So he drops the smallest/biggest element, and moves straight on to the growth into a tree; and as Matthew had begun to change Mark's present-tense parable into a story, with his 'which a man took and sowed', he presses on with the aorists 'grew' and 'became' for consistency. Similarly Matthew, having relapsed into Mark's presents, ends 'so that the birds of heaven come/came (ἐλθεῖν) and nest in its branches'; while Luke keeps up the 'story' to the end, 'and *the birds of heaven nest*ed *in its branches*'.

13.20f. The worldwide mission of the Church is conveyed as powerfully by Matthew's companion-piece, the Leaven, as by the Mustard-seed; for if God's kingdom is like leaven, the three measures of meal must stand for the world in which it is 'hidden', and the leavening of the whole can mean nothing less than the bringing of the word of God to every nation under heaven. Luke reopens with a further pleonastic question (§ 1.7): 'And he said again, To what shall I liken the kingdom of God?', repeating a part of v. 18. The brief parable is identical with Mt. 13.33, save Luke's plain ἔκρυψεν for Matthew's compound ἐνέκρυψεν: perhaps he thought ἐνέκρυψεν εἰς sounded clumsy.

Bultmann (pp. 12f., 62) saw that the three controversial healing stories, Mk 3.1-6, Lk. 13.10-17, 14.1-6 were all variants of the same; he supposed an isolated saying in v. 15 here as the original core round which the stereotyped healing story formed, Luke adding the final touch in v. 17. Dibelius (pp. 94f.) and Lohse (*TDNT*, VII, pp. 25f.) see the correlation between the loosing of the animals in v. 15 and of the woman in vv. 12, 16, and speak of novelistic expansion in the oral period. But the close relation to the development of Mk 3.1-6 in Mt. 12.9-14 suggests that it is Luke who is the 'novelist', adapting Matthew's sheep to ox and ass for the sake of the loosing parallel; as does the Lucan phrasing. J. Roloff (*Kerygma*, p. 67) argues that rabbinic rulings were more strict than Luke implies; this is disputed by Marshall, but it would be entirely in line with Luke's inaccuracy on Judaica.

The Mustard-seed is the traditional copy-book instance of a Q piece preserved virtually intact in Luke, which is then 'conflated' by Matthew with the Marcan version: so Streeter, pp. 246-48; Schmid, pp. 300f.; Schulz, pp. 298-309. There is only hesitation over 'in his garden', for which Polag (pp. 66f.) prints Matthew's ἐν τῷ ἀγρῷ αὐτοῦ: Jeremias (*Parables*, p. 27 n. 11) cites Theophrastus for the growing of mustard in Greek gardens, while that is forbidden in Palestine. However, Schmid points to Matthew's introduction of the same phrase in the preceding parable, 13.24—*embarras de richesses* once more. The argument has been particularly appealing because Mark has a straight description of nature in the present tense, and Luke a straight story in the aorist, while Matthew starts with 'a man took and sowed' and later veers back to Mark's present. Also Luke does not have the less-than/greater-than phrases, where Matthew agrees with Mark, and he does have the grown-tree-branches elements where Matthew disagrees with Mark. Hence the picture of Matthew the conflator, sandwiching phrases from Mark and Q: see pp. 41f.

However, further enquiry is less encouraging to the conflation theory. Dupont (*NRT* [1967]) is right to insist that the point of its being *mustard*-seed is that mustard *is* so small, and was proverbial among the Jews for being so: so the Marcan form, with its smallest/greatest contrast, is earlier than the Q-Lucan form, which lacks it. Dupont also argues convincingly that 'Q' has dropped the smallest/greatest line in favour of the tree because by his time the Church has become a world-wide organism, like the world-tree in Ezekiel 17 and 31, and Daniel 4; and he thinks that Mark took it in the same way. But surely the point is that the birds of heaven who nest in or under the tree's branches are symbols of the nations of the world in these OT parables, and are said to be (Ezek. 31.6; Dan. 4.22). So whether or not Jesus taught the parable, or in whatever form, by the time it had the birds of heaven in it, it envisaged the Church as a world-organism. Now whoever first thought of the Church as comparable to the empires of Pharaoh and Nebuchadnezzar, can hardly be supposed to have done so in the 50s when the Greek, Asian and Galatian churches were only just founded. Such a concept arises when these churches are established, and the later into the 60s the better. But such thinking is in Mark and 'Q' alike; so the standard idea of a parable of Jesus which developed early into two independent forms (or three, including Thomas, with Crossan, *JBL* [1973]) looks impossible.

Now Dupont argues further that the Leaven parable (as we now have it) exactly follows the sentence-form of the Mustard-Seed, and has been formed to be its companion-piece. He conjectures an earlier form of it, but the present form, culminating in 'until the whole was leavened', was understood by the evangelists of the whole world being transformed by the Church. But if the Q leaven is formed on the basis of the Q mustard-seed with its tree-and-birds, Church-and-Gentiles ecclesiology, then the present form never meant anything else but this.

So the Q form of the mustard and the leaven was a later development of the Marcan form of the mustard, made by a Christian who had witnessed the worldwide expansion of the Church, and the adherence of the Gentiles. As we know that Matthew re-wrote Mark, and was an enthusiastic witness of the Church's Gentile mission, we cannot but ask whether the Q developments bear the stamp of his style. We may notice first the false logic of inferring from Matthew's mixture of aorists and presents the conflation of two sources: Matthew is by common consent rewriting Mark alone in most of the Passion narative, and constantly shifts between his own preferred aorist and Mark's preferred historic present (e.g. 26.20ff./31, 37/38, 44/45). So Matthew could be developing Mark alone here also; retaining the general Marcan presents, 'is smaller... is greater', but glossing in his own story line, 'sowed... grew... came...'; in the context γίνεται δένδρον should probably be taken as a historic present, 'it became a tree'.

In favour of this we may note (1) the close similarity of the preceding parable. Mark has straight nature parables all through Mk. 4, of which the second is the Seed Growing Secretly. He has an ἄνθρωπος in it who sows the seed and sleeps and awakes, but the parable is in the present with the seed germinating, growing and bearing fruit, till in the end he harvests it. Matthew has turned the parable into the much more human story of the Tares: his ἄνθρωπος is active, with a staff and enemies. He has an ἄνθρωπος as hero of the Treasure and Pearl, too, and a number of other parables. Furthermore, we have to compare 13.24, ἀνθρώπῳ σπείραντι ... ἐν τῷ ἀγρῷ αὐτοῦ, with 13.31 ἄνθρωπος ἔσπειρεν ἐν τῷ ἀγρῷ αὐτοῦ. (2) The opening formula of the Mustard and Leaven, ὁμοία ἐστὶν ἡ βασιλεία occurs only here in Luke, never in Mark, but ×7 in Matthew—with the Treasure (13.44M), Pearl (13.45M), Net (13.47M) and Labourers (20.1M), as well as at 11.16QD, cf. 13.52M. (3) Matthew includes clauses of the form, ὅν-aor. nom. part.-subject-verb, in other parables: ὅν λαβὼν ἄνθρωπος ἔσπειρεν (13.31, ἔβαλεν Lk.), ἥν λαβοῦσα γυνὴ ἐνέκρυψεν (13.33), ὅν εὑρὼν ἄνθρωπος ἔκρυψεν (13.44M), ὅν ἐλθὼν ὁ κύριος αὐτοῦ εὑρήσει (24.46QC). (4) 13.31, 33 are particularly Matthaean because of the use of λαβών, -οῦσα cf. Mt. 25.16, 18, 20M; 25.1, 3M; 20.11M. (5) ἕως (οὗ) is normally found with the subjunctive in the Gospels: the only other exceptions are at Mt. 1.25 ἕως οὗ ἔτεκεν υἱόν, 2.9 and 24.39QD. (6) It is Matthew's Gospel where the grand scale is to be found, talents and servants by the dozen, despots and torturechambers; and here even Mark's little mustard-plant is said (by hyperbole) to become a tree, and the woman makes bread enough for more than a hundred people. Over so short a span, that is a lot of Matthaean characteristics: even the doubling of the little parables has its parallel with the Treasure and the Pearl.

13.10 ἦν + part., ἐν-μιᾷ-τῶν*.

13.11 ἀσθενεία, ἔτος*, ἦν + part., A—καί-μή non-A. Hapaxes: συγκύπτειν (cf. ἀνα -), παντελής. ἀνακύπτειν 21.28R. εἰς το π. goes naturally with ἀ.: 'stand up straight'. Luke sees the affliction as the work of a spirit 'ever bowing down her back', cf. 4.39.

13.12 προσφωνεῖν*, εἶπεν, ἀσθενεία. γυναί 22.57R.

13.13 παραχρῆμα*, δοξάζειν-τὸν-θεόν*. Hapax: ἀνορθοῦν (Acts 15.16R).

13.14 σάββατον, ἡμέρα, δεῖ, ἐρχόμενος*, A—καί-μὴ-non-A, τῇ-ἡμέρᾳ-τοῦ-σαββάτου*. Hapaxes: ἐργάζεσθαι (Deut. 5.13), ἀγανακτεῖν.

13.15 ὁ-κύριος = Jesus*, εἶπεν, ἔκαστος + part. gen., σάββατον, βοῦς. Hapaxes: ὄνος, ποτίζειν. The ox and ass are the animals mentioned in the fourth commandment, but the LXX ὑποζύγιον is replaced by Lk. with the more specific ὄνος.

13.16 Ἀβρααμ, ὤν, ἔτος*, δεῖ, τῇ-ἡμέρᾳ-τοῦ-σαββάτου*.

13.17 ταῦτα, pleon. πᾶς (×3), χαίρειν*, τά + part., γίνεσθαι. Hapax: καταισχύνεσθαι. οἱ ἀντικείμενοι 21.15R. ἔνδοξος 7.25R. τά γινόμενα ὑπ᾽ αὐτοῦ cf. 23.8.

13.19 ἐαυτοῦ, (γίνεσθαι). Hapaxes: κῆπος, (κατασκηνοῦν), (κλάδος). γίνεσθαι εἰς LXX. Note *m.Kil.* 3.2, 'Heterogeneous seeds may not be sown in a garden-bed, but heterogeneous vegetable (-seeds) may be sown therein': the seed/vegetable contrast may seem rather Jewish to Luke. For the interpretation (*contra* Fitzmyer), cf. Soncino Talmud *ad loc.* The final clause goes back to Greek Daniel: ἐν τοῖς κλάδοις αὐτοῦ κατεσκήνουν τὰ ὄρνεα τοῦ οὐρανοῦ (4.21Th.). Grässer (p. 142) says that the Q growth theme and the nesting of the birds symbolize the growth of the Church and the Gentile mission; which would fit well with Matthew's attitudes. Schulz (pp. 301, 307) concedes the loss of 'apocalyptic' edge, and assigns to a later strand of Q.

13.20 εἶπεν. πάλιν, rare in Lk., is probably due to similar use in Mt. 13.45, 47; but Luke uses it for repetition, not resumption.

13.21 Hapaxes: (ἄλευρον), (σάτον), (ζυμοῦν). Dodd (pp. 191ff.) and Jeremias (pp. 148f.) see the parable as Jesus' own, and the 'whole' as Israel: but the growth element seems again to be implied (Schulz, p. 309), and the world mission of the 70s is a natural background.

Dahl, N.A., 'The Parables of Growth', *ST* 5 (1951), pp. 132-66.
Dupont, J., 'Les paraboles du sénevé et du levain', *NRT* 89 (1967), pp. 897-913.
Crossan, J.D., 'The Seed Parables of Jesus', *JBL* 91 (1973), pp. 244-66.
Zingg, P., *Das Wachsen der Kirche* (OBO 3; Göttingen, 1974), pp. 100-15.

SECTION 6—THE SECOND HALF OF THE JOURNEY
(13.22–18.8: Mt. 25–16)

41. *Israel and the Gentiles*, 13.22–14.24

a. *The Condemnation of Israel*, 13.22-35

Luke has now worked through the greater part of the Matthaean *Galilee* material. He has followed the Matthaean sequence fairly closely from Mt. 9.35 through to the end of Matthew 16, with certain minor adjustments. Matthew 17 is almost all Marcan material used in Luke 9: Matthew 18 is an expansion of Mk 9.42-50, which still lies ahead. The only chapter to be skipped was Matthew 13, and the non-Marcan elements have at least just received a notice with the Mustard and Leaven parables of the last unit. So the evangelist may breathe more easily. Furthermore, he has in the course of expounding Mt. 9.36-16.28 taken the opportunity to include considerable sections of the *later* Matthaean teaching expansions, especially in Matthew 23-25. Most of the Woes discourse has been used in Luke 11, and the Marriage, Thief, and Servant parables, and other matter, in Lk. 12.35-13.9. Luke has no stomach for Matthew's impressive Assize despatching almost all the Gentile world to hell (Mt. 25.31-46); and the Talents (Mt. 25.14-30) he is keeping for a later context (19.11-27). So he has for practical purposes reached the end of the Matthaean additions to Mark. He has of course omitted many interesting items, especially in Matthew 17-24, as he is well aware, and to these we shall turn in the coming pericopae; but the back of the work is now broken, and in the coming chapters there is a freer atmosphere. In traditional terms there is now more L, less Q; on my alternative paradigm there is more Luke, less Matthew.

With the Mustard Seed and the Leaven Luke has adumbrated a new topic, and one that is dear to his heart, the judgment of Israel and the coming of salvation to the Gentiles. Israel's rejection of the gospel had been most poignantly expressed in the Lord's lament over the city, 'Jerusalem, Jerusalem, how often. . . '; and with this in mind

Luke restates his journey theme in the opening verse, 'And he was journeying. . . making his journey to Jerusalem'. The pericope thus has an effective inclusio (§2.3), with its climax the Jerusalem, Jerusalem logion; and we can tell that Luke has turned to Mt. 23.37-39 for the latter, as he has 48 out of 53 words in common there, but looser contacts with other Matthaean passages. These other texts are drawn in for a variety of reasons. Some are included as being in the scroll still open at Matthew 25—the door that will be closed (Mt. 25.10), and even the two days leading up to the Passion (Mt. 26.2). Others are taken by turning back to the Sermon: Luke included the cutting down of the unfruitful tree (Mt. 7.19) in his Fig-Tree (13.9); he now moves on to the 'many' who will plead to the Lord in vain (Mt. 7.22f.), and to the coming of Gentiles from east and west to the Messianic feast (Mt. 8.11f.). These texts do not always dovetail very neatly into each other, and as Luke also works in suitable pieces from Matthew 14 and 20, it is not surprising if the whole passage has that over-compressed, hammered look which we noticed in 6.39-49, and which is notorious in 16.14-19.

13.22. Luke begins his restatement with a further echo of the text from which he began, Mt. 9.35, 'And Jesus went round all the towns and villages teaching in their synagogues'. He writes, 'And he was travelling through *towns and villages teaching*, and making his journey to Jerusalem'. Jerusalem has not been mentioned since 9.53 (10.30), nor journeying since 10.38. The return to this underlying movement not only leads up to 13.34f., but also signals the coming of a new policy now that the main Galilaean matter in Matthew has been covered—a policy that will become clear in the pericopae ahead.

13.23. Of the Matthew 25 material, Luke has used the Bridesmaids parable in part with his 'Let your loins be girded. . .' (12.35-37); but the climax of the occasion was untouched, and is germane to his present interest. Mt.25.10ff, '. . . and the door was shut', recalls an earlier Matthaean charge to enter through the narrow gate (7.13): for there were few who would find life through that narrow gate (v. 14), and many would end in destruction (vv. 22f.). Luke accordingly adapts the gate of Matthew 7 to the door of Matthew 25, and begins with a foil question (§1.4), 'And one said to him, Lord, are they *few* that are saved?' But that is a question to which Luke would rather not give a direct reply, so the Lord answers, 'Strive to *enter through the narrow door, for many*, I tell you, will seek to enter and will not be able'. Matthew had two gates and two roads in ch. 7, and his listeners had to *choose* between them; and life is like that. He had a single door in ch. 25, and his listeners had to *be ready* so as to go in while it was open; and life is like that too. Luke has once more embarrassed himself by combining two Matthaean images. The single door offers no choice, and its narrowness makes being ready irrelevant; so he solves the dilemma with ἀγωνίζεσθε. Paul did indeed say that the Christian life was like a man competing (ἀγωνιζόμενος, 1 Cor. 9.25); but Luke's picture of salvation as a competition to push through a narrow door is not felicitous. Nonetheless it corresponds, he might feel, to spiritual reality; for salvation depends on faithful perseverance at great personal cost (8.15; 14.25ff, etc.).

13.25. With v. 25 he turns to develop the Matthew 25 image; we do best to read a comma after v. 24, and to think that pushing does no good once the door is shut—otherwise there is no main verb to the sentence. Matthew wrote: '. . . and the door was shut (ἐκλείσθη). Later the other girls come saying, Lord, lord, open to us; but he answered and said, Amen, I say to you, I do not know you' (25.10-12). Luke continues, '. . . once the master of the house rises and *shuts the door* (ἀποκλείσῃ), and you begin to stand outside and to knock on the door *saying, Lord, open to us*; and he will *answer and say* to you, *I do not know you*, where you are from'. Matthew's girls belonged in the marriage context and are unsuitable; Luke turns the occasion into a dinner-party, and supplies an οἰκοδεσπότης from Mt. 24.43. He thinks of him as reclining at table with the guests who come on time, but then 'rising' to shut the door; and has the late-comers 'beginning to stand outside and to knock on the door' (Luke's pejorative ἄρχεσθαι, § 3.2). This has the effect of piling on the agony, and is effective preaching.

13.26f. So Luke has begun with the 'few' of Mt. 7.14, and the fusion of the shut door of Matthew 25 with the narrow gate of Mt. 7.13; but the 'Lord, lord' and 'I do not know you' of Matthew's Bridesmaids come also in the continuation of the Matthew 7 passage, and beckon him further. 'Many' entered by the broad gate in Mt. 7.13, and 7.22f. takes up their fate: 'Many will say (ἐροῦσιν) to me in that day, Lord, lord, did we not prophesy in your name and cast out demons in your name, and do many miracles in your name? And then (τότε) I will confess to them, I was never acquainted with you.

Go away from me, you who work lawlessness'. Luke follows this three-fold sentence-pattern with his next sentence: (a) '*Then* (τότε) you will begin to *say*, We ate and drank before you, and you taught in our streets; (b) And he will say (ἐρεῖ), I tell you, I do not know where you are from—(c) Away *from me*, all *work*ers of iniquity'. Matthew was concerned with the false Christian prophets of 7.15, with their charismatic marvels and their immorality: he writes 7.22f. as he wrote 5.19f. to warn such people that they could not enter the kingdom. Luke is adapting his words to apply to the Jewish people at large, who had not responded to Jesus' ministry—or Luke's: the only plea they can offer is that they ate and drank at the same gatherings where Jesus was, and that he taught in their towns. So again, Matthew, who composed the piece, can produce a plausible if unjustified set of arguments for the miscreants: Luke's amendment leaves a transparently feeble and unconvincing excuse (§4.5). He amends the second sentence more effectively, repeating his previous 'I do not know where you are from', but dropping the object 'you', and prefixing the emphatic 'I tell you': the impression is hard and final. Matthew's third sentence was a version of Ps. 6.9 LXX:

Ps. 6.9	ἀποστῆτε ἀπ' ἐμοῦ πάντες	οἱ ἐργαζόμενοι τὴν	ἀνομίαν
Mt. 7.23	ἀποχωρεῖτε ἀπ' ἐμοῦ	οἱ ἐργαζόμενοι τὴν	ἀνομίαν
Lk. 13.27	ἀποστῆτε ἀπ' ἐμοῦ πάντες	ἐργάται	ἀδικίας

Luke begins by assimilating Matthew to the Psalm with ἀποστῆτε and πάντες; but his charge against Jewry is not that they broke the law (ἀνομία) but that they fundamentally disregarded God, for which he uses the term ἀδικία (16.8; 18.6; Acts 8.23). Nor is it that they are presently engaged (ἐργαζόμενοι) in wrong action, but that it has become part of their character (ἐργάται). So although Luke has so few words in common with Matthew 7 in 13.26f., we can see his motives for developing the passage in the way he has.

13.28f. Luke has already introduced the theme of the Gentiles displacing the Jews in the Mustard-seed, and few texts in the tradition set this out as clearly as Mt. 8.11f., which so soon follows on Mt. 7.22f. Jesus has not found faith like this Gentile centurion's in Israel: 'and I say to you that many shall come from east and west, and shall recline with Abraham and Isaac and Jacob in the kingdom of heaven; but the sons of the kingdom shall be cast out into outer darkness—there shall be weeping and clenching of teeth'. It is in this direction that Luke now wishes to push the exposition, and he opens with '*there shall be weeping and clenching of teeth*'; perhaps because it is that text in Mt. 25.30 which draws his mind to Mt. 8.13, perhaps because 'Away from me. . . ' suggests the implication of agonized rejection. Anyhow, that is where he begins, and we should note that he does not say they go to hell, nor does he think it. There is no Matthaean eternal fire, or furnace, or Gehenna; only weeping and clenching of teeth, as they, Jesus' Jewish public, 'see *Abraham and Isaac and Jacob* and all the prophets *in the kingdom of* God, and yourselves being *cast out*'. Faithless Jewry will suffer the anguish of exclusion from the Messianic banquet, but hell is another matter (see on 13.35). 'All the prophets', who had taken God's side in the OT period, and suffered for it (6.23; 11.49), will be there at table— Matthew had left them out in his haste, and Luke supplies the lack. He ends, 'And *they will come from east and west* and from north and south, *and will recline in the kingdom of* God'; dotting Matthew's i with the two missing points of the compass. The clumsy doubled 'in the kingdom of God', and the clumsy '*there* shall be weeping. . . *when* they see', and the weak expansions, are all signs of Lucan secondariness.

13.30. Paul had taught that the gifts of God were without repentance, and that the fulness of Israel would be saved at the last; and despite the forbidding sound of 'I know you not' in the preceding verses, Luke believed the same. He has avoided mentioning hell so far, and he now turns to a promising-sounding verse, Mt. 20.16, 'So the last shall be first, and the first last'. Did the evangelist not mean that the Christian 'last', who had given up all (19.27-30), would be first in the next life (19.28), and that the wealthy and Pharisaic 'first' would be last, and only just squeeze into the kingdom? I am afraid that he didn't think they would get in at all; but it reads as if he did, and Luke amends circumspectly, 'And lo, there are *last* who *will be first, and* there are *first* who will be *last*'. He means: there are some Gentiles who will hear the gospel late, but who will be high among the saints, and there are some Jews who will (as the Chinese say) catch the last ferry. Only really awful rich Pharisees like Dives end up in the Lucan hell.

13.31. Luke wants now to press on to a climax for the pericope with Matthew's 'Jerusalem, Jerusalem. . . '; but he needs to prepare for this (13.34f.) with some word from Jesus of his going to the place (v. 33). Matthew is thin on comments of this kind, and Luke picks out and expands two. The first is from Matthew's account of the

Baptist's death: 'At that time Herod the tetrarch heard the report of Jesus, and he said to his servants, This is John... and wanting to kill him (John), he feared the people... And his (John's) disciples approached and... told Jesus. And when Jesus heard he withdrew from there... and going out he saw a great crowd' (14.1-14). Herod wanted to kill John, and it seems to be implied that, thinking Jesus to be John redivivus, he wanted to kill Jesus too; John's disciples came and told Jesus of their master's death, and of the threat to his own life, and Jesus moved on. This theme suits Luke's purpose, for it enables him to keep Jesus on the move to Jerusalem; but he is not keen to include the Baptist's disciples—they were troublesome in his own community (Acts 19.1-4), and he has been rid of the Baptist for six chapters (7.18-35). So he puts, '*In that* very hour certain Pharisees *approach*ed saying to him, *Go out* and depart *from* here, for *Herod wish*es *to kill* you'. The disciples of John and the Pharisees were associated in his mind, with their frequent fasts and prayers (5.33); so he credits the warning to 'certain Pharisees', thinking perhaps that there were Pharisees in the Baptist's movement as there were in the Church (Acts 15.5).

13.32. So Jesus is on the way once more; but Matthew 14 is of no help with his response to Herod's threat. Luke still has Matthew 25 open before him, and his eye falls on the words following the Assize scene: 'And it came to pass when Jesus had completed (ἐτέλεσεν) all these words, he said to his disciples, You know that after two days is the Pasch, and the Son of Man is betrayed to be crucified'. This can be rephrased, for it is a logion peculiar to Matthew, and Luke will be following Mark in the context. He prefaces his version with 'Go and say to that fox': Mt. 23.37 has Jesus and his own described as a hen and her chickens, and the enemy of the hen and chickens was the fox then as now. He goes on, 'Lo, I cast out demons and perform (ἀποτελῶ) healings today and tomorrow, and the third day I am perfected (τελειοῦμαι)'. The theme of two days and then the Passion is developed from Mt. 26.2; the ἐτέλεσεν of Mt. 26.1 has been influential on both ἀποτελῶ and τελειοῦμαι, the latter unique in this sense in L-A, though there are similar uses in Heb. The exorcisms and healings which fill the two intervening symbolic days are probably suggested by Mt. 7.23, which Luke has just been citing, '... and in thy name *cast out demons*, and in thy name do many miracles'. Such influences (unlike that of Mt. 26.2) are likely to be subconscious.

13.33. Symbolic days are all very well, but it is real days, and a real journey to Jerusalem, which concern Luke; so he adds, 'But I must travel today and tomorrow and the next day, for it is not possible for a prophet to perish outside Jerusalem'. He is already rolling the scroll back to find 'Jerusalem, Jerusalem. . . ' at Mt. 23.37ff., and there are the verses he has already used at 11.49ff., on Abel and Zechariah, who *perished* (Luke said) between the altar and the house. The πορεύεσθαι takes up the warning Pharisees' πορεύου (and Luke's normal usage); today and tomorrow and the next day have become the creeping petty pace of everyday life; and the saying can end on the high note of Jesus' destiny to die where the prophets died before him.

13.34. The link is thus made smoothly to Mt. 23.37f., which Luke virtually transcribes: '*Jerusalem, Jerusalem, which kills the prophets and stones those sent to her, how often would I have gathered* (ἐπισυνάξαι) *your children as a bird her* brood (τὴν ἑαυτῆς νοσσιάν) *under her wings, and you would not*'. Neither change is significant. Luke has been building up his onslaught on the Jewish people for their rejection of Jesus' preaching, and no text is more effective to this end than the present, where the national 'leaders' at the capital were rebuked for their hard hearts—and the crowds who followed them. Judgment must await such obduracy.

13.35. Luke continues, close to Matthew, '*Lo, your house is left. But I say to you, you shall not see me till* it shall come when *you say, Blessed is he who comes in the name of the Lord*'. Again the changes are small (and their MS authority doubtful). The judgment that he foresees for the Jewish people is not hell-fire but the disaster of 70. Hell is conspicuously absent, even from v. 28. What is coming is the destruction of the temple, which is the meaning of οἶκος to Luke, as in 11.51R; and this is exactly the same judgment foretold in 11.50f. Matthew sites the saying after Jesus' entry into Jerusalem, and there is no doubt that he refers in the final clause to the second coming— whether for judgment to hell, as the context suggests, or to last minute repentance, as the wording suggests. But Luke has sited the saying in the Journey before Jesus' coming to the city; and as his coming is greeted by precisely these words (19.38, with 'the king' added) from 'the whole multitude of the disciples', it is difficult to escape the conclusion that this is Luke's meaning. Hence his opening δέ perhaps: the judgment is over with v. 35a, and the rest of the verse is on another (irrelevant) topic.

Luke felt hardly about the Jews' refusal of the Gospel, and the many sufferings they had imposed on his master Paul, as well as on his Lord (as he saw it). He closes the Acts with the bleak prophecy of Isa. 6.9f., and the comment that 'this salvation of God is sent to the Gentiles'. But this should not blind us to Jesus' prayer that they should be forgiven in 23.34 (cf. J. Leslie Houlden, *JSNT* [1984]), and the careful wording of 13.28 supports this. The Jews' punishment was limited to this world, and to the misery of seeing the Gentiles enjoying the Messianic banquet from which they would be excluded. But even Messianic banquets do not go on for ever.

Critical opinion is much divided over this passage. Verse 22 is generally allowed to be Lucan, but the question in v. 23 is disputed. Bultmann (pp. 359f.), Hoffmann (*ZNW* [1967], p. 193n) and Schulz (p. 310) take it to be Lucan, against Schmid (p. 244), Jeremias (p. 195 n.9), Manson (p. 124); both language and foil question form are on the side of the former group. The narrow door verse (vv. 24f.), with affinities to Mt. 7.13f. and 25.11f., are similarly divisive. Hoffmann (*ZNW*, pp. 195f.) thinks the Lucan form may be the earlier; Jeremias (pp. 95f.) and Schulz (pp. 309ff.) argue for Lucan development of Matthew; Manson (pp. 124f.), and Wrege (pp. 132-35) suppose two independent traditions. The same is partly true of vv. 26f., but here Hoffmann (*ZNW*, pp. 200ff.) and Schulz (pp. 424ff.) see Matthew as developing the Lucan form to deal with an ecclesiastical situation—another instance of the Lucan priority fallacy, for Matthew may well have developed 7.22f. on his own, and Luke adapted it to his context of God's judgment of Israel. For the banquet verses, vv. 28f., Strecker (p. 100) and Trilling (p. 89) follow Schmid in thinking the compact Matthaean form a development of the loose Lucan one, while Harnack (pp. 56f.), Schulz (pp. 323ff.) and Marshall take it the other way round. Verse 30 is usually ascribed to Q, but further conclusions are muted.

The Herod passage, vv. 31-33, has been divisive on different lines. It is commonly attributed to L, and often thought to go back to sound tradition (cf. Harold Hoehner, pp. 214-24). However, Bultmann (pp. 35, 66) and Dibelius (pp. 162f.) note the duplication of v. 32 and v. 33, and suggest either the attachment of a loose saying, or taking v. 31 as a Lucan construction; Steck (p. 44) sees v. 33 as a Lucan preparation for vv. 34f., as I do. More radical approaches are made by A. Denaux and Martin Rese (*BETL* [1975]), both of whom see Luke's redactional hand throughout, though for different purposes. Denaux thinks the Pharisees are hostile as usual in Lk., and hypocritical (12.1), while Herod is being traduced, being as usual in Luke merely neutral to Jesus; Luke has worked the passage up from Mark 6, esp. 6.19, 'Herodias *wished to kill* (John)'. If so, the attitudes of both Pharisees and Herod are very obscure, and Matthew 14 is a much better parallel, where Herod wishes to kill John, and by implication Jesus. Rese thinks the Pharisees are portrayed as friendly (cf. Acts), and that vv. 32f. have been built up on the basis of the Transfiguration—mission concluded by exodus/fulfilment at Jerusalem: the absence of mention of preaching is then due to the Herod threat. Both Rese and Denaux show the unity of the section, and the Lucan nature of the language; but perhaps neither gives a very clear motivation for Luke's supposed activity.

'Jerusalem, Jerusalem. . . ' (vv. 34f.) is nearly identical in the two Gospels, and therefore attributed to Q. This is the only agreed Q section, and we may notice the usual Matthaean features. (1) Matthew imposes a doubled geographical vocative, 'Land of Zabulon and land of Naphtali', on the text of Isa. 8.23 (4.15), like 'Jerusalem, Jerusalem' here. Cf. also the redactional parallel at 2.6, 'And thou, Bethlehem, land of Judah'—the Semitic Judah is preferred to the normal Judaea as Ἰερουσαλημ is here to Ἰεροσόλυμα. (2) With 'Jerusalem. . . your children, and you would not', compare Mt. 2.18, 'Rama. . . Rachel weeping for her children, and she would not be comforted'. (3) Mark 12.1ff. describes in allegory God's sending the prophets and Israel's killing them, and Mt. 21.33 glosses, 'one they killed and one they stoned'; so here, 'which kills the prophets and stones those sent to her'. (4) The hen and chickens form a pair of animal symbols along with dogs and swine, wolves and sheep, gnat and camel, and other Matthaean pairs (cf. my *Alternative Approaches*, pp. 19f.). (5) With λέγω ὑμῖν οὐ μή . . . ἕως (ἄν), cf. 24.34R; 5.18M; 10.23; 16.28Mk.

13.22 διαπορεύεσθαι, κατά + acc., πόλις. Hapax: πορεία (cf. πορεύεσθαι). ποιεῖσθαι 5.33R, ×4 Acts. Ἰεροσόλυμα perhaps under the influence of Mt. 20.17, cf. 16.19. διαπορεύεσθαι anticipates vv. 31, 33.

13.23 εἶπεν-δέ*, τις. οἱ σωζόμενοι Acts 2.47. εἰ interrog. 22.49R. κύριε, εἰ. . . Acts 1.6.

13.24 ζητεῖν, ἰσχύειν. Hapaxes: ἀγωνίζεσθαι, (στενός). The striving is quite different from the Pharisees' forcing of the kingdom in 16.16 (*pace* Hoffmann, *ZNW*, pp. 196f.); and it is only the exigencies of his narrow door image which have made him suggest that competitive striving is the way to heaven.

13.25 ἀφ'οὖ, κρούειν*. Hapax: ἀποκλείειν (Mt. κλείειν). We have to choose between (1) dividing v. 24 from v. 25 with a comma, 'they will not be able, once the master. . . '; (2) making v. 25 an anacoluthon, with no main verb; (3) making ἐρεῖ the main verb, with καί = even. The last is improbable, as καί has so little force as 'even', and naturally means 'and'. Luke is not above writing anacoluthons (13.9), but ἀφ'οὖ/ἧς does not elsewhere begin a

Lucan sentence (7.45; 24.21; Acts 24.11). Perhaps (1), with its long, rambling sentence, is the least bad solution. The imagery is also unclear. Marshall thinks the householder 'closes the door of his house once he knows that all his guests are present'—but did his guests just happen to coincide with the hard pushers, and did he 'rise' from table, having begun before they had arrived?

13.26 ἄρχεσθαι-λέγειν, φαγεῖν-καὶ-πιεῖν*.

13.27 ἀφιστάναι*, πάντες pleon., ἀδικία*. B reads ἐρεῖ λέγων, which is printed by N-A²⁶; but the combination is without parallel in L-A (cp. Metzger, p. 163). οὐκ εἰδέναι πόθεν cf. 20.7R.

13.28 ᾽Αβρααμ, πάντες-οἱ-προφῆται. Hapaxes: (κλαυθμός), (βρυγμός). Black (p. 82) sees 'yourselves being cast out' as an Aramaic circumstantial participle, but Luke writes ὁρᾶν + part. at Acts 8.23.

13.29 Hapax: βορρᾶς.

13.31 ἐν-αὐτῇ-τῇ-ὥρᾳ*, τις, πορεύεσθαι. προσῆλθαν with weak aorist ending, cf. BDF 81(3), also Acts 14.19, ἐπῆλθαν. ἐντεῦθεν also at 4.9QD only in the Gospels. The Pharisees are associated with the Herodians in plans to kill Jesus at Mk 3.6. It is an error to speak of Jesus' departure from Galilee; this is not said, and is contradicted by 17.11. τινες Φαρισαῖοι, cf. 11.27; Acts 5.34.

13.32 εἰπεῖν (×2), πορεύεσθαι. Hapaxes: ἴασις (cf. ἰᾶσθαι), ἀποτελεῖν. The structure of the saying, . . . ἐν τῇ τρίτῃ . . ., is familiar from the Passion predictions, e.g. Mt. 20.19, which Luke may have looked at (cf. Mt. 20.16/Lk. 13.30). The fox is often taken to be symbolic of low cunning (_b. Ber._ 61b) or of contrast with the lion (_m. Ab._ 4.15); but neither of these suggestions is implied by the text, while threat to the life of the hen is there. τελειοῦσθαι of being perfected in death, Wis. 4.15.

13.33 πλήν*, δεῖ, πορεύεσθαι, Ἰερουσαλημ*. Hapax: ἐνδέχεται (cf. 17.1 ἀνενδεκτόν). ἐχομένη = next, Acts 20.15; 21.26 (ἡμέρα).

13.34 ἑαυτῆς sandwiched*. Hapaxes: (λιθοβολεῖν), (ποσάκις), νοσσιά. ἐπισυνάξαι: the weak aorist was increasingly common in Koine (BDF, p. 75) and Hoffmann (p. 191n) thinks Luke may be secondary. Majority opinion is heavily the other way, partly because the form is a hapax. It is unclear why Luke writes τὴν νοσσιάν for Matthew's τὰ νοσσία—perhaps the collective corresponds to Jerusalem, or to the Church, or perhaps Luke just prefers collectives, cf. 14.35, κοπριά, a dung-heap.

13.35 οἶκος, ὄνομα. Luke drops Matthew's ἔρημος; perhaps echoing Jer. 12.7, 'I have deserted τὸν οἶκόν μου, ἀφῆκα my inheritance'. Despite brackets in N-A²⁶ both δέ and ἥξει ὅτε should be read. The former dissociates the final sentence from what precedes, as is required, and will have been dropped due to its absence from Matthew. The latter involves apparently extraordinary syntax, but ἥξει ὅτε is a kind of parenthesis; cf. 17.22 ἐλεύσονται ἡμέραι ὅτε. See Metzger (p. 163).

Tyson, J.B., 'Jesus and Herod Antipas', *JBL* 79 (1960), pp. 239-46.
Hoffmann, P., 'πάντες ἐργάται ἀδικίας', *ZNW* 58 (1967), pp. 188-214.
Zeller, D., 'Das Logion Mt 8,11f/Lk 13,28f und das Motiv der "Völkerwallfahrt"', *BZ* 15 (1971), pp. 222-37, 16 (1972), pp. 84-93.
Denaux, A., 'L'Hypocrisie des Pharisiens et le dessein de Dieu', in F. Neirynck (ed.), *L'Evangile de Luc* (1973), pp. 245-85.
Rese, M., 'Einige Überlegungen zu Lukas XIII, 31-3', in J. Dupont (ed.), *Jésus aux origines de la Christologie* (1975), 201-25.
Hoehner, H.W., *Herod Antipas* (SNTMS Cambridge, 1972).
Denaux, A., 'Der Spruch von der zwei Wegen', in J. Delobel (ed.), *Logia* (1982), pp. 305-35.
Houlden, J.L., 'The Purpose of Luke', *JSNT* 21 (1984), pp. 53-65.
Zeller, D., 'Entrückung zur Ankunft als Menschensohn', in *Fs* J. Dupont (1985), pp. 513-30.

b. *The Dropsical Man at Dinner*, 14.1-14

In the previous unit I noted the extent of Luke's achievement with the Matthaean additions to Mark, and the work that still remained to do. With minor exceptions he had worked through Matthew's Galilean additions in Mt. 9.36-16.28, and had glossed in substantial amounts of Matthew 23-25 besides: but this policy had inevitably resulted in the omission of numerous valuable sayings and parables in Matthew 17-25. In that this material is all teaching, Luke may reasonably feel that its order is not significant (p. 453): but he has no intention of wasting it. We have just seen him in 13.22-35 adapting the end of the Bridesmaids from Mt. 25.10ff., and the two-days-and-then-the-Passion logion from Mt. 26.2; and then rolling back his Matthaean scroll to Mt. 23.37-39, and copying out the Jerusalem logion, as well as drawing in sayings from elsewhere from memory. What we are to observe in the present unit is the development of a group of sayings from earlier in Matthew 23—on the lawyers and Pharisees and their oppressive rulings (23.2-4), on their love of chief seats (23.6), and on the demotion of the proud and exaltation of the humble (23.12).

The suggestion of this series of Matthaean references is that Luke is unrolling his scroll of Matthew *backwards*, and taking the Matthaean texts he has missed *in reverse order*. At first perhaps this was an expedient rather than a policy. He has worked forward as far as Mt. 26.2, where the Passion begins, and he now works back through the scroll looking for the Jerusalem logion in 23.37ff. But thereafter an innocent necessity commends itself as a valuable method, for it is only by handling a text sequentially that one can be sure of not missing things. It does not matter in which direction Luke goes the second time over the Matthaean land, but it does matter that he should go systematically if he is to gather everything in his gleaning. Matthew's sayings are jewels, and no diamond must be lost from the Matthaean tiara.

That Luke has in fact adopted such a systematic procedure may be seen from setting out a list of the principal Matthaean passages on which he has drawn:

Luke		*Matthew*
13.22-33	Closed door, Two days to Passion	25.10ff.; 26.2
13.34f.	Jerusalem, Jerusalem	23.37ff.
14.1-14	Pharisees, chief seats, proud/humble	23.2ff., 6, 12
14.15-24	Great Dinner	22.1-14
14.25-35	Tower-builder	21.33
15.11-32	Father and Two Sons	21.28-32
16.1-13	Steward remitting Debts	(18.23-35)
17.1-10	Offences, Forgiveness, Faith	18.6-21; 17.20
17.20–18.8	The coming of the Son of Man	16.4-28, with 24

These are not all the references, but they are the most obvious ones, and almost all of them are Mt.R. Their combined impact makes a Lucan policy of reverse gleaning through Matthew 25–16 very probable.

In. ch. 11 Luke covered most of the second half of Matthew 23— vv. 23-36—and as much as he wished on synagogue seats and greetings (11.43; Mt. 23.6-11), shutting the kingdom (v. 52; Mt. 23.13), and oaths (nothing, Mt. 23.16-22). He did however carefully leave out 'the chief places at dinners' (v. 43; Mt. 23.6a), and the reason now becomes clear: he means to exploit this weakness in the present context more fully. He begins accordingly, 'And it came to pass as he entered the house of one of the rulers of the Pharisees on a sabbath to eat bread' (v. 1), and goes on in vv. 7f., 'marking how they chose *the chief places*, (he said). . . do not sit down in *the chief place*'; and speaks in v. 12 of making a *dinner*. Mt. 23.12 had concluded, 'And whoever shall exalt himself shall be humbled, and whoever shall humble himself shall be exalted', and Luke applies this lesson to the chief seat question, 'For everyone who *exalts himself shall be humbled, and* he who *humbles himself shall be exalted*' (v. 11).

Matthew had more serious things against the scribes and Pharisees, and Luke has already taken up (11.46) their binding heavy burdens on men—indeed he took this to be a piece of gross hypocrisy, since in his version it is not that they will not move them (from other men), but that they will not touch them themselves. He returns to this charge now. The critics of his healing are not just synagogue officials as they were in the similar story in 13.10-17, but 'lawyers *and Pharisees*', the Lucan equivalent of Matthew's 'scribes and Pharisees'. They bind a burden hard to bear on the dropsical man, in that they would deny him healing on a sabbath day; and yet any of them would be quick enough to pull up their son or their ox if they fell in a well on sabbath. So Luke has his eye on the unused, or undeveloped material at the beginning of Matthew 23—vv. 2, 4, 6 and 12.

14.1-6. To make the point, however, he requires an example, and for this he falls back on the model of Mt. 12.9-13, which he has already used once at 13.10-17. In Mt. 12 Jesus went into their synagogue; here 'it came to pass that he *went into* a Pharisee's house'. There, 'and behold a man with a dry hand'; here '*and behold a man* with dropsy'. There they asked, 'Is it lawful to heal on the sabbath?'; here it is Jesus who puts the question, '*Is it lawful to heal on the sabbath* or not?' (§4.6). There Jesus replies, 'What man will there be of you who will have one sheep, and if this falls on the sabbath into a pit, will not take and raise it up?' Here he continues, '*Which of you*'s son or ox will *fall into* a well, and he *will not* at once pull him up *on the sabbath* day?' In both stories the sufferer is healed, and the critics confounded into silence. Luke adds at the beginning that they were watching him, and at the end that they were silent, as in the Marcan version of the incident (3.2, 4; Lk. 6.7).

So much matter in common with the Matthaean redaction of Mk 3.1-6 makes a prima facie impression of Lucan re-writing: but what account can be given of the differences? I have already suggested that the dinner situation and the lawyers-and-Pharisees are due to Matthew 23; and we may add that the scene with an individual Pharisee inviting Jesus to a meal and then slighting him is familiar from Lk. 7.36 (ἠρώτα δέ τις αὐτὸν τῶν Φαρισαίων ἵνα φάγῃ μετ' αὐτοῦ, καὶ εἰσελθὼν εἰς τὸν οἶκον...), and 11.37, alone in the

Gospels. For the dropsy, Luke is probably developing themes in Matthew 12. He knows that Jesus healed every disease (Mt. 9.35), and the man with the dry (ξηράν) hand suggests as his antithesis the man with the water disease (ὑδρωπικός). Greek medicine from Hippocrates on (e.g. Airs Waters and Places) worked on the theory of the humours, and excessive dryness and wetness were believed to underlie much disease. In ch. 7 living in a wet area is said to make people ὕδρωπες. Further, Jesus' comment on the pit is likely to have been pointed, for a pit is normally dry, and so suited to compare with a dry hand: if then Jesus was faced with a man whose body was inflated with water, he will have asked his opponents if they would not rescue an animal from the water, i.e. a well. He had said too in Matthew, 'How much more then is a man worth than a sheep!', so he includes a man with his animal; and since the point at issue is the Fourth Commandment, he drops the sheep, as he did at 13.15, and substitutes 'a son or an ox', which are actually mentioned in the sabbath law. ἀνασπᾶν recurs in Acts 11.10 only in the NT, and 'the sabbath day' is Lucan, as is much of the remaining language (see below).

14.7-11. The silence following this scene enables Jesus to take the initiative on the chief seats issue, as we have noted; but Luke can see that the Matthew 23 material is thin, and he accordingly continues to roll his Matthaean scroll back, past the Marcan stories in Mt. 22.15-46, to the new material in 22.1-14, the Wedding Feast. This has a lesson of its own, to which Luke will devote the next pericope; but he takes some details from it now as well. Matthew speaks of those invited to the wedding (κεκλημένους εἰς τοὺς γάμους), so Luke has Jesus begin, 'When you are *invited* by anyone *to* a *wedding*. . . '; and he goes on to speak of a more honourable man being invited (κεκλημένος). In a moment Matthew will say that the king has made ready his ἄριστον; so Luke continues, 'When you make an ἄριστον or a dinner' (v. 12).

However, the point about chief places is only really explored in the Old Testament: Prov. 25.6f. counsels, 'Do not put yourself forward in the King's presence, or stand up in the places (τόποις) of the great: for it is better for you that it be said, Come up (ἀνάβαινε) to me, than to be humbled before the great'. This is the development that Luke is looking for, for it embraces both the chief seats of Mt. 23.6 and the exalting/humiliating contrast of 23.12. These texts direct the exposition: 'When you are *invited* by anyone *to* a *marriage* (Mt. 22), do not sit down in *the chief seat* (Mt. 23), lest a more honourable man than you be invited; and he who invited you both will come and say to you, Give *place* to this man (Prov.), and then you will begin with shame to take the lowest place (Mt. 23). But when you are invited, go and sit in the lowest place (Prov.), that when he who has invited you comes he will say, Friend, *come up* (προσανάβηθι) higher (Prov.); then you will have glory before all your fellow-guests (Mt. 23)'. We may notice an exact parallel to the structure of the two sentences vv. 8-10 in Lk. 14.12ff.: '*when you* make a luncheon... *do not* invite... *lest* they too... *But when you* make a party, invite... and blessed will you be...'.

It is often urged (Jeremias, pp. 191-93; Schweizer; Marshall) that the verses are in origin an eschatological parable of warning, and not a piece of worldly wisdom advising subtlety rather than effrontery in pursuit of kudos. But the text gives no hint of so high a spiritual level. Luke says Jesus noticed them picking the chief seats, and παραβολή means a *mashal* like the one in Proverbs 25 (cf. Lk. 6.39). Luke himself is not above a little worldly wisdom, as is notorious in 16.1-8, and noticeable in 14.28-32. But it is a cul-de-sac into which Mt. 23.6 and Proverbs 25 have drawn him: the point of the verses (and of the preceding ones) is summed up in v. 11—the Jewish leadership is constantly exalting itself, and God will humble it (cf. 16.15). It thus reinforces the theme of the condemnation of Israel in 13.22-35, and looks forward to the Gentile mission in 14.15-24.

So the theme is Lucan, and so are the structure and the worldly wisdom; and we may add the topic of shame. Shame is mentioned in Luke's Gospel only—'all who opposed him were ashamed' (13.17), 'to beg I am ashamed' (16.3), 'yet because of his shamelessness' (11.8). The language in general is congenial to Luke, and with the Matthaean texts to hand on the scroll, it seems clear that Luke has composed the piece.

14.12-14. The same is true of the final sub-section. Luke found in Mt. 22.1-10 not just the words καλεῖν and ἄριστον, but the command to go to the crossroads and invite to the wedding anyone who should be found (v. 9). Such liberality to *the poor*, and pretermission of *the rich*, is exactly in line with Luke's own instincts. We have seen him praise God for filling the hungry with good things and sending the rich away empty at 1.53, and look forward to the filling of the hungry and the hunger of those now full at 6.21, 25. How natural then if he should add now Jesus' counsel to his host not to invite his wealthy friends, but the poor! *Friends and relations and neighbours* are congenial to Luke too: Elizabeth's neighbours and relations came to share in her happiness (1.58), and the owners of the lost sheep and coin both invite their friends and neighbours to celebrations (15.6, 9); Joseph and Mary sought Jesus among their relations and acquaintance (2.44). We have also met before Luke's love of *quartets* (§23): good measure, pressed down, shaken together, running over; relax, eat, drink, be merry; friends and brethren and relations and neighbours; poor, lame, halt, blind. The latter four we meet again at v. 21. We have just had the same structure of double sentence in vv. 8-10, '*When you* are invited. . . *do not* sit. . . *lest* a more honourable. . . *But when you* are invited, go and sit. . . then you will have glory. . . ' We find the same *counsel* not to do good to those who will return it, but to those who cannot, that we may be blessed by God, at 6.32ff. The words are different from Matthew's, and 6.35 gathers the matter together: 'But love your enemies and do good and lend, expecting nothing back; and your reward will be great'. It was failure to observe this principle which cost Dives eternal life. Luke likes *parties* too (§4.4); and he has eleven *macarisms* in the Gospel outside the Beatitudes, against Matthew's four; and *the resurrection of the just* is a Lucan concept too (20.35f.R only). It is difficult to find anything which is not characteristic of the evangelist.

The similarity of the healing of the dropsical man with that of the man with the withered hand in Matthew 12 requires an explanation. Schürmann (*TU*, p. 213) suggests Q; Bultmann (pp. 12, 62) thinks that v. 5 was a variant of Mt. 12.11, and that the church has composed the story to fit it on the basis of Mk 3.1-6 and Lk. 13.10-17 (so also Roloff, pp. 66-69); Grundmann and Marshall opt for accident; Gundry thinks Matthew has borrowed details from the dropsy story, which he has omitted. If we follow Schürmann and Gundry, Q becomes an enormous and speculative catch-all. Bultmann is more plausible: but then why not allow that Mt. 12.11 is Mt.R, like so many other minor additions to Mark? This is only disregarded because Bultmann accepted the dogma that Luke did not know Matthew. 'The church' can then become Luke, to whom Bultmann credited only v. 1.

Bultmann (pp. 104, 108) notes the worldly wisdom of vv. 8-10, and its deep roots in Jewish thinking, including Proverbs 25; he wonders how it came to be included in the Gospel. This seems more straightforward than

Jeremias (pp. 191-93), whose eschatological warning view appears forced; nor is it strengthened by honouring the version in Mt. 20.28D as the more original form of the same saying (pp. 35f.; Black, pp. 171-75). The Aramaic retranslation does not adequately account for δόξα/χρήσιμον, as *shivḥa* could never be translated 'useful'; the D verse is a later Greek paraphrase of Luke. Bultmann's problem is solved if Luke is seen as developing the chief seats and humble/exalt themes from Matthew with the aid of Proverbs 25.

Conzelmann (pp. 110f.) sees 'the resurrection of the just' as pre-Lucan, taking Acts 24.15, 'there will be a resurrection of just and unjust', as Luke's own counterblast. Conzelmann discriminates three phases of Christian thought: (1) a general cosmic resurrection, (2) an individual, hopeful, resurrection of the just, (3) Luke's message of judgment without time. This seems speculative; for Luke contains all three emphases himself. There is no need to read Acts 24.15 as polemical: the resurrection is a 'hope' only for the just, who therefore are mentioned apart from the unjust. Conzelmann does not comment on Luke's redaction in 20.35f. The just alone are mentioned here, because it is only they who have been entertaining the poor, and so will share in the Messianic Feast.

14.1 καὶ-ἐγένετο-ἐν-τῷ-(inf.)-αὐτὸν. . .καί*, οἶκος, τις, ἄρχων, σάββατον, αὐτοί nom., ἦν + part, παρατηρεῖσθαι.

14.2 τις. Hapax: ὑδρωπικός. ἔμπροσθεν 5.19R; 21.36R?; 19.27QD.

14.3 εἶπεν-πρός*, οἱ-νομικοί*, σάββατον.

14.4 ἐπιλάβεσθαι*, ἰᾶσθαι*. ἡσυχάζειν 0/0/2+2, 23.56R.

14.5 εἶπεν-πρός*, βοῦς, ἡμέρα-τοῦ-σαββάτου*. Hapaxes: φρέαρ, ἀνασπᾶν (Acts 11.10). εὐθέως Lucan alacrity (§3). Matthew's βόθυνος normally = *paḥath*, a pit (dry); it is a pool only at 4 Kgdms 3.16. φρέαρ means a dug well. υἱὸς ἢ βοῦς is both the best testified reading and the one inviting a change by its clumsiness. Regulations concerning children and animals falling into pits are to be found in *m. B.K.* 5.6f. It is unclear whether sabbath rescues were permitted in the first century; for the third century see *b. Sab.* 128b. Black (pp. 168f.) argues for an original Aramaic with assonance between *bᵉra* (son), *bᵉ'ira* (cattle) and *bera* (well). But *bᵉ'ira* means cattle, not an ox, so that an original has to be supposed which agrees with neither Luke nor Matthew. Neirynck (pp. 640) takes vv. 1-6 to be nearly all Lk.R: but what of the similarity of v. 5 to Mt. 12.11R?

14.6 ἰσχύειν*, πρός + vb. dicendi*, ταῦτα. Hapax: ἀνταποκρίνεσθαι (ἀντι- 2/0/13+7).

14.7 λέγειν-παραβολήν*, πρός + vb. dicendi* (×2), ἐκλέγεσθαι*, καλεῖν. Hapax: ἐπέχειν (Acts 3.5).

14.8 καλεῖν (×2), τις, κατακλίνειν*, εἶναι + part. ἔντιμος 7.2.

14.9 καλεῖν, τόπος (×2). Hapax: αἰσχύνη (cf. 13.17; 16.3). τότε ἄρξῃ in a hostile sense, 'then you will start...', 13.26QD; 23.30. κατέχειν 8.15R. There may be an echo of Mt. 20.16 again, first/last.

14.10 καλεῖν (×2), πορεύεσθαι, ἀναπεσεῖν, τόπος*, δόξα, ἐνώπιον*, πάντες pleon. Hapaxes: προσαναβαίνειν (double compounds 12/14/31+35), ἀνώτερον. ἵνα + fut. 20.12R, BDF, p. 369(2). φίλε 11.5.

14.11 (ἑαυτόν) ×2.

14.12 δὲ-καί*, καλεῖν, δεῖπνον, φίλος*, συγγενής*, γείτων, πλούσιος*, καί= also, αὐτός nom., γίνεσθαι. Hapaxes: ἀντικαλεῖν, ἀνταπόδομα (ἀντι-2/0/13+7, cf. vb. ×2 v. 14). ἄριστον 11.38.

14.13 καλεῖν, πτωχός. δοχή 5.29R. φωνεῖν is a welcome variation after 8× καλεῖν.

14.14 οὐκ-ἔχειν + inf.*, ἀνάστασις.

Meeus, X. de., 'Composition de Lc., XIV et genre symposiaque', *ETL* 37 (1961), pp. 847-70.
Ernst, J., 'Gastmahlsgespräche: Lk 14, 1-24', in *Fs* H. Schürmann, 57-77
Neirynck, F., 'Jesus and the Sabbath', *Evangelica*, 637-80.
Cavallin, C., 'Bienheureux seras-tu...à la résurrection des justes', *Fs* J. Dupont, pp. 531-46.

c. *The Great Dinner*, 14.15-24

The first of Luke's three pericopae described the condemnation of Israel and the sharing of Gentiles in the Messianic banquet. The second foresaw the humbling of the legalistic and self-seeking Pharisee, and the raising of the humble and generous, as yet unspecified. The third continues the dinner theme, expounding in the famous parable the Church's double mission, first to the poor of Israel and second to the Gentiles without.

Matthew's Dinner parable, 22.1-14, is still open on the scroll. It is a sparkling tale, but has a number of aspects with which Luke (and some more recent exegetes) have felt uncomfortable. First, it is an allegory, and an allegory where the story is marred: it suddenly appears that all the guests to the king's wedding-feast live in a town together, and that they are slaughtered by his armies, and their town burned; meanwhile the king's oxen and fatlings are put in the freezer. Second, the characters are flat, and Luke likes his characters to be people (§4). Third, the reader is left in considerable doubt over the king, who seems over-harsh in exacting such punishment on the entire population, and despotic and even unjust to the guest in the wrong clothing. Finally there is the scale of the story, away in the realms of fantasy, while Luke likes his parables down to earth, and with situations such as his congregation were familiar with (§5).

14.15. He reopens the scene, therefore, with a remark of one of the guests at the Pharisee's party: this has the regular Lucan function of providing Jesus with a foil against which his parable can stand out (§1.4). The remark is itself characteristic of the evangelist in its lampooning of vacuous piety; cf. the woman at 11.27, 'Blessed is the womb. . . ' It is Luke also who is so fond of macarisms—outside the Beatitudes he has eleven, where Matthew has four and Mark none. 'Eating bread in the kingdom of God' takes up the reference to the Messianic banquet: Gentiles were to sit with the patriarchs in the kingdom of God at 13.29, and the open-handed of 14.12ff. would find their blessing there at the resurrection of the just.

14.16-24. For all Luke's alterations, the parable retains Matthew's structure: (1) The host gave a big reception; (2) *he sent his servant(s) to* summon *those invited*, saying the meal was *ready*; (3) the guests rudely ignored the message, *going off* to see to their *farm* or business purchases; (4) *then* the host was *angry* at their behaviour (matters are worse in Matthew), and said to *his servant(s)* to *go out into the streets* and bring in anybody; (5) in this way there would be guests at the banquet. There are only eighteen words in common between the two stories; but the presence of Matthew's τότε and ἀγρός (16/7/9, 13.31R) among them may suggest which way the wind is blowing.

Luke's major alteration is the removal of the royal setting, with which the most unfortunate parts of the allegory are associated. The king thus becomes a commoner, Luke's standard ἄνθρωπός τις, and he is giving a big dinner in place of the prince's marriage. Luke has already shunted off the marriage theme to 14.7, and he wants to concentrate the thought of the parable on the Gentile mission, which is his present topic, rather than on Jesus as the bridegroom/the marriage feast of the lamb. He is not at home with parables about kings, and his own attempt at such an allegory in 19.11-27 is not a success. He knows the world of middle-class dinner-parties, and fills in at ease the excuses at which Matthew hints so sparsely with 'one to his farm, another to his business'. Matthew's king, of course, has servants by the score, enough for two multiple embassies, and the second group (= the church) can be insulted and murdered; this then leading to an army of reprisal (= Titus), and the reduction of the offenders' city (= Jerusalem) to flames (= 70). This is just the kind of thing Luke is glad to be without. His 'certain man' has a single servant for this kind of duty, and works him hard. He must go the round of the guests 'at the hour of dinner', and they are said to be 'many'; he is despatched a second time to go round the streets and lanes of the town, and escort in the blind and the lame—no mean task; and finally he is sent to scour the highways and hedges for tramps. The poor man must have been exhausted; but then such slave-driving of the single worker is what we find in Lk. 17.7-10, and Luke's vineyard-owner has only one man in 13.6-9. He knew what life was like working for the petit-bourgeoisie (§5).

But although Luke is pleased to dispense with the top-heavy allegory of the Jewish War, he is perfectly happy to accept, and even to elaborate, Matthew's final point on the mission to the Church. No doubt Matthew's own church was mainly Jewish and his concern was a pastoral stress on righteousness; but Luke is interested in the entrance of the Gentiles, to which his thought has been tending for a chapter. He cannot, however, take over Matthew's 'as many as you find' without some clarifying expansion; nor has he any wish to ignore the existence of the large and influential Jewish church. So he takes up the Matthaean detail of the crossroads/roads, and provides for a double mission. The first time his servant is sent to 'the streets and lanes of the town', i.e. within the bounds of the Jewish community; and he is to bring in the poor and halt and blind and lame i.e. the Jewish Christian church. The (wealthy) Pharisaic movement and other Jewish leaders had been resistant to the gospel; those who had accepted the apostolic preaching had included a good number on the bread-line (Gal. 2.10; Rom. 15.26), and within a couple of generations the Jewish Christian community would be known as the Ebionim. But the Gentile mission is then provided for by a second despatch of the servant: this time to the highways and hedges, that is outside the town, and so outside the Jewish community. For only so would the master's 'house be filled with guests'. By including a first circuit of the streets and lanes, Luke has been able to give an allegorical force to Matthew's ὁδούς. To Matthew 'as many as you find' on the roads and at the crossroads meant the laity of the (whole) Church, 'bad and good' (v. 10): Luke has this taken care of in two sendings—the contrast of streets with 'highroads', and especially with the 'hedges' that line them, shows that Luke is making space for the great Gentile mission that had been his life's work.

So Luke has dropped the greater part of the Matthaean allegory, but has not been above supplying an allegorical twist of his own (§6); as he does with the Pounds, and the Fig-Tree. But he is never content with a colourless allegory, and at every point adds life and humanity to his Vorlage (§4). Matthew has no *oratio recta* until after the burning of the city. Luke has the master's first sending in direct speech, 'Come, for it is now ready', and all the three excuses are given in direct speech; the master uses *oratio recta* twice to the servant, and he replies. This is part of the standard Lucan liveliness, which enables us to see into the *characters* of the people (§4.2). Thus the master is courteous in his first message; and his anger expresses itself, not in Matthaean vindictiveness, but in generosity to the poor (v. 21). The servant is faithful and willing—'Sir, it is done as you have commanded, and there is still room'. The *excuses* are the transparent lies of which Luke is such a master (§4.5). 'One to his farm', said Matthew: 'I have bought a farm', says Luke, 'and I must needs go and see it'. Really? ἀνάγκη? 'Another to his business (ἐμπορίαν)', said Matthew: 'I have bought five yoke of oxen, and am going to test them', says Luke. At dinner time? 'I have married a wife', comes the Lucan addition (no doubt with an eye on Deut. 20.7), 'and therefore I cannot come'—Luke's devastating weak 'cannot' (§4.5): 'the door is shut and my children are with me in bed: I cannot get up and give you', 'I cannot dig'. The progressive rudeness is itself masterly: 'I must needs. . . please have me excused', 'I am going. . . please have me excused', 'I cannot come'. In Luke the Jewish people tried to excuse themselves on the ground that they had eaten in Jesus' presence, and he had taught in their streets!

We may see Luke's hand behind some other details of the story. The oxen are a Lucan *handful* (§12): five sparrows, five in a house, five hundred dinars and fifty. With 'they all began to excuse themselves. . . have me excused', compare Luke's 'I will say to my father, Father', 'How can you say to your brother, Brother?' 'Go out quickly into the streets' is Lucan *promptitude* (§3): 'Take your bill and sit down quickly', 'will not pull him up at once on the sabbath day?' 'The poor and halt and blind and lame' are a Lucan *quartet*

(§23): 'good measure, pressed down, shaken together, running over', 'relax, eat, drink, be merry', or the same four at 14.13. The added conclusion, 'For I say to you that none of those men who were invited shall taste of my dinner', is the Lucan motif of the exclusion of the unbelieving Jews from the Messianic banquet. We had the same doctrine at 13.28, 'and yourselves being cast out', at 13.30, 'there are first who will be last', and 14.11, 'Everyone who exalts himself will be humbled'. For the *hostility to marriage* of 14.20, cf. 14.26QD; 18.29QD.

Such an account of Luke's redaction of Matthew involves an independent explanation of Mt. 22.1-14: I have offered such an explanation, seeing Matthew as giving a second version of the Husbandmen (Mt. 21.33-44) in the light of the book of Esther (*MLM*, pp. 415ff.). To standard theorists, the existence of common structure and language in the two parables shows they both took over a Q parable; and (on Jülicher's principle, that Jesus' parables had a single point) this can be recovered by stripping away both the Matthaean allegory in the body of the story and the Lucan allegory at the end. Polag (pp. 70f.) is thus left with the featureless rump to which the Q hypothesis inevitably tends.

Jeremias (pp. 63ff., 67ff., 176ff.) proposes an elaboration of this. There was in circulation at the time the story of a wealthy tax-gatherer called Ma'yan, who invited the wealthy to dinner and was snubbed by them; so he filled the places at his banquet with beggars, and died in his moment of charity. Jesus adapted the story to the message of the gospel: 'God's banquet is full of publicans and sinners', he told his opponents, 'you are too late'. This tale is in part reflected in the Lucan version, and in part in Thomas 64 with an unembellished 'dinner'. The double mission was a pre-Lucan expansion, whose only intention was to stress that every place must be taken. Thereafter churchly embellishment and allegorization have silted over the original situation. This amazing reconstruction (for which Jeremias gives credit to his pupil, W. Salm) rests upon a complex of hypotheses: the Ma'yan story is first found in *j. Sanh.* 6.23c/*Hag.* 2.77d, and no argument is offered to suggest it was known half a millennium earlier; nor for the often repeated assertion that Jesus' parables were addressed to his opponents. The Thomas version is entirely explicable as an encratite form of Luke, with a hostility to trade. There is nothing to show (see below) that the double mission predates Luke. For the dependence of Thomas on Luke, see Schürmann, *TU* pp. 228-47; B. Dehandschutter, *BETL* 32, pp. 287-97.

The problems of providing an original setting with Jesus may be seen by comparing this with the views of Hahn (*Fs* Stählin, pp. 51-82), and Vögtle (pp. 171-218). Perhaps Jesus was speaking of his rejection by the pious Jews, and his acceptance by the publicans and sinners. But then the parable would be totally misconstrued by its first tradent, Luke, as he makes the invited to be well-to-do and their replacements to be beggars, whereas the publicans and sinners were often in the money, and the pious are often supposed to be poor. Or perhaps Jesus was threatening the Jewish people that they would be replaced by the Gentiles, and the Church turned this into a prophecy of the Gentile mission. But then where would be the basis for thinking of the Jews as well-to-do and the Gentiles as poor? (Marshall). Derrett (pp. 126-55) has provided a welcome contrast with a reconstruction which combines all the major features of Luke and Matthew instead of removing them; but the impression left is of brilliance rather than plausibility.

14.15 ἀκούσας-δέ, τις, ταῦτα, εἶπεν. φαγεῖν ἄρτον 14.1, cf. 7.33R; τῶν συνανακειμένων 14.10; μακάριος 14.14—the language as well as the thought of the Messianic banquet links on to the preceding verses.

14.16 εἶπεν, ἄνθρωπός-τις*, δεῖπνον, καλεῖν. ἐποίει δεῖπνον μέγα, cf. 5.29R ἐποίησεν δοχὴν μεγάλην. ἐκάλεσεν πολλούς—perhaps influenced by Mt. 22.14, πολλοὶ γάρ εἰσιν κλητοί.

14.17 δεῖπνον, (καλεῖν). τῇ ὥρᾳ τοῦ δείπνου, cf. 1.10 τῇ ὥρᾳ τοῦ θυμιάματος, Acts 3.1; 10.30. There is no proper Palestinian evidence of a practice of so sending a servant round at Jerusalem dinner-parties (*pace* Jeremias, p. 176). *Lam. R.* 4.2 explains 'the precious sons of Zion' by, 'None of them would attend a banquet unless he was invited twice'. Requiring two invitations is not the same thing as being summoned at dinner-time; and in any case the paragraph is fanciful—another explanation offered is, 'When a man of another Palestinian town married a woman of Jerusalem, he gave her weight in gold' (cf. Billerbeck's scepsis, I, p. 880). The detail is carried over from Mt. 22.4, which has in turn taken it from Esth. 6.14, along with the royal setting, the wedding, the dinner and the unworthy guest. Another sign of dependence on Matthew is ἔτοιμά ἐστιν, which has no subject—cp. Mt. πάντα ἔτοιμα. p75 א L Θ read ετοιμα εισιν (printed by Greeven), which is even more peculiar without πάντα.

14.18 εἶπεν, ἐρωτᾶν*. Luke's hostile ἤρξαντο = 'they started', cf. 3.8QD, §3.2. ἀπὸ μιᾶς is taken by Black (p. 113) to be a literal translation of the Aramaic *min h^ada*; but BAG, *s.v.* ἀπό VI, says this would yield ἀφ'ἑνός, and conjectures the omission of γνώμης, etc., as does BDF (p. 241) (6). Luke understands a noun at 9.18; 12.47f.; Acts 19.19, also. παραιτεῖσθαι Acts 25.11. ὁ πρῶτος ... ἕτερος, cf. Pounds, 19.16, 20QD, 16.5, 7. ἀγρὸν ἠγόρασα, Morgenthaler, *LGZ* 20, *Klangfigure*. ἀνάγκη 21.23R; cf. 1 Cor. 7.37.

14.19 ἕτερος*, εἶπεν, πορεύεσθαι, ἐρωτᾶν*. Luke has interpreted Matthew's ἐμπορίαν as purchase rather than business, and associates the farm with the means to work it. According to Dalman, *AuS* II, pp. 40, 47f., a normal size of farm could be worked by two yoke of oxen, but the letter of Aristeas 116 gives a hundred *arurae* (seventy acres) as normal, and this would require three. Papyrus evidence from Egypt supports Aristeas (H.T. Andrews' note in Charles, *A&P* II, p. 106). Thus Luke's scale is, as usual, comfortable middle-class, 60% richer than the average (§5), and the man is by no means 'a larger landowner' (Jeremias, p. 177). δοκιμάζειν 12.56(2), ζεῦγος, a pair, 2.24.

14.20 ἕτερος*, εἶπεν, πόλις, πτωχός. γυναῖκα ἔγημα, *Klangfigure*, cf. on v. 18; Luke has the Attic aorist, Matthew and Mark the Hellenistic ἐγάμησα, Paul both (BDF, p. 101).

14.21 παραγίνεσθαι*, ταῦτα. Hapax: ῥύμη (Acts 9.11; 12.10). ἀπήγγειλεν ταῦτα 24.9R. οἰκοδεσπότης, 13.25QD. πλατεῖαι and ῥύμαι are a natural pair, Isa. 15.3; Tob. 13.17f.; Mt. 6.2, 5. ἔξελθε εἰς τὰς πλατείας τῆς πόλεως, cf. 10.10QD πόλιν. . . ἐξελθόντες εἰς τὰς πλατείας αὐτῆς. Cf. 9.41R; 19.27, for εἰσάγαγε ὧδε; Mt. 22.12 εἰσῆλθες ὧδε.

14.22 εἶπεν, ἔτι, τόπος. γίνεσθαι = be done, 13.17; 23.8.

14.23 εἶπεν-πρός*, οἶκος. Hapaxes: φραγμός, ἀναγκάζειν (Acts ×2). φραγμοί were planted round vineyards, etc., to keep thieves out (Mk 12.1). ἀνάγκασον gives Lucan vitality to the story; Jeremias (p. 177) prefers the beggars' 'oriental courtesy'. γεμίζειν 15.16 v.l., γέμειν 11.39. μου before the noun 7.44f.; 10.29; 14.24, 26, 27, 33.

14.24 ἀνήρ*, καλεῖν, δεῖπνον. Forms an inclusio with v. 15 (Leaney). μου before the noun, see on v. 23.

Haenchen, E., 'Das Gleichnis vom grossen Mahl', *Die Bibel und Wir*, pp. 135-55.
Hahn, F., 'Das Gleichnis von der Einladung zum Festmahl', in *Fs* G. Stählin, pp. 51-82.
Vögtle, A., 'Die Einladung zum grossen Gastmahl und zum königlichen Hochzeitsmahl', *Das Evangelium und die Evangelien*, pp. 191-218.
Ballard, P.H., 'Reasons for Refusing the Great Supper', *JTS* NS 23 (1972), 341-50.
Resenhöfft, W., 'Jesu Gleichnis von den Talenten, ergänzt durch die Lukas-Fassung', *NTS* 26 (1980), pp. 318-31.

42. *The Cost of Discipleship*, 14.25–16.13

a. *Leaving All*, 14.25-35

Matthew's Marriage-Feast parable expounded with transparent clarity the replacement of Judaism by the Church; but it left its author uneasy at the thought of those 'both bad and good' who were presently enjoying the royal bounty. It was to resolve this unease that he added the final verses. Matthew's God requires not just faith but righteousness, not just the invitation to the feast but wearing the marriage garment of obedience. For it will be found at Judgment Day that many were called into the Church, but the elect who have done what the Lord said are few.

Luke too believes that God's invitation and our response in faith are primary (14.16-24), and he is as uneasy as Matthew at the suggestion that all that is required of a Christian is baptism; but he does not believe that salvation depends upon our keeping a higher law, and appearing in robes of righteousness. Even unfaithful Christians will be saved (12.41-48). What then is it which distinguishes the true from the false disciple? Luke saw it in the response of the first disciples of all: 'they left all and followed him' (5.11). So too Levi 'leaving all, arose and followed him' (5.28). This was the essence of the Christian life for the Twelve, similarly; 'Blessed are the poor. . . ' (6.20f.) is a macarism on those who have nothing because they have left all. Those who came to follow Christ in 9.57-62 have the same challenge put to them: to have nowhere to lay their head, to let go even family burial rites and saying farewell to those at home. They must be like Elisha, leave all and go. It is this message which is so powerfully developed in Luke 12. It is the soul which matters, and gaining the whole world is of no avail: sell your possessions and give alms, and lay up an imperishable treasure (vv. 33f.).

This is accordingly the leitmotif of the present trio of Lucan pericopae. In 16.1-13 both parable and exposition will urge the wisdom of trading off present possessions against a welcome above: the lesson is for *disciples* (καὶ πρὸς τοὺς μαθητάς) who are still attached to their money. The two earlier lessons are for those still without. To the *Pharisees* (15.1-3), the cost is a spiritual one: to leave their pride and share God's joy in the repentance of sinners. For the '*crowds*' (14.25), that is the uncommitted attenders whom Luke's eagle eye could descry week by week 'journeying with' his congregation, the call is for commitment. Jesus' call is to leave all and follow him: without this is no discipleship. The demand is put with conviction and eloquence.

As Luke is changing the point of Matthew's teaching, it is not surprising that there is little overlap of wording. Nonetheless there are themes in the present Matthaean pericope, the Marriage-Feast, and in its predecessor and companion, the Husbandmen, which can be developed, as we shall see; nor is there any lack of texts from elsewhere in Matthew which are to his purpose.

14.25. He begins with his standard, rubrical verse, on the 'many crowds' on the road with Jesus, to whom the words are addressed: perhaps they are entirely Luke's own creation, though, if he needed it, the similar sayings in Mk. 8.34 are addressed to the crowd (Mt. diff.).

14.26f. For the opening line and theme of his unit, however, he makes free use from memory of a compound of several Matthaean sayings:

> Mt. 10.37 The lover of *father* or *mother* over me, is not worthy of me, and the lover of son or daughter over me is not worthy of me; and he *who does not* take *his cross and* follow *after me* is not worthy of me. He who finds *his soul*... Mt. 16.24 *If anyone* wishes to *come after me,* let him deny himself and take up *his cross* and follow me. For whoever wishes to save *his soul*... Mt. 19.29 And everyone *whoever* has left houses or *brothers* or *sisters* or *father* or *mother* or *children* or lands for my sake, shall receive... Lk. 14.26f. *If anyone comes* to *me,* and does not hate his *father* and *mother,* and wife and *children,* and *brothers* and *sisters,* and *his* own *soul* also, he cannot be my disciple. *Whoever does not* carry *his cross and come after me,* he cannot be my disciple.

The 'If anyone comes to me' form is closest to Mt. 16.24 (cf. Mk 8.34): 'come to' signifies intending discipleship also at 6.47QD, and is a preliminary to 'coming after'. The relations to be hated are nearly the same as in Mt. 19.29 (= Mk 10.29): Luke has paired them, and added 'and wife', as he does at 18.29, his regular ascetic tendency (cf. 14.20). His asceticism leads him to use strong language: he uses the LXX comparative μισεῖν (cf. esp. Deut. 21.15-17, 'the hated wife') for Matthew's οὐ φιλῶν, and ἀποτάσσεται follows in v. 33. Similarly, 'he cannot be my disciple' is much stronger than 'he is not worthy of me'. Luke is nailing his colours to the mast: no commitment, no salvation. The later part of the double logion is closest to Mt. 10.37ff.

14.28ff. Luke's doctrine is thus stated, and he will take it from wherever in Matthew it may come. But doctrines need illustration, and he turns again now to the open scroll in front of him for further inspiration. Before the Marriage-Feast in Mt. 22.1-14 came the

Husbandmen in Mt. 21.33-46, and the φραγμούς of Lk. 14.23 may make us think that Luke's eye has already strayed thus far; for Matthew began, 'There was a householder who planted a vineyard, and set a φραγμόν around it, and dug out a winevat in it, and built a tower (ὠκοδόμησεν πύργον). At Lk. 20.9 this is reduced to 'A certain man planted a vineyard': the hedge and the tower are omitted. Now for one in search of an illustration for counting the cost of discipleship, the building of a tower has an immediate appeal, and Luke feels the need to expound this detail of the Husbandmen on its own. For he has just relayed two Matthaean sayings which stress the price which a new disciple must undertake; and the investment required in so considerable a building as a tower involves exactly the same principle.

The mode of the illustration parable is as Lucan as usual. It is not, of course, an exposition of God's action, like the Marcan, and most of the Matthaean parables, but an *imperative*, hortatory parable, challenging the would-be Christian to commitment (§8). With this in view, it opens with the 'Which-of-you' formula, whereby such challenges can be introduced: cf. 'Which of you will have a friend?', 'Which man of you having a hundred sheep?' (QD), 'which of you having a servant?'. θέλων is taken over from Mt. 16.24, εἴ τις θέλει; πύργον οἰκοδομῆσαι from Mt. 21.33. 'First sitting down' is the obverse to Lucan *alacrity*. Luke's characters do not always act quickly, with haste, or at once; they not only rise up (ἀναστάς), they also sit down when occasion requires—'what king. . . will not first sit down?', 'take your bill, sit down quickly and write fifty' (§3.1). The *scale* of the investment is such as Luke's middle-class congregation could encompass: those with five yoke of oxen to work their farms, and mortgages of five hundred dinars, would be familiar with the need for an orchard-tower from which thieves could be spotted. The laying of *foundation-stones* was a Lucan interest: he introduced this element into the Matthaean Builders, despite the presence of perfectly adequate bedrock (6.48QD). θεντὸς θεμέλιον is another instance of Morgenthaler's *Klangfiguren*, like ἀγρὸν ἠγόρασα or γυναῖκα ἔγημα. With 'laying a foundation *and not being able* to finish', 'he began to build but was not able to finish', compare Luke's 'silent and not able to speak', 'bent and not able to stand straight', 'blind and not seeing the sun'. The appeal to *shame* is Lucan too: with 'all who see begin to deride him', compare 'all his adversaries were ashamed', 'then shall you begin with shame to take the lowest place'. The hostile ἄρξωνται is Luke's too: 'do not begin to say, We have Abraham', 'then you will begin to say, We ate' (§3.2). Finally there is Luke's *oratio recta repetition of the moral*: 'lest having laid a foundation and not being able to finish, all who see begin to deride him saying, This man began to build and was not able to finish'. Compare, 'He goes after the lost one till he finds it. . . saying to them, Rejoice with me, for I have found my sheep that was lost' (QD), 'he came seeking fruit on it and found it not. And he said to his vinedresser, Lo, these three years I come seeking fruit on this fig-tree and find it not', 'This my son was dead and is alive again, he was lost and is found. . . this your brother was dead and is alive again, and lost and is found' (§11).

14.31f. Short illustrations or parables of this kind tend to come in pairs in Luke, as in Matthew: mustard and leaven, lost sheep and lost coin, Noah and Lot. So Luke returns to his Vorlage for the suggestion of a second theme, and there, in Mt. 22.7, is the detail he has so far omitted, on the king who sent (πέμψας) his army. Luke is content to draw on Matthew's Marriage-Feast over several pericopae, just as he did with the Bridesmaids (12.35ff.; 13.25ff.): he had the marriage meal at 14.8, the dinner parable itself at 14.16-24, the king sending his army now, and the sacrificing of the fatling is held over to 15.23. Of course Matthew's motive for the king's expedition will not suit Luke's purpose, and must be amended; but the suggestion of sending (ἀπέστειλεν, Mt. 21.34, 36, 37; 22.3, 4) an embassy to negotiate with a strongly placed adversary, is a repeated theme of both the Husbandmen and the Marriage. The second parable can then be aligned with the first with the moral of counting the cost, and virtually writes itself.

'Which of you. . . does not first sit down?' is answered by 'Or what king. . . does not sit down first?' The king, and the military setting, are foreign to Luke, and taken over from Matthew 22; his only other royal parable, the Pounds, is in exposition of Mk 11.10, 'the coming kingdom'. In his discomfort, there comes to him the recollection of some campaign of David's where the Syrian king had an army of twenty thousands εἴκοσι χιλιάδας, 2 Kgdms 8.4), and king Thoou sent (ἀπέστειλεν) his son to king David to ask him terms of peace (ἐρωτῆσαι αὐτὸν τὰ εἰς εἰρήνην, 8.10). So Luke's king takes counsel, like his tower-builder working out a budget, whether with ten thousand troops he can meet an invader with twenty thousands (εἴκοσι χιλιάδων); otherwise he must send (ἀποστείλας) an embassy and ask terms for peace (ἐρωτᾷ τὰ πρὸς εἰρήνην). The *scale* once more is such as Luke is used to. Jesus had preached to crowds in the ten thousands at 12.1, and these are nearly the smallest armies numbered in the Bible. At its lowest ebb the Israelite army was ten thousand (4 Kgdms 13.7), and the Chronicler's hosts rise to a million. The turns of phrase are often Lucan (see below): with εἰ δυνατός ἐστιν, cf. Acts 20.16, εἰ δυνατόν εἴη; with 'while he is still far away', cf. the Prodigal, 'while he was still a long way off' (15.20), and even the Centurion, 'when he was now not a long way off' (7.6QD); the combination εἰ δὲ μή γε is Lucan; and Luke likes abstracts in - εία, πρεσβεία, πορεία, θεραπεία.

14.33. It remains to sum up the challenge with a οὕτως sentence, as Luke does at 15.10; 17.10; 21.31. He takes up the opening 'which of you?' from the Tower-builder with 'any of you'. The form of the two main statements with which he began was 'If anyone/whoever . . . does not. . ., he cannot be my disciple', and he returns to this now, 'any of you who does not. . . he cannot be my disciple'. The two main challenges were to hate one's family (compared to the Lord), and to take up one's cross, and these are now restated in fine Lucan language, ἀποτάσσεται πᾶσι τοῖς ἑαυτοῦ ὑπάρχουσιν, to renounce all that belongs to us. We have had ἀποτάσσεσθαι before in a similar context at 9.61, and τὰ ὑπάρχοντα comes again with the same force at 12.33. In a way Luke means it. Commitment is everything, and commitment had perhaps led him to leave his family and not to marry; certainly it had done both to Paul his master, and brought him to a martyr's death. Commitment might mean poverty for any Christian, and he must be prepared for that. But in a way it is also the good preacher bidding up the price: some of Luke's congregation were not that badly off, and when it came to the point he would settle for a percentage—'but for what is within, give alms, and lo, all is pure to you', 'sell your belongings' (no 'all' this time) 'and give alms'. He did not think Aquila needed to leave Priscilla to be a disciple. Lagrange (p. 412) notes sagely that the demand has softened noticeably from one's family and the cross in vv. 26f. to one's possessions in v. 33.

14.34f. A further saying springs to mind on the valuelessness of half hearts.

Mk 9.50 *Salt is good; but if the salt* becomes unsalty, *with what will* you *season* it? Mt. 5.13 You are *the salt* of the earth; *but if the salt is blunted, with what will it be* salted? It is *no* longer good for anything, but being *cast out* to be trampled by men. Lk. 14.34f. *Salt is good; but if even the salt is blunted, with what will it be seasoned?* It is fit neither for land nor for dung-heap: they *cast it out.*

Matthew has fitted Mk 9.50 into his 'You are. . .' series—'Blessed you are. . . You are the salt of the earth. . . You are the light of the world'. He adapts 'becomes unsalty' to the standard proverbial form which we find in the mouth of R. Joshua (c. AD 90), 'Salt, when it becomes feeble (s^eri, Jastrow), wherewith shall it be salted?' (*b. Bek.* 8b). Pure salt cannot become unsalty; but it is commonly gathered in Palestine from dried pools by the Dead Sea, where it is never pure: when it is used, say for the preservation of meat, the salt dissolves and the remaining chemical forms a scum, which is then useless, and is thrown out into the street (Jeremias, p. 169). 'Good' salt is sharp (ὄξυς), and Matthew renders s^eri with its opposite, μωρ(άνθῃ), a root he is fond of (7/0/1). He also improves Mark's style with the passive 'be salted', and expounds the consquences with his accustomed menace: being cast out (into outer darkness, the sea [13.48], etc.) is the normal Matthaean symbol for hell. Trampling (καταπατεῖν) underfoot recurs in Mt. 7.6 as a figure for total rejection, and οἱ ἄνθρωποι = men is a favourite Matthaean expression (27/5/10, 9.8R, etc.).

Luke has combined the two forms, Mark predominating at first (καλὸν τὸ ἄλας, ἀρτύειν), Matthew later. He cannot easily begin with Matthew's 'you are the salt of the earth', and then say salt residue is no good for the earth; but he follows Matthew's μωράνθῃ, his future passive, and the form of his final clause, 'It is no (good) for. . . cast out'. Thus he takes over the Matthaean μωρ- and the Matthaean ἔξω βάλλεσθαι, though he does not mean this so allegorically. Matthew's worthless Christian is cast out of heaven; Luke's cannot be a disciple at all. He rephrases the sentence. Matthew said the residue εἰς οὐδὲν ἰσχύει, and he began with the salt τῆς γῆς: Luke develops the suggestion, 'it is fit neither εἰς γῆν nor for dung-heap'. He used εὔθετος in the similar context at 9.62, 'not fit for the kingdom of God'. He knows about dung (13.8); and land and dung-heap are Lucan near-duplicates here (§22). There is no need to think that anything positive is implied about beneficial use of salt for the land, a practice unknown in Jewish sources according to Jeremias (27). Luke was enough of an agriculturalist (§30.2) to know that farmers did not use salt-waste for fertilizing and he is correctly stating a negative fact.

Luke really minds about commitment, so he signs the pericope off with the traditional impressive 'he that hath ears. . . ' He used the same form at 8.8, cf. Mk 4.9. Perhaps his mind was drawn to it by Mt. 21.33, 'ἀκούσατε another parable'; but perhaps not.

For 14.26f., the consensus (apart from Harnack, p. 62) is that the Lucan outline is original except for the insertion of γυναῖκα. . .ψυχήν, ἑαυτοῦ, and βαστάζει: so Polag, pp. 70f; Schmid, p. 27; Schulz, p. 446. Such a judgment arises from (a) the Matthaean language of Mt. 10.37f., and (b) the radical demands of the Lucan μισεῖ and 'cannot be my disciple', which Matthew supposedly weakens to 'love more', 'is not worthy', and refers to Jesus personally—'more than me' (Bultmann, p. 160). The first argument is the standard Matthaean vocabulary fallacy (see pp. 11-15); and involves some of the standard embarras de richesses difficulty, in that Matthew has his favoured λαμβάνει (53/20/22, 16.7R etc.). For Mt. 10.37f. as Matthew's expansion of Mk 8.34, see *MLM*, p. 351. Schulz (p. 447) notes that ἔρχεσθαι πρός με is paralleled in Lk. 8.47QD and so may be Lk.R; but does not note how close in addition the opening is to Mt. 16.24R. The second argument depends on the assumption that Jesus was the only radical in the Christian movement, and the Church had a monochrome tendency to water his radicalism down. Not only is this absurd in view of the encratite movements already evidenced in 1 Corinthians, Colossians and the Pastorals, but Luke shows himself consistently hostile to marriage and money throughout the Gospel. His 'hating' of one's family (compared to Christ) is of a piece with his addition of 'leaving all' at 5.28R, and 'or wife' at 18.29R; and was, as an expression, available to him in this context in Deut. 21 LXX, and also in Mt. 6.24 = Lk. 16.13. Luke's 'cannot be my disciple' refers the issue to Jesus personally no less than Matthew's 'more than me', and again is more radical.

The two parables, Tower-Builder and King's Embassy, have no apparent parallel in Matthew, and are therefore credited to L: for their Lucan mode and message see above.

The situation with the salt logion, vv. 34f., is similar to vv. 26f. The Matthaean version is agreed to be largely Mt.R, so Polag (pp. 72f.) virtually prints the Lucan version as Q (om. καί; ἁλισθήσεται = Mt.) This then involves assuming that Q began 'Salt is good', like Mark (Schulz, pp. 470ff.). Q will also have been familiar with Jewish proverbs in the same way that Matthew was; and will have threatened his converts with being cast out, as Matthew did. So we are repeatedly involved in explaining by hypotheses about an unknown source what we can perfectly easily explain out of the documents in front of us; and ἀρτυθήσεται tells us that Luke is under the influence of Mark.

14.25   συμπορεύεσθαι, στραφείς*, εἶπεν πρός*.

14.26   εἰ. . .οὐ*, ἔτι, δὲ-καί, ἑαυτοῦ in sandwich*. εἰ. . .οὐ. . .οὐ δύναται, cf. Acts 15.2; 27.31. μου before noun, see on 14.23.

14.27   βαστάζειν, ἑαυτοῦ.

14.28   (οἰκοδομεῖν), οὐχί. Hapaxes: ψηφίζειν, δαπάνη (-ᾶν, cf. 10.35; 15.14, Acts 21.24), ἀπαρτισμός (cf. Luke's liking for ἀσπασμός, διαλογισμός). Loose εἰ = whether, 6.7Mk. ἔχειν = have enough, 7.42; 14.14.

14.29   ἰσχύειν. θεντὸς θεμέλιον 6.48. ἐκτελέσαι, cf. τελεῖν, ἀποτελεῖν 13.32. πάντες οἱ θεωροῦντες cf. πάντες οἱ ἀκούοντες/-σαντες 1.66; 2.18, 47.

14.30   οὗτος-ὁ-ἄνθρωπος*, οἰκοδομεῖν, A-καὶ-οὐ-non A, ἰσχύειν.

14.31   πορεύεσθαι, ἕτερος*, οὐχί. Hapaxes: βουλεύεσθαι + εἰ δυνατός (Acts 27.39 + εἰ δύναιντο), εἴκοσι. συμβάλλειν 2.19, ×4 Acts. ὑπαντᾶν 8.27Mk. ἐν = with, 14.34Mk; 22.49QD; 1.51. ἤ τίς βασιλεύς; cf. 15.7 ἤ τίς γυνή; χιλιάς Acts 4.4. (ἐξ)έρχεσθαι ἐπί 21.35; 22.52Mk.

14.32   εἰ-δὲ-μή-γε*, ἔτι, ἐρωτᾶν*, τὰ + prep.*, εἰρήνη*. πρεσβείαν ἀποστείλας, cf. 19.14 ἀπέστειλαν πρεσβείαν. πόρρω, cf. 24.28, πορρώτερον, 17.12 πόρρωθεν. τὰ πρὸς εἰρήνην, 19.42: there are differences in the MSS over the text, but Metzger's Commentary accepts τα προς without discussion.

14.33   τὰ-ὑπάρχοντα*, ἑαυτοῦ in sandwich*. ἀποτάσσεσθαι + dat., 9.61; Acts 18.18, 21.

14.34   δὲ-καί*. Hapaxes: (μωραίνειν), (ἀρτύειν).

14.35   Hapax: κοπρία. The passage has given rise to proposals of Aramaic originals: Black (pp. 166f.) offers three word-plays, *tpl* = (a) unsavoury, (b) fool (μωραίνειν), *tpl/tbl* salt, *'ar'a* land, *re'a* dung, *ra'ra'* trample. The last involves making a compendious version of Mt. and Lk. Jeremias (p. 168) regards the first two as certain, on account of the 'strange locution "If the salt becomes foolish"': but Liddell and Scott give μωρός = insipid. Com. anon. 220, Diosc. 4.19. For the chemistry, cf. E.P. Deatrick, *BA* (1962); for the original force of the salt metaphor, cf. W. Nauck, *ST* (1953).

Nauck, W., 'Salt as a Metaphor in Instructions for Discipleship', *ST* 6 (1952), pp. 165-78.

Dinkler, E., 'Jesu Wort vom Kreuztragen', in *Fs* R. Bultmann (1954), pp. 110-29.

Deatrick, E.P., 'Salt, Soil, Savor', *BA* 25 (1962), pp. 41-48.

Derrett, J.D.M., 'Nisi Dominus aedificaverit domum: Towers and Wars (Lk. xiv. 28-32)', *NT* 19 (1977), pp. 241-61.

b. *Joy at Repentance*, 15.1-32

The Tower-builder took Luke back from Mt. 22.1-14 to Mt. 21.33; and before that comes Mt. 21.28-32, the parable of the Two Sons. Matthew has his parable addressed to the Jewish authorities, and he expounds the meaning. The first son, who said No, but afterwards repented and went to work, was a figure for the publicans and whores who repented at John's preaching—John and Jesus have been linked in the preceding story. The second son, who said, I will, sir, but did not go to work, or do the father's will, stood for 'the chief priests and elders' (21.23), 'the chief priests and the Pharisees' (21.45), who had not believed John nor repented. The parable is Matthew at his starkest, but the repentance theme is one that Luke can use: for the cost of discipleship is repentance for all, and the acceptance of our fellow-sinners besides. As for the two sons and their father, Luke has seen a way to make of them his masterpiece.

15.1-3. Luke means to give himself room this time. He links his own Sons parable on to what goes before with a mere εἶπεν δέ at 15.11, and despite the thirty-two verse unit, we have no option but to follow his indication, and take the chapter together. The three-verse setting is itself a sign of the same expansiveness. The last chapter ended, 'He who has ears to hear, let him hear', and Luke begins this one, 'All the publicans and sinners were drawing near *to hear* him'. These are the 'poor and maimed and blind and halt' who came to the Great dinner in 14.21. He prefers the more general *'publicans and sinners'* to the 'publicans and whores' of Mt. 21.31f.; he uses 'sinner' again in the same sense at 7.37—perhaps he thought 'whores' a bit strong for church members.

The response of the disreputable, and the criticism thereof by the respectable, were most memorably exemplified in the scene at Levi's house (5.27-39); and it is this story, which Luke takes to be typical, that provides the setting to illuminate his Two Sons parable. Here is the proud Jewish leadership of Mt. 21.28-32, but now in their more familiar form: 5.30, 'And the Pharisees and their scribes were murmuring (ἐγόγγυζον) ... saying'; 15.2, *'And* both *the Pharisees and* the *scribes were murmuring* (διεγόγγυζον), *saying'*. They are scribes, not Luke's normally preferred lawyers; and he uses διαγογγύζειν again in a precisely similar context at 19.7. The complaint is similar, too: 5.30, 'Why do you eat and drink with publicans and sinners?'; 15.2, 'This man receives *sinners* and *eats* with them'. The eating is an intrusive feature now: 15.1 implied a scene of Jesus preaching to sinners. There is an opening ὅτι, and a third-person verb ἐσθίει, in the parallel Mk 2.16 as in 15.2, against διὰ τί and ἐσθίετε in 5.30. Jesus also responds with a 'parable' in both passages: 5.36, 'And he also spoke a parable to them'; 15.3, '*And he spoke to them* this *parable*'. The phrasing is Lucan in v. 3, Lucan with a background of Mk 2.15f. in vv. 1f.

15.4-7. A part of Luke's art is to set his main teaching in relief by the technique of a foil introduction (§1.4). Often this is a question or comment from the crowd; but it also takes the form of a pair of sayings of the Lord himself to lead up to the decisive parable. Thus, 'Man, who made me a judge. . .', and 'Beware and keep yourselves. . .' lead up to the Rich Fool; the Galilaeans and the Siloam Tower lead up to the Fig Tree; scandals and faith as a grain of mustard lead up to the Servant of all Work; and here Luke prepares the way for his Two Sons by the artfully contrasted Lost Sheep and Lost Coin. The Sheep is from the still unused Matthaean treasure-chest in Matt. 18.12-14: the Coin is Luke's own creation.

15.4. Matthew 18 is given to instructing 'the disciples' on the running of the church. They are to care for 'the little ones' (vv. 1-9=Mk 9.33ff., 42ff.) and this care is described in specific detail in vv. 15-20: in between comes the similitude of the lost sheep. Matthew often thinks of Christians as sheep, and the pastoral image was an OT commonplace. Much of the language is the evangelist's; but whether he composed the whole (*MLM*, pp. 398ff.), or edited a traditional form, is not our concern here. He begins, 'What do you think? If a man has a hundred sheep and one of them wanders, will he not leave the ninety-nine on the hills and go and seek for the wanderer?' The situation fits the Matthaean context exactly: the church leader has a congregation and one of them sins, so he is to leave the rest and 'gain' the sinner (v. 15).

To Luke the similitude of the lost sheep has immediate appeal. His topic in the Two Sons is repentance, and here is the Lord picturing a sinner as a lost sheep being brought back to the fold: what better illustration could there be to lead into the coming parable? He sets off accordingly, 'What *man* of you having *a hundred sheep and* losing *one of them* does not abandon *the ninety-nine* in the desert *and go* after the lost one until he find it?' He follows Matthew in the rhetorical appeal-question opening, though he prefers his own τίς ἐξ ὑμῶν form, still in his head from 14.28 (cf. 11.5; 17.7). He carries over, by accident, Matthew's ἄνθρωπος, which is quite plethoric. The structure of the sentence, which is the same in the two Gospels, and the succession of four identical or closely similar phrases in the same order (ἕκατον πρόβατα καὶ, ἐξ αὐτῶν/ἕν, τὰ ἐνενήκοντα ἐννέα, καὶ πορεύ(εται) guarantee a close relationship. Luke often writes ἔχειν in the first line of a parable (11.5; 13.6; 15.8; 16.1; 17.7; ἔχων in 15.8 and 17.7). He does not like Matthew's πλανᾶν (8/4/ 1+0), but has read of the lost (ἀπολωλότα) sheep of the house of Israel; he can represent Jesus' mission as the seeking and saving of the lost (τὸ ἀπολωλός, 19.10); and losing and finding are to be the keynotes of the present chapter. καταλείπειν is a word he likes; he inserted it in the Levi story which is in his mind (5.28R), and has it ×6 in Acts. He adapts Matthew's πορεύ(εται) with an ἐπί and so saves the unnecessary 'seek'.

15.5f. Matthew continued: 'And if it happens that he finds it, truly I say to you that he rejoices over it more than over the ninety-nine that did not wander'. Again the aptness of the image to the reality is striking. 'If it happens that. . .' represents a sober estimate of the pastor's chances of reclaiming the errant; the ninety-nine who did not wander stand for the normally virtuous majority in any congregation; and the joy is that happiness in the restoration of his community which is his principal reward. It is this last feature which appeals to Luke: '*And find*ing it he lays it on his shoulders *rejoic*ing; and coming home he calls together his friends and neighbours, saying to them, Rejoice with me, for I have found my sheep which was lost'. It is joy in the sinner's repentance which he wishes to emphasize, in contrast to the meanness of the elder brother/Pharisee in the coming Two Sons. We may note at once the Lucan *vividness* of imagination (§4.8). The shepherd is not a Matthaean clergyman-in-disguise, but heaves the hulking animal, with its damaged leg, on to his shoulders. As the finding is imagined, so is the rejoicing, with a further Lucan *party* (§4.4). Friends and neighbours are asked in, like the neighbours and relatives who came to rejoice with Elizabeth in 1.58 (συνέχαιρον), or the friends and brethren, relatives and rich neighbours, who were likely to be invited at 14.12, or the relations and friends of 21.16R.

Luke ends with the *repetition* of his point *in oratio recta*, 'he goes after the lost one until he finds it. . . I have found my sheep that is lost'. We have just seen the same feature with the mocking of the Tower-builder, and it recurs with the Fig Tree, the Coin and the Sons (§11).

15.7. Matthew appended the application: 'So it is not the will before your Father in heaven that one of these little ones should be lost'—God does not wish any Christian to go to hell. Luke is making a rather different point: '*I say to you that so* there will be joy *in heaven over one* sinner who repents rather *than over ninety-nine* righteous, who have no need of repentance'. οὕτως, ἐν οὐραν(ῷ) and ἕν are taken over from Mt. 18.14; λέγω ὑμῖν ὅτι (dropping the ἀμήν), χαρά/χαίρει ἐπί, ἤ ἐπὶ ἐνενήκοντα ἐννέα from the previous verse. The moral he is after is the divine joy over the turning of sinners' hearts, in contrast to the ungenerous response of the murmuring Pharisees. He regularly signs his parables off with λέγω ὑμῖν: 11.8; 12.37; 14.24; 15.10; 16.9; 18.8, 14. He adapts Matthew's 'ἔμπροσθεν your Father in heaven' to 'in heaven', avoiding the stock Father-in-heaven as usual: ἔμπροσθεν will become ἐνώπιον in the Coin below. 'One sinner who repents' is more Lucan, and more suited to the pre-Church situation than 'one of these little ones'. The ninety-nine who 'did not wander', are similarly brought into real life as 'righteous who have no need of repentance'. Luke's eye is back on Levi's home, with 5.31f, 'The well *have no need of* a doctor. I came not to call the *righteous* but *sinners* to *repentance*'. The assimilation is done with a sparkling skill, but the Matthaean situation sticks out uncomfortably through the Lucan gloss none the less. The ninety-nine who did not wander have a natural meaning in Matthew's church life: but to Luke, and in the setting Luke has given them, there is not one of the ninety-nine Pharisees who is not in need of repentance. We may note similarly that Matthew's situation is neatly in parallel with the pastor who goes out to find the single sinner; while in Luke, Jesus is reclaiming 'all the publicans and sinners', and it is they who are 'drawing near' to him.

15.8ff. Matthew's ἄνθρωπος of 18.12 suggests a parallel illustration with a γυνή, and the woman's realm is the house as the man's the land, and her charge the keeping of the savings he has won. So Luke's second lead-in follows naturally: 'Or *what* woman *having* ten drachmas, if she *lose one* drachma, does not light a lamp and sweep

the house, and seek carefully *until* she *find* it?' The shape of the
sentence is formed after v. 4, but with Matthew's οὐχί and ζητεῖ. 'Or
what woman. . .?' recalls 'Or what king. . .?' from 14.31. We have
Luke's introductory 'having' once more (see above on v. 4). The ten-
to-one proportion is Luke's favourite: ten lepers and one grateful, ten
servants and one *mna* apiece, five hundred dinars and fifty (§12).
Drachmas are the standard monetary unit in Luke's Greece, in
contrast to the similarly valued dinar which we find elsewhere in the
Gospels. We see Luke's imagination at work again in the searching,
as we did in the finding of the sheep (§4.8): perhaps he has even left
the ζητεῖ over deliberately from Mt. 18.12, in order to expound it in
his second illustration. Lighting a lamp comes again at Lk. 8.16R;
11.33QD, taking care (ἐπιμελῶς) with the Good Samaritan (10.34f.,
ἐπιμελεῖσθαι), and Paul's friends at Sidon (Acts 27.3, ἐπιμέλεια).
The scale is humbler than other Lucan parables like the Tower-
builder and the Two Sons, where there are much larger liquid savings
implied; but it is still respectable. There is no warrant by centuries
for the claim that the drachmas were in the woman's head-dress, or
that they betoken 'a very poor creature', or that she lived in 'a
miserable, windowless dwelling' (Jeremias, p. 135): she would be
much hurt by such aspersions.

The rest of the Lost Drachma is formed in parallel with the Lost
Sheep: '*and finding* it, she *calls together* her *friends and neighbours
saying, Rejoice with me, for I have found* the drachma which I had
lost'. It is simply a feminine counterpart to the shepherd's recovery of
his sheep, with a feminine Lucan party, and the joy expressed in
Lucan *oratio recta*, with Lucan friends and neighbours. The brief
narrative carries home the point Luke wishes to make with happy
force: the Church is a community of forgiven sinners, lost ones
whom God has found, and in whose finding we are to rejoice and not
to be Pharisees.

15.10. He expresses this in a final parallel with v. 7: '*So, I say to
you*, there is *joy* before the angels of God *over one sinner who repents*'.
This time he omits the unfortunate 'more than over nine righteous
who have no need ' (cf. Mt. 18.14). 'Before the angels of God' puts
the joy at two removes of reverence from the Most High: Luke's
ἐνώπιον is his preference to Matthew's ἔμπροσθεν in 'before your
Father in heaven' (18.14); his angels are taken from the little ones'
angels who always behold God's face in Mt. 18.10. He used the same
periphrasis, with similar encouragement, at 12.8f.

The matter in common with Matthew 18 is so limited that Streeter (p. 265) and Manson (p. 282) supposed two overlapping sources (L and M). However it has been sufficiently impressive to persuade most critics that we have Q material in the Lost Sheep: the discussion has been which version is the more original. Schmid (pp. 305-308), Jeremias, (*Parables*, pp. 38-40, 132-35) and Jan Lambrecht (pp. 37-42), opt for a Lucan original version, while Bultmann (p. 171), Eta Linnemann (pp. 67-70) and Schulz (pp. 387ff.) for a Matthaean. It is easy to see with Schmid that the Matthaean text is well suited to Matthew's theme of the little ones, and he is influenced (p. 308) by his general view of Matthew as an adapter of Q. Jeremias takes the same arguments further. Matthew is a pattern instance of a change of audience, from opposition to disciples, with allegorizing of details: Luke gives the original setting, for Jesus really did eat with sinners, and respond to Pharisaic critics for doing so. In *Parables* (p. 40), Jeremias found an Aramaic *ra'awa* underlying both Luke and Matthew; later this is withdrawn in favour of an alliterative *ḥedhwa. . . hᵃdha haṭᵉya*, from Black (p. 184). The detail in Luke corresponds both to Palestinian life and to Jesus' own message of God's joy in the turning of sinners.

There is little force to this. Matthew's allegory fits his church situation so well that it is likely to have been made for it. Luke will then be the first of many to think of Jesus as the Good Shepherd, encouraged by the well-known theme of Mk 2.13ff., etc. Jeremias himself (*Sprache*, p. 243) allows that Lk. 15.1-3 is only a free version of 5.29f., and most of his other 'Trad' claims are to be found in Matthew (λέγω ὑμῖν, οὕτως, ἤ, numeral before noun phrase). The Aramaic proposal from Black is certainly better than the earlier suggestion, but it remains no more than a speculation: alliterations are not that rare, and there is no 'haṭᵉya' in Matthew. The Palestinian background features—common moorland (ἔρημος), counting sheep, second shepherds, etc.—are found elsewhere also. A serious weakness of Jeremias's position is v. 7: can 'who have no need of repentance' really mean 'who have not committed any gross sin' (p. 135)? Bailey's suggestion that this is ironic (p. 155) is equally weak: it is an unwary carry-over from Mt. 18.13, where the meaning is straightforward. An even more serious weakness is the failure to notice the manifold Lucan mode—the vivid imagination, party, friends and neighbours, oratio recta repetition of the moral, etc.

If the Lucan Sheep had been original, then the Drachma could have been its companion-piece from the beginning (?Q, Schmid, p. 306): but if it is not, and the colourful material is all Luke's addition, as Linnemann and Schulz persuasively argue, the so closely similar Drachma will have to be Lk.R also; and this is Bultmann's conclusion (p. 171). Linnemann (p. 73) naturally prefers the option that Luke has amended Matthew's Sheep into line with his own Drachma; but then what becomes of the Lucanness of the Drachma?

15.1 ἦσαν + part., ἐγγίζειν*, πάντες pleon., τελωνής, ἁμαρτωλός. Publicans-and-sinners as in 5.30 = Mk 2.15f.

15.2 τε, οὗτος, προσδέχεσθαι*. Hapax: συνεσθίειν (Acts 10.41; 11.3). διαγογγύζειν 19.7; cf. 5.30R (δια-20/19/44+46). προσδέχεσθαι has its common meaning of 'welcome' (Rom. 16.2; Phil. 2.29), not that he was host to them (cp. Jeremias, p. 100)—how would he be that on the road? Elsewhere in Lk. it means 'expect'.

15.3 εἶπεν-δὲ-πρὸς*, -παραβολήν*. παραβολήν sing. is followed by several 'parables' at 5.36 also.

15.4 ἔχειν in parable openings, (πορεύεσθαι), εὑρίσκειν. ἀπολέσας: no fault is implied; he is missing a sheep, cf. 8. A hundred sheep is probably rather a big flock, as befits a Matthaean shepherd: Jeremias (p. 133) compares Jacob's flocks of 200 head and more, but Jacob is portrayed as rich—Bailey (I, p. 148) says a normal family today has 5-15 sheep, and Dalman (VI, p. 246) gives a span of 20-200. καταλείπειν 4/3/4+6. Luke substituted ἔρημος for τὰ ὄρη at 8.29/Mk 5.5: no Aramaic original is required.

15.5 (εὑρίσκειν), (χαίρειν). Hapax: ὦμος. χαίρων part., 19.6, 37R; Acts 5.41; 8.39 (Marshall).

15.6 οἶκος, συγκαλεῖν*, φίλος*, γείτων, εὑρίσκειν. συγκαλεῖν act. = invite to a party, cf. 14.12, 13, 16 etc. καλεῖν; med. = summon, 9.1R; 23.13; cp. Acts 5.21. συγχαίρειν + dat. 1.58. ἀπολωλώς 2/0/5, 19.10R; but cf. Mt. 10.6 τὰ πρόβατα τὰ ἀπολωλότα.

15.7 ἁμαρτωλός, μετανοεῖν, μετάνοια. χαρὰ ἔσται 1.14; γίνεται in v. 10 shows there is no stress on the future. ἕν/99, cf. 12.52R, five in ἑνὶ οἴκῳ. ἤ = μᾶλλον ἤ, Mt. 18.13.

15.8 ἔχειν in parable opening, δέκα*, οὐχί, ἅπτειν*, ζητεῖν, ἕως-οὗ, εὑρίσκειν. Hapax: ἐπιμελῶς (v.s.). σαροῖ τὴν οἰκίαν cf. 11.25QC οἶκον. . . σεσαρωμένον. The only early evidence for the wearing of coins by women is *m. Kel.* 12.7, where a single damaged dinar is used as a pendant for a girl's necklace.

15.9 εὑρίσκειν (×2), συγκαλεῖν*, φίλος*, γείτων.

15.10 γίνεσθαι, ἐνώπιον*, ὁ-θεός, ἁμαρτωλός, μετανοεῖν.

And so to the main topic, the father and his two sons of Mt. 21.28-32. Matthew began, 'A man had two children', and Luke can follow him thus far: '*A* certain *man had two* sons'. He writes his standard ἄνθρωπός τις, and correctly specifies Matthew's τέκνα as sons. But thereafter the characterlessness of the Matthaean family, and the unpersuasiveness of the too-allegorical plot, are an offence to him: he drops the allegory, as so often (§6), and turns the characters into real people (§4).

The plot he rewrites in the light of his own introduction in vv. 4–10. The insistent themes of both Sheep and Coin illustrations were losing and finding, and the joy consequent on the latter; and the new story arises simply from the combination of these with the situation of the Matthaean family. The first son, symbolic of Matthew's sinners, is 'lost'—that is, he goes abroad and leads a sinful life. The πορναί of Mt. 21.31f. can suitably have their place in this (15.30). There he must come to a change of mind (μεταμεληθείς, Mt. 21.29); and 'chastening', hard times, are the normal method of inducing such better thinking in the Bible (Deut. 21.18; Jer. 31.18, etc.), and until very recently. Impoverishment and hunger are thus needed to bring about his repentance; and once he has come home repentant, the father can rejoice and throw a party, like the shepherd and the woman with the drachma. At this point then Matthew's second, two-faced son can be introduced, the counterpart of the Pharisees. In place of the unrealistic Matthaean cipher, saying he would work, and not doing so, Luke can paint him as 'slaving for years' (v. 29), and resentful of his brother's welcome. It is this attitude which, to Luke, characterized the Pharisees (v. 2). They never transgressed God's commandment at one level, but at another (11.42) they missed the whole point: for the love of God was about joy at repentance, and it is joy in the repentance of our fellow-sinners which is an essential part of the price of discipleship.

Jacques Dupont (*Béatitudes* II, p. 239), Marshall and others, have suggested that the attitude of the elder son has something in common with the workers in the Vineyard of Mt. 20.1-16; for they murmured (ἐγόγγυζον λέγοντες) as Luke's Pharisees διεγόγγυζον λέγοντες in v. 2; they resented the generosity of the householder to the undeserving (Mt. 20.12); they protested their own faithful service ('we have borne the burden and heat of the day', cf. 'Lo, so many years have I been serving you'); and they thought they might have been better treated ('they thought they should receive more', cf. 'you never gave me a kid'). Despite the lack of verbal correspondence, we may think this right. The two Matthaean parables are linked by both being concerned with working in a vineyard (20.2f. ἐργατῶν

... ὑπάγετε εἰς τὸν ἀμπελῶνα; 21.28 ὕπαγε σήμερον ἐργάζου ἐν τῷ ἀμπελῶνι); and are divided by an unbroken sequence of Marcan stories which Luke will use in 18.31-20.8. Luke is following the policy which we have seen him adopting since the end of ch. 13: he is going back through his copy of Matthew and picking out the Matthaean additions he has missed. He has already used 'So the last shall be first...' at 13.30, and he does not want two parables contrasting Christians and Pharisees and their work. So he allows the Matthew 21 parable to provide the structure of his story, and the Matthew 20 parable to give the Pharisee's situation, and his resentment; which are far better suited to the reality than the second son's hypocrisy in Mt. 21.30. We may also suspect the influence of Matthew 20 in some further details. Luke's workers are μίσθιοι here, but he drifts into calling them δοῦλοι in v. 22, and παῖδες in v. 26, and these are his words for worker elsewhere: Mt. 20.1-16 is the only Matthaean parable to use the words μισθοῦσθαι, μισθός, which come three times. Similarly, Luke is reluctant to use ἐμός, which comes only in 9.26=Mk 8.38, and 22.19=1 Cor. 11.25 (never in Acts); he has πάντα τὰ ἐμὰ σά ἐστιν in v. 31, which may well reflect τὸ σόν ... τοῖς ἐμοῖς from Mt. 20.14f.

There, then, is the skeleton of the plot; and Luke's imagination goes to the Old Testament to put flesh on it, whether consciously or no, as it does with the Unjust Judge to Ecclus 35, or with the King's Embassy to 2 Kgdms 8. Moses famously tells of a lost son, Joseph, and the joy of his father Jacob at his recovery, and the envy of his brothers. Joseph was thought to be dead (Gen. 37.33ff.), and the means to the family's reunion was a severe famine (41.57; 43.1). Through this he rose to greatness in Egypt: 'And Pharaoh took the ring from his hand and put it on Joseph's hand, and he put on him a linen robe' (41.41f.). His brothers came to buy corn, and at length tell Jacob, 'Your son Joseph is alive' (45.26). The old man goes down to Egypt, and Joseph 'went up to meet Israel his father in the town of Heroes, and when he was seen by him he fell on his neck and wept with much weeping'.

Luke has already shown his familiarity with the Joseph story (12.42; cf. Acts. 7.9-15), and he proceeds to apply here as much as is to the point. He has a younger son like Joseph who goes to a far country, and ends the tale in the centre of his father's affections, displacing his jealous older brother(s). There was a great *famine* in that country, which ultimately brings the family together once more. When the father *saw* the prodigal returning, he 'ran and *fell on his neck and* kissed him'. He tells his servants, 'Bring out the first *robe* and *put* it *on him*, and place a *ring on* his *hand*', He concludes twice, 'This my *son* was dead and came to *life* (again)' (vv. 24, 32). It is not, I think, likely that so much detail should be in common without a relationship at some level, not necessarily that of conscious intention; in particular we might have expected 'a ring on his *finger*', and the double stress on 'he was dead and came to life' has sometimes been thought exaggerated.

The story is full of Lucan characteristics—first the evangelist's lively *imagination* (§4.8). The younger boy's impatience for 'his' share, the division (no doubt providing for the older boy after the father's death), the 'not many days', the prodigal's realising of his assets, the distant land, the pigs, the carob-pods, and so many other details, are far removed from the Matthaean/Marcan parabolic mode, where as many items as possible can be related to the underlying 'meaning'. Luke, as usual, has his mind on the story and not its spiritual counterpart: where his predecessors have on average three points out of four consistent with the allegory, Luke here has perhaps one out of four. Even though the father represents God in the story, the force of the human situation drives a wedge between them in the prodigal's confession, 'Father, I have sinned against heaven and before you'. In this respect it is to be aligned with the Good Samaritan, Dives and Lazarus, and other colourful Lucan parables.

A corollary of the vividly imagined human story is the realistic human *character* of the participants (§4): it would be hard to think of a clearer contrast than that of Matthew's cardboard father and sons with Luke's realistic human beings. Each of the three emerges from the brief conversation pieces as a many-sided person, not black and white at all. The prodigal is impatient ('Father, give me. . . '), decisive ('after not many days. . . '), adventurous ('a far country'), improvident ('he wasted his substance'), unprincipled ('riotous living', 'whores'), independent ('he went and joined one of the citizens. . . '), realistic ('coming to himself'), humble ('I will say to him, Father, I have sinned. . . make me as one of your hired servants') and trustful in his father's affection. The father is weak ('he divided. . . '), warm-hearted ('his heart was moved and he ran. . . '), generous (the fatted calf), exaggerated (the best robe, the ring, 'was dead and has come to life'), tactful ('he came out and entreated him', 'Child, you are always with me'), balanced and restrained ('all that is mine is yours: it was right to make merry. . . '). The elder son is cautious ('calling one of the servants, he enquired. . . '), resentful ('he was angry and would not go in'), hard-working ('See how many years I have slaved for you'), obedient ('I never transgressed your commandment'), mean-spirited ('you never gave me. . . but when this your son. . . ') and slanderous ('devoured your living with whores'). All three are real people, and not ciphers for the sinner, God and the Pharisee, as they are in Matthew.

A further part of the story's realism is its everyday *scale*. Luke is not at home in palaces, and where money comes by the talent, as Matthew is. The setting here is a prosperous middle-class farm, one of many such jewels in the crown of the early Principate. The father's 'substance' is in line with the capital of other Lucan heroes, the creditor of 7.41 or the tower-builder; not so well off as the Rich Fool, or Dives, or the Steward's master, but then the first two of these were too rich (§5). The younger son's share (estimated optimistically by Derrett, 107, at two-ninths) suffices to keep him in riotous living for an unspecified period; but there is not enough to spare for the faithful older boy to be allowed a kid now and again. There is an indoor staff (v. 22) as well as those in the fields; but the lowest of them (v. 17) is hired. There are no slaves, there is no steward, and the elder son works in the fields (v. 25). The family assets rise to a ring, symbolic perhaps of authority; otherwise we hear only of 'the first robe' (not 'my') which anyone can wear, and a spare pair of shoes for the barefoot wanderer. The barn is cleared for a Hardyesque scene of rustic merriment, plough and sickle being laid aside for horn and pipe. Bailey (I, pp. 186f.) reckons that the fatted calf would have been enough for a hundred, and that the whole village is invited.

The parable is characteristic of Luke in other ways. The prodigal *soliloquizes* (§4.1): 'How many hired servants. . . '; and his soliloquy embodies a resolution, 'I will arise and go. . . ', like the resolutions of the Rich Fool, 'I will pull down. . . ', the Steward, 'I know what I will do', and the Judge, 'I will vindicate her'. Twice key messages are *repeated in oratio recta*: 'I will say to him, Father, I have sinned against heaven and before you, I am no more worthy to be called

your son. . . . His son said to him, Father, I have sinned against heaven
and before you, I am no more worthy to be called your son'; 'Let us
make merry, for this my son was dead and has come to life again, he
was lost and is found. . . It was right to make merry and be glad, for
this your brother was dead and came to life, he was lost, and is
found'. We found the same feature in the Fig-tree, the Tower-builder,
the Sheep and the Coin (§11). There is also Lucan *alacrity* (§3):
'After not many days', 'he realized all' (cp. 'he abandoned all'!), 'I will
get up and go', 'he got up and went', 'he ran and fell on his neck',
'Quickly bring out the first robe'.

It is hard to resist the conclusion that the parable has a double
message, for the listener is made to feel first the relief and happiness
of repentance, and then the propriety (ἔδει) of rejoicing in the
turning of sinners. Both messages are *hortatory* (§8); they are not
indicative, descriptive of the actions of God, but imperative, urging a
proper line of conduct on the Christian, like so many other Lucan
parables. Furthermore repentance is a favourite Lucan *doctrine*; the
topic of another Lucan parable, the Pharisee and Publican (again
with the appropriate contrast), and the basis of the Church's
preaching (24.47; Acts 2.38). The early pages of Acts are full of the
joy that arises from κοινωνία in the church (2.46; 5.41; 8.8, 39; 13.52,
etc.). So both halves of the story carry a Lucan message; and with the
whole manner of the parable so characteristic of Luke in the many
ways outlined, and with a matrix available in Mt. 21.18ff., it seems
obvious that it is Luke's own creation.

This is not the standard conclusion; rather, the parable has been seen as
Jesus' own parable, conveyed to Luke by L. This is assumed rather than
argued for in earlier critics, e.g. Manson (pp. 284-90); sometimes the naive
suggestion that so fine a piece of artistry must come from Jesus underlies the
discussion, cf. Bailey, I, p. 158. The principal defenders of dominical
authorship have been Schweizer, *TZ* (1948, 1949); Jeremias, *TZ* (1949),
Parables, pp. 128-32, *ZNW* (1971), pp. 172-81, *Sprache*, 248-255; and Otfried
Hofius, *NTS* (1978). Schweizer and Jeremias discussed a variety of alleged
Semitisms and other 'non-Lucan' language. The former are still maintained
by Charles Carlston, *JBL* (1978); but in his later writings Jeremias mentions
only two of his earlier claims, and many of these can be read as
Septuagintalisms. Black (p. 63) comments on the frequent use of non-
Aramaic participles. In *Parables*, p. 130, Jeremias still suggests that ἀναστὰς
πορεύσομαι is a translation of Aram. *ᵃqum wᵉ'ezel*; but this seems a frail
hope in view of Luke's love of ἀναστάς, and his liking for πορεύεσθαι.

Sprache, p. 253, maintains only an Aram. *ha-* behind ἰδοὺ + nom. of time: the same locution comes at 13.7. The 'non-Lucan' words are arrived at by circular argument (cf. above, pp. 15ff.): for instance ἐπιθυμεῖν + inf. is claimed as a stylistic pecularity of the Lucan source, but it is also found at 16.21, 17.22QD and 22.15R). It is of course possible that Luke had a single source (*Sonderquelle*) with a consistent style, giving parallels to some Matthaean and Marcan stories as well as L matter; but the hypothesis is not advanced by assuming it.

Hofius' argument is drawn from the number of OT passages which he claims underlie the parable, all of which (nearly) depend on the Heb.: Hos. 2.9; Exod. 10.16; Gen. 33.4 (especially); 41.42; 1 Sam. 28.24f.; Ps. 31.13; Deut. 26.13; Prov. 29.3. If the author is so familiar with the Hebrew OT, then he is not Luke, who knows the LXX. The argument is not strong. No doubt the author is steeped in the OT, but conscious influence is another matter: why should he think of Israel-Gomer going back to her husband, or compare the forgiving father to Esau? There are fatted calves sacrificed in Mt. 22.4, where the language and the passage are nearer to Luke's hand than 1 Samuel 28; and the same sequence 'fell on his neck and kissed him' is natural to Luke at Acts 20.37, as well as coming in the Esau and Jacob stories. An array of other OT echoes is described by Derrett (pp. 116-21) and Drury (*Tradition*, pp. 75-77); but the centrality of the Jacob/Joseph story, which Drury has emphasized more recently (*Parables*, pp. 144f.) seems plausible both on account of the general similarity of the two narratives and in view of the detailed correspondences in Greek.

Earlier Wellhausen, and more recently J.T. Sanders (*NTS* [1969]) have sought to divide the parable, but have not carried general conviction. A more radical proposal has been made by Luise Schottroff (*ZTK* [1971]): the whole parable is composed by Luke himself. The main argument is that the picture of the Pharisees is a Christian caricature which no Pharisee would have recognized: indeed, it is the Pauline caricature which is mirrored in Luke. The whole parable is addressed by Luke to the Church, the second half to the Pharisees in the Church. This has been disputed, e.g. by Carlston and by Ingo Broer (*NTS* [1974]). Broer reads the second half of the parable as without criticism of the elder son, and takes this to be the attitude to the ninety-nine in 15.7 also: there is thus no achievement-claim by the elder son, the feature which Luke so objects to in 16.14f. and 20.20. Both 15.7 (= Mt.) and the parable are thus pre-Lucan, and correspond well with Jesus' agreed attitude to sinners. But although the father's words are gentle, and permit Broer's reading, few readers escape the feeling that a criticism is implied; and did not Luke himself read it so, in view of vv. 1-3R? For v. 7 see above. Carlston objects that repentance elsewhere in Luke has a more strongly moral tone than here; but it is difficult to make much of this, cf. 24.47; Acts 2.38. Once the parable is seen as a development of Mt. 21.28ff., with the story being allowed to take charge, in the Lucan way, there is no obstacle to seeing two favourite Lucan doctrines as its point: first the necessity of repentance, and secondly the contrast between God's joy in the acceptance of sinners and (? Christian) Pharisaic stand-offishness. Of course this was a major part of Jesus' message; but then Luke knew that from Mark and Matthew, and that is why so many scholars ascribe the parable to Jesus.

15.11 εἶπεν-δέ*, ἄνθρωπός-τις*, (ἔχειν opening a parable*).

15.12 πάτερ, voc.*, μέρος sing. Hapax: διαιρεῖν (cf. ἀν -, ἀφ-, περι-), οὐσία [and in v. 13]. ὁ νεώτερος 22.26R. 'He said to his father, Father', cf. 6.42R, 'say to your brother, Brother', cf. 11.5. ἐπιβάλλειν is standard for an inheritance 'falling to' one, Tob. 3.17; 6.11. βίος = livelihood, 21.4Mk; 8.43R (N-A²⁶ prints in parenthesis). Derrett (pp. 105-12) gives a clear account of the legal arrangements.

15.13 ἅπας, χώρα, ζῆν. Hapax: ἀσώτως (cf. Eph. 5.18 ἀσωτία). μετ' οὐ πολλὰς ἡμέρας, cf. Acts 1.5, οὐ μετὰ πολλὰς ἡμέρας, 27.24. The language has been influenced by the Talents story in Mt. 25: ἀπεδήμησεν, Mt. 25.15, συνάγειν/διασκορπίζειν Mt. 25.24, 26, εἰς χώραν μακράν Lk. 19.12R, in the Lucan Pounds.

15.14 γίνεσθαι, κατά + acc., χώρα, καί-αὐτός. Hapax: δαπανᾶν (Acts 21.24; cf. Lk. 14.28; 10.35). ἐγένετο λιμὸς ἰσχυρά, cf. 4.25 ἐγένετο λιμὸς μεγάς; Acts 11.28 λιμὸν μεγάλην, fem. ὑστερεῖν 22.35R?: ἤρξατο is genuinely inceptive.

15.15 πορεύεσθαι, χώρα, πέμπειν*. ἐκολλήθη = joined ×5 Acts. πολίτης 19.14R; Acts 21.39. εἰς τοὺς ἀγρούς. . . βόσκειν χοίρους cf. 8.32, 34, Mk. εἰς + gen. = τις, 5.3R; 11.46QD; Acts 23.17; 1.22. Luke does not repeat the subject when the meaning is clear, cf. Acts 14.10; 23.20. The pigs do not imply a Palestinian origin: Luke knew it was degrading for a Jew to feed pigs.

15.16 ἐπιθυμεῖν*, ὅς in attraction*. Hapax: κεράτιον. N-A²⁶ reads χορτασθῆναι, with which cf. Lk. 16.21 ἐπιθυμῶν χορτασθῆναι: Greeven, and many critics, prefer the coarse γεμίσαι τὴν κοιλίαν—if so, Luke had γεμίζειν at 14.23QD, and κοιλία has figures 3/1/8+2, though elsewhere of the womb. Bailey (I, pp. 172f.) identifies the pods with an especially nasty wild carob, but the siliqua ceratonia is bad enough: his wages are not enough to slake his hunger in a time of high prices, and nobody gave to him, i.e. took pity on him, and invited him to a meal. διδόναι without obj., 6.4Mk, 30, 38QD.

15.17 ἑαυτόν. εἰς ἑαυτὸν ἐλθών is to be compared to ἐν ἑαυτῷ γενόμενος, Acts 12.11. φάναι 17/6/8+24. περισσεύειν, Acts 12.15. ὧδε 9.12R, 9.41R.

15.18 ἀναστάς*, πορεύεσθαι, πάτερ voc.*, ἐνώπιον*, '. . . father, and I will say to him, Father', see on v. 12. ἀναστὰς πορεύεσθαι 1.39; 17.19; Acts 22.10; cf. 8.26. ὁ οὐρανός = God, cf. 15.7QD.

15.19 καλεῖν. οὐκέτι εἰμὶ ἄξιος Acts 13.25R. εἰς + gen., see on v. 15.

15.20 ἀναστάς*, ἑαυτοῦ, ἔτι*. ἔτι δὲ αὐτοῦ μακρὰν ἀπέχοντος, cf. 14.32 ἔτι αὐτοῦ πόρρω ὄντος, 7.6, ἤδη δὲ αὐτοῦ οὐ μακρὰν ἀπέχοντος. εἶδεν αὐτὸν καὶ ἐσπλαγχνίσθη, cf. 7.13, 10.33, ἰδὼν ἐσπλαγχνίσθη. δραμών, 24.12. ἐπιπίπτειν 0/1/2+6: cf. Acts 20.37 ἐπιπεσόντες ἐπὶ τὸν τράχηλον τοῦ Παύλου κατεφίλουν αὐτόν.

15.21 εἶπεν-δέ*, πάτερ voc.*, καλεῖν, ἐνώπιον*.

15.22 εἶπεν-δὲ-πρός*, πούς. Hapaxes: ταχύ (Acts 17.15), ἐκφέρειν (×4 Acts 5), δακτύλιος. δότε: Luke needs a general word to cover both ring and shoes—he uses διδόναι vaguely for bring, provide at 7.44; 12.51; cf. Acts 19.31.

15.23 εὐφραίνεσθαι. ὁ μόσχος ὁ σιτευτός, cf. Mt. 22.4 τὰ σίτιστα. Note Luke's familiar four-verb sequence, bring-sacrifice-eat-celebrate, cf. 12.19, relax, eat, drink, celebrate; here too there is no καί between the first two, but the imperative sequence is lost. θύειν 1/1/4+4. φέρειν with a view to sacrifice, Acts 14.13.

15.24 ἦν + perf. part., εὑρίσκειν, εὐφραίνεσθαι. Hapax: ἀναζῆν. ἀπολωλώς/ εὑρ- carried over from 15.4. K.H. Rengstorf (*Die Re-Investitur*) suggested that the son had been formally declared dead in the Jewish ceremony of qᵉṣaṣâ, but this is not referred to, and seems out of character with the father's informal affectionate ways.

15.25 ὡς = when*, ἐρχόμενος with a verb*, ἐγγίζειν. Hapaxes: συμφωνία, χόρος. ἀγρός sing. 17.7; 23.26Mk without article. συμφωνία probably = music, but cf. BAG ad voc.

15.26 εἴη*, ταῦτα. προσκαλεσάμενος ἕνα τῶν cf. 7.18R προσκαλεσάμενος δύο τινὰς τῶν, 16.5; 18.16R. παῖς = δοῦλος 7.7QC; 12.45QD. τί εἴη ταῦτα 8.9R; 9.46R; esp. 18.36R ἐπυνθάνετο τί εἴη τοῦτο and Acts 21.33. πυνθάνεσθαι 0/0/2+7.

15.27 ὑγιαίνειν*, ἀπολαμβάνειν*. ἥκειν, 4/1/5+0, 13.35QD; 19.43.

15.28 δὲ-καί*. ὀργίζεσθαι 14.21QC. καὶ οὐκ ἤθελεν 18.4; 13.34QC; perhaps influenced by Mt. 22.3 καὶ οὐκ ἤθελον ἐλθεῖν. παρεκάλει αὐτόν 7.4QD, ×3=Mk, often in Acts.

15.29 ἔτος*, φίλος*, εὐφραίνεσθαι. Hapax: ἔριφος. τοσοῦτος 7.9QC, ×2 Acts. δουλεύειν 16.13, 13QC. οὐδέποτε ἐντολήν σου παρῆλθον is formed on the basis of Israel's confession in Deut. 26.13, οὐ παρῆλθον τὴν ἐντολήν σου. παρέρχεσθαι metaph. 11.42QD.

15.30 οὗτος contemptuous. κατεσθίειν 8.5Mk; 20.47Mk. βίος = livelihood, see v. 12. 'Your': it is still the father's, even if he has convenanted it to the elder son after his death (v. 12). ὅτε δέ ×7 Acts.

15.31 τέκνον voc. abs. (cf. πάτερ, ἀδελφέ, φίλε abs.). πάντοτε 18.1R?: ἀεί is never used in the Gospels, and comes only once in Acts.

15.32 εὐφραίνεσθαι*, χαίρειν*, δὲ-καί*, δεῖ, ζῆν, εὑρίσκειν. ἔδει: the imperfect implies ἡμᾶς; for a reproach σέ would be needed, and preferably the present.

Schweizer, E., 'Zur Frage der Lukasquellen. Analyse von Luk. 15,11-32', *TZ* 4 (1948), pp. 469-71.

Jeremias, J., 'Zum Gleichnis vom verlorenen Sohn, Luk. 15,11-32', *TZ* 5 (1949), pp. 228-31.

Schweizer, E., 'Antwort', *TZ* 5 (1949), pp.231-33.

Rengstorf, K.H., *Die Re-Investitur des verlorenen Sohnes in der Gleichniserzählung Jesu: Luk. 15.11-32* (Köln, 1967).

Sanders, J.T., 'Tradition and Redaction in Luke xv. 11-32', *NTS* 15 (1969), pp. 433-38.

Jeremias, J., 'Tradition und Redaktion in Lukas 15', *ZNW* 62 (1971), pp. 172-89.

Schottroff, L., 'Das Gleichnis vom verlorenen Sohn', *ZTK* 68 (1971), pp. 27-52.

O'Rourke, J.J., 'Some Notes on Luke xv.11-32', *NTS* 18 (1972), pp. 431-33.

Broer, I., 'Das Gleichnis vom verlorenen Sohn und die Theologie des Lukas', *NTS* 20 (1974), pp. 453-62.

Carlston, C.E., 'Reminiscence and Redaction in Luke 15:11-32', *JBL* 94 (1975), 368-90.

Grelot, P., 'Le père et ses deux fils: Luc xv,11-32', *RB* 84 (1977), pp. 321-48, 538-65.

Hofius, O., 'Alttestamentliche Motive im Gleichnis vom verlorenen Sohn', *NTS* 24 (1978), pp. 240-48.

Peterson, W.L., 'The Parable of the Lost Sheep in the Gospel of Thomas and the Synoptics', *NT* 23 (1981), pp. 128-47.

c. *The Unjust Steward*, 16.1-13

Luke has now rewritten the two vineyard parables of Mt. 21.28ff. and Mt. 20.1-16, and he rolls his scroll back through Matthew 19: once again, it is Marcan material, almost unamplified. The saying on the thrones (Mt. 19.28) is not germane to his present theme, and is postponed to the Last Supper. Just now Luke is concerned with the conditions for entering the kingdom, rather than ruling in it, and his focus of attention is the parables, which fill so much of Luke 14–16. Before our Matthew 19 stands the last Matthaean parable in Matthew 25–18, the Unforgiving Debtor.

In its essence, the story appeals to Luke: it is about a middleman who is called upon to give account (λόγον) for money entrusted to him, and whose future hereafter turns upon his treatment of his own debtor. He calls on the man to pay what he owes (ἀπόδος εἴ τι ὀφείλεις), and as he is unable to, imprisons him; and when this reaches the ears of his own creditor, the king, he finds himself similarly penalized. How unwise, says Matthew, to insist upon our debts here on earth! If we do not remit such amounts, how can God be expected to remit what we owe him? Luke does not care for the Matthaean scale of operations, his kings and his millionaire-satraps, still less for his oriental torture-chamber; he moves the mode into his own more middle-class world, with more everyday figures and more imaginable people. His middleman is the steward of an estate, called upon to give account (ἀπόδος τὸν λόγον) of his stewardship. He realises that his position hereafter will depend upon his treatment of the estate's debtors, and summons them, asking how much they owe (πόσον ὀφείλεις;). By diminishing the amounts, he ensures his acceptance when his position is gone. How wise, says Luke, to remit the debts while he had time! If we look to our future similarly, we shall be accepted in heaven.

Luke has not felt bound by the plot of the Matthaean parable (any more than he was by Matthew's two sons), nor is much of the language the same; but the basic situation is the same, a middleman with both debts and debtors, and the basic teaching is the same, the vital importance of ensuring our future with God hereafter in our handling of money/'debts' in this life. For the rest, he is feeling increasingly confident in his treatment of the Matthaean text, with a succession of triumphant successes in the 'new parables' of chs. 14–15, and more to come. The present parable would have been nearly as memorable if only he could have foreborne to gloss it with a second theme in vv. 10-13.

Once more, the Lucan mode of the parable is inescapable. First, the *scale* (§5) is away from fairy-tale kings and talents, here in the real world. The estate-owner is a Lucan ἄνθρωπος πλούσιος, like the Rich Fool and Dives; but his wealth is not enormous, and his estate is capable of being managed by a single οἰκονόμος, who has not been able to make enough out of it to retire without anxiety. The debts are the largest in the Gospel: Jeremias (p. 181) values a hundred baths of oil at 1,000 denarii, and a hundred cors of wheat at 2,500. The remissions are thus 500 denarii in each case, the amount of the larger debt remitted in Luke 7; we may contrast the 10,000 talents of

Matthew 18, sixty million denarii. Farmers may often have owed the Lucan figures, and might hope to pay off the whole in a good year; on Jeremias's figures again (pp. 177, 181), the oil was the produce of about 150 trees, and the wheat of 100 acres, the average farm being sixty.

Again, the central figure of the parable, the steward, is a real *human being* (§4). Matthew's king is an Olympian cipher for God, moving between mercy and judgment; his 'servant' is a cipher for the unforgiving Christian, moving without motive from grovelling to violence. Luke has made the latter into a steward as he did at 12.42, and this time an all too believable prudent rascal. He has been living it up at the expense of the estate (v. 1), and he thinks up a policy for looking after his future, also at the expense of the estate. There is nothing black and white about him. He is a thorough swindler, an unjust steward, on the one side, but he has the virtue of far-sighted common sense on the other. In this way he is like the many-sided characters of Luke's other parables. Like them, too, he *soliloquizes*, 'What shall I do. . .? I know what I will do'—how many Lucan characters reflect upon their predicament, and similarly resolve on a solution (§4.1)! We may think especially of the lord of the vineyard in whose mouth Luke puts the new words, 'What shall I do?' (20.13), or the Rich Fool's, 'What shall I do. . .? I will do this'. In this way Luke has provided a *dubious hero* (§4.7); in place of Matthew's (and Mark's) respectable kings, householders and businessmen, we are asked by Luke to identify with crooked stewards and judges, publicans and Samaritans. Characteristic too are some features of the dialogue. 'I cannot dig' is a Lucan *feeble excuse* (§4.5), like 'I cannot rise and give you', or 'I have married a wife, and so I cannot come'. Luke likes *digging* too—'who dug and deepened', 'I will dig round it and dung it'. 'I am ashamed to beg' brings in Luke's awareness of *shame*: cf. 'yet because of his shamelessness he will rise', 'all who opposed him were ashamed', 'with shame to take the lowest place'. Lucan *alacrity* is in evidence once more with 'Sit down quickly' (§3); and Lucan kings and tower-builders also *sit down* to business.

The characterization of the parable has often been misread through critics' expectation that it would follow the stereotyped Matthaean mould; but we must let the text speak for itself. The man is an οἰκονόμος, a term limited in the Gospels to Luke. It is rash to import details from a specialized knowledge of Jewish law, which Luke is unlikely to have known: he is probably thinking of the ordinary estate manager who is a familiar figure across the Roman world, and whose honesty was a cause of anxiety to many a landowner. The steward has been 'wasting the owner's goods', that is, misappropriating, peculating, and otherwise taking advantage of his position. The master dismisses him, and calls for an account—a statement of the value of stores and other assets, of debts outstanding, creditors, etc. There is no question of the steward foregoing profits/ interest which would have come to him. He says to the first debtor, 'How much do you owe *my lord*?'; all that is done is to change (falsify) his debt to the owner. Neither Roman vilicus nor Jewish *shaliaḥ* ran estates on contract, nor does the parable imply this, nor is interest either implied or disapproved. The steward says, 'Take (δέξαι) your contract (γράμματα)', passing him the IOU from the pile. The loser is the owner, now as before.

But the question is bound to arise at once in the listener's mind, What then did the owner feel about that? In a village where a number of tenants have suddenly received a large bonanza, it is unrealistic to suppose that he will not hear what is happening in a matter of hours, especially as v. 2, 'What is this I hear about you?', shows him to have his ear close to the ground. So Luke adds, 'And the master commended the unjust steward because he had acted prudently'. ὁ κύριος is much better taken as the master of the parable, 'my master' of vv. 3, 5, because 'And I say to you' in v. 9 is Luke's regular bridge from parable to application (11.9; 14.24; 15.7, 10; 18.14); and the story is unfinished unless we are told if the steward got away with it. In fact there is not much the owner can do. The documents are falsified, and he can only accept the loss, with good or bad humour. He chooses the former: 'Good for him! For (ὅτι) he has acted prudently; for (ὅτι) the sons of this world are more prudent towards their generation than the sons of light!' Both ὅτι's justify the praise; the first is natural after ἐπαινεῖν (cf. 1 Cor. 11.2, 17), and the second is required because the reason is insufficiently clear (cf. 10.21QC). So the Lucan master is seen as a relaxed, philosophical fellow, with two sides to him (how unlike Matthew's stern, just, God-like masters!). He is careful enough of his property to dismiss a dishonest manager, but willing to accept the additional loss with a quip. There is some similar ironic realism at 14.11 (ὅτι with a proverb), and 18.5.

16.9. It is possible, then, to read the parable as a Lucan re-writing of Matthew's parable of the remission of debts—on a Lucan scale, with two-sided Lucan people, soliloquies, feeble excuses, etc. But what about the point? The point to which the story tends, and which Luke draws from it, is in v. 9: 'And I say to you, make yourselves (ἑαυτοῖς ποιήσατε) friends from the mammon of unrighteousness, that when it gives out (ἐκλίπῃ) they may receive you into eternal habitations'. This is comfortingly familiar. First it is an *imperative*, hortatory conclusion as with so many other Lucan parables (§8). Luke said in v. 1 that the parable was addressed to the disciples; and there is every sign that it was designed to carry this message. Second, we have met the contrast between temporal and eternal wealth in Luke before: 'ποιήσατε ἑαυτοῖς purses that wax not old, a treasure in the heavens that does not give out' (ἀνέκλειπτος, 12.33QD). It looks therefore as if the meaning of the two sayings will be the same: '*dispose of your money* in this life so as to make friends of the angels above, for they will look after you for ever'. This moral fits the parable: the only apparently uncomfortable slide is with the phrase ἐκ τοῦ μαμωνᾶ τῆς ἀδικίας, and that arises from Luke's feeling about money. 'The mammon of unrighteousness' is not an exact translation of any Aramaic phrase we know: Billerbeck's *mamon disᵉqar* means 'the mammon of fraud' (presumably ἀπάτης: II, p. 220), and Jeremias' *hon hariŝ'a* (p. 46) would hardly come out as 'mammon' at all. Rather we should see Luke as taking mammon from Mt. 6.24 (= Lk. 16.13), and adding his own gloss τῆς ἀδικίας, as in the previous verse or 18.6. What the steward has done is to make himself friends by means of his dishonest handling of money, so as to have a home after his dismissal: what the disciple is to do is to make friends similarly in heaven by giving away his money on earth. Luke does not mind the pejorative and misleading phrase 'the mammon of unrighteousness', because he is at heart a radical, and agrees with Proudhon that property is theft; a committed Christian will leave all, say farewell to all his possessions.

The conclusion in v. 9 thus fits the parable very well; alas, there is a similar-sounding reflection in Matthew's Talents, and Luke adds that for good measure. But unfortunately the point is not the same, and commentators have been swift to see the appending of an alien interpretation. It is, however, far from uncharacteristic of Luke to create a *muddle* (§9) by combining two sources; and there are famous instances of his parables not matching the conclusions with which he provides them, in the Two Debtors of ch. 7 and the Good Samaritan of ch. 10.

16.10. The Talents contains a situation comparable with the present parable, in that there is again a wealthy owner giving the stewardship of his affairs into the hands of an agent, from whom he requires an account. The rich man commends his first two agents with the words, 'Well done, good and faithful servant, you were faithful over a few things (ἐπὶ ὀλίγα ἦς πιστός), I will set you over much (πολλῶν)' (Mt. 25.21, 23). In the Lucan version of the Talents, the Pounds, the king commends the first servant, 'Well done, good servant, for you were faithful in a very little (ἐν ἐλαχίστῳ πιστὸς ἐγένου)' (19.17); and he is given charge over ten cities, with a reward of a *mna* for himself (v. 24). Luke accordingly continues in the present context, 'He who is *faithful in a very little* (ὁ πιστὸς ἐν ἐλαχίστῳ) is faithful also in *much*'; and he adds the converse, 'and he who is dishonest in a very little is dishonest also in much' (v. 10). It is likely that the latter is a version of the master's words to the bad (πονηρός) servant who had hidden his talent/pound; but it is restyled into an antithesis with v. 10a, with the Lucan ἄδικος carried over from ἀδικίας. Luke's thought is that the faithful disciple who has been a good steward of God's money and given it away to the poor, will be faithful discharging the larger responsibilities God will give him in heaven. Those who have been 'unjust', and spent God's money on themselves, do not deserve a larger trust.

16.11f. This leads on to a double reflection. The first part is a clarification of the preceding: 'If then you were not faithful (πιστοὶ οὐκ ἐγένεσθε) with the unrighteous mammon, who will entrust you with the true wealth?' πιστὸς γένεσθαι comes as naturally to Luke as it does at 19.17R. As in v. 9, the unrighteous mammon means no more than our 'filthy lucre'. Luke is a spiritual man, and deeply distrustful of the stuff; it will inevitably corrupt its owner—rich men are always bad—but he does not mean that it has been fraudulently obtained. The aim is merely to stress the preceding half-verse: if you are not faithful with God's money, in giving it away, you cannot expect to be entrusted with the real wealth of heaven (whatever that may be). The thought is then carried further with, 'And if you were not faithful with another's goods, who will give you your own?' The faithful servant of the Pounds was not merely entrusted with ten cities (= true wealth), but also was given his faithless colleague's *mna* (= your own). It is not clear quite what heavenly realities Luke has in mind behind his symbolism.

16.13. The mammon theme which Luke has been developing since v. 9 was familiar to him from Mt. 6.24, and he now rounds off the pericope with a virtual citation: '*No* house-servant *can serve two masters: for either he will hate the one and love the other, or he will hold to the one and despise the other. You cannot serve God and mammon*'. This is exactly what he has been trying to say. A disciple has to choose, either God or money; the love of money and the holding to it are the end of effective discipleship for those who try to have it both ways. The opening section (14.25-35) of Luke's present trio warned the crowd that discipleship meant hating one's own and saying farewell to all one had. The middle section addressed the Pharisaic opposition, that it meant welcoming sinners into the Church. The topic is now concluded with the renewing of the challenge to hate money, when one is a disciple (v. 1): Luke has added οἰκέτης to show that the worker belongs to the Christian household (οἶκος). He knew that the temptations of money were a net about our feet all this life long.

The Steward has been a 'riddle' to so many readers partly because of a reluctance to allow so ambiguous a character to be our model: hence the attraction of theories that he was really sacrificing his own profit, or remitting usury. But even when it is seen that ambiguous characters are part of Luke's way, there remains a profound tension from the introduction of a second view of money. Luke himself was a radical, with money as with marriage; it is not for nothing that he is Thomas' favourite Gospel. He thought the rich would hunger and weep hereafter, and that no apologia was required for seeing Dives into torment in Hades. The only thing to do with money was to give it away in large amounts: to leave all, to say farewell to all our possessions, to sell what we have and give alms. This, Luke's own view, is expressed in the conclusion with which he draws the parable's moral: money fails (ἐκλίπῃ), you cannot take it with you, it is 'the mammon of unrighteousness' which will corrupt you even if you have inherited it, or earned it honestly. By giving it away, you will ensure your eternal home. Matthew, however, held to the more normal biblical view: money was both a spiritual peril and a divine reward. We must not lay up treasure for ourselves, we must have the generous eye and take no anxious thought for the morrow; and if we do, all these things will be added unto us, our heavenly Father will give us good things. The very images he uses betray a sympathy for the business life: we must come to terms with our creditors, and remit our debts, the religious life is like making an enormous sum of money. Small wonder if Matthew has been a congenial Gospel to a Church run by businessmen, and if Luke is the Gospel for liberation theologians. But no man can rend a piece of a new garment and put it on an old one—the new will not agree with the old; and nor will a piece of Matthew's genial theology agree with Luke's firm line. In v. 9 we are to make ourselves eternal friends out of our filthy lucre—that is (12.33), we are to give it away. In vv. 10-12 a patch is tacked on from Matthew's Talents: money is a trust, God wants us to husband his treasure faithfully, be a good steward. But faithfulness and unrighteous wealth do not really go together: you cannot in fact serve the Lucan God and be a steward of Mammon.

Since Jülicher (II, pp. 495-514), it has been increasingly popular to discard the concluding verses as mistaken interpretations, whether composed by Luke or introduced ready-made from tradition: the parable can then be taken on its own (vv. 1-7), and can yield an eschatological warning—act while you may, the hour of account is here! So Dodd, pp. 29ff.; Jeremias, pp. 45ff., 181f.; Schneider. The original text will then end at v. 8a, 'And the Lord (i.e. Jesus) praised the steward. . . ' This seems multiply forced: (1) The parable has no ending; we are not told if the steward got away with his stratagem. Every other Lucan parable that starts 'A certain man. . . ' keeps him in the story to the end. The reader here wants to know how he reacted. (2) ὁ κύριος absolute refers naturally to the master in the parable, as at 12.37, 42. (3) If v. 8a is outside the parable, we require 'he said' before 'I say to you'. (4) 'And I (ἐγώ) say to you', is not only Luke's normal rubric for moving to comment, but the ἐγώ seems to stand against the approval of the master in v. 8. (5) Jeremias' parallel in 18.6 covers none of these objections: there ὁ κύριος cannot refer to a character in the story, there is an εἶπεν, and the λέγω ὑμῖν in 18.8 merely emphasizes the point of 18.7. Without Jesus in 16.8a there is no evidence for the 'crisis' interpretation—not that that disturbs Jeremias in many other contexts, and it is quite normal to assume both dominical authorship and the crisis view without requiring evidence.

Many other attempts have been made to solve the 'riddle' of the parable. One of the most attractive has been that of Derrett (pp. 48-77, with *JTS* [1972]), who is followed by Fitzmyer: the amounts the steward remits are the interest which he has illegally charged, and the remission not only pleases the debtors, but (by its propriety) wins the master's commendation. But surely it would be necessary to mention so key a feature? Luke could not assume a knowledge of interest-components evading Torah from his Gentile congregation, and would have to supply, 'the master, knowing that the money was usury', or some similar phrase. There is the additional feature, too, that in 19.23 Luke seems to accept interest payments in parables without compunction; and this seems to undermine the whole proposal. Besides, if one could borrow wheat at 25% interest, or oil at 100%, who would borrow oil? Everyone would borrow wheat, sell it and buy oil. Otherwise one can avoid the scandal of the owner's approval by supplying question marks at the end of v. 8 and v. 9 (R. Merkelbach, *VC* [1979]), or by conjecturing a double Aramaic mistranslation (the master cursed him for acting craftily, Günther Schwarz, *BZ* [1974]). Other options are legion.

Older commentators like Lagrange and Klostermann followed the traditional line of Augustine, which saw the parable as an exhortation to give away money, and so go to heaven; and this has been supported by Francis E. Williams more recently in *JBL* (1964). Such a position cannot be maintained, however, for the whole unit as the teaching of Jesus, in view of the tensions between v. 9 and vv. 10-12; we need a radical view of money as 'the mammon of unrighteousness' to remove the tension between v. 9 and the parable; and we require an author for the parable who likes ambiguity in his characters, dishonest but provident, firm but philosophical. On such terms, or in other words with Lucan authorship of the whole, the old is best.

16.1   λέγειν-πρός*, ἄνθρωπός-τις*, πλούσιος*, ἔχειν opening parables, καὶ-οὗτος*, τὰ-ὑπάρχοντα*. Hapax: διαβάλλειν (cf. διάβολος). ὡς of allegation 23.14R; Acts 3.12. διασκορπίζειν 15.13.

16.2   εἶπεν, ἀκούειν-περί, ἔτι*. Hapax: οἰκονομεῖν (cf. -ος, -ία). φωνήσας = summoning, Acts 9.41; 10.18. ἀποδοῦναι τὸν λόγον Acts 19.40 (no art. + περί): Lk. adds article as a man's stewardship will always have ended with the (customary) account. 'The account *of* your stewardship' without περί is natural. οὐ δύνῃ ἔτι cf. 20.26R οὐδὲ γὰρ ἀποθανεῖν ἔτι δύνανται. Luke writes δύνασαι 5.12Mk; 6.42QC, δύνῃ here only, cf. Mk. 9.22, Rev. 2.2.

16.3   εἶπεν-δὲ*, ἑαυτόν, τί-ποιήσω*, ἀφαιρεῖν, ἰσχύειν*. Hapax: αἰσχύνεσθαι (κατ- 13.17). σκάπτειν 6.48R; 13.8; ἐπαιτεῖν 18.35R. εἶπεν-ἐν-ἑαυτῷ 7.39; 18.4.

16.4   τί-ποιήσω*, δέχεσθαι, οἶκος, ἑαυτόν. Hapax: μεθιστάναι(×2 Acts cf. σταθείς). δέχεσθαι εἰς τοὺς οἴκους cf. 2.28 ἐδέξατο εἰς τὰς ἀγκάλας, cf. 16.9.

16.5   προσκαλεσάμενος-ἕνα, ἑαυτόν. χρεοφειλετής 0/0/2, 7.41. ὁ πρῶτος . . . ἕτερος 14.18ff.QD; 19.16, 20QD. εἷς-ἕκαστος, 4.40R, ×6 Acts.

16.6 εἶπεν (×2), δέχεσθαι, καθίσας, γράφειν. Hapax: βάτος. βάτος and κόρος are Graecized, like Σόδομα and ʼΙεροσόλυμα in Acts. Luke uses the Semitic measures, partly for local colour, partly because Greek ones were small. γράμματα 0/0/3+2 = document, Acts 28.21. ταχέως 14.21QD. The numeral precedes the measure for stress; it is soon to be altered. σου carries a similar stress; there is a queue (cf. 14.23).

16.7 ἕτερος*, εἶπεν (×2), δέχεσθαι, γράφειν. Hapaxes: ἔπειτα, κόρος.

16.8 ἀδικία*, ποιεῖν + adv., ἑαυτόν. Hapax: ἐπαινεῖν. υἱός metaphorical, τοῦ αἰῶνος τούτου 20.34R. ὑπέρ + acc. 6.40QC, Acts 26.13 (not comparative). ὁ. τῆς ἀδικίας cf. v. 9, 18.6,

16.9 ἑαυτόν, φίλος*, ἀδικία*, ἐκλείπειν, δέχεσθαι. Cf. 12.33. σκηνή a heavenly dwelling, cf. Heb. 8.2; Lk. 9.33. αἰώνιος in contrast to this αἰών (v. 8), where there is ζωὴ αἰώνιος; cf. *4 Ezra* 2.11. 'They may receive you', indef. = the angels, as in 12.20; expressly, 16.22.

16.10 ὁ + phrase + adj., καί = also (×2). ἐν ἐλαχίστῳ 19.17.

16.11 γίνεσθαι. Hapax: ἀληθινός. πιστεύειν = entrust, here alone; the suggestion comes from πιστός. Luke does not normally write rhetorical questions, but cf. 6.39QD; 6.46QD; 12.51QD; 13.18QD (double) = Mk. ἀληθινός = eternal, cf. Heb. 8.2 again, τῆς σκηνῆς τῆς ἀληθινῆς.

16.12 γίνεσθαι. Hapax: ἀλλότριος (Acts 7.6R). ὑμέτερος 0/0/2+1, 6.20QD; Acts 27.34; for ἡμέτερον BL, see Metzger, p. 165.

16.13 (ἕτερος ×2)*, (θεός anarthrous). Hapaxes: (ἀντέχεσθαι), (καταφρονεῖν), οἰκέτης (Acts 10.7). οὐδείς + noun 4.24; Acts 25.18; 27.22.

Williams, F.E., 'Is Almsgiving the Point of the Unjust Steward?', *JBL* 83 (1964), pp. 293-97.
Derrett, J.D.M., '"Take thy Bond . . . and write Fifty"'. *JTS* ns 23 (1972), pp. 438-40.
Schwarz, G., '". . . lobte den betrügerischen Verwalter"', *BZ* 18 (1974), pp. 94f.
Topel, L.J., 'On the Injustice of the Unjust Steward: Lk. 16:1-13', *CBQ* 37 (1975), pp. 213-27.
Molina, J.P., 'Lc. 16,1-13: l'injuste Mammon', *ETR* 53 (1978), pp. 371-75.
Fuchs, E., 'L'Evangile et l'argent: La parabole de l'intendant intelligent', *Bulletin du Centre Protestant d'Etudes* 30/2 (1978), pp. 51-63.
Feuillet, A., 'Les paraboles de Luc 16', *Esprit et vie* 89 (1979), pp. 241-71.
Merkelbach, R., 'Über das Gleichnis vom ungerechten Haushalter (Lucas 16,1-13)', *VC* 33 (1979), pp. 180-81.
Scott, B.B., 'A Master's Praise: Luke 16, 1-8a', *Bib* 64 (1983), pp. 173-88
Focaut, C., 'Tromper le Mamon d'iniquité', in *Fs* Dupont (1985), pp. 547-69.

43. *The Law and the Gospel*, 16.14-17.19

a. *Dives and Lazarus*, 16.14-31

The remission of debts is only one aspect of the great parable in Mt. 18.23-35; there is also the dreadful warning of the wealthy man who had no mercy and was handed over to the tormentors (βασανισταῖς). 'Should you not have had mercy (ἐλεῆσαι) on your fellow-servant', says the king, 'even as I had mercy on you?' (v. 32). A little earlier in Matthew 18 there is the further repeated threat of hell—eternal fire (v. 8), the gehenna of fire (v. 9). This is the penalty for 'scandalizing one of these little ones (ἕνα τῶν μικρῶν τούτων) who believe in me', and it is said, 'See that you do not despise one of these little ones; for I tell you that their angels' have access to God (v. 10)—a Matthaean addition to Mark.

Luke has counselled 'the disciples' to look to their eternal future by giving away the unrighteous mammon; but the strong suggestion of the Matthaean text is an exposition of the other side of the coin. Luke is a reluctant preacher of hell-fire, but he is by no means reluctant to stress the future penalties of wealth (1.53; 6.24-26), and he has repeatedly said that salvation is dependent on its abandonment (12.33; 14.33; 16.9; cf. 19.9). He feels led therefore to tell a parable of his own on the rich man who ended 'in torments' (βασάνοις, 16.23), 'in this place of torment' (βασάνου, v. 28), 'in anguish in this flame' (v. 24). But to Luke the μικροί were not Matthew's junior church-members, but the unimportant of society: 'all from unimportant to important (ἀπὸ μικροῦ ἕως μεγάλου) gave heed to him' (Acts 8.10), 'testifying both to the unimportant and the important' (Acts 26.22). So he interprets Dives' fault as in not having mercy on the least important of all in ancient society, the beggar, and so 'scandalizing' him; and Dives calls in vain to Abraham to have mercy on him (ἐλέησόν με, v. 24). When the parable is over, the disciples are warned that drowning is better than '*scandalizing one of these little ones*' (17.2): if the word 'these' is to be allowed any reference, it can be only to the likes of Lazarus. It is the angels who bear Lazarus to Abraham's bosom also.

16.14f. Those in need of such a warning are, to Luke, 'the Pharisees who were fond of money'. He had taken over the Matthaean tradition that scribes and Pharisees were hypocrites, full of graspingness within (11.39 QD), and he has himself made his stereotyped wealthy host-figures into Pharisees at 7.36; 11.37 and

14.1 (with wealthy friends, 14.12). He makes his usual foil introduction therefore (§1.4), with the Pharisees scoffing at the challenge to choose between God and Mammon: Luke has the rulers 'scoff' again, at Jesus on the cross (23.35R). But Matthew had set the God-and-Mammon logion, and its associated matter on treasure in heaven (6.19-24) in a larger context; for in the preceding verses the 'hypocrites' do their righteousness (δικαιοσύνην)—that is, their alms, prayer and fasting—before men ((ἔμπροσθεν τῶν ἀνθρώπων), and such will receive no reward from 'your Father who sees in secret' (6.1-18). There is no doubt in the mind of either evangelist who these hypocrites are (Mt. 5.20; 23.5), and Luke accordingly has Jesus say to his Pharisees: 'You are those who justify (δικαιοῦντες) yourselves before men (ἐνώπιον τῶν ἀνθρώπων), but God knows your hearts; for what is exalted among men is abomination before God'. Luke prefers ἐνώπιον to Matthew's ἔμπροσθεν and the verb δικαιοῦν to Matthew's noun, which gives a Pauline Christian the shudders. He is expressing the same disgust with piety for show; the Lucan God knows the hearts where Matthew's Father sees in secret.

16.16. Matthew had not only revealed in 5.20 that the hypocrites of ch. 6 were Pharisees; he had also set out there the principle that to inherit the kingdom one must do more than the law—'Unless your righteousness exceed that of the scribes and Pharisees, you shall not enter the kingdom of heaven'. This was to Luke the basic error of Pharisaism—works-righteousness, self-justification from works of the law, boasting, all those elements in the Lutheran interpretation of Paul which E.P. Sanders has been at such pains to correct. But he combines another Matthaean text with it: 'From the days of John the Baptist until now the kingdom of heaven suffers violence, and men of violence force it. For all the prophets and the law prophesied until John' (Mt. 11.12f.). Mt. 5.20 says we need to do more than the law to enter the kingdom; Mt. 11.12f. says that the period of the law ended with John; after that came the kingdom, and subject to much violence.

Luke adapts, no doubt from memory, taking the logically prior point first: '*The law and the prophets* (were) till *John*; from then *the kingdom of* God *is* evangelized, and everyone *makes his way violently* (βιάζεται) *into* it'. Matthew had been citing Malachi (11.10), so he found it natural to write, 'For all the prophets prophesied till John', and he added clumsily, '... the prophets *and the law* prophesied ...':

John marks the end of an epoch governed by the law even more than by the prophets, though strictly speaking the law did not prophesy. Luke puts the law before the prophets, as is normal (24.44; Acts 13.15; 24.14), but finds himself caught in the same syntactical impasse as his predecessor. He does not want to say that the law prophesied, so he drops the verb altogether. The second half of the sentence he rewrites with a freer hand. Matthew had been commenting on 'men of violence' like Herod who had imprisoned John (11.2), but this is irrelevant in Luke's context. He is making the simpler point, that there is a time of the Old Testament and a time of the kingdom, and he writes, 'the kingdom of God εὐαγγελίζεται', with an eye on the near-by Mt. 11.5, 'the poor εὐαγγελίζονται'. These are the only two contexts where εὐαγγελίζεσθαι is used in the passive. His ἀπὸ τότε is drawn from yet another Matthaean context: after John's baptising of Jesus in Matthew 3, and his arrest in Mt. 4.12, comes Mt. 4.17, 'ἀπὸ τότε began Jesus to preach. . . The kingdom of heaven has come'. ἀπὸ τότε here is Mt. R; it is inserted again into the Marcan narrative at Mt. 16.21 and 26.16.

However, this leaves out Matthew's triple stress on violence, and Luke has a use for his 'the kingdom of heaven suffers violence' (βιάζεται, passive). He takes this to mean the Pharisees, of whom Mt. 5.20 said that they were trying to enter the kingdom, and would not succeed, and he writes, 'and everyone βιάζεται (middle) into it'. Their legalistic piety and their scoffing at Jesus' teaching on money were just an attempt to force their way in. That was how it seemed to Luke, but it is rather a wayward interpretation of Matthew's clear wording, and it is no wonder that it has caused trouble.

16.17. The use of Mt. 5.20 has been rather slight: we can be confident of its influence partly because it sets out the principle underlying Mt. 6.1-18, and so gives the thread of thought in Lk. 16.15f.; and partly because Luke then goes on to Mt. 5.18. This runs, 'Until heaven and earth pass away, one iota or one tittle shall not pass away from the law, till all come to pass'; and Luke writes, 'But it is easier for *heaven and earth* to *pass away* than for *one tittle* of *the law* to fall'. The 'but' (δέ) is essential. Verse 16 might easily give the impression that after John the law was no longer valid, and v. 17 supplies the reassurance that this is not so. Whatever relaxations the Holy Spirit might sanction for the future Gentile church, Luke was in no doubt that the Bible was the word of God for the Jews; and he paints the good people of Luke 1-2 and 23-24 as observant of it, no less than the Jerusalem Christians of Acts. For the rest, he improves Matthew's uncomfortable wording, with its two 'until' clauses, and the second one obscure. He uses the formula εὐκοπώτερόν ἐστιν. . . ἤ, perhaps a reminiscence of Mt. 19.24/Mk 10.25. He retains Matthew's favoured 'heaven-and-earth' (15/1/6), but slims down the rhetorical pair, 'one iota or one tittle', just as he puts 'moth' for Matthew's 'moth nor rust', or 'mint and rue' for his 'mint and anice and cummin'. He retains κεραία, the 'crown' on the Hebrew letters, as being smaller than the yod/iota. He varies Matthew's repetition of παρέλθῃ with his favoured πεσεῖν.

16.18. When the first Christians spoke of the law and the gospel as affecting practical living, two points seemed to be primary, as perhaps they have remained: sexual ethics and money ethics. Paul treats of the sanctification of the Thessalonians with warnings against first πορνεία (1 Thess. 4.2ff.) and then πλεονεκτεῖν (vv. 6-8); and he similarly rebukes the Corinthians first for their πορνεία (1 Cor. 5.1) and then as πλεονεκταί (5.10f.; 6.1-10). The same double emphasis was there in the Jewish tradition earlier: 'Guard yourselves therefore, my children', says Judah, 'against sexual promiscuity and love of money' (*T.Jud.* 18.2). Luke is able to select the same from Matthew's Sermon. The validity of the law, and the requirement of more by the gospel, were laid down in Mt. 5.17-20; then came six illustrations in 5.21-48, including the remarriage rule at 5.32; and then the call to private piety, that led on to the choice between God and Mammon. Luke has just glanced through Matthew 19 too, where the remarriage issue is covered in 19.2-12, and the money issue in 19.16-30. His pericope is about money (16.14, 19-31), but he includes the sexual rule too as an example of the law-and-gospel principle from its other main field. He is quite content with a brief ruling, such as is given at Mt. 5.32: if he thought that marriage is hardly allowable for a disciple (14.26; 18.29), we cannot be surprised if a second attempt receives short shrift.

Luke was familiar with three versions of the gospel ruling. Mt. 5.32 πᾶς ὁ ἀπολύων τὴν γυναῖκα αὐτοῦ παρεκτὸς λόγου πορνείας ποιεῖ αὐτήν μοιχευθῆναι, καί ὃς ἐάν ἀπολελυμένην γαμήσῃ μοιχᾶται. Mt. 19.9 runs, in the ℵ text, printed by N-A[26]: ὃς ἄν ἀπολύσῃ τὴν γυναῖκα αὐτοῦ μὴ ἐπὶ πορνείᾳ καὶ γαμήσῃ ἄλλην μοιχᾶται. The B text, printed by Greeven, adds καὶ ὁ ἀπολελυμένην γαμῶν μοιχᾶται. Mk 10.11f.: ὃς ἂν ἀπολύσῃ τὴν γυναῖκα αὐτοῦ καὶ γαμήσῃ ἄλλην μοιχᾶται ἐπ' αὐτήν, καὶ ἐὰν αὐτὴ ἀπολύσασα τὸν ἄνδρα...μοιχᾶται. Luke himself writes: πᾶς ὁ ἀπολύων τὴν γυναῖκα αὐτοῦ καὶ γαμῶν ἑτέραν μοιχεύει, καὶ ὁ ἀπολελυμένην ἀπὸ ἀνδρὸς γαμῶν μοιχεύει. He begins with the first six words of Mt. 5.32, adding the (necessary) remarriage phrase from Matthew 19/Mark 10, with his preferred ἕτερος. Being a radical, he drops Matthew's 'except' clause, the high-road to compromise and muddle. He twice writes μοιχεύει for μοιχᾶται, after the Seventh Commandment οὐ μοιχεύσεις. His second clause reverts to Mt. 5.32, or perhaps, if he knew it, Mt. 19.9B, which has the participial form. He does not concern himself with women's divorce (Mk 10.12), an even rarer and more unpalatable possibility; though Mark's ἄνδρα may have influenced his ἀπὸ ἀνδρός. He is content to have made the point in the clearest and starkest manner possible.

There is no break in the sense with v. 19, 'And there was a certain rich man...' We may recapitulate the train of Luke's thought thus: 'Jesus said to the money-loving Pharisees, God loathes your self-justification. His kingdom is being proclaimed now (though the law is still valid), and you all try to force your way in. Your so-called remarriage is just adultery. There was a rich man who went to hell for his neglect of the poor, and Abraham refused to send word to his brothers; if they did not hear the law, neither would they one risen from the dead'. I will not maintain that it is his clearest piece of writing, but once we see that he is using Matthew, it is totally comprehensible; and the method of combining epigrams from here and there in an earlier writing is bound to lead to obscurity, as we have seen in 6.39-44 or 12.1-12. We may at least defend his consistency. The Church saw the Pharisaic movement as defying both the law (Gen. 2.24) and the gospel over remarriage (Mk 10.1-12; Mt. 19.2-9); as ignoring the Torah principle of care for the poor, and the plain evidence of God's hand in the Resurrection.

16.14 ἀκούειν-δέ in transition, ταῦτα, ὑπάρχειν*. Ηapax: φιλάργυρος. ταῦτα πάντα 12.30R; 24.9R. φιλ-compounds 0/0/2+3; ἐκμυκτηρίζειν 23.35R.

16.15 εἶπεν, δικαιοῦν*, ἑαυτόν, ἐνώπιον, ὁ-θεός, τό + phrase, ἐνώπιον-τοῦ-θεοῦ*, θεὸς/ἄνθρωποι. Ηapax: βδέλυγμα. ὑμεῖς-ἐστε-οἱ 22.28R; Acts 3.25. God as καρδιογνώστης Acts 1.24; 15.8. God's hostility to self-exaltation 14.11; 18.14; cf. 1.52f. Creed, correctly, 'You do indeed give alms, but you only do so to justify yourselves before men'. Marshall, 'It fits in with the criticism made in Mt. 6.1-4', but missing the dependence.

16.16 εὐαγγελίζεσθαι-τὴν-βασιλείαν-τοῦ-θεοῦ*. Hapaxes: (βιάζεσθαι), μέχρι (×2 Acts). πᾶς abs. = everyone, 6.40QD, 11.4QD.

Verses 16ff. have been much commented on: for a recent review of literature see Stephen Wilson, pp. 43-51. Wilson himself suspects three discrete sayings without a consistent approach to a common theme (p. 51). Harnack (pp. 182f.) and Lührmann (pp. 27f.) take the Matthaean setting to be original, but Schmid (pp. 284f.) and many prefer the Lucan setting. The argument that the Lucan setting is earlier because it is difficult (and made easier by Matthew) merely pushes the difficulty back one stage. Schulz (p. 261), Schmid and Lührmann take the Lucan form of v. 16a to be original; but Hoffmann (pp. 53-56) sees the teaching of the turn of the age with John as Lucan (cf. Luke 1-2). Schulz lists most authorities as taking v. 16b to be a Lucan development; but again some Matthaean redaction is visible (e.g. ἡ βασιλεία τῶν οὐρανῶν). The verse has been the lynch-pin of Hans Conzelmann's enormous hypothesis; but its position here seems too casual to carry such weight (Werner Kümmel, *Fs* Stählin); and Walter Wink (pp. 51-55) has argued convincingly that Luke's general position is to include John Baptist in the Gospel era.

Frederick Danker, *JBL* (1958): 'In all the parallels cited by Wetstein of βιάζεσθαι followed by εἰς, hostile intent is expressed' (p. 234): he cites Polyb. 1.74.5, Appian, Syr. 45, B.C. 1.103; and none of the references given by G. Schrenk (*TDNT* I, pp. 609-14) modifies this judgment. Danker argues persuasively that the δέ in v. 17 also requires a hostile meaning ('Everyone tries force, but the law is still valid'); that in this way the whole passage is about the Pharisees; and that the lawbreaking πᾶς of v. 18 will be the same as that in v. 16. This seems conclusive against the view that 'everyone' was the Lucan outcasts pressing into the kingdom (Kümmel, *ibid.*, p. 96). The only implausible thing in Danker's article is the speculation on the logion's original setting.

Schürmann (*TU*, pp. 126-36) argues that Q here included an extended parallel to Mt. 5.17-20, running on to 'examples such as are adduced in Mt. in 5.21-48', as well as the substance of Mt. 6.1-4. This begins to look like my own hypothesis that Luke knew the Sermon on the Mount. Wilson (pp. 49f.) criticizes it as not accounting for Luke's omission of Mt. 5.19; but Luke does not think the Pharisees relaxed the commandments, but that they broke them (11.46).

16.17 Schulz (p. 114) counts six redactoral uses of πεσεῖν in Luke, but none elsewhere is metaphorical. He takes the Matthaean form to be in general earlier, but (with many) thinks Luke's 'one tittle' is from Q, to which Matthew has added the iota. But Luke tends to abbreviate cliché pairs (cf. Harnack, p. 43, 'superfluous'). Matthew, in my view as well as in that of most, wrote the second ἕως clause himself; its clumsiness and obscurity could well lead to Luke's omitting it.

16.18   ἕτερος*, ἀνήρ*. See Schulz, p. 116, for the Matthaean nature of much of Mt. 5.32; Matthew has included the brief statement of principle among his examples of the 'fulfilment' of the law in ch. 5, as well as the full Marcan controversy in ch. 19 (cf. *MLM*, pp. 290f.).

Schrenk, G., Βιάζομαι, *TDNT*, I, pp. 609-14.
Danker, F.W., 'Luke 16.16—an Opposition Logion', *JBL* 77 (1958), pp. 231-43.
Bammel, E., 'Is Luke 16, 16-18 of Baptist's Provenance?', *HTR* 51 (1958), pp. 101-106.
Schürmann, H., '"Wer daher eines dieser geringsten Gebote auflöst. . ."', *BZ* 4 (1960), 238-50 = *TU*, pp. 126-36.
Braumann, G., '"Dem Himmelreich wird Gewalt angetan"', *ZNW* 52 (1961), pp. 104-109.
Menoud, P.H., 'Le sens du verbe Βιάζεται dans Lc 16,16', in *Fs* B. Rigaux, (1970), pp. 207-12.
Kümmel, W.G., '"Das Gesetz und die Propheten gehen bis Johannes"', in *Fs* Stählin (1972), pp. 89-102.
Moore, W.E., 'Βιάζω, ἁρπάζω and Cognates in Josephus', *NTS* 21 (1975), pp. 519-43.
Catchpole, D.R., 'The Synoptic Divorce-Material as a Traditio-Historical Problem', *BJRL* 57 (1974-75), pp. 92-107.
Descamps, A., 'Les textes evangéliques sur le mariage', *RTL* 9 (1978) pp. 259-86, 11 (1980), pp. 3-50.

16.19-31. So the two Matthaean contexts, the alms-Mammon context in Matthew 6 with Matthew 5 behind it, and the fire-torment context in Matthew 18, combine to beckon Luke into a familiar path—that of the blessedness of the poor, and the woes of the rich, which he has already trodden in the Beatitudes and Woes, and the Magnificat. We have in addition a more accidental echo of Matthew in the coming Parable. Luke's dogs (κύνες), and the poor man's wish to be filled ἀπὸ τῶν πιπτόντων ἀπὸ τῆς τραπέζης of the rich man, recall the κυνάρια of Mt. 15.27, eating ἀπὸ τῶν ψιχίων τῶν πιπτόντων ἀπὸ τῆς τραπέζης of their masters (Mk diff.).

So Matthew suggests a parable in which the ungodly ends in the torments of hell for his lack of mercy (18.33f.), in eternal fire for his treatment of the little ones (18.7-10), for his preferring Mammon to God (6.24). Dives and Lazarus can be seen emerging in Luke's imagination. But another familiar OT text has also made its contribution, and that is Isaiah 61, which has already left its mark on Luke's programmatic sermon (4.18ff.) and his Beatitudes. There the prophet foretold the good news for the πτωχοί, the day of requital (ἀνταπόδοσις), to comfort (παρακαλέσαι) all who mourn. Many commentators note the absence of the idea of the reversal of fates in the rabbis, but it is there in Isaiah 61, and is already worked out in Luke's Beatitudes and Woes. Those who hitherto had oppressed Israel would now (said the prophet) stand and feed their flocks: 'you shall be called the priests of the Lord,. . . you shall eat the wealth of the nations. . . Instead of your shame you shall have a double portion, instead of dishonour you shall rejoice. . . yours shall be everlasting joy' (vv. 1-7). Luke knew what this meant. The πτωχός (poor-and-faithful, as in Isaiah) would be comforted (παρακαλεῖται, v. 25) for his shame and dishonour in this world; the rich would weep and mourn. The reversing of fates, the requital which is the essence of Luke's parable, is absent from Matthew, but is present in Isaiah. The only thing that the prophet has not made plain, but which the evangelic tradition had, was that the reversal would not take place in this world, but in the world to come.

The parable is in many ways characteristic once more of Luke. It is an *illustration-parable*, without a heavenly counterpart; like the Samaritan, the Rich Fool, and the Pharisee and Publican—all in Luke, and no instance of the genre elsewhere. It is full of *colourful touches*: purple and fine linen, a portico-gate, sores, dogs, crumbs, brothers. The pathetic detail of Lazarus's desire to be filled with the dogs' food reminds us of the Lucan Prodigal's desire to be filled with the pigs' food. The central character is said to be a rich man, but he is only rich to Luke's *middle-class* standards of wealth. He is clothed in purple and fine linen (ἐνεδιδύσκετο πορφύραν καὶ βύσσον), such as the good wife of Proverbs provided for herself (ἐκ δὲ βύσσου καὶ πορφύρας ἑαυτῇ ἐνδύματα, Prov. 31.22). He entertains daily (Lucan εὐφραίνεσθαι), just as the Rich Fool says to his soul, εὐφραίνου; and he has a portico-gate, a πυλῶν to his house, like Mary the mother of John Mark in Acts—a far cry from Matthew's millionaires. He is a *two-sided* character too, like the Lucan Steward, or Judge, or Publican, and in contrast to Matthew's caricatures (§4). He is a bad man in that he neglects the poor; he is a good man in that even in hell he remembers his brothers. Lazarus, on the other side, is a Lucan *scandalous hero*: where his predecessors have the wealthy and reputable for heroes of their parables, Luke includes a Samaritan and a publican, an embezzling steward, a widow and a beggar.

The *eschatology* is Lucan too. In Mark and Matthew, life ends with the coming of the Son of Man, but in the new Lucan parables people just die—the Rich Fool in ch. 12, poor and rich alike here (a sure sign too that the parable is late). Angels bear Lazarus away at his death, just as 'they' require the rich fool's soul, and welcome the prudent children of light into eternal habitations—a feature not found in the other Gospels. Lazarus's blessedness is pictured as reclining next to Abraham, in the position of honour at the paradisal banquet ('in Abraham's bosom', cf. Jn 13.23), while Dives beholds from afar in anguish; like the Jews in 13.28, who will weep to see Abraham and the patriarchs and Gentiles from every quarter at table in God's kingdom, and themselves cast out. Luke seems also to have Abraham and Lazarus in a sub-division of Sheol, divided by a chasm from the area where Dives is in torment; just as Paradise is implied to be in the underworld in 23.43, 'Today you will be with me in Paradise'. If so, this would be at variance with paradise being in the third heaven in 2 Cor. 12.2, 4.

The *five* brothers are a Lucan handful; cf. five sparrows, five yoke of oxen, five in a house (§12). The replies of Abraham to Dives are the *themes of Acts*. With 'they have Moses and the prophets: let them hear them', cf. Acts 15.21, 'Moses has had in every city those who preach him, for he is read every sabbath in the synagogues'. With 'Neither will they be convinced though one should rise from the dead', cf. Acts 2, 3, 4, and many chapters on to 28. The central doctrine of the parable is the *blessing of the poor* and the woeful *fate of the rich*, without specification of their respective virtue and vice, faith or unbelief; exactly as we find in the Lucan Beatitudes and Woes, and in the Magnificat, and not elsewhere in the Gospels. The best we can say is that Dives' contempt of the poor is portrayed, and that 'one of these little ones' in 17.2 refers to Lazarus, and assumes his faith from Mt. 18.6.

The cumulative weight of these features is decisive for Lucan authorship; and the words listed below as not uncharacteristic are a high proportion (31%). The only feature seriously alleged against this are the two historic presents, ὁρᾷ in v. 23 (Rehkopf, p. 99), and λέγει in v. 29. But Luke occasionally uses the historic present with verbs of seeing in dramatic situations (βλέπει, 24.12R; cf. Mk 16.2 θεωροῦσιν;

θεωρεῖ Acts 10.11); and he has historic present verbs of saying seven other times in the Gospel (three in parables), and eleven times in Acts (Neirynck, *MA*, p. 229).

H. Gressmann adduced as a possible background to the parable the Egyptian story of similar reversal of fates, which is known in Jewish literature (*j.Sanh.* 6.23c/*j.Hag.* 2.27d). Jeremias (pp. 182-87) and many commentators rely on this as a contemporary folk-tale on which Jesus drew, with its poor scholar by the streams of paradise, watched by the erstwhile rich publican unable to reach the water. It is, however, very doubtful if we should accept such influence. The Jewish evidence is in the Palestinian Talmud, and neither the features of the Egyptian story (e.g. stress on the contrast of the two funerals), nor those of the Jewish version (e.g. the publican, the streams) recur in Luke. Jeremias appeals to the Great Supper as further evidence of Jesus' familiarity with the tale, but I have questioned it there also. Still less should we follow him in laying all the stress on the 'second half' of the story ('The parable is about the five brothers', p. 186).

A. Feuillet stresses the link with the Unjust Steward; but it is pressing the point to speak of the debtors of 16.5ff. as poor, and, as O. Glombitza rightly says, account needs to be given of the difficult intervening verses.

Gressmann, H., 'Vom reichen Mann und armen Lazarus: Eine literargeschichtliche Studie', *Abhandlungen der königlichen phil. Akademie der Wissenschaften*, phil.-hist. Kl. 7 (Berlin, 1918) (not seen).
Derrett, J.D.M., 'Fresh Light on St Luke xvi: II Dives and Lazarus and the Preceding Sayings', *NTS* 7 (1960), pp. 364-80, = *Law*, pp. 78-99.
Cadbury, H.J., 'A Proper Name for Dives', *JBL* 81 (1962), pp. 399-402.
Grobel, K., '. . . Whose Name was Neves', *NTS* 10 (1964), pp. 373-82.
Evans, C.F., 'Uncomfortable Words—V ". . . Neither will they be Convinced"', *ET* 81 (1970), pp. 228-31.
Glombitza, O., 'Der reiche Mann und der arme Lazarus', *NT* 12 (1970), pp. 166-80.
Dupont, J., 'L'après-mort dans l'œuvre de Luc', *RTL* 3 (1972), pp. 3-21.
Feuillet, A., 'La parabole du mauvais riche et du pauvre Lazare (Lc 16, 19-31)', *NRT* 101 (1979), pp. 212-23.
Schnider, F. and W. Stenger, 'Die offene Tür und die unüberschreitbare Kluft', *NTS* 25 (1979), pp. 273-83.
Kremer, J., 'Der arme Lazarus: Lazarus, der Freund Jesu', in *Fs* Dupont (1985), pp. 571-84.

16.19 Hapaxes: ἄνθρωπός-τις*, πλούσιος* (cf. 16.1), εὐφραίνεσθαι*, καθ'ἡμέραν*. Hapaxes: ἐνδιδύσκειν, πορφύρα, βύσσος. λαμπρῶς cf. -ός, 23.11R; Acts 10.30, -ότης Acts 26.3. Marshall, 'A costly mantle of wool such as would be worn by royalty', in defiance of Prov. 31.22, which he cites.

16.20 πτωχός, τις with a noun*, ὀνόματι*. Hapaxes: ἑλκοῦν, πυλῶν (×5

Acts). ἐβέβλητο plup. pass. Lazarus is the only named character in a Gospel parable; but cf. Jerusalem and Jericho, 10.30, and Zacchaeus, Mary and Martha named in Lucan stories. Jeremias (p. 185) suggests that the meaning of the name, 'God helps', explains it; but it is not likely that Luke's Greek readers would have the Hebrew to translate the full form of the name, Eleazar, let alone the apocopated Lazarus. Derrett (*NTS* [1961], p. 7) suggested an identification with Eliezer, Abraham's servant, which gives a link, though of a far-fetched kind, and the evidence from *Exod.R.* is very late. The name remains a surd, for which however, the Isaiah 61 reference provides a possible solution. There the poor are promised, 'You shall be called priests of the Lord'; and the first of Israel's priests was called Eleazar. The name was Graecized to Lazarus at the period (Vermes, pp. 53, 190). It is conceivable that we have an echo of this in the name Finaeus (= Phinehas?, Ps.-Cyprian, *de Pasch. comp.* 17)/Phinees (Priscillian, Tract 9), since Phinehas is a pair to Eleazar as a priest's name: p^{75} Νέυης, and sah. Nineveh, would be progressive corruptions (cf. Cadbury, *JBL* [1962]).

16.21 ἐπιθυμεῖν*, τράπεζα, πλούσιος*, ἀλλὰ-καὶ, ἐρχόμενος + verb*. Hapaxes: κύων, ἕλκος, ἐπιλείχειν. ἀπό. . .τραπέζης cf. Mt. 15.27, χορτασθῆναι cf. 6.21, + ἀπό 15.16.

16.22 ἐγένετο + inf.*, πτωχός, Αβρααμ, δὲ-καὶ*, πλούσιος*. Hapax: ἀποφέρειν. Luke is often thought to have concepts of life after death which were out of line with contemporary orthodoxy. But this is doubtful, as ideas were in considerable flux at the time (cf. Cavallin). Angels escorting the dead are testified from the 2nd Century (SB II, pp. 233ff.); Abraham welcomes the Jewish martyrs in *4 Macc.* 13.17; the division at death of the righteous and the wicked in Sheol is in *1 Enoch* 22, with torments for the latter beginning at once, cf. Wis. 3.1. But Luke's infernal paradise (which would contradict 2 Cor. 12.1ff.) is not clear from this text; *TDNT* παράδεισος.

16.23 ἐπάρας-τοὺς-ὀφθαλμούς, ὑπάρχειν*, Αβρααμ. τῷ ᾅδῃ, cf. τοῦ ᾅδου 10.15R. ὁρᾷ, see above.

16.24 καὶ-αὐτός nom.*, φωνεῖν = cry out*, εἶπεν, Αβρααμ, πέμπειν*. Hapaxes: βάπτειν, ἄκρον, καταψύχειν. ἐλέησον × 4. Lucan interest in parts of the body: ἄκρον δακτύλου, γλῶσσα, κόλπος. Dives is saying within himself, 'I have Abraham to my father' (3.8).

16.25 εἶπεν-δὲ*, Αβρααμ, τεκνόν, voc., μιμνήσκεσθαι, ἀπολαμβάνειν*, ὁμοίως*, νῦν*. cf. τὰ ἀγαθά μου 12.18L; παρακαλεῖσθαι 6.24/Mt. 5.4Q. The parable could have closed here, but at the cost of Luke's subtlety. Evans (*ET*, p. 81) sees, against Jeremias, that the second half is ancillary to the first; and in fact takes up the theme of the law and the prophets (v. 16; Ellis, p. 201).

16.26 ταῦτα, στηρίζειν. διαβαίνειν. διαπερᾶν: compound δια-verbs 20/19/ 44+46. καὶ ἐν πᾶσι τούτοις, cf. 24.21, καὶ σὺν πᾶσι τούτοις.

16.27 εἶπεν-δὲ*, ἐρωτᾶν*, πάτερ*, πέμπειν*, εἰς-τὸν-οἶκον + gen. ἐρωτᾶν-ἵνα 7.36, + final clause 0/1/4+1, ἐρωτῶ-σε 14.18f. L.

16.28 ἔχω first word*, διαμαρτύρεσθαι, καὶ-αὐτοί*, τόπος.

16.29 Αβρααμ, ἔχω first word*, Μωϋσῆς-καὶ-οἱ-προφῆται*. ἀκουσάτωσαν 3rd pers. impv. ἀκ. αὐτῶν, cf. Deut. 18.15ff. 'αὐτοῦ ἀκούσεσθε. . .ἀναστήσω a prophet ἐκ τῶν ἀδελφῶν αὐτῶν, and the man who does not ἀκούσῃ whatever that prophet says. . . I will punish him'. This text may have found an echo in Luke's mind for the second half of the parable. λέγει see above. Moses-and-the-prophets is not a rabbinic expression (SB IV 1, pp. 415-17).

16.30 εἶπεν, οὐχί, Αβρααμ, τις, πορεύεσθαι, μετανοεῖν.

16.31 εἶπεν-δὲ*, εἰ. . .οὐ, Μωϋσῆς-καὶ-οἱ-προφῆται*, τις, πείθεσθαι. Evans (*ET*, pp. 81, 231) notes the closeness to the Acts theme of the rejection of the resurrection, and suggests Lucan authorship in consequence. I take it that this verse has affected the writing of John 11, and not vice versa (cf. Barrett, *John*, pp. 46, 389). J. Kremer (*Fs* Dupont) argues in the opposite sense, Lazarus being the only name introduced into a parable: but then it is also the only name of a sufferer in John.

b. *Faithfulness*, 17.1-10

17.1. Luke has now presented his version of Mt. 18.23ff., both as a parable of the remission of debt (16.1-13), and as an exposition of the wealthy in torment (16.19-31), and he moves on backwards up the Matthaean scroll. In Mt. 18.1-22 Jesus teaches 'the disciples', first about humility (vv. 2-5) and not scandalizing those young in the faith (vv. 6-10), then on shepherding the lost sheep (vv. 11-14), and then on the treatment of offenders, rebuking them (vv. 15-20), or forgiving them if offended oneself (vv. 21-23). So Luke begins, 'And he said to his disciples', omits the scene with the child, which he has already given in its Marcan context (9.46-48; Mk 9.33-37), and so reaches Mt. 18.6f., 'Whoever shall scandalise one of these little ones. . . ' Without the previous section this is too abrupt, so he reverses the order of the two verses, taking Mt. 18.7 first: 'It is necessary that scandals should come, but woe to the man through whom the scandal comes'. He replaces Matthew's ἀνάγκη with the impressive ἀνένδεκτον (cf. 13.33 οὐκ ἐνδέχεται), which results in a clumsy double negative, 'impossible. . . not' (Marshall).

17.2. He then moves back to Mt. 18.6, which again runs more smoothly with a reversal of order, 'It is to his advantage that a millstone. . . ' (18.6b) being placed before 'he scandalise one of these little ones. . . ' (18.6a), and linked by 'rather than that'. 'These little ones' have no clear context in Luke: he is thinking of Lazarus (Grundmann). The unnatural phrase has simply been imported from the Matthaean context, though the qualifying 'who believe in me' has been dropped. With these changes of order and improvements, he takes his eye off the scroll, and in creep some phrases from the ever more familiar Mark, εἰ, περικεῖται (περὶ) for Matthew's κρεμάσθῃ, '(thrown) into the sea' for Matthew's 'drowned in (its) depth'. But both Mark and Matthew have μύλος ὀνικός, an asses' millstone, a great heavy stone requiring animals to move it, for which practical Luke substitutes λίθος μυλικός, a hand-millstone turned by women; such would be much more easily handled, and equally effective.

17.3. The rest of Matthew's paragraph was concerned with being cast into hell, and Luke has had enough of hell for the moment; nor can he easily use the Lost Sheep, which he has taken at 15.3ff. So he presses on to the topic of offences: Mt. 18.15, 'If your brother sins. . . ' But Matthew's zeal for church order—first a private call, then with two churchwardens, then a public hearing in church, followed if necessary by an excommunication—is just the kind of thing to leave Luke cold, and he contents himself with a personalized 'rebuke him, and if he repents, forgive him'. Matthew's 'If your brother sins' meant 'if a Christian in your community misbehaves', and the disciple (= apostle) was then authorized to bind or loose (Mt. 18.18). But Luke is as little interested in excommunication procedures as he is in divorce regulations or food rules. To him religion was a personal matter, and 'if your brother sins' implies 'against you' (17.4). He prefaces the saying with a Lucan personal warning, προσέχετε ἑαυτοῖς, changes Matthew's legal-sounding ἔλεγξον for a Lucan personal ἐπιτίμησον, 'reprove', and closes with the prospect of Lucan repentance and Lucan forgiveness. The Matthaean context leaves its traces behind: first in the reader's sense of disorientation as he moves from 17.1f., where he is not to offend the poor, the 'little ones', to 17.3f., where he is concerned with rebuking and forgiving; and second in a typical instance of Lucan fatigue (§19.2). Matthew in 18.15 used the weak aorist ἁμαρτήσῃ, which Luke improved at 17.3 to the strong ἁμάρτῃ; but in 17.4 he lapses back into Matthew's ἁμαρτήσῃ.

17.4. The personalizing of Mt. 18.15 means that the whole
following passage, including 18.19f. on corporate prayer, is out of
context, and Luke moves on to 18.21f., where the topic of forgiveness
is resumed. 'How often', asks the Matthaean Peter, 'shall my brother
sin against me and I forgive him? Till seven times?'; and he receives a
Matthaean hyperbole in reply, 'seventy times seven'. Luke rewrites
the sentence in Jesus' mouth in parallel with 17.3, but retains
Matthew's future (ἀφήσω) in his ἀφήσεις, now a command, in place
of the normal Lucan imperative (cf. ἄφες, 17.3). He does not like
Matthew's astronomical figures, and as usual brings the business
down to earth: 'seven times in the day' is not less strict than 490
times (in a lifetime)—not that either figure is meant literally—and
has the advantage both of being imaginable, and of being scriptural
(Ps. 119.164). Of the new language, ἐπιστρέφειν, μετανοεῖν and their
combination (Acts 3.19; 26.20) are all Lucan.

17.5f. The evangelist has now arrived at the Debtor parable again
(Mt. 18.23ff.), and has only four verses to his credit from Mt. 18.1-22;
so he turns back to Matthew 17. He does not wish to teach his church
to subscribe to the Jerusalem Temple, so Mt. 17.24ff. is of little
interest; and all the rest of the chapter is Marcan, save the saying on
faith in Mt. 17.20, 'If you have faith as a grain of mustard seed, you
will say to this mountain, move hence. . . ' Here, Luke feels, is the
theme to expound, πίστις. It is as faith*fulness* that he goes to expound
the saying, with his Servant parable; but of course the meaning of the
word in Mt. 17.20, and so in Lk. 17.6, is 'faith', belief that prayer will
work miracles. It is in consequence of this simple ambiguity that the
reader receives the impression of a paragraph of staccato, unrelated
elements.

A further sign of the Matthaean background is the change from
Luke's normal 'his disciples' in 17.1 to 'the apostles' in v. 5
(elsewhere in the Gospel used only at their calling, sending and in the
Passion). But 'the disciples' of Matthew 18 are not any disciples, but
the Twelve who are given with Peter the power to bind and to loose;
Luke has been aware of this, and now clarifies their identity.
(Perhaps neither evangelist thought that miracles of the dimension of
Lk. 17.6 could be done by rank-and-file Christians). Luke introduces
the saying with a Lucan foil introduction (§1.4), 'The apostles said to
the Lord, Increase our πίστις', of which almost every word is Lucan.
He has also to amend the wording itself, for Matthew's 'this

mountain' referred to the mount of Transfiguration, and Luke's Jesus is on the Galilee-Samaria border (17.11), However, the saying has a near duplicate at Mt. 21.21, 'If you have faith and never doubt, you will not only do what has been done to this fig-tree (συκῆ), but even if you say to this mountain, Be taken up and cast into the sea, it will be done'. Luke's 'If you have faith as a grain of mustard seed' comes from Mt. 17.20; the συκαμῖνος and the moving to the sea from Matthew 21. The sycamine is not actually the same as the fig-tree, but of the same family: Luke makes the change because the sycamine is bigger—*m. BB* 2.11 implies a span of 25m—and its removal thus more impressive. Its planting in the sea would be more impressive still—a miracle indeed. The combination of being rooted up and being planted also occurs in Mt. 15.13, whence Luke may have introduced it here.

Faith, to Luke, however, is more to do with plodding on than with working wonders, and he turns now to expound the theme of faithfulness in his own words. Matthew had spoken of the disciple as caring for (his Master's) lost sheep (18.11-14), and although the verb ποιμαίνειν does not occur there, it does come in the Isaiah 61 passage which we have seen to underlie 16.19ff., and ploughing beside it: 'And aliens shall come keeping your sheep (ποιμαίνοντες), and foreigners shall be your ploughmen' (ἀροτῆρες, 61.5). So Luke sets off with his standard 'Which of you hav(ing). . . ', and continues '. . . a servant *plough*ing or *keeping sheep*. . .?' He keeps to the familiar Lucan level of *restricted wealth* (§5): the master has only one man to plough, keep sheep, cook and serve his dinner—so unlike the Matthaean householders with their talents and their major-domos. He sets his seal with the characteristic Lucan note of *urgency*, which has marked so many parables (§3): 'Come *at once* and sit down at table'—cf. 'Go out quickly', 'Sit down quickly', 'that they may open to him at once' (12.36). The scene echoes the parable of 12.36ff. in a number of other ways: 'Blessed are those *servants*. . . he will *gird himself* and sit them down, and will *come and serve* them (παρελθὼν διακονήσει)'. The same hand wrote both parables. Luke likes *eating-and-drinking* too; and *thanks* are a theme very congenial to him (χάρις 0/0/8+17)—'what thanks have you?', 'he is kind to the unthankful', 'he fell. . . giving him thanks'. The tone of the teaching has to our liberal ears a *slightly unhealthy self-abasement*: 'When you have done all. . . say, We are unprofitable servants'—like the Lucan steward who was flogged lightly for what he did not know was wrong, or the Lucan thief who felt that he deserved to be crucified. There is an echo of Matthew's Talents in the δοῦλοι ἀχρεῖοι (Mt. 25.30), but the meaning and the substance of the parable seem to be Lucan in every way.

If even vv. 5f. and 7-10 seem to lack a genuine connection, what are we to say of the unity of the whole paragraph? We can of course reply that it is a rump of Matthaean logia, with a Lucan parable tacked on; so what unity can be expected? Nonetheless, our experience has been that throughout the Journey Luke has taken a topic for each of his trios of pericopae; and it appears proper to look for the same thing here too. In 16.16 he introduced (unnecessarily) the idea of the gospel as a step beyond the law; so perhaps this idea has been in his mind throughout 16.14-17.19. Deuteronomy and Isaiah told us to care for the poor; it is the gospel which elevates this command to a criterion of salvation. Forgiveness is occasionally counselled in the Old Testament (e.g. Ecclus 28.2): it is the gospel which expects forgiveness to be indefinite. Judaism seemed to Luke a require a circumscribed righteousness of tithes and fasting, mint and rue; the gospel lifted our eyes to judgment and the love of God, with whom we cannot justify ourselves, but are unprofitable servants. Its concern is not with law but with faith.

17.1 εἶπεν-δὲ-πρὸς*, τοῦ + inf.*, πλήν*. Hapaxes: ἀνένδεκτον, (σκάνδαλα).

17.2 (περί). Hapaxes: λυσιτελεῖ, μυλικός, (περικεῖσθαι). περί is read at Mt. 18.6 by ℵ B etc., and is accepted by N-A²⁶, but regarded as an assimilation by Greeven, who reads εἰς with most MSS. For ῥίπτειν cf. 4.35R, ×3 in Acts. For μύλος cf. Bauer; Luke thinks of grinding as a job for women, 17.35.

17.3 προσέχετε ἑαυτοῖς, ἐπιτιμᾶν, μετανοεῖν.

17.4 ἡμέρα, ἐπιστρέφειν, μετανοεῖν. ἐπιστρέφειν + μετανοεῖν, Acts 3.19; 26.20; ἐ. + πρὸς, Acts 9.40. Bultmann (p. 151), followed by Lührmann (pp. 111ff.), Schulz (pp. 320ff.) and almost all opinion, takes Luke to be close to the Q formulation, which has been expanded by Matthew, or his church, into a set of rules. The view assumes that all development is in the same direction; it ignores Luke's evident dislike of church legislation, e.g. in omitting the Marcan ruling on divorce, which is much fuller than Lk. 16.18; and the general absence of such rulings from his Gospel.

17.5 εἶπαν, οἱ-ἀπόστολοι*, ὁ-κύριος = Jesus*, προστιθέναι.

17.6 εἶπεν-δὲ*, ὁ-κύριος = Jesus*, φυτεύειν. Hapaxes: συκαμῖνος, ἐκριζοῦν.

εἰ ἔχετε may be a reminiscence of Mk 11.22 א D etc., cf. H.-W. Bartsch, *NTS* 27, p. 587; but Luke prefers εἰ 55/36/55+36 to ἐὰν 66/35/29+11. For the sycamine, etc., see C.-H. Hunzinger, *TDNT*, VII, pp. 289f. It is the sycomore, fig-mulberry, which has the reputation for living six centuries, and being deep-rooted: but others besides Luke in the ancient world seem to have been in two minds which was which.

17.7 ἔχειν* opening parable, ἀναπεσεῖν. Hapaxes: ἀροτριοῦν, ποιμαίνειν. In common with 12.36f.: δοῦλος, περιζωννύναι, παρελθὼν, διακονεῖν, εὐθέως.

17.8 οὐχὶ, ἑτοιμάζειν, δειπν-, eat-and-drink (2), μετὰ-ταῦτα*, σύ after verb*.

17.9 μὴ interrog., χάρις*, τὰ + part., διατάσσειν (cf. 3.13; Acts 23.31).

17.10 καὶ also, τά + part., διατάσσειν. Hapax: ἀχρεῖος. οὕτως applying a parable, cf. 14.33; 15.7, 10 (Marshall).

Minear (*JBL* [1974]) takes the parable to refer to the attitude required of apostles, who were pastors and ploughmen (1 Cor. 9), and should be faithful servants (1 Cor. 4). But surely Jesus did not intend them to be such, and Luke would not be interested in the duties of men long dead? Also his separation of v. 10 from vv. 7-9, 'The Parable of the Unrelenting Master', seems a little pedantic.

Jeremias (pp. 193) takes the parable as a challenge to the Pharisees, etc., as the apostles would not have owned farms and slaves; but the parabolist may be allowed some licence! He suggests, on the basis of 2 Sam. 6.22 LXX, that ἀχρεῖοι means 'unworthy', a claim widely repeated. But the meaning there is 'abased, contemptible'; cf. *Ep. Jer.* 17; Isa. 33.9 Sym., Th.; Ezek. 17.6 Th.

Minear, P.S., 'A Note on Luke 17.7-10', *JBL* 93 (1974), 82-87.

c. *The Ten Lepers*, 17.11-19

17.11. Matthew had added to his faith logion of 17.20 a topographical note, 'And as they were gathering in Galilee...' (17.22); and this encourages Luke to remind his reader that that is where his gentle Journey is still in progress—'And it came to pass as he was going to Jerusalem, that he was passing along the frontier of (διὰ μέσον) Samaria and *Galilee*'. Luke has had Jesus moving slowly eastwards along the Samaria-Galilee border since the unpleasantness of 9.52-6 (*q.v.*). Mark had already sent him on his way at Mk 9.30, 33 (cf. 10.1), but Luke cannot have him actually leave Galilee till he has finished with the Galilean matter in Matthew; and it is this loyalty to his predecessors which has caused him to lose his reputation as a geographer with the wise and understanding. But the end is nearly in sight now, with Matthew 16, from which he made the great leap forward, almost in view. A reminder is timely, for once the Matthaean material is done (18.8), Jesus will soon be in Jericho (18.35), and at the gates of Jerusalem.

The remainder of Matthew 17 is Marcan, and already used: the Transfiguration and the Possessed Boy (Lk. 9.28-43). However, Luke is looking for a third pericope on the topic of the law and the gospel, and he feels drawn into supplying a substitute for the healing, as he has done so often before (see on Lk. 7). Jesus had laid down the permanent validity of the law in Mt. 5.17-19, and the extra required by the gospel in 5.20-48; and he had then illustrated the principle in his own healing ministry. In Mt. 8.1-4 he had healed a leper, telling him to report to the priest with his offering, as laid down in Lev. 14; in Mt. 8.5-13 he had healed a Gentile. It is this combination of faithfulness to the law, and graciousness beyond it, which Luke is in quest of. Now two features suggest that Luke substitute the Matthew 8 complex for the Matthew 17 story. One is their strong similarity. Matthew 8: 'As he was coming down from the mountain, great crowds followed him; and lo, a leper approaching worshipped him... A centurion approached him, saying, Lord, my boy is laid at home paralysed, terribly tormented...' Mt. 17.9, 14, 'And as he was coming down from the mountain... when they came to the crowd, a man approached him, kneeling to him and saying, Lord, have mercy on my son, for he is moonstruck and suffers badly'. The second is that Mt. 11.5 told Luke that Jesus had healed more than one leper ('lepers are cleansed'), just as it had vouched for the raising of more than one dead person. Luke has, as we saw, substituted in ch. 7 for all the healings on Galilaean territory in Mt. 8-9 but the leper, and he feels it proper to supply that lack now.

Luke's narrative is a compound of these elements, and of motifs of his own, including the story of the healing of Naaman, to which he alluded in the Nazareth sermon in 4.27. He mentions the border between Samaria and Galilee because he means to introduce the healing of one beyond the bounds of Israel and its covenanted law; he has had a full Gentile with the Centurion's servant, and the location of the Journey supplies the suggestion that the man should be a Samaritan. Luke himself is sympathetic to Samaritans. The rejection in the Samaritan village was his interpretation of Matthew's 'enter no town of the Samaritans' (see on 9.52ff.); he has included a merciful Samaritan in ch. 10, and a successful mission in Acts 8.

17.12-19. There are ten lepers because Luke is fond of the one-in-ten proportion—one coin lost out of ten, one faithless servant out of ten, five hundred dinars and fifty, one thankful leper out of ten (§12).

The lepers meet Jesus as he is going into the village, and stand far off, because Lev. 13.46 directs that they dwell apart, outside the camp—and no doubt this was how such hapless people lived. They lift up their voice like the Lucan woman in the crowd at 11.27, or the apostles at Acts 4.24 (also in petition). They say, 'Jesus, master, have mercy on (ἐλέησον) us', because in Mt. 17.15 the father says, 'Lord, have mercy on (ἐλέησον) my son'; and Jesus replies, 'Depart and show your*selves to the priests*' because in Mt. 8.4 (= Mk 1.44) he said, 'Go show yourself to the priest'. In the earlier story the man was cleansed before the command to go and show himself, but Naaman was not healed until he had obeyed the prophet's word: so now, as they obey and go, they are cleansed. One of them returns (ὑπέστρεψεν, v. 15) glorifying God with a loud voice, as Naaman returned (ἐπέστρεψεν) to Elisha and said, 'Lo, I know that there is no God in all the earth but in Israel' (4 Kgdms 5.15). He falls at Jesus' feet, like Matthew's leper (προσεκύνει), and Matthew's father (γονυπετῶν, 17.14), all *before* the miracle: falling at the feet is more dramatic in Luke than kneeling, as with Sapphira (Acts 5.10) and Cornelius (Acts 10.25). He thanks Jesus (v. 16) like Naaman again, who said 'and now accept a thank-offering' (εὐλογίαν *ibid.*); and he is a foreigner like Naaman too (ἀλλογενής). We have seen the poor and their comforting from Isaiah 61 in Lazarus, and the ploughing and shepherding of Isaiah 61 in the Servant of all work—perhaps Isa. 61.5 has been influential here too, 'And there shall come ἀλλογενεῖς. . .' The Nazareth sermon already foreshadowed a future when the Jews would give no thanks for Christ's works, but faith would be found among strangers—beginning from Samaria (Acts 8). Mt. 17.17 bemoaned Israel as a faithless generation, while Mt. 8.10 spoke of such faith as the Gentile's not being found in Israel; so Luke concludes 'Rise and go: your faith has saved you', as he did at 7.50.

The story has seemed to many e.g. Bultmann (p. 33), Creed, Pesch (*Taten*, pp. 114-34)—to be an elaboration of the Leper story in Mark 1. Marshall maintains its historicity, but it is difficult to deny not merely that the story has been created, but that the creation is by Luke. The proportion of vocabulary congenial to Luke is particularly high—45%. So are the Lucan themes: the Naaman echoes from 4.27, the faith of the foreigner/Samaritan, thankfulness, the one-in-ten proportion. Marshall says it is untypical of Luke to have doublets in his narrative, but this is not so: he has two raisings from death, and two exorcisms, and two missions.

Hans-Dieter Betz (*JBL* [1971]) has proposed a possible account of the growth of the story from an oldest layer of the healing of ten lepers, one of whom was thankful; but no evidence can be offered for such reconstructions, and they ignore the Lucan nature of the whole fabric. His claim that the church is interested in a salvation beyond the healing is right: such was the interest of Luke, e.g. 19.11. There is an exhaustive discussion of the pericope in W. Bruners's monograph, in which credit is given to Luke for his full part in the creation of the present story: 'Luke is the author of the whole narrative' (p. 298). Bruners is not misled by the claims of pre-Lucan language (see above, pp. 15ff.) which deceive even Fitzmyer.

17.11 καὶ-ἐγένετο*, ἐν-τῷ*, πορεύεσθαι, Ἰερουσαλήμ*, καὶ-αὐτός*, διέρχεσθαι*, μέσος. καὶ-ἐγένετο and Γαλιλαία are also in Mt. 19.1. Creed and others take διὰ μέσον as 'between', i.e. on the frontier. Conzelmann, 60ff, takes the verse as evidence of Luke's geographical ignorance, and is followed by many: but Rengstorf (hesitantly but correctly) sees that Luke means the plain of Jezreel.

17.12 τις + noun*, δέκα*, ἀνήρ*, ἔστην = stood*. Hapax: ἀπαντᾶν. cf. 10.38 ἐν δὲ τῷ πορεύεσθαι αὐτοὺς αὐτὸς εἰσῆλθεν εἰς κώμην τινά. πόρρω(θεν) 1/1/3.

17.13 καὶ-αὐτοί*, φωνή, ἐπιστάτα*. ἦραν φωνήν Acts 4.24, ἐπάρασα Lk. 11.27.

17.14 εἶπεν, πορεύεσθαι, ἑαυτούς, καὶ-ἐγένετο* ἐν τῷ. Hapax: ἐπιδεικνύναι (3/0/1+2). ὑπάγειν 19/15/5, but 8.42R: cf. Mt. 8.4; Mk 1.44. 'The priests' may imply Jewish and Samaritan priests.

17.15 ἰᾶσθαι*, ὑποστρέφειν*, φωνή, δοξάζειν-θεόν. φωνή-μεγάλη 3/4/7+6.

17.16 πεσεῖν-ἐπί, παρὰ-τοὺς-πόδας*, εὐχαριστεῖν, καὶ-αὐτὸς-ἦν*. ἔπεσεν ἐπὶ πρόσωπον 5.12R.

17.17 εἶπεν, οὐχί, δέκα*, ποῦ. οὐχί ℵ etc. Aland: οὐχ BL Greeven.

17.18 εὑρίσκειν + part.*, ὑποστρέφειν*, δόξα, ὁ-θεός. Hapax: ἀλλογενής. δοῦναι δ. τῷ θεῷ, cf. Acts 12.23 οὐκ ἔδωκε δ. τῷ θεῷ.

17.19 εἶπεν, ἀνιστάναι = get up*, πορεύεσθαι.

Betz, H.D., 'The Cleansing of the Ten Lepers (Luke 17:11-19)', *JBL* 90 (1971), pp. 314-28.

Bruners, W., *Die Reinigung der zehn Aussätzigen und die Heilung des Samariters* (Forschung zur Bibel, 23; Stuttgart, 1977).

44. The Coming of the Son of Man, 17.20–18.17

a. The Son of Man's Day, 17.20-37

Synopses and commentators (see below) tend to treat Lk. 17.20-37 as a development of Q, with a smoother parallel in Matthew 24. The problem with the Lucan passage is then in part to account for the harder sequence of thought (as well as for the verbal differences); but in part the difficulty is also to explain the presence of two verses which are not in Matthew 24 at all, but which have parallels in Matthew 16. Lk. 17.20-24 warns that there will be no signs of the Son of Man's coming (vv. 20-23), but it will be like lightning (v. 24), and in vv. 26-30 follow the Noah and Lot comparisons, which carry the same message of sudden judgment. But the thread of thought is apparently broken by v.25: 'But first *he must suffer many things*, and be rejected *from* this generation'. The closest parallel to this is Mt. 16.21R, 'he must... suffer many things from the elders and chief priests and scribes': for the significance of the ἀπό see above p. 00. Second, there is a wavering of the thought in vv. 31-33, especially v. 33. Down to v. 30 the message has been that the Son of Man's coming will be sudden and inescapable, and this is resumed with the Matthew 24 matter in vv. 34-37 on those taken and left, and on the vultures. But in v. 33 comes the surprising, '*Whoever* seeks to gain *his life shall lose it, and whoever loses* it will bring it to life'; there is surely hardly time or occasion for losing one's life when the Son of Man is arriving. Again the closest parallel is at Mt. 16.25, 'For whoever wishes to save his life shall lose it, and whoever loses his life for my sake shall find it'.

The reason for these 'intrusions', and for other features of the passage, is supplied by the Lucan policy which we have been tracing since Lk. 13.34f. Luke has been working his way back through the Matthaean scroll from Matthew 23, including, altering or amplifying all the additions which Matthew made to Mark. With Lk. 17.1-19 he has been treating Matthew 18 and 17, the latter rather scantily as it is mostly Marcan. So he has now reached Matthew 16 again, the point from which he began his long leap forward in Luke 12 (the leaven of the Pharisees, the saving of the soul, the Son of Man and his angels, the signs of the time). He has closed the gap, and can round off his prolongued 'Galilean journey' section: that is why (44) is the last non-Marcan piece, and Luke can rejoin Mark at Lk. 18.15=Mk 10.13. The Coming of the Son of Man is the topic of Mt. 16.27f., 'For the Son of Man will come in the glory of his Father... till they see the Son of Man coming in his kingdom'; and Luke expounds this with the aid of the matter which he has carefully left over from Matthew 24. He continues with the same theme right up to 18.17 (drawing in the Marcan Children): we shall find the Unjust Judge reaching its point with, 'But when the Son of Man comes, will he find faithfulness on earth?' (18.8), and the humility of the penitent and the child as the price of exaltation in the kingdom (18.14, 17).

17.20f. Luke begins from Matthew 16 also. In Mt. 16.1-4, the Pharisees and Sadducees asked (ἐπηρώτησαν) Jesus to show them a sign from heaven, and he answering said to them that an evil and adulterous generation sought for a sign, and would not be given one. Hence Luke's proem: 'And being *asked* (ἐπερωτηθείς) by *the Pharisees* when the kingdom of heaven was coming, *he answered them* and *said...*' He is slightly changing the meaning (§20). Matthew's Pharisees were asking for a sign to vindicate Jesus' claims: Luke's Pharisees are warned that there will be no sign of the coming of the kingdom. But at least we have an explanation for a third much canvassed problem of the section—why should an address to the disciples (v. 22) be introduced by a question from the Pharisees? The answer is, Luke was drawing on Mt. 16.1-4.

The presence of the Pharisees serves to clarify the structure of Lk. 17.20-37. It does not follow exactly the (excellent) order of Matthew 24 because Luke is drawing on Matthew 24 only secondarily: what is open before him is Matthew 16, and it is the order of that chapter which he follows. This may be set out in a table:

Matthew 16	Matthew 24	Luke 17
1 Pharisees ask a sign		20 Pharisees ask of kingdom
4 No sign	23f. Lo here or here	21 No sign. 'Lo here'
	26 Lo in the desert	22f. 'Lo there', do not go
	27 Like ἀστραπή	24 Like ἀστραπή
21 He must suffer		25 He must suffer
	37-39 As Noah	26f. As Noah

	40 Two in field	28-30 As Lot
	17f. Roof, go back	31f. Roof, go back, Lot's wife
25 Save/lose life		33 Save/lose life
	41 Two grinding	34f. Two in bed/grinding
	28 Vultures	37 Vultures
27f. Son of Man comes	44ff. Coming finds	18.8 Coming will he find?

The order is sufficiently close to Matthew 24 to make it likely that Luke referred to that, though the wording is not very close: I will suggest that variations from the two Matthaean passages arise from thoughts latent in them.

Mt. 16.4 said that no sign would be given to this generation, but by the end of the chapter Jesus is speaking of the Son of Man coming in his kingdom. Hence Luke's, 'being asked. . . when *the kingdom of God was coming*'—it is almost always God's kingdom in Luke. But the sort of signs which both evangelists are concerned with for the coming of the kingdom are nationalist revolts, the Judases and Theudases who had just found their disastrous climax in 66–70. So rather than use the misleadingly grand σημεῖον, Luke says the kingdom does not come by watching for it, παρατήρησις; and develops this from his predecessors' words on false Christs and prophets—Mk 13.21, ἴδε ὧδε ὁ χριστός, ἴδε ἐκεῖ; Mt. 24.23R ἰδοὺ ὧδε ὁ χριστός, ἢ ὧδε.

There is however a difference of emphasis between Matthew and Luke about the Lord's coming. Matthew wishes to warn his church against any false signs, but he is heart-whole in looking for Jesus' coming, and only occasionally implies the weakening doctrine that the kingdom is already here ('if I by the Spirit of God. . . ', 12.28). Luke also still looks for the Son of Man's coming (18.8; 21.34ff.; and long passages from the tradition), but there are many signs of his embarrassment over the delay, as Conzelmann has argued, and he adds a note of weak 'realised eschatology' here, as at 11.20, 'if I by the finger of God. . . ' Here as there the comment is to Pharisees: 'for, lo, the kingdom of God is in your midst'. Luke uses the hapax ἐντός rather than his usual ἐν μέσῳ, which might be more suited to disciples (22.27; 24.36) than to Pharisees.

17.22. Mt. 16.1-4 was a conversation with the Pharisees, but the words on the Son of Man's suffering and coming (16.21-28) are spoken to Jesus' disciples, so Luke now says, 'And he said to *the disciples*'. Matthew's words are unhappily direct: 'There are some of those standing here who will not taste of death till they see the Son of Man coming in his kingdom' (16.28). This is just the doctrine of the imminent Parousia which Luke now knows history to have falsified. Earlier he has glossed the Marcan version—Mk 9.1, . . . till they see the kingdom of God come in power'; Lk. 9.27, 'till they see the kingdom of God'. The omission of Mark's final phrase leaves open a 'realized' interpretation. Luke will again stress that the Lord's coming was not to be immediate at 19.11 and Acts 1.6f., but there too his meaning is partly veiled. This time he makes sure there is no misunderstanding. Jesus had told the disciples that the days would come when they would want to *see* one of the days of *the Son of Man*, but they would be disappointed. There never was any question of the Parousia in the disciples' lifetime. The rather clumsy phrase, 'one of the days of', arises from Luke's introduction of 'Days will come. . . ': in the days of persecution ahead they would comfort themselves with the thought of the days of blessedness after the Son of Man's coming. Unhappily, in v. 26 'the days of the Son of Man' means the period immediately *before* his Coming; but that meaning is excluded here. The conjunction of the coming of the Son of Man, the kingdom, and the expectation of the disciples' seeing them, makes it most likely that Luke is 'interpreting' Mt. 16.28 where these themes are concentrated; he is modifying them in the light of history.

17.23f. Luke justifies his amendment of Mt. 16.28 by drawing in the Lord's warning against those who may say, 'Lo here. . . ', a second time, just as they come a second time in Mt. 24.26. Matthew of course was speaking of *false* Christs, but Luke makes the words refer to the real Christ's return; so where Matthew warns the disciples not to 'go out' (into the desert), or to 'believe' (stories of inner rooms), Luke has to make changes to 'go away' and 'pursue', vague expressions for going to greet the Lord at his coming. Mt. 24.27 had gone on conveniently to speak of the suddenness and ubiquity of the Parousia: 'For just as the ἀστραπή comes forth from the east and shines as far as the west, so will be the Parousia of the Son of Man'. Perhaps Matthew meant by ἀστραπή the light (Lk. 11.36) of the sun, which really does shine forth from east to west: if he meant the lightning, his observation was defective. But Luke can see that lightning is an ideal image for the suddenness of the event, which is alone his concern: he writes ἀστραπὴ ἀστράπτουσα that there be no mistake, and has it (seen) to flash 'from one end of the world to the other'. He drops Matthew's Parousia, also, a word that had only caused trouble (and which Paul had dropped in middle life), replacing it with 'the Son of Man in his day'—Lucan ἡμέρα.

17.25. Then, returning to Matthew 16 he adds, 'But first the Son of Man *must suffer many things* and be rejected *from* this generation' (Mt. 16.21; cf. Lk. 9.22 with the same ἀπό). He has another πρῶτον δέ at 9.61QD. The intrusion is not so inapt as is sometimes thought: between the present phase of the kingdom 'in your midst' and the lightning-like Day of the Son of Man must come the Passion. Nonetheless, it is without force for Luke's own time, and its interruption of the themes of Matthew 24 is a sure sign of the presence of Matthew 16 on Luke's table as he writes. 'This generation' is an abbreviation for the elders, etc., who feature in other forms of the saying; it is likely to stem from the 'wicked and adulterous generation' which we have already noted from Mt. 16.4.

17.26f. The principal addition that Matthew had made to the Marcan prophecy of the Son of Man's coming had been in a series of scriptural parallels, beginning with Noah. Luke follows him with enthusiasm. He cuts the repetitious 'For as were the days of Noah, so will be the Parousia of the Son of Man. For as they were in those days before the flood. . . ', to a brisker, 'And as it happened in *the days of Noah, so shall it be* also in the days *of the Son of Man*'. 'As it happened', 'in the days of' and 'also' are all Lucan expressions—'in the days of Herod the king', 'in the days of Elijah', 'in the days of the census'. Matthew emphasizes the barbarity of that generation 'chewing and drinking', for which Luke substitutes his characteristic 'they ate, they drank'; and for Matthew's two pairs, 'chewing and drinking, marrying and giving in marriage', he writes a Lucan anarthrous four, 'they ate, they drank, they married, they were given in marriage'—cf. 'good measure, pressed down, shaken together, running over', 'rest, eat, drink, celebrate', 'the poor, the halt, the lame, the blind' (§23). He cuts Matthew's now irrelevant 'they knew not until. . . ', and improves his 'the flood took them all away (ἦρεν)' to '. . . destroyed them all', perhaps because he is to use ἆραι more positively at 17.31. Otherwise he copies the Matthaean version almost verbatim.

17.28. Noah alone was named in Mt. 24.37ff.; but the evangelist had continued, 'Then two shall be in the field; one is taken and one is left' (24.40). The thought was of Lot and his wife, who had fled from Sodom to the open country; the angels had warned him, 'Do not look back; escape to the mountains lest you *be taken* with them (συμπαραλήμφθῃς)' (Gen. 19.17)—but his wife had looked back and been taken, while Lot himself had been left. Lot was a pair with Noah as 'righteous men' saved from heaven-sent catastrophe (Josephus *Ant.* 1.2.3; 2 Pet. 2.5-8), and the influence of the Lot story was in this context at least as early as Mark: 'Let them flee to the mountains' (Mk 13.14). Luke accordingly builds an antistrophe on Lot to match his strophe on Noah; much as he adds an Elisha illustration to match his Elijah reference at 4.25-27, or Judas to Theudas in Acts 5, or the Coin to the 'Q' Sheep at 15.3ff. He structures the second sentence exactly on the lines of the first. Of 'Likewise as it happened in the days of Lot; they ate, they drank, they bought, they sold, they planted, they built', every expression is favoured by Luke except 'Lot', 'they bought' and 'they sold'. He drops the marrying and giving in marriage because Sodom was not actually famous for marriage: its inhabitants were more given to making money, no doubt, building houses (v. 31a) and planting in the fields (v. 31b).

17.29. Verse 29 similarly is structured exactly on the lines of v. 27c: 'in the day that Lot went out of Sodom' balances 'till the day that Noah went into the ark'; 'fire and brimstone rained from heaven' is an abbreviation of Gen. 19.24 LXX, and balances 'the flood came'; both sentences end 'and destroyed them all'. In just the same way does Luke structure his 'there were many lepers in Israel in the time of Elisha. . .' on the preceding 'there were many widows in the days of Elijah in Israel. . .' (4.25ff.). The parallel with the Son of Man is Lucanised this time, with κατὰ τὰ αὐτά and ἀποκαλύπτεσθαι (1/0/3); he uses the somewhat similar ἀναφαίνεσθαι at 19.11.

17.31f. The Lot theme had not just been present in Mt. 24.40, as I have said, but latent also in Mark's charge to flee to the mountains. It is no use fleeing to the mountains when the Son of Man's day comes as suddenly as the lightning, and Luke's whole anxiety is to end the disappointments that come from looking for signs; but Christians should certainly lift up their heads and make ready to greet their Lord, not go back home for a change of clothes. He therefore takes up the Matthaeo-Marcan saying 'he that is on the roof. . . and he that is in the field. . ' (Mk 13.15f./Mt. 24.17f.). He is noticeably closer to the Matthaean redaction, with τὰ (σκεύη) for Mark's τι, with 'let him not go down to take. . . ' uninterrupted by Mark's 'nor enter', and ἐν ἀγρῷ for Mark's εἰς; but he ends with Mark's full εἰς τὰ ὀπίσω, where Matthew just has the adverb. In a sense it was the εἰς τὰ ὀπίσω for which the saying was included, for Lot was warned not to look round εἰς τὰ ὀπίσω in Gen. 19.17, and the line of thought moves on accordingly in v. 32 to 'Remember Lot's wife'. But it is evident now that vv. 31f. have been brought in from a foreign context (Mt. 24.17f. being concerned with the great tribulation, while 24.37ff. is about the Parousia): Luke began by saying that the Son of Man's day would be like lightning, and he will soon tell us of pairs of people asleep or grinding and suddenly parted. The Lot story imports the incompatible thought of an attempt to escape.

17.33. Verse 33 takes the incompatibility a step further. Lot and his family were trying to save their lives, and there in the Matthaean passage before him is Mt. 16.25, 'For whoever wishes to save his life will lose it; and whoever loses his life for my sake will find it'. Luke copies the text in, with Lucan ζητήσῃ for Matthew's θέλῃ, and compounds περιποιήσασθαι (Acts 20.28) and ζῳογονήσει (Acts 7.19) for Matthew's simple 'save' and 'find'. But in the day the Son of Man comes like the lightning, it will be too late to be thinking of saving one's life, or of losing it. As in 16.1-13 Luke has combined three Matthaean passages from different contexts, and the result is incoherent.

17.34f. With v. 34 Luke returns to Mt. 24.40f., two men in the field, two women at the mill, and to his real message. We should not be looking for signs of Christ's coming, for it will be sudden—and traditionally in the night (Mk 13.33ff.; Mt. 24.43; 25.6; 1 Thess. 5.2, etc.), at least by the images used. It would be better therefore to think of the two men not as at work in the field, but as in bed—families slept together in Lk. 11.7, and until relatively modern times. Matthew had the two women grinding at the mill, i.e. at their day-time labours while their husbands were in the fields. Luke has them at home 'grinding together': he thinks of them using small hand-mills in the evening, just as he avoids the ass-turned millstone at 17.2. He turns Matthew's graphic presents, 'one is taken and one is left' into more polished futures following 'two shall be. . . ', and uses the

Lucan ὁ εἷς . . . ὁ ἕτερος and their feminine form. His introductory 'on this night' comes as rather a surprise after so many uses of 'day', but is easy to understand.

17.37. With Mt. 24.41 Luke has reached the Thief in the Night, and other parabolic matter which he has used in ch. 12; most of the earlier part of the chapter was in Mark 13, and is reserved for its customary recital and exposition the Sunday before Passover. One text from Matthew he had not used, however, on the carcass and the eagles—perhaps by accident, perhaps by design. He uses it now, in any case, as his closing epigram. As it does not follow smoothly from v. 35, he supplies it with a foil introduction (§1.4). It was futile to enquire when the kingdom would come (v. 20), and it is equally futile to enquire where. The Son of Man will come in a moment like the lightning, and he will come everywhere, like the vultures on the carrion.

The passage has been much discussed: there is a classic article by R. Schnackenburg in *Fs* Rigaux (1970), and monographs by J.-D. Kaestli (1970), J. Zmijewski (1972) and R. Geiger (1973) give considerable space to it. Opinion is divided on a number of questions. (1) Do 17.20f. belong with the rest? (2) Are the verses which do *not* have counterparts in Matthew 24 (a) derived from Q (Matthew having for some reason dropped them), or (b) taken from Luke's special source, or (c) Luke's own creation? (3) Does the Q form follow Matthew's or Luke's form and order?

17.20 εἶπεν. Hapax: παρατήρησις (παρατηρεῖν 0/1/3+1, 20.20R). ἡ βασ. τοῦ θ. ἔρχεται 22.18R, 11.2QC.

17.21 ἰδοὺ-γάρ*. Hapax: ἐντός. Bultmann (p. 25) and Fitzmyer think vv. 20f. were originally independent; Schnackenburg (pp. 214ff.), Kaestli (p. 28), and Schürmann (p. 237) take them as a unit with 17.22-37 (18.8) in Q. The change from the coming of the kingdom of God to the coming of the Son of Man is not evidence against unity if Luke has a major hand in the work, as the two are synonymous in Lk. 21.27, 31, 36. Mussner and Riesenfeld take παρατήρησις to mean looking for signs, and the former (and many) correctly stress the present force of 'is in your midst'; cf. Aquila, Exod. 17.7, 'Is Yahweh ἐντός ἡμῶν?', Job 2.8. But the saying is not a riddle, but is intended for the Church (Strobel). Both ἰδού (62/7/57+23) and ἤ (67/33/45+35), which are in common with Mt. 24.23 against Mk 13.21, are often inserted by Matthew redactionally, and look like Mt. R here.

17.22 εἶπεν-δὲ-πρός*, ἡμέραι-ἐλεύσονται*, ἐπιθυμεῖν*, ἡμέρα. μία τῶν ἡμερῶν 8.22R; 20.1R; it is future, like 'the days of Messiah' (Schnackenburg, pp. 227f.). ἐπιθυμεῖν always elsewhere of desiring things yet to come, and 'they shall say' (v. 23) makes a desire for the past, earthly days of Jesus (Dodd, *Parables*, p. 81; Leaney, Conzelmann, p. 96) very unlikely. Schnackenburg takes the verse as Lk.R.

17.23   διώκειν is a hapax in this colourless sense, 'go after'. Greeven prints ἰδοὺ ἐκεῖ ἰδοὺ ὧδε with L 33 etc.; N–A²⁶ adds ἤ in parenthesis with p⁷⁵B— but this looks like an assimilation to v. 21. μὴ ἀπέλθητε without connection suggests a clumsy adapting of Matthew's ἐάν. . .μή. . .

17.24   ἡμέρα, τήν/τῆς + prep. phrase. Hapax: λάμπειν (Acts 12.7). ἀστράπτουσα 24.4R; cf. ἐξαστράπτων 9.29R. ὑπὸ τὸν οὐρανόν, Acts 2.5; 4.12. Schulz (p. 279) sees Luke's reason for changing Matthew's phrasing on the ἀστραπή (cf. Manson, p. 141); Fitzmyer takes Matthew to be 'simplifying' Q=Lk., seeming not to notice the difficulty over the 'lightning' in Matthew.

17.25   Schnackenburg calls this verse a strange insertion (as good as certain by Luke), and this view is general, with no parallel in Matthew, and the connection broken. Various weak explanations are offered: Luke's insistence on passion before glory,cf. Acts 14.22 (Schnackenburg); 'the Son of Man' means the Church (Manson, pp. 142ff.); although Jesus suffered, yet he will come again (Marshall). But Mt. 16.1, 4, 21, 25, 28 are the thread on which the Matthew 24 sequence is strung. Perhaps also, though, Luke knew of traditions that Jesus had expected the kingdom in his lifetime (cf. 19.11), and wished to discount them.

17.26   καθώς, γίνεσθαι, ἐν-ταῖς-ἡμέραις + gen. (2)*, καί = also. καθώς-ἐγένετο, 11.30QD; 17.28. This time the days of the Son of Man are *before* the Parousia, cp. v. 22 (Schnackenburg). οὕτως-ἔσται is a Matthaean expression (12/2/2).

17.27   ἐσθίειν/πίνειν*, (ἄχρι*), (ὅς in attraction*), (ἡμέρα). Hapaxes: (κιβωτός), (κατακλυσμός). With ἐγαμίζοντο Luke introduces a feminine subject, where Matthew viewed marriage exclusively from the male angle (Marshall); as often Luke thinks of women.

17.28   ὁμοίως*, καθώς, γίνεσθαι, ἐν-ταῖς-ἡμέραις + gen.*, ἐσθίειν/πίνειν*, οἰκοδομεῖν, φυτεύειν. καθώς-ἐγένετο, 11.30QD; 17.26QD. Lot was combined with Noah in many Jewish documents, from Wis. 10.4-6; *TNaph* 3.4f. (J. Schlosser, *RB* [1973]; Lührmann, pp. 75-83). The present combination could have been made by Jesus (Marshall), Q (Bultmann with Q^Lk, p. 117; Schnackenburg; Manson, pp. 143f.), or by Luke, whether from L (Fitzmyer) or his own hand (P. Vielhauer, *Aufsätze*, p. 67). But, as Bultmann says, Matthew would hardly have omitted it if it stood Q ('by mistake', Schnackenburg); elsewhere he has all the Q antistrophes (6.25ff.; 11.16ff.

21ff.; 12.41f.). It would seem rather a happy coincidence for two such parallel logia to have been preserved in two independent sources, L and Q. Luke seems to have constructed the Coin himself in parallel with the Sheep (q.v.). Note also Luke's hostility to trade (14.18, 19, and the reduction of the money in 19.12-27, §5).

17.29 ὅς in attraction*, ἡμέρα. Hapax: (θεῖον). The virtual quotation of Gen. 19.24LXX is in the Lucan manner.

17.30 ὅς in attraction*, ἡμέρα. κατὰ-τὰ-αὐτά 6.23QD, 26QD. ἡ ἡμέρα ἀποκαλύπτεται, cf. 1 Cor. 3.13 (see above, ch. 4).

17.31 ἡμέρα, ὁμοιῶς*, (ἐπιστρέφειν). σκεῦος 1/2/2+5 (elsewhere sing.). ἐν-ἐκείνῃ-τῇ-ἡμέρᾳ 6.23QD; cf. 10.12QD; 21.34R.

17.32 Hapax: μνημονεύειν (Acts 20.21, 35). Bultmann (p. 117), Schnackenburg, etc. take the verse to be Lucan creation.

17.33 ζητεῖν. Hapaxes: περιποιεῖσθαι (Acts 20.28), ζῳογονεῖν (Acts 7.19). Schnackenburg says that the wording is adapted from Q = Mt. 10.39, but Mt. 16.25 is markedly closer (ὃς ἐὰν θέλῃ/ἀπολέσῃ, cf. Lk. ὃς ἂν ζητήσῃ/ ἀπολέσῃ: cp. Mt. 10.39, ὁ εὑρών/ὁ ἀπολέσας). Zmijewski (pp. 479ff.) says the dependence is on Mk. 8.35, which is closer, but Luke's ἀπολέσῃ = Mt. 16 against Mk 8 ἀπολέσει.

17.34 ὁ-εἷς ... ὁ-ἕτερος*. ταύτῃ-τῇ-νυκτί, 12.20; Acts 27.23: this night of which I am speaking; cp. v. 31, ἐκείνῃ τῇ ἡμέρᾳ. Schnackenburg thinks Luke is original here because the night/bed detail agrees with Christ's coming in the night; but Luke himself thought Christ would come in the night (12.35QD; 21.36R), and is adapting after the day-time activities on the roof and in the field (v. 31 = Mk, Mt.). Schulz (p. 280) follows Wellhausen in thinking that the couple in bed are original, as a man and wife, and so a pair. But such arguing is futile—even if they are man and wife, Luke could have introduced the pair for that very reason. But the two women grinding make it likely that Luke has two brothers in mind, or something similar. Marshall has the farmer and his wife in bed while the household begin their tasks: some farmer! Zmijewski (pp. 497ff.) sees that Luke is improving Matthew's picture.

17.35 ἐπὶ-τὸ-αὐτό, ἡ μία...ἡ ἑτέρα. Hapax: (ἀλήθειν). Hand-grinding could be done by night; cf. *Anth. Pal.* 11.251, νυκτὸς ἀληλέκεναι.

17.37 ποῦ, εἶπεν, καί = also. Hapax: (ἀετός). Luke avoids πτῶμα at the Mk 15.45 context also. ἐπισυναχθήσονται echoes Mt. 24.31; cf. 2 Thess. 2.1; Mk 13.27.

Noack, B., *Das Gottesreich bei Lukas: eine Studie zu Luk. 17,20-24* (Uppsala, 1948).

Roberts, C.H., 'The Kingdom of Heaven (Lk. xvii.21)', *HTR* 41 (1948), pp. 1-8.

Strobel, A., 'Die Passa-Erwartung als urchristliche Problem in Lk 17,20f' *ZNW* 49 (1958), pp. 163-74.

—'"In dieser Nacht" (Lk 17,34)', *ZTK* 58 (1961), pp. 16-29.

—'Zu Lk 17,20f', *BZ* 7 (1963), pp. 111-13.

Rüstow, A., 'ΕΝΤΟΣ ΥΜΩΝ ΕΣΤΙΝ: zur Deutung von Lukas 17,20-21', *ZNW* 51 (1960), pp. 197-224.

Mussner, F., '"Wann kommt das Reicht Gottes?"', *BZ* 6 (1962), pp. 107-11

Sneed, R.J., ' "The kingdom of God is within you" (Lk 17,21)', *CBQ* 24 (1962) pp. 363-82

Vielhauer, P., *Aufsätze zum Neuen Testament* (München, 1965).

Rigaux, B., 'La petite apocalypse de Luc (XVII,22-37)', in *Fs* Philips (1970), pp. 407-38.

Schnackenburg, R., 'Der eschatologische Abschnitt Lk 17,20-37', in *Fs* Rigaux (1970), pp. 213-34.

Schlosser, J., 'Les jours de Noe et de Lot; A propos de Luc xvii, 26-30', *RB* 80 (1973), pp. 13-36.

Léon-Dufour, X., 'Luc 17,33', *RSR* 69 (1981), pp. 101-12.

b. *The Unjust Judge*, 18.1-8

Luke has been expounding the Coming of the Son of Man from Matthew 16 and 24.23-41 and he means this to be the subject of his whole triple unit. At 24.20 Matthew had had Jesus instruct his disciples to pray (προσεύχεσθε); at 24.31 he had spoken of the Son of Man's gathering of his elect (ἐπισυνάξουσιν τοὺς ἐκλεκτοὺς αὐτοῦ), the very verb with which Luke has just closed his seventeenth chapter; and after the two women at the mill (24.41) Matthew had moved on to the need to be ready for the Son of Man's coming (vv. 42-44) and the Faithful Servant (vv. 45-51). Luke will treat the Son of Man's coming to redeem his own more fully in the Marcan sequence at Luke 21, and the readiness theme and the Servant he has taken already in Lk. 12.35-48. But the need for prayer in face of the Lord's delayed coming is urgent, and Luke's eye is caught by the congenial words in Mt. 24.44ff., ὁ υἱὸς τοῦ ἀνθρώπου ἔρχεται . . . πιστός. . .ἐλθών. . .εὑρήσει. . . So he expands the Matthaean teaching into a parable of his own, which will teach the need of praying (προσεύχεσθαι) that God will soon vindicate his elect, τῶν ἐκλεκτῶν αὐτοῦ—a phrase not occurring elsewhere in L-A. He closes the prayer with a rhetorical question which shows whence he draws his inspiration, '*Will the Son of Man coming find faith*fulness on earth?' (ὁ υἱὸς τοῦ ἀνθρώπου ἐλθὼν ἆρα εὑρήσει τὴν πίστιν. . .;).

So the theme of Luke's parable comes from Matthew 24; and the imagery comes from the Old Testament, from Ecclus 35, with its memorable picture of the widow at prayer. 'Do not pester with gifts (δωροκόπει)', says ben Sira, '. . . for the Lord is judge (κύριος κριτής), and with him is no respect of persons. He will not accept any person against a poor man, and he will listen to the prayer of him that is wronged. He will in no wise despise the supplication of the fatherless, nor the widow (χήραν) if she poureth out her tale. Do not the tears of the widow run down her cheek? Is not her cry (καταβόησις) against him that causeth her to fall?. . . The prayer of the humble pierceth the clouds; and till it come nigh, he will not be comforted: and he will not depart till the Most High shall visit; and he shall judge righteously, and execute judgment. And the Lord will not (οὐ μή) be slack, neither will he be longsuffering (μακροθυμήσῃ) towards them (ἐπ' αὐτοῖς), Till he have crushed the loins of the unmerciful; and he shall repay vengeance (ἐκδίκησιν) to the heathen. . . Till he repay to a man according to his doings (κατὰ τὰς πράξεις αὐτοῦ)' (Ecclus 35.11-22LXX). The similarity between the two passages is too close to be accidental: it extends not only to the central picture of enduring prayer as like a widow pleading her cause, and of the certainty of divine response, but also to some striking elements of the language. Luke's parable is about a χήρα, and a κριτής who is a figure for God. She prays, ἐκδίκησόν με, and God's ἐκδίκησις of his elect is promised in v. 7, as the judge vows, ἐκδικήσω αὐτήν in v. 5. She pesters him (κόπον), not with gifts but with her continual coming, and is a figure for the good Christians βοώντων to God night and day. Luke sums the matter up with the same double negative οὐ μή, and the same striking phrase μακροθυμεῖ ἐπ' αὐτοῖς. The very problem of being sure of Luke's meaning here is a testimony to the wording having been brought in from a source. Ben Sira meant, 'God will not *be slow* till he exacts vengeance, *being patient over them*, the wrong-doers'; to Luke the αὐτοῖς are the praying Christians, and his μακροθυμεῖ carries the meaning, 'and *he is slow, delaying over them*'. We have met Luke retaining his source's language but changing the meaning before (§ 20).

We may well wonder what drew Luke's attention to Ecclus 35. Perhaps it is just a liking for ben Sira: the Rich Fool is sometimes thought to contain echoes of his book, and so is the Prodigal Son, since Ecclus 33 warns the prudent father not to distribute money to his children till he is on his death-bed. But we may notice also Mt. 16.27, since Luke has been working over that chapter. Matthew writes, 'he shall render to each according to his doing (κατὰ τὴν πρᾶξιν αὐτοῦ)', and the closest OT text is Ecclus 35.22, 'he will render back to a man according to his doings (κατὰ τὰς πράξεις αὐτοῦ). (The other similar LXX texts, Ps. 62.13 and Prov. 24.12, both have ἔργα.) So it is possible that even the line to Ecclesiasticus was provided by Matthew.

But even granted that the suggestion of the topic comes to Luke from Matthew, and the image for the parable from Ecclesiasticus, may the parable itself not come from Jesus? Linguistic considerations are given in the notes, but they can hardly prove more than that Luke has, or has not, put the parable in his own words. For a choice between Jesus (Jeremias, Catchpole, and most) and Luke (Linnemann, Drury, Freed), we have to consider more general aspects of the unit.

The *doctrine* of the parable seems to be very close to the meaning which Luke ascribes to it in v. 1. The widow is forever pleading, and does not faint. Without an unjust judge there would be no plot, for a just judge would give her justice at once, and the parable would lose its point. Her continual coming, and bothering him, and threatening to wear him out, are the structure of the story, and answer to the need to persevere in prayer. The judge must be a figure for God (and is said to be in v. 7); but God is not to be thought of as an unjust judge at all. His lack of principle is thus entailed by the story, which requires delay, and so perseverance. But a situation in which there is delay, and the need to persevere in prayer, is much more like Luke's situation than Jesus'. Jesus (it is thought) preached that God had acted, and men should respond. Luke was writing in the 80s when the flame of eschatological hope was guttering, and perseverance, faithfulness and prayer were the message. So the structure of the parable in vv. 2-5, as well as the conclusion in vv. 7-8, point to a composition in Luke's time rather than sixty years before.

This is confirmed by a number of features of the parable. (1) It is an *imperative* parable, teaching the hearer how to behave, rather than an indicative parable intimating God's action. Such imperative parables are virtually limited to Luke's Gospel (§8). A parable teaching that we should always pray is like a parable teaching us not to covet, or to love our neighbour as ourselves, or to accept our forgiven brother. (2) Luke is particularly concerned with *prayer*. He has a second parable on the subject, in the Friend at Midnight, which has a number of details echoing the Judge. Just as the Judge says, 'this widow bothers me (παρέχειν μοι κόπον)', so does the Friend in bed say, 'Do not bother me (μή μοι κόπους παρέχε)'. The Judge expresses his change of heart with a sentence in the form εἰ καὶ οὐ...διά γε..., and the Friend's change of heart takes exactly the same form. This is only an instance of a more general stress on prayer in Luke.

(3) There is a family likeness also with a second Lucan parable, the *Unjust Steward*. The phrase, ὁ κριτὴς τῆς ἀδικίας recalls the parallel τὸν οἰκονόμον τῆς ἀδικίας, with his mammon τῆς ἀδικίας (cf. Lk. 13.27QD ἀδικίας). Both parables turn on the change of mind of an unprincipled protagonist; and (even though 'the Lord' has a different reference), there is a striking likeness in the phrasing—'The Lord (Jesus) said, Hear what the unjust judge says', 'The lord (owner) commended the unjust steward'. (4) These are the only two parables in the Gospel tradition in which the central character is a crook: we may distinguish them with their story format from the similitude of the thief. But this is part of a larger contrast, for Lucan parables have a spread of *disreputable heroes*, Samaritans, beggars, etc. (§4.7), where Marcan and Matthaean parables have only nice people for their central characters. (5) The widow is similarly (by her poverty) not quite up to standard either. But *widows* are a Lucan concern. A widow who stands for God's elect, who cry to him day and night, recalls the Lucan widow Anna of 2.37, who served with fasts and prayers day and night; and also the twelve tribes who served night and day in Acts 26.7. Luke speaks of Elijah's widow, and the widow at Nain, and the widow's mite (dropped by Matthew), and the daily provision for widows in Acts, and the widows by Dorcas' deathbed. (6) A corollary of having a bad man as a figure for God is that the conclusion of the parable has to take the form of *quanto potius*, 'how much the more...': if the unjust judge gives in to persistent pleading, how much the more will God! We have the same logic with the Steward: if the sons of this world look after their future prudently, how much more should the sons of light! The Friend is similar: if a man in bed will give in to persistent knocking, how much more will God! There is no parable outside Luke which uses this logic. Matthew's heroes (and Mark's) are born just and merciful, *like* God.

(7) We may note also the judge's *soliloquy* (§4.1). He says within

himself, 'Though I fear not God...' This is a strikingly regular feature of the Lucan parables, not much found in Mark and Matthew, and enables us to see the man's character. (8) As with other Lucan parable-characters, we note his *two-sidedness* (§4). The man is a rogue, but he is not a bleak baddie, like Matthew's bad Servant or unforgiving Debtor. He is rather likable despite all: he does not reverence God or regard man, but there is a certain ironic realism in him—he can see that the widow has got him cornered by never giving up. The atmosphere again recalls the Steward, this time with the ironic realism of the owner. (9) Finally, we may notice the *oratio recta repetition* of the key words (§11): 'There was a judge who feared not God nor regarded man... Give me justice... Though I fear not God nor regard man... I will give her justice'. Cf. 'Father, I have sinned...', 'This your brother was dead...', 'This man began to build...'

The OT inspiration for the parable tells neither way. The Marcan Husbandmen is rooted in Isaiah 5 and Cant. 8.11; and Luke sometimes has parables with OT backgrounds, like the Embassy, the Two Sons or the Samaritan. But the pervasive Lucanness of the mode of the parable, exemplified in the nine points above, really puts the question of its authorship beyond cavil. One can shunt off the Lucan phrasing (which is also extensive), and suppose an earlier form without it: but what is left of the parable if one removed the nine points of its mode?

It has been normal to attribute the parable to L (*Sondergut*) without question: it is not in any of the other sources so that is where Luke must have taken it from. So G. Delling (*ZNW* [1962]), and recently Schneider and Fitzmyer. D. Catchpole (*NT* [1977]) notes the links with 17.22ff., and with Mt. 24.44-46 and 13.16f., and so with Q. He can hear 'the voice of the historical Jesus' behind it, as can Delling and Jeremias (pp. 154-57). Earlier, the parable, vv. 2-5, had been split from the conclusion, but Jeremias, Delling and Catchpole justify vv. 7-8 as dominical too: πίστις would then mean 'a right relation to God' rather than faithfulness, according to Catchpole. Eta Linnemann (pp. 119-24) argued against such approaches, and for Lucan authorship, and in this she is followed by John Drury (*Parables*, pp. 152f.) and Edwin Freed in a detailed examination to be published in *NTS* (I am grateful to him for an advance copy).

18.1　ἔλεγεν-δὲ-παραβολήν*, δεῖ, Α-καὶ-μὴ-non-A. Hapax: ἐγκακεῖν. With 'pray and not faint', cf. 'dumb and not able to speak', etc. πρὸς-τό here alone, but cf. διὰ-τό, μετὰ-τό etc. + inf. Bultmann (pp. 209, 360) and Jeremias (p. 156) take v. 1 as Luke's addition to turn an eschatological parable into an exhortation; but Drury correctly stresses that the eschatology of the parable implies a strong element of delay.

18.2 κριτής*, τις + noun (2), πόλις, τὸν-θεὸν-φοβεῖσθαι, θεός/ἄνθρωπος. ἔν τινι πόλει cf. 7.37. Noun + τις-ἦν 16.1, 19.

18.3 χήρα*, ἐν-τῇ-πόλει. ἐν-τῇ-πόλει-ἐκείνῃ Acts 8.8.

18.4 χρόνος, μετὰ-ταῦτα*, εἶπεν, ἑαυτόν, τὸν-θεὸν-φοβεῖσθαι, θεός/ ἄνθρωπος. ἐπὶ + acc. of time, 4.25. οὐκ ἤθελεν = 'he would not'—no reason is given.

18.5 διὰ-τό*, γε*, παρέχειν*, χήρα*, οὗτος contemptuous, ἐρχόμενος + verb*. Hapax: ὑπωπιάζειν. παρέχειν μοι κόπον/ους, 11.7. ὑπωπιάζειν is uncomfortable. Its literal meaning is 'give a black eye to', and this is defended by Creed, Delling and C. Spicq (*RB* [1961]); and it is not impossible, since Luke has personal violence in his teaching at 6.29QD; 10.30; 12.45QD; 13.24QD; 14.23QD. The widow could be young, and driven to desperation (εἰς τέλος, 'in the end'). Fitzmyer follows Jeremias's 'wear me out completely', but there is no real parallel for this translation. Paul uses the verb to mean 'pommel' (1 Cor. 9.27), and the metaphorical 'smear my reputation' found in Greek sources is unhelpful. Derrett (*NTS* [1978]) suggests a Hebrew original; but Hebrew originals are in doubt.

18.6 εἶπεν-δέ*, ὁ-κύριος = Jesus*, κριτής*, ἀδικία*. ἀκούσατε Acts 2.22; 7.2; 15.13; 22.1. ὁ κριτὴς τῆς ἀδικίας cf. 16.8f.

18.7 ὁ θεός, βοᾶν, ἡμέρα. Hapax: μακροθυμεῖν. βοᾶν in prayer 9.38R, 18.38R. ἡμέρας καὶ νυκτός Acts 9.24. A. Wifstrand (*NTS* [1964]) provides parallels from Chrysostom where μακροθυμεῖν clearly means 'delay'; and for participles followed by καί and a main verb in Jer. 14.15LXX; 2 Jn 2; Rev. 3.7; Jn 5.44. This gives good sense, 'who call on him day and night, and he delays over them'. So Leaney. Catchpole shows that this is the normal biblical meaning for Gentiles, but that with Israel it is 'longsuffering'; but the latter meaning reads unnaturally here. Jeremias's rendering (p. 156), 'God listens to their cry with unwearied patience', might be felt by the suffering Lucan church to be a bit thick!

18.8 πλήν. Hapaxes: τάχος, ἄρα. ἐν τάχει Acts12.7; 22.18; 25.4, always 'quick', 'soon', as throughout LXX (C.E.B. Cranfield, *SJT* [1963]), never 'suddenly' (Jeremias). Cranfield points out against Conzelmann that Luke here imports the idea of an imminent eschatology: but it is only imminent after prayer and delay. Perhaps Luke's ἄρα was suggested by ἄρα in Mt. 24.45.

Spicq, C., 'La parabole de la veuve obstinée et du juge inerte, aux décisions impromptues', *RB* 68 (1961), pp. 68-90.

Delling, G., 'Das Gleichnis vom gottlosen Richter', *ZNW* 53 (1962), pp. 1-25.

Cranfield, C.E.B., 'The Parable of the Unjust Judge and the Eschatology of Luke-Acts', *SJT* 16 (1963), pp. 297-301.

Ljungvik, H., 'Zur Erklärung einer Lukas-Stelle (Luk. xviii. 7)', *NTS* 10 (1964), pp. 289-94.

Wifstrand, A., 'Lukas xviii.7', *NTS* 11 (1964), pp. 72-74.

Derrett, J.D.M., 'Law in the New Testament: The Parable of the Unjust Judge', *NTS* 18 (1972), pp. 178-91.

Catchpole, D.R., 'The Son of Man's Search for Faith (Luke xviii.8b)', *NT* 19 (1977), pp. 81-104.

Zimmermann, H., 'Das Gleichnis vom Richter und der Witwe', in *Fs* Schürmann (1977), pp. 79-95.

Freed, E.D., 'The Parable of the Judge and the Widow (Luke 18.1-8)', *NTS* 33 (1987), pp. 38-60.

SECTION 7—UP TO JERUSALEM
(18.9–21.38; Mk 10.13–13.37; Mt. 19.13–25.30)

44. *The Coming of the Son of Man*, 17.20–18.17 (cont.)

c. *The Exaltation of the Humble*, 18.9-17

With the texts on the coming of the Son of Man in 17.20–18.8, Luke has completed his gleaning movement through the later chapters of Matthew. I suggested that in the second half of the Journey, from 13.22 on, he was rolling his Matthaean scroll backwards, with the intention of covering all those elements of teaching between the end of Matthew 25, to which he has leaped forward, and Matthew 16, which he had been expounding in Luke 12. As this is so signal an achievement, and as it is a novel element of exposition, it may seem proper to pause a moment and review the extent of what Luke has done.

On p. 582 I set out an outline table of the more obvious references to Matthew in Lk. 13.22–18.8. But it will have become clear to the reader, that the 'reverse-order' hypothesis accounts for not just most, but the whole of the Lucan outline through these chapters. From the Closed Door (Mt. 25.10ff.), and the two-days-and-then-the-Passion logion (Mt. 26.2), Luke moves back to 'Jerusalem, Jerusalem. . .' (Mt. 23.37-39). In 14.1-14 he has Jesus in controversy with lawyers and Pharisees on their hard rulings (Mt. 23.2-4), their looking for chief seats (Mt. 23.6), and the exalting of the humble (Mt. 23.12); and with points about invitations to a wedding or a breakfast (Mt. 22.3f.). In 14.15-24 he has the parable of the great Dinner (Mt. 22.1-10); and in 14.25-34 he has the casting out of the unworthy (Mt. 22.11-14), the building of the tower (Mt. 21.33), and the king's army (Mt. 22.7) and embassy (Mt. 21.34).

Luke 15 uses the Lost Sheep parable of Mt. 18.12-14 as an introduction to his main parable, the Father and his Two Sons (Mt. 21.28-32), which has been glossed with the Labourers in the Vineyard (Mt. 20.1-16). The great parable of the Unmerciful Debtor

(Mt. 18.23-35) he used twice. In 16.1-13 he drew on the theme of the middle man with his master and his debtors, and the remission of debt (glossing in the stewardship theme from Mt. 25.21, 23). In 16.14-31 he expounded the torments awaiting the unmerciful, with Mt. 18.6-10 to help, including the angels who watch over the little ones. 17.1-10 saw a somewhat staccato rendition of the topics of scandal (Mt. 18.6), forgiveness to the end (Mt. 18.15-23), and faith (Mt.17.20). 17.11-17 is the only section not directly dependent on the next preceding passage in Matthew: and even here the Ten Lepers can be seen as a substitute for Mt. 17.14-20. Our present sequence on the Coming of the Son of Man is a reexposition of the Pharisees' request for a sign (Mt. 16.1-4), and Jesus' prediction of his suffering (Mt. 16.21) and coming (Mt. 16.25-28), glossed with the detail from Matthew 24.

In this way *every* Lucan pericope can be seen as developed from a matrix in Matthew; and as the sequence in Luke is exactly the reverse of that in Matthew, the hypothesis of reversed-order gleaning seems almost inescapable. In addition we can see how logical it was for Luke to bring his gleaning to an end at Matthew 16, because it was Matthew 16 that he had reached in his forward progression to Luke 12. Furthermore the critic can hardly discern any non-Marcan text in Mt. 16-25 which Luke has omitted, except where his reasons may be obvious (Pharisaic oath-rules, etc.). It seems suitable therefore to salute our evangelist as he leaves his Matthaean scroll for the last time. He has not only developed his source with genius; he has also worked through it with exemplary care and proper system.

With the Matthaean matter complete, Luke is free to rejoin his main source Mark once more—and Matthew follows in tandem for the rest of the road. He left Mark at the Strange Exorcist (Mk 9.40; Lk. 9.49f.), and has since briefly covered Scandals (Mk 9.42-48; Lk. 17.1f.), Salt (Mk 9.49f.; Lk. 14.34f.) and Divorce (Mk 10.1-12; Lk. 16.18). The Marcan pericope following is the Children (Mk 10.13-16), and this can be made quite a suitable end to the Lucan theme for the day. We began with the Pharisees asking when the kingdom of God was coming. We have heard that it will come in a moment, and that the Church can pray faithfully for its coming; no preacher can be content without stressing that the humble will be welcome in the kingdom, but pride and Pharisaism will not.

18.15-17, 14. Luke takes Mark's story much as it comes. He makes Mark's children 'babes' in v. 15, but this is not significant because he has drifted back to 'children' in v. 17 (fatigue, §19.2). He cuts out Jesus' indignation with the disciples, in order to preserve the reputations of the latter, as often. Because he is not interested in the story of the children for itself, but only for the moral of humility, he leaves out Mark's final verse, 'And taking them in his arms. . . ', and finishes with the challenging, 'Whoever will not receive the kingdom of God as a child shall not enter it'. He means 'as a child does', with a child's humility.

There are minor agreements with Matthew's version of the story,—e.g. '*and* forbid them not': but, more significant, there is an echo of the Matthaean version of the earlier, similar story in Mt. 18.1ff., where Jesus stood a child in the disciples' midst as a warning against pride. There Matthew wrote προσκαλεσάμενος παιδίον (18.2R): here Luke amends Mark, προσεκαλέσατο αὐτά. It is really this story, commending child-like humility, which is closer to Luke's point. Matthew had continued, 'so he who will humble himself (ταπεινώσει ἑαυτόν) as this child, shall be great in the kingdom of heaven' (18.4R). This is what Luke wants to say, so he prefaces the Children with the words, 'Everyone who exalts himself shall be humbled (ταπεινωθήσεται), and he who humbles himself (ταπεινῶν ἑαυτόν) shall be exalted' (v. 14). The wording is closest to Matthew's other rendering of the same idea at 23.12; but the accuracy is not bad for a reminiscence.

18.9-14. The children story is too short, and not forceful enough to carry Luke's point with conviction: so he does what we have found him doing a number of times before (§10), prefacing Matthaean teaching with a newly wrought parable of his own—the Friend at Midnight before 'ask and you shall receive. . . ', for example, or the Rich Fool before '. . . nor gather into barns'. He would like a parable that would gather up the theme of the spiritual failing of the Pharisees from 17.20, at the beginning of his triple unit; and the topic of prayer suggests itself from 18.1-8. Since proud Pharisees are to Luke a stock contrast with repentant publicans, we might think that he put the two characters together himself; or maybe the phrase 'let him be to you *like* (ὥσπερ) the Gentile and *the publican*' (Mt. 18.17) stuck in his memory (or his gullet). At any rate he writes the parable first, with the conclusion, 'for everyone who exalts himself shall be humbled. . . '; and links the Children on with, 'And they *also* brought him the babes. . . '

But could he not have found a convenient parable in the tradition? Well, it is rather Lucan. It is a hortatory parable, such as are nearly peculiar to Luke (§8). It commends penitence, like the Prodigal Son, and rejects self-justifying pride, like that of his elder brother. The sinner in Luke 7 is another Lucan penitent contrasted with a proud Pharisee, and the theme is the centre of Luke's theology through both books. The 'parable' is in fact an illustrative story, like three others only in the Gospel tradition, the Good Samaritan, the Rich Fool and Dives and Lazarus—all in Luke (§7). The characters soliloquize, as Luke's characters so often do (§4.1); this time in prayer, but even the Pharisee prays 'to himself'. For all that their stock positions allow little freedom to characterize them, both emerge as real people, and very unlike Matthew's publican and Pharisee in his two sons, who are sheer cardboard: 'I fast twice a week, and give tithes on all I get' is specific like the Lucan excuses at the Dinner, the purchased farm, and five yoke of oxen, or the debts owed to the Steward in wheat and oil (§4.8). The man is disgustingly unctuous, as only Luke in our tradition knows how to make him. The parable is about prayer, too, a topic covered only by Luke, and by him three times: the Friend at Midnight, the Unjust Judge, and here.

The details are as characteristic of Luke as the general mode. The 'certain who trusted in themselves that they were righteous' recall the Jewish authorities in Lk. 20.20R who 'pretended that they were righteous'. Pharisees regularly 'despise others' in Luke: they despised Jesus for not knowing the woman to be a sinner in 7.39, and for eating with sinners in 15.2. 'Two men went up into the Temple to pray' reminds us of Peter and John in Acts 3.1, who 'went up into the Temple at the hour of prayer'. Only Luke has individual Pharisees, Simon in ch. 7, other dinner-hosts in chs. 11 and 14. The three nouns, ἅρπαγες, ἄδικοι, μοιχοί occur together in 1 Cor. 6.9-10, which can hardly be accidental—one more sign of Luke's close familiarity with 1 Corinthians (Ch. 4). The Pharisee's claim to tithe *all* that he gets probably implies the same error that Luke betrayed at 11.42, 'you tithe mint and rue and every herb'. The publican 'standing afar off' recalls Jesus' acquaintance of 23.49R, who 'stood afar off', and 'he smote his breast' like the crowds at the crucifixion

at 23.48R, who 'went away smiting their breasts'. For further verbal
Lucanisms, see the notes below. In this way Luke has achieved the
transfer from Matthew to Mark with perfect smoothness. His three-
unit homily on the Coming of the Kingdom of God/Son of Man has a
satisfying chiastic conclusion. Pharisees asked at the beginning when
the kingdom of God was coming: at the end, the Pharisee who trusts
in himself that he is righteous is shown as unjustified. He will be
humbled when the kingdom comes: it is the humble sinner who will
be exalted. Of such penitents and of children is the kingdom of God,
and anyone who does not receive the kingdom of God with a child's
humility will not enter into it. So when we pray for the Lord's
coming, brethren, let it be as downcast sinners, and without
Pharisaic works-righteousness, as Luther said.

18.9 εἶπεν. . .πρὸς. . .παραβολήν*, τις, ἑαυτόν, οἱ-λοιποί. πεποιθέναι ἐπί
11.22QD, ἐξουθενεῖν 23.11L, Acts 4.11 LXX R. Jeremias (pp. 139) rightly
'trusted in themselves (instead of God)'; but hardly 'because'—ὅτι + pres. =
'that' at 18.37 and often. Luke explains the parable with a preamble as at
18.1; 19.11 (Marshall).

18.10 ὁ-εἷς. . .ὁ ἕτερος*, Φαρισαῖος sing.*, τελώνης (approvingly).
ἄνθρωποι δύο cf. ἄνθρωπός τις 0/0/8.

18.11 Φαρισαῖος sing.*, σταθείς*, ταῦτα, πρός of speech, ἑαυτόν, ὁ-θεός,
τελώνης, εὐχαριστεῖν, οἱ-λοιποί, οὗτος contemptuous. Hapaxes: ἅρπαξ,
μοιχός 1 Cor. 6.9f. ἄδικοι θεοῦ βασιλείαν οὐ κληρονομήσουσιν. . .οὔτε
μοιχοί. . .οὔτε ἅρπαγες. ὁ θεός vocative only here and 18.13; but cf. ὁ πατήρ
10.21Q. ἤ-καί 1/0/3 (11.12, 12.41, both QD; Mt. 7.10). Black (p. 59) points to
asyndeta in vv. 11, 12, 14 as evidence of an Aramaic original (cf. Jeremias,
p. 140, 'such profusion'). But had Luke written δέ in v. 11, he would have
weakened the δὲ in v. 13. The unlinked ἅρπαγες, ἄδικοι, μοιχοί are like
Luke's unlinked fours, 'good measure, shaken together, pressed down,
running over', 'take your ease, eat, drink, rejoice', etc. (§23). 'I fast. . . I
tithe. . . ', without connections, gives the artistic impression of a disgusting
catalogue of self-congratulation; cf. the similar staccato impression of the
Prodigal's confession in 15.18f.
N-A[26] reads σταθεὶς πρὸς ἑαυτὸν ταῦτα with AW etc.; Greeven and
Diglot read the order 1423 with p[75]א[2] B etc. Jeremias (p. 140) prefers N-A[26]
as alone being Semitic, and assumes an Aramaic reflexive *leh*: 'he took up a
prominent position and uttered his prayer'. But one cannot just assume
translation from the Aramaic, and in fact all four words are typical of Luke.
Greeven has the better attestation, but both texts can mean 'he prayed thus
to himself'—Lucan soliloquy too.

18.12 σαββάτον, plethoric πάντα. Hapax: δίς. πάντα-ὅσα 18.22, κτᾶσθαι 1/0/2+3, ἀποδεκατοῦν 11.42. Jeremias (p. 142) takes as an instance of contemporary Pharisaic hypocrisy the prayer of R. Neḥunia on leaving the Beth-hamidrash (b. Ber. 28b): but that is not much more offensive than 'There but for the grace of God goes John Gilbert'. We have no evidence that Pharisees despised repentance: see the just strictures of E.P Sanders, *Paul and Palestinian Judaism*, Pt.I.

18.13 τελώνης, ἐπαίρειν*, τοὺς-ὀφθαλμοὺς-(ἐπ-)αίρειν, οὐρανός sing., τύπτειν, ὁ-θεός. Hapax: ἱλάσκεσθαι. ἁμαρτωλός; μακρόθεν ἐστὼς... ἔτυπτεν τὸ στῆθος, cf. 23.48R. The Prayer of Manasseh is closer to the text than Ps. 51, whose influence is suggested by Jeremias (p. 144) and Marshall.

18.14 δικαιοῦν*, εἰς-τον-οἶκον-Χ, παρά comparative*, plethoric πᾶς, ἑαυτόν (2). δεδικαιωμένος is perhaps an echo of Luke's old master; cf. Acts 13.38. Jeremias (p. 141) suggests an Aramaic *min* behind παρά; but this should be ἀπό, and Luke favours παρά for comparisons. He is right that the Pharisee is not justified at all.

18.15 καὶ = also, βρέφος*, ἰδόντες (δὲ). Marshall sees the link of theme between the parable and the Children pericope, and the links to Mt. 18.2, 4, but does not draw my conclusion.

18.16 (κωλύειν).

18.17 (δέχεσθαι). Neirynck (p. 134) gives four Minor Agreements, but three are very minor.

Schottroff, L., 'Die Erzählung vom Pharisäer und Zöllner als Beispiel für die theologische Kunst des Überredens', in *Fs* H. Braun (1973), pp. 439-61.

Hengel, M., 'Die ganz andere Gerechtigkeit: Bibelarbeit über Lk 18,9-14', *Theologische Beiträge* 5 (1974), pp. 1-13.

Merklein, H., '"Dieser ging als Gerechter nach Hause"', *BK* 32 (1977), pp. 34-42.

Schnider, F., 'Ausschliessen und ausgeschlossen werden', *BZ* 24 (1980), pp. 42-56.

Feuillet, A., 'Le pharisien et le publicain (Luc 18, 9-14)', *Esprit et vie* 48 (1981), pp. 657-65.

45. Riches and Poverty, 18.18–19.10

a. The Rich Ruler, 18.18-30

After the Children in Mark comes the Rich Man. Few subjects are more congenial to Luke than the threat which riches pose to the spiritual life. The subject has been a regular leitmotif through the Journey, and the Marcan story of the man who refused Christ's challenge to sell his all and give to the poor is just to the point. Luke has already warned his congregation more than once that one must resign all one has to be a disciple (6.20/24; 14.33): the Marcan tale is the classic example of this truth. He sharpens the point by omitting Mark's sphinx-like final verse, 'Many that are first shall be last. . .' (Mk 10.31, of which he has given a version at 13.30), and so leaving an emphatic inclusion. 'Good teacher', asks the man in v. 18, 'what shall I do to inherit *eternal life*?': 'there is no one', ends Jesus in vv. 29f., 'who has given up all, but he shall receive it back manifold in this life, and in the world to come *eternal life*'.

In the main Luke follows the Marcan text faithfully. He calls the 'one' in Mark a ruler (Lucan ἄρχων), as his wealth implies. He does his best, both in Gospel and Acts, to draw some distinction among the Jewish people between 'the people' who were responsive, and the 'rulers' who were not, and it is no accident that Mark's rich man has now become an ἄρχων. A second Lucan tendency can be seen in the addition of 'or wife' to the Marcan list of relations the disciple must be prepared to leave. Mark has house, brothers, sisters, mother, father, children and lands; Luke has house, wife, brothers, parents and children. The wife was also included at 14.26QD. Otherwise he puts fornication before murder, following the LXX order of the commandments, and drops Mark's, 'Do not defraud', which is not in Exodus 20/Deuteronomy 5. He improves Mark's Greek in various trivial ways, and by including better-class words like τρῆμα, a hole, and βελόνη, a needle.

Luke has followed Mark without reference to Matthew, who added the thrones logion at Mt. 19.28—unless he has noted it down to use at 22.30. He does have reminiscences of the Matthaean version, but it is hard to show the MAs to be significant. (1) He has ἐφύλαξα active in v. 21 = Mt. 19.20, against Mark's middle. But Luke prefers the active of φυλάσσειν. (2) He has οὐρανοῖς, plural, in v. 22 = Mt. 19.21, against Mark's singular. In general Luke prefers the singular, so this is interesting; but he has the plural in the similar phrase, 'treasure in the heavens' at 12.33 where the Matthaean parallel at 6.20 has a singular. The influence of the memory of Mt. 19.21 on both Lucan passages seems likely, but cannot be shown. (3) There is too much textual uncertainty over the needle's eye logion to make any argument. (4) More hopefully, in v. 26 Luke defines the vague Marcan οἱ δέ as οἱ ἀκούσαντες; and this is surprising, as the aorist would be natural only at the end of a conversation (cf. 2.18; 18.23; cp. the present οἱ ἀκούοντες, 2.47; 11.28). Matthew has ἀκούσαντες δέ οἱ μαθηταί. (5) Mk 10.28 has the aorist ἀφήκαμεν followed by the perfect ἠκολουθήκαμεν; Mt. 19.27 improves with a second aorist ἠκολουθήσαμεν; Lk. 19.28 writes the participle ἀφέντες so that he does not need to change Mark's perfect, but in fact like Matthew he writes ἠκολουθήσαμεν.

18.18   τις + noun*, ἄρχων.

18.19   (εἶπεν)-δέ*, (ὁ-θεός).

18.20   Hapaxes: (φονεύειν, κλέπτειν, ψευδομαρτυρεῖν, τιμᾶν).

18.21   (εἶπεν), (ταῦτα), φυλάσσειν*. Hapax: (νεότης).

18.22   ἀκούσας-(δέ), εἶπεν, ἔτι, πάντα pleth., (πτωχός). Hapaxes: λείπειν, (δεῦρο).

18.23   ταῦτα, γίνεσθαι, πλούσιος*. Hapaxes: περίλυπος, σφόδρα (Acts 6.7).

18.24   ἰδὼν-δέ, εἶπεν. Hapaxes: (δυσκόλως, χρήματα).

18.25   (πλούσιος*). Hapaxes: (κάμηλος), τρῆμα, βελόνη. Mark's τρυμαλιά comes in the LXX and Plutarch, Luke's τρῆμα goes back to Aristophanes and Plato (and, famously, Hippocrates). But Hippocrates also has the Marcan ῥαφίς, which is found in the papyri; Luke's βελόνη also goes back to Aristophanes. Cf. BAG.

18.26   εἶπον -(δέ)*.

18.27   εἶπεν, (ὁ-θεός). Hapax: (ἀδύνατος).

18.28   εἶπεν-δέ*.

18.29   γονεύς. ἴδιος 6.41QD, × 15 Acts.

18.30   οὐχί, ἀπολαμβάνειν*. Hapax: πολλαπλασίων.

b. *The Blind Beggar*, 18.31-43

Mark went on from the Rich Man to the third of the Passion Predictions, and the claim of the sons of Zebedee to sit beside Christ in heaven. Luke has two good reasons for leaving the latter out: it tarnishes the reputation of two of the best-known apostles, and it is irrelevant to the theme of money and salvation which he has introduced with the rich Man. So he omits it as a story, while quarrying the more edifying parts of it: the baptism that Jesus was baptised with (12.50), the primacy of service (22.25ff.), and (as we shall shortly see), the Son of Man's coming to save (19.1-10). But the Marcan story following, the healing of blind Bartimaeus, provides a far better foil to the Rich Man. The latter had been wealthy, and had been called by the Lord to sell all and follow him, but he would not; how hard, Jesus had said, for those with money to enter the kingdom, so that the disciples wondered who could be saved. Now in contrast we have a poor man, a blind beggar by the road; Jesus' passing is his moment of hope, and of blessing, and he clamours for it; the Lord told him, 'Your faith *has saved you*'; and *he followed him*, glorifying God. Riches and poverty, refusal and discipleship, sorrow and joyful praise, loss and salvation: the two stories could not stand in finer contrast.

Luke takes some of the colour out of the Marcan account to make his contrast the starker. We are not now given the beggar's name, nor that of his father, nor his casting away of his cloak and leaping up, etc. We have 'a certain blind man' to go against 'a certain ruler'; he is begging where the other was very rich; he hears the crowd and enquires what this might be, while the other could go straight to Jesus with his question. Blind, he can see that Jesus is David's son, where the ruler's 'Good teacher' is inaccurate and perhaps insincere. Told to be silent, he cries the louder for the act of mercy, where the ruler bandies words. The robust urgency of his need, says the preacher, is a pattern for us all. His faith saved him where the rich man could not enter the kingdom and be saved. ἠκολούθει αὐτῷ answers to ἀκολούθει μοι in v. 22, and ἠκολουθήσαμέν σοι in v. 28. His glorifying and the crowd's praise make a happy antithesis to the περίλυπος rich man of vv. 23f.

Perhaps Mark had intended another contrast: the spiritual blindness of the Zebedaids with the insight of Bartimaeus. Luke is omitting the sons of Zebedee, but he does develop the Passion prediction in the same direction. In Mark the Passion prediction leads on with obvious force to the story of the apostles who had not taken in about Jesus' coming baptism, and the cup he is to drink: when the latter is removed, the Passion prediction lacks any obvious connection with the blind man. Luke retains the former, however, and makes the link with a new verse, v. 34, 'And they understood none of these things, and the matter was hidden from them, and they did not know what was being said'. So although the Passion prediction interrupts Luke's sequence of stories on wealth, poverty and salvation, he retains it as a lead-in to the Blind Man. The twelve, for all their privileges, still did not understand the central mystery of the Gospel, Jesus' sufferings and resurrection, as foretold in the prophets. It took a blind man to see that Jesus was the son of David.

Jan Lambrecht ('Reading and Re-Reading Lk 18.31-22.6', in *Fs* Dupont 1985], pp. 585-612) argues that 18.31 marks the beginning of a new long section going up to Jerusalem for the Passion; with Jesus' Return constantly expected, not too far ahead; and with the Jewish people punished for rejecting Jesus, while Gentile salvation is forgotten. Although the ἐγένετο δέ of 18.35 looks like the intended beginning of a pericope, he cites 16.22, 17.14 and 19.15 as cases where this formula does not begin a pericope; and this seems to be justified by Luke's composing of 18.34 which gives a unity to 18.31-43. But Lambrecht overlooks what seems to be a more obviously intended sequence of Lucan thought: (1) the Rich Man who refused salvation, (2) the poor blind man who was saved by faith, (3) the rich toll-collector who repented, and salvation came to his house. Luke has added (3) to the tradition, and omitted the interjacent Marcan story of the Zebedaids. If we begin from 18.18, we can have Lambrecht's unity, and this as well.

18.31   εἶπεν-πρός*, Ἰερουσαλημ*, τελεῖσθαι, pleon. πάντα, τὰ + part., γράφειν.

18.32   Hapax: (ἐμπτύειν).

18.33   (ἡμέρα). Hapax: (μαστιγοῦν).

18.34   καὶ-αὐτοί*, ἦν + part., τὸ-ῥῆμα-τοῦτο*, τὰ + part. In a way the verse is Luke's substitute for the Sons of Zebedee story.

18.35   ἐγένετο-δέ*, ἐν-τῷ + inf.*, ἐγγίζειν*, τις, (παρά). Mark began the story, 'And they enter Jericho', but says that Bartimaeus was healed as they left the town. Luke changes this detail, so as to accommodate a second Jericho incident, Zacchaeus (Marshall).

18.36   (ἀκούσας)-δέ, διαπορεύεσθαι, πυνθάνεσθαι, τί-εἴη*.

18.37   ἀπαγγέλλειν. Hapax: Ναζωραῖος (×7 Acts). Mark: 'It is Jesus the Nazarene', Matthew 'Jesus παράγει', Luke: 'Jesus of Nazareth παρέρχεται'—a possible MA.

18.38   βοᾶν.

18.39   σιγᾶν, αὐτός nom. Hapax: προάγειν (cf. Mk 10.32).

18.40   σταθείς*, ἄγειν, ἐγγίζειν*. Hapax: κελεύειν (×17 Acts).

18.41   (εἶπεν).

18.42   (εἶπεν).

18.43   παραχρῆμα*, δοξάζειν-τὸν-θεόν*, πᾶς pleon., λαός*, ὁ-θεός. Hapax: αἶνος.

c. *Zacchaeus*, 19.1-10

The first of Luke's three pericopes told of the Rich Ruler whose attachment to his money debarred him from the kingdom: how hardly would the rich enter—yet with God all things are possible, and even the rich can be saved. The second told of a blind beggar by contrast, whose ready faith saved him. In his third story Luke gives an instance of a rich man, a chief publican (ἀρχιτελώνης), whose heart God turned to give away his wealth, ill and well gotten alike; so that the Lord could say, 'Today salvation has come to this house'. Jesus told the ruler to sell all and give away to the poor, and he became sad, for he was very rich: Zacchaeus was rich, and he received Jesus with gladness, giving half of his possessions to the poor as well as multiple restitution. The evangelist's third incident tellingly points the moral he draws from their two Marcan predecessors.

Did Luke find so suitable a tale in L, or did he, as Bultmann supposed (pp. 33f.), create it out of the call of Levi in Mk 2.13ff.? Marshall objects that Luke does not create Son of Man sayings like 19.10, and it seems to me that there are details in the story Bultmann does not explain: but they are nearer to hand than Marshall thinks. Luke has omitted the folly of the Sons of Zebedee (Mk 10.35-45); but there are precious features of the story no evangelist would wish to lose, especially the famous conclusion, '*The Son of Man came. . .* to give his life a ransom for many'. The atonement doctrine is not Luke's own, and he steadily avoids it all through the early sermons in Acts, though he is honest enough to ascribe it once to his master Paul (Acts 20.28). Luke thought the good news was God's free forgiveness (24.47 and passim), and, like many a more recent theologian, he could not see why God should require a redemption price in the blood of the innocent; so he substitutes, in line with 15.4ff. (and 9.56D?), 'The Son of Man came to *seek* and to save *the lost*'. Just as this is drawn from Mk 10.45, so the passing through Jericho and the crowd are drawn from elements omitted in Mk 10.46b, 'And as he. . . and a large crowd were leaving Jericho'.

Luke's gospel of the forgiveness of sins is characteristically realized in the conversion of publicans: Levi in 5 (Mark), with the Baptist (3.12R; 7.29R), and with Jesus (7.34QC; 15.1ff.L), even in a parable (18.9-14L). So Luke sees the Son of Man as bringing salvation to a publican here, too; but ordinary publicans were poor men—to make his contrast with the Ruler, Luke needs a wealthy publican, and so an ἀρχιτελώνης (here only in the Gospels). Bultmann cannot be far wrong in sensing the matrix of the Zacchaeus story in Mark 2/Luke 5. There a *publican by name* Levi is called by Jesus and leaves his all; he gives a large party in his house, where the Pharisees *murmured* (ἐγόγγυζον) because Jesus ate with publicans and *sinners* (Lk. 5.27ff.). Luke has in fact already elaborated this scene once in 15.1ff., where the same carpers *murmured* (διεγόγγυζον, as in 19.7) for the same reason, and Jesus spoke of the shepherd going after *the lost* sheep, and the woman *seeking* her coin, and of both *rejoicing*. Nonetheless I think Bultmann is a little wrong, and that the source of the story is more exactly in Mt. 9.9ff. Matthew, 'a man named Matthaeus'; Mark, 'Levi the son of Alphaeus'; Luke, 'a man by name called Zacchaeus'. Matthew, 'And seeing, the Pharisees said. . . Why does your teacher eat with publicans and sinners?'; Mark, 'And the scribes of the Pharisees, seeing that he ate with publicans and sinners, said, Why, etc.'; Luke, '*And seeing* they all murmured, saying, He has gone in to stay with a sinner'. Luke has told the Levi story once; now he is adapting the Call of Matthew. Both end, 'I *came*. . .'. The names Ζακχαῖος/ Ματθαῖος are strikingly alike.

Bultmann speaks boldly of a Lucan creation: but we have seen before that when Luke is telling a synoptic story the second time, using the Matthaean rather than the Marcan form, he tends to a rather imaginative exegesis of his text, to give a differentiated narrative. Thus the raising of the ruler's daughter of Mt. 9.18ff. appeared, with the adduction of other passages, as the raising of the Widow's Son in Luke 7; the Sinner of the same chapter was a very developed form of the anointing narrative of Mark 14; the Dropsical Man of Luke 14 is a version of the man with the dry hand of Matthew 12. In all these cases Luke is forming a 'substitute' narrative by following some suggestion in the given text. We must, accordingly, ask whether the same process is not at work here: Luke has described the call of Levi, following Mark—he would hardly be content with the virtually identical call of Matthew.

Two details seem to have been influential here. First, Mt. 9.9 speaks of Matthew as 'sitting ἐπὶ τὸ τελώνιον'. There is no doubt that the intended meaning is '*at* the toll-office'. But Greek use permits ἐπί with acc. to carry the meaning '*over*'; cf. Rev. 7.15, 'He who sits on the throne will make his tabernacle over them' (ἐπ' αὐτούς, cf. BAG III. 1 ζ). So it is open to Luke to think that for some reason the toll-collector has climbed up into some eminence, and is sitting over the toll-office.

A second text comes in the Marcan Sons of Zebedee story, of which Mk 10.45 is to provide the basis for the pronouncement in Lk. 19.10, 'The Son of Man came. . . ' Mk 10.43, 'He who would be great among you, he shall be your minister'; and this is a recurrent gospel theme, of which Luke has already given a version at 9.46, 'He who is least (μικρότερος) among you all, he shall be great'. The point about ministering he will expound at 22.26f., but the 'littleness' is also significant to him, for he speaks of the easily despised outcasts who have come into the church as 'these little ones' at 17.2. Taken together the two hints make the suggestion of just such a colourful tale as appealed to him. Zacchaeus will have been physically μικρός, in stature. The presence of a large ὄχλος (Mk 10.46) will have made it impossible for him to see Jesus. Jesus went into Jericho and out of it (Mk 10.46), so he must have gone through it (διέρχεσθαι, 19.4). If Zacchaeus was over (ἐπί) the toll-office, he must have found a large tree near-by; and a suitable large tree, as at 17.6, would be a fig-mulberry, συκομορέα. It seems that we can watch the creative mind at work.

In a number of ways the story is typical of Luke. Its hero is a *disreputable* character (§4.7), a publican like the hero of the Pharisee and Publican (or, substantially, of the Prodigal Son). He *repents* as they do; and he finds a cure for the problem of wealth by giving it in *alms*, as at Lk. 12.33, 'Sell your possessions and give alms. . . ', 11.41, 'But as for what is within, give alms, and lo all is pure to you'. There is the customary crowd of *murmuring* critics (15.2R; cf. 13.14; 14.1, etc.). Zacchaeus is a pattern of Lucan *alacrity*: 'And running on ahead. . . Zacchaeus, hasten and come down. . . and he hastened and came down' (§3). He *rejoices* and *entertains* Jesus: there is no party this time, but 'he received him' (ὑπεδέξατο) recalls Martha at 10.38. The emphasis on *today* is Lucan also: 'Today I must stay in your house. . . Today salvation is come to this house' (cf. 2.11; 4.21; 23.43, etc.). *Salvation* itself, as a noun (σωτηρία/-ιον) is exclusively Lucan in the Gospels (0/0/7+7); it comes three times in the Benedictus, where it is also linked with *Abraham*, as here. Zacchaeus is a son of Abraham as the Bent Woman was a daughter of Abraham (13.16), and so an heir of the promises to Abraham (1.55, 73). We have already noted Luke's interest in the *seeking* of *the lost* in the Sheep and Coin, and the Prodigal was lost too. But the tale is not just Lucan in its concentration of theological themes. It sparkles with Lucan *life* (§4.8): Zacchaeus's name (cf. Martha, Lazarus, Jericho in the parable), his shortness, the 'sycamore', the specific generosity of his response with half the money given away as well as fourfold restitution—far more than was legally required. Somehow Zacchaeus's words achieve that level of *positive emotion* which is only to be found in Lucan stories like the Samaritan and the Prodigal: we are hearing the authentic joyful note of the man who had nothing to lose but his golden chains, and who has just seen them fall from his wrists.

Most commentators take the passage to come to Luke from L, and this is supported in modern times by Jeremias's claims of pre-Lucan language: for a critique of these, see pp. 15ff. But for the Lucanness of the whole, see W.P. Loewe, *CBQ* (1974), and Drury, *Tradition*, pp. 72-75. Drury's typological claims for Joshua and Rahab should be treated with caution. A variant line of interpretation has been proposed whereby Zacchaeus is seen not as repenting—'Lo, the half of my goods I (will) give. . .'—but as defending himself—'Lo, the half of my goods I give (regularly). . .': so R.C. White, Fitzmyer. This seems forced: why does he say, 'Lo', when there is nothing to see, and how can Jesus speak of salvation today when all he has done is to have Jesus for the night? The traditional view is Luke all over, even if 'repent', 'forgive', etc. are not used: the 'lo' stands for a present pledge, which his critics can witness, and it is 'today' when the vital turning point in his life takes place. He will restore fourfold not money gained in future extortions, but what he has taken improperly in the past. Bultmann (p. 33) thinks vv. 8 and 10 are later additions, since Jesus' reference to 'he' answers to the critics' comments in v. 7: but they are much more meaningful in the light of Zacchaeus's action in v. 8.

19.1 διέρχεσθαι*. Jericho was the first town on the road from Peraea into Judaea, and is very likely to have had a major customs post. The Beggar has been moved by Luke from western ('departing', Mk 10.46) to eastern ('approaching', 18.35) Jericho for the sake of the thematic order: faithless rich man, faithful poor man, penitent rich man.

19.2 ἀνήρ*, ὀνόματι*, καλούμενος*, καὶ-αὐτὸς-ἦν*, καὶ-αὐτὸς*, πλούσιος*, καὶ-ἰδού. Hapax: ἀρχιτελώνης. Luke was interested in the meaning of names, and thought Barnabas significant as 'Son of Exhortation'. He correctly says that Tabitha means a gazelle (Dorcas); so he may have known that *zakai* means 'to be innocent, justified'—compare the δεδικαιωμένος publican of 18.14. If so, the change from Ματθαῖος to Ζακχαῖος would be very apt. Perhaps, similarly, Martha = mistress: cf. §25.3. A connection between Zacchaeus and *Matthias* is as old as Clement Alex. *Strom.* IV.6.35.2.

19.3 ζητεῖν. ἐζήτει ἰδεῖν τὸν ῾Ι., 9.9R; object + ind. question, cf. 13.25. ἡλικία 2.52; 12.25QC.

19.4 ἤμελλεν*, διέρχεσθαι*. Hapaxes: προτρέχειν, συκομορέα. ἐκείνης (ὁδοῦ), 5.19. ἔμπροσθεν adv. 19.28R.

19.5 ὡς = when*, τόπος, εἶπεν-πρὸς*, σπεύδειν, σήμερον, οἶκος, δεῖν, μένειν. Bultmann (pp. 33f.) sees the scene as 'manifestly imaginary', based on Mk 2.14ff.

19.6 σπεύδειν, χαίρειν*. ὑπεδέξατο, 10.38; Acts 17.7.

19.7 ἁμαρτωλός, ἀνήρ* (combined of Peter, 5.8). καταλύειν = lodge 9.12R, 0/0/2, cf. -λυμα 0/1/2.

19.8 σταθείς*, εἶπεν-πρὸς*, ὁ-κύριος*, τὰ-ὑπάρχοντα*, πτωχός, τις (×2). Hapaxes: ἡμίσυς, τετραπλοῦς. συκοφαντεῖν, 3.14. The Law required restitution + 20% (Lev. 6.1-5): fourfold repayment occurs at Exod. 22.1 over the theft of sheep, but is here symbolic of prodigal generosity, the sign of full-hearted conversion. See Derrett, *Law*, 278-285, esp. p. 284, for other instances of fourfold restitution.

19.9 εἶπεν-δὲ-πρὸς*, σήμερον, σωτηρία*, οἶκος, γίνεσθαι, καὶ-αὐτός*, Αβρααμ. καθότι 0/0/2+4. The address to Zacchaeus followed by a sentence referring to him in the third person is due to the context: v. 9a is a response to Zacchaeus in v. 8, v. 9b to the critics in v. 7. It is quite likely that we should see a Pauline overtone to Luke's 'son of Abraham': Z. too is a son of Abraham, and not by birth only but now, as he has demonstrated, by faith also. Otherwise why καθότι?

19.10 ζητεῖν, ἀπολωλός.

Loewe, W.P., 'Towards an Interpretation of Lk 19:1-10', *CBQ* 36 (1974), pp. 321-31.
White, R.C., 'Vindication for Zacchaeus?', *ET* 91 (1979), 21.
O'Hanlon, J., 'The Story of Zacchaeus and the Lukan Ethic', *JSNT* 12 (1981), pp. 2-26.

46. *Into Jerusalem*, 19.11-48

a. *The Pounds*, 19.11-27

We have had three incidents around Jericho, on the themes of wealth and poverty, faith and salvation: now we are to have three incidents approaching Jerusalem, on the themes of Jesus' kingship, and the fate of the city that refuses him. The first is the Pounds parable, told 'because he was near Jerusalem' (though the opening phrase, 'as they heard these things' implies that he was still in Jericho). The second is the Entry into Jerusalem. In the third he weeps over the city before cleansing the Temple.

Mark moves direct from Bartimaeus to the Entry, with its messianic overtones, and its 'Blessed be the coming kingdom of our father David'—just the kind of comment which Luke deplored as misleading and the cause of embarrassment. No doubt Jesus had actually expected the kingdom soon in power, whether before or after his death; and Luke's repeated protestations may make us suspect that there were those in his community who had heard about this. For not only does he write here, 'he told a further parable, because he was near Jerusalem, and they thought that the kingdom of God was to appear immediately'; but he also makes the apostles' first question in Acts, 'Lord, will you at this time restore the kingdom to Israel?' At all events, he removes the offensive 'the coming kingdom' (19.38; Mk 11.10), and inserts the Pounds to save any possible misunderstanding.

Matthew had contained some suitable material which emphasized the delay between Christ's passion and his parousia: the Servant, the Bridesmaids and the Talents all contain this theme, though Luke has used the Servant in ch. 12, and adapted the Bridesmaids in both ch. 12 and ch. 13. But the master who entrusted money to his servants and went away, and came 'after a long time' (Mt. 25.19) is in many ways suited to the present juncture. Unfortunately Luke is thinking of the Marcan text about the coming kingdom, and he notices that the matter following the Talents in Matthew is the Great Assize, when the king, who is Christ, like the master in the Talents, sends his disobedient subjects to hell. Luke is not good at combining stories. He nearly made a chaos of the Centurion's Boy by bringing in reminiscences of Cornelius and Jairus; he wrought confusion at the end of the Unjust Steward by mixing the remission of debts theme from Matthew 18 with the Talents; and this time he has produced a disaster, an unhappy blend of inconsequence and absurdity.

The 'man' of Matthew's parable he makes a noble, and sends him to 'a far country' (cf. Matthew's 'after a long time'), to receive a kingdom and return, as Jesus does for the Assize. Given the scale on which Matthew thinks, with money laid out by the talent, nobles and kingdoms would not be out of place: but Luke has an aversion from big business, and he reduces the investments to a *mna* apiece, 100 denarii, three months wages (§5). The stingy feel which this gives to the story is in no way redeemed by his increasing the number of 'servants' to ten—one master, ten servants, Luke's familiar proportion of 10:1 (ten lepers, one Samaritan; ten silver pieces, one lost, §12). However his interest is not commercial at all, but political: it is the kingdom the Lord has gone to receive which prompted the parable, and in v. 14 we move to a group of people unrelated to the servants— the 'citizens' who send an embassy to stop the appointment.

When the nobleman returns, his kingship confirmed, his first thought is his money (v. 15): Matthew's *parable* was about money, and this for the moment pushes out the political interest. The first servant has made ten *mnae* out of his one (10:1 *again*, v. 16), and in view of his commercial reliability, is made surprisingly (and unsuitably) governor of ten cities. Both here and with the second servant who has made five (five yoke of oxen, five sparrows, five in a house, etc., §12), the political aspect of the story makes an uncomfortable mix. By v. 20 Luke has forgotten that he had ten servants, and in place of 'the third' writes 'the other'; like the many guests at the great dinner in ch. 14, who turn out to be only three. In fact the whole structure of the parable implies the three Matthaean servants. Being the trustee for so small a sum of money, this 'other' servant is supplied with one of Luke's colourful details (§4.8), a napkin in which to hide it; and he changes Matthew's beautiful balance, 'reaping where you did not sow, and gathering where you did not scatter' (§21) to 'taking what you did not lay down. . . '. Matthew's master is accused fairly of taking the return from the land without working for it; Luke's master is accused unfairly of taking (profit) from (investments) he had not made, when he has actually 'laid out' ten *mnae* in this instance. Luke is not at home with business (§30.3). His master then reprimands the servant, and commands to give his *mna* to the man with ten: but the man actually has eleven, not ten, and he is now governor of ten cities too, so a *mna* is an absurd sum, a tip. The bystanders object that he already has ten *mnae*; compare the Lucan insertion at 20.16, 'When they heard this they said, "God forbid"'. Although the bystanders are speaking, Luke goes steaming on, 'I tell you. . . ', which he intends to be spoken by Jesus (cf. 7.29f., 31). He gives us the moral, 'To everyone that has. . . ', but he forgets to deal with the wicked servant, as he hastily recollects the rebels of v. 14, whom he commands to put to the sword.

So, sadly, Luke's last great parable from a base in Matthew is a disappointment. Why then has Homer nodded? From falling between two stools: he has neither followed his *Vorlage* closely, as he does with Mark's Husbandmen, nor elaborated as we have seen him do so many times with brilliance. He has superimposed the kingship theme on the Matthaean Talents, an uneasy combination. His preference for manageable sums of money does not fit the scale of his royal allegory. His liking for ten-to-one proportions does not fit the structure of a parable which has two good servants and one bad. Even the allegory is not properly worked out, for the noble's return as king corresponds to Christ's return as king—but the slaughter of the unwilling citizens is likely to answer to the great massacre of 70 (11.50f.; 13.35a). It is this theme which is to recur so forcibly in the present triple unit (19.41-44), and again at 20.16 and 21.20-24: it is hard to find any clear teaching in Luke that consigns the Jewish λαός, for whom he shows so much sympathy, to eternal destruction.

Critical evaluation of the parable has tended towards the conclusion for which I have argued, that the royal elements are Luke's own redaction of an earlier ('Q') version preserved more exactly in Matthew; though it has not quite reached so clear and simple an answer. Manson (pp. 312-17) thought the Matthaean and Lucan versions to be so different that they must come from different sources, M and L; and a similar line is followed by Schneider, Weiser (p. 255) and Lambrecht. But at the same time the verbal similarities are strong enough to require a common source at an earlier stage: so some version of the Q hypothesis is needed in the end. Most critics have accordingly opted for a straightforward Q solution. As Matthew is fond of kings and grandeur, it is not likely that he has cut these elements out of a Q=Lucan version: so either Luke has combined two different parables, a money parable and a royal parable, or he has glossed the second on to the first.

The hypothesis of two parables combined was defended by Harnack; (*Sprüche*, pp. 84f.) and Wellhausen (p. 106); but the version of the theory most familiar in modern times is that of Jeremias (*Parables*, pp. 58-60). The royal parable is there seen as based upon the journey of Archelaus to Rome to claim the title of king on Herod's death, pursued by an embassy of protesting Jews (Josephus *Ant.* 17.9.1-3, *B.J.* 2.2.2): Jesus told it to the

Pharisees as a warning against false security. We may concede that some memories of Archelaus underlie the parable, but that does not tell us that it was Jesus' parable, still less that it was addressed to Pharisees. The evidence we have in the Lucan text, with the noble's absence in a far country, seems to point to a situation in which the Church needs reassurance because the Parousia has not yet happened. This is the very same emphasis which comes in the Matthaean Talents—'after a long time', Mt. 25.19—and suggests the post-70 period for both.

These considerations have led many moderns—Bultmann (p. 190), Creed, Dodd (p. 146), Grässer (p. 116), Lührmann (pp. 70f.), M. Didier (*De Jésus*, pp. 248-71), Schulz (p. 288), Fitzmyer—to the view that the royal elements are substantially Luke's own gloss: so we have come close to the new paradigm view, where Luke is straightforwardly editing the Matthaean version. It is, however, usually objected that the Q version was not quite our Matthew, reliance being made on the dubious generalization that the smaller figures in Luke must be earlier than the larger ones in Matthew.

It is vain to speculate on an original meaning which the parable had for Jesus. Dodd and Jeremias can fit it into their general theory: the emphasis is all on the day of reckoning, when the bad servant (= the pious Jew/Pharisaic scribe) will be condemned for his complacency. Fitzmyer follows Didier in the view that Jesus spoke the parable to the disciples: the *mna* is the secrets of the kingdom which have been entrusted to them. Our only evidence is the parable which Matthew passed on to Luke, since the Lucan additions are all the evangelist's: and Matthew himself is reassuring his church about the delayed Parousia. I have argued elsewhere (*MLM*, pp. 440ff.) that the Matthaean version is one of a sequence of expansions of the Marcan Doorkeeper: and that itself is a warning to the Church to keep awake against the Lord's delayed Return.

Ignace de la Potterie (*Fs* Dupont) follows L.T. Johnson (*NT* [1982]), in suggesting that Luke thought the appearance of the kingdom was near. He thought the kingdom had come already (11.20; 17.21), and would be revealed shortly—in Johnson's view, in judgment in the Entry to Jerusalem in 19.38, in de la Potterie's at Pentecost. But 19.11 reads like a distancing from the imminent view, and Pentecost is never Jesus' coming in Luke.

19.11 ταῦτα, προστιθέναι*, λέγειν-παραβολήν*, διὰ-τὸ, Ἰερουσαλημ*, δοκεῖν = think, παραχρῆμα*, μέλλειν. Hapax: ἀναφαίνεσθαι (Acts 21.3). For introduction cf. 16.14, ἤκουον δὲ ταῦτα..., 20.45. Motive supplied for parable, cf. 18.1, 9. ἐγγυς-εἶναι + place ×3 Acts.

19.12 εἶπεν, ἄνθρωπός-τις*, πορεύεσθαι, χώρα, ἑαυτόν, ὑποστρέφειν*. εἰς-χώραν-μακράν 15.13 (cf. Mt. ἀπεδήμησεν). Hapax: εὐγενής (Acts 17.11).

19.13 (καλεῖν), δέκα (×2)*, ἑαυτοῦ, εἶπεν-πρός*. Hapax: πραγματεύεσθαι (cf. v. 15). ἐν-ᾧ ἔρχομαι, while I am coming, cf. 5.34R, where ἐν ᾧ = while; cf. ἐν οἷς, 12.1. ἔρχομαι: cf. Mt. 25.19, ἔρχεται

19.14 τοῦτον contemptuous. πρεσβείαν-ἀποστεῖλαι 14.32, πολῖται 15.15 (note that the king's subjects come from a πόλις, cf. Mt. 22.6), βασιλεύειν-ἐπί 1.33; 19.27.

19.15 καὶ-ἐγένετο-ἐν-τῷ + inf. . .καὶ*, εἶπεν. Hapax: διαπραγματεύεσθαι (cf. v.13). ἐπανελθεῖν cf. 18.40, δεδώκει plup.

19.16 παραγίνεσθαι*, δέκα*. Παrax: προσεργάζεσθαι (cf. Mt. 25.16 ἠργάσατο). ὁ πρῶτος. . .ἕτερος 14.18ff.; 16.5, 7.

19.17 εἶπεν, γίνεσθαι, δέκα*, πόλις. Hapax: εὖγε (often punctuated εὖ [= Mt.] γε*). πιστὸς ἐν ἐλαχίστῳ. . .ἐγένεσθε, cf. 16.10f. Luke avoids Matthew's double epithets, good-and-faithful, bad-and-slothful (v. 22), faithful-and-wise (12.42; cp. Mt. 24.45).

19.19 εἶπεν-δὲ*, καὶ = also (×2), γίνεσθαι, πόλις. καὶ-σύ 10.37; 22.58 (Mk?). Luke avoids Matthew's repetitiveness (cf. 8.6R; 20.12R).

19.20 ἕτερος*. Hapaxes: ἀποκεῖσθαι, σουδάριον. ἣν εἶχον ἀποκειμένην, cf. 14.18f. ἔχε με παρῃτημένον. σουδάριον Acts 19.12, Jn 11.44; 20.7. Jeremias (p. 61) claims that keeping money in a cloth was a Palestinian custom, and so reflects an early form of the story. But *b. Ket.* 67b. says, 'R. Abba used to bind his money in a scarf, sling it on his back, and so place himself at the disposal of the poor'; and *m. BM* 3.10 similarly implies that the cloth is on the man's back. But in Luke the money is *stored* (ἀποκειμένην) in the cloth, cf. the English 'in an old sock'. It is only the Matthaean safekeeping by burial which is Jewish, cf. S–B, *ad loc.* Luke is not too fond of Latin words (23/19/16+18), but he does include αὐστηρός QD (19.21f.) and καισαρ 23.2R.

19.21 ὃ = that which (×2). ἐφοβούμην cf. Mt. 25.25 φοβηθείς. αὐστηρός (cf. v. 20) is less offensive than Matthew's σκληρός (Schulz). αἴρειν/θεῖναι is usually taken to be drawn from banking; but it is quite likely to be a weak repetition of reaping/sowing, a Lucan synonym for a Matthaean parallel (§22).

19.22 ὃ = that which (×2). ᾔδεις reflects Matthew's ἔγνων (25.24; Schulz, p. 292). λέγει is an uncommon Lucan historic present, but cf. 13.8; 16.7, 29 in parables; 7.40; 11.37, 45; 24.36 in other conversations (Neirynck, *MA* p. 229), and ×11 in Acts (verbs of saying).

19.23 τράπεζα (cf. Mt. τραπεζίταις), (σύν*), πράσσειν*. Hapax: (τόκος).

19.24 εἶπεν, (δέκα*). τοῖς παρεστῶσιν Acts 23.2; cf. v. 4; Mk 14.70; Lk. 1.19.

19.25 εἶπαν, δέκα*. Foil interposition, cf. 20.16bR (§1.4).

19.26 (πᾶς pleonastic). The Matthaean form of the parable is presumed, with more money for the successful.

19.27 πλὴν*, τούτους contemptuous, ἄγειν. Hapax: κατασφάζειν.

Dupont, J., 'La parabole des talents ou des mines', *RTP* 3/9 (1969), pp. 376-91.
Weinert, F.D., 'The Parable of the Throne Claimant (Luke 19.12, 14-15a, 27) Reconsidered', *CBQ* 39 (1977), pp. 505-14.
Resenhöfft, W., 'Jesu Gleichnis von den Talenten, ergänzt durch die Lukas-Fassung', *NTS* 26 (1980), pp. 318-31.
Johnson, L.T., 'The Lukan Kingship Parable (Lk 19.11-27)', *NT* 24 (1982), pp. 139-59.
de la Potterie, I., 'La parabole du prétendant à la royauté (Lk. 19.11-28)', in *Fs* Dupont (1985), pp. 613-41.

b. *From Jericho to Olivet*, 19.28-38

At 19.11 Jesus was outside Jericho and 'near Jerusalem', when Luke inserted his form of the Matthaean Talents. Now he is 'going up to Jerusalem' (v. 28), 'nearing Bethphage and Bethany by the Mount called of Olives' (v. 29), 'nearing the descent of the Mount of Olives' (v. 37); he is rejoining Mark for the stories of the ass, and of the disciples' acclamation (vv. 29-38). But although the use of the Marcan *Vorlage* is clear, Luke's phrasing is less close than often; and opinion has been divided whether, with Creed, Schneider and Fitzmyer, we should think of Luke's free re-writing (and L for vv. 39f, with Fitzmyer), or whether with Manson (pp. 317-19), Schramm (pp. 144-49) and H. Patsch (*ZTK* [1971]), we should think of a second source, especially for the last two verses.

The evidence of a second source is in part a series of MAs.

(1) Mt. 21.2	λύσαντες		ἀγάγετέ μοι
Mk 11.2	λύσατε	αὐτὸν καί	φέρετε
Lk. 19.30	λύσαντες	αὐτὸν	ἀγάγετε

Luke agrees with Matthew both in the participle λύσαντες and in the substitution of the aorist imperative of ἄγειν for Mk's present imperative φέρετε. Matthew very often combines aorist participles with aorist imperatives (e.g. 2.13, 20; 9.6R, 13R), but Luke is quite tolerant of two imperatives linked by καί (e.g. ἀνάστηθι καί, Acts 8.26; 9.6, 34; 26.16, ×4 out of ×12). He uses φέρειν of bringing an animal at 15.23 (φέρετε, impv), Acts 14.13. ἤγαγον comes again in v. 35 = Mt. 21.7MA: but for bringing an animal, without Matthew Luke uses φέρειν.

(2) Mt. 21.6 πορευθέντες   δὲ οἱ μαθηταί
    Mk 11.4 καὶ ἀπῆλθον   καὶ   εὗρον
    Lk. 19.32 ἀπελθόντες   δὲ οἱ ἀπεσταλμένοι εὗρον καθὼς εἶπεν

Matthew has inserted the long fulfilment of Zech. 9.9 at 21.4f., and requires the restated subject. In Luke the story just follows on, as in Mark. In the closely similar story of the Passover preparation Luke writes just ἀπελθόντες δὲ εὗρον καθώς without a resumptive subject. For further MAs in v. 36, see below: it may also be that Luke's insertion of ἐπεβίβασαν at v. 35 owes something to Matthew's citation of ἐπιβεβηκώς from Zech. 9.9 (Marshall).

Much more forceful, however, is the correspondence with the following scene in Matthew; for when the latter has described the cleansing of the Temple, he elaborates a second scene of enthusiasm, with cries of 'Hosanna to the son of David'. Commentators on Matthew note the Matthaean style (Allen, McNeile, Gundry), and ascribe to Mt. R. The new material consists of (1) the healing of blind and lame, (2) the authorities' indignation, ἰδόντες. . .τὰ θαυμάσια, (3) and the children crying (κράζοντας) Hosanna; (4) the authorities said to Jesus, 'Do you hear what these say?', (5) and Jesus cited Ps. 8 in reply, 'From the mouth of infants didst thou perfect praise (αἶνον)'. Now all these five points have echoes in Lk. 19.37-40. (1-2) 'The disciples praised God for all the acts of power (δυναμέων) which they had *seen*' (v. 37). The response is somewhat mysterious (Creed, Manson), because 'the whole multitude of his disciples' seems to have gathered recently, and the only miracle Jesus has done for quite a long time in Luke is the healing of the blind beggar. (2/4) 'And certain of the Pharisees from the crowd said to him, Teacher, rebuke your disciples' (v. 39). The authorities were chief priests and scribes in Matthew, but the request to curb his followers is peculiar to these two passages. (3) 'If these will be silent, the stones will *cry out* (κράξουσιν)' (v. 40). There is an echo from Hab. 2.11 perhaps, 'The stone will shout (βοήσεται) from the wall', but κράξουσιν echoes the children κράζοντας (but also Mk 11.9). (5) 'The whole multitude of the disciples began αἰνεῖν τὸν θεόν (v. 37); cf. Matthew's αἶνον from Ps. 8. αἰνεῖν is perfectly Lucan, but not so common as δοξάζειν. We may add (6) that Jesus' prophecy of Jerusalem's doom in 19.42-44 could similarly be a reflection of Mt. 21.22, 'This is the *prophet* Jesus of Nazareth' (see the next section). The combined force of these points is considerable. Fitzmyer, 'They seem to be a form of Mt. 21.15-16', appeals to Bultmann (p. 34), who thinks Luke and Matthew drew on a common source; but he does not mention Q, and Polag does not make the attribution even in his list of possibilities. Cf. Schneider, p. 385, 'However one may judge the relation of the two verses to Mt. 21.15f...' It is best to say that Patsch's lost source is the Gospel of Matthew: we have here one more instance of Lucan substitution.

Otherwise, Luke is content with Mark. The only doctrinal need is to remove 'the coming kingdom of our father David' (Mk 11.10). Luke inserts ὁ βασιλεύς after 'he that comes': the king is here, but not yet the kingdom (19.11; Acts 1.6). For the same reason he removes the cutting of branches, which were part of the Tabernacles symbolism of the kingdom of God: they were specifically ordered to be waved at the recital of the Hosanna verse from Ps. 118 (*m. Sukk.* 3.9).

19.28 εἰπών*, ταῦτα, πορεύεσθαι. ἀναβαίνων-εἰς-Ἰεροσόλυμα carried over from Mk 10.32/Mt. 20.17 (cf. Mk 11.1). ἔμπροσθεν probably 'in front' = Mark's προάγων (Marshall).

19.29 καὶ-ἐγένετο-when*, ὡς = when* (καὶ-ἐγ.-ὡς 1.23, 41; 2.15), (ἐγγίζειν*), καλούμενος*.

19.30 εἰπών*, (εὑρίσκειν), (ἄγειν). Hapaxes: (κατέναντι), πώποτε.

19.31 ἐρωτᾶν*, (ὁ-κύριος = Jesus*). ὁ κύριος probably means Jesus in all three Synoptics.

19.32 (εὑρίσκειν), (καθώς). ἀποστέλλεσθαι καθὼς εἶπεν advanced from Mk 11.6, but note καθὼς προσέταξεν in the proper parallel position in Mt. 21.6. ἀπεσταλμένοι pf. pass. part.

19.33 εἶπαν-πρός*. κύριοι pl. Acts 16.16, 19; Lk. 16.13Q = Mt. 6.24.

19.34 (εἶπαν), ὁ-κύριος*. The edifying oratio recta of v. 31 is repeated.

19.35 (ἄγειν). Hapax: ἐπιρρίπτειν. ἐπιβιβάζειν ἐπὶ 10.34; Acts 23.24; so any link with Mt. 21.5/Zech. 9.9 LXX is insecure. ἐπιρρίπτειν cf. ρίπτειν 3/0/ 2, 4.35R; 17.2R.

19.36 πορεύεσθαι. Hapax: ὑποστρωννύναι.

Mt. 21.8a	ἔστρωσαν ἑαυτῶν	τὰ ἱμάτια	ἐν τῇ ὁδῷ
.8b	ἐστρώννυον		ἐν τῇ ὁδῷ
Mk 11.8	τὰ ἱμάτια αὐτῶν ἔστρωσαν		εἰς τὴν ὁδόν
Lk. 19.36	ὑπεστρώννυον	τὰ ἱμάτια	ἐν τῇ ὁδῷ

Lk. 19.36 ἑαυτῶν ABWΘ: Greeven. αυτων א DL fam. 1, 13: N-A²⁶, Diglot. ἑαυτῶν is preferable, as Luke has αὐτῶν τα ἱμ. at 19.35. But in any case the order, the imperfect, and ἐν τῇ ὁδῷ are all reminiscences of Matthew.

19.37 ἐγγίζειν*, ἅπαν-τὸ-πλῆθος*, χαίρειν*, αἰνεῖν-τὸν-θεόν, φωνή, περί, πᾶς pleon., ὧν in attraction*, δύναμις = act of power*. πρὸς + dat. is unique in L-A. Hapax: καταβάσις. But Schramm (pp. 145-49) exaggerates the evidence for a *Nebenquelle*: 14 words out of 28 (none of which is from Mark) are Lucan. Note Luke's accurate topography.

19.38 (εὐλογεῖν*), (ὄνομα), οὐρανός sing., εἰρήνη*, δόξα, (ὕψιστος*). Luke distracts his hearer from the familiar Marcan message of hope now, 'the coming kingdom of our father David', with pie in the sky. At 2.14 the angels said, 'Glory to God in the highest, and on earth peace. . .', but now the peace is limited to heaven too: no doubt, if pressed, he would refer us to 10.18. Jn 12.13 takes over Lk.R's βασιλεύς.

Patsch, H., 'Der Einzug Jesu in Jerusalem: Ein historischer Versuch', *ZTK* 68 (1971), pp. 1-26.
Fitzmyer, J.A., 'The Use of ἄγειν and φέρειν in the Synoptic Gospels', in *Fs* F.W. Gingrich, ed. E.H. Barth, *et al.* (Leiden, 1972), pp. 147-60.

c. *The Cleansing of the Temple*, 19.39-48

Jesus was 'near Jerusalem' at 19.11, he came down the Mount of Olives in 19.28ff., now he enters both city and the Temple itself (v. 45). Luke's handling of the story is determined by an uncomfortable tension in his sources. Mark told of the Cleansing of the Temple, flanking the incident on either side with the Fig-tree, and attendant matter; but Matthew has both parts of the Fig-tree *after* the Cleansing, and he has an apparently fuller version of the Temple scene—Jewish authorities indignant with Jesus for permitting his followers' over-enthusiasm (21.15f.), the crowds hailing Jesus as a prophet (21.11), the healing of blind and lame (21.14). So Luke leaves aside the Fig-tree, whose main message he has already given (13.6-9; 17.6), and provides his own version of the extra Matthaean material. (cf. above, p. 686).

In Matthew the scribes, etc., said to Jesus, 'Do you hear what these say?', as the children cried out (κράζοντας): in Luke some Pharisees from the crowd said to him, 'Teacher, rebuke your disciples'. They thus make the standard Lucan foil introduction (§1.4) for Jesus' prophetic reply, 'If these shall be silent, the stones will cry out' (κράξουσιν). Luke is adapting Hab. 2.11, 'The stone shall shout from the wall': he means they will cry out God's praise (v. 37). But the great hammer of the Temple and the great prophet of the fall of Jerusalem, had been not so much Habakkuk as Jeremiah, and it was Jeremiah whose mantle Jesus had assumed in the earlier Gospels, calling the place 'a den of robbers' (Jer. 7.11). This whole section of the prophecy had been against 'the Temple of the Lord, the Temple of the Lord' (7.4), and bitterly its author wept at his message (8.18, 23 LXX, κλαύσομαι). Prophet and priest had dealt falsely, saying Peace, peace, when there was no peace (εἰρήνη, 6.13f.; 8.10.); they would be overthrown at the time of their visitation (ἐν καιρῷ ἐπισκοπῆς αὐτῶν, 6.15), when a siege mound would be cast up against Jerusalem (6.6). It is this which inspires Luke to provide the message implied by Matthew's 'Jesus the prophet'. He *weeps* over the city: had it but known even now the way to its *peace*! But it knows not the *time of its visitation*; and *siege bank, encirclement* and *hemming in on every side* will be its fate. The χάραξ, κύκλος and συνέχειν come from Jeremiah's description of the siege (52.4f., περιεχαράκωσαν, κύκλῳ, συνοχή); the *razing* of town and *children* from Ps. 136.9LXX. The Romans' not leaving one stone upon another is from the Lord's own words in Mk 13.2=Lk. 21.6.

So now we see why peace was limited to heaven in v. 38: Jerusalem knows not the things that belong to her peace. We can see too why Luke has so drastically abbreviated the actual Cleansing, reducing it to two brief verses (45f.), and omitting purchasers, money-changers, dove-sellers, passers-by, Gentiles, etc. Luke's Jesus knows that the Cleansing is an empty gesture: Jerusalem knows not to repent, it is hidden from her eyes. Now he is re-enacting the prophecy of Jeremiah: soon the real cleansing in blood and fire will fulfil the disaster of 587.

N-A[26] and some commentators take vv. 39f. with vv. 28-38; but they belong better with the present pericope. Not only do the λίθοι of v. 40 lead on to those of v. 44, but Luke has a liking for Pharisaic objections with which to open his units (e.g. 14.1; 15.2; 16.14; 17.20). With 'certain Pharisees from the crowd', cf. 'a certain woman from the crowd' (11.27), and 'a certain man from the crowd' (12.13), each of whom opened their respective unit.

There is a strong wish among commentators to see an original oracle of Jesus underlying vv. 40-44 (so Dodd, *JRS* [1947]; Manson, p. 320; Fitzmyer; even David Tiede, *Prophecy*, pp. 78-86, whose actual argument seems to support

Lucan authorship), and Lloyd Gaston, *Stone*, 359, attributes it to a pre-Lucan phase. The arguments used to defend this are not strong. (1) Jeremias (*Sprache*, pp. 281f.) counts seven uses of καί linking main verbs, and eight enclitic uses of σε, σου, σοι; a pattern different from Acts. Surely such arguing is blinkered: vv. 42-44 consist of a piled up sequence of prophecies of disaster spoken to Jerusalem, a feature not found in Acts, and that is why the verbs are joined by 'and', and addressed to 'you'. (2) Dodd showed that 'there is no single trait of the forecast which cannot be documented directly out of the Old Testament' (p. 79). It would be natural for Jesus to couch his prophecy in OT terms: should we not expect a post-70 form of the prophecy to contain echoes of the actual event, such as the firing of the Temple gates and other details given by Josephus? I do not think we should. Luke is unlikely to have read Josephus: he regarded Jeremiah and Ps. 137 as prophecies of AD 70, and more accurate than any account he may have heard. (3) There were other prophecies of the fall of Jerusalem, e.g. by Jesus ben-Ananias, so there is no reason for thinking that our Jesus' words here are *post eventum*. It is indeed fallacious to infer that all true prophecies are *post eventum*; and Sanders has argued that it is extremely likely that Jesus spoke against the Temple (*Jesus and Judaism*, pp. 61-76). But that does nothing to support the claim that the present passage comes from tradition. (4) Gaston finds a tension between Proto-Luke and Luke: but this is disputed by Tiede (pp. 68-70), and does not seem to me to be substantial.

In favour of Lucan authorship are (1) the coincidence of so many words with LXX prophecies of the fall of Jerusalem. As Luke regularly approximates his OT references to the LXX, this would incline us to think of Lucan authorship. (2) There is a fair sprinkling of words congenial to Luke (see below, 19 out of 102), and nothing that strikes the reader as alien: Jeremias' claims that ἐγγίζειν and ἥξουσιν ἡμέραι are pre-Lucan (*Sprache*, pp. 181f.) lack a sound basis (cf. above, pp. 80ff.). (3) The cumulative argument in favour of free Lucan writing elsewhere (ch. 3) leads to scepsis over the frequent unargued claim, 'Luke drew this from L'.

19.39 τις, εἶπαν-πρός*.ἀπὸ τοῦ ὄχλου 9.38R, ἐκ 11.27; 12.13.

19.40 εἶπεν. Habakkuk prophesied the coming of the Chaldaeans to punish Israel, like Jeremiah. For other views of the significance of the stones' cry, see Marshall.

19.41 ὡς=when*, ἐγγίζειν*, πόλις, κλαίειν*. Cf. 23.28f. L, 'weep not for me. . .'

19.42 σύ following verb*, ἡμέρα, τὰ + prep.*, εἰρήνη*, νῦν*. For the dependence on Jeremiah in these verses cf. Hastings, pp. 116-120. τὰ πρὸς εἰρήνην 14.33. Ignorance as the ground of ill-doing is Lucan, 12.47f.; 23.34; Acts 3.17.

19.43 ἥξουσιν ἡμέραι. . .καί, συνέχειν*. ἥξει ὅτε 13.35 QD; καί = that, σ.ψ. ἐγένετο. Hapaxes: παρεμβάλλειν, χάραξ, περικυκλοῦν, πάντοθεν (but παρεμβολή 0/0/0 + 6, double preposition compounds 12/14/31+45, and cf. siege vocabulary in Jer. 52 detailed above).

19.44 ἀνθ᾽ ὧν. Hapaxes: (ἐδαφίζειν), (ἐπισκοπή).

19.45 Mark's 42 words are reduced to 19.

19.46 (γράφειν), (οἶκος ×2). Hapax: (σπήλαιον). Luke, like Matthew omits 'for all nations', and has the same word-order 'but you make/made it'.

19.47 τὸ + prep.*, καθ᾽ ἡμέραν*, (ζητεῖν), λαός*. οἱ πρῶτοι (τοῦ λ.) Acts 13.50; 25.2; 28.17. Opening clause, cf. Mk 14.49.

19.48 εὑρίσκειν, τὸ + ind. questions*, τί - ποιήσω (-σιν)*, λαός*, ἅπας. Hapax: ἐκκρεμαννύναι. 'The people' are favourable to Jesus through most of Luke's Passion.

Dodd, C.H., 'The Fall of Jerusalem and the "Abomination of Desolation"', *JRS* 37 (1947), pp. 47-54 = *More New Testament Studies* (Grand Rapids, 1968), pp. 69-83.
Tiede, D.L., *Prophecy and History in Luke-Acts* (Philadelphia, 1980).

47. *Temple Controversies*, 20.1-26

a. *Authority*, 20.1-8

Luke now follows Mark closely through the controversies in the Temple. He is still concerned to group his material in clusters of three, and his source needs no serious adaptation now to that end: Mark provided controversies over authority and tribute, with Jesus' Husbandmen parable between. In Mark the authority question was posed by the chief priests and the scribes and the elders, and it is to 'them' that Jesus addresses the Husbandmen; 'they' then send Pharisees and Herodians to ask about the tribute. Luke follows for the first two scenes; in the third 'they' send questioners unspecified to catch him in his talk.

Two-thirds of the words in the Authority story come from Mark: there is, however, a rather considerable number of MAs, for which Schmid (pp. 137-39) offers individual explanations. The more serious of them are as follows. (1) In Mk 11.27 Jesus is walking in the Temple, and the question, 'By what authority do you do these things?' clearly refers to the Cleansing. Matthew has Jesus teaching (διδάσκοντι) in the Temple (21.23), and the question then refers to that. Luke also has him teaching (διδάσκοντος) and evangelizing in the Temple (v. 1), with the same effect. Schmid: 'a generalisation which was obvious as being factually likely'. (2) Mk 11.29 'ἐπερωτήσω you one question': both Matthew and Luke replace with ἐρωτήσω. Luke uses ἐπερωτᾶν ×17, always with the sense, 'ask a question', 3.10R, 14R, cf. 17.20; ἐρωτᾶν ×15, of which 11 have the meaning 'request'. There are instances (9.45; 19.31) where he writes ἐρωτᾶν into Mark with the sense 'ask a question', but he much more commonly retains the compound.

20.1 καὶ-ἐγένετο*, ἐν-μίᾳ-τῶν*, ἡμέρα, ὁ-λαός*, εὐαγγελίζεσθαι*, ἐφιστάναι*, σύν*.

20.2 εἶπαν (×2), λέγειν-πρός*, (ταῦτα).

20.3 εἶπεν-πρός*, εἰπεῖν, (ἐρωτᾶν*).

20.4 (οὐρανός sing.).

20.5 (ἑαυτόν), (εἰπεῖν), (οὐρανός sing.). Hapax: συλλογίζεσθαι.

20.6 (εἰπεῖν), ὁ-λαός*, (ἅπας), πείθεσθαι. Hapax: καταλιθάζειν.

20.8 (εἰπεῖν), (ταῦτα).

b. *The Wicked Husbandmen*, 20.9-19

Claims have been made, on the strength of different lines of evidence, that Luke had a tradition of the Husbandmen independent of Mark. Dodd (*Parables*, pp. 124-32), maintained that there had been a pre-Marcan form without Mk 12.4, with a simple three-point climactic sequence of two servants and the owner's son; and this received apparently dramatic confirmation with the discovery of the Gospel of Thomas, which has exactly this form of the parable (Th. 65). Jeremias (*Parables*, pp. 70-77) expanded and fortified Dodd's arguments. The earliest form of the story underlies the hardly allegorized versions of Th. and Luke, and Mark and Matthew have imported into it allegorical details from Isa. 5.1ff. LXX, with the servants assimilated to the prophets, the son to Christ, his death to the crucifixion outside the city, etc. The priority of the Thomas version has been accepted by J.E. Ménard, J.D. Crossan (*JBL* [1971]), Fitzmyer and others.

Jeremias's account is in fact a sleight of hand. On p. 72 he tells us that 'we are no longer in a position to say whether (Luke's) sober restraint is merely due to his sense of style, or to oral tradition'; but nine lines further down he says that 'nothing remains (in Matthew) of the original simple story as we read it in the Gospel of Thomas *and in Luke*' (my stress). So it appears that oral tradition was in fact the answer. But in note 84, at the bottom of the same page, 'According to the evidence furnished by linguistic and stylistic studies, the faultless symmetry of Lk. 20.10-12 is Luke's work...' Jeremias knows perfectly well that a very high percentage of the differences of Luke from Mark can be accounted for as characteristically Lucan (46% on my count), but he allows this first to be clouded with doubt and then (at once) to be forgotten. In this way he is able to force the parable on to his enormous graph, in which every parable begins by being 'simple' and without allegory, and ends by being ecclesiasticized and misunderstood.

As usual, we should understand Luke as preferring the story to its meaning. He leaves out the details from Isaiah 5—fence, vat, tower— partly because he is not writing a vineyard = Israel allegory, but also because he has already given his own development of the man who built a tower in 14.28ff. He reduces Mark's stream of servants, beaten, hit on the head, killed, to a sequence of three, beaten, disgraced and wounded. In this way he loses the allegory with the prophets, but he gains a better progression, with an unspoiled climax in the son's murder; we are reminded too of the three excuses in the Lucan Supper. Marshall is right to dispute the claim that allegory underlies the son's being cast out of the vineyard *before* his death; Jesus' death 'outside the gate' is found significant in Heb. 13.12 by parallel with the sacrificial animals which are burned outside the camp. There is no sign of such thinking behind Luke, and it is natural to take the vineyard as a symbol for Israel, not Jerusalem. So the Lucan differences from Mark are in line with Luke's general preference for telling a story rather than an allegory.

Schramm (pp. 150-67) also argues for a second, non-Marcan source for Luke. In part he bases this, like Jeremias, on Thomas, giving detailed verbal parallels with Luke; like the opening, 'A (good) man had/planted a vineyard', without elaboration. But nothing can be made from Thomas. As B. Dehandschutter (*Marc* [1974]) has pointed out, Thomas is following Luke both in sequence and in a number of details at this point: Thomas 63 is a form of the Rich Fool in Luke 12; Thomas 64 of the great δεῖπνον in Luke 14; Thomas 65 of the Husbandmen in Lk. 20.9-16; and Thomas 66 of the Stone logion of Lk. 20.17. So detailed parallels with Luke are to be expected: Thomas is following Luke, and he knows the 'perhaps' which Luke has added at v. 13b to save the suggestion of divine error (W. Schrage, p. 140; cp. J.E. Ménard, p. 167). It is easy, too, to be over-impressed by Dodd's coup in prophecy. He thought a simple three-point climax would be natural to folklore: two servants and the son, like priest, Levite and Samaritan. And so it is, but that does not imply that it is original. Luke is not interested in allegory and he cuts Mark's servants down to three; Thomas is not interested in the Old Testament, or for that matter in the cross, and he cuts them down to two. He is for ever abbreviating the Gospel material for the sake of his gnostic mystifications (cf. W.R. Schoedel, *CTM* [1972]).

Schramm is, however, on firmer ground when he notes the points at which Luke agrees with Matthew against Mark. (1) Mk 12.2, 'And he sent to the farmers at the season a slave'; Mt. 21.34, 'And when the season of fruits drew near, he sent...'; Lk. 20.10, 'And in season he sent...' The advancing of καιρῷ seems unnatural (cp. 12.42), and may be an echo of Matthew's clause. (2) Luke adds a second οἱ γέωργοι in the same verse ('unnecessary', Marshall), which may also be a reminiscence of Matthew. (3) He agrees with Matthew in changing the Marcan order, (a) killed, (b) threw out, in Mk 12.8. As the allegory explanation is so weak for this, remembrance of Matthew is the best reason available. (4) Most important of all is the whole of 20.18, the parallel to which should be read with N-A^{26} at Mt. 21.44 (see below), 'And he who falls on this stone...' Luke does indeed have a *Nebenquelle* beside Mark for the pericope: but that second source is Matthew.

20.9 λέγειν-παραβολήν*, πρός*, ὁ-λαός*, (φυτεύειν), χρόνος, ἵκανος. χρόνοι ἵκανοι 8.27; 23.8. [τις*] AWΘ etc. N-A^{26} Hapax: (ἐκδιδόναι). 'for considerable times' is inserted to give time for the story, and is not connected with the delayed parousia (Grässer, p. 113).

20.10 ἐξαποστέλλειν*. ἵνα followed by the future δώσουσιν αὐτῷ is extremely rare in Luke (14.10 only elsewhere), and may be an echo of Mt. 21.41 ἀποδώσουσιν αὐτῷ.

20.11 προστιθέναι*, ἕτερος*, πέμπειν*, ἐξαποστέλλειν. Hapax: (ἀτιμάζειν) (also Acts 5.14).

20.12 προστιθέναι*, πέμπειν*, καί = also. Hapax: τραυματίζειν (also Acts 19.16).

20.13 εἶπεν-δέ*, τί-ποιήσω;*, πέμπειν. Hapax: ἴσως. 'The lord of the vineyard' is borrowed forward from Mk 12.9. Luke characteristically extends the soliloquy (§4.1) with his tell-tale τί ποιήσω; ἴσως saves the impression that God was wrong.

20.14 ἰδόντες-δέ, (πρός* of speaking), ἀλλήλων, γίνεσθαι. Hapax: (κληρονόμος).

20.15 Vineyards are places in intensive cultivation with little space between the rows for crowd action: Matthew imagines the lynching as taking place more naturally outside, and Luke follows him. There is perhaps also the thought of Naboth, who was stoned (Mt. 21.35) outside the city (3 Kgdms 21.13).

20.16 τούτους contempt., ἀκούσαντες-δέ, εἶπαν, γίνεσθαι. Luke inserts a foil protest (§1.4), with Lucan optative.

20.17 εἶπεν, τὸ-γεγραμμένον*, (οἰκοδομεῖν), (γίνεσθαι). Hapax: (γωνία). The citation of Ps. 118 is abbreviated, the not so pointful 'This was from the Lord. . . ' being dropped to smooth the transition to 'Everyone who falls on *that stone. . . '*

20.18 πεσεῖν-ἐπί + acc. (×2). Hapaxes: συνθλᾶν, λικμᾶν. Neither the image of falling on a stone, nor the verb συνθλασθήσεται recalls Dan. 2, which is echoed only in the second half of the verse, with the stone in motion, and the surprising λικμήσει, winnow (2.(35), 44 Th.). A similar saying is attributed to R. Simeon b. Jose, c.200, 'In this world Israel is compared to the rocks (Num. 23.9; Isa. 51.1), and the stones (Gen. 49.24; Ps. 118.22), and the nations of the world to potsherds (Isa. 30.14). If the stone fall on the pot, woe to the pot! If the pot fall on the stone, woe to the pot!. . . Even so, in Nebuchadnezzar's dream (Dan. 2.45). . . ' (*Midr. Esth.* 3.6 [94b]).

If the parallel verse is read at Mt. 21.44, that would in itself be a sizeable nail in Q's coffin. It is read there by all the Greek uncials but D, and all the principal cursives but 33; in the Latin tradition by q, the Vulgate and Augustine; by the Syriac versions apart from Syr. sin, and by Afrahat and Ephrem; and by the Coptic. It is omitted by D 33, eight old Latin MSS, Irenaeus, Origen, Eusebius and three of five references in Chrysostom. N-A[26] prints it in a single bracket ('authenticity probable'), UBS[3] in a double bracket, rated C ('an accretion' [Metzger, p. 58]).

The verse should be read for the following reasons. (1) Matthew is insistent on the doctrine of hell. There is no other parable in Matthew where the wicked are mentioned without being consigned there: under the symbol of the fallen house (7.27), the burned tares (13.30), the discarded fish (13.48), the tormented debtor (18.34), the excluded wedding guest (22.13), the wicked servant cut in pieces (24.51), the excluded bridesmaids (25.12), the worthless man with the talent (25.30). Where such parables are given supplementary comments (in almost every case), the fear of hell is instilled there also: 'So also will my heavenly Father do unto you. . . ', 'there men will weep and gnash their teeth', etc. So here. Matthew has already given the double moral of the parable at 21.41, (a) 'he will wretchedly destroy those wretches', (b) 'and let out the vineyard to other tenants. . . ' After Mark's stone logion he resumes the conclusion: (b) 'Therefore I tell you that the kingdom of God will be taken away from you and given to a nation. . . '; (a) 'and he that falls on this stone will be shattered. . . ' Here is one more symbol, supplied by Mark, for the destruction of the damned: the parable is incomplete without it. (2) The occurrence of the double saying on the stone and the potsherd in the rabbinic tradition, and its link with both Ps. 118.22 and Dan. 2.44 there, are striking; just the sort of tradition Matthew is familiar with, and Luke not. (3) The hypothesis of assimilation from Luke is not straightforward. Luke has πᾶς ... ἐκεῖνον, where Matthew has καὶ ... τοῦτον (there is some MS variation). (4) It is easy however to see how the verse could be dropped from Matthew, since 21.43 seems to form a natural conclusion in parallel to 21.41. (5) The MS support for inclusion is strong, and the omitting witnesses are those long dignified as support for Western 'non-interpolations', now more straightforwardly called omissions.

20.19   (ζητεῖν), ἐπιβάλλειν-τὰς-χεῖρας, ἐν-αὐτῇ-τῇ-ὥρᾳ*, ὁ-λαός*, (εἶπεν-παραβολήν*).

Hengel, M., 'Das Gleichnis von den Weingärtnern Mc 12,1-12 im Lichte der Zenonpapyri und der rabbinischen Gleichnisse', *ZNW* 59 (1968), pp. 1-39.

Crossan, J.D., 'The Parable of the Wicked Husbandmen', *JBL* 90 (1971), pp. 451-65.

Schoedel, W.R., 'Parables in the Gospel of Thomas: Oral Tradition or Gnostic Exegesis?', *CTM* 43 (1972), pp. 548-60.

Newell, R.R. & J.E., 'The Parable of the Wicked Tenants', *NT* 14 (1972), pp. 226-37.

Snodgrass, K.R., 'The Parable of the Wicked Husbandmen: Is the Gospel of Thomas Version the Original?', *NTS* 21 (1974), pp. 142-44.

Dehandschutter, B., 'La parabole des vignerons homicides (Mc., XII,1-12) et l'évangile selon Thomas', in M. Sabbe (ed.) *Marc* (1974), pp. 203-19.

Lowe, M., 'From the Parable of the Vineyard to the Pre-Synoptic Source', *NTS* 28 (1982), pp. 257-63.

c. *Tribute Question*, 20.20-26

The Marcan sequence continues, and a little over half Luke's words come from Mark. There is one rather clear reminiscence of the Matthaean version, however, in v. 21. Mark had (1) 'Teacher, we know that you are true', (2) 'and you care for no one, for you regard not the face of men', (3) 'but teach the way of God in truth'. Matthew reverses the order of (2) and (3): (1) 'Teacher, we know that you are true', (3) 'and teach the way of God in truth', (2) 'and you care for no one...' Luke writes, (1) 'Teacher, we know that you say *and teach* rightly', (2) 'and accept not face', (3) 'but teach the way of God in truth'. He keeps the Marcan order, abbreviating (2), but he has διδάσκεις twice, once in the Marcan position in (3), and once at the end of (1), where Matthew had put it: the expression is 'somewhat redundant' (Marshall). Luke also agrees with Matthew in δείξατε (Mt. ἐπιδείξατε) for Mark's φέρετε in v. 24; in the insertion of a word for 'therefore' (τοίνυν, Mt. οὖν) and in the word-order in v. 25; and in θαυμάσαντες (Mt. ἐθαύμασαν) in v. 26, if we are to take the Marcan text as ἐξεθαύμαζον with N-A[26]. The passage is also an object-lesson in the perils of the hapax argument: of 56 words taken over from Mark, one is a hapax; of 44 redactional words, four are hapaxes.

20.20 παρατηρεῖν, ἑαυτόν, ἐπιλάβεσθαι*. Hapaxes: ἐγκάθετος, ὑποκρίνεσθαι. Mark says the questioners were Pharisees and Herodians: Luke has some (?remote) Herodian connections (8.3; Acts 13.1), and limits himself to saying that they were hypocrites. So he absolves the Pharisees also as in 11.39-44; cp. 16.14f; 18.11; cf. Mk 12.15). The use of the question to hand Jesus over to the governor is made clear at 23.2.

20.21 ὀρθῶς, (ὁ-θεός).

20.22 φόρος for borrowed Latin κῆνσος, cf. 23.2.

20.23 κατανοεῖν*, (εἶπεν-)πρός. Hapax: πανουργία.

20.24 Hapax: (εἰκών).

20.25 (εἶπεν-) πρός*, (ὁ-θεός ×2). Hapax: τοίνυν.

20.26 ἰσχύειν, ἐπιλάβεσθαι*, ῥῆμα*, ἐνάντιον, ὁ-λαός*, (θαυμάζειν-ἐπί*), σιγᾶν.

48. *More Temple Controversies*, 20.27-21.4

a. *The Sadducees' Question*, 20.27-38
Luke continues his Marcan sequence, and for the greater part of the pericope sticks close to the Marcan wording: but vv. 34-36 and v. 38b diverge markedly from Mark, and have led to suggestions by Grundmann, Rengstorf, Schramm (pp. 171f.) and others, of an independent source. The evidence offered by 'strongly Semitizing language' does not, however, seem very convincing. 'The sons of this age' could count as 'semitizing', but it is found elsewhere only once in the NT, and that at Lk. 16.8, so it could be Lucan: 'that age' is not found as a synonym for 'the age to come' in rabbinic writing. Creed draws attention to some forceful parallels with *4 Maccabees*, whose doctrine of immortality is close to Luke's. 'Believing that they do not die to God, just as our patriarchs Abraham and Isaac and Jacob do not, but they live to God' (*4 Macc.* 7.19, cf. Lk. 16.25) is close to v. 38b, 'For they all live to him' (sc. God, following the saying on Abraham, Isaac and Jacob). *4 Macc.* 18.3, 'They were found worthy (κατηξιώθησαν) of a divine portion' is similar, too, to v. 35a, 'those found worthy of that age'. So, as elsewhere, Luke seems to be amplifying Mark from his *4 Macc.* background (Neirynck, *Luc*, pp. 176f.), even though Lucan vocabulary is thin.

There is, however, a formidable cluster of Minor Agreements with Matthew. (1) Matthew improves Mark's opening ἔρχονται to his favourite προσῆλθον, Luke to προσελθόντες. Luke has προσελθεῖν 8 times in the Gospel + 7 in Acts against Matthew's 50; but in the Marcan (and Q) matter he never uses it except in agreement with Mark (9.12) or Matthew (8.24, 44; 20.27; 23.52). In other words he never inserts it redactionally into Marcan matter except in agreement with Matthew (×4). (2) Mark follows 'Sadducees' with a relative clause, 'who say there is no resurrection'. Matthew changes this to a weak participle λέγοντες, with the same meaning. Luke improves Mark to 'some of the Sadducees', and follows this with οἱ ἀντιλέγοντες . . .: the article is an improvement on Matthew's naked participle, but unfortunately it should be in the genitive, agreeing with Sadducees, since all, not some, of them deny the resurrection. The error is most easily explained by the attraction of a Matthaean echo. (3) Matthew and Luke both write ἐπηρώτησαν for Mark's imperfect. Of course they both often do this, but not by any means always: Luke retains Mark's imperfect at 20.40, and inserts one of his own at 20.14. (4) Mark has 'If anyone's brother dies and leaves a wife. . . ', and Luke changes this rather clumsily to 'dies having (ἔχων) a wife'. Matthew has 'not having (ἔχων) children' at the same point. (5) If we accept the N-A²⁶/UBS³ text, the whole structure of the sentence of vv. 29-31 agrees with Matthew rather than Mark.

Mt.	The first, marrying, perished, and having no seed left his
Mk	The first took a wife, and dying left no seed;
Lk.	The first, taking a wife, died childless;

Mt.	wife to his brother; likewise	also the second,
Mk		and the second took her and
Lk.		and the second,

Mt.		and the third		up to the
Mk	died, leaving no seed,	and the third likewise,		and the
Lk.		and the third took her, and	likewise also the

Mt.	seven.		Later	the woman		died.
Mk	seven left no seed.		Last of all	the woman also		died.
Lk.	seven left no children and died.		Later		the woman also	died.

Luke joins Matthew in an opening aorist participle for the marriage, and a main verb for the death, where Mark has 'took a wife, and dying. . . '; and Luke and Matthew both write καὶ ὁ δεύτερος καὶ ὁ τρίτος without Mark's intervening clause. (6) Matthew replaces Mark's ἔσχατον πάντων with his favourite ὕστερον, and Luke follows him with ὕστερον. This is a striking MA, as Luke never uses ὕστερον elsewhere: the figures are 7/1/1+0. Schmid lists these points rather than explaining them (142f). He says that adverbial ἔσχατον is little used, but the same phrase ἔσχατον πάντων is used by Paul in 1 Cor. 15.8; cf. Num. 31.2; Prov. 29.21.

With a variety of further small points in vv. 33-35 (οὖν, the joint omission of 'when they rise', and inclusion of τῆς ἀναστασέως (τῆς) ἐκ νεκρῶν [v. 35; Mt. 22.31]), the cumulative case for Lucan knowledge of Matthew in this pericope seems strong.

20.27 τις, (ἀνάστασις). Hapax: (Σαδδουκαῖοι). ἀντιλέγειν 0/0/2+3. Sadducees here only in Luke, ×5 in Acts.

20.28 (γράφειν), (τις). Hapax: (ἐξανιστάναι). The wording is not close to the Deut. 25.5f. law, but approximates to Gen. 38.8 at the end, following Mark. ἄτεκνος here only, not in LXX.

20.31 δὲ-(καὶ)*.

20.32 Hapax: (ὕστερον = Mt.).

20.33 (ἀνάστασις), γίνεσθαι.

20.34 (εἶπεν = Mt.). Hapax: γαμίσκεσθαι. οἱ υἱοὶ τοῦ αἰῶνος τούτου, Lk. 16.8. The verse is inserted as an emphasizing introduction to 'they neither marry nor are given in marriage'; cf. 12.4f., 10. If the reading is right, Luke prefers the spelling γαμίσκεσθαι on his own account, but returns to Mark's γαμίζεσθαι in v. 35.

20.35 (ἀνάστασις). Hapaxes: καταξιοῦν, τυγχάνειν. καταξιωθέντες, cf. Acts 5.41 κατηξιώθησαν, Lk. 7.7QD ἠξίωσα. τυχεῖν = reach ×3 in Acts. ἡ ἀνάστασις ἡ ἐκ νεκρῶν, Acts 4.2, cf. Lk. 16.31; 24.46.

20.36 ἔτι, ἀνάστασις. Hapax: ἰσάγγελος. cf. 16.2 οὐ γὰρ δύνῃ ἔτι οἰκονομεῖν. 'Sons of God', i.e. with him eternally, cf. 'sons of the Most High', 6.35. 'Sons of the resurrection', cf. 10.6QD 'a son of peace': υἱός metaph. 10/2/9. The verse is an exposition of Mark's 'they are as angels in heaven', a little prosy in the Lucan manner.

20.37 (ὁ-θεὸς), (θεὸς ×2), (Αβρααμ), καὶ = also. Hapax: μηνύειν (+ Acts 23.30).

20.38 (θεός), (ζῆν), ζῆν. The last clause should not be translated 'For all live to him' (since Luke only means the just as sons of the resurrection, 14.14), but 'For they all. . .', viz. Abraham, Isaac and Jacob; cf. *4 Macc.* cited above.

b. *David's Son*, 20.39-44

Luke has already taken the next Marcan unit, The Great Commandment, in another context at 10.25ff., so he moves on to the pericope
following, David's Son; but he prefaces the latter with a version of
the conversation that closes the former, 'The scribe said to him, You
have spoken well. . . And no one dared question him any more' (Mk
12.32, 34). That Luke set these verses with David's Son may be seen
from v. 41a, 'He said to them', viz. 'certain of the scribes' of v. 39;
changed from Mark, who has Jesus teaching (the people) in the
temple. Thus one story is linked on to the next, in the usual Lucan
way.

Two thirds of the wording of the story is Marcan; but there are
echoes of Matthew. Mark's scribe becomes 'certain of the scribes', cf.
Matthew's plural 'the Pharisees'. In v. 44 Luke agrees with Matthew
in omitting αὐτός, in adding οὖν second word, in writing καλεῖ for
λέγει and πῶς for πόθεν, and in the order of the final words, υἱός
ἐστιν for ἔστιν υἱός.

20.39   τις, (εἶπον ×2). Maddox (*Purpose*, p. 40) correctly notes that the
scribes' comment shows Lucan approval of Pharisaism only insofar as it is
against Sadducee doctrine, and on the resurrection issue only. The passage is
not very friendly towards the scribes, but they were on the Lord's side
here.

20.40   Hapax: τολμᾶν.

20.41   εἶπεν-δὲ-πρός.

20.42   (αὐτός nom.), (εἶπεν), (anarthrous κύριος = God). λέγει cf. v. 37. ἐν
βίβλῳ ψαλμῶν Acts 1.20, cf. Lk. 3.4.

20.43   (πούς). ὑποπόδιον reverts from Mark's ὑποκάτω to LXX, and is a
hapax.

20.44   (καλεῖν). See above for five Matthaean Agreements.

c. *Scribes and Widows*, 20.45–21.4

Luke follows Mark still, combining Jesus' criticism of scribal
hypocrisy over widows with the story of the widow's mites, as his
predecessor had done. Only the former comes in Matthew, in the
much expanded discourse of Matthew 23. Luke is close to the
Marcan wording of Jesus' words in this first element, but is twice
influenced by Matthew. In Mark Jesus warns the crowd against the

scribes, and at Lk. 14.7, where there is similar Pharisaic jostling for the best seats, Jesus also speaks generally 'to those invited'; but in Mt. 23.1 he spoke to 'the crowds and his disciples', and the τοῖς μαθηταῖς recurs in Lk. 20.45. Luke sometimes restricts the teaching similarly elsewhere 'to the disciples', but he does not have to. More strikingly, Mark has 'who wish to walk in long robes and (for) salutations. . . and chief seats at dinners'. Matthew has 'and they love (φιλοῦσιν) the chief seat at dinners. . . and salutations'. Luke has 'who wish to walk in long robes and love (φιλούντων) salutations. . . and chief seats at dinners'. φιλεῖν meaning love (not kiss) has figures of 4/0/1+0, so it looks like a Matthaean introduction carried over into Luke. Hawkins (p. 137), followed by Schmid (p. 46), correctly says that the new verb averts the 'rather strange sound' of the Marcan sentence, where θελόντων governs both 'to walk' and 'salutations'; but Luke did not have to use Matthew's φιλεῖν—other verbs were to hand, including his favourite ἐπιθυμεῖν, which is closer to Mark's meaning.

20.45 ἀκούοντος-δὲ, παντὸς-τοῦ-λαοῦ*, εἶπεν.

20.46 (ἀσπασμός*), (δεῖπνον). προσέχετε-ἀπὸ cf. 12.1; Mt. 16.6 on Pharisaic corruptions.

20.47 (χήρα*), (μακρός). Hapaxes: (κατεσθίειν), (πρόφασις).

21.1 (πλούσιος*). Hapax: (γαζοφυλακεῖον). ἀναβλέψας cf. 19.5.

21.2 τις, (χήρα*). Hapax: πενιχρός.

21.3 (εἶπεν), ἀληθῶς-λέγω-ὑμῖν, (χήρα*), (πτωχός).

21.4 ἅπας (×2), ὁ-θεός, (βίος*). Hapax: ὑστέρημα.

49. *The Discourse on the End*, 21.5-38

Luke has been following Mark consistently through Lk. 20–21.4, and it is not in dispute that he continues to follow Mark through the Discourse of 21.5-38. What is in dispute is whether he now has a second source: for clearly the wording is much less close to Mark than it has been in ch. 20, for instance in the persecutions, siege of Jerusalem and final sub-sections.

For many commentators, including Bultmann (p. 129), Klostermann, Creed and Conzelmann (pp. 116-24), it has seemed sufficient to suppose that Luke was rehandling the Marcan tradition himself; and

this has also been the conclusion of the authors of massive
monographs on the topic, E. Grässer (pp. 152-68), J. Zmijewski
(pp. 59-65, 311) and R. Geiger (pp. 150f.). No second source need be
posited. On this view Luke has followed some such policies as these:
(a) he has rephrased Marcan sentences which he has already given in
the Q/Matthaean version, like 'Do not be anxious what you are to
speak. . .' (Mk 13.11), which he already has at 12.11f., or 'He that is
on the rooftop. . .' (Mk 13.15), which he has at 17.31; (b) similarly he
has omitted Mark's false prophets sub-section (Mk 13.21-23), which
he has in substance at 17.23 and which breaks the thread of thought;
and 'Of that day or hour no one knows. . .' (Mk 13.32), of which he
supplies a variant and less offensive version at Acts 1.7; etc.; (c) he
has filled in the detail of Mark's persecutions paragraph from his
knowledge of the Church's sufferings given in Acts; (d) writing some
15-20 years after Mark, he tones down the eschatological associations
of the siege of Jerusalem, which he makes a clear historical event
leading up to the redemption of the Church, rather than the opening
of the eschaton; (e) he has added an ethical exhortation to end the
Discourse, perhaps because the delay in the Parousia required such a
stress.

There has been no lack, however, of supporters of a second source:
Taylor (*Behind the Third Gospel*, pp. 101-25), Manson (pp. 323-27),
Lloyd Gaston (pp. 355-65), Lars Hartman (pp. 226-35), Schramm
(pp. 171-82), and others. In part this is based upon three general facts
about the Discourse, and in part on particular points, which are
handled below. The three general facts are: (1) there is a marked
difference in the freedom with which Mark is treated here by
contrast with Lk. 18.15-21.4. There nearly 60% of Luke's words were
Marcan, here less than 40%. (2) In the non-Marcan words there is a
much lower count of standard Lucan expressions than in 18.15-21.4,
and a slightly higher count of hapaxes. Thus in 18.15-21.4 the
'Lucan' expressions were about 40% of the R words overall, while
here they are around a quarter: there the hapaxes were one word in
17, here one in 15. (3) The differences have been seen as more
significant than can be shown by word-counts. Taylor writes, 'Mk xiii
supplies the ground-plan on which the Lucan Discourse is built; but
in the Discourse, as in the Passion narrative, non-Markan matter is
given the preference, and into it Markan extracts have been inserted'
(p. 125). Marshall says, 'When the Marcan material is set aside, we

are left with a reasonably continuous discourse instead of a set of *disiecta membra*' (p. 756).

I do not think there is any force in these general arguments (nor indeed in most of the particular points when we come to them). Luke has been broadly content to reproduce Mark since 18.15. But sometimes he has, by common consent, been adding his own gloss to Mark, as in the expansion of the reply to the Sadducees in 20.34-36; and it is arguable that he has sometimes added larger glosses, perhaps with some suggestion from Matthew, as in the approach to Jerusalem (19.37-44), or Zacchaeus (19.1-10). Even the first (20.34-36) shows that Luke can be free with his *Vorlage* when he wishes, and the difference in date would give him ample reason for partially rewriting Mark 13. In the—admittedly very short—passage 20.34-36 there are 35 non-Marcan words out of 46, and only two of these are 'Lucan' while four are hapaxes. The slightly obvious truth is that when Luke writes to a familiar theme, as he does with Zacchaeus, the 'Lucan' words are a high proportion (36%) and the hapaxes few, one in 28; when he writes on a less usual topic, as in 19.39-44, with military technical terms and echoes of the LXX, the 'Lucan' words drop to 20% and the hapaxes are one in 17. Our passage also has military and other technical terms, and LXX echoes in plenty, so it is not surprising if the 'Lucan' words are fewer and the hapaxes slightly up.

Claims of a second continuous source parallel to Mark 13, as made by Taylor and Marshall, have been hard to sustain: the non-Marcan pieces have constantly to be filled in from Mark, who alone, for example, has the coming of the Son of Man. Thus it becomes more economical to appeal to loose sayings from L rather than to a continuous discourse: so Fitzmyer, who accepts many of the changes as Lk.R, and limits the L matter to vv. 18, 21b, 22, 24, 28 and 34-36. But of these, in v. 22 'Lucan' "proof from prophecy" may be at work', and v. 24 with its OT allusion 'could also easily be attributed to Lucan composition' (p. 1328); while v. 18 '(about the hairs of the head) is clearly a proverb' (p. 1327), and if so hardly needs to have come from L. So we are left with rather a rump of confident claims of L origins. Verse 21b, on leaving Jerusalem and not entering it, 'is substituted for Mk 13.15 because of concern not to create a doublet of 17.31'; 'instead of Mark 13.27 Luke substitutes v. 28, probably derived from L' (p. 1328); and vv.34-36 'is clearly an ending to the discourse which Luke has substituted for Mark 13.33-37. . . to avoid a doublet of 12.38-40' (p. 1326). But is it not rather a striking coincidence that whenever Luke has covered a point earlier in the Gospel and wishes not to repeat himself, there in L is a second version of the same saying, waiting for him to use? Surely (unless an enormous L is posited, much of which Luke did not use) such a series of happy chances is most unlikely. We may agree with Fitzmyer that Luke wants to avoid writing the same saying twice, but it is much more likely that he simply composed the new matter himself. Verse 28 has quite a proportion of Lucan phrasing, and vv. 34-36 is a deliberate expansion of Mark's paraenesis, in line with 1 Thessalonians 5 (cf. above pp. 141f.).

21.5-7. The first problem, then, that Luke feels with the Marcan Discourse is its setting. Mark had 'one of his disciples' comment on the Temple buildings 'as he was leaving the Temple' (13.1), and Jesus then delivers the speech 'on the Mount of Olives opposite the Temple' to Peter, James, John and Andrew (v. 3). But to Luke throughout the Gospel it has been important that Jesus' teaching should have been heard by the people: the Sermon on the Plain was spoken to the disciples in the hearing of the people, and many times on the Journey the address has switched from the disciples to the crowd and back. In the same way in Acts the word has first to be addressed to Israel, even though as a people they were destined to reject it. So it seemed anomalous to restrict Jesus' most impressive warning of all to a group of four disciples alone on the hillside. This was not done in a corner. Indeed, Mark himself reports Jesus' words at his arrest, 'I was daily with you teaching in the Temple' (14.49), and the false witness that he had spoken (publicly) of the destruction of the Temple. So now Luke omits mention of Jesus' leaving the Temple, or of the Mount of Olives; and his addition of offerings (ἀναθήμασιν) to the fine stones admired as adorning the building, implies that it is being seen from inside. The interlocutors, similarly, are no longer disciples but merely τινων (5) and 'they' (7); and they address Jesus as διδάσκαλε, like other polite strangers in Luke. At the end of the Discourse Luke says, 'He was teaching by day in the Temple' (cf. Mk 14.49), and camped by night on the Mount of Olives (which thus receives its bow); 'and all the people came early in the Temple to him to hear him' (vv. 37f.). The Lucan Jesus fires his Parthian shot in public, in the heart of the enemy stronghold.

21.8-11. A more difficult problem arises over the sequence of the Marcan signs that 'all these things are to be consummated'. The first sign in Mark, the beginning of birthpangs, had been a complex of messianic pretenders, wars, famines and earthquakes (13.5-8), and these had been followed by the persecution of the church (vv. 9-13), and the Abomination in the Temple (v. 14), which would initiate the Great Tribulation (vv. 15-23), and so inaugurate the End (vv. 24-27). Luke does not have a very accurate knowledge of public affairs before his time (§29), but he is aware of history in a way that Mark is not, and he feels uncomfortable about the 'beginning of birthpangs'. The previous century had seen a procession of enormous wars, civil, servile and foreign, but since the defeat of Varus by the Germans there had been peace on the earth as there had not been since the days of creation. At a pinch Luke knows of a famine which came to pass in the days of Claudius Caesar (Acts 11.28); but modern research does not know of it. At the same time, Luke does know (as do other Christians) that persecution began almost as soon as the Church started preaching. It would seem more logical therefore to omit the dubious preliminary signs, and start with the trials of the Church, as from Acts 4. On the other hand wars and revolutions (ἀκαταστασίαι) had been a dramatic feature of the later 60s, with the Jewish War and the Year of the Four Emperors within the memory of all; and as for earthquakes, one of the greatest eruptions of recorded history took place at Vesuvius in 79, when the mountain was reduced to nearly half its earlier height in a convulsion which still awes the visitor at Pompeii. Surely then (Luke feels) it is 'these things' which the Lord was prophesying, and he turns Mark's 'beginning of pangs' into an introductory account of the whole sequence. This he achieves with marvellous simplicity, by prefacing the persecutions section with the words, 'But before all these things. . . ' The persecutions thus come first, and the Marcan pangs can be allowed really to hurt by being coloured in to match later reality. Mark's 'wars and rumours of wars' become 'wars and revolutions' to recall AD 69-70 at Jerusalem and Rome; 'nation shall rise against nation, and kingdom against kingdom' is allowed to stand, covering these and other works of violence. Mark's 'earthquakes in places' become 'great earthquakes. . . ' to suit Vesuvius; his λιμοί become λιμοὶ καὶ λοιμοί for the assonance; and Luke adds 'and there shall be terrors and signs from heaven' as an equivalent to the 'signs in sun and moon and stars' that will herald the Son of Man in 21.25. The transfer of meaning while retaining nearly the same words (§20) is made with a slickness that easily deceives the eye.

21.5 τις, περί, (εἶπεν). Hapax: ἀνάθημα Cf. 2 Macc. 9.16, καλλίστοις ἀναθήμασιν κοσμήσειν...

21.6 (ταῦτα), ἐλεύσονται-ἡμέραι*. ταῦτα nomin. pendens, cf. Acts 7.40. θεωρεῖτε cf. Mk 12.41 (Marshall). ὃς-οὐ-καταλυθήσεται = Mt.

21.7 (ταῦτα) ×2, (μέλλειν), γίνεσθαι. διδάσκαλε from Mk 13.1. Jesus is addressed as διδάσκαλε 11 times, the Baptist once, in Luke, always by polite outsiders: disciples call him κύριε or ἐπιστάτα. As in Mark, the destruction of the Temple is the turning point in the events leading to the End. There is no significance (contra Conzelmann, p. 128) in the change from Mark's συντελεῖσθαι to γίνεσθαι: both are in synonymous parallelism (§22) with 'When shall these things be'?—Luke assimilates to Dan. 2.28, cited at 21.9, δεῖ ταῦτα γενέσθαι, and he likes γίνεσθαι.

21.8 (εἶπεν) (= Mt.), (ὄνομα), ἐγγίζειν, πορεύεσθαι. Hapax: (πλανᾶν). Luke gives little hint of whom he meant by 'many... saying, I am'—perhaps Simon Magus (Acts 8.9f.) and Dositheus, whom later orthodoxy accused of messianic and divine pretensions (Clem. *Hom.* 2.22-24; *Rec.* 2.7-12, Orig. *Hom.* Luc. 25, *Comm. Mt.* 33 (ad. 24.4f.); *comm. Joh.* 13.27). His gloss, 'and, The time has come' is a stock expression: this, and the succeeding 'go not after them' are echoes of Luke's weak version of Mt. 24.26 at 17.24, 'They shall say to you, Lo there, lo here; go not away, nor follow' (so Taylor, Schramm, etc.). Cf. ἔρχεσθαι ὀπίσω, 9.23; 14.27.

21.9 ταῦτα, (γίνεσθαι). Hapax: ἀκαταστασία. ἀκατ. ×3 in 1-2 Cor.: it has been thought to refer to events in Rome (Creed, Holtzmann, Grundmann), Palestine (Leaney), or either (Marshall). πτοεῖν 24.37, more graphic, 'panic'. Mark: ἀλλ' οὔπω τὸ τέλος; Luke: ... πρῶτον, ἀλλ' οὐκ εὐθέως... The difference is significant, but only in that Luke has lived to see the disasters of 66-70 as a part of the lead-up to the End, not as the trigger of the End. He has not postponed the End indefinitely (vv. 31f.). Mark's οὔπω marked the interval between the *preliminary* wars, etc., and the fall of Jerusalem which would inaugurate the End.

21.10 Luke's intrusive τότε ἔλεγεν αὐτοῖς has seemed to Schramm, Marshall and others a clear sign of the arrival of the second source. 'Für eine Unterbrechung liegt keinerlei Grund vor' (Schramm, p. 175): he criticizes Conzelmann's distinction between a principle ('grundsätzliche Aspekt') and its systematic exposition ('die gliedernde Ausführung', p. 119) requiring a new start, as an unproven postulate without any analogy. τότε ἔλεγεν αὐτοῖς is not typically Lucan. But the real distinction is not between principle and exposition, but between warnings, μὴ πλανηθῆτε (v. 8a), μὴ πορευθῆτε (v. 8b), μὴ πτοηθῆτε (v. 9), and the prophecies in the future tense, which run from 'Then he said to them' (v. 10) on till v. 27. Luke often breaks a discourse with some such remark, e.g. this Discourse again at 21.29, or the Sermon on the Plain at 6.39. He uses ἔλεγεν as here meaning 'he went on to say' at 13.19; and τότε ἄρξονται λέγειν is used, without implying a second source presumably, at 23.30. It is in any case an unpromising place for the *Nebenquelle* to begin, as v. 10 is otherwise word for word identical with Mark. Taylor's second source does not begin till v. 12.

21.11 μέγας (×2), (τόπος), (λιμός*), τε* ×2, οὐρανός sing. Hapaxes: λοιμός, φόβητρον. The last phase of world history as seen around AD 90 in the light of Mk. 13.19-25: vast eruptions like Vesuvius, famine-and-pestilence (cf. Ezek. 4-5; Rev. 6), prodigies and astronomical abnormalities. The ancient world was superstitious, and Luke expects the same quota of two-headed calves born, year-long comets, etc., as Livy reports before Cannae or Josephus of the siege of Jerusalem (*B.J.* 6.289) (cf. Manson).

21.12-19. We have seen above the inadequacy of Taylor's case for a second source behind these verses. The much greater volume of verbal change and the difference of tone are alike due to Luke's difference of attitude from Mark. Mark's Gospel had been a challenge to martyrdom in the world's last hours, and his Jesus had foretold nothing but persecution, trial, hatred, betrayal and death: while to Luke the generation of the apostles had been one of triumphant obedience to grace, every persecution leading inevitably to a further advance of the Word. He has therefore in some measure rewritten Mk 13.9-13 in the light of the vision of the Church's story he tells more fully in Acts. Of course the Lucan crowd-audience is now forgotten: the 'you' is the Marcan apostles, and remains so to the end of the Discourse.

21.12f. 'They will lay hands on you', Luke begins, as they did on the apostles (Acts 5.18), or James and Peter (Acts 12.1); 'they will persecute you', as Saul persecuted the Church, and so its Lord (Acts 9.4f., etc.). Mark had, 'they will hand you over to sanhedrins and synagogues', but Luke says 'synagogues and prisons', thinking of where the Sanhedrin had put the apostles (Acts 5.19), and Herod Peter (Acts 12.1-12), and Saul the Jerusalem church (Acts 8.3). The hearers will be 'led away' to their fate (cf. the end of Herod's guards in Acts 12.19). This will be 'before kings and governors': Mark had 'governors and kings', thinking perhaps of the Emperor as the final court of appeal, but Luke thinks of 'the kings of the earth and the rulers. . . Herod and Pontius Pilate' as gathered against the Lord and his Anointed in his Church (Acts 4.26f.). This will be not 'for my sake' (Mark), but 'for my name's sake', since it was by the name of Jesus that the apostles healed, and in which they were forbidden to preach, and for which they were found worthy to suffer in Acts 3–5 (esp. 5.28, 40, 41). Mark said such trials would be 'for a testimony to them', and Luke rephrases ἀποβήσεται ὑμῖν εἰς μαρτύριον, 'it will turn out for you as an (opportunity for) witness'. The οὖν in v. 14 links v. 13 to the 'word and wisdom' which they will be given, and Acts 4.33 shows the apostles giving τὸ μαρτύριον with power after persecution.

21.14f. After this initial verse on the Church's persecutions, Mark says, 'And the gospel must first be preached to all the nations'; and Schramm takes it to be 'schlechterdings undenkbar' (p. 176) that Luke should have omitted a theme so close to his heart. But again, the Acts story seems to give us a window into Luke's mind; for there the mission of the Twelve, and especially of Peter, is to Israel and to Gentiles in Palestine, while the Gentile mission proper was reserved to one not yet converted. We find the same distinction in Matthew: equally concerned for the movement to all nations, Matthew's Jesus bids the Twelve go not on a Gentile road but keep to the lost sheep of the house of Israel (10.5-23). So here the Gentile mission may be pretermitted partly because it is not the Twelve's concern, and partly because it breaks the thread between their being accused in vv. 12f. and making their defence in vv. 14f.

Mk 13.11 promised the gift of the Holy Spirit in such accusations, but Luke has already reproduced this verse in the Matthaean form and context at Lk. 12.11f. Again his thoughts go to Acts, for 'I will give you a mouth and wisdom which all your adversaries will not be able to withstand or oppose (ἀντειπεῖν)' recalls Stephen—'they could not withstand the wisdom and the spirit with which he spoke' (Acts 6.10). The high priestly court, similarly, could not oppose (ἀντειπεῖν) the apostles when they saw the lame man standing healed (Acts 4.14). It is not (again *pace* Schramm) surprising that Luke omits the Holy Spirit, his favourite doctrine, for he believed that it was Jesus who had poured out the Spirit at Pentecost (Acts 2.33), and it was in fact 'the Spirit of Jesus' (Acts 16.7); it was Jesus who healed in the Church (Acts 9.34), and Jesus who was persecuted (Acts 9.5).

21.16ff. With vv. 16f. Luke returns to the Marcan wording more closely. For Mark's three pairs of relatives who hand each other over, brothers, father and child, children and parents, Luke substitutes his standard set of four (§23)—parents and brothers and relations and friends: the last two are Lucan favourites. But where Mark had, 'and they shall put them to death', Luke writes '. . . some of you': he is thinking of James, martyred in Acts 12.2, and perhaps Peter and others. The world's hatred follows, as in Mark, and then Luke adds, 'And not a hair shall perish from your heads'. Schramm is right this time that there is a contradiction with v. 16, 'they shall put some of you to death!' But is the *Nebenquelle* more than Acts 27.34, 'Not a hair shall perish from the head of any of you'? A second *Gospel* tradition does nothing to ease the contradiction, which Luke has plainly not noticed. Geiger (pp. 189f.) may be right to refer the muddle to Lk. 12.7, where 'the hairs of your head are all numbered' comes shortly before 'when they bring you before synagogues. . . '; but the truth (which Schramm, and many other respectful exegetes are reluctant even to consider) is that Luke is a confirmed muddler (§9), and does not require a second source to get his wires crossed. He means, 'But you will come to no (ultimate) harm in God's hands': but that is not unfortunately what he has said. He closes the paragraph by turning Mark's 'But he who endures (ὑπομείνας) to the end will be saved' into an exhortation, 'By your endurance (ὑπομονῇ) win your souls!' Luke's penchant for exhortation is testified more fully at vv. 34-36; ὑπομονή he introduced at 8.15, and the gaining of souls at 17.33. The age of apostolic persecution was to extend, not to the End, but to AD 70.

21.12 ἐπιβάλλειν-τὰς-χεῖρας, ὄνομα. πρὸ δὲ τούτων πάντων cf. Acts 5.36; 21.38.

21.13 ἀποβήσεται, cf. Phil. 1.19 μοι ἀποβήσεται εἰς σωτηρίαν. The meaning could be, 'Your sufferings will be a testimony in your favour (on Judgment Day)'; cf. Hartman, p. 217, Zmijewski, pp. 161-69, Maddox, p. 116: but why should Luke wish to change the Marcan sense?

21.14 Hapax: προμελετᾶν. θεῖναι ἐν ταῖς καρδίαις; cf. 1.66; 9.44 R; Acts 5.4; 19.21. ἀπολογεῖσθαι, 12.11QD. Cf. A. Fuchs, *SUML*, pp. 171-91 for Luke's substitution of a rewritten version of Mk 13.11 which he has already in substance at 12.11f.

21.15 ἐγὼ-γάρ, σοφία, ἅπαντες, ἀντειπεῖν, (ἀντιλέγειν). Hapax: ἀνθιστάναι. στόμα cf. Exod. 4.11, 15; Ezek. 29.21. οἱ ἀντικείμενοι ὑμῖν cf. 13.17, οἱ ἀντικείμενοι αὐτῷ. For the Christological emphasis, cf. Grässer, p. 160.

21.16 δὲ-καί*, (γονεύς)*, συγγενής*, φίλος. Hapax: (θανατοῦν). ἐξ ὑμῶν, sc. ἕνα, cf. 22.58.

21.17 (ὄνομα).

21.19 For Luke's stress on perseverance, cf. Schuyler Brown. ψυχαὶ pl. ×8 in Acts. ψ. σῶσαι 1/2/3. κτᾶσθαι 1/0/2+3.

21.20-24. It is the section on the siege of Jerusalem which has attracted the strongest assertions of a second Lucan source. Schramm (pp. 178-80) puts together the arguments of Manson (pp. 328-30) and C.H. Dodd (*JRS* [1947]) under five heads; none of which, however, can be considered decisive.

(1) The verses are very close to the siege of Jerusalem prophecy in 19.42-44, which is *Sondergut*. But the argument is circular: both passages could equally well be written by Luke, and display the same redactoral interest—cf. above, p. 690.

(2) '20-24 have not the slightest verbal resemblance to Mark' (Dodd, pp. 48f.), apart from v. 21a and v. 23a, which are virtual transcriptions. However, this leaves an uncomfortable similarity of sentence structure in vv. 20-23 in common between Mark and the lost source. Both began ὅταν δὲ ἴδητε. . .τότε. . .; both had the hapax ἐρήμωσις in the protasis; both went on to a rhythmical parallelism, 'Let not him/them. . . and he/they that is/are. . . let him/them not. . .'; in both, the second half of this parallelism was a warning to those in the country to keep out of danger; both then ended with a prophecy of dire trouble beginning with the words ἔσονται/ἔσται γάρ. This is much more than a slight verbal resemblance.

(3) The Marcan v. 21a breaks the thread of sense, for the following αὐτῆς, αὐτήν refer to Jerusalem in the non-Marcan v. 20, not Judaea in v. 21a. But such breaks in sense are liable to occur whenever a source is re-written, with or without a second source: Luke rewrites the introduction to the Paralytic himself (5.17) and forgets that he has not mentioned that Jesus was in a house, without a second source to distract him.

(4) 'Luke has succeeded in throwing his rewriting into poetic form' (Manson, p. 329), which, says Schramm (lest we should miss the irony), is 'höchst unwahrscheinlich'. But why should this be

unlikely? A prophecy of this kind falls naturally into the parallel cola of the OT prophets; the Marcan Discourse is similarly in rough 'poetic form'; many people think Luke wrote the Woes in ch. 6 and other poetic passages; and he may well, as I have argued, have been the composer of the Canticles in chs. 1-2.

(5) All the details of the siege may be found in a variety of OT passages, especially those referring to the fall of Jerusalem in 586 BC and Daniel; so they may well come from a document earlier than AD 70. Yes, they may, but they need not. We should hardly expect Luke to seek out historical details in the way Josephus did. He knew the outline of events, and he also knew that this, like everything else, had been foretold by God in scripture (v. 22); so it would not be surprising if he put his trust in the word of God to give him the best phrasing.

So the claims of Taylor, Manson, Dodd and others seem unnecessary, if an exegesis can be provided on the assumption of Luke's reworking Mark alone, Since Mark wrote under the actual impact of events (13.14), and Luke two decades later, it is no wonder if there is a difference of perspective. The blasphemy in the Temple had not, as Mark anticipated, inaugurated the dire times of the end: Luke does what history compelled him to do, relegates the whole episode to the scenario of preliminaries, of which it now becomes the last. This is achieved with characteristic skill, which is a joy to behold.

21.20. Mark had begun, echoing Daniel, 'When you see the abomination of desolation (ἐρήμωσις). . . '. Luke, as elsewhere (§20), keeps the word but changes the meaning: 'When you see Jerusalem surrounded by camps, know that her desolation (ἐρήμωσις) has arrived'. This is not the ἐρήμωσις spoken of by Daniel but by Jeremiah the prophet (4.7; 7.34; etc.), and Jeremiah spoke too of Nebuchadnezzar's στρατόπεδον (41.1) encircling Jerusalem (κύκλῳ, 52.7). He foretold also (Lk. 21.24, πεσοῦνται στόματι μαχαίρης, καὶ αἰχμαλωτισθήσονται) that the people of Jerusalem would fall by the sword (πεσοῦνται ἐν μαχαίρᾳ, 20.4), and would go into captivity (ἒν αἰχμαλωσίᾳ, 20.6), and would be slaughtered by the mouth of the sword (ἐν στόματι μαχαίρας, 21.7). As in 19.41-46, Luke has used the LXX of Jeremiah to give colour to the Lord's prophecy of the event. Jeremiah spoke, not of 586, but of 70.

21.21-23. Luke leaves unaltered Mark's 'Then let those who are in

Judaea flee to the mountains': the echo of Lot is fainter, the practical peril more real (cf. 1 Macc. 2.28). But Mark's warning to those on the roof or in the field not to collect their things from the house makes the situation too eschatological for credibility; Luke subtly substitutes, 'and let those in the midst of her (sc. Jerusalem) go out, and those on the farms not enter her'. He is still thinking of Jeremiah, who was at liberty to leave the city and pass the Babylonian lines; the peril now is to the besieged in Jerusalem, not, as in Mark, to 'all flesh'. This is the fulfilment of all the divine vengeance promised to Israel from Deut. 32.35 and on (ἐν ἡμέρᾳ ἐκδικήσεως, Lk. ἡμέραι). In this situation Mark's woe to the pregnant and the suckling retains all its force; but his universal θλῖψις from Dan. 12.1 is reduced to a more historical ἀνάγκη μεγάλη on the γῆ (sc. of Judaea), and wrath against 'this people'. His 'Pray that it be not in the winter' is dropped, as the ἀνάγκη befel in August, 70 (Fitzmyer).

21.24. Although Luke's downplaying of the cosmic has reduced his emphasis on Daniel, and introduced the more prophetic Jeremiah, as we have seen, yet Luke sees himself still as interpreting Daniel. These things must be (v. 9, Dan. 2.28), and the desolation of v. 20 recalls Dan. 9.27; 12.11, just as the ἀνάγκη interprets Dan. 12.1. The question has arisen how we should interpret the last clause of v. 24, 'Jerusalem shall be trampled by the Gentiles till the times of the Gentiles are fulfilled'. Is this to be seen as placing a limit on Roman oppression, or as pointing to the Gentile mission, which Luke saw as the event of his own day (Acts 28.28), and which was in the Marcan Discourse (13.10) (Zmijewski, pp. 216-20; Maddox, p. 120)? We should prefer the first, for the trampling of Jerusalem is also in Daniel (8.13), and is immediately followed by a time-limit of days, interpreted in 8.23 as 'when the sins (of the Gentile kings) are fulfilled (πληρουμένων)'. Mk 13.20 also refers to a divine limit on the tribulation, and it is this verse which Luke is rewriting.

21.20 Ἰερουσαλημ*, γνῶτε-ὅτι, ἐγγίζειν. Hapaxes: κυκλοῦν cf. 19.43 περικυκλοῦν; στρατόπεδον, στρατ-4/1/8+24; (ἐρήμωσις).γνῶτε is perhaps suggested by Mark's ὁ ἀναγινώσκων (Marshall).

21.21 ἐν-μέσῳ, χώρα. Hapax: ἐκχωρεῖν (NB play with χώρα). χώρα = farm 12.16, αἱ-χῶραι Acts 8.1. ἐν = Mt. 24.18.

21.22 (ἡμέρα), (ἐκδίκησις), τοῦ + inf.*, πιμπλάναι*, pleth. πάντα, τὰ-γεγραμμένα*. πιμπλάναι = fulfil ×5 of time, here only of scripture.

21.23 (ἡμέρα), ὁ-λαός*. ἀνάγκη 1 Cor. 7.26, θλ.καὶ ἀν. 1 Thess. 3.7, ἔσται γὰρ θλ. μεγάλη Mt. 24.21, (ὁ-λ. -οὗτος, 9.13R; Acts 13.17; 28.26.

21.24 Pleth. πάντα, Ἰερουσαλημ*, ἄχρι*, εἶναι + part. Hapax: αἰχμαλωτίζειν. πατεῖν, 10.19 (cp. Ps. 90.13 LXX καταπ.); καταπ. 8.5R; 12.1R; καιροί pl. 1/0/ 1+4; πληροῦν of time, 0/1/1+5. Hartman (pp. 226-35) argues that a second source underlies Luke 21, using not only general arguments considered above (somewhat diffidently), but also the use of the Hebrew, non-LXX, OT. This is especially the case for the Jerusalem section, where he suggests the underlying use of Isa. 10.3-6 (day of visitation-flee-prisoners-slain-anger-people of my wrath-tread down), 13.4-15 (day of Yahweh-destruction-wrath-anger-desolation-visit-flee-fall by the sword), and Zeph. 1.7-15 (day of Yahweh-visit-waste-wrath-distress and anguish-ruin and devastation). As Luke normally uses the LXX, the non-LXX catenas of words imply non-Lucan authorship. But Hartman asks too much. Almost every word is accounted for above, as Marcan, Matthaean, characteristic of Luke, or drawn from the Jeremiah siege passages; and it is one thing to have the echoes of passages like Isaiah 10 ringing in the back of your head, and another to be citing them verbally from the Hebrew.

21.25-28. With the 'times of the Gentiles' Luke has reached his own day. Jerusalem is being trampled under the Roman heel; in God's μακροθυμία the last act will open. Mk 13.21-23 had spoken of the coming of false Messiahs and prophets, but Luke has already touched on this topic in v. 8, and he hastens on to history's climax, which is the next thing to come. Mark had described the trials ahead in the bright apocalyptic colours of Isa. 13.10f. and 34.4: the sun would be darkened and the moon not give her light, the stars would fall and the heavenly powers shudder. But Luke is too much a child of the enlightenment for this. He tells us that the darkness at Jesus' death was due to an eclipse, and at v. 11 he spoke only of 'great signs from heaven': so now, 'there shall be signs in sun and moon and stars'—eclipses, comets and so on. With his human imagination (§4) he moves on to think what the reaction to this would be 'on earth' (cf. v. 23), and he draws on the LXX to fill in the details. The primary passage, as it later turns out, is Isaiah 24, where the Lord destroys the world (τὴν οἰκουμένην, v. 1, Lk. 21.26), and shakes the foundations of the earth (v. 18; Lk. 21.26), bringing fear (φόβος) and bewilderment (ἀπορία, v. 19; Lk. 21.25) on mankind, with the stirring of the water of the sea (θαλάσσης, v. 14; Lk. 21.25). The sea is introduced as an echo of the primaeval struggle of God with Rahab, Luke's σάλος being drawn from Ps. 89.10, 'Thou rulest the power τῆς θαλάσσης, thou stillest τὸν σάλον of its waves'; and there is a hint too of Ps. 65.8f., 'Who confounds the hollow τῆς θαλάσσης, ἤχους of its waves: τὰ ἔθνη shall be troubled'. As it was in the days of Noah, so will it be in the days of the Son of Man; who is seen coming on a cloud in v. 27.

21.28. Luke closes the great prophecy with a line of parenesis. Jesus was asked in v. 7, 'What is the sign when *these things* are *to happen?*', and he closes his prophetic speech, 'When *these things* begin *to happen...*' ('These things' in v. 7 were actually the sack of the Temple from v. 6, but they have extended to τὸ τέλος by v. 9). But Luke is in fact merely summing up the short Marcan paragraph he is about to reproduce. 'When you see ταῦτα γινόμενα', says Mark at 13.29, 'know that he is ἔγγυς': 'when τούτων begin γίνεσθαι', says Luke, 'lift up your heads because your redemption ἐγγίζει'. Almost all the words have Lucan associations (see below): only ἀπολύτρωσις is a hapax, but Luke has λύτρωσις at 1.68; 2.38 and λυτροῦσθαι at 24.22 for Israel's 'deliverance'—the compound form comes ×3 in Paul, excluding Eph.-Col.

21.25 Hapaxes: (σελήνη) (σάλος Ps. 89.10) ἄστρον (×2 Acts), συνοχή (but συνέχειν 1/0/6+3), ἀπορία (Isa. 24.19, but ἀπορεῖσθαι 24.4; Acts 25.20, διαπορεῖν 0/0/1+3).

21.26 φόβος, ἐπέρχεσθαι, (ἡ-οἰκουμένη), (σαλεύειν). Hapaxes: ἀποψύχειν (ἐκψ. ×3 Acts), προσδοκία (Acts 12.11, προσδοκᾶν 2/0/6+5). φόβου, cf. φόβητρα in v. 11. τῇ οἰκ., Isa. 13.11. αἱ δυνάμεις τῶν οὐρ. = Mt. 24.29, Mk αἱ ἐν τοῖς οὐρ.

21.27 δόξα. νεφέλη sing. for the single Son of Man. δόξης πολλῆς = Mt. 24.30

21.28 ταῦτα, γίνεσθαι, ἐπαίρειν*, διότι, ἐγγίζειν. Hapax: ἀπολύτρωσις (see above). ἀνακύπτειν 13.11, παρακ. 24.12; 'look up' and 'raise your heads' are an extension of ὄψονται (v. 27).

21.29-36. Luke may have 'delayed the Parousia' in the sense that he knows it did not come in the wake of the Fall of Jerusalem; but for his own day it is 'drawing near' now these things have begun (v. 28), and he goes on remorsely with Mark that it is ἔγγυς (v. 31). We must concur with Maddox (pp. 121f.) that Luke's expectations in his day are the same as Mark's had been earlier: the delay is twenty years, not indefinite.

21.34ff. At first Luke is content virtually to reproduce the memorable Marcan parenesis: the fig-tree, 'this generation shall not pass...', 'my words...' The uncomfortable statement of Jesus' ignorance of the day and hour (13.32) alone he pretermits, substituting a less offensive form at Acts 1.6. But when he reaches Mark's closing verses (watch and pray, the nightwatchman), he is faced with a difficulty. He has already given the fuller Matthaean version of this teaching—the Thief in the Night, the Faithful and Wise Servant, and forms of the Return from the Wedding, the Talents and the Judgment in chs. 12-13, 19; and does not want to end with the weaker Marcan parable. He contents himself therefore with an expanded version of Mark's single verse of exhortation. 'But περὶ τῆς ἡμέρας ἐκείνης', wrote Mark, '...βλέπετε ἀγρυπνεῖτε; for you know not when ὁ καιρός is': 'προσέχετε ἑαυτοῖς', says Luke, 'lest...ἡ ἡμέρα ἐκείνη come on you suddenly...ἀγρυπνεῖτε praying at every καιρῷ'.

He changed Mark's βλέπετε to προσέχετε ἑαυτοῖς in the same way at 12.1/Mk 8.15; he has expanded both this (see below) and ἀγρυπνεῖτε in traditional ways ('watch and pray' belong together in Mk 14.38, and in some MSS at Mk 13.33); he has retained Mark's καιρός, but changed its meaning from 'the appointed time' to 'every time' (§20)

The means of expanding this simple Marcan thought is threefold; he draws on Matthew, on Paul and on Isaiah 24 (once more). It is Matthew 24 which makes him give warning against drunkenness and cares of this life, for the bad servant there ate and drank with the drunkards, and gave no thought for his lord's coming (vv. 48f.); and it is Matthew 25 which makes him end, 'that you may be able... to stand (σταθῆναι) before (ἔμπροσθεν) the Son of Man'—for Matthew ends his Discourse with the Great Assize, when all nations will be gathered before (ἔμπροσθεν) the Son of Man, and he will stand (στήσει) the sheep on his right. Luke tends to write ἐνώπιον (0/0/ 22+13) rather than ἔμπροσθεν (18/2/10+2—two of the Lucan uses are as adverbs, and five have Matthaean parallels).

But the parenesis which associated carelessness at the Lord's coming with drunkenness was earlier than Matthew, and is to be found in 1 Thess. 5.7. Having described Christ's coming from heaven in 4.13ff., the apostle turns at 5.1ff. to the times and καιρῶν: 'When they are saying, Peace and safety, then destruction is coming upon them suddenly (αἰφνίδιος αὐτοῖς ἐφίσταται) like birth-pangs on the pregnant, and they shall not escape (ἐκφύγωσιν)' (5.3). 'Take care of yourselves', says Luke, 'lest. . . that day come upon you suddenly (ἐπιστῇ ἐφ'ὑμᾶς αἰφνίδιος). . . praying that you may be able to escape (ἐκφυγεῖν). αἰφνίδιος and ἐκφεύγειν are both hapaxes in Luke, and the concurrence of rare words with the given topic cannot be an accident. Hartman (pp. 192f.) thinks it is 'necessary to assume that 1 Thess. uses the same tradition as Lk. 21.34ff', but he does not treat seriously the cumulative evidence we have seen in ch. 4 for Luke's knowledge of at least 1 Corinthians and 1 Thessalonians. The simplest and most probable thesis is that Luke is drawing on 1 Thessalonians here direct.

When so many OT prophecies contain reference to the punishment of Israel, fall of Jerusalem, signs in heaven, etc., it is not easy to be confident which is uppermost in Luke's mind. However, we have noted the rather rare word ἀπορίᾳ in 21.25, and linked this with Isa. 24.19, 'With shaking shall the earth be shaken, and with ἀπορίᾳ the earth ἀπορηθήσεται'. Isaiah continues, 'The earth reels. . . as the drunkard and the carouser (ὡς ὁ μεθύων καὶ κραιπαλῶν, v. 20), and it is this combination which inspires Luke's ἐν κραιπάλῃ καὶ μέθῃ in v.34. Furthermore Isa. 24.17 cries, 'Fear and a pit and a snare upon you (παγὶς ἐφ' ὑμᾶς)', and he who escapes one shall fall into the next; and it is this which lies behind Luke's 'that day come ἐφ' ὑμᾶς suddenly, like a snare (ὡς παγίς)', as well, perhaps, as the φόβος of v. 26. These verbal echoes are enough to show that Isaiah 24 is a significant source for Luke in ch. 21, and suggests that other expressions have come from the same chapter. 'Lo, the Lord destroys the world (τὴν οἰκουμένην)' (Isa. 24.1a) probably lies behind τῇ οἰκουμένῃ in v. 26; 'and he will lay it waste (ἐρημώσει) and lay bare the face of it (τὸ πρόσωπον αὐτῆς), and scatter them that dwell therein' (24.1b) looks like the source for Lk. 21.35, 'like a snare; for it will come upon all who dwell on the face of all the earth (τοὺς καθημένους ἐπὶ πρόσωπον πάσης τῆς γῆς)'. Luke writes καθημένους not ἐνοικοῦντας or κατοικοῦντας (τὴν γῆν) (Isa. 24.1, 5, 6, 17), but then he makes the same substitution at 1.79 against Isa. 9.1 κατοικοῦντες.

21.29 εἶπεν-παραβολήν. 'and all the trees': it is the fig whose branches are bare of leaves when other trees have begun to shoot, and whose sudden foliage makes the Marcan parable so pointful. Luke is thinking of the mustard-tree which he added to the fig at 13.19.

21.30 ἑαυτῶν. Hapaxes: προβάλλειν (Acts 19.33), (θέρος). βλεπ. ἀφ' ἑαυτῶν, cf. 12.57.

21.31 (ταῦτα), (γίνεσθαι), (γινώσκετε-ὅτι). The Marcan text suggests no subject for ἐγγύς ἐστιν, and Luke supplies the normal topic for parables, the kingdom of God, rather than 'he' (Christ). The meaning is the same.

21.32 (γίνεσθαι). ἕως-ἄν = Mt. 24.34: ἀμὴν λέγω ὑμῖν...οὐ μὴ...ἕως ἄν 5/1/1—Luke has ἕως ἄν only in Marcan parallels 9.27; 20.42; and here; never in Acts. The verse is a clear statement of Luke's expectations, even if the survivors of 'this generation' were rather sparse by AD 90 (Maddox, 111-15).

21.33 (οὐρανός, sing.).

21.34 προσέχετε-ἑαυτοῖς, (ἐφιστάναι = 1 Thess. 5.3), ἐφ'-ὑμᾶς*, (ἡμέρα). Hapaxes: κραιπάλη, μέθη (cf. Isa. 24.20), βιωτικός (1 Cor. 6.3f. cf. Lk. 8.14R, μεριμνῶν...ἡδονῶν τοῦ βίου), (αἰφνίδιος) = 1 Thess. 5.3 (cp. Mk 13.36, ἐξαίφνης). βαρεῖσθαι cf. 9.32R. Luke concludes his prophecy of the End with an exhortation to prayer and faithfulness, as he followed 17.20-37 with 18.1-8 (Ott, pp. 73-75).

21.35 Pleon. πάσης. Hapaxes: (παγίς) (Isa. 24.17), ἐπεισέρχεσθαι (cf. ἐπερχομένων, v. 26, 0/0/3+4, double prep. compound verbs 12/14/31+35).

21.36 δεῖσθαι*, ταῦτα, μέλλειν, γίνεσθαι, pleon. πάντα. Hapaxes: (ἀγρυπνεῖν), (ἐκφεύγειν) = 1 Thess. 5.3. ταῦτα πάντα τὰ μέλλοντα γίνεσθαι takes up the opening question that set off the Discourse, 'What is the sign when μέλλη ταῦτα γίνεσθαι?' The continual prayer recalls Lk. 18.1, 7. Prayer (προσεύχεσθε) may be at Mk. 13.33 (א ACL etc.: Greeven, cf. Lambrecht, pp. 242f.). κατισχύσητε, 23.23, cf. Isa. 24.20 κατίσχυσεν.

21.37f. Mark had taken Jesus out of the Temple, and had made the Discourse available to the four disciples only on the Mount of Olives. Luke has the Discourse given publicly in the Temple (cf. on 21.5-7), and he now justifies this by reference to Mk 14.49, 'I *was daily* with you *in the temple teaching*'. For the Mount of Olives he goes back to Mt. 21.17, where, following his Cleansing of the Temple, Jesus 'went out outside the city to Bethany and lodged (ηὐλίσθη) there'. Jesus is still at Bethany the night of his betrayal, so Luke feels justified in saying, 'and for the nights *he went out and lodged* (ἐξερχόμενος ηὐλίζετο) on the Mount of Olives. These are the only two uses of αὐλίζεσθαι in the NT. Further, Matthew (diff. Mark) begins the account of Jesus' following day in the Temple, πρωΐ (21.18); and Luke continues, 'All the people came early (ὤρθριζεν) to him in the Temple'.

21.37   (ἡμέρα), το-καλούμενον*. Hapax: (αὐλίζεσθαι = Mt.).

21.38   πᾶς-ὁ-λαός*. Hapax: ὀρθρίζειν (but ὄρθρινος 0/0/1; ὄρθρος, 0/0/1+1).

In the preceding dozen sections (since 9.51), there has been a unity of theme (e.g. Mission, Temple Controversies), subdivided in each case into three sub-sections which form the more obvious pericopae. In 21.5-38 it is the unity which is obvious: if Luke for some reason tended to think of his teaching units in sub-sections of three, we should have to think of 21.5-38 dividing into (a) vv. 5-19 Preliminaries (the persecution of the Church), (b) vv. 20-28 The Climax (Fall of Jerusalem, Signs in heaven, the Son of Man), (c) vv. 29-38 Paraenesis. Both (a) and (b) end with a line of exhortation (v. 19, v. 28), and (c) opens with 'And he spoke a parable to them'.

Taylor, V., *Behind the Third Gospel* (Oxford, 1926).
Dodd, C.H., 'The Fall of Jerusalem and the "Abomination of Desolation"', *JRS* 37 (1947), pp. 47-54.
Kümmel, W.G., *Promise and Fulfilment* (London, 1957).
Bartsch, H.-W., *Wachet aber zu jeder Zeit!* (Hamburg, 1963).
Hartman, L., *Prophecy Interpreted* (Con. Bib. 1; Lund, 1966).
Lambrecht, J., *Die Redaktion der Markus-Apokalypse* (An. Bib. 28; Rome, 1967).
Pesch, R., *Naherwartungen: Tradition und Redaktion in Mk 13* (Düsseldorf, 1968).
Gaston, L., *No Stone on Another* (NT Suppl. 23; Leiden, 1970).
Zmijewski, J., *Die Eschatologiereden des Lukas-Evangeliums* (BBB 40; Bonn, 1972).
Geiger, R., *Die lukanischen Endzeitsreden* (Bern/Frankfurt, 1973).

SECTION 8—THE PASSION AND RESURRECTION
(22-24; Mk 14-16; Mt. 26-28)

50. *The Passion*   Passover 6 p.m.

a. *The Last Supper*, 22.1-23

The Lucan Church now moves on to its Paschal celebration, which is divided, as in the earlier Gospels, into three-hourly units, stated or implied (cf. pp. 155ff.). In one respect, as we have found earlier, the Lucan liturgical arrangements are less elaborate than those implied in Mark and Matthew. Just as we found indications that Luke's congregation had only Sunday services over the autumn festal season, where his predecessors provided lessons for the actual days (pp. 397ff.), so here: they both described a supper at the house of Simon the leper on the night before Passover, and Luke has transferred this story to ch. 7. It would seem therefore that the earliest (Marcan) and Jewish (Matthaean) churches opened the Paschal season a day before the feast, with the story of the woman's gift of ointment told 'in memory of her'; but that Lucan Christians did not begin the celebration of the Pasch till Passover evening itself. On the other hand, we shall note throughout the story expansions of the earlier tradition, and once more it is easy to divide the opening unit into three: (a) vv. 1-6 Judas' Betrayal, (b) vv. 7-13 Passover Preparations, (c) vv. 14-23, The Opening of the Supper, with the Institution. Both the Betrayal and the Preparation pericopae lead up to the Supper (with its Woe to the betrayer), and the time of the Lucan liturgy is implied at v. 14, 'When the hour (of sundown) had come'.

Whereas for ch. 21 the weight of scholarly opinion was heavy in favour of Mark alone as the source for Luke, and the evidence, it seemed, equally so, matters are not the same for the passion story. I have already commented in ch. 3 on the arguments of Taylor, Schürmann and Rehkopf, and the general weakness of the proposals for a second Lucan source, into which the evangelist has inserted occasional phrases and sentences of Mark. But there are, of course, a number of short 'L' paragraphs without any Marcan parallel, as well as pieces with sharp differences from Mark in wording and order, and we shall need to examine with care the alternatives of *Sondergut* tradition and free Lucan rewriting/expansion.

22.1-13. At least it is agreed by almost everyone that Luke begins by following Mark. More than half the words in the Betrayal and Preparation stories are Marcan; and parallels are available from elsewhere in the Lucan writings for much of the redaction. Schramm's parting shot (pp. 132f.) is to suggest that 'Satan entered into' Judas is drawn from the *Nebenquelle*: after this he feels his case is established by others. But it is not right to suggest that Luke would have written 'the devil' rather than Satan, for we have a closely similar use in Acts 5.3, 'Ananias, why has Satan filled your heart. . .?', besides the still to be discussed 22.31L, 'Satan demanded to have you'. Schuyler Brown (pp. 84-97) has argued plausibly that Judas presented a problem to Luke, insofar as he had been chosen by Jesus to be one of the Apostles; and that he resolves this disappointment of the Lord's choice by the hypothesis of Satanic intervention. The similar Satanic possession of Ananias in Acts 5, also corrupted by money, accounts for backsliding in the idealized, Spirit-filled, primitive church, and looks like Luke at work again; although he has changed Mark's 'Satan' to 'the devil' at 8.12, he has introduced it himself at Acts 26.18, and the figures are 4/6/5+2. Nor is it a significant argument that almost the same phrase occurs in Jn 13.27: as so often, John gives a heavily embroidered version of a simple Lucan theme, with Satan entering Judas as he eats the morsel.

The Betrayal does, however, also contain two rather striking Minor Agreements with Matthew:

Mt. 26.14   ὁ λεγόμενος Ἰούδας Ἰσκαριώτης
Mk 14.10   Ἰούδας ὁ Ἰσκαριώθ
Lk. 22.3   Ἰούδαν τὸν καλούμενον Ἰσκαριώτην

At Mk 3.19 pars., Mark and Luke both have Ἰουδαν Ἰσκαριώθ, and Matthew has Ἰούδας ὁ Ἰσκαριώτης, without any word for 'called'. This time Matthew has again written the Greek form—ώτης, but with his familiar λεγόμενος (×13 with names); and Luke has also put the Greek form -ώτης, with *his* familiar καλούμενος (0/0/11+13). The second case is even more impressive:

Mt. 26.16   ἐζήτει εὐκαιρίαν ἵνα αὐτὸν παραδῷ.
Mk 14.11   ἐζήτει πῶς αὐτὸν εὐκαίρως παραδοῖ.
Lk. 22.6   ἐζήτει εὐκαιρίαν τοῦ παραδοῦναι αὐτὸν. . .

Matthew and Luke have agreed here in changing Mark's adverb unto an accusative of the related noun, which is a hapax in both Matthew and L-A. Schmid (p. 58) accounts for this as a common change of a Marcan vulgarism, but the adverb is used by Xenophon, Philo and Josephus, and the noun is as well testified among the papyri (M-M). It is not an explanation to list it as a change of vocabulary (Neirynck, p. 285). Luke often has occasion to use expressions meaning 'seek an opportunity to', and commonly writes ζητεῖν with inf. or noun clause. At Acts 24.25 he uses καιρὸς. The coincidence of hapax is due to Luke's reminiscence of Matthew.

22.1   ἐγγίζειν. 'The feast of Unleavened Bread' lasted a week, as Luke well knew (Acts 12.3; 20.6), and he uses πάσχα interchangeably in Acts 12.4 also; cf. Jos. *Ant.* 3.249; 14.21; 17.213. This was not accurate (§26), as Passover is only a single day (sometimes counted as two). With Lk.'s rare ἡ λεγομένη π., cf. Mt. 26.3 τοῦ λεγομένου Καϊάφα: perhaps a reminiscence.

22.2   (ζητεῖν), τὸ + ind. qn.*, ἀναιρεῖν, (ὁ-λαός)*. An improvement on Mark's muddling μὴ ἐν τῇ ἑορτῇ. . .; the ἑορτή has been transferred to v. 1.

22.3   καλούμενος*, ὤν. Hapax: ἀριθμός (0/0/1+5). Judas follows smoothly on the conspiracy.

22.4   τὸ + ind. qu.* στρατηγοὶ, sc. τοῦ ἱεροῦ (22.52), 0/0/2+3. The plural is inaccurate (§26): the chief disciplinary officer of the Temple was called the *sagan*, a title translated by Josephus ὁ στρατηγὸς τοῦ ἱεροῦ, *B.J.* 6.5.3 (Jeremias, *JTJ*, p. 161). Luke uses the singular in Acts. συλλαλεῖν 4.36R.

22.5   (χαίρειν*). Hapax: συντιθέναι (+ Acts 23.20).

22.6   (ζητεῖν). Hapax: (εὐκαιρία = Mt.). ἐξομολογεῖν, a rare use meaning 'he consented': Schuyler Brown notes the ring of blasphemy arising from the context of 12.8f. ἄτερ, 22.35.

22.7   ἦλθεν-(ἡμέρα)*, δεῖν, θύειν. 'The day of Unleavened Bread' is a loose expression for 14th Nisan, when houses were cleansed of leaven (§26), and 'the pasch had to be sacrificed': but Mark is not much better, and is followed by Matthew.

22.8   εἰπών*, πορεύεσθαι, ἑτοιμάζειν. Luke gives Jesus the initiative, while still basing the wording on Mk 14.12b. He supplies the name Peter at 8.45, and has Peter-and-John seven times in Acts: they are the obvious 'two of his disciples' mentioned by Mk.

22.9   εἶπαν, (ποῦ), (ἑτοιμάζειν).

22.10   (εἶπεν), (πόλις), (βαστάζειν). Hapax: (κεράμιον). ὁ-δὲ-εἶπεν = Mt. 26.18. συναντᾶν, 9.37R + 2 Acts.

22.11   (ποῦ). Polite ἐρεῖτε, 19.31.

22.12   (ἑτοιμάζειν). Hapaxes: (ἀνάγαιον), (στρωννύειν).

22.13   (εὑρίσκειν), (καθώς), εἰρήκει (plup.)*, (ἑτοιμάζειν).

22.14-23. With 22.14 the Last Supper begins, and the close agreement with Mark falters. The variations from Mark are so striking at the Institution of the eucharist that it is clear that a second source must be predicated. What is not clear is whether we should take a minimizing position, that Luke is accommodating the Marcan story to the tradition of 1 Corinthians 11, in his own words (Creed, Leaney, Schneider, etc.); or if we should rather think of an independent source into which Luke has inserted the occasional reminiscence of Mark (Taylor, Schürmann, Rehkopf). I shall argue for the former.

22.19f. The core of the passage in both Mark and Luke is Jesus' eucharistic words. The position is complicated by the omission of Lk. 22.19b-20 by Dabeff²il: that is, the phrase 'which is given for you', the command 'do this. . . ', and the whole verse on the cup. The tendency today is towards the longer text (N-A[26], Greeven; the UBS committee gave a C rating by majority vote, Metzger, pp. 173-77, which Fitzmyer [p. 1388] thinks 'far too low'). The authorities for that include all the ancient text-types, including some Western representatives; and it is possible that the Western scribe stopped short at τὸ σῶμά μου, where Mark and Matthew end the words over the bread; and that he omitted the verse on the wine because v. 17 already described Jesus taking a cup. This line of argument seems mildly, if not completely satisfactory; at least it is more convincing than the defence of the shorter text as (a) better because shorter, (b) suspiciously like 1 Cor. 11.24f., and (c) containing non-Lucan features. It seems entirely plausible that Luke should have lengthened the text by assimilating it to that familiar to his Pauline church—and the more so in view of his familiarity with 1 Corinthians argued in ch. 4; and if so, it will not be surprising if the combination is not completely smooth. Henry Chadwick (*HTR* [1957]) cites two un-Lucan locutions: (a) the omission of the copula, and (b) the final phrase being in the nominative rather than dative. For (a), however we may have some mitigation from the Pauline text:

1 Cor. 11.25 τοῦτο τὸ ποτήριον ἡ καινὴ διαθήκη ἐστὶν ἐν τῷ ἐμῷ αἵματι

Lk. 19.20 τοῦτο τὸ ποτήριον ἡ καινὴ διαθήκη ἐν τῷ αἵματί μου

It would be understandable if Luke did not introduce ἐστίν after ποτήριον, and omitted it where it would interrupt the phrase 'the new covenant in my blood'; nor would the omission be unparalleled, cf. 2.12, καὶ τοῦτο ὑμῖν τὸ σημεῖον and other texts below. Chadwick himself agrees that (b) is not final, and that the difficulty of the shorter text has to be explained whichever option is preferred.

A complete account can then be given of vv. 19-20. Luke opens, following Mark, 'And taking bread, he gave thanks, broke it and gave it to them, saying, This is my body'; his only changes are εὐχαριστήσας (= 1 Cor. 11.24) for εὐλογήσας, and λέγων for καὶ εἶπεν (= v. 20a). Mark stops the words over the bread here; but Luke continues with the familiar τὸ ὑπὲρ ὑμῶν from his Pauline liturgy (= 1 Cor. 11.24), and carries the latter on, first with 'This do in my remembrance', and then with the whole sequence, 'And the cup likewise after dining, saying, This is the new covenant in my blood'. He makes three trivial changes in the Pauline wording. He brings ὡσαύτως from first to fourth word, thus opening the sentence with 'And (the) cup. . . ', as Mark does; he omits the copula ἐστίν, as at 24.17, 48; 1.42 (×2); 2.12; 4.36, etc.; and he puts Mark's μου for 'my' in place of the Pauline ἐμῷ. He closes with τὸ ὑπὲρ ὑμῶν ἐκχυννόμενον, which is based on Mark's τὸ ἐκχυννόμενον ὑπὲρ πολλῶν; but the ὑμῶν follows the Pauline ὑμῶν over the bread, and the order follows the Matthaean τὸ περὶ πολλῶν ἐκχυννόμενον. This combination of Mark with the Pauline liturgical formulae involves the minor misfortune that it is the cup rather than the Lord's blood which is poured out; but, as Chadwick says, there is not so much difference between a cup and its contents. In addition he balances the ἐκχυννόμενον in the second verse with διδόμενον in the first, which correctly goes with 'my body'.

22.14-18. The possession of two sharply differing accounts of the eucharistic words, Marcan and Pauline, places Luke in further embarrassments which are not resolved by the clever fusion which I have just outlined. He begins straightforwardly with Mk. 14.17f. He drops Mark's ὀψίας γενομένης as usual (6/5/0+0), putting his favoured ὅτε ἐγένετο (0/1/3+3) with 'the hour' (cf. ὅτε ἐγένετο ἡμέρα, 6.13R; Acts 27.39). ἀναπεσεῖν, 'the apostles' and σύν are among Luke's preferred expressions too (see below). But the complications are upon him at once, for Mk. 14.18 and 14.22 both say ἐσθιόντων αὐτῶν, 'while they were eating', the latter being the occasion of the eucharistic words; and these, since Luke is giving preference to his own Pauline tradition, were said μετὰ τὸ δειπνῆσαι, after the eating was finished. Nor has Mark even remembered to indicate that the meal was a Passover! All the Paschal references in Mark are in the Preparation paragraph. Luke therefore clarifies his predecessor's text, as so often, drawing partly on the preceding Marcan matter, partly on what follows. 'Where do you want (θέλεις) us to go and prepare for you to eat the Passover (φάγῃς τὸ πάσχα)?', asked the disciples in Mk 14.12: 'With desire have I desired to *eat* this *Passover* (τὸ πάσχα φαγεῖν) with you', says the Lucan Jesus. θέλειν has been strengthened into ἐπιθυμεῖν, a word recurrent in Luke (2/0/ 4+1; 17.22QD), and which does not at all imply disappointed desire (16.21); the combination with ἐπιθυμίᾳ is a Septuagintalism paralleled at Acts 5.28 and 23.14. '. . . to *eat* this *Passover with* you" draws also on Mk 14.16, '. . . where I may eat the Passover with my disciples'. Luke's final πρὸ τοῦ με παθεῖν, 'before I suffer', is a reflection of the opening words of Jesus at the Marcan supper, 'One of you will betray me. . . The Son of Man must go. . . ' (Mk 14.18-21): πρὸ τοῦ + inf. is paralleled at 2.21; Acts 23.15, and παθεῖν (infin.) is on the Lucan list.

22.16. Even if the Marcan Jesus had made no explicit reference to his Last Supper being a Passover, yet he had implied that it was: 'Amen I say to you that I shall not again drink from (ἐκ) the fruit of the vine till that day when I drink it new in the kingdom of God' (Mk 14.25). The 'new' wine will be drunk at the Messianic feast celebrating mankind's redemption, the fulfilment of the paschal feast on earth celebrating Israel's redemption. So Luke writes a careful pair to the saying, to cover the eating as well as the drinking: 'for *I say to you that I shall not* eat it *until* it is fulfilled *in the kingdom of God*'. We may compare the careful pairing of the bread and cup sayings in vv. 19f. which we have just examined; or Luke's composition of the Lost Coin to match the Lost Sheep, or of Lot to match Noah. Of the changed words ἕως-ὅτου is frequent in L–A (4/ 0/6+4), and πληρωθῇ is a verbal equivalent to καινόν. The logic of Luke's 'for' is not too plain because of the compressed style: he means, I wanted very much to eat this Passover with you because it will be our last meal together until we eat it fulfilled in heaven.

22.17f. Having made use of the form of Mk 14.25 for eating of the meal, Luke is virtually compelled to move on to the original for the drinking of the wine. Mark represents the words as being said *after* the eucharistic sentences of 14.22-24; but he also says that this took place 'while they were eating' (14.22). Luke sees a way to resolve this difficulty, for he knows enough of Jewish ways (§26) to be aware that a succession of (four) formal cups were drunk at a Jewish Passover (*m. Pes.* 10.2). Two of these were at the beginning of the meal, while the 'cup of blessing' (*kos shel beraka*) closed the meal (*m. Pes.* 10.7). The same pattern is likely to have been normal at Christian eucharistic services with which Luke was familiar. The *agape* of the Pauline churches included wine (1 Cor. 11.21f.), over which there must have been a grace said, while the 'cup of blessing' (1 Cor. 10.16) will have been at the climax of the service. So it must appeal to Luke to solve his problem by understanding the cup of Mk 14.23 and the subsequent saying on the new wine of 14.25 as if they were at the *beginning* of the Supper. Mk 14.24, on the blood of the covenant, he must take 'after the dining' with 1 Cor. 11.25: but the rest he adapts now.

Mk: καὶ λαβὼν ποτήριον εὐχαριστήσας ἔδωκεν αὐτοῖς καὶ ἔπιον. . .πάντες
Lk.: καὶ δεξάμενος ποτήριον εὐχαριστήσας εἶπεν λάβετε τοῦτο καὶ διαμερίσατε εἰς ἑαυτούς

Dependence—one way or the other—is plain: (1) καί, (2) aor. part., 'taking', (3) ποτήριον without the article, (4) εὐχαριστήσας as a second unlinked participle, (5) λάβετε τοῦτο is also the Marcan wording over the bread in 14.22. Despite Schürmann, straightforward dependence of Luke on Mark seems the easier. Marcan καί opens the sentence, just as Luke took it over in 22.15 and v. 19. He uses δεξάμενος as a variation for λαβών in view of the coming λάβετε— cf. 16.6f., where δέχεσθαι is similarly used for taking from someone else. No doubt the cup was handed to the president of the Lucan eucharist as it is by the server to the Priest today; cf. the Jewish Passover practice, 'After they have mixed for him the third cup. . . '

(*m. Pes.* 10.7). Mark often has two participles without καί as he has here λαβὼν. . .εὐχαριστήσας ἔδωκεν: e.g. 14.39, 57, 60 and especially v. 67 ἰδοῦσα τὸν Πέτρον. . .ἐμβλέψασα λέγει. 'He said, . . . divide this among yourselves' is Luke's oratio recta form of Mark's 'and they all drank of it': Mt. 26.27 also has oratio recta, 'saying, Drink of it, all of you'. διαμερίζειν and ἑαυτούς are both Lucan. The Lucan version of Mk 14.(22-)23 then continues into Mk 14.25, '(For) I say to you that I shall not drink. . . ' Luke puts his favoured ἀπὸ τοῦ νῦν for Mark's οὐκέτι; he puts ἀπό for Mark's ἐκ, since one drinks *from* the fruit of the vine rather than *out of* it; and his familiar ἕως οὗ again. Marshall suggests that the final clause, 'ἕως οὗ the kingdom of God ἔλθῃ' may be modelled on 1 Cor. 11.26, ἄχρι οὗ (ὁ κύριος) ἔλθῃ; which seems very plausible. So Luke has contrived to include all the matter on the cup which Mark says took place while they were eating; except only for the eucharistic words on the cup which Paul says were spoken after the meal, and which now follow in 22.19f.

22.21ff. If the Marcan order, (a) eucharistic words (14.22-24), (b) 'I will drink no more' (v. 25), has been reversed in this way in Luke on account of the tradition in Paul, the same is likely to be true of a second reversal, that of the words on the Traitor. For these precede the eucharistic words in Mark (14.18-21), but follow, in a variant form, in Luke (22.21-23); and there is something rather similar in 1 Cor. 11.27ff. It is after Paul has cited the words of institution that he goes on to speak of the one who eats and drinks unworthily, and of the sickness and death that will ensue; Luke has already made Satan enter Judas, and he will later describe his grisly death (Acts 1.18). It is he who makes plain for the first time that Judas received the sacramentalized elements, and this may best be explained as Luke's reading of 1 Cor. 11.27-29 (cf. p. 140), backed, no doubt, by the general tendency in the Church to blacken Judas. Any eating and drinking so unworthy as to incur death must be unworthy indeed; and what more evident example of such conduct could there be than Judas's treachery? It tells in favour of this explanation that John has so dramatically connected Judas's damnation with his reception of the morsel (Jn 13.26-30). Both the later evangelists thus stress Judas's reception of the sacramentalized food in a shocking way not found in the earlier two Gospels; but once more the highly symbolic Johannine account is easily read as a dramatized version of the same theme first found nascent in Luke.

We may also note that the whole unit, 22.1-23, opened with the story of the Traitor (vv. 1-6), and closes with Jesus' words on the Traitor (vv. 21-23), thus giving a satisfying inclusio (§2.3). Luke has contrived two lesser inclusios in the same passage. The Betrayal section opened with Mark's plot to destroy Jesus away from the people (22.1f.), and Luke closes it with Judas's engagement to betray him ἄτερ ὄχλου, an addition of his own (v. 6). Similarly, he closed the next paragraph with Mark's 'and they prepared the Passover' (22.13), to which he has provided his own counter with the opening dominical instruction, 'Go and prepare us the Passover. . . '(v. 8). So there is a secondary, stylistic reason for closing with the Traitor.

22.21-23. The transfer requires some adjustment to the wording. In Mark they were eating when Jesus introduced the topic, 'One of you παραδώσει με, he who is eating μετ' ἐμοῦ', and this is later specified as 'he who dips (Matthew adds τὴν χεῖρα) μετ' ἐμοῦ in the dish'. But the meal is now over in Luke, and the eating finished; the eucharistic words have been spoken over the concluding cup μετὰ τὸ δειπνῆσαι, So he is restricted to the more general, 'But lo, ἡ χεὶρ τοῦ παραδίδοντός με μετ' ἐμοῦ at the table'. πλήν is frequent in Luke, as is ἰδού. τράπεζα is neutral: the same ἐπὶ τῆς τραπέζης recurs at 22.30, another verse that may be L or R. Mark's 14.21 then follows in a slightly Lucanized form: '*For the Son of Man* goes his way according to what is destined, but *woe to that man through whom he is betrayed*'. Luke prefers πορεύεται to Mark's more vulgar ὑπάγει, and his connective πλήν, as in v. 21, is a grander form of Mark's δέ. κατὰ τὸ ὡρισμένον is characteristic both in the κατὰ τὸ + part. form, and in the notion of divine predestination. In Mark the disciples enquired who Jesus meant in oratio recta before 'For the Son of Man goes. . . ', and in Matthew both before and after. As Luke is abbreviating the sequence, he has no option but to place the enquiries after the saying. He uses the indirect form (cf. 22.2/Mk 14.2), with thoroughly Lucan phrasing (see below).

A plausible liturgical setting can be provided for the whole unit, 22.1-23, by supposing that the Lucan church met on the Paschal Eve at 6 p.m., and heard the stories of Judas's treachery, the preparation and the Supper. The syntax (and other considerations) make it impossible to break the unit at v. 20, 'And after dinner likewise. . . '; but there is a fresh introduction at v. 24. It is the first watch of a long vigil.

22.14 γίνεσθαι, ἀναπεσεῖν, οἱ-ἀπόστολοι*, σύν*. Schürmann is right in seeing the verse as straight redaction of Mark, *Pmb* (pp. 104-10) against Rehkopf (p. 90). ὥρα only means 'the appointed hour', as at 1.10; 22.53; Acts 3.1, not 'God's hour', which would be unique. 'The apostles' dignifies the occasion more than Mark's 'the Twelve'.

22.15 (εἶπεν)-πρὸς*, ἐπιθυμεῖν*, παθεῖν (inf.). Hapax: ἐπιθυμία. The context, with v. 16/18 linked to v. 15 by 'for', and the evidence that Luke composed the verse, show that the meaning is 'I wanted very much to do what we are now doing'. ἐπιθυμία does not have to mean a frustrated desire, cf. Mk 4.19; Jn 8.44; for ἐπιθυμεῖν cf. Lk. 16.21—why should Lazarus sit by Dives' gate if he was never given any crumbs? πάσχα is the whole Paschal meal now about to begin, as this is what Peter and John were sent to prepare (Schürmann, *Pmb*, pp. 8f.). πρὸ τοῦ + inf., 2.21; Acts 23.15.

22.16 ἕως-ὅτου. Jeremias (*EWJ*, pp. 207-18) takes the words as a vow to abstain from the meat (and later wine), so as to intercede for the Jewish people; but it is not a vow formula, and no intercession is implied. However, he is right (pp. 122-25) that the words refer to fulfilment in the Messianic banquet, not the eucharist; and may well be right that each year brought the expectation that Christ might return this Passover (see above pp. 152f.).

22.17 δέχεσθαι, (εὐχαριστεῖν), διαμερίζειν*, ἑαυτῶν. Schürmann (*Pmb*, pp. 23-34) argues that Luke is not dependent on Mark here, but vice versa; however, the argument is circular—δέχεσθαι = 'take' occurs also in Lk. 16.6f., where it may well be Luke's own writing rather than evidence of a pre-Lucan source. The context (ἀνέπεσεν) implies clearly that to Luke all vv. 14-19 take place at (the beginning of) the meal, so the cup is the first of the four (cf. L. Goppelt, *TDNT*, VI, pp. 153f. for the occurrence of 'the fruit of the vine' at this point in the liturgy, though it is common in such blessings). εἰς ἑαυτούς, 7.30R.

22.18 ἀπὸ-τοῦ-νῦν*, (ἕως)-οὗ. Hapaxes: (γένημα), (ἄμπελος). Jeremias (*EWJ*, p. 211) takes ἀπὸ τοῦ νῦν to mean 'from this moment on', but it means 'hereafter' at 1.48; 22.69R etc. Luke has ἀπό/ἐκ 127+114/87+84, Mark 47/67. 'The kingdom of God comes' is a standard expression, occurring in the Lord's Prayer and at 17.20,?R: as all the non-Marcan expressions are thus paralleled in Luke, Schürmann's argument (*Pmb*, pp. 34-45) for an independent source is weak.

22.19 (εὐχαριστεῖν). Hapax: (ἀνάμνησις).

For the textual problem, cf. Metzger, pp. 174-77. The Shorter Text, ending at 'This is my body' (v. 19a) is supported by Daff²il, and also by be with a different order of verses; and it is familiar to the tradition behind syr^sc with variation of order and assimilation to 1 Cor. 11.24. It is printed by WH,

Diglot, NEB, and has been defended in recent years by H. Chadwick (*HTR* [1957]), Leaney (pp. 72-75), A Vööbus (*NTS* [1969], *ZNW* [1970]), and M. Rese (*NTS* [1975]). Its testimony is described by Chadwick as worthy of respect, and by Rese as 'miserable'; but Rese is surely right to say that the matter must be resolved neither by adding and weighing MSS nor by counting heads, but by arguments. It is necessary to explain the origin of the two main traditions. The Longer Text is accepted by most modern commentators, and has been most fully defended by Jeremias (*EWJ* [=3rd German edn], pp. 139-59) and Schürmann (*Untersuchungen*, pp. 159-92).

Unfortunately the lines of defence taken by Jeremias and Schürmann are quite different, and neither is well supported. Jeremias appeals to the Church's *disciplina arcani*: Luke wrote the Longer Text, but it was felt to be undesirable for all and sundry to have access to it, so scribes cut out the two institution directives, and the words on the cup between. But the Shorter Text is likely to go back to the second century, and was the *disciplina arcani* so early? And why has no scribe interfered with 1 Cor. 11.24f., etc.? Schürmann reckons on two abbreviations, both arising from liturgical practice: v. 19b dropped out because of a church use which lacked 'which is given for you', and 'Do this. . .'; v. 20 because scandals with wine made it desirable to separate the Eucharist from the agape with its wine, described in vv. 15-19a. But two abbreviations make a difficult hypothesis; and we are often speculating about second century liturgical practice.

Chadwick and Rese have thus little difficulty with their opponents; but their own theories are less successful. Chadwick supposes an independent lost source for Lk. 22.14-18, which would then be misunderstood by Luke; he thought it was a eucharistic text which had left out words over the bread, which he supplied in v. 19a from Mark—and a scribe supplied vv. 19b-20 from a further misunderstanding. This leaves out of account the close relation between vv. 14-18 and Mark, which is well set out by Rese. Rese thinks Luke was re-writing Mark so as to turn an institution of the Eucharist into a farewell Passover meal: he does not believe in the atoning force of the cross, and this alien doctrine has been wished on to him by vv. 19b-20.

Rese's fine article does not explain why in re-writing Mark Luke should put the Traitor logia last and the 'I shall no more' logia first; and he really assumes that Luke has Mark only, and not 1 Corinthians besides. This leaves no entirely satisfactory solution: the assimilation to Mark and Matthew proposed above is all right for v. 19b, but a second, weaker, hypothesis is required for v. 20. Perhaps we have to concede that scribal omissions are not always satisfyingly explicable. What does seem clear is that Luke is adapting Mark to suit a second tradition; and that second tradition has shown repeated signs of being 1 Corinthians 11.

22.20 ὡσαύτως is second word at 13.5, as here, but first at 20.31R; the similar ὁμοίως is usually first word, but second at 16.25. Reminiscence of Mk 14.27 may have been influential: cp. Schürmann, *Esb*, pp. 34-36, 83-85. ὑμῶν makes Mark's πολλῶν specific: Christ died for the Church. H. Patsch is persuasive in arguing against Schürmann for the priority of the Marcan form—where Schürmann makes points, they would count for the priority of the Pauline form—the Lucan differences all seem secondary.

22.21 πλήν*, τράπεζα. For Rehkopf's arguments for an independent source here, see pp. 81ff. The context requires a literal meaning for ἡ χείρ, not the OT 'hand' of a hostile person. ὁ παραδιδούς is a stock phrase, Mk 14.42, 44.

22.22 κατὰ-τὸ + pf. part. pass.*, ὁρίζειν, πορεύεσθαι, πλήν*. Rehkopf (p. 15) is right to draw attention to μέν in the third word position, a unique phenomenon in the NT: but cf. Heb. 7.28 ὁ λόγος δὲ τῆς ὁρκωμοσίας. Marshall offers loose parallels at Acts 3.21; 21.39. The move is perhaps due to the contrast with the following τῷ ἀνθρώπῳ.

22.23 καὶ-αὐτὸν*, πρός of speech*, ἑαυτῶν, τὸ + ind. qn.*, τίς εἴη*, μέλλειν, πράσσειν*. συζητεῖν 24.15; Acts 6.9; 9.29 (but dropped at Mk 1.27 par.): συζήτησις ×2 Acts. ἑαυτῶν is used reciprocally at 7.49. τίς ἄρα cf. Acts 12.18 τί ἄρα.

Schürmann, H. 'Lk 22,19b-20 als ursprüngliche Textüberlieferung', *Bibl* 32 (1951), pp. 364-92, 522-41, = *TU*, pp. 159-92.
Schürmann, H. *Der Passamahlbericht Lk 22,(7-14.) 15-18* (Münster, 1953).
Schürmann, H. *Der Einsetzungsbericht Lk 22,19-20* (Münster, 1955).
Chadwick, H., 'The Shorter Text of Luke XXII.15-20', *HTR* 50 (1957), pp. 249-58.
Jeremias, J., *The Eucharistic Words of Jesus* (ET London, 1966 = *Die Abendmahlsworte Jesu*, 3rd edn, 1960, revised 1964).
Vööbus, A., 'A New Approach to the Problem of the Shorter and Longer Text in Luke', *NTS* 15 (1969), pp. 457-63.
Vööbus, A., 'Kritische Beobachtungen über die lukanische Darstellung des Herrenmahls', *ZNW* 61 (1970), pp. 102-10.
Patsch, H., *Abendmahl und historischer Jesus* (Stuttgart, 1972).
Rese, M., 'Zur Problematik von Kurz- und Langtext in Luk XXII.17ff', *NTS* 22 (1975), pp. 15-31.

b. *The Farewell Discourse*, 22.24-38   Passover, 9 p.m.

We have already seen Luke quietly making a sermon out of Judas' treachery: he had, as Paul taught the Corinthians, eaten and drunk to his own damnation (1 Cor. 11.29), and his death (1 Cor. 11.30) is soon to follow. But there is a much more important text to expound from the supper, which gives the significance of the whole: 'This cup is the new covenant in my blood, which is shed for you'. It is this which is Luke's central preoccupation through the Farewell Discourse.

The words raise many echoes, and it is for this reason that the thread of Luke's mind is not easy to follow. The first is with the story of James' and John's request in Mk 10.35-45, which Luke omitted in ch. 18; he spared their blushes there, only to bring disgrace on the apostolic college at this most holy moment. For then Jesus had said, 'The cup which I drink you shall drink' (Mk 10.39), and now he has drunk of the cup, and they also. So the first lesson which the Lucan church must learn is that to drink Christ's cup is to share his humility.

22.24f. Luke assimilates the contretemps to the earlier discussion on the road, who was greatest (τίς μείζων, Mk 9.34), and describes the occasion with another word from the context of the Corinthian eucharist—φιλονικία (1 Cor. 11.16, 'If anyone seems to be φιλόνεικος'). He then returns to Mk 10.42-44, 'Those who are supposed (δοκοῦντες) to rule over the Gentiles lord it over them, and their great men exercise authority over them'. The δοκοῦντες has gone into Lk 22.24, 'which of them δοκεῖ to be μείζων'; the rulers become kings (cf. 10.24QD, 'prophets and kings'); the κατα-compounds (κατακυριεύειν, κατεξουσιάζειν) are dropped in a citation from memory; and Luke is able to display his knowledge of Egyptian history with 'are called Benefactors'. There was a Ptolemy the Benefactor in the second century BC, though the point Luke was supposed to be making was about arrogant ruling, not good reputation—rather a Lucan muddle (§9).

22.26f. Mark continued, 'But it is not so among you, but he who wishes to be great among you shall be your διάκονος, and he who wishes to be first among you shall be the slave of all': Luke is thinking of the various orders in his church, and he writes, 'let him be as the νεώτερος' (like the νεώτεροι who buried Ananias and Sapphira, Acts 5.6, 10, or the νεανίσκοι of 1 Jn 2), '...as ὁ διακονῶν' (Acts 6.2). The moral is then drawn with an inclusio: who is μείζων, the ἀνακείμενος (Mk 14.18) or the διακονῶν? But Jesus was among them as ὁ διακονῶν, like the Son of Man who came διακονῆσαι in Mk 10.45. Luke has been beguiled into introducing the Pauline atonement theology into his Gospel with the two ὑπὲρ ὑμῶν's of vv. 19f., but nothing will induce him to copy out the 'ransom in place of many' from the second half of the verse in Mark. Service means service to death, but not substitution.

The embarrassing scene with the sons of Zebedee had begun with their request to sit beside the Lord *in his kingdom* (Mt. 20.21, cp. Mark 'glory'). Jesus made no undertaking then, but now he has just said (Mt. 26.29, diff. Mk.) that he will *drink* the fruit of the vine with the apostles *in his Father's kingdom*; and furthermore, on another occasion he had said that '*you who* followed me, at the rebirth when the Son of Man sits on the throne of his glory, you too *shall sit on* twelve *thrones judging the twelve tribes of Israel*' (Mt. 19.28). This then, in Luke's understanding, is the διαθήκη which Jesus has made at his Supper. They are not to seek for greatness, but to serve (vv. 24-27); and (δὲ) he on his side will reward them.

22.28f. '*You* are *those who* (ὑμεῖς ἐστε οἱ) have' not merely followed, but have 'continued with me in my trials'—the Lucan concept of an apostle as one who 'accompanied us during all the time that the Lord Jesus went in and out among us, beginning from the baptism of John' (Acts 1.21f.). πειρασμοί are Lucan too.'.... And I covenant (διατίθεμαι) to you even as *my Father* covenanted (διέθετο) to me a *kingdom*'. That is the force of Mt. 26.29. The kingdom is both Jesus' (Mt. 20.21) and his Father's, and the covenant of Mt. 26.28, sealed in his blood, is seen as bringing this kingdom to the apostles. ὁ πατήρ μου is rare in Luke: for the form of sentence cf. 6.36QD, 'Be merciful καθὼς καὶ ὁ πατὴρ ὑμῶν is merciful'. For God's covenant, cf. Acts 3.25, 'τῆς διαθήκης which God διέθετο to your fathers'.

22.30. The Lucan vision of the kingdom is entailed by the passages which he is following. It is a Messianic banquet, at which they will be (eating and) *drinking* the 'new' fruit of the vine (cf. 13.29 also) with Christ; 'at his table' as at 22.21, *in his kingdom* where James and John hoped to sit. But, alas, there is also the picture of Mt. 19.28, where the apostles were to sit not at dinner but on thrones of judgment with the twelve tribes before them, and Luke has already begun on this tack with his 'You... who' (v. 28). So we have an uncomfortable combination of sources: the Twelve are discovered sitting round the banquet table of the age to come eating and drinking, and on thrones deciding the eternal fate of their fellow-Jews, in the same half-sentence (§9, 15).

22.24 γίνεσθαι, δὲ-καί*, τὸ + ind. qn.* Hapax: φιλονικία (1 Cor. 11.16). Schürmann (*JAr*, pp. 63-99) and Taylor (*PNL*, pp. 61-64) argue for an independent source for Luke in this passage; Finegan (pp. 13f.) for Lucan redaction of Mark. Schürmann concedes that Luke's source for vv. 24-26 is secondary to Mark; but the differences seem explicable as Luke's own work.

He argues that Luke would not have introduced an apostolic quarrel here if it had not been in his source; but a much more pointed apostolic quarrel was attached to 'The cup which I drink you shall drink', which is Luke's probable source here. Life with Paul had taught Luke that quarrels were a feature of eucharistic life (1 Cor. 11), and he aims to edify by being realistic. Although he keeps most of the Marcan order, he has transferred some other Marcan pericopes, the First Apostles, the Mother and Brothers and the Anointing.

22.25 εἶπεν, καλεῖν. Hapaxes: κυριεύειν, ἐξουσιάζειν, εὐεργέτης. The omission of the κατα's from κατακυριεύειν and κατεξουσιάζειν makes the Marcan verbs less oppressive, and may be part of Luke's *piano* approach to authority, cf. to 'Agrippa the king' in Acts 26. εὐεργέτης, cf. -εῖν Acts 10.38, -εσία Acts 4.9, may be a similar toning down.

22.26 γίνεσθαι. Hapax: ἡγεῖσθαι. There is a slight shift from who seemed to be greatest, i.e. most important, to ὁ μείζων, i.e. the actual church leaders: if so, shifts are familiar from the Lucan Sinner, Good Samaritan, etc. (§9). The wording is close to Mt. 23.11, ὁ δὲ μείζων ὑμῶν ἔσται ὑμῶν διάκονος. ὁ-μείζων is unique in Luke, but redactional at Mt. 18.4: Mt. 23.11 seems to be Matthew's own writing. ὁ ἡγούμενος means the Church leader at Acts 7.10; 14.12; 15.22.

22.27 οὐχί, ἐν-μέσῳ. Bultmann (p. 144) and Schürmann (*JAr*, pp. 79-92) regard this as an earlier form of Mk 10.45b. But (1) the Lucan form provides a suitable close to the topic; (2) it takes up the Marcan ἀνακείμενος (Mk 14.18), which has been missing from Luke so far; (3) there is a dramatic Lucan parallel to the form of the sentence in 6.39 QD:

μήτι δύναται τυφλὸς τυφλὸν ὁδηγεῖν;   οὐχὶ ἀμφότεροι εἰς βόθυνον ἐμπεσοῦνται;
τίς γὰρ μείζων, ὁ ἀνακ. ἤ ὁ διακ.;   οὐχὶ ὁ ἀνακείμενος;

The foot-washing in John 13 is a further example of a short Lucan saying being developed into a symbolic Johannine story, cf. p. 323; and John has also developed the Lucan Farewell Discourse in his own majestic manner.

22.28 πειρασμός. διαμεμενηκότες, cf. 1.22: the perfect implies trials throughout Jesus' ministry (S. Brown, pp. 8f., *contra* Conzelmann). Schulz (pp. 330f.) argues for the secondariness of the Lucan form. Mt.'s ἀκολουθήσαντες will be the Q form—but that seems to be Mt.R; cf. 19.27!

22.29 καθώς. ὁ-πατήρ-μου comes at 2.49L; 10.22=Mt.; 24.49L.

22.30 ἔσθειν-καὶ-πίνειν*, τράπεζα. Schulz (pp. 331f.) notes the difference of meaning of 'kingdom' in v. 29 and v. 30, and the combination of the meal and judgment themes, as double signs of Lucan secondariness: the change from subjunctive to future also shows that Matthew's form was original. The 'twelve' thrones have been dropped, perhaps for Judas's absence. ἔσθειν for ἐσθίειν: also in BD at 7.33, 34; 10.7 in combination with πίνειν.

22.31-34. The prophecy of Peter's Denial, which follows, is at least in the first three verses even further from the Marcan version than is the previous section. Finegan (pp. 14f.) argues for redaction of Mark, but is a lone voice against Schürmann (*JAr*, pp. 99-115) (for vv. 31f.), Manson (pp. 339f.) and Taylor (*PNL* pp. 65f.) (for vv. 31-33), Rengstorf and Rehkopf (pp. 84) (for vv. 31-34), and many others; nevertheless he is right.

The Marcan tale had nothing to commend it to Luke: it was merciless to the apostles, who would be made to stumble and scattered like sheep; it foretold their post-resurrection encounter with Jesus in Galilee, while Luke took this to have happened in Jerusalem (24.6; cp. Mk); and it made the worst of Peter, who is represented as doubly and vainly boastful (14.29, 31), and as contradicting the Lord. As Luke elsewhere regularly whitewashes the Twelve, and especially Peter, and suppresses the whole Galilee expedition, it would be no surprise if he did the same here. He cannot reasonably pretend that the apostles did not desert Jesus, or that Peter did not deny him, but a more charitable presentation is possible, and incumbent.

22.31. He begins, as Mark does, with the Twelve ('you shall all be made to stumble'/'Satan demanded you [all]'), but like Mark makes Peter's denial the central topic. The doubled 'Simon' recalls Luke's 'Master, master' (8.34R), 'Martha, Martha', 'Saul, Saul', and is a feature found only in Luke. As at 22.3R he introduces Satan (cf. 10.18; 13.16; Acts 5.3; 26.18): in both cases this heightens the effect, though in different ways. Satan entered into Judas, and this increases the horror of the listener at his treachery: Satan demanded the Twelve for sifting, and this increases the hearer's sympathy for them—they are no longer quite responsible, but are pawns in the hands of supernatural powers, like Job for whom Satan treated with God. The introduction of Satan can be justified, for the apostles were about to enter temptation (πειρασμός, Mk 14.38), and it is Satan who puts us to the trial (Mt. 6.13; Job 1-2); and the two most obvious metaphors for such testing were the crucible (1 Pet. 1.7) and the threshing-floor (Lk 3.17). Luke has more chaff at 20.18, and goes for the same image here: the sieve has the advantage, as a metaphor, of pressing the point of the Twelve's testing, and leaving in convenient obscurity the question of whether they passed the test. The story to come (and v. 22b) imply that they were chaff; but later experience, to Luke, shows them to have been wheat indeed.

22.32. The apostles' hope of surviving their trial lay in prayer (Mk 14.38), and it was their—and especially Peter's—failure to pray which resulted in their partial downfall. But when Satan stands before God for the soul of man, it is ultimately not their prayers which are effective, but those of God's Son; and if Peter and the Apostolic College were in the end to show themselves heroes, that will have been through the intercession of the Lord. So Luke can depend that Jesus will have prayed for them (Lucan δέεσθαι, Lucan prayer περί, 6.28QD; Acts 8.15; 12.5); and his prayer will have been that their πίστις (=faithfulness) fail not. It is Luke who twice introduces πιστεύειν in the sense of 'persevere, be faithful' into the Sower (8.12, 13); who follows the apostles' 'Lord, increase our πίστις' (17.5) with the parable of the faithful servant-of-all-work; and who asks if the Son of Man will find πίστις = faithfulness on the earth (18.8). Luke alone favours the notion of the unfailing (ἐκλίπῃ) quality of the genuinely spiritual: treasure ἀνέκλειπτος in the heavens (12.33), eternal tabernacles when mammon ἐκλίπῃ (16.9). Luke's eyes are not on Peter's coming peccadilloes of Paschal night, but further ahead, ποτε. After the crucifixion it is he who will be the first to turn to God (ἐπιστρέφειν in this sense Acts 3.19), and then he will strengthen (Lucan στηρίζειν) his brethren. That Peter in fact did this is implied in 24.34, 'The Lord is risen indeed, and has appeared to Simon', and is described fully in the opening chapters of Acts.

22.33. The same distraction from the harsh Marcan present to the shining future of Acts continues into v. 33. Peter's vain and shameful boast, 'If I must die with you, I will not deny you' (Mk 14.31), is replaced with the loyal and truthful, 'Lord, with you I am ready to go both to prison and to death'. Peter was to back those courageous words with his life in the events of Acts 5 and 12, and his eventual martyrdom (which Luke here implies): the quickness of Luke's mind once more deceives the ear.

22.34. But the present cannot be entirely glossed over, and he closes with Jesus' prophecy of Peter's denial before cockcrow, almost in the Marcan form. The opening vocative, 'Peter', is inserted though (perhaps from Mk 14.29), and looks like an intended contrast with 'Simon, Simon' of v. 31. Maybe Luke is recalling the 'Simon bar-Jonah. . . thou art Peter' of Mt. 16.17f. Not for him the interpretation of Peter as the rock of Church order, with powers to bind and excommunicate: his Peter was the rock of the Church of Acts, strengthening his colleagues with his leadership, zeal and devotion to death, however faint might be his first beginning.

The ascription of part or all of this material to L is very unhelpful. We have to suppose a prophecy, stated in v. 34, implied in v. 32b, without an accompanying account of its fulfilment, since no case can be made for an L account of the Denial. We have to postulate an L with a strong motive to whitewash all the apostles, and with a special interest in saving the reputation of Peter; and he has to do this with concepts and language favoured by Luke. Where is Occam's razor?

22.31 τοῦ + inf.* Hapaxes: ἐξαιτεῖσθαι, σινιάζειν. We should probably read an introductory εἶπεν δὲ ὁ κύριος with ℵ DWΘΨ fam 1, 13 and most MSS: despite their absence from p⁷⁵BL syr^sin, it would be remarkable for a copyist to have written both Lucan εἶπεν-δὲ and Lucan ὁ-κύριος = Jesus. ἐξαιτεῖσθαι, cf. αἰτεῖσθαι, med. 5/7/3+8.

22.32 δέεσθαι*, περί, ἐκλείπειν, ἐπιστρέφειν, στηρίζειν. Hapax: ποτέ. δέεσθαι + ἵνα, 9.40R; 21.36R; cf. 8.32R; 7.36; 16.27 (contra Schürmann, *JAr*. 106). Opinion is divided on whether πίστις means faith or faithfulness here. Bultmann (p. 267), E. Fuchs (*TDNT* VII, p. 292) and Marshall favour faithfulness; Schürmann (*JAr*, p. 112) S. Brown (pp. 60f.) faith (which may 'fail' and be recovered by 'conversion').

22.33 εἶπεν, πορεύεσθαι. Cf. Paul, 'I am ready (ἑτοίμως) not only to be bound but also to die', Acts 21.13. .

22.34 εἶπεν. Note that Peter does not 'deny Jesus' absolutely, as in Mk 14.30, which would be unforgivable (12.9): he just denies 'that he knows him', a happy Lucan prevarication.

22.35-38. The final section of the Farewell Discourse, on the Two Swords, has been the occasion of much puzzlement: Manson (pp. 339-41) thinks Jesus is being ironic; Conzelmann that the 'but now' marks the crucial change from Jesus' time to the time of the Church; H.W. Bartsch (*NTS* [1974]) that Jesus intended his disciples to arm for the eschatological struggle. Only Finegan, as usual, sees the verses as a Lucan construction; and a strong case can be made out for this.

Jesus was speaking in v. 31 of Satan's demand to sift the apostles, but attention soon focussed on Peter, who received a thorough whitewashing—or as thorough at least as the facts permitted. We should expect Luke to do the same for the other members of the College, who are shortly to be found sword in hand at the Arrest. One mitigation is suggested (not very forcefully) by Jesus' remark to the authorities, 'But (this all took place, Mt.) that the scriptures (of the prophets, Mt.) might be fulfilled' (Mk 14.49). Luke takes this up with enthusiasm: it was not only foretold in the Bible that Jesus should suffer, but that he would be reckoned with the lawless (Isa. 53.12), and that, of course, is how the disciples must have appeared, attacking the police. But in fact this was not only the will of God, as Isaiah had said, but it was in obedience to Jesus' own command. We may see here once more Luke's anxiety to show the Church as a peaceful organization, without threat to the imperium. Normally, throughout the ministry, they had gone unarmed and had come to no hurt: the fact that they had been armed at the Arrest had nothing to do with Zealotry—Jesus had expressly withdrawn his earlier ban on provisions, and even on a sword, for the Pasch (νῦν), as a simple measure of prudence.

The general tenor of the passage can thus be ascribed to three standard Lucan interests: the blamelessness of the apostles, the fulfilment of the scriptures and the Church's innocence of offence against Rome.

22.35f. It begins without question as Luke's own writing, since it takes up the Lucan redaction of the Q Mission (10.4), 'Behold, I send you. . . carry no purse, no bag, no shoes': the same items in the same order with the same single syllable between. βαλλάντιον is Lucan, and the unexplained interdict on shoes is repeated (see on 10.4). Nor is it uncharacteristic of Luke to have slightly muddled the issue (§9), forgetting that he described this ban at the sending of the Seventy-Two, not of the Twelve at all. But the evangelist of the poor cannot simply write, 'But now take your purse. . . ', for the poor have no purse. So he has recourse to the same 'he who has'/'he who has not' contrast that he wrote into John Baptist's teaching in 3.11, and at 19.26QC, and to the buying-and-selling that he wrote into 17.28; in this way Jesus can take responsibility for the buying of the sword. The sentence is constructed on the model of 17.31, 'he who shall be on the roof. . . let him not go down. . . and he that is in the country likewise let him not turn back'.

22.37. Luke moves now to his Isaiah citation, and very Lucan is the framework he gives it (see below). The wording itself varies a little from the LXX, which has καὶ ἐν τοῖς ἀνόμοις ἐλογίσθη, to Luke's καὶ μετὰ ἀνόμων ἐλογίσθη: and this has led to suspicions that the citation was from a non-LXX source, as he is normally fairly accurate in citing the Greek OT. But this is very unlikely: *mnh* is used some 25 times in the Hebrew Bible, and only translated twice by λογίζειν, and *pš'* is rendered only four times by ἄνομος. The translation is thus basically the LXX, and Bartsch suggests sensibly that the μετὰ removes the possibility that Jesus might be one of (ἐν) the lawless. It is possible to exaggerate Luke's accuracy of citation (cf. T. Holtz, pp. 41ff.): for instance, neither of the two Psalms citations in Acts 1.20 is quite accurate. But Luke can also make deliberate changes, as in Acts 7.43, ἐπέκεινα Βαβυλῶνος.

22.38. So it came to pass that Jesus was reckoned with law-breakers (Minear, *NT* [1964] correctly sees these to be the apostles); and if law-breakers in the plural, at least two of them must have had swords—we have suspected the same literalism with the two raisings, many lepers, etc. out of Mt. 11.5. Jesus replies to their comment that such they have, with a gruff ἱκανόν ἐστιν (Lucan ἱκανός). The words are non-committal, and not very meaningful, like v. 68. Luke keeps his plural swordsmen in v. 49.

22.35 εἶπεν/αν, βαλλάντιον, τις. οὐθέν, 23.14, ×3 Acts. ὑστερεῖν 15.14; ἄτερ 22.6R.

22.36 εἶπεν-δὲ*, νῦν, βαλλάντιον, ὁμοίως*, καὶ = also. αἴρειν 9.3=Mk, 17.31=Mk, Acts 21.11 in this sense, 'take'. The verse presents insoluble problems to most theories. It is unbelievable that most early Christians went about armed: so how could such a saying be either produced or retained by the community? Minear is right in seeing the saying as mitigating the scene to come, but thinks the disciples disobeyed Jesus—despite the tendency of Luke in vv. 21-24. Marshall thinks it 'a call to be ready for hardship and self-sacrifice', but all such 'symbolic' interpretation is as unconvincing as the 'ironic' theory.

22.37 τὸ-γεγραμμένον*, δεῖ, τὸ + prep.*, περί, τελεῖσθαι. Hapaxes: (ἄνομος), (λογίζειν). cf. 18.31R τελεσθήσεται πάντα τὰ γεγραμμένα. λέγω γὰρ ὑμῖν ὅτι 14.24; 22.16, 18; cf. 19.26QD. Bartsch can hardly be right that the text was applied by Luke to the two malefactors: why should he then put it in this context? Schürmann (*JAr*, pp. 126-28) objects that Luke does not elsewhere introduce citations into the Gospel, and that he passes Mark's references to Isaiah 53 by. But Mk 14.49b suggests a citation, and Luke leaves this out at 22.53; and he does not care for Mark's Atonement theology. τὸ introduces a citation here only, but cf. 22.4, 23.

22.38 εἶπαν/-εν, ἱκανός. ἰδοὺ. . .ὧδε, 17.21, 23. κύριε, cf. v. 33.

One change that Luke has made to Mark in this section requires comment: the move of Peter's Denial Prophecy from after to during the Upper Room scene—and indeed the development of the conversation at the Supper into a short Farewell Discourse. The motive for this change is most easily sought in a liturgical arrangement of the Lucan Passion narrative. Passover began with the story of the Last supper at 6 p.m.: that is, the Treachery, the Preparation and the Supper narrative, vv. 14-23. At v. 20 Luke includes a note of time, 'After supper', but the story is in mid-flow, and cannot be broken till v. 23. The post-Supper conversation may be suitably taken in Luke's church at 9 p.m., 'late', and is also in three parts: the 'cup of the covenant' exposition, Peter's coming Denial, and the Two Swords. We shall see that the triple sub-section scheme is a feature that continues, and since we have found so long a sequence of triple sub-sections following 9.51, we can speculate that the same may underlie the Passion. Any attempt to keep vigil through the night of the Passion (ἀγρυπνεῖτε, Mk 13.33; Lk. 21.36; γρηγορεῖτε, Mk 13.35, 37; 14.34, 38; Mt. 24.42f.; 25.13; 26.40f.) is likely to lead to edifying 'fillers' for the time; and an obvious move is to extend the Last Supper conversation, since Jesus' words must be limited thereafter. A regular feature of the Lucan passion story, right up to the moment of Jesus' death, is in fact the supply of dominical words and gestures to interpret the Marcan story. The brief Lucan Farewell Supper Discourse may be seen as the precursor of the more ambitious John 13-17. Whether the triple sub-divisions imply an *hourly* narrative (cf. 22.59) must be left open.

Dupont, J., 'Le logion des douze trônes (Mt. 19,28; Lc 22,28-30)', *Bibl* 45 (1964), pp. 355-92.
Minear, P.S., 'A Note on Luke xxii 36', *NT* 7 (1964-65), pp. 128-34.
Roloff, J., 'Anfänge der soteriologischen Deutung des Todes Jesu (Mk. x.45 und Lk. xxii.27)'' *NTS* 19 (1972), pp. 38-64.
Bartsch, H.-W., 'Jesu Schwertwort, Lukas xxii.35-38', *NTS* 20 (1974), pp. 190-203.
Guillet, J., 'Luc 22,29: Une formule johannique dans l'évangile de Luc?', *RSR* 69 (1981), pp. 113-22.
Schlosser, J., 'La genèse de Luc, XXII,25-27', *RB* 89 (1982), pp. 52-70.

c. *Gethsemane*, 22.39-53   Passover, Midnight

With Gethsemane, it becomes more obvious that Luke is just giving his version of Mark: to the faithful Finegan we may add Creed and

Eta Linnemann (*Studien*, pp. 11-40) for this view, though Taylor, Grundmann, Rehkopf (p. 84) and others argue for a second source still. But we can account for the Lucan wording with Mark and Lucan tendencies and vocabulary.

22.39f. Luke has already transferred to the Farewell Discourse as much as he wants of Mark's conversation en route to Gethsemane; so he begins with Mark's comment that the party went out to the Mount of Olives. He drops Mark's 'hymn', the Paschal Hallel, for which the time is now past; and adds κατὰ τὸ ἔθος, a characteristic phrase. This he does partly because he takes it that Jesus is spending the nights in a tent (ηὐλίζετο) on the side of the Mount of Olives (21.37, whereas Matthew, from whom he got the word, understood it to mean that Jesus was *lodging* at Bethany, Mt. 21.17); and partly because it is easy for the listener then to understand how Judas knew where to come. Mark says they went to a hamlet called Gethsemane, but Luke leaves this out because he is envisaging Jesus encamped on the hillside, as he had no doubt seen pilgrims encamped himself (§28; Josephus, *Ant.* 17.217, Jeremias, *JTJ*, p. 61); and the Marcan description implies open ground, not a village. Mark also says that he told the disciples to sit there while he prayed (v. 32), and that he told Peter, James and John to watch (v. 34), which is later specified as 'Watch and pray that you come not into temptation' (v. 38): Luke comes down to brass tacks as once with 'Pray not to enter temptation' (Matthaean εἰσέλθητε, 26.41), but as usual he keeps the odium away from Peter (James and John), who receive an honourable non-mention.

22.41. The scene is thus set for Jesus' noble acceptance of his Father's will, while the Twelve are edifyingly at prayer. The earlier tradition was that Jesus 'went on a little', and Matthew had said, 'while I go yonder (ἐκεῖ)'. Luke infers (§13) that the distance was 'about a stone's throw', because that explains how the disciples could observe what was to follow; and ὡσεὶ λίθου βολήν may be an echo of ὡσεὶ τόξου βολήν in Gen. 21.16, where Hagar leaves Ishmael in the hour of her trial, and is comforted from heaven. ἀποσπασθ(έντας) ἀπ' αὐτῶν is a phrase occurring also in Acts 21.1, where it has a strong meaning, 'tearing ourselves away from them', and it probably means the same here: Luke is stressing Jesus' attachment to the warmth of his community (ἐπιθυμίᾳ ἐπεθύμησα . . .) and the wrench it was to go and face his fate on his own. θεὶς τὰ γόνατα προσηύ(ξα)το also comes at Acts 20.36, in the same scene.

22.42. Luke has Mark's formulation of Jesus' prayer before him with its 'take this cup from me'; but the familiar echoes of the Matthaean form have nearly taken over, λέγων, πάτερ μου, εἰ δύνατόν ἐστιν...πλὴν... (Mt. 26.39). The λέγων and πάτερ, on its own, Luke might have written without suggestion, but the εἰ clause, in place of Mark's 'all things are possible to thee' looks like a Matthaean prompting. Matthew had 'if it is possible', following Mark; Luke knows anything is possible with God and substitutes 'if you will', Lucan βούλεσθαι/βουλὴ τοῦ θεοῦ. He forms his second clause, 'not my θέλημα but thine γινέσθω', differently from Mark's 'not what I will but what thou (dost)' (Mt., 'as...as'); but it looks uncomfortably like Mt. 26.42, γενηθήτω τὸ θέλημά σου, a phrase found also in the Matthaean, but not the Lucan Lord's Prayer. Dodd (*HTFG*, pp. 363f.) suggests the influence of oral tradition, but Marshall is right in saying, 'Luke was indebted to another source than Mk at this point'—only why should the source not be Matthew?

22.43f. The first sub-section thus reaches its climax in Jesus' great prayer of submission: in the second, vv. 43-46, he receives strength from heaven in his hour of trial. Verses 43f., on the angel and the sweat, are missing from p⁷⁵ℵ ABNRTW f syrˢⁱⁿ copt Marc Clem Orig, and are testified in ℵ*DLΘ fam.1 latt syrᶜᵘʳ Justin Iren. and most MSS. They are put in double brackets by N-A²⁶, and were omitted by WH. Metzger gives them a C rating (cf. Aland, *NTS* [1966]), but they are printed in the Diglot and by Greeven. Metzger (p. 177) argues that it is unlikely that they would have been deleted in so many different areas of the Church so early. However (1) the witnesses for them also cover many areas of the Church: Egypt(L ℵ*), the West (Justin, Iren., D, all the Old Latin but f), Caesarea (Θ fam 1 565 700), Syria and Byzantium. (2) It is not difficult to explain their omission from an early MS. Epiphanius mentions that some of his contemporaries thought them incompatible with the divinity of Christ, and they are the verses most offensive to a Christian tending to Docetism or other gnostical belief, of any in the Gospel. Marcion did not read them. (3) If they were written by someone other than Luke, he has a marvellous gift for imitating Luke's style. They begin ὤφθη δὲ αὐτῷ ἄγγελος; but then 1.11 also begins ὤφθη δὲ αὐτῷ ἄγγελος, and Acts 7.30 says of Moses ὤφθη αὐτῷ...ἄγγελος. ὤφθην is in fact a Lucan favourite: 1/1/3+10 beside here. With an angel ἀπ' οὐρανοῦ, cf. the great signs ἀπ' οὐρανοῦ at 21.11R. ἐνισχύειν is the verb used of the angel who strengthens Daniel in Dan. 10.18 Θ, the only strictly comparable passage in the OT. γενόμενος ἐν ἀγωνίᾳ recalls the same participle used for changes of emotion at Acts 10.4; 16.29; 19.28. ἐκτενέστερον προσηύχετο recalls even more sharply προσευχή that was made for Peter ἐκτενῶς at Acts 12.5: the adjective/adverb come only twice elsewhere in the NT, in 1 Peter—the noun ἐκτενεία comes only at Acts 26.7. ὡσεί is Lucan. For ἐπὶ τὴν γῆν cf. 5.11; 6.49QD; 8.27R. (4) We have already seen Luke twice put the Passion in a supernatural setting. Satan entered Judas, and he demanded the Twelve to sift. It would be entirely in keeping with this if Jesus himself were under the influence of angelic force. Furthermore, we have seen Jesus in an earlier πειρασμός, at the close of which the devil left him for a season (4.13), and that there Luke omitted Matthew's note, 'and lo, angels came and ministered to him' (Mt. 4.11). It would be in the Lucan manner (§17) to hold over such a note for later use. (5) Without vv. 43f. Luke would have omitted Jesus' profound grief from Mk 14.33f., for which there is no obvious motive. The agony shows the cost of the cross, and is needed dramatically and theologically. Thus the case for including vv.43f. seems overwhelming.

But why has Luke reversed the Marcan order distress-submission? Probably Mt. 4.11 has been the influence: first Jesus overcame temptation, then the angels came, there as here. Their ministration now is to lend their weight in his further turmoil: Mark mentions more than one phase of Jesus' prayer, and it might seem too easy if even his initial response of obedience was prompted from on high. The ἀγωνία may mean either the traditional 'agony', or perhaps 'conflict': the sense is not very different. The sweat is compared to drops of blood probably for size and flow: as with the stone's throw, Luke is being specific (§13). If the verses have been suppressed by docetist scribes as too offensive, we may have to reckon with a deliberate move by Luke to stress the starkness of the Lord's suffering, just as he stresses the physicality of the Spirit at his Baptism, or of his body after the Resurrection: they would then be Luke's form of Ignatius' ἀληθῶς ἔπαθεν (*Smyrn.* 2.2).

22.45f. If the effect of the Lucan version is to heighten Jesus' anguish, it is also, as usual, to diminish Mark's harshness on the apostles. Their threefold failure in Mark is reduced to once. Jesus rises (Lucan ἀναστάς) from prayer (Lucan ἡ προσευχή), and comes and finds them 'sleeping from grief': the comical and transparent whitewashing is paralleled in 24.41, 'while they still disbelieved from joy', cf. Acts 12.14, 'she did not open the gate from joy'. The hurt Marcan 'Simon, are you asleep? Could you not watch one hour?' becomes the kindly 'Why do you sleep? Rise (Lucan ἀναστάντες) and pray. . .': Jesus' only concern is that they be fortified for their hour of trial—their support for him is nothing. Mark's 'the spirit is willing, but the flesh is weak' is omitted: there was nothing wrong with the Apostles' flesh or spirit, as the Acts was to show. So both changes and omissions serve standard Lucan interests.

22.39 πορεύεσθαι, κατὰ-τὸ-ἔθος, καὶ = also. The harsh Marcan comments on the shepherd and the flock may be contrasted with the much more positive use of the same images in the Farewell Discourse by Paul in Acts 20.38—perhaps another case of Lucan transfer to Acts of a theme missing from Mark (§17).

22.40 γίνεσθαι, τόπος, εἶπεν,(πειρασμός*). Cf. γενομέναι ἐπὶ τὸ μνημεῖον, 24.22; Acts 21.35; ἐπὶ τὸν τόπον, 23.33; γενόμενος κατὰ τὸν τόπον, 10.32. Pray + inf., Acts 26.3.

22.41 καὶ-αὐτός*, ὡσεί. Hapaxes: ἀποσπᾶν, βολή. ἀποσπᾶν, Acts 20.3; 21.1 (cf. Mt. 26.51), cf. ἀνεσπάσθη, Acts 11.10. θεὶς τὰ γόνατα, 0/0/1+4, with προσεύχεσθαι, Acts 9.40; 20.36; 21.5.

22.42 πάτερ*, (πλήν), γίνεσθαι. Hapax: (παραφέρειν). τοῦτο τὸ ποτήριον (for 312), cf. v. 20. τὸ θέλημα. . .τὸ σὸν γινέσθω, cf. Acts 21.14, τοῦ κυρίου τὸ θέλημα γινέσθω. βούλεσθαι ×14 Acts.

22.43 ὤφθην, οὐρανός sing. J. Duplacy (*Fs Metzger*, 1981) suggests a variety of motives for suppressing, and also for interpolating vv. 43f., but prefers the former. T. Lescow (*ZNW* [1967]) accepts both verses, but takes v. 43 to be R and v. 44 *Vorlage*: but the ideas, and much of the language of v. 44 are Luke's.

22.44 γίνεσθαι (×2), ὡσεί. Hapaxes: ἀγωνία, ἱδρώς, θρόμβος. Luke has as many parts of the body as any other evangelist (cf. *MLM*, p. 103): with 'drops of blood', cf. 'the tip of his finger', 'a hair of your head'. γενόμενος ἐν ἀγωνίᾳ, cf. Acts 22.17, γενέσθάι με ἐν ἐκστάσει. With ἱδρώς cf. Luke's interest in tears and weeping: Jesus weeps at 19.41. ὡσεί = like 24.11, ×3 Acts.

22.45 ἀναστάς*, ἡ-προσευχή, εὑρίσκειν. Hapaxes: κοιμᾶσθαι, λυπή. κοιμᾶσθαι 2/0/1+3: κοιμώμενος, Acts 12.6. πρὸς τοὺς μαθητάς, Mt. 26.40.

22.46 εἶπεν, ἀναστάντες*, (πειρασμός*). εἰσέλθητε = Mt. 26.41. 'Could you not (ἴσχυσας/-ατε) watch (with me) one hour?', is dropped from reverence to the apostles; but has perhaps helped to suggest the angelic 'strengthening' (ἐνίσχυσεν).

For the Arrest scene, vv. 47-53, the defenders of a non-Marcan source are joined by Rehkopf (pp. 31-82); but the Marcan framework seems secure in vv. 47, 50, 52-53a, and the new material several times has echoes of Matthew, as well as good Lucan colouring. Finegan (pp. 20f.) and Creed are on sounder lines arguing for (rather heavy) Lucan redaction.

22.47. Luke has suppressed the second and third visit of Jesus to the sleeping apostles (Mk 14.39-42), but, as we shall see, he does not omit all the matter of these verses. For the moment, he links the arrest on to Jesus' saddened counsel of v. 46 with Mark's 'while he was still speaking', and not even a δέ. He retains Mark's 'Judas. . . one of the Twelve', and the 'crowd', but he envisages the latter as comprising chief priests, temple generals, etc. (v. 52), and it is on these people, the Jewish leaders, that Luke places responsibility for the crucifixion in Acts. He accordingly puts the crowd first, and 'he who was called Judas' (ὁ λεγόμενος Ἰούδας, cf. 22.1R ἡ λεγομένη πάσχα) is reduced to 'guiding them'—the same rather humble office that he exercises (ὁδηγοῦ) in Acts 1.16. He omits Mark's 'from the chief priests', etc., because he takes these people to be present for so important a moment; and he also leaves out the explanation, 'the traitor had given them a sign. . . ', as being unnecessary. Thus he can continue his sentence about Judas, 'and he drew near (ἤγγισεν) to Jesus to kiss him'. The first expression is taken from Mk 14.42, 'He who betrays me ἤγγικεν'; 'to Jesus' comes from Mt. 26.49; the uncompounded φιλῆσαι from φιλήσω in Mk 14.44.

22.48. Mark gave no hint of Jesus' attitude to Judas, but Matthew supplied the laconic, 'Friend, (?do) what you are here for' (Matthew's cold use of ἑταῖρε, cf. Mt. 20.13; 22.12); and Luke, as throughout the Passion story, clarifies the Lord's mind. He opens with ᾿Ιησοῦς δὲ εἶπεν αὐτῷ, all four words occurring in Mt. 26.50, but then makes the rebuke plain, 'Judas, with a kiss do you betray the Son of Man?' Mark had 'the hour has come, lo, *the Son of Man is betrayed*. . . ' at 14.41, and '*the betrayer* had given them a sign, saying, He whom I *kiss*. . . ' (v. 44); so the creativity required was not amazing. He had also written himself at v. 22, 'the Son of Man goes. . . but woe to that man through whom he is betrayed'. He omits Mk 14.46, leaving the actual arrest to come: Jesus cannot touch the wounded man's ear if his arms are pinioned.

22.49f. The story now moves on to the disgraceful incident of the apostles' violence, but Luke is once more at hand with the whitewash bucket. He prefaces, 'And when those about him saw what was to be, they said, Lord, shall we smite with a sword?' The whole thing was a misunderstanding: Jesus had expressed himself rather ambiguously in vv. 35-38, and they asked permission before drawing it, but in the heat of the moment, with commendable loyalty and at great personal risk. . . The plural, 'Shall *we* smite. . . ', is continuous with the *two* swords which Luke discovered in the ἀνόμων of Isaiah 53. Most of the expressions are Lucan (see below), and those that are not can be explained. In particular, πατάξομεν/ἐπάταξεν in v. 50, used here only in Luke, are taken from πατάξας in Mt. 26.51. Otherwise the cutting off of the high priest's servant's ear follows Mark closely. The distinction of the man's master is marked by putting the genitive first, and should be rendered 'the servant of the high priest himself': the apostles were wrong, but were doing their best. Luke adds the 'right' ear, as he did at 6.6R: the right limb is often taken to be the more significant (cf. Mt. 5.39).

22.51. Here again Mark leaves Jesus' attitude unclear, while Matthew inserts the rebuke, 'Put up your sword. . . '. But to Luke, rebukes are not enough. Surely the great healer, who had such δύναμις, and who had gone about doing good and healing so many that were oppressed, would have wished to undo the harm his followers had done in their haste! If we may be sure of the wish, and we may be sure of the power, then we may be sure of the deed. The act of touching the sick seems natural (5.13; 7.14; 8.43ff.), and ἰᾶσθαι is the Lucan word for healing. Jesus needs his captors' permission to perform the cure, and says, 'Let (me) go as far as this (fellow)': they do not actually lay hands on him till v. 54, but he could hardly be thought to move about without their allowing him.

22.52f. Jesus now reproves the leaders of the arresting party, in nearly the Marcan words; but they turn out to be much higher class people than Mark had led us to suppose—indeed, they are 'the chief priests and officers' of the Temple who interviewed Judas in 22.4R, together with elders who Mark said had sent the party (14.43). This was not done in a corner. Mark said the arrest was to fulfil the scriptures (v. 49), but Luke has already cited Isa. 53.12 on this point, and wants to keep the spotlight away from the apostles. So he goes back to Mk 14.41, 'The hour has come; lo, the son of Man is betrayed into the hands of sinners': this is their *hour* then, and the power of darkness. Once more Luke discerns the hand of Satan behind the Paschal event: Satan's ἐξουσία comes in 4.6 also, and Acts 26.17. But darkness is mentioned rather than Satan because Luke takes the hour of the arrest to be midnight: after the three hours (v. 59) of Peter's denial, the cock crows. As a final act of piety to the Twelve, Luke suppresses Mark's 'and they all forsook him and fled'. He has really done them proud.

22.47 (ἔτι), ἐγγίζειν. ὁ λεγόμενος 13/1/2+2 (22.1R); perhaps Luke wishes to imply he was not a true Judah—Iscariot was paired with a new Judah, son of Jacob, at 6.16. ἰδού, Mt. 26.47.

22.48 (εἶπεν). φίλημα 7.45.

22.49 ἰδόντες-δὲ, περί, τὸ + part.*, εἶπαν. ἐσόμενος here only, but ἔσεσθαι ×5 Acts: for the phrase, cf. 21.36; Acts 20.22. κύριε, cf. vv. 33, 38. Interrogative εἰ (direct only): Acts 1.6; 7.1; 19.29; 21.37; 22.25, Mt. 19.3. Instrumental ἐν = Heb. *b^e*, 1.51; 10.27 ×4; 11.20: πατ. ἐν μαχ. 4 Kgdms 19.37.

22.50 (τις)-ἐξ, (ἀφαιρεῖν). τις-ἐξ-αὐτῶν/ἡμῶν 11.15QD; 24.22; Acts 11.20; 15.2, 24; 17.4. Gen. before noun not uncommonly, e.g. 12.16, 30QD, 35; 13.21, 34QD; 14.23, 26, 27QD; 26.53. οὕς is 'better' Greek than Mark's diminutive ὠτάριον, cf. πλοῖον/πλοιάριον.

22.51 εἶπεν, ἐᾶν, ἰᾶσθαι. Hapax: (ὠτίον). ὠτιον: Luke reverts to Matthew's form of the dimin. (26.51). The context makes better sense if the words are to those arresting him about the wounded man (οὗτος = 'this fellow' commonly in Lk., e.g. 23.2, 18), than if to the disciples, whether meaning 'No more of this' (RSV), or 'Let them have their way' (NEB).

22.52 εἶπεν-δὲ-πρὸς*, παραγίνεσθαι*. παραγενομένους, cf. Mk 14.43. Anarthrous Ἰησοῦς 3.21R; 4.1QD; 22.48; Acts 5.30; 7.55.

22.53 (καθ'ἡμέραν*), ὤν. πρός = with, Lk. 9.41Mk. only; Luke prefers σύν, μετά. κρατεῖν 12/15/2+4; stretch forth/lay τὰς χεῖρας ἐπί, 1/1/4+4.

Lescow, T. 'Jesus in Gethsemane bei Lukas und in Hebräerbrief', *ZNW* 58 (1967), pp. 215-39.

Barbour, R.S., 'Gethsemane in the Tradition of the Passion', *NTS* 16 (1970), pp. 231-51.

Feuillet, A., 'Le récit lucanien de l'agonie de Gethsémani (Lc xxii.39-46)', *NTS* 22 (1976), pp. 397-417.

Stanley, D.M., *Jesus in Gethsemane* (Ramsey, NJ, 1980).

Duplacy, J., 'La préhistoire du texte en Luc 22.43-44', in *Fs* Metzger (1981), pp. 77-86.

d. *Peter's Denial*, 22.54–65   Passover, 3 a.m.

The Denial pericope faces the standard paradigm with its most acute crisis, for twice in the course of eleven verses there are striking combinations of words in which Luke agrees with Matthew against Mark; one of these I have commented on in ch. 1 above (pp. 6-9). At the same time the correlation between Luke and Mark is rather loose, with frequent differences of wording; but the structure of the sentences is often the same, and there is interchange between the phrasing of the different denial forms. This leads to disagreement among commentators. Finegan (pp. 23f.) Linnemann (*Studien*, pp. 97-101), Creed and Schneider (*Verleugnung*, pp. 73-104), stick out for Lucan redaction, with some recourse to copyists' errors, evidenced and otherwise, for the MAs. Grundmann, G. Klein ('Verleugnung', pp. 290-94), D.R. Catchpole (*Trial*, pp. 160-74), and Marshall have full-scale parallel written sources. Taylor (*PNL*, pp. 77f.) has Lucan redaction for the Denial, eked out with some oral tradition; he and Fitzmyer return to L for the mocking. The only satisfactory solution, however, is to amplify Lucan reworking with knowledge of Matthew.

22.54. 'Having arrested him' (συλλαβόντες) is carried over from συλλαβεῖν in Mk 14.48; at last the deed can be done. Mark's ἀπήγαγον becomes the clumsy ἤγαγον καὶ εἰσήγαγον; Mark's 'to the high priest' has to become 'to the high priest's house'—Jesus is not to be tried before the high priest now, in the middle of the night, as he was in Mark, but at dawn. Mark and Matthew had then briefly turned their attention to Peter, and it is the latter whose wording comes to Luke, ὁ δὲ Πέτρος ἠκολούθει (Mt. has also αὐτῷ ἀπὸ) μακρόθεν. Mark then brings Peter into the courtyard, and has him sit with the servants warming himself 'by the blaze' (πρὸς τὸ φῶς). Luke infers how this came to be (§13): 'when they had lit a fire in the middle of the courtyard. . .'—περιάπτειν for a big fire, cf. Lucan ἅπτειν, ἀνάπτειν; Lucan ἐν μέσῳ. For 'he sat', he uses Matthew's ἐκάθητο; elsewhere in the Gospel he has the doubly augmented form only at 18.35=Mk (cf. Acts 14.9), preferring ἦν καθήμενος, etc. (5.17; 22.69R; Acts 2.2; 8.28).

22.56. Mark and Matthew leave Peter at this point, and describe Jesus' trial before the Sanhedrin. Luke however continues with the Denial story. This has clear liturgical advantages, for Peter's Denial was at cockcrow, and Luke is thus able to take the story without intermission as the single topic for the 3 a.m. watch. His predecessors had described two meetings of the Sanhedrin, one for the Trial, before the Denial, one at dawn, after, to hand Jesus over to Pilate. So what Luke has done not merely concentrates all the Petrine material, but also all the Sanhedrin material, the latter beginning at v. 66, 'And when it was day. . . ' Thus we have a neat gathering of the story by topic for exposition through the two watches of the vigil. There is however something more to the transposition than this. As we shall see, the Lucan Sanhedrin hearing is not really a trial at all. Luke has 'interpreted' the two meetings in such a way as to remove any mask of legality or dignity from the Jewish authorities. Their proceedings are summary (vv. 66f.), they ignore their victim's dignified replies (vv. 70f.), they deny the need for evidence (v. 71), and their accusations to Pilate are lies (23.2). It is all part of Luke's tendency to portray the Jewish leaders in the worst light possible.

Luke takes the story on, then, from Mk 14.67/Mt. 26.69. He takes over Mark's παιδίσκη, and the form of the sentence:

Mk: And seeing Peter warming himself, looking at him she says. . .
Lk.: And seeing him sitting by the blaze and gazing at him she said. . .

'Sitting. . . by the blaze (πρὸς τὸ φῶς)' is carried over from Mk 14.54. The other words are all Lucan but 'him'. In Mark she said, 'You too were with the Nazarene, Jesus' the first time, but the second time, 'This man was one of them': Luke combines the two, 'This man too was with him' (Lucan σύν)—he is going to drop the girl in favour of a man, so her two sentences go happily into one.

22.57. Poor Peter, so rattled in Mark ('But he denied saying, I neither know nor understand what you say'), sounds a little more dignified here: 'But he denied him, saying, I do not know him, madam'. As at v. 34, Peter is not really *denying* Jesus; he's just denying that he *knows* him, if you see what St Luke means.

22.58. No one could pretend that Peter had acted courageously during the present episode, but Luke feels that it is unnecessary to portray him as being frightened of a girl. Mark had mentioned two remarks of the girl (which we have seen Luke telescoping), before going on to 'the bystanders': it would seem charitable to think of Peter quailing twice before them then, and once before her, to make up the triple denial. That this is what he has in fact done, may be seen from the parallel structure of Luke's second with Mark's third accusation:

Mk: And a little while after. . . they said to Peter, Truly ἐξ αὐτῶν εἶ.
Lk.: And a short while after another. . . said, You also ἐξ αὐτῶν εἶ.

Luke's ἰδών echoes Mark's ἰδοῦσα from the second accusation, but in both the brief intermission and the oratio recta he is following the third. He prides himself on his ἀκρίβεια, and would not dream of attributing a woman's words to a man. Peter replies with wise brevity, 'Man, I am not' (ἄνθρωπε, 5.20R): Mark's 'he denied' is dropped this time.

22.59. Having borrowed so much forward, Luke is at liberty to introduce the third accusation himself. He can do with a second interval, and 'about an hour' (Lucan ὡσεί of time) suggests itself, since the three denials occupied the period from 'the hour of darkness' to cockcrow; and 'another' of those standing by can suitably 'asseverate' (Acts 12.15), to form something of a climax. But Luke has not spent all the words of the Marcan men's accusation in a hurry, but has kept half back for the present hour of need. Mark had, 'ἀληθῶς you are of them, καὶ γὰρ Γαλιλαῖος εἶ': Luke writes, 'ἐπ' ἀληθείας he too was with him, καὶ γὰρ Γαλιλαῖός ἐστιν'. He did the same with Matthew's Bridesmaids at 12.35-38 and 13.25-27. Peter's response in Mark had been to curse and to swear, but Luke's charity once more comes to his aid with a mere, 'And Peter said'. The over-vehement Marcan wording, 'I do not know this man of whom you speak', becomes 'Man, I do not know what you are speaking of' (cf. Mk 14.68): the same vocables, with slightly different cases and syntax, yield a less offensive and more dignified sense—cf. 'What you have said in the dark. . . ' (12.3QD), 'Remember what he said to you when he was still in Galilee' (24.6R) (§20). Peter is not really denying acquaintance with Jesus now, is he? The cockcrow follows at once (Luke adds 'while he was still speaking', cf. v. 47Mk); but even this Luke has reduced from twice to once, as Matthew had before him.

22.61f. In Mark the second cockcrow brings Peter to 'remember the word, how Jesus said that, Before the cock crow twice you shall deny me thrice'; Luke has the sentence virtually unchanged (with τοῦ λόγου τοῦ κυρίου for Mark's ῥῆμα, cf. Acts 20.35 below), but he provides additional dramatic motivation for Peter's repentance. He knows that Jesus had a searching gaze that pierced the heart, for Mark had described him as 'looking upon' the rich young man (ἐμβλέψας, Mk 10.21); and since, in his account, Jesus has not yet been taken before the Sanhedrin, but is still in the courtyard, he prefaces to Peter's remembering, 'And the Lord turned and looked upon (ἐνέβλεψεν) Peter...' With Lucan ὁ κύριος and Lucan στραφείς, the addition must stem from Luke: he inserted a similar piercing look (ἐμβλέψας) at 20.17R. Mark describes Peter's remorse with the brief, 'And as he thought thereupon he wept', but Luke prefers Matthew's fuller, 'And going out outside, he wept bitterly', five more words in sequence, further nails in Q's coffin. Streeter's appeal (p. 323), to a Western MS tradition which omits the verse, followed by Schneider (pp. 95f.) is refused by Metzger, who approves the verse (with a C); and this seems highly probable, as Luke can hardly have left Peter impenitent, when tears of repentance mean so much to him (7.38, 44).

22.63ff. Luke's neat concentration of the material, with the Denial at cockcrow, and the Trials at dawn, leaves one loose end; for if the Sanhedrin is to question Jesus at daylight, and hand him on to Pilate, who is then to pass him to Herod before receiving him back for judgment, there can be no leisure for the beating and blindfolding which Mark describes after the high priest's trial. Luke accordingly inserts it here, where, between 3 and 6 a.m., Mark had placed it— only now it is after Peter's Denial and before the Sanhedrin scene, instead of vice versa. Mark had 'certain' spit on him, blindfold his face, hit him (κολαφίζειν, probably with the fist), say Prophesy!, and receive him with blows, ῥαπίσμασιν, whether of hand or stick. Luke specifies, 'the men who held him'—Lucan ἄνδρες, Lucan συνέχειν, though the 'him' is loose. Then he provides a general statement, 'they mocked him, beating him': he uses his preferred δέρειν, taking the ῥαπίσματα to be with a cane. Finally he recalls that where Mark has the short, 'to say to him, Prophesy', Matthew has the fuller and clearer, 'saying, Prophesy to us, you Christ, who is it who struck you?'; and writes, 'Prophesy, who is it who struck you?'. That gives seven words in order in common with Matthew, only one of which occurs in Mark; and the word for 'struck', παίειν, is a hapax in L–A, although the Marcan text might have suggested κολαφίζειν or ῥαπίζειν, and there is Luke's favourite τύπτειν. Streeter's notorious apologia (pp. 325-28) followed by Schmid and Tuckett (*NTS* [1983]), is founded on no manuscript, version or patristic citation at all. Luke concludes, 'And many other things spoke they blasphemously against him'. The blaspheming is lifted from βλασφημίας in Mk 14.64, the adjacent verse (where it was Jesus who was accused of it). For the conclusion we may compare Luke's close to the Baptist's preaching: πολλὰ μὲν οὖν καὶ ἕτερα παρακαλῶν εὐηγγελίζετο τὸν λαόν (3.18).

22.54 συλλαμβάνειν*, ἄγειν, εἰσάγειν. ἄγειν and ἀπάγειν (Mt.) are interchangable at Acts 23.17f. ἀκολουθεῖν abs. 9.49R; Acts 21.36 (*contra* Catchpole, p. 163).

22.55 ἐν-μέσῳ, μέσος. Hapaxes: περιάπτειν, συγκαθίζειν. ἅπτειν = light 0/0/4+1 (8.16R), ἀνάπτειν 12.49. συγκαθισάντων cf. Mk συγκαθήμενος; καθίζειν 8/8/7+9. Indefinite subject, cf. 14.35 QD. μέσος nom. = in the midst of, is unique in L-A, though the word is Lucan; it is written for variety, following ἐν-μέσῳ in v. 55a. Mk's 'warming himself. . . ' is omitted as unhelpful to Peter's image.

22.56 (ἰδοῦσα-)δὲ, τις, εἶπεν, (καὶ = also), (οὗτος contemptuous), σύν*. Schneider (pp. 80f.), Dietrich (pp. 144f.), and many puzzle at the change of person from the girl's first accusation in Mark, not noting that Luke has combined her two challenges. τις for μία (Cadbury, p. 193). ἀτενίζειν 0/0/2+10.

22.57 γύναι, 13.12L, cf. ἄνθρωπε in vv. 58, 60. Marshall cites vocatives at the end of sentences at 5.8; Acts 2.37; 26.7, against Rehkopf, p. 98.

22.58 ἕτερος*, καὶ = also. Hapax: βραχύς. βραχύ, Acts 5.34; 27.28. φάναι, 17/6/8+24, usually in conversations in Acts. Peter does not, as in Mark, go out to the forecourt, and thus remains throughout under Jesus' all-seeing eye (v. 61). ἕτερος = a second (person) as at 20.9 (*contra* Catchpole, p. 173).

22.59 ὡσεί of time*, τις, καὶ = also, οὗτος contemptuous. Hapax: διϊσχυρίζεσθαι (Acts 12.15). ἐπ' ἀληθείας 0/2/3+2. διαστάσης cf. διαστῆμα Acts 5.7. ἄλλος, cf. Mt. 26.71 ἄλλη. The third challenge is the same as the first, with μετὰ for σύν for variety, ἐξ αὐτῶν εἶ having been used for the second.

22.60 εἶπεν-δὲ*, ὅς in attraction*, παραχρῆμα*, ἔτι. ἔτι αὐτοῦ λαλοῦντος cf. 9.42R; 24.41; Acts 10.44.

22.61 στραφείς*, ὁ κύριος (×2) = Jesus*, (εἶπεν), σήμερον. Hapax: ὑπομιμνήσκεσθαι (Luke likes compound verbs [Cadbury, pp. 166f.]; ὑπο-compounds 6/5/15+16). With ὑπεμνήσθη ὁ Πέτρος τοῦ ῥήματος τοῦ κυρίου ὡς εἶπεν, cf. Acts 11.16 ἐμνήσθην δὲ τοῦ ῥήματος τοῦ κυρίου ὡς ἔλεγεν,

Acts 20.35, μνημονεύειν τε τῶν λόγων τοῦ κυρίου ᾽Ιησοῦ ὅτι αὐτὸς εἶπεν. σήμερον cf. 22.34.

22.62 (κλαίειν). Hapax: (πικρῶς). Tuckett (*NTS* [1983], p. 137) says the MS evidence for omitting the verse is 'admittedly weak'; but 'if v. 62 is included, there is a very abrupt change of subject from v. 62 ('he' = Peter) to v. 63 (the men holding 'him' = Jesus). Without v. 62 the text runs on more smoothly, since in v. 61b Jesus is the speaker'. This is very misleading: in v. 61b the main clause is 'Peter remembered', and a literalist would, if v. 62 were not there, still construe 'him' in v. 63 as Peter. But Luke quite often writes a loose αὐτόν at the beginning of a sentence, meaning Jesus, when the previous subject was someone else, e.g. 9.10 (Herod); 23.27 (Simon), 23.49 (the centurion).

22.63 ἀνήρ*, συνέχειν*. ἐμπαίζειν 18.32 (14.29L; 23.11L). δέρειν 1/3/ 5+3, 12.47f.L. In favour of an an L-source here it is said: (1) v. 63 is not Marcan at all, (2) the loose αὐτῷ presupposes a referent in the source, (3) Luke is interested in the Servant Songs, but has missed the reference to Isa. 50.6, the spitting, which comes in Mark. But (1) the vocabulary is explicable as Lk.R, and Luke needed to specify the subject; (2) for parallels to the loose αὐτῷ cf. on v. 61; (3) the 'Servant Songs' are a modern invention—Luke's concern with the prophecies of Isaiah 53 do not imply an extension to Isaiah 50. In any case vv. 63-65 are out of the Marcan sequence, and agree more closely with Matthew—they are very likely to have been written without re-reading the Marcan text.

22.64 Hapaxes: (περικαλύπτειν), (παίειν). ἐπηρώτων λέγοντες, 3.10, 14; the imperfects are because the actions are being repeated. For a discussion of Streeter's textual emendation, see pp. 6f., 9f. Fitzmyer (p. 1458) ascribes both 'Who is it who smote you?', and 'And going out outside he wept bitterly' to L. This gives ten out of twenty-five consecutive words which also occur in Matthew to a non-Marcan source, in two sequences of five, and with two rare words (πικρῶς, παίσας): how many words should we need to conclude that the non-Marcan source was Matthew?

22.65 ἕτερος*. Speaking εἰς = against, 12.10QD ×2, cf. Acts 6.11. The parallel concluding text at 3.18 is clearly Lk.R with εὐαγγελίζεσθαι and ὁ-λαός.

c. *The Trials*, 22.66–23.12   6 a.m., Passover

Mark (and Matthew) had described two gatherings of the Sanhedrin, one with a full-scale trial, before Peter and the cockcrow, the other a brief meeting at dawn, to hand Jesus over to Pilate. The trial is formal, being conducted by the high priest, with witnesses, the rending of garments at Jesus' 'blasphemy', and a unanimous verdict of condemnation. This trial Luke omits for a complex of reasons which I have suggested above: it is topically and liturgically convenient to have the Denial material together at cockcrow, and the Trial matter together at dawn; and it suits the Gospel's tendency to denigrate the Jewish authorities if their proceedings appear not as a properly constituted trial but as a 'kangaroo' travesty of justice. He cannot have the Sanhedrin deliver Jesus to Pilate without some proceedings, and he gives the occasion an air of disreputableness, consonant with his conviction that 'our chief priests and rulers' were responsible for Jesus' death (24.20; Acts 3.17; 7.52, etc.). But the substance of his hearing is provided by rewriting parts of his predecessors' Trial scenes: many of the remaining details—the false witnesses, the accusation of blasphemy, the tale that Jesus would destroy the Temple—turn up in the story of Stephen (Acts 6.11-14, §17).

22.66. Luke's introduction is a compound of the opening verses of Mark 15 and Matthew 27, with some reminiscence of Mt. 26.57, which began the Sanhedrin trial. His 'when it was day' is a Lucan form of Mark's 'early'; he has Mark's chief priests and scribes, and he makes from Mark's πρεσβυτέρων a πρεσβυτέριον (Acts 22.5) comprehending both. Mark's Sanhedrin, i.e. the members, becomes a Lucan συνέδριον, i.e. a council chamber, as in Acts 4.15. But Luke's 'presbytery of the people' is an echo of Matthew's 'elders of the people' (27.1); his συνήχθη recalls Matthew's συνήχθησαν (26.57); and his ἀπήγαγον is in both Mt. 26.57 and Mk 14.53.

22.67f. In Mark and Matthew the crisis of the trial had come with the high priest's challenge, '(Mt., Tell us if) you are the Christ, the Son of the Blessed (Mt. God)'. The combination is uncomfortable for Luke. 'The Christ' is a political title in part, easily misrepresented as meaning a Messianic trouble-maker (23.2, 5, 35, 39). 'The Son of God' is a religious title, and the essence of what every Christian believes (1.32; 3. 22; 9.35). It seems best therefore to separate the two halves of the claim. First then the Lucan sanhedrists say, 'If you are the Christ, tell us': the 'tell us' is moved to the end, but otherwise the wording is from Mt. 26.63. Luke's introduction, 'they led him away, saying. . . ', gives the impression of disorderliness, and lack of proper chairmanship. But he cannot allow Jesus to permit any currency to the dangerous suggestion that he is a political Messiah, and so makes him give an entirely non-committal reply. 'If I tell you' (taking up the 'tell us') 'you will not believe', is entirely apposite, and in line with the whole later Jewish response to the gospel in Acts; '. . . and if I ask you will not answer' is quite inappropriate, and is Luke's usual clumsy attempt at a parallelism (§21). It is drawn from Mk 14.61, 'he *answered* nothing. Again the high priest *asked* him'—Luke's habit of retaining the words and changing the sense (§20).

22.69. In Mark and Matthew, Jesus' response to the high priest had led on to the prophecy, 'You shall see the Son of Man sitting at the right hand of power, and coming with the clouds of heaven'. They are thinking of the parousia soon, and that will not quite do for Luke: it is 90, and the elders of the 30s are all dead. But it is true that the Son of Man will sit at God's right hand, even if they do not see him. Luke drops the 'you will see'; amends Matthew's ἀπ' ἄρτι to the Lucan ἀπὸ τοῦ νῦν (for 'from now on' that is where he will be); keeps the Matthaean order καθήμενον(ς) ἐκ δεξιῶν; and glosses 'of power' with τοῦ θεοῦ, as he does at Acts 8.10. The whole 'coming' clause he suppresses as unsuitable.

22.70f. The elders are now able to resume battle with the religious half of the question: 'Are you then the Son of God?'—Matthew's phrasing again (26.63). Luke adds to the impression of unparliamentary behaviour: 'They all said. . . '—it was like Her Majesty's Opposition scenting blood. Here Mark had given Jesus the unequivocating, 'I am', and Matthew the ambiguous σὺ εἶπας. Luke combines the two, with 'You say that I am', which is straightforwardly equivocal. But the Lucan elders are not interested in listening to the answer to their questions. They hear what they want to hear: 'we have heard it ourselves from his mouth'. They have no need of evidence at their hearings: 'What need have we still for witness?' μαρτυρία is from Mk 14.59; αὐτοί is Lucan, and 'from his mouth' can be paralleled. He leaves out the rending of clothes, the high priest's appeal for a verdict, and the unanimous vote of death. This has not been a trial, and they would not be suitable.

22.66 ὡς = when*, γίνεσθαι, ἡμέρα, (ὁ-λαός*), τε*. Hapaxes: πρεσ-βυτέριον (Acts 22.5), (συνέδριον). σ. = council-chamber in Acts 4.15; 6.12, 15, and perhaps often when preceded by ἐν and εἰς. Mark's πρωΐ means 'at dawn' (cf. Mk 13.35; Mt. 27.1, πρωΐας δὲ γενομένης): Luke similarly writes ἡμέρα γίνεσθαι at 4.42 (Mk πρωΐ ἔννυχα λίαν), 6.13R; Acts 12.18; 23.12; 27.39, ὡς ἐγένετο 1.44; 4.25. συν. αὐτῶν Acts 23.28, priests and scribes are linked unclearly to the πρεσ. τοῦ λαοῦ: at Acts 22.5 Luke writes, 'The high priest and all the π.', so perhaps τε means 'and' here (cf. Bauer *ad voc*. 1ab for numerous references), the scribes being viewed like Catholic *periti*. But cf. 20.19; 22.2, where 'the high priests and scribes' *are* the Sanhedrin.

22.67 (εἶπον), (εἶπεν)-δέ*. Luke also suppresses the suggestion that Jesus had a Jewish *trial* at 18.32, omitting Mark's 'he shall be handed over to the high priests and scribes, and they shall condemn him to death' (Paul Winter, p. 28); though he seems to imply it at Acts 13.27f. (Catchpole, pp. 184f.), a typical lapse of memory (§9). John gives a version of the verse at 10.24f. with Johannine παρρησία and 'I told you. . . ' (3.7; 6.36; 8.24). οὐ μὴ πιστεύσητε may be an echo of Hab. 1.5, cited at Acts 13.41. Despite Catchpole (p. 196), the language is not untypical: οὐ μή 19/10/18 (18.30QD; 21.18R), πιστεύειν 11/14/9+37, ἐὰν 66/35/29 (17.4QD)+11.

22.68 (ἀπὸ)-τοῦ-νῦν*, ὁ-θεός. ἔσται καθήμενος, cf. Luke's periphrastic imperfects. ἡ δύναμις τοῦ θεοῦ Acts 8.10, cf. Lk. 1.35; 5.17: for epexegetic τοῦ θεοῦ, cf. 9.20R.

22.70 εἶπαν-δέ*, πάντες, πρὸς with verb of saying*. The concepts Christ-Son of Man-Son of God are linked naturally by Luke at 9.20; 9.22, 26; 23.35, and so give οὖν its normal force here. Christ and Son of God are identified at 4.41R; Lk. 9.20, 22.

22.71 εἶπαν, (ἔτι), αὐτοί. Hapax: μαρτυρία (cf. Mk 14.59). ἀπὸ τοῦ στόματος αὐτοῦ cf. 4.22 (ἐμαρτύρουν!), 11.54R?, 19.22QD. Cp. Catchpole, pp. 200-202.

Blinzler, J., *The Trial of Jesus* (ET *Der Prozess Jesu*, 2nd edn; Westminster, 1959).
Schneider, G., *Verleugnung, Verspottung und Verhör Jesu nach Lukas 22,54-71* (München, 1969).
Catchpole, D.R., *The Trial of Jesus* (SPB 18; Leiden, 1971).
Donahue, J.R., *Are You the Christ?* (SBLDS 10; Missoula, 1973).
Winter, P., *On the Trial of Jesus* (2nd edn revised by T.A. Burkill and G. Vermes; St. Jud. 1; Berlin/New York, 1974).
Juel, D., *Messiah and Temple* (SBLDS 31; Missoula, 1977).
Delorme, J., 'Le procès de Jésus ou la parole risquée (Lc 22,54-23,25)', *RSR* 69 (1981), pp. 123-46.

23.1. Mark and Matthew now return from Peter to the Sanhedrin, which holds a dawn meeting to hand Jesus over bound to Pilate. Luke is able to continue the story of the Sanhedrin without intermission, though having no conviction they cannot bind Jesus. He opens with his favourite ἀναστάν, and ἅπαν τὸ πλῆθος is Lucan too—the phrase extends the impression of unparliamentary disorder.

ἤγαγον αὐτόν is probably an echo of Matthew's αὐτὸν ἀπήγαγον (diff. Mk).

23.2f. With the hearing before Pilate, Luke's sensitive political antennae come into operation. First, Mark opens the trial with Pilate addressing Jesus as if he were a well-known trouble-maker—'Are you the king of the Jews?'—and the chief priests append their accusations. That will never do. Luke puts the accusations first, and he formulates them in such a way that the listener is struck by their unfairness. They have the gall to say, (a) 'he prevents the payment of taxes to Caesar', when in 20.25 Jesus' words were 'pay what is Caesar's to Caesar', and (b) 'he says that he is Christ a king', when he has just declined to make that claim in so many words (22.67). The iniquity of the Jewish leadership, and their deception of Pilate, are thus made plain for all to see. This can then lead on to a virtual transcription of Mk 15.2, Pilate's question to Jesus: Luke has formed the accusations to lead up to this, 'Christ, a king' being the equivalent of 'the king of the Jews', and the taxation issue being a plausible mischief-making chapter and verse. Jesus answers Pilate, as in Mark, with an ambiguous σὺ λέγεις.

23.4. But there are further questionable features about the trial in Mark. In Mk 15.4 Pilate asks Jesus courteously if he has no reply to the chief priests' charges, and Jesus makes no reply to him either. This reads like arrogant rudeness and contempt of court. Further, at the end of the trial (Mk 15.16-20), Pilate apparently permits Roman legionaries to maltreat Jesus in the Praetorium, a procedure which reflects no credit either on the reputation of the imperial forces, or on the image of their prisoner, whom Luke wishes to represent as respected by Roman authority. He therefore transfers these features to a subsidiary hearing, before Herod. The present scene can then be brought to a climax with the first of Luke's ringing claims that Rome found Jesus innocent, 'I find no guilt in this man'. Pilate repeats the verdict at v. 14 and v. 22R; Herod said the same (v. 15), as does the centurion (v. 47R), and the idea runs like a thread through Acts.

23.5. Luke's rather forceful manipulation of Mark is made plain by the phrase, 'Pilate said to the chief priests and the crowds'. The crowds have appeared from nowhere, being drawn from a little further on in the Marcan story (15.8). The persistence of the chief priests comes from Mk 15.11, 14b, too, and so does the verb 'he stirs up', ἀνασείειν being found only here and at Mk 15.11 in the NT:

Luke has again kept the words and changed the meaning (§20). 'The people', 'beginning from', and 'Judaea' in the sense of Judaea-and-Galilee, are all Lucanisms.

23.1 ἀναστάς*, ἅπαν-τὸ-πλῆθος*, ἄγειν. τὸ πλῆθος for the Sanhedrin, Acts 23.7. ἄγειν ἐπὶ a court, cf. 21.12; Acts 9.21.

23.2 οὗτος contemptuous, εὑρίσκειν, κωλύειν, ἑαυτόν. ἤρξαντο δὲ κατηγορεῖν αὐτοῦ λέγοντες cf. Acts 24.2 αὐτοῦ ἤρξατο κατηγορεῖν ὁ Τ. λέγων. διαστρέφειν Acts 13.8, 10 cf. ἀποστρ. 23.24. τὸ ἔθνος ἡμῶν 7.5QD, nowhere else in the Gospels. τὸ ἔθνος = Jews 0/0/2+6. φόρος 20.22R. λέγων ἑαυτὸν εἶναι..., Acts 5.36; 8.9. Χριστὸν βασιλέα εἶναι cf. 2.11, ὅς ἐστι Χριστὸς κύριος.

23.3 ἐρωτᾶν*. λέγων, ἔφη, Mt. 27.11.

23.4 εἶπεν-πρός*, οὐδὲν-αἴτιον, εὑρίσκειν, ὁ-ἄνθρωπος-οὗτος.

23.5 ὁ-λαός*, ἀρξάμενος-ἀπό. Hapaxes: ἐπισχύειν, (ἀνασείειν). ἐπισχύειν cf. ἰσχύειν, 4/4/8+6, ἐνισχύειν 22.43, κατισχύειν 23.23. οἱ δὲ ἐπ. λέγοντες cf. v. 23 οἱ δὲ ἐπέκειντο...αἰτούμενοι. καθ᾽ ὅλης τῆς Ἰουδαίας, cf. Acts 9.31, and esp. 10.37, καθ᾽ὅλης τῆς Ἰουδαίας ἀρξάμενος ἀπὸ τῆς Γαλιλαίας. ἡ Ἰουδαία including Galilee, 4.44.

23.6. The hearing before Herod has presented a puzzle. It is remotely unlikely that it is historical, since it is not in Mark, and Pilate will hardly have sent Jesus up to Herod for trial (ἀναπέμπειν is so used of Festus sending Paul up to Caesar, Acts 25.21): and the substance of the story—Jesus' silence under Jewish accusation, and his mockery by soldiers with fine clothing—is a less convincing form of the same features in Mk 15.4f., 16ff., whence Luke omits them. Martin Dibelius (*ZNW* [1915]) suggested that Luke derived the story from Ps. 2.1, since he cites this verse in a prayer of the Church in Acts 4.25, and proceeds to interpret the 'kings of the earth and rulers' as Herod and Pontius Pilate; the story would thus have its origin in 'cultic language' (p. 126). But, although Dibelius is supported by Bultmann (p. 273), Creed and others, the force of the incident, as Grundmann says, is to provide a second testimony to Jesus' innocence (v. 15), not to describe a conspiracy against the Lord's Anointed at all. So Ps. 2.1 is an unconvincing origin for the incident, and is more likely to have been applied at a secondary stage to a story already believed to be true, and with a new interpretative twist, just as Acts 4 says.

But where, then, will Luke have got the story from? We have already seen his motivation for removing the discreditable features of the trial, Jesus' silence and the soldiers' mockery, away from Pilate; but he cannot simply have manufactured a hearing before Herod from nothing. He might think it believable that Pilate should so have acted, because he records a hearing before Herod Agrippa II authorized by Festus in the case of Paul (Acts 25–26); and he believed (erroneously) that in legal matters the place of a person's origin was important (Lk. 2.1-4; cf. Acts 23.34). But he would still need authority for his present historical assertions.

There are two hints in the wording of the story. Luke uses ἀποκρίνεσθαι frequently, always in the aorist, 46 times in the Gospel, 20 times in Acts; of these 44+19 use the passive form ἀποκριθῆναι, and 2+1 the middle form ἀποκρίνασθαι. One of these latter is at 23.9 οὐδὲν ἀπεκρίνατο: and at Mt. 27.12 the same phrase occurs, οὐδὲν ἀπεκρίνατο. There is no Marcan parallel here, and Mark writes οὐδὲν ἀπεκρίθη at 15.5. Secondly, Luke says that Herod rejoiced λίαν (v. 8); and λίαν is a word coming ×4 in Mark which Luke alters or omits on each occasion. It is a hapax here in L–A; and it also occurs in the parallel pericope in Matthew, ὥστε θαυμάζειν τὸν ἡγεμόνα λίαν (Mt. 27.14). So it looks as if Luke might have drawn on Matthew for the story.

Now Matthew follows the Marcan wording quite closely through the trial, but he makes one significant change fairly regularly: he calls the Marcan 'Pilate' by his title 'the Governor' (ὁ ἡγεμών). Luke also uses this title for Roman governors in Acts, but it is a more general term, and is used of the princes of Edom in Exod. 15.15, or of Teman in Job 42.17d; and ἡγούμενος is used of Joseph in Egypt (Acts 7.10), and of an Israelite king at Mt. 2.6. So, since both Matthew's trial scene and his mockery scene begin with reference to ὁ ἡγεμών, it is open to Luke to understand this prince as Herod; and the indications are that he has accepted this possibility. He takes the Marcan story of Pilate's trial first (23.1-5), breaking it off at Mk 15.2, 'Thou sayest'. Then he moves over to the Matthaean story of the ἡγεμών's trial: first the 'prince' questioned Jesus (ἐπηρώτησεν αὐτὸν ὁ ἡγεμών, 27.11 = Lk. 23.9a, ἐπηρώτα δὲ αὐτόν); but Jesus does not reply (οὐδὲν ἀπεκρίνατο, 27.12 = Lk 23.9b); despite the accusations of chief priests and elders (27.12)/chief priests and scribes (Lk. 23.10; Mark has chief priests alone). He then transfers the later item on the 'prince's' soldiers (Mt. 27.27) to the present context, with its mockery (ἐνέπαιξαν, 27.31 = Lk. 23.11) and fine clothing (27.28f.; Lk. 23.11). Mt. 27.13, 'Then *Pilate* said to him...' tells Luke that the session with the 'prince' is now over, and the scene is transferred back to Pilate's court (Lk. 23.13). But the 'prince' has evidently come too, and is much surprised at Jesus' comportment (27.14); so Luke feels entitled to infer warm relations between him and Pilate, in place of the notorious hostility obtaining before (Lk. 23.12, § 13, Philo, *Leg.* 299-305).

Luke's interpretation of Matthew here is a tour de force, and would not have been undertaken without the pressing desirability of keeping Caesar's representative above reproach, and his prisoner likewise. Loisy was probably right in suggesting that even Luke's 'splendid garment' has been substituted for the purple/red cloak of tradition, lest there be the least hint of lèse-majesté; and the whole passage hailing Jesus as king (Mt. 27.29f.) has been smoothed over.

23.6 εἰ with questions, direct and indirect (often uncertain which), 5/4/ 9+11. ἐπηρώτησεν is used in the parallel passage, Acts 23.34.

23.7 ὤν, καί-αὐτός*, ἐν-ταύταις-ταῖς-ἡμέραις*. ἐπιγνοὺς ὅτι...Ἡρώδου ἐστίν, cf. Acts 19.34, ἐπιγνόντες ὅτι Ἰουδαῖός ἐστιν, 22.29 ἐπιγνοὺς ὅτι Ῥωμαῖός ἐστιν. ἐξουσία = jurisdiction, 4.6; Acts 1.7; 5.4. ἀναπέμπειν 0/0/ 3+1 (23.11, 15). Although Lk. prefers Ἰερουσαλήμ to Ἰεροσόλυμα, the latter comes 4× in Lk., 23× in Acts. Herod might be expected to be in J. for the feast (2.41; cf. Acts 12.1ff.).

23.8 χαίρειν* = rejoice. ἦν + part., χρόνος, ἱκανός, διὰ-τό*, ἀκούειν-περί, ἐλπίζειν, τις, γίνεσθαι. Hapax: (λίαν). For Herod and Jesus, cf. 9.9R. χρόνοι ἱκανοί, cf. 20.9R, 8.27R, Acts ×4. σημεῖα γίνεσθαι ὑπό Acts 2.46; 4.13. If ἐξ ἱκανοῦ is read with p75, cf. Acts 20.11.

23.9 ἱκανός, αὐτός nom.

23.10 εἱστήκει = he stood. Hapax: εὐτόνως (Acts 18.28)

23.11 καί also, σύν*. Hapaxes: στράτευμα (Acts 23.10, 27), λαμπρός. Cf. Acts 10.30 ἐν ἐσθῆτι λαμπρᾷ, Lk. 24.4 ἐν ἐσθῆτι ἀστραπτούσῃ. 16.19 λαμπρῶς. ἐξουθενεῖν 18.9; Acts 4.11R.

23.12 γίνεσθαι, φίλος*, τε*, αὐτῇ-τῇ-ἡμέρᾳ, ἀλλήλων, ὤν. Hapaxes: προϋπάρχειν (Acts 8.9), ἔχθρα. To be ἐν an emotion, cf. 22.44; Acts 22.17.

Dibelius, M., 'Herodes und Pilatus', *ZNW* 16 (1915), pp. 113-26.
Hoehner, H.W., 'Why did Pilate Hand Jesus over to Antipas?', in E. Bammel, ed., *The Trial of Jesus* (London, 1970), pp. 84-90.
Corbin, M., 'Jésus devant Hérode', *Christus* 25 (1978), pp. 190-97.

f. *The Sentence of Crucifixion*, 23.13-32   Passover, 9 a.m.
Luke continues the steady process of establishing Jesus' innocence
and exculpating Pilate: he rewrites the Judgment scene in his own
words, with both a preface, vv. 13-16, twice stating the themes, and
an appendix, vv. 27-32, on the road to the cross. The latter is part of
Luke's ambivalence towards the Jewish people. If Pilate is to be, so
far as possible, cleared, then the Jews must bear the responsibility,
and in Acts they reject the Gospel; but Luke would like to restrict the
guilt to the Jewish leadership, and display the common people as
sympathetic.

23.13-16. So Pilate summons the accusers to resume the trial—the
chief priests, as before, 'the' (Lucan) 'rulers' for the scribes (22.66;
23.10), and 'the' (Lucan) 'people' for the crowds (v. 4), Mark's
bloodthirsty audience. He restates Jesus' innocence in unequivocal
terms, the repetition of the phrase from v. 4 dinning the message into
the hearer's ear: he had found no guilt in 'this man' for the
subversion they alleged. Furthermore Herod, an independent
witness, and unprejudiced and well-informed (Pilate having deferred
to him, as Festus does to Agrippa), also found him innocent. He had
done nothing to deserve death: the Governor generously offers to
buy off their malice with a mild thrashing (παιδεύσας).

23.18-22. But they will have none of it. They shout (cf. Mk 15.13,
'they shouted again'), 'Away with this fellow', as they do with Paul at
Acts 21.36; 22.22; 'release us Barabbas' is Mk 15.11b in oratio recta.
As Luke has skipped over Mark's explanation of who Barabbas was,
this has now to be inserted; one of his clumsy afterthoughts (§19.1).
The sedition and murder are from Mark: 'happened' and 'in-the-city'
are Lucan. Pilate's good-heartedness shines the brighter from the
context. Mt. 27.21, 'Whom do *you wish* of the two that I *release* to
you?': Lk., '*Pilate* spoke again, *wishing* to *release* Jesus' (§20, italics
for emphasis). The Roman Governor was all good will; it was the
Jews who responded, 'Crucify, crucify', doubling the single Marcan
verb: cf. Luke's 'Martha, Martha', 'Simon, Simon', 'Saul, Saul'. This
then leads into Pilate's third resounding proclamation of Jesus'
innocence: the same words reassure the listener, no guilt of death
was found in him, and the Governor repeats the proposal to let him
off with a flogging.

23.23. But the pressure was too much. The Jews insisted with loud
voices, and their voices prevailed; Pilate gave judgment that they

should have 'their request', and handed Jesus over to 'their will'. So it requires a critical mind to see the Governor as weakly betraying his trust, and unjustly delivering a man to a terrible death to court popularity; Luke has touched up the Marcan account with art and effectiveness. Any middle class reader will know that the state was on Jesus' side, and that the Jews preferred a revolutionary and murderer from the jail to the Author of Life (cf. Acts 3.14). The Lucan tendencies are as pervasive as the Lucan language.

23.13 συγκαλεῖν*, οἱ-ἄρχοντες*, ὁ-λαός*. συγκαλεσάμενος, 9.1R, ×2 Acts.

23.14 εἶπεν-πρὸς*, ὁ-ἄνθρωπος-οὗτος*, (×2) ὁ-λαός*, ἐνώπιον*, οὐθὲν-αἴ-τιον, εὑρίσκειν, ὅς in attr. Hapaxes: ἀποστρέφειν, Acts 3.26, cf. δια- v. 2; ἀνακρίνειν 0/0/1+5. ὡς = alleged to be, 6.22QD; 16.1. προσφέρειν, 23.36R? οὐθέν, 22.35, ×3 Acts.

23.15 εἶναι + part., πράσσειν*. ἀλλ' οὐδέ, Acts 19.2. ἀναπέμπειν, vv. 6, 11. ἄξιον θανάτου, ×4 Acts, ἄξιον πληγῶν, 12.48.

23.16 The whole verse recurs at v. 22d. παιδεύσας is nicer Greek than Mark's φραγελλώσας (15.15), but the meaning is equally nasty.

23.18 οὗτος contemptuous. Hapax: παμπλήθει (cf. ἅπαν τὸ πλῆθος v. 1). ἀνέκραγον strong aorist for Mark's 'low' ἔκραξαν.

23.19 εἶναι + part., γίνεσθαι, ἐν-τῇ-πόλει, τις. ὅστις, στάσις, φόνος from Mk 15.7; 'cast in prison' (cf. v. 25) implied by Mark's 'bound', cf. Acts 16.23, 37.

23.20 προσφωνεῖν*. πάλιν is taken over from Mark against Luke's practice: 17/28/3+5.

23.21 Hapax: ἐπιφωνεῖν (×3 Acts). Luke is usually careful with aorist imperatives, and may use the present σταύρου for the lingering death; but cp. 18, αἶρε.

23.22 εἶπεν-πρὸς*, οὗτος contemptuous, οὐδὲν-αἴτιον, εὑρίσκειν. Hapax: τρίτον (cf. πρῶτον). τί γὰρ κακὸν ἐποίησεν = Mt. 27.23, the last two words being reversed from Mark. v. 22d = v. 16.

23.23 φωνή (×2). ἐπικεῖσθαι, 5.1; Acts 27.20. φωνὴ μεγάλη, 2/4/7+6. αἰτεῖσθαι, Mk 15.6, 8. κατισχύειν, 21.36, cf. ἐπ-, ἰσχύειν.

23.24 γίνεσθαι. Hapaxes: ἐπικρίνειν (cf. ἐπιφωνεῖν v. 21, ἐπικεῖσθαι v. 23, ἐπι-, 25/22/45+46), αἴτημα (cf. θέλημα, v. 25, ὑστέρημα, 21.4R).

23.25 ἀπέλυσεν...τὸν (Β.)...τὸν δὲ Ἰησοῦν παρέδωκεν = Mt. 27.26, Mk similar. The structure of the sentences from v. 20 is the same as in the other two Gospels, although the phrasing has been heavily touched up. θέλημα, of man's will, 0/0/4.

Mark says that the soldiers 'led him away' (15.16), and then, after the mocking, which Luke has transferred to Herod's troops, that they impressed Simon of Cyrene to carry Jesus' cross (v. 21). Luke continues to wrap the matter in the old miasmal mist: his 'they led him away' seems to follow on from 'Pilate delivered him to *their* will', and so to be about the Jews—if Herod is said to have στρατεύματα, and Jesus was arrested by Temple officials calling themselves στρατηγοί, whose servants carry swords, then why should anyone think of the execution being carried out by the Romans? Mark's ἀγγαρεύουσιν, the Roman impressment, is suppressed for the Lucan ἐπιλαβόμενοι.

Luke is not happy, however, to leave the matter so. He has steadily portrayed Jesus throughout the Gospel as a bringer of good news to ordinary people, who were not made to stumble by him; and he does not wish to lose that image now. But further, there was an important addition made to the tradition in Mt. 27.25 (alas, later generations may feel, a fatal addition): for in Matthew Pilate had ceremonially washed his hands clean of the guilt of the crucifixion, and 'the whole people' had accepted the guilt with the doom-laden words, 'His blood be on us and on our children (ἐφ' ἡμᾶς καὶ ἐπὶ τὰ τέκνα ἡμῶν)'. Pilate's freedom from guilt is now established by Luke also, and he prefers to place the prophecy in Jesus' mouth rather than the people's; so the Matthaean sentence becomes a Lucan prophecy to the same effect—Jesus' death shall be atoned for by the destruction of the next generation in the fall of Jerusalem.

23.27f. Luke first supplies a large crowd, such as was normal at crucifixions; and since their children are to be mentioned, he includes women beating their breasts and mourning. We hear of wives (Manson, p. 343) and daughters (Bultmann, p. 37 n. 3) mourning at such occasions, so he might feel his construction to be justified. Jesus then says to them, putting the Matthaean words to use, 'Weep not for me, but weep *for* yourselves *and for your children* (ἐφ' ἑαυτὰς κλαίετε καὶ τὰ τέκνα ὑμῶν)': the 'weep not for... but weep for' is a Lucan form of sentence as at 10.20, 'rejoice not because... but rejoice because', 14.12, 'do not ask... but invite...' The address,

'Daughters of Jerusalem', has a good Septuagintal ring (Cant. 2.7; 3.10; 5.16; 8.4).

23.29. The thought of the coming suffering of women and children in AD 70 takes Luke's mind back to 21.23, 'These are the days of vengeance... Woe to those with child and those giving suck in those days'; but now the anguish is not in flight but in slaughter. He reverses the statement: 'The days are coming in which they will say, Blessed are the barren, and the wombs that bare not, and the breasts that fed not'. He pairs κοιλία and μαστοί at 11.27 also, and has a preference for the former, 3/1/8+2.

23.30. If Jesus prophesied the bereavement of Israel, his words will have been in line with the words of God in the OT; and here Hosea especially springs to mind—'Even if they rear (ἐκθρέψωσιν) their children (τέκνα), they will be made childless by men... Give them a childless womb and dry breasts (μαστοὺς ξηρούς)... If they bear (γεννήσωσιν), I will kill the darlings of their womb (κοιλίας)' (Hos. 9.12, 14, 16). In fact some words from the following verses of Hosea express eloquently the distress of 'those days', and these Luke places on Jesus' lips: 'They will say to the mountains, Cover us, and to the hills, Fall on us' (but he gets the two clauses reversed).

23.31. The Jewish people said in Matthew, 'His blood be on us, and on our children'; and he and Luke could not but reflect that, if Jesus had suffered so terribly in innocence, the blood-baths of AD 70 were only to be expected for the guilty. 'To destroy the moist with the dry' was a phrase in Deut. 29.19, interpreted by the LXX as 'that the sinner bring the sinless to destruction with him'. The link of thought may still be through Hosea, 'Ephraim is dried up to the roots, he shall bear no more fruit': but the meaning is a simple extension of Mt. 27.25, 'If they treat the righteous so, what will be the fate of sinners?' Luke and Matthew taught the same lesson with the requirement of the blood of the innocent from this generation (11.50f., par.).

23.32. Luke includes the two malefactors at this early stage, on the road to the cross: he means to make something of them.

23.26 ὡς = when*, ἐπιλαμβάνεσθαι*, (τις). ἀπήγαγον is from Mk 15.16 rather than Mt. 27.31. ὡς = while, 12.58QD; 24.32 ×2 (Marshall). Σίμων τις, cf. Acts 19.24; 21.16, etc. 'Bear the cross ὄπισθεν Jesus', cf. of the disciple, 9.23; 14.27 (ὀπίσω).

23.27 πολύ*, πλῆθος*, ὁ-λαός*. ἠκολούθει δὲ αὐτῷ 22.39R? πολὺ πλῆθος, 5.6; 6.17Mk; Acts 14.1; 17.4; πλῆθος τοῦ λαοῦ 4.17R, Acts 21.36. Women come often in Luke. κόπτεσθαι, 8.52R; θρηνεῖν/κλαίειν 7.32.

23.28 στραφεὶς-πρὸς*, εἶπεν, Ἰερουσαλήμ*, κλαίειν (×2)*, πλήν*, ἑαυτόν. κλαίειν-ἐπί 19.41.

23.29 ἡμέραι-ἔρχονται*, κοιλία*. A second Lucan lament over Jerusalem, cf. 19.41-44. θυγατέρες in an extended sense, 1.5; 13.16. 'The days will come when...' is a septuagintalism (Manson), liked by Luke, not an Aramaism (Bultmann, p. 116). στεῖρα 1.7, 36. ἐροῦσιν, κοιλία, γεννᾶν, μαστοί, (ἐκ)τρέφειν all in Hos. 9.12-16; 10.8. Thomas (79) has combined the text with Lk. 11.27 (quite suitably), and is seen to be secondary by Robin Wilson (*Gnosis*, p. 72).

23.30 (πεσεῖν-ἐπί). τότε ἄρξονται λέγειν as an alternative to ἐροῦσιν, 13.25f.QD.

23.31 ταῦτα, γίνεσθαι. Hapax: ὑγρός (opp. to ξηρός). Manson cites the comment of R. Jose ben Jo'ezer on his way to crucifixion, 'If it is thus with those who do his will, how much more with those who anger him' (*Gen. R.* 65.22). The sentiment is courageous, and the coincidence accidental: cf. Prov. 11.31; 1 Pet. 4.17. ἐν ὑγρῷ/ξηρῷ = *bᵉ*, a Lucan septuagintalism.

23.32 ἄγειν, δὲ-καί*, ἕτερος, σὺν*, ἀναιρεῖν. κακοῦργος cf. πανουργία 20.23R.

Käser, W. 'Exegetische und theologische Erwägungen zur Seligpreisung der Kinderlosen Lc 23,29b', *ZNW* 54 (1963), pp. 240-54.
Neyrey, J.H., 'Jesus' Address to the Women of Jerusalem (Lk. 23.27-31)–A Prophetic Judgment Oracle', *NTS* 29 (1983), pp. 74-86.

g. *The Crucifixion*, 23.33-43   Passover, Noon

Luke's account continues to diverge considerably from Mark's, with at least one major 'L' section over the Penitent Thief, as well as many smaller differences. These lead Taylor, Marshall and many to postulate an independent Lucan source here too; while Creed (rather hesitantly), Finegan (pp. 31f.) and Wolfgang Schenk (*Passionsbericht*, pp. 93-102) look to continuous Lucan redaction. The case made by the last group can be strengthened, once it is understood that Luke is interpreting Matthew as well as Mark.

23.33. The sense of the three Gospels is the same in bringing Jesus to Golgotha, but Luke is closer to Matthew, in (1) 'when they came', cf. Mt. 27.33, 'having come', diff. Mk, 'they bring him', and (2) 'the place called a Skull', cf. Mt., 'a place named Golgotha', cp. Mk, 'the

Golgotha place, which is interpreted The Place of a Skull'. As usual, Luke leaves out the foreign name. He postpones the offering of the wine, which comes next in Mark and Mt., so as to make that a part of the soldiers' mockery, and moves straight to the crucifying.

23.34. The manuscript tradition is divided on the following saying, πάτερ, ἄφες αὐτοῖς, οὐ γὰρ οἴδασιν τί ποιοῦσιν. Although the current tendency is to bracket the half-verse (see below), the linguistic evidence is that it should be retained, and ascribed to Luke himself; for the style and the doctrine are alike his. He likes to write 'father' (0/0/7), as he does 'Brother' (6.42QD), and 'Child' (1/0/3); he has 'Father' for God in the Lord's Prayer, QD, Gethsemane (22.42R) and 'Father, into thy hands...' Forgiveness is the keynote of his gospel (24.47, and *passim*), and the same sentiment is on the lips of the dying Stephen (Acts 7.60). He writes ἄφες αὐτῷ at 17.3QD, and ἄφες ἡμῖν in the Lord's Prayer (QC). It is Luke alone who associates forgiveness with ignorance, and he does so several times: 'he who did not know and did things worthy of blows shall receive few stripes' (12.48); 'And now, brethren, I know that you did it in ignorance... repent that your sins may be wiped out' (Acts 3.17ff.); 'the times of ignorance God overlooked' (Acts 17.30); cf. also Acts 13.27. So if the verse has been interpolated by a scribe, he has a fine mastery of Lucan style and teaching. The problem is rather how such splendid words could ever have been omitted, and here we may be driven to Harnack's theory (*Probleme*, p. 255) that the thought of forgiveness for Jews was too much for some; but I should prefer to suppose that Luke himself inserted them in a revised version of his book. We could think of him as constantly trying to imagine Jesus' thoughts, as he has at 22.15, 48 and often; and he need not have completed the task by his first edition.

The story continues starkly, with Mk and Mt., 'But dividing his clothes, they cast lots': his forgiveness was of no concern to them. The action was a fulfilment of Ps. 22.19, and this psalm had been much meditated on in the early church, for the bystanders' 'shaking their heads' in Mk and Mt. had come from Ps. 22.8, and Matthew's 'He trusted in God...' from the following verse.

23.35. Luke takes up the line of the psalm, now that he has begun on it: the eighth verse begins, 'All they who watched me (θεωροῦντες) derided me (ἐξεμυκτήρισαν)', and he exploits this to his purpose. Mark had three groups of people who mocked Jesus: the by-passers, the chief priests and scribes, and the robbers. Luke can improve that. He begins, 'And the people stood *watching* (θεωρῶν)'—they were sympathetic, and only fulfilled the psalm in innocence—'and the rulers also it was who *derided* (ἐξεμυκτήριζον)'—they, with the verb first, were the ones with malice. The rulers' words carefully follow the chief priests' in Mark: Luke copies 'he saved others', and puts 'let him save himself' for Mark's 'he cannot save himself. . . let him come down'. In Mark they called him 'Christ, the king of Israel': Luke says, 'if this fellow is the Christ', and glosses, in Lucan manner 'of God' (9.22; cf. 2.26), 'the elect' (cf. 9.35).

23.36-38. Having exculpated the people, Luke needs another group of mockers, and thinks of the man with the spear who had given Jesus (ἐπότιζεν) a spongeful of vinegar (ὄξος), with a sarcastic remark about Elijah (Mk 15.36). The vinegar is seen as a fulfilment of another psalm, 69.22, 'They gave me for my food gall (χολήν), and for my drink they gave me (ἐπότισαν) vinegar (ὄξος)'; and is aligned by Luke with the soldiers in Matt. 27.34, 'who gave him to drink wine mixed with χολῆς'. There was no kindness in any of these men, and the psalm-verse makes Luke think that only one action was involved, and not necessarily just before Jesus' death. He concentrates the two Ps. 69 moments as he did the two Ps. 22 fulfilments, and earlier the two Sanhedrin hearings in Mark (§15). But the soldiers' words he takes from the Marcan passers-by, whom he will not make 'the people' (did not the soldiers παραπορεύεσθαι? They are παρεστηκότες at Mk 15.35). 'And saying. . . Save yourself' comes from Mk 15.29f, '. . . if you are. . . ' from Mt. 27.40, '. . . if you are the Son of God'. Luke's soldiers say, '*if* you *are* the king of the Jews', because that was what was written on the cross, and he now proceeds to tell us about that, having kept it till the section about the soldiers. It would be their task to put on the inscription, so those are the words they will have thrown in the Lord's teeth.

23.39f. And so finally to the malefactors. Matthew says that 'they cast the same (τὸ αὐτό) reproach at him' (27.44), so the careful Luke repeats, 'Are you not (Lucan οὐχί) the Christ? Save yourself and us'. He has been as scrupulously accurate as he promised in 1.3, and as skilful in rearranging his material as he was with the three Denials. But the presence of two dying sinners on Jesus' either side strikes the warm-hearted evangelist with a familiar note. Will not the crucified king of the Jews, who even in happier days drew so many sinners by the preaching of his kingdom, have reached the heart of one of these two now? Matthew's 'they reproached him' surely only means that there were reproaches from them too. Luke knew that one of them repented as certainly as he knew that Jesus must have healed the high priest's servant's ear. So he gives us a final pair of homiletic models, the obdurate and the penitent, to go with so many in his Gospel: Simon and the woman who was a sinner, the elder brother and the prodigal, the Pharisee and the Publican, the rich ruler and Zacchaeus. Once more he turns Matthew's stereotypes into differentiated real people—like the builders, the refusers of invitations, the debtors and the sons, who are so flat in Matthew and so three-dimensional in Luke.

23.41-43. The repentant ill-doer's words are a compound of Lucan piety, Lucan apologetic and Lucan cosmology. Fearing God is Lucan piety, practised by Cornelius and by the patriarchs (1.50), abjured by the Unjust Judge. Suffering as the desert of the sinner is accepted by the servants who knew and who did not know their master's will (12.47f.); indeed the over-acceptance of the harshness of life—'we indeed justly'—is paralleled only in Luke, where the servant who has ploughed and cooked and served, without either thanks or refreshment, is a model for the motto, 'We are unprofitable servants'. 'Jesus, remember me' similarly recalls God's remembering his mercy (1.54) and his covenant (1.72), and Cornelius' prayers which were remembered before God (Acts 10.31): there is no remembering in heaven in the other Gospels. Jesus' kingdom is mentioned because he has just been derided as the king of the Jews, but Luke has told us that there will be no end of his kingdom (not God's) at 1.33, and that the apostles would eat and drink in his kingdom (22.29f.). Salvation 'today' is Lucan too—'Today is born a Saviour', 'Today this scripture has been fulfilled', 'Today salvation has come to this house'.

But the apologetic is Lucan too: 'we receive the due reward (ἄξια) of our deeds; but this man has done nothing amiss'. Pilate has already testified three times that 'this man' had done nothing worthy (ἄξιον) of death, and Herod the same: now even a criminal says it, and the centurion will soon follow. Furthermore, there seems to be a somewhat distinctive Lucan cosmology implied in v. 43. Jewish speculations of the fate of the soul after death were various, but it was normal to imagine the souls of the righteous as going to Paradise, or the Garden of Eden, thought of as in the heavens (cf. 2 Cor.

12.2f.): so G.F. Moore (II, pp. 390f.). Sometimes however, a place is set apart for the souls of the righteous in a section of Sheol, as in *1Enoch* 22 (Cavallin, pp. 41, 49); and other texts leave the point ambiguous, as when the dying R. Johanan b. Zakkai said, 'Before me lie two ways, one leading to the Garden of Eden, and one to Gehenna' (*b. Ber.* 28b). Now the normal Christian belief of NT times is that the righteous (= Christian) dead *sleep* (κοιμᾶσθαι) in the underworld between death and judgment, and Luke uses this verb of Stephen and David (Acts 7.60, 13.36 = fall asleep). It is easily understandable then that he should take the *Enoch* 22 view rather than the more widely attested one, and think of Paradise as a section of Hades; and this seems to be what he has done both here and at 16.25 (*q.v.*). Jesus and the penitent criminal are to go together to Paradise in the underworld 'today', Good Friday; whence Jesus will arise on Easter Day, and his companion at the Parousia. Luke is singular in thinking of the righteous dead as in bliss rather than as asleep, and that in both Gospel passages; so here too we may speak of the thinking as Lucan, and ascribe it in the first instance to the evangelist.

23.33 ὁ-καλούμενος*. Hapax: ἀριστερός. ὅτε 6.13R; καὶ ὅτε ἦλθον, cf. Acts 1.13 καὶ ὅτε εἰσῆλθον. ἐκεῖ 21.2R; 10.6QD. κακοῦργοι to avoid the Zealot associations of Mk's λῃσταί. ὁ μὲν ... ὁ δὲ, 8.5 Mk; Acts 14.4; 17.32; 27.44; 28.5, 24. ἀριστερός is changed from Mk's εὐώνυμος, the standard LXX pair being δέξιος/ἀριστερός (×23), cp./εὐώνυμος ×3; cf. also 2 Cor. 6.7.

23.34 (διαμερίζειν*), πάτερ*. Hapax: (κλῆρος). The authorities for v. 34a are split: p⁷⁵ א¹BW 579 sa bo^pt against, א*²L bo^pt Clem. Or. for; Dav against, ce Ir. Tat. for; Θ syr^s against, 565, 700, fam. 1, 13, syr^cph for. WH, Aland bracket; Kilpatrick, Greeven print. Metzger (p. 180) awards C rating, with the remarkable comment, 'the logion, though probably not a part of the original Gospel of Luke, bears self-evident tokens of its dominical origin'. κλῆροι pl. R, cf. Acts 1.26.

23.35 εἱστήκει, ὁ-λαός*, (καὶ = also), οἱ-ἄρχοντες*, (ἑαυτόν), οὗτος contemptuous, ὁ-θεός. ἐκμυκτηρίζειν, 16.14. Luke drops Mark's 'It was the third hour'; he has the incidents at the crucifying together at the sixth hour (v. 44).

23.36 καὶ = also. Hapax: (ὄξος). ἐνέπαιζον from Mk 15.30 ἐμπαίζοντες. προσερχόμενος, 9.42R; Acts 7.31.

23.37 εἰ σὺ εἶ 22.67.

23.38 δὲ-καί, (οὗτος contemptuous). Metzger (p. 180) gives a B rating to the shorter text, without 'written in letters of Greek and Latin and Aramaic'. ἦν γεγραμμένη would be Lucan Greek; γράμματα, 16.6, ×2 Acts.

23.39 οὐχί. Hapax: κρεμαννύναι (Acts 5.30; 10.39 of cross). ἐβλασφήμει from Mk 15.29.

23.40 ὁ-ἕτερος*, φοβεῖσθαι-τὸν-θεόν*, σύ following verb*. οὐδέ; 6.3R, ὁ-αὐτός, 5/1/6+7.

23.41 ὃς in attraction*, πράσσειν ×2*, ἀπολαμβάνειν, οὗτος contemptuous. Hapaxes: δικαίως, ἄτοπος. Cf. δίκαιος, 17/2/11+6, 20.20R; 23.50R. ἄτοπος, Acts 25.5; 28.6, μηδὲν ἄτοπον.

23.42 μιμνήσκεσθαι*. μνήσθητι, 24.6R, 0/0/3. Better sense is given by Greeven's reading ἐν τῇ βασιλείᾳ (with most MSS) than Aland's εἰς (p⁷⁵BL): Jesus could hardly be thought of as remembering the thief when he enters his heavenly realm at the Ascension (24.26), but rather when he comes in his kingdom to judge mankind (22.30). Not at the parousia, says Jesus, but today.

23.43 εἶπεν, σήμερον. Hapax: παράδεισος. ἀμήν σοι λέγω 4.24R?; 12.37QD; although Luke often drops Semitic words, he sometimes introduces them, e.g. μαμωνᾶς.

Daube, D., '"For They Know Not What They Do": Luke 23,34', *Studia Patristica* 4 (TU 79, Berlin, 1961), pp. 58-70.

Grelot, P., '"Aujourdhui tu seras avec moi dans le Paradis" (Luc XXIII, 43)', *RB* 74 (1967), 194-214.

h. *Jesus' Death*, 23.44-56a		Passover, 3 p.m.

23.44f. Luke returns to Mark for the three hours' darkness, for which, however, he supplies an explanation, 'the sun suffering an eclipse'. He has sought for many explanations throughout the book, starting with the taxation as a reason for Jesus' birth at Bethlehem; he is no more fortunate this time, as eclipses cannot coincide with a full moon. It is conceivable that he had heard of the eclipse of 29th Nov., AD 29 (J.F.A. Sawyer, *JTS* [1972]). He brings the rending of the Temple veil forward, so as to have the portents together: both signify God's anger with Jewry, the second the coming destruction of the Temple.

23.46. In Mark Jesus gives two 'loud cries', the first with the words, 'My God, my God. . .', the second his death-cry. Luke combines the two, so as to suppress the anxious-making thought that the Lord might have lost his faith. He would prefer a more serene Psalm-text, and happily this is suggested by Matthew: 'And Jesus cried again with a loud voice and let his spirit go' (26.50). ἀφῆκεν τὸ πνεῦμα: surely the familiar psalm-verse from the evening prayer (S-B, II, p. 269) will have been in his mind, 'Into thy hands will I commend my πνεῦμα'. Luke prefaces his favourite 'Father', and changes the tense for appropriateness.

23.47-49. Once more Luke divides the onlookers into three groups, and once more he manipulates the Marcan tradition for his own purposes. First comes Mark's centurion: but Luke fears to mislead his hearers if he were to give the Marcan words, 'Truly this man was son of God'. Such confessions come, in his experience, from hearing the word of God, and repenting; and should perhaps be better reserved for another centurion and his friends, who were to hear the word from Peter in Acts. So Luke contents himself with the now standard testimony to Jesus' innocence: 'Really this man was righteous'. Then he wishes to portray the crucifixion as attended by a large and sympathetic crowd of wellwishers, who had not been in evidence in Mark; so he takes the Marcan θεωροῦσαι away from the women, and uses it twice—'all the crowds who were present at the θεωρίαν', 'θεωρήσαντες what happened, they went home beating their breasts'. This did not happen in a corner; and it was only the rulers who really wanted it. Thirdly, there are Mark's women, amplified with 'all his acquaintance': the addition not only swells the crowd of the loyal and grieving, but recalls (a little distantly) Ps. 37.12 LXX οἱ φίλοι μου καὶ οἱ πλησίόν μου . . . οἱ ἔγγιστά μου ἀπὸ μακρόθεν ἔστησαν.

23.44　ὡσεί, (γίνεσθαι). **Hapax**: (ἔνατος). ὡσεὶ ὥρα + ordinal, Acts 10.3. ἤδη (if read, with Aland), cf. 24.29; perhaps cf. Mk 15.42. Luke may have taken the suggestion of ἡλίου from Mark's Ηλιας, or Matthew's ηλι.

23.45　ἐκλείπειν, μέσος. **Hapax**: (καταπέτασμα). ἐσχίσθη μέσον, cf. Acts 1.18 ἐλάκησε μέσος.

23.46　(φωνή), εἶπεν, πάτερ*, εἰπών*. **Hapax**: (ἐκπνεῖν). φωνήσας φωνῇ μεγάλῃ, cf. Acts 16.28, ἐφώνησε δὲ μεγάλῃ φωνῇ.

23.47　(ἰδὼν-δέ), (γίνεσθαι), δοξάζειν-τὸν-θεόν*, ὁ-ἄνθρωπος-οὗτος*. ὄντως, 24.34.

23.48　Pleon. πάντες, τὰ + part., γίνεσθαι, τύπτειν, ὑποστρέφειν*. **Hapaxes**: συμπαραγίνεσθαι (double compounds, 12/14/31+35, παραγ. 3/1/

8+20), θεωρία, cf. Mk θεωροῦσαι. τύπτοντες τὰ στήθη in pious grief, 18.13.

23.49 εἰστήκει, pleon. πάντες, ταῦτα. Hapax: συνακολουθεῖν (συν- 21/24/ 41+47). γνωστοί, 2.44, -όν × 10 Acts.

23.50f. And so to the Burial. Mark began by noting that it was now evening, and Luke postpones this. There is far too much to get done before sabbath if it is evening already, and he wants no suspicion of sabbath-breaking (v. 56); he needs the full three hours implied by v. 44. Joseph is loaded with Lucan virtue, 'a good and just man', cf. Simeon (2.25), Cornelius (Acts 10.22), Barnabas (Acts 11.24), or the fine and good of heart of 8.15; the description is Luke's interpretation of Mark's εὐσχήμων, which can mean noble=virtuous as well as noble=wealthy (cf. Creed on Phrynichus, p. 309). But if he was indeed good and just, it can be inferred with confidence that he had not been in agreement with 'their' (the Sanhedrin's) kangaroo trial, and pressure on Pilate: so Luke exculpates him as carefully as he did the Governor.

23.52f. The description of Joseph's actions follows Matthew more closely than Mark. Fifteen out of the next sixteen words (all but καθελών, Mk) are identical with Matthew. οὗτος προσελθὼν τῷ Πιλάτῳ includes Matthew's favoured resumptive οὗτος and προσελθών. Luke, like Matthew, drops the Marcan τολμήσας, and the whole sentence on Pilate's confirmation of the death, and the purchase of the linen. He uses Matthew's ἐνετύλιξεν for Mark's ἐνείλησεν, and has αὐτό for the object with Matthew, against Mark's αὐτόν (cp. v. 53b, ἔθηκεν αὐτόν). He says that no one had ever yet lain in the tomb, echoing Matthew's καινῷ.

23.54. But for Luke, as for all the evangelists, the burial is but the preparation for the Resurrection story; and the vital witnesses here are the women. Mark's story remains Luke's prime authority, but it raises two anxieties as it stands. First, there seems to be some muddle over who the women were, with three slightly differing lists at Mk 15.40, 47 and 16.1; so for the moment Luke contents himself with a general description, 'the women who had accompanied him from Galilee'—faithful counterparts to the men who 'accompanied us all the time the Lord Jesus went in and out among us' (Acts 1.21), and so were eligible to be apostles. Secondly, Mark speaks as if the women had gone out and bought the ointments *after* the sabbath

(16.1); and although this might be physically possible it sounds difficult, and raises the suspicion of sabbath-breaking. Luke's first Christians are as faithful to the Law as the characters of his Infancy narratives, and he firmly omits the purchasing altogether, and has the preparation on the Friday afternoon. Mark said the burial took place on Preparation day, Friday, and Luke puts this note of time now, adding, 'and sabbath ἐπέφωσκεν'; he means it was drawing on, but it is an unparalleled use, as the verb means to dawn (φῶς). The source of this solecism is a misreading of Mt. 28.2, the only other place in the NT where the word occurs. Matthew wrote ὀψὲ δὲ σαββάτων τῇ ἐπιφωσκούσῃ εἰς μίαν σαββάτων, which the context shows to mean, 'After the sabbath, as (the night) was dawning into Sunday': but the prepositional use of ὀψέ (after) is rare, the adverbial use (late) being normal. So Luke took the meaning to be 'Late on the sabbath, as (the day) was drawing into Sunday'. Mt. 28.1 and Mk 15.47 alike speak of the women seeing Jesus' burial-place, and that is the message of Lk. 23.55 also: he follows Mark as usual, who clearly gives the proper time (Friday before sundown), while his unique use of ἐπιφώσκειν shows that he is also using, and has misunderstood, Matthew. (See further note below.)

23.55f. The women see the tomb, and *how* the body was laid; so they know that further anointing will be required, and where to come. They then go home, like other Lucan characters, where they make ready the ointments; Luke adds 'and myrrhs', thinking perhaps of Cant. 1.3, 'The scent of the μύρων is beyond any ἀρώματα'—it was he who introduced the daughters of Jerusalem also (Cant. 2.7, etc.). Then they rest on the sabbath according to the commandment, as good Lucan people do.

23.50 ἀνήρ ×2*, ὀνόματι*, ὑπάρχων*. Hapax: (βουλευτής). ἀνὴρ ὀνόματι Ἰ. cf. Mt. 27.57, ἄνθρωπος. . .τοὔνομα ᾽Ι.

23.51 εἶναι + part., πόλις, (προσδέχεσθαι). Hapaxes: πρᾶξις, συγκατατιθέναι (double compound, cf. v. 48). πόλις τῶν ᾽Ιουδαίων, cf. 1.26; 4.31; 8.26, etc. βουλή × 7 Acts.

23.53 εἶναι + part., κείμενος*, οὔ. Hapaxes: (ἐντυλίσσειν), (σινδών), λαξευτός. μνῆμα 24.1, 0/2/3+2. λαξευτός: Mk and Mt. use λατομεῖν, which however is normally used for digging pits in LXX (a tomb at Isa. 22.16)— Luke prefers λαξεύειν = hew stone (×22 LXX). οὐκ ἦν οὐδεὶς οὔπω cf. Acts 8.16 οὐδέπω ἐπ᾽ οὐδένι. For the MAs, see further my *NTS* (1978) article (pp.

230f.) and C.M. Tuckett's reply (*NTS* [1984], pp. 138f.). There are in fact six points of agreement with Matthew in the sentence (vv. 52f.); of which ἐνετύλιξεν may seem striking, and προσελθών and the neuter αὐτό significant. Tuckett is content to insist that Luke could have made the same change as Matthew each time independently, and makes no account of a cumulative argument. As for ἐνετύλιξεν, 'Matthew and Luke may have objected to Mark's verb because of its bad associations'. These unspecified bad associations are cited as going back to Abbott in the last century, and are a last resort. Mark's ἐνειλεῖν is used by Plutarch, Philostratus, Dio Chrysostom and others, of wrapping children in swaddling-bands or lion-skins; and if they *did* both wish to change the verb, they had several alternatives to choose from.

23.54 ἡμέρα, σάββατον. Hapaxes: (παρασκευή), (ἐπιφώσκειν). 'The day of Preparation', cf. 'the day of sabbath', 0/0/4+2. For ἐπιφώσκειν see further my *NTS* (1978) articles (pp. 237ff.) and Tuckett's response (*NTS* [1984], pp. 139f.). Although not disputing the absence of any instance of the word in the sense of 'evening drawing on' before Luke, Tuckett feels that 'we can reasonably expect of Luke of all the NT writers' that he would not take over a 'lexically strange usage' uncritically. Such confidence is of course unfalsifiable, as all counter-instances can be treated in the same way; but it is not borne out by general experience, which shows educated people constantly taking over mis-usages, infer for imply, disinterested for uninterested, derisory for risible. Luke took the word over from Matthew as a perfectly familiar *word*, and (on my view, once he has read it so in Matthew) in a given, if novel *sense*. It seems a bit much for Tuckett to excuse himself from 'providing *any* explanation', and then to accuse me of being 'somewhat speculative'!

23.55 εἶναι + part. Hapax: κατακολουθεῖν (Acts 16.17). συνέρχεσθαι, 5.15R, ×16 Acts. θεᾶσθαι, 5.27R. ἐτέθη, cf. Acts 7.16, ἐτέθησαν ἐν τῷ μνήματι.

23.56a ὑποστρέφειν*, ἑτοιμάζειν.

Broer, I., *Die Urgemeinde und das Grab Jesu* (SANT 31; Munich, 1972).

Sawyer, J.F.A., 'Why is a Solar Eclipse mentioned in the Passion Narrative (Luke xxiii.44-45)?', *JTS* 23 (1972), pp. 124-28.

Lange, J., 'Zur Ausgestaltung der Szene vom Sterben Jesu in den synoptischen Evangelien', in *Fs* Schnackenburg (1974), pp. 40-55.

Schreiber, J., 'Die Bestattung Jesu', *ZNW* 72 (1981), pp. 141-77.

51. The Resurrection, 23.56b–24.53

a. *The Empty Tomb*, 23.56b–24.12   Easter Day

The debate on the independent source continues: Bultmann (pp. 284-87), Finegan (pp. 86f.), C.F. Evans (pp 92ff.), H. Grass (p. 35), J. Kremer (pp. 96-112), and Neirynck (*Ev.*, pp. 297-312; *NTS* [1984]) see merely a thorough Lucan editing of Mark, where Grundmann, Taylor (*PNL*, pp. 106-109), and Marshall see evidence of a second lost source. But the new material is often Lucan in interest and language, and (as throughout 24) the realization that Luke had Matthew as well as Mark solves outstanding problems.

24.1-3. This is the Resurrection, and Luke uses his powers of inference (§13) to fill in some of the details. Mark seems to haver between 'extremely early' (i.e. in the half-light) and 'when the sun had risen' (16.3), so Luke rephrases to 'in the deep dawn'—he mentions the dawn again three times. Mark said, the women 'see that the stone has been rolled back, and on going into the tomb saw an angel': but then, the big thing was not what they saw, but what they did not see. Luke keeps Mark's structure, but adds the second crucial clause: 'they found the stone rolled away from the tomb, but on going in they did not find the body of the Lord Jesus'. He is 'the Lord Jesus', now that he is risen; as so often in Acts.

24.4. A third point over which there is some tension is the angelic revelation. Mark speaks of a young man sitting on the right inside the tomb, wearing a white robe; while Matthew describes the angel of the Lord as sitting on the stone, with his face like lightning and his clothing white as snow. Luke sees these as two separate angels, then, and combines the description of their apparel—'behold, two men in lightening clothes'; just as he combined the two Sanhedrin hearings, or the two wine incidents at the crucifixion (pp. 753, 766). Of course Luke sometimes has angels in pairs, as at the Ascension ('behold, two men in white apparel'), like Moses and Elijah at the Transfiguration ('behold, two men', 9.30) or many earthly pairs of messengers (10.1; 19.29; 22.8); but angels are found singly also (quite often), and without their clothes lightening, and Luke would hardly have presumed on the second angel if he had not been able to 'discover' it in Matthew.

24.5. Mark says the women were amazed, but Matthew implies that they were frightened, with the angel saying, 'Fear you not'; this is more the reaction which Luke anticipates from the vision of an angel (1.12, 29; 2.9), so he writes a favourite phrase for them, ἐμφόβων γενομένων. Matthew also suggests an appropriate expression of fear a few verses further on, for at 28.9f. Jesus meets the women and says to them, 'Fear not', and they are clasping his feet and worshipping him. Luke elsewhere has Peter, at a similar moment of awe, 'fall at Jesus' knees' (5.8), or the thankful leper 'fell on his face at his feet' (17.16; cf. 5.12); so it is natural to him to add, 'and bending their faces to the earth'. The brilliant light alone might bring them to their knees (cf. Acts 9.4). In Mark, the angel said, 'You seek Jesus of Nazareth, the crucified': Luke makes the comment more pointed by taking it as a question, 'Why do you seek the living among the dead?' He twice gives us the same living/dead contrast of the Prodigal Son, and at 20.38; Acts 10.42; 25.19.

24.6f. The next verse owes everything to Mt. 28.6. Not only are the opening words in Matthew's order, 'He is not here, (but) he is risen' (diff. Mk), but it is Matthew only who continues, καθὼς εἶπεν, words which have a quite different reference at Mk 16.7 (seeing Jesus in Galilee). In Matthew the reference is to 'Jesus the crucified. . . is risen'; and Luke would very much rather speak of that than the Marcan suggestion of a trip to Galilee. In his belief the apostles stayed in Jerusalem at first, as Christ willed (24.47, 49; Acts 1.4, 8); but he has not just travestied his tradition, as is so often maintained. Matthew's 'as he said' becomes, 'Remember that he spoke to you while still in Galilee, saying of the Son of Man that he must be betrayed into the hands of sinners, and crucified, and on the third day arise'. 'Crucified' comes nowhere in the passion-prophecies (where 'killed' is used), and is taken from Mk 16.6. 'The Son of Man is to be betrayed into the hands of men' comes in 9.44; 'the Son of Man must. . . rise on the third day' comes in 9.22; both prophecies are in Galilee, and there is no need to think of the verse as a bold instance of a deliberate change of Mark's meaning at all.

24.8f. Being women, the receivers of this message do not presume to rise to faith before the apostles, but limit themselves to remembering his 'sayings' (a Lucanism), and scuttling off to the Eleven. For all his feeling for women, Luke comes from a world of male chauvinists. Mark is now drawing his book to a close on its puzzling note, 'They said nothing to anyone', and Luke turns again to Matthew, whom he follows for both structure and content. Mt. 28.8, 'And departing quickly from the tomb. . . they ran to inform his disciples'; Luke, 'And returning from the tomb, they informed the Eleven of all this'. Although ἀπαγγέλλειν is a word congenial to Luke, he could have used a much more common word like εἶπαν (Mk 16.7) or ἔλεγον (Luk. 24.10). Luke alone speaks of 'the Eleven' absolutely (24.33; Acts 2.14), and he has a larger group with them here as at Acts 1.15. These include Cleopas and his friend.

24.10f. Luke appends the names of the women at the end of the story, as he does at the Ascension (Acts 1.13), or with Cleopas, who appears as an afterthought at 24.18, or Simon the Pharisee at 7.40. Mary Magdalene and Mary wife of James come from Mk 16.1: Luke's contact, Joanna wife of Chuza, Herod's steward, takes second place as she did at 8.3, and Salome has to join 'the others with them'. Luke thinks of only the three named women as being at the tomb—how could there be room for more inside? They informed the Eleven in v. 9, and 'the others' joined 'with them' in trying to get the news accepted; ἔλεγον, they kept saying it, but to no purpose. Luke has a bigger group with his central women, as he has with his men (cf. 8.3, 'and many others'). The apostles do not credit the story (ἠπίστουν, v. 11); 'these sayings' appeared 'before' them as a joke. Such is to be the pattern throughout the Resurrection story, disbelief turning reluctantly to conviction; for only so can the hearer be reassured that his vital witnesses are hard-headed and trustworthy men, and not credulous simpletons. Now the Eleven disbelieve, but Peter goes to the tomb and 'wonders at what had happened'; Cleopas and his companion were slow of heart to believe, but at length their eyes were opened and they knew him; in the evening the disciples think the Lord is a ghost and disbelieve (ἀπιστούντων) for joy, but their touching and his eating bring confidence in time.

24.12. The absence of v. 12 from certain Western MSS, and the development of its theme at length in John 20, caused earlier critics, under the influence of Hort, to exclude it from the text; but modern opinion (Aland, *NTS* [1966], Metzger, p. 184) has moved to accept the verse. This is partly in view of its support by newly discovered MSS; partly because it is echoed in vv. 23f.; partly because it counterbalances the apostles' disbelief (Kremer, pp. 105f., see on v. 11); and partly because of its strongly Lucan language (Neirynck, *Ev.*, pp. 310-34).

But if the verse is integral to Luke's text, did its substance come to him from L? Fitzmyer's appeal to John 20, and so a lost Luke-John source, should as usual be discounted: John is a development of Luke (and Matthew) (Neirynck, *NTS* [1984]). Kremer's point suggests that Luke needs something like a Petrine visit to the tomb, and that it functions in two ways to give his resurrection stories a climax:

Appearance	*Disbelief*	*Faith*
Angels to Women	The Eleven: a joke	Peter at tomb: wonder
Christ on Emmaus road	Cleopas: slow of heart	Breaking of Bread
Christ to disciples	Disbelief for joy	Commissioning

Not only is the visit required to give a positive end to the first scene: it gives the minimum response of faith, which is then to rise to increasing heights in the second and third scenes. For 'wonder' is so often for Luke the first step to faith, and all Peter sees is the grave-clothes; Cleopas and his friend will see Jesus, and know him in the breaking of bread, if for a moment; the apostolic company will touch him, eat with him, be commissioned by him, and see him away to heaven.

So (especially as Matthew does not know of such), a Petrine visit is likely to be a Lucan construction. Luke knows that the angel said to the women, 'tell his disciples and Peter' (Mk 16.7), and the implication is that Peter was not quite in the same category as the others. Luke sees Peter as being the first to turn, and then to strengthen his fellows (22.32); and it was common Christian knowledge that Peter had been the first to see the Lord (1 Cor. 15.5, familiar to Luke, 24.34). But Luke knows of no detail of the Petrine appearance either. He may however feel entitled to infer that someone among the Twelve made a positive response to the women's report, and to infer that that someone was Peter (§13). He has him get up (Lucan ἀναστάς), and run (ἔδραμεν, cf. Mt. 28.8, ἔδραμον, of the women) to the tomb. Mk 16.4 said of the women, 'looking up they behold (ἀναβλέψασαι θεωροῦσιν) that the stone has been rolled away': the Lucan Peter goes a step further, 'peering he sees (παρακύψας βλέπει) the grave-clothes on their own (μόνα)'. He has retained the structure of the Marcan phrase (Neirynck, *Ev.*, pp. 329-34), and uses παρακύπτειν in the standard Biblical sense of 'look' (*ibid.*, pp. 401-40). Peter takes the first step towards faith by 'wondering at what had happened', and (like so many Lucan characters) ends up by going home. On examination, most of the words in the verse bear the Lucan stamp (see below).

23.56b (σάββατον). ἡσυχάζειν, 0/0/2+2. ἐντολή, 1.6; κατὰ τὴν ἐντολήν cf. κατὰ τὸν νόμον, 0/0/2+4.

24.1 ὑπὸ τὸν ὄρθρον, Acts 5.21, ὀρθρίζειν, 21.38, ὄρθρινος, 24.22. βαθύς, Acts 20.9; cf. 5.4; 6.48. 'They came φέροντες' Acts 5.16; Lk. 5.18; Mk 23.26R, 6/15/4+10.

24.2 εὑρίσκειν. Hapax: (ἀποκυλίειν).

24.3 εὑρίσκειν, ὁ-κύριος* = Jesus. τοῦ κυρίου Ἰησοῦ is missing in most Western MSS, but is justified by Metzger, p. 183; the phrase is associated with the resurrection in Acts 4.33; cf. 2.36. It comes ×17 in Acts.

24.4 καὶ-ἐγένετο-ἐν-τῷ...καὶ*, περί, ἀνήρ*, ἐφιστάναι*. Hapax: ἀπορεῖσθαι: cf. Acts 25.20 ἀπορούμενος...τὴν περὶ τούτων ζήτησιν; διαπορεῖν 9.7R, ×3 Acts. ἐπέστη(σαν) of divine visitants, 2.9; Acts 12.7; 23.11. ἐσθής 23.11, 0/0/ 2+3: (ἐξ)αστράπτων cf. 9.29R. Standard explanations of why Luke has doubled the Marcan angel to two are not too convincing. If it is a folk-motif of legend (Bultmann, pp. 314-16; Grass, p. 32), why are there so many single angels in Luke–Acts (Zechariah, Mary, the Shepherds, Gethsemane, the Apostles in prison, Philip, Cornelius, Peter in prison, the Shipwreck)? If two witnesses are required (Morgenthaler, *LGZ*, II, pp. 7ff.; Bode, p. 60), what is Peter doing on his own in v. 12?

24.5 γίνεσθαι, κλίνειν*, εἶπεν-πρὸς*, ζητεῖν, ζῆν. A slight rebuke is to be felt, as with Cleopas, v. 25. ἔμφοβος γενόμενος, v. 37; Acts 10.4; 24.25. ζῆν in this context, 24.26; Acts 1.3; 25.19.

24.6 μνησθῆναι*, ὤν, ἔτι. μνησθῆναι ὡς, 22.61; Acts 11.16.

24.7 δεῖ, ἁμαρτωλός. λέγειν + acc., 9.31; cf. Acts 13.32f. τὰς χεῖρας τῶν ἁμ. cf. Mk 14.41.

24.8 μνησθῆναι*, ῥῆμα.

24.9 ὑποστρέφειν*, (ἀπαγγέλλειν), pleon. πάντα ×2, ταῦτα, οἱ-λοιποί.

24.10 οἱ-λοιποί*, σύν*, speak πρός*, οἱ-ἀπόστολοι*, ταῦτα. ἦσαν δὲ + names, Acts 13.1. ἡ Μαγδαληνὴ Μαρία unique in this order; cf. Acts 20.4, Ἀσιανοὶ δὲ Τύχικος καὶ Τ.

24.11 ἐνώπιον*, ὡσεί, τὰ-ῥήματα-ταῦτα*. Hapax: λῆρος. ἐφάνησαν, cf. 9.8R. ἀπιστεῖν 24.41; Acts 28.24, not in Mk or Mt.; cf. Acts 12.13f. for general resemblance.

24.12 ἀναστάς*, ἑαυτόν, θαυμάζειν, τὸ-γεγονός*. Hapaxes: παρακύπτειν (cf. ἀνα- ×2), ὀθόνια. ἀναστάς normally first word, but Peter's name takes precedence for emphasis. ἔδραμεν, cf. 15.20, transferred from Mt. 28.8. ὀθόνια, cf. ὀθόνη ×2 Acts; Luke thinks of the Marcan σινδών (23.53) as being in strips. βλέπει, hist. pres., rare in Luke, is justified by Neirynck (*Ev.* pp. 329-34) as a carry-over from Mk 16.4, ἀναβλέψασαι θεωροῦσιν, and by John Muddiman (*ETL* [1972]) as giving special emphasis. Aland reads μόνα but not κείμενα, which would be Lucan. ἀπῆλθεν πρὸς ἑαυτόν, cf. Acts 28.16, μένειν καθ' ἑαυτόν. θαυμάζειν + acc., 7.9QD; Acts 7.31.

b. *The Road to Emmaus*, 24.13-35   Easter Day
The Emmaus Road story has been a nest of problems. As a special Lucan unit, it has been widely ascribed in its original form to the Lucan Sondergut/L; but Lucan ideas and language are so pervasive that it has proved difficult to isolate clearly any tradition from the redaction. This has led some bolder critics, like Hans-Dieter Betz (*ZTK* [1969]) and Christopher Evans (*Resurrection*, pp. 92-115), to see the whole story as a legend created by Luke. But commentators usually make the attempt to discriminate tradition from redaction, and there are full-length analyses by John Alsup (pp. 190-200), J. Wanke (pp. 23-126), R.J. Dillon (pp. 69-155), J.-M. Guillaume (pp. 67-159), and Jacob Kremer (pp. 112-36), among others. The difficulty, as Alsup confesses (p. 192) is the inadequacy of criteria. As a minimum traditional element, Wanke proposes to include the names Emmaus and Cleopas, and the appearance of Jesus as one unknown who is later recognized. Kremer (p. 131) adds the association of the recognition with a meal. Fitzmyer (p. 1558) gives further points, even crediting Mk 16.12f. as pre-Lucan.

Kremer also gives a list of problems facing the exegete. Why was a Cleopas/Emmaus appearance repeated in the Lucan church—did it legitimate some non-apostolic authority? How is it that this story comes to be described so graphically, whereas the story of Jesus' appearance to Peter remains confined to a formula? Is there a liturgical interest behind the recognition in the bread-breaking? Why did Luke himself think an appearance to non-apostles sufficiently important to describe at such length? No account of the pericope is going to be satisfying that does not give a plausible answer to these questions.

By 24.12 Luke has completed the Marcan material, with one small exception. I noted above (p. 775) that the Marcan angel's instruction to go to Galilee was not *changed* (as is often said) into a reminiscence of teaching in Galilee, but *replaced* by a fuller statement of the reminiscence in Matthew. The Marcan instruction is therefore still outstanding, and Luke's handling of Mark hitherto encourages us to think that he is more likely to have rewritten it than to have suppressed it. The Marcan words were, 'You seek Jesus the Nazarene (Ναζαρηνόν), the crucified. He is risen (ἠγέρθη), he is not here: behold the place where they laid him. But go, tell his disciples and Peter that he goes before you to Galilee: there you shall see him, as he told you' (Mk 16.6f.). Jesus had 'told them' in 14.28, in virtually the same words.

Now there are three expressions which Mark uses in this message which are not congenial to Luke. (1) He uses the Latinized form Ναζαρηνός (cf. Romanus), as he does elsewhere (1.24; 10.47). While Luke retains this the first time (4.34/Mk 1.24), he changes it the second time to the better Greek form Ναζωραῖος (18.37R, cf. Ἀθηναῖος); and this is the form that he uses all eight times in Acts. (2) Mark uses the verb σταυροῦν ×8, and Matthew ×10, but Luke retains only four of these, and has the verb only twice in Acts. He prefers to use ἀναιρεῖν of Jesus' death (Acts 2.23; 10.39; 13.28), or ἀποκτείνειν (Acts 3.15), no doubt because they cause less scandal to his middle-class audience. (3) Luke never uses the passive ἠγέρθη in Acts, but always the active, 'God ἤγειρεν him'; it comes where there are synoptic parallels in the Gospel, at 9.22 and 24.6. Luke prefers ἀναστῆναι for 'he rose again'—24.7R; 16.31; 24.46; Acts 9.40; 10.41; 17.3. Now all three of these expressions come in the Emmaus road story. At 24.19 the travellers say, 'The things concerning Jesus the Nazarene (Ναζαρηνοῦ)', at 24.20 they say, 'They crucified him (ἐσταύρωσαν)'. At 24.34 the disciples say, 'The Lord ἠγέρθη indeed, and appeared to Simon'.

These indications are not a lot to go on, but they may be a hint of the working of Luke's mind. Luke knows that Peter was the first of the apostles to see the Lord (1 Cor. 15.5), and he believed that the first appearances happened soon, while the apostles were in Jerusalem (24.48). Here in Mark is the unquestionable angelic assurance that the disciples and Peter would see Jesus following his resurrection; and it is really inevitable that Luke should equate the Petrine appearance (ἠγέρθη. . .ὤφθη, 24.34), with the angelic prophecy (ἠγέρθη. . .ὄψεσθε, Mk 16.6f.). But what then is to be made of 'he goes before you to Galilee: *there* you shall see him'? The words allow of two understandings. One—and much the more natural, and no doubt the one intended by Mark—is that the disciples and Peter would see him *in Galilee*. Unfortunately this goes against Luke's conviction that the first appearances were on Easter Day, and in the environs of Jerusalem. So he may have preferred to opt for a second interpretation: 'he *is going* before you to (προάγει ὑμᾶς εἰς) Galilee'—there they would see him, *on the road to Galilee*. But this would of course raise further questions. 'The disciples' are mentioned *before* Peter in Mk 16.7. But Peter was the first of the apostles to see the Lord. Was there then an appearance to other, non-apostolic disciples at the same time as the Petrine appearance, or before? The presence of the three non-Lucan expressions from Mk 16.6f., and the possibility of such a reading of the text by Luke, make it attractive to think that Mark is once more the foundation-stone of his pericope.

In this way we should have access to the fundamental tradition which gave Luke the bare outline of the story. Mark's 'the disciples and Peter' have become Luke's 'And lo, two of them' and 'Simon'— the 'them' being τοῖς λοιποῖς of v. 9. Mark's 'he is going before you to(wards) Galilee' becomes 'they were travelling to a village called Emmaus, sixty stades from Jerusalem'. Although there is some doubt of where Emmaus was (see below), it is most likely that Luke thought of the place as the first night's stop from Jerusalem to the north. There is no sign that Cleopas and his friend lived there, and the impression we have is that they are Galileans like the rest of the party. They speak of the women as ἐξ ἡμῶν (v. 22), and the women had followed Jesus from Galilee (8.3; 23.49, 55); and if only the apostles were there for the Last Supper (22.14), an experience of one of the Galilean feedings seems to be implied by 'he was known to them in the breaking of bread' (v. 35). Mark said προάγει: Luke says ἐγγίσας συνεπορεύετο αὐτοῖς—he is on the Galilee road ahead of the apostles and the women. Mark said they would see him there: Luke that their eyes were held from recognizing him. Mark said that the angel told the women, 'He is not here; behold the place where they laid him', and that they were seized with ἔκστασις. Luke says, 'Certain *women* of us amazed (ἐξέστησαν) us, having been early at the tomb, and not finding his body, they came saying that they had even seen a vision of *angels*, who said that he was alive'. The wording (see below) is a Lucan version of the Marcan substance: only ἐξέστησαν, act., is unique in Luke-Acts, and may be influenced by Mark's ἔκστασις.

We may see Luke, then, as deriving the framework of his story from Mk. 16.6f.; but this framework has been filled in from somewhere. One likely source is the Old Testament. Bultmann (p. 286) cites Hermann Gunkel for the suggestion that it is a typical legend, based on similar stories from the OT of God walking the earth in the form of a man, like Genesis 16 and 18. There are indeed features recalling Genesis 18—the 'man' who is a divine figure, who is entertained to a meal by humans unawares; 'λήμψομαι ἄρτον, and you shall eat'; and the opening words, ὤφθη δὲ αὐτῷ ὁ θεός. In Genesis 16 the angel of the Lord found Hagar ἐν τῇ ὁδῷ of Shur, and said to her, ποῦ πορεύου; and Hagar said, 'I have openly seen ὀφθέντα μοι'. In Genesis 19 the two angels came to Sodom ἑσπέρας, and Lot constrained them (κατεβιάσατο) to come in with him. He gave them a meal, and worshipped with his face to the ground (τῷ προσώπῳ ἐπὶ τὴν γῆν), and said, 'You shall depart early (ὀρθρίσαντες) on your way'. Most of the commentators note such parallels, and in many cases allow that Luke has drawn inspiration from them (e.g. Alsup, Wanke, Kremer). Such a conclusion may indeed seem obvious in a story where Jesus expounds the things concerning him in *all* the scriptures, beginning from Moses.

Nevertheless, there is still more colour to the Lucan narrative than can be provided from all the OT types available; and important as these stories are for giving both the atmosphere and some of the detail, Luke can hardly have created so much from so little. I should like therefore to add a further suggestion. Luke has followed his Marcan source faithfully from 1.1 to 16.7(8), but there was a considerable section which he omitted, Mk 6.45-8.26, as covering Jesus' mission outside Galilee, a topic which he was reserving for Acts. Some part of the incident he has in fact drawn in from this Long Omission, especially in the controversy over washing (11.37-54; Mk 7.1-23). But the greater part has been unused, from the Walking on the Water in Mk 6.45ff., which has often been seen as a kind of parable of Christ's walking the water of death, to the blindness theme of 8.14-26, the physical blindness of the Bethsaidan and the spiritual blindness of the disciples. I would propose that Luke has allowed this unused material to provide the suggestion both for his Emmaus road story, and for the evening appearance story following.

The Emmaus story turns on the disciples' blindness: 'their eyes were held from recognizing him. . . O foolish (ἀνόητοι) and slow of heart (τῇ καρδίᾳ) to believe. . . Was it not necessary that the Christ should suffer?. . . Their eyes were opened, and they recognized him'. This seems first to echo the conversation in the boat in Mk 8.14-21, and then the following story of Peter confessing Christ, who sees but still does not see (8.27-33): 'Do you not yet understand (νοεῖτε)? Have you your heart (τὴν καρδίαν) hardened? Having eyes do you not see?. . . You are the Christ. . . It is necessary that the Son of Man should suffer' (Mk 8.17f., 29, 31). The word Luke uses for their eyes being opened, διηνοίχθησαν, is the word Mark uses for the opening of the ears of the stammerer, 'Ephphatha, διανοιχθῆτι' (Mk 7.34); and 'they recognized him' (ἐπέγνωσαν, cf. v.16 ἐπιγνῶναι αὐτόν) also comes in Mk 6.56, where the crowd runs round ἐπιγνόντες αὐτόν. Furthermore, the disciples' failure to see in the Marcan boat is related to the Feeding stories. It follows directly on from the Four Thousand in Mk 8.1-9, and it is by appeal to his breaking the loaves (ἄρτους ἔκλασα) on these two occasions that Jesus tries to bring them to understand. We seem to have an evocative parallel to this in the climax of the Emmaus story, when Jesus is known to the travellers τῇ κλάσει τοῦ ἄρτου (v. 35).

It is perhaps not possible to be sure where Luke's intentions end and where sub-conscious influence begins; but the extent of the parallels makes it plain that if there is any L tradition behind the story it will have been of a vestigial kind. Luke took it that Mark 16 indicated a second appearance alongside that to Peter, which took place also on Easter Day on the way to Galilee; and the themes of the disciples' initial failure to recognize Jesus, and of their enlightenment in the breaking of bread, have their origin in a meditation on the 'omitted' passages from Mark 8. But of course Christ's being known in the breaking of bread, and his immediate vanishing, are a part of the weekly experience of every Christian at the Eucharist. So the story is also structured like a Lucan eucharist as pictured in Acts 20.7-12. There the breaking of bread (κλάσαι ἄρτον) consists of Paul's extended λόγος, followed by his breaking the bread (κλάσας τὸν ἄρτον) and eating, with conversation (ὁμιλήσας). As the Pauline λόγος was an exposition of the fulfilment of the scriptures in Christ, so does the risen Jesus expound to the travellers the things concerning himself in all the scriptures, beginning from Moses and all the prophets (v. 27). Then, when they are seated at Emmaus, 'taking the bread he blessed, and breaking he gave it to them' (v. 30).

Does anything then remain for L to have provided? And what is to be said about Kremer's problems? Of the two names, Emmaus and Cleopas, I do not think that the former is very significant, for reasons hinted above. It is inconvenient for us that we are not quite sure where the place was, but it is very likely to have been Josephus' Ἀμμαοῦς (*B.J.* 7.217), the modern Kaloniyeh (Schürer, I, pp. 512f.), four miles out of Jerusalem on the Joppa road. It is only just over half Luke's sixty stades from the city, but four miles is a believable distance for the couple to have covered after sitting down to supper there. Galilean pilgrims may have travelled to and from Jerusalem by a variety of routes, and the Joppa road route would have the advantage of being flatter along the plain, and it would also avoid the main Samaritan centres on the hill-road. But in any case the most natural conclusion is that Luke thinks of the couple as Galileans (see above), and that he understands Emmaus to be the natural place to stop for the first night out of Jerusalem on the way to Galilee. So there is no need to suppose any L tradition for its association with the story: it may have been as familiar a gathering point for first-night-out pilgrims as the Tabard at Southwark was to Canterbury pilgrims in Chaucer's day.

The name Cleopas, however, probably is significant. It is usually taken that Cleopas is to be indentified with Clopas in Jn 19.25 ('Mary of Clopas'), though Fitzmyer points out that Cleopas is a shortened form of Cleopatrus, and Clopas an Aramaic name: but dual names of similar sound are too common to be a problem. The interest arises from the mention of a Clopas by Hegesippus (c. 160): 'And after James the Just had suffered martyrdom, as had also the Lord on the same account. . . the son of his uncle, Simeon the son of Clopas, was appointed bishop; whom all put forward, being a cousin of the Lord, as the second (bishop)' (ap. Eus. *H.E.* 4.22.4). The accepted date for James' martyrdom is 62, so the Clopas mentioned as James' uncle is likely to fit quite well as the Clopas of John 19 and the Cleopas of Luke 24: (1) family ties are clearly important in the nascent Christian community, and he is a close relative of Jesus, his uncle; (2) although he is a generation higher than Jesus, he has a son who became 'bishop' of Jerusalem in 62, and continued in the office for a long period (Eus. *H.E.* 3.32); so he is likely to have been not much older than Jesus; (3) the mention of Clopas in John 19 is likely to imply that he was a familiar name.

Clearly our evidence here is insufficient to justify confidence; but the possible identification would do much to resolve Kremer's difficulties. For Luke was a Pauline Christian, and Paul had been forced frequently to defend himself as an apostle against the supporters of Peter (Gal. 2; 1 Cor. 1-4; 2 Cor. 10-12). Peter remained the symbolic leader of Jewish Christianity in some of its forms for many years after his death: in the *Kerygmata Petrou* he debates with a Paul thinly disguised as Simon Magus, and the lowered image of Peter in the Fourth Gospel is probably also a reflection of epigonal struggles. In such a situation Luke was bound to have an ambivalent relation to Peter. On the one side he had been the Church's rock, who had strengthened his brethren in the early days, and behaved like a hero; but on the other, Luke cannot wait to push him into the background. As soon as he has converted Cornelius, he virtually disappears from the story, with the aid of Herod's persecution: when he takes part in the Council in Acts 15, he plays second fiddle to James, and is patronized by him, in a way that surprises the reader of Gal. 2.7f. Otherwise no more is heard of him: the reader of Acts understands that Paul had taken over the Church's mission. In Peter's place stands James, who is already understood to be leading the Jerusalem church in Acts 12.17, and even more at 21.18. Thus Luke has used the Jerusalem church, with its 'elders' and James, as a means of pushing Peter into the shadows, even though historically James was as much a threat to Paul as Peter (Gal. 2.12).

This visible ambivalence towards Peter in Acts may then account for the phenomena in Luke 24. Peter was unquestionably the first of the apostolic witnesses of the risen Lord, and his experience should be included. But there is no call to emphasize it: there are grievous wolves about, not sparing the flock (Acts 20.29), whom I have argued to be Jewish Christians (see on 6.39-49 above). Mark mentioned an appearance to Jesus' disciples as well as to Peter on the way to Galilee (16.6f.); and it will do more good to lay the stress there. Aside from the Eleven and the women, the only faithful group in Luke's eyes were Jesus' family, 'Mary the mother of Jesus and his ἀδελφοί' (Acts 1.14), so Luke is confined to thinking of his Emmaus travellers as Jesus' 'brethren': indeed, the same seems to be implied by Jesus' words in Mt. 28.10, 'Go and tell my brethren'. ἀδελφοί may be used by Luke in the standard elastic biblical way to include Jesus' male relatives like Cleopas. Of all the 'brethren' of Jesus, Luke might be thought to have a special motive for thinking of Cleopas, for he was father of Simeon, Luke's contemporary, bishop of the church that had been in Jerusalem, and that was now in weakness in Pella or elsewhere. Just as he used the Jerusalem elders and James to ease Peter out of the centre in Acts, so he might be pleased to use the father of James' successor, Simeon, to perform the same office over the Resurrection. A divine appearance to the father would not be out of Lucan character either: he began the Gospel with an angelic appearance to John's father, and he may suitably end with an appearance of the Lord to Simeon's father. We may note that Origen believed the companion of Cleopas to have been his son Symeon (*c.Cels.* 2.62, 68); so the link was familiar into the third century.

In such matters our evidence is limited, and the account I have just offered is inevitably speculative. Its attraction is that it offers an explanation for the features picked out by Kremer. The Emmaus story was told in the Lucan church in preference to a Petrine story because of the confrontation in Luke's day between Pauline Christians like Luke and Jewish Christians giving authority to Peter. Luke cannot deny Peter's position (nor does he wish to): but he has given pride of place, and his utmost art, to describing a non-Petrine appearance. We have a parallel in Acts for his transferring the attention to the Jerusalem church, and we have evidence which makes it plausible to think that Cleopas was father of that church's leader in Luke's day. The weakness of the Jerusalem church in the 80s would make the honouring of its leadership a harmless exercise.

For the rest, we seem to have nothing but Lucan thinking. As Evans says (pp. 93f.), the whole scene reads like a sermon from Acts. Jesus had been a prophet, mighty in deed and word before God and all the people (v. 19). It is Luke who tells us that in Jesus a great prophet had arisen (7.16), and that he was first preached as the prophet like Moses (Acts 3.22f.); he has Stephen speak of Moses as 'mighty in his words and deeds' (Acts 7.22), Zechariah and Elizabeth righteous 'before God' (1.6, cf. v. 8), and Jesus escape arrest 'before the people' (20.26R). He had been crucified by 'our chief priests and rulers' handing him over (v. 29)—the standard Lucan piling of the guilt on to the authorities' shoulders, leaving the people sympathetic. 'We hoped that this was he who should redeem Israel' (v. 21): Anna had spoken of Jesus to all who were expecting the redemption of Jerusalem in 2.38, and at the End the Lucan disciple is to lift up his head, for his redemption draws near (21.28). The cross is not spoken of as atoning for sins, but (as so often in Luke) as necessary in the providence of God: 'ought not the Christ to suffer?' (v. 26). All this is triumphantly proclaimed as foreshown in the Bible: 'And beginning from Moses and all the prophets he expounded to them in all the scriptures the things concerning himself' (v. 27). Nor were these things done in a corner (Acts 26.26): 'Are you the only person staying in Jerusalem and unaware of what has happened there in these days?' (v. 18). At the end of the ministry stands the Ascension, as usual in Luke: 'ought not the Christ to suffer and to enter his glory?' Perhaps we should add the Eucharist as a Lucan emphasis also.

But the Emmaus story bears the Lucan stamp as much by its art as by its doctrine. Dupont, in a famous essay, drew out the parallels with the Ethiopian Eunuch in Acts 8: the puzzlement, the explanation of scripture by a heaven-sent messenger, the moment of enlightenment, the climax with sacrament and joy. But the reader feels something more pervasively characteristic besides, which sets the mode of telling apart from the dry Matthaean appearance of Mt. 28.17-20, or the symbol-laden John 21. It is that concern with human feelings which we have seen in the Prodigal Son and the Samaritan and other Lucan stories, and which I have illustrated under §4, with all the excuses and soliloquies and parties and the rest. Of our NT authors none could express the disciples' unhappiness so subtly as is done with 'And they stood still, downcast' (v. 17); nor, by contrast, their joyful alacrity, 'And getting up that very hour...'; nor the emotive power of 'Was not our heart burning within us?'

24.13 εἶναι + part., πορεύεσθαι, ἐν-αὐτῇ-τῇ-ἡμέρᾳ*, ἀπέχειν of distance, Ἰερουσαλήμ*, ᾗ-ὄνομα. Hapaxes: στάδιον, ἐξήκοντα.

24.14 καὶ-αὐτοί*, speaking πρός*, ἀλλήλους, περί, pleon. πᾶς, ταῦτα, τὰ + part. ὁμιλεῖν, 0/0/2+2. Hapax; συμβαίνειν, but cf. Acts 3.10, ἐπὶ τῷ συμβεβηκότι αὐτῷ, +2 Acts.

24.15 καὶ ἐγένετο ἐν τῷ + inf.* + καὶ*, αὐτός nom.*, ἐγγίζειν*, συμπορεύεσθαι. συζητεῖν, 22.23, ×2 Acts, Mk 8.11.

24.16 τοῦ + inf.*. τοῦ μή, 4.42, 0/0/2+5. κρατεῖσθαι, Acts 2.24, only.

24.17 εἶπεν-δὲ-πρός*, speaking πρός*, ἀλλήλους. Hapaxes: ἀντιβάλλειν (ἀντι—2/0/13+7), σκυθρωπός. τίνες οἱ λόγοι οὗτοι, cf. 4.36R, τίς ὁ λόγος οὗτος; οἱ-λόγοι-οὗτοι, 24.44 +2 Acts.

24.18 ὀνόματι*, εἶπεν-πρός*, Ἰερουσαλημ*, τὰ + part., γίνεσθαι, ἐν-ταῖς-ἡμέραις-ταύταις*. Hapax: παροικεῖν (Gen. 19.9, cf. -ος, Acts 7.6, 29, -ία Acts 13.17). For Cleopas cf. Zahn, pp. 712-14.

24.19 εἶπεν ×2, τὰ + prep.*, περί, γίνεσθαι, ἀνήρ*, ἐνάντιον, ὁ-θεός, pleon. πᾶς, ὁ-λαός*. ἀνήρ + noun, Acts 3.14 and common ἄνδρες ἀδελφοί. cf. Acts 7.22 δυνατὸς ἐν λόγοις καὶ ἔργοις αὐτοῦ. ποῖος, cf. 5.19R.

24.20 τε*, οἱ-ἄρχοντες*. ὅπως τε, cf. καὶ ὡς v. 35. The suggestion that the crucifixion was carried out by Jewish authorities is in line with 23.25 and other texts.

24.21 ἐλπίζειν, αὐτός nom., μέλλειν, γε*, σύν*, καὶ also, pleon. πάντα, ταῦτα (×2), ἡμέρα, ἄγειν, ἀφ'οὗ, γίνεσθαι. καί γε Acts 17.27. ἄγειν in this impersonal sense is unique. σὺν πᾶσι τούτοις, cf. 16.26 ἐν πᾶσι τούτοις. Hapax: λυτροῦσθαι.

24.22 ἀλλὰ-καί, τις, γίνεσθαι. Hapax: ὀρθρινός (cf. 24.1; 21.38). ἐξιστάναι act. Acts 8.9; cf. perhaps ἔκστασις, Mk 16.8. ἐπὶ τὸ μν. 24.12R.

24.23 μή + part., εὑρίσκειν, καὶ = also, ζῆν. ὀπτασίαν ἑωρακέναι 1.22; ὀπτ. Acts 26.19; ἑωρακέναι, 0/0/2+2.

24.24 τις, ὁ + prep.*, σύν*, εὑρίσκειν, καθώς, καὶ = also, εἶπαν. Vague τινες = one, cf. Acts 17.28, where τινες = Aratus.

24.25 καὶ-αὐτός*, εἶπεν-πρός*, τοῦ + inf.*, ὅς in attraction*, pleon. πάντα. Hapaxes: ἀνόητος (cf. Mk 8.17), βραδύς (cf. Acts 27.7). ὦ 2/1/2+4. πιστεύειν ἐπί, Acts 9.42; 11.17; 16.31; 22.19.

24.26 οὐχί, ταῦτα, δεῖ, δόξα. 'To enter his glory' may refer to the Ascension.

24.27 ἀρξάμενος-ἀπό, Μωϋσῆς-καὶ-οἱ-προφῆται*, pleon. πᾶς (×2), τὰ + prep.*, περί, ἑαυτόν. Hapax: διερμηνεύειν (cf. Acts 9.36, ×5 1 Cor. 12-14).

24.28 ἐγγίζειν*, οὗ, πορεύεσθαι (×2), καὶ-αὐτός*. Hapax: προσποιεῖσθαι. πορρώτερον, cf. πόρρω, 14.32, -θεν, 17.12.

24.29 μένειν (2), κλίνειν*, τοῦ + inf.*, σύν*. Hapaxes: παραβιάζεσθαι (Acts 16.15; Gen. 19.3A, 9), ἑσπέρα (0/0/1+2, cp. ὀψία, 7/5/0+0). Cf. ἡμέρα ἤρξατο κλίνειν, 9.12R, ἑσπέρα ἤδη, Acts 4.3.

24.30 καὶ ἐγένετο-ἐν-τῷ + inf.*, κατακλίνειν*, εὐλογεῖν, ἐπιδιδόναι. Cf. 7.36, εἰσελθὼν. . .κατεκλίθη.

24.31 διανοίγειν*, καὶ-αὐτός*, γίνεσθαι. Hapax: ἄφαντος. Cf. 4 Kgdms 6.17 διανοῖξον δὴ τοὺς ὀφθαλμοὺς τοῦ π., where the general situation of spiritual blindness is similar.

24.32 εἶπαν-πρός*, ἀλλήλούς, οὐχί, εἶναι + part., ὡς = when/while (×2)*, διανοίγειν*. καιομένη ἦν, 12.35; cf. Ps. 38.4 ἐθερμάνθη ἡ καρδία μου...καὶ ἐκκαυθήσεται πῦρ. διανοίγειν of scriptures, Acts 17.3.

24.33 ἀναστάς*, αὐτῇ-τῇ-ὥρᾳ*, ὑποστρέφειν*, Ἰερουσαλήμ*, εὑρίσκειν, ὁ + prep., σύν*. Hapax: ἀθροίζειν, cf. 11.29, ἐπαθροίζεσθαι. The eleven and companions, as at 24.9; the same tendency which puts Peter in the shade will not allow the Twelve a monopoly.

24.34 ὁ-κύριος = Jesus*, ὤφθη. ὄντως, 23.47. ὤφθη Σίμωνι, cf. 1 Cor. 15.5, ὤφθη Κηφᾷ: an anarthrous dative of a proper name is, I think, unexampled elsewhere in L-A, and suggests that Luke has retained the structure of the original phrase. Dupont (*Fs* Ubach, p. 353) says Luke wishes 'by this archaism to preserve its stereotyped character to the ancient announcement of faith'; Dietrich (p. 159), 'Σίμωνι belongs to an early layer in the history of tradition, like 22.31 and 5.1ff.'. But at 5.1ff. Peter has not received his surname, and a contrast of a deliberate kind may have been introduced by Luke at 22.31. So perhaps here: surely the early Church knew Peter as Cephas, and will have used the Pauline form—the Lucan 'Simon' takes the edge off it a little, just as does its position as postscript to the Emmaus appearance. Luke knows 1 Cor. (ch. 4).

24.35 καὶ-αὐτοί*, τά + prep.*. Hapax: ἐξηγεῖσθαι (0/0/1+4). τῇ-κλάσει-τοῦ-ἄρτου, Acts 2.42. ἐγνώσθη αὐτοῖς, cf. Acts 9.24, ἐγνώσθη τῷ Σαύλῳ.

c. The Appearance in Jerusalem, 24.36-53   Easter Day

Luke knew that Jesus had appeared at least six times to apostolic men (1 Cor. 15.5ff.): first to Cephas, then to the Twelve, then at a mass appearance, then to James, then to all the apostles, and finally Paul. The appearance to Paul he describes in Acts 9, and that to all the apostles, who are named in Acts 1.13, as at the Ascension. He knew that the Pauline appearance had taken place some time after such events had generally ceased ('as to one born out of due time'), and he signifies the distinction by formally closing the main sequence 'after forty days': his form of the appearance 'to all the apostles' is marked off as a permanent parting till Jesus' coming, *the* Ascension (Acts 1.11). Luke is not anxious to encourage Jewish Christians by mentioning any experience of James, so he contents himself by referring to the two middle appearances with the general statement, 'he showed himself to (the apostles) alive after his passion by many proofs' (Acts 1.3). He has already mentioned the appearance to Simon; and that to the Twelve (or more accurately the Eleven) can provide a suitable climax to his Gospel. In this way the Lucan

account of the appearances can be seen to square quite satisfyingly
within the Pauline tradition: indeed, it is hardly credible that he
should not have known that tradition, or have wished to contradict
it, even without the evidence that he knew 1 Corinthians. An
important corollary of this general dovetailing is that our present
passage is seen by Luke as the second of the sequence of six
appearances, that 'to the Twelve': it is not the fifth and last (excludng
Paul), and it is *not* the Ascension. This appearance took place on
Easter Day in the evening, that forty days later; and Luke uses a
diferent verb for Jesus' (temporary) departure.

24.36-43. It is likely that historically whatever experience the
Twelve had will have taken place when they came together to eat in
the evening; and with church meetings in the evening (Acts 20.7), an
evening meal setting must have seemed inevitable to Luke. But here
for once we have no reason for scepsis about tradition. It is only
when we come to the details of the occasion that the tradition hypothesis weakens. For the numerous coincidences with John 20 cannot
be shown to go back to a common tradition, but are explicable as a
Johannine expansion of Luke: cf. Neyrinck (*Fs* Dupont). Rather, we
are struck with the similarities with a second unit from the Long
Omission from Mark, Jesus' Walking on the Water. Perhaps from the
beginning this story was something of an allegory of the resurrection.
Dennis Nineham (*Mark*, p. 181) cites A.E.J. Rawlinson: 'To the
Roman Church. . . it must have indeed appeared that *the wind was
contrary*. . . They are to learn from this story that they are *not*
forsaken, that the Lord watches over them unseen, and that He
Himself—no phantom but the Living One, Master of winds and
waves—will surely come quickly for their salvation, even though it
be *in the fourth watch of the night*' (Rawlinson, *Mark*, p. 88). It looks
as if Luke has transferred the colours of the Marcan story to his own
resurrection situation. In Mark they thought (ἔδοξαν) he was a ghost
(φάντασμα); in Luke they thought (ἐδόκουν) they were seeing a
spirit. 'Be of good cheer', says Jesus in Mark, 'It is I (ἐγώ εἰμι), fear
not', for they were troubled (ἐταράχθησαν). Luke says they were
startled and frightened, and Jesus said, 'Why are you troubled
(τεταραγμένοι)?. . . See my hands and my feet that it is I (ἐγώ εἰμι)
myself'. Mark says they did not understand about the loaves, but
their heart (sing.) was hardened: Luke says, 'Why do questionings
arise in your *heart* (sing.—see below)?. . . He opened their mind to

understand the scriptures'. In Mark Jesus has blessed the bread and portioned (ἐμέρισεν) the fish: in Luke he blesses the bread at Emmaus and eats a *portion* (μέρος) of the *fish* now. It seems likely that Luke has filled in an otherwise colourless tradition of the appearance to the disciples from the similar Marcan story of the Lake.

Apart from the bare traditional fact, and the parallels with Mark 6, the opening part of the scene (vv. 36-43) contains little that is not specifically Lucan. It follows the same basic structure which we have seen with the Empty Tomb and Emmaus incidents. Jesus appears with a greeting (v. 36), as he did on the road, and the angels did at the tomb; the disciples respond with panic and fear to the supernatural presence, as the women had, and with misunderstanding (a spirit), as on the road (a stranger); they are reassured first by Jesus showing them his hands and feet, and then by his eating the fish before them. This is the final reassurance which Luke's hearers are to receive, so it not only transcends Peter's seeing of the empty grave-clothes and the breaking of bread and word at Emmaus: it is a doubled and ultimate reassurance, in being tangible. Jesus said, 'Touch me and see', and still they disbelieved for joy: then he actually ate in their presence. So the story follows Luke's essential Resurrection pattern: appearance, disbelief-misunderstanding, reassurance. So important is this dynamic that both the evangelist and his audience have forgotten that Peter and the Emmaus disciples have already seen the Lord, and have no business to be panic-stricken and disbelieving.

A particular Lucan stress is on the physicality of Jesus' resurrected body. We have already found something similar with the physicality of the Holy Spirit at Jesus' baptism, as the earnest of its reality: not Mark's, 'he saw the Spirit descending', but 'the Holy Spirit descended in bodily form like a dove' (3.22R). So here the reality of the resurrection is testified by its physicality: Jesus was not a spirit without flesh and bones, but one could touch him, and he could eat. The touching comes in Mt. 28.9 too, when the women 'took hold of him by his feet', though nothing is made of it; and it is elaborated in John 20 with the Thomas story. But only Luke has Jesus actually eat, and he returns to the point in Acts 1.4 and 10.41. The purpose of this emphasis is not entirely plain, but it may be related to the Docetism which Ignatius opposes with the aid of Lk. 24.39. In a rough citation, 'Lay hold and handle me. . . ' Ignatius presses home his conclusion,

'he suffered truly, as also he raised himself truly' (*Smyrn*. 2f.): see
Neyrinck again (*Fs* Dupont, pp. 572-77). But whether this is Luke's
interest or not, physicality is a theme of L–A especially. So bound up
is he in it that he forgets to note that the disciples came to faith, even
after the fish; they are left 'still disbelieving for joy'—like the Lucan
Rhoda, who did not open the door for joy (Acts 12.14), or the
disciples who sleep for grief (22.45).

24.44-48. So Luke has enough from Paul and Mark and his own
thinking to provide for the incident of the appearance: what he still
needs is a farewell message from the Lord, and for that he turns to
Matthew. Matthew had provided three new post-Resurrection
stories: the Lord's meeting with the women, the plot to say Jesus'
body was stolen, and the appearance to the Eleven in Galilee. The
first of these is nearly identical in content with the women's meeting
with the angel, and the second was relevant to Matthew's church
alone, perhaps. But the third scene is of interest to Luke; and of great
interest because it is an encounter between Jesus and the Apostles,
such as he is in process of describing. It provides the two things that
he needs to close the Gospel on a climactic note, an assurance of
Jesus' power on the one side ('All authority. . . '), and a commission
on the other ('Go therefore and make disciples. . . ').

Unfortunately Matthew seems to say that it took place on a
mountain in Galilee, but as with Mk 16.7 Luke is convinced that this
had not been so, and he once more applies his powers of exegesis.
Matthew said, 'The eleven disciples ἐπορεύθησαν εἰς Galilee, to the
mountain where Jesus commanded them' (28.16); but there is no
mention anywhere in Matthew of his having specified some
mountain in Galilee. It seems likely rather that Jesus told them
during the course of his present meeting that they should come with
him to Bethany on the Mount of Olives, where he had lodged his last
week (Mt. 21.17; Lk. 21.37). ἐπορεύθησαν εἰς will then mean 'they
went *towards*': Luke uses the same phrase himself in this meaning—
9.53, 'his face was πορευόμενον εἰς Jerusalem'; 17.11, ἐν τῷ
πορεύεσθαι εἰς Jerusalem'; cf, also Acts 27.6 'a boat πλέον εἰς Italy',
though it never gets there. He understood the εἰς of Mk 16.7 in the
same sense. This reading enables Luke to tack the Matthaean
appearance to the Eleven on to the scene he already has. He takes
Mt. 28.16f. as Matthew's account of the action at the end of the
evening: the Eleven went with Jesus to the Mount of Olives on the

way to Galilee, as he told them (24.50). 'They worshipped when they had seen him' (Mt. 28.17): Luke says, 'And when they had *worshipped* him they returned' (24.52)', after the parting at Bethany.

For the rest, Luke understands Jesus' last words in Matthew to take place in the room in Jerusalem: indeed, Mt. 28.18 seems to resume from the beginning, 'And Jesus approaching spoke to them, saying'. Matthew's comment οἱ δὲ ἐδίστασαν also agrees well with the scene of doubt and disbelief which Luke has just described. Matthew gives four substantial points in Jesus' Farewell, and Luke accepts and adapts all four:

(1) Jesus *assures* the disciples, 'All authority in heaven and on earth is given to me' (v. 18b). Although this is sometimes disputed, it seems likely that Matthew is giving a verification of Jesus' repeated prophecies that the Son of Man must suffer but will rise again, for the words of the prophecies and the assurance seem to be combined in Dan. 7.13f., '(one) like a son of man came on the clouds of heaven. . . and there was given to him authority, and all the nations' (LXX). Matthew's meaning will then be: Daniel 7 is fulfilled—Jesus suffered but now has all authority, and will come on the clouds in judgment. Luke begins Jesus' words with his expounding scripture to the group (vv. 44f.); 'and he said to them that thus it is written that the Christ should suffer and rise from the dead the third day' (v. 46). It is the same prophecy, based on Dan. 7, which Luke gave at 9.22 and 18.31-33 with the words 'the Son of Man', and to which he now refers with 'These are my words which I spoke with you while still with you. . . '

(2) Jesus *commissions* the universal mission: 'Go therefore and make disciples of all nations (πάντα τὰ ἔθνη), baptizing them in the name of the Father and of the Son and of the Holy Spirit' (Mt. 28.19). Making disciples and baptizing are the language of Jewish, churchy Matthew. In Lucan language this means 'that repentance for remission of sins should be proclaimed to *all nations* (πάντα τὰ ἔθνη) *in his name*. Making disciples is done by proclaiming forgiveness, and baptism will then follow repentance. Jesus adds that he will send 'the promise of my *Father*', which is power from on high, thus pointing forward to the coming of the Holy Spirit at Pentecost, and at baptism.

(3) The Church's *message*: 'teaching them to observe all that I command you' (Mt. 28.20a). Here the evangelists diverge in content,

for the gospel to Matthew was much concerned with the keeping of all Jesus' commandments. But to Luke, as we have just seen, what has to be proclaimed is a message of the fulfilment of scripture, Christ's passion and resurrection, repentance and forgiveness: those were 'my words which I spoke with you while still with you' (v. 44). The phrasing is not far from Matthew's 'all that I commanded you', but this time the meaning is quite distinct.

(4) Jesus' *permanent presence*: 'and lo, I (καὶ ἰδοὺ ἐγώ) am with you always. . . ' (Mt. 28.20b). Luke believed no less than Matthew in the reality of the divine presence with the Church, but he thinks of this presence as rather that of the Holy Spirit: so he ends Jesus' words, 'And lo, I (καὶ ἰδοὺ ἐγώ) send the promise of my Father upon you. . . power from on high'. Thus all the four themes of the Matthaean Farewell recur in Lucanized form in the Lucan Farewell; with enough phrases in common to support the dependence, but without perhaps making it obvious.

It is a commonplace that the themes of Jesus' Farewell in Luke are favourite ideas of the evangelist: the fulfilment of scripture, the call to repentance for the forgiveness of sins (cf. especially Acts 10.43, 'to him bear all the prophets witness that everyone who believes in him receives forgiveness of sins through his name'), the world-wide mission beginning from Jerusalem (cf. Acts 1.4, 'not to leave Jerusalem, but to wait for the promise of the Father which you heard from me'), the coming of the Spirit and the witness of the apostles (cf. Acts 5.32, 'we are witnesses of these sayings, and the Holy Spirit').

24.50-53. Luke now uses his interpretation of Mt. 28.16f. to round off his story, and to close his Gospel. Matthew's 'The eleven disciples went towards Galilee to the mountain where Jesus told them' becomes Luke's 'He led them out outside as far as to Bethany'. That was the way Jesus had come in from Galilee, and in 19.29 Bethany and the Mount of Olives are mentioned together. Bethany is below the peak, whence Jesus' Ascension will take place (Acts 1.12). He raises his hands in blessing, the only imaginable farewell gesture; was parted from them (διέστη) and was carried up (ἀνεφέρετο) to heaven. Luke grades his verbs for the parting at his post-Resurrection scenes. At Emmaus 'he became invisible from them' (24.31)—Jesus is only just risen, and is constantly visible to his own, at least three times in the day. Now there is a more formal parting with a blessing, and he is carried up to heaven. It is the end of the Gospel. For

Ascension Day Luke has an even more dignified and gentle movement: he is lifted up (ἐπήρθη) and a cloud receives him out of their sight. Angels are then at hand to explain that this is the last time till he comes again. For the Ascension alone Luke uses the formal, time-honoured ἀνελήμφθη, Acts 1.2, 11; Lk. 9.51.

Matthew says the eleven disciples worshipped Jesus—προσεκύνησαν, the verb he has so often used with Jesus for object through the Gospel. Luke has used it twice only, in QC matter in the Temptation; and he uses it four times in Acts, twice of true worship of God at festivals (Acts 8.27; 24.11), twice of false worship (Acts 7.43: 10.25). So his προσκυνήσαντες here (see below) is probably a reminiscence of Matthew; as perhaps is also his μετὰ χαρᾶς μεγάλης, which comes of the women in Mt. 28.8. For the rest, we have Luke's typical ὑπέστρεψαν at the end of his tale; and the Gospel ends in the Temple, where it began, and where the disciples will spend so much of their time in the early chapters of Acts. With so much evidence of Lucan themes, not too much non-Lucan matter remains to be explained.

'However', says Kremer (p. 151), 'it would be wrong to take the whole pericope as a mere invention of the evangelist'. He gives as traces of pre-Lucan tradition: tension with the Emmaus story, as in v. 34 both groups of disciples are confident of the resurrection while here they are frightened and unbelieving (including 'Simon'!); failure to mention the disciples' faith after Jesus' eating; the presence of traditions about an appearance to the Eleven in 1 Corinthians, Mk 16.7 (implied), Mt. 28.16-20, and above all in John; the presence of similar statements of the kerygma in Pauline letters, especially 1 Cor. 15.3-10; and the recurrence of Jerusalem and Bethany in Acts 1 as the site of a final departure of Jesus, which is also assumed by Paul's 'and last of all to me. . . ' (1 Cor. 15.8). Actually, Kremer and I are near to agreeing. I also think the pericope is not a mere invention, but that Luke has sources, one of which is 1 Corinthians. We differ in that I think he is using 1 Corinthians itself and Mt. 28.16-20 itself, and not a lost tradition common to various NT authors; I see no evidence for denying John's knowledge of Luke, and much evidence that Luke is drawing on the Long Omission. His regular pattern of Appearance–Disbelief (Fear, Lack of Understanding, etc.)–Assurance, which in this case draw in the themes of the Walking on the Water, entail some tension with the joyful close of the Emmaus story; and (whether by art or by muddle) Luke has kept the disciples' joy and praise of God to the end of the tale (vv. 52f.). We have seen often enough that Luke does not require a lost source to contradict himself.

Note on the Text

There is more difficulty over the text of Luke 24 than over any other chapter, with the Western tradition (normally Dabdeff²lr¹ with some other support) frequently giving a shorter text. I have already noted the similar situation at 22.19b-20, but the following omissions over against the Egyptian tradition are notorious in ch. 24:

v. 3	τοῦ κυρίου	v. 6	οὔκ ἐστιν ὧδε ἀλλὰ ἡγέρθη
v. 12	ὁ δὲ Πέτρος ... (whole verse)	v. 36	καὶ λέγει αὐτοῖς Εἰρήνη ὑμῖν
v. 40	καὶ τοῦτο εἰπὼν ...(whole verse)	v. 49	ἰδού
v. 51	καὶ ἀνεφέρετο εἰς τὸν οὐρανόν	v. 52	προσκυνήσαντες αὐτόν

These differences have been often discussed, seven of them (omitting v. 49) being taken together, with 22.19b-20 and Mt. 27.49, by Westcott and Hort (II, pp. 175-77) as 'Western Non-Interpolations'. After a century in which there was a general willingness to justify the Western readings, the pendulum has now swung back, largely due to the presence of most of the longer forms in p⁷⁵. For the arguments see Metzger, pp. 184-93, and Aland, *NTS* (1966).

The argumentation above is in part dependent upon reading the longer text. Fortunately all the words in common with Mark 6 are undisputed; and even an agreed gloss, 'It is I, be not afraid' in v. 36 GPW c, which occurs in the Walking on the Water at Mk 6.50, shows that the link was still present in the minds of copyists (Kremer, p. 139; cf. D's φάντασμα for πνεῦμα in the same verse, = Mk 6.49). The only partial exception is the singular ἐν τῇ καρδίᾳ (= Mk 6.52), which is read by p⁷⁵BD it sa against the major MS tradition with ταῖς καρδίαις. But the argument for Luke's use of Matthew would be weakened considerably without ἰδοὺ in v. 49 and προσκυνήσαντες αὐτόν in v. 52, both of which are missing in the Western texts. It is therefore convenient for me that all these disputed words are printed in N-A²⁶.

If the discovery of p[75] has turned the scale on the attestation issue, it seems that the study of Lucan style has also been important. I have already noted the Lucan style of v. 12, and of τοῦ κυρίου in v. 3: so now λέγει, εἰρήνη ὑμῖν in v. 36 recalls 10.5, λέγετε, εἰρήνη τῷ οἴκῳ τούτῳ (uniquely); εἰπών in v. 40 has figures of 0/0/6+20, and καὶ τοῦτο εἰπών is paralleled at Acts 1.9; 7.60; 19.41; there are enough parallels for the historic present λέγει (6+2, Neirynck, *MA*, p. 229); and even ἀνεφέρετο which is a hapax, looks right, since Luke would not want ἀνελήμφθη, which is reserved for the Ascension, and there is no closer passive verb. So it seems that we can drop the muddling phrase 'non-interpolations', which has darkened counsel so long, and speak of 'Western omissions'. The Western text often does omit (Metzger, p. 192 n. 3), and the concentration of omissions in Luke 24 may be due to nothing more exciting than fatigue.

24.36 ταῦτα, αὐτός nom., ἔστην*, ἐν-μέσῳ, εἰρήνη*. εἰρήνη ὑμῖν, see note above.

24.37 γίνεσθαι, (δοκεῖν = think). πτοεῖσθαι 21.9R, ἔμφοβος γενόμενος, 24.5R, 0/0/2+2, πνεῦμα = ghost, Acts 23.8.

24.38 εἶπεν, εἶναι + part., διαλογισμός*-(τῇ-καρδίᾳ). δ. ἀναβαίνουσιν ἐν τῇ καρδίᾳ ὑμῶν, cf. Acts 7.23, ἀνέβη ἐπὶ τὴν καρδίαν αὐτοῦ. For the links with Mark 6, cf. F.W. Danker, *New Age*, p. 252. καρδία sing. + gen. pl. 1/6/6.

24.39 πούς, αὐτός nom., καθώς. Hapaxes: ψηλαφᾶν (Acts 17.27), ὀστέον. Hands-and-feet, Acts 21.11.

24.40 εἰπών*, πούς. If ἐπιδεικνύναι is read, cf. 17.14, 0/0/2+2. καὶ τοῦτο εἰπών, see above.

24.41 ἔτι, θαυμάζειν, εἶπεν, τις. Hapaxes: βρώσιμος (cf. βρῶμα, 1/1/2), ἔνθαδε, 0/0/1+5. ἀπιστεῖν, 24.11R, Acts 28.44.

24.42 ἐπιδιδόναι*, μέρος sing. Hapax: ὀπτός (cf. verbal adjectives like γνωστός).

24.43 ἐνώπιον*.

24.44 εἶπεν-δὲ-πρός*, speak πρός*, ἔτι, ὤν, σύν*, δεῖ, pleon. πάντα, τὰ-γεγραμμένα*, Μωϋσῆς-καὶ-οἱ-προφῆται*. οὗτοι οἱ λόγοι of Jesus' necessary Passion and Resurrection, 9.28, 44; cf. 24.8, (17). ἔτι ὤν, 24.6: the phrase looks back on Jesus' life from a distance (Kremer, p. 142). πληροῦν of scripture, 4.21 ×3 Acts. ὁ-νόμος-Μ. 2.22, 0/0/2+3. ψαλμοί, 20.42R, 0/0/2+2. Bultmann (p. 289): 'It is now quite clear that the fashioning of the (missionary) motif in Mt. 28.16-20; Lk. 24.44-49; Acts 1.4-8, with all the Johannine stories, is a quite late achievement of Hellenistic Christianity. For these stories presuppose the universal mission'. But Bultmann thought of a common lost source, and only Finegan (pp. 91f.) sees that Luke could have expanded it all from material in Matthew, even the mountain; and he not very clearly. Marshall represents orthodoxy, with ominous confidence, 'It cannot be doubted that common traditions underlie these accounts'.

24.45 διανοίγειν*, τοῦ + inf.*. Hapax: νοῦς (cf. ἀνόητοι, v. 25). νοῦν/ συνιέναι cf. Mk 8.17, οὔπω νοεῖτε οὐδὲ συνίετε (p. 783).

24.46 εἶπεν, γέγραπται, ἡμέρα. ἀναστῆναι ἐκ νεκρῶν 0/3/3+5; 24.26, cf. v. 7.

24.47 ὄνομα, μετάνοια, ἄφεσις-ἁμαρτιῶν, ἀρξάμενοι-ἀπό, Ἰερουσαλημ*, (πάντα pleon). ἐπὶ-τῷ-ὀνόματι-X, 3/3/5+6. Isa. 2.2-4 is usually suggested as a basis for a prophecy of a mission from Jerusalem. For the loose ἀρξ. ἀπὸ I., cf. Acts 1.22.

24.48 ταῦτα. For Lucan omission of copula (with N–A²⁶), cf. 24.17, 44 etc. μάρτυς, 2/1/2+13.

24.49 ἐφ᾽ ὑμᾶς*, ἐν-τῇ-πόλει, ἕως-οὗ. Hapax: ἐπαγγελία (×8 Acts). ἐξ-ύψους, 1.78. ἐνδύειν metaph. here only in Gospels, ×4 1 Cor. 15.

24.50 ἐπαίρειν*, εὐλογεῖν. Hapax: ἐξάγειν (×8 Acts). ἕως + prep., Acts 17.17; 21.5; 26.11. The blessing forms a natural end to the scene, but is omitted at Acts 1.9. It is remarkable that many commentators take this scene as identical with the Ascension: in recent years P.A. van Stempvoort (*NTS* [1958]), Stephen Wilson (pp. 96-107), even Marshall. But Luke clearly says that this took place on Easter Day, that forty days later; and carefully does not use the final ἀνελήμφθη of scripture here.

24.51 καὶ-ἐγένετο-ἐν-τῷ*, εὐλογεῖν. Hapax: ἀναφέρεσθαι (see above). διέστη, 0/0/2+1 (other senses); cf. ἔστη, ἀνέστη. εἰς τὸν οὐρανόν, Acts 1.11 (×3).

24.52 καὶ αὐτοί*, ὑποστρέφειν*, Ἰερουσαλήμ*. μετὰ-χαρᾶς-μεγάλης Mt. 28.8; also cf. 2.10; 8.13; 10.17.

24.53 εἶναι + part., εὐλογεῖν, ὁ-θεός*. διὰ-παντός, 0/0/1+3, Acts 2.25 LXX; 10.2; 24.16.

Dupont, J., 'Les pèlerins d'Emmaüs (Lc 24,13-35)', in R.M. Diaz, ed., *Miscellanea biblica B. Ubach* (Montserrat, 1953), pp. 349-74.

Schubert, P., 'The Structure and Significance of Luke 24', *Fs* Bultmann (Berlin, 1954), pp. 165-86.

van Stempvoort, P.A. 'The Interpretation of the Ascension in Luke and Acts', *NTS* 5 (1958), pp. 30-42.

Grass, H., *Ostergeschehen und Osterberichte* (2nd edn; Göttingen, 1962).

Betz, H.D., 'The Origin and Nature of Christian Faith according to the Emmaus Legend (Luke 24.13-35)', *Interpretation* 23 (1969), pp. 32-46.

Bode, E.L., *The First Easter Morning* (Ana. Bib. 45; Rome, 1970).

Evans, C.F., *Resurrection and the New Testament* (SBT 2.12; London, 1970).

Lohfink, G., *Die Himmelfahrt Jesu* (SANT 26; Munich, 1971).

Fuller, R.H., *The Formation of the Resurrection Narratives* (New York, 1971).

Wanke, J., *Die Emmauserzählung* (Erfurter th. St.31; Leipzig, 1973).

Alsup, J.E., *The Post-Resurrection Appearance Stories of the Gospel Tradition* (Calwer th. Mon.5; Stuttgart, 1975)

Kremer, J., *Die Osterevangelien—Geschichten um Geschichte* (Stuttgart, 1977).

Dillon, R.J., *From Eye-Witnesses to Ministers of the Word* (Ana. Bib. 82; Rome, 1978).

Guillaume, J.-M., *Luc interprète des anciennes traditions sur la résurrection de Jésus* (Paris, 1979).

Neirynck, F., *Evangelica* (BETL 60; Leuven, 1982), Part II, pp. 181-488.

Neirynck, F., 'John and the Synoptics: the Empty Tomb Stories', *NTS* 30 (1984), pp. 161-87.

Neirynck, F., 'Lc 24,36-43: Un récit lucanien', in *Fs* Dupont (1985), pp. 655-80.

A Lucan Vocabulary

The expressions below are 'Lucan' either in the sense that they are
introduced by Luke redactorally, or in the sense that they occur with
a markedly greater frequency in Luke than in Mark and Matthew,
and in at least three different contexts: for discussion see pp. 79-86.
Figures represent number of uses in Matthew/Mark/Luke+Acts.
Unmarked references are to Lucan redactions of Mark; those marked
'Q' to passages where Luke differs from Matthew (=QD elsewhere in
this book). If two references are given, there may be further
redactoral instances. Expressions marked * pass Hawkins' criteria: at
least four uses in different contexts, and at least twice the combined
number of uses in Mark and Matthew.

Ἀβρααμ	7/1/15+7	
ἀγαλλιᾶσθαι/-σις	1/0/4+3	10.21Q
ἀγαπᾶν	8/5/13+0	
ἄγειν	4/3/13+26	19.30, 35
ἅγιος	7/10/20+53	4.1Q, 10.21Q
* ἀδικία(cf. -ος,-εῖν)	0/0/4+2	13.27Q
αἰνεῖν-τὸν-θεόν	0/0/3+3	
οὐδὲν-αἴτιον	0/0/3+(1)	23.22
ἀκούειν-περί	0/2/4	9.9; 7.3Q
ἀκούσας(etc.)-δέ	5/0/9+16	18.22, 36
ἀληθῶς-λέγω-ὑμῖν	0/0/3	9.27; 12.44Q
ἀλλὰ-καί	1/0/3+4	12.7Q
ἀλλήλων	3/5/11+8	4.36; 6.11
ἁμαρτία	7/6/11+8	11.4
ἁμαρτωλός	5/6/18	24.7
* ἄν + optative	0/0/4+5	9.46
ἀνά + numbers	(2)/0/3+0	9.3, 14
ἀναπεσεῖν	1/2/4+0	22.14
* ἀναστάς/άντες	2/6/17+18	5.25, 28
ἀνάστασις	4/2/6+11	20.36
* ἀνήρ	8/4/27+100	5.12, 18
ἀνθ'ὧν	0/0/3+1	12.3Q

* ἄνθρωπε	0/0/4+0	5.20; 22.58
* ἄνθρωπός-τις	0/0/8+2	14.16Q; 19.12Q
* ὁ-ἄνθρωπος-οὗτος	0/2/6+8	23.4, 47
ἀντιλέγειν/ἀντειπεῖν	0/0/3+4	20.27; 21.15
ἅπας	3/4/11+10	3.26; 5.26
ἀπέχειν, of distance	1/1/3	7.6Q
* ἀπὸ-τοῦ-νῦν	0/0/5+1	22.18, 69
* ἀπολαμβάνειν	0/1/4	6.34Q
ἀπολλύναι = lose	7/3/13	15.4, 6Q
ἀπολωλός	2/0/5	15.4, 6Q
ἀποστέλλεσθαι, pass.	2/0/5+4	4.43; 19.32
* ἀπόστολος	1/1/6+28	6.13; 22.14
* οἱ-ἀπόστολοι	1/1/4+15	22.14; 24.10
* ἅπτειν, light (cf. ἀν-, περι-)	0/0/4+1	8.16; 22.55
ἄρχεσθαι-λέγειν	2/4/9	3.8Q; 12.1Q
ἀρξάμενος-ἀπό	1/0/3+2	
ἄρχων	5/1/8+11	8.41; 18.18
* οἱ-ἄρχοντες	1/0/4+6	23.35
* ἀσθενεία	1/0/4+1	5.15
* ἀσπασμός	1/1/5+0	
αὐξάνειν	2/1/4+4	
αὐτός, nom.	12/15/46	
* αὐτὸς-ὁ	1/1/11+1	10.7Q; 20.19
* ἐν-αὐτῇ-τῇ -ὥρᾳ/ἡμέρᾳ	0/0/8+2	20.19
* ἐπὶ/κατὰ-τὸ-αὐτὸ	1/0/4+6	17.30, 34.
* καὶ-αὐτός	4/5/41+8	3.23; 4.15
* καὶ-αὐτός-ἦν	0/0/6+1	5.17
* ἀφαιρεῖν	1/1/4+0	
ἄφεσις	1/2/5+5	
-ἁμαρτιῶν	1/1/3+5	
* ἀφιστάναι(-ἀπό)	0/0/4+6	8.13
ἀφ' οὗ/ἧς = since	0/0/3+1	13.25Q
* ἄχρι	1/0/4+15	21.24
βαλλάντιον	0/0/4	10.4Q; 12.33Q
βαστάζειν	3/1/5+4	10.4Q; 14.27Q
cf. δυσβάστακτος		
* βίος	0/1/4	8.14, (43)
* βοᾶν	1/2/4/+3	9.38; 18.38
βοῦς	0/0/3	14.19Q
* βρέφος	0/0/5+1	18.15
* Γαλιλαῖος	1/1/5+3	

* γε	4/0/8+4	5.36; 37MA
εἰ-δὲ-μή-γε	2/0/5	5.36; 37MA
γείτων	0/0/3	15.6Q
γεννᾶν, of women	0/0/4, cf. γεννητός	
γίνεσθαι	75/55/129+124	20.14, 16
* ἐγένετο. . .καί	1/0/11+1	(cf. Fitzmyer,
* ἐγένετο + fin. vb	5/2/22+0	pp. 118f.)
* ἐγένετο + infin.	0/1/5+16	
* γίνεσθαι + ἐπί	1/1/6+5	4.36
* τὸ γεγονός	0/1/4+3	8.34; 24.12
* καὶ-ἐγένετο	7/5/24+4	9.18, 29
* ἐγένετο-δὲ	0/0/17+19	6.6, 12
* γινώσκειν-τίς	1/0/4+2	10.22Q
γ(ι)νώ(σκε)τε-ὅτι	2/1/4	21.20, 31
* γονεῖς (pl.)	1/1/6	8.56; 18.29
γράφειν	10/10/21+12	18.31; 20.17
* τὸ-τὰ γεγραμμένον/-α	0/0/5+2	20.17; 21.22
δαιμόνιον	11/11/23+1	4.33, 35
δάκτυλος	1/1/3	11.20Q
* δὲ-καί	3/2/25+7	4.41; 5.36
δέησις	0/0/3+1	5.33
δεῖ	8/6/18+22	4.43; 22.7
* ἔδει	3/0/6+4	22.7
δεῖπνον, cf. δειπνεῖν	1/2/5	14.16Q
* δεῖσθαι	1/0/8+7	5.12; 8.28
* δέκα	3/1/11+1	19.13Q
δέρειν	1/3/5+3	22.63
δέχεσθαι	10/6/18+9	8.13; 22.17
(incl. δεκτός: cf. also ἀποδ.,		
προσδ., ὑποδ.)		
διά-τὸ + inf.	3/3/7+7	9.7
* διαλογισμός	1/1/6	5.22; 6.8
+ καρδίαι	0/0/3	3.15; 9.47
* διαμερίζειν	1/1/6+2	11.17Q; 12.52Q
(cf. διαμερισμός)		
* διανοίγειν	0/1/4+3	
διαπορεύεσθαι	0/0/3+1	6.1; 18.3
* διατάσσειν	0/1/4+5	8.55
* διέρχεσθαι	1/2/10+21	5.15; 9.6
* δικαιοῦν	2/0/5+2	7.29Q
διότι	0/0/3+5	21.28
δοκεῖν = think	4/2/8+3	8.18; 12.51Q
δόξα	7/3/13+4	9.31, 32

δοξάζειν	4/1/9+5	5.25; 18.43
* δ.-τὸν-θεόν	2/1/8+3	5.25; 18.43
* δύναμις, of Jesus' healing		
power	0/1/5+2	5.17; 6.19
ἐᾶν	1/0/3+7	4.34, 41
ἑαυτόν	32/24/58+22	9.47; 20.20
* ἑαυτοῦ, sandwiched	1/0/5	9.60Q; 11.21Q
ἐγγίζειν	7/3/18+6	19.37; 22.1
ἐγὼ-γάρ	0/0/3+3	8.46; 21.15
κατὰ-τὸ-ἔθος	0/0/3	22.39
(ἔθος ×7 Acts)		
* εἰ-δὲ-μή-γε	2/0/5	5.36; 10.6Q
* εἰ-οὐ	1/1/6+1	11.8Q; 12.26Q
* εἶναι, prep. + art. + ἑ.	0/0/7+3	5.12; 9.18
* + dat.	3/2/15+10	8.30, 42
+ part.	16/31/62+46	4.31; 23.51
* εἴη	0/0/7+4	3.15; 9.46
ὤν	5/7/15+32	20.36; 24.6
εἰπεῖν	182/84/294+124	8.4; 20.34
* εἶπεν/-ον/-αν-δέ	0/0/59+15	9.9, 13
* εἰπών	0/1/6+20	9.22; 22.8
* εἶπεν-παραβολήν	0/1/7	6.39Q; 15.3Q
εἴρηκεν/-ται	1/0/3+6	22.13; 4.12Q
* εἰρήνη	4/1/13+7	11.21Q; 19.38
* ὁ εἷς...ὁ ἕτερος	1/0/4+1	17.34Q
εἰσάγειν	0/0/3+6	22.54
* εἰσφέρειν	1/0/4+1	5.18, 19
ἕκαστος + part. gen.	0/0/3+5	4.40
* ἐκλέγεσθαι	0/1/4+7	6.13; 9.35
ἐκλείπειν	0/0/3	22.32; 23.45
(cf. ἀνέκλειπτος)		
ἐλάχιστον (noun)	0/0/4	12.26Q
ἔλεος	3/0/6	
* ἐλήλυθα	0/0/4+4	5.17, 32
ἐλπίζειν (cf. ἐλπίς)	1/0/3+2	6.34Q
* ἐν-μιᾷ-τῶν	0/0/5	5.12, 17
* ἐν- τῷ + inf.	3/2/32+7	3.21; 5.12
ἐνάντιον (cf. ἔναντι)	0/0/3+2	20.26
* ἐνώπιον	0/0/22+13	5.18, 25
ἐξαποστέλλειν	0/0/3+7	20.10
* ἐξέρχεσθαι-ἀπό	5/1/13+1	4.35, 41
* ἐπαίρειν	1/0/6+5	6.20Q; 21.28
- τοὺς-ὀφθαλμούς	1/0/3	6.20Q

ἐπέρχεθαι	0/0/3+4	11.22Q; 21.26
ἐπί + dat.	17/16/35+27	9.43; 23.38
+ acc., of time	1/0/3+12	
ἐπιβάλλειν-τὴν/τὰς-χεῖρα(ς)	1/1/3+4	9.62Q; 20.19
ἐπιγινώσκειν-ὅτι	0/1/3+4	
ἐπιδιδόναι	2/0/5+2	
* ἐπιθυμεῖν	2/0/4+1	17.22Q; 22.15
* ἐπιλάβεσθαι	1/1/5+7	9.47; 20.26
* ἐπιστάτης	0/0/7	8.24, 45
ἐπιστρέφειν	4/4/7+11	8.55; 17.4Q
ἐπιτρέπειν	2/2/4+5	8.32
αἰ-ἔρημοι	0/0/3	5.16; 8.29
* ἐρχόμενος + vb.	0/0/4	
* ἐρωτᾶν	4/3/15+7	4.38; 8.37
* ἐσθίειν-καὶ-πίνειν	5/0/14+3	5.30, 33
* ἕτερος	9/1/33+17	3.18; 4.43
ἔτι	8/5/16+5	9.42; 20.36
ἑτοιμάζειν	7/6/14+1	23.56; 24.1
* ἔτος	1/2/15+11	3.1, 23
* εὐαγγελίζεσθαι	1/0/10+15	3.18; 20.1
-τὴν-βασιλείαν	0/0/3	4.43; 8.1
εὐλογεῖν	5/5/13+2	6.28Q
εὑρίσκειν	27/11/45+35	5.19; 6.7
+ acc. part. immediately		
following	1/0/6+3	8.35; 12.43Q
* εὐφραίνεσθαι	0/0/6+1	
εὐχαριστεῖν	2/2/4+2	22.17?
ἐφ᾽ ὑμᾶς	2/1/7+2	10.9Q; 21.12
* ἐφιστάναι	0/0/7+11	4.39; 20.1
* ἔχειν, opening parable	1/0/6	15.4Q
* ἔχω, lst word in clause,		
pres. ind. act.	0/0/5	19.25Q
* ἔχειν + inf.	1/0/5+6	12.4Q
οὐ/μὴ ἔχειν + noun cl.	3/3/6+3	12/4Q
ἕως-οὗ/ὅτου + subj.	4/0/6+4	22.16, 18
ζῆν	6/3/9+13	10.28Q; 24.5
ζητεῖν	14/10/25+10	5.18; 6.19
ἡμέρα	45/27/83+94	4.42; 5.17
* ἐν ταῖς-ἡμέραις -ταύταις	0/0/4+3	6.12
* ἐν-ταῖς-ἡμέραις + gen.	0/0/7+3	17.26Q
* ἡμέραι-ἔρχονται/ἥξουσιν	1/1/5+0	17.22Q, 21.6
* καθ᾽ἡμέραν	1/1/5+6	9.23; 11.3Q
* ἥτις	3/0/10+4	8.26, 43

θαυμάζειν	7/4/12+5	8.25; 9.43
* -ἐπί	0/0/4+1	9.43; 20.26
θεός	51/48/122+166	6.12;9.43
anarthrous	6/2/10+3	3.2
/ἄνθρωποι	2/2/7+5	16.15Q
* θεραπεύειν-ἀπό	0/0/4	5.15; 6.18
θύειν	1/1/4+4	
* ἰᾶσθαι	4/1/11+4	6.19; 9.2
* ἰδού-γάρ	0/0/5+3	6.23Q; 17.21Q
ἰδών/-όντες-δέ	10/5/15+4	5.12; 18.15
* Ἰερουσαλημ	2/0/27+36	5.17; 6.17
ἱκανός	3/3/9+18	8.27, 32
* ἔστην = I stood.	1/1/8+5	6.17; 8.44
σταθείς	0/0/3+6	18.40
ἰσχύειν	4/4/8+6	8.43; 20.26
καθίσας	2/2/4+4	
καθώς	3/8/17+11	5.14; 6.31Q
* καί in apodosis	0/0/4+1	11.34
καὶ-αὐτός see αὐτός		
καὶ-οὗτος, etc.	0/1/7+1	8.41; 20.28
καὶ-γάρ	2/2/8+1	6.32Q; 11.4Q
καί = also	60/36/124+91	4.41; 5.33
κἀκεῖνος	2/2/4+3	22.12
καλεῖν	26/4/43+18	19.29; 21.37
* καλούμενος	0/0/10+13	6.15; 23.33
κατὰ + acc.	21/16/37+74	8.1, 39
distrib.	2/3/7+12	8.4; 9.6
* -τὸ + pf. part.	0/0/4+2	4.16; 22.22
-τὰ-αὐτά	1/0/3+1	6.23Q; 17.30Q
* κατακλίνειν	0/0/5+0	9.14, 15
* κατανοεῖν	1/0/4+4	12.24Q; 20.23
* κεῖσθαι	3/0/6	23.53
* κείμενος	1/0/4	23.53
* κλαίειν	2/4/11+2	6.21Q, 25Q
* κλίνειν	1/0/4	9.12; 24.5
* κοιλία = womb	1/0/7+2	
* κριτής	3/0/6+4	
* κρούειν	2/0/4	12.36Q; 13.25Q
* ὁ-κύριος = Jesus	0/0/13	22.61 ×2
κύριος anarth. = God	18/4/15+11	5.17
κ.-ὁ-θεός	3/2/7+3	20.37
κωλύειν	1/3/6+6	6.29Q; 23.2

* λαλεῖν-περί	0/0/4+3	9.11
λαλεῖσθαι, pass.	1/2/5+8	
λαός	12/2/36+48	3.18; 6.17
πᾶς/ἅπας-ὁ-λ.	1/0/10+6	3.21; 8.47
λατρεύειν	1/0/3+5	
λέγειν-παραβολήν	0/1/14	5.36; 21.29
ἔλεγεν-δὲ-π.	0/0/5	5.36
* ἡ λιμνή	0/0/5	8.22, 33
* ὁ-λόγος-τοῦ-θεοῦ	1/1/4+13	8.11, 21
(+ ἀκούειν)	0/0/3+1	5.1; 8.21
οἱ-λοιποί	4/2/6+6	8.10; 24.9
* λυχνός	2/1/6	11.36Q; 12.35Q
ἤμελλεν, -ον	0/0/4+4	9.31; 7.2Q
μένειν	3/2/7+13	8.27
μέσος	7/5/14+10	4.35; 8.7
ἐν μέσῳ	3/2/7+6	8.7; 21.21
μετὰ-ταῦτα	0/0/5+4	5.27; 10.1Q
μετανοεῖν	5/2/9+5	15.7Q; 17.2Q
μετάνοια	2/1/5+6	5.32; 15.7Q
μή + part.	16/4/24+12	9.33; 7.30Q
* Α-καὶ-μὴ-non-Α.	2/0/6	12.21Q
* μήν	0/0/5+5	
* ἐν-μιᾷ-τῶν	0/0/5	5.12, 17
* μνησθῆναι	3/0/6+2	24.6, 8
μονογενής	0/0/3	8.42; 9.38
Μωϋσῆς-καὶ-οἱ-προφῆται	0/0/4	
νομικός	1(?)/0/6	7.30R; 11.45Q
νῦν	4/3/14+25	6.21Q; 11.39Q
ἀπὸ-τοῦ-νῦν	0/0/5+1	22.18, 69
ὁ + phrase + noun	2/3/7+19	9.37; 19.30
τὸ + ind. q.	0/0/7+2	9.46; 22.2
* τὸ + pf. part.	1/1/11	8.34, 56
* τὸ/τὰ + prep.	1/2/8+15	8.15; 10.7Q
τὰ + part.	7/2/15	9.7; 18.31
* τοῦ + inf.	6/0/20+18	21.22; 22.6
οἰκοδομεῖν	8/4/12+4	7.5Q; 17.28Q
οἶκος	10/12/33+25	7.10Q; 10.5Q
* = household	2/0/7+7	10.5Q
εἰς-τὸν-οἶκον + gen.	4/6/15+5	5.28; 8.41
ἡ-οἰκουμένη	1/0/3+5	4.5Q; 21.26
* ὁμοίως	3/2/11+0	5.33; 17.31Q
ὄνομα	22/15/34+60	5.27; 23.50
* ᾧ/ᾗ ὄνομα	0/0/6+1	8.41
* ὀνόματι	1/1/7+22	5.27; 23.50

ὤφθην	1/1/4(?)+10	9.31
ὄρθρος, -ινος, -ίζειν	0/0/3	21.38; 24.1
ὀρθῶς	0/1/3	10.28Q; 20.21
* ὅς in attraction	2/1/11+23	3.19; 9.36
οὗ = where	3/0/5+8	10.1Q; 23.53
* οὐαὶ-ὑμῖν-τοῖς	0/0/5	6.24Q; 11.42Q
gnomic οὐδείς	3/5/10	4.24; 8.16
οὗτος contemptuous	4/4/15+8	21.4; 23.2
τοῦτο. . .ὅτι	0/0/3+2	12.39Q
* καὶ οὗτος/αὕτη	0/0/7	8.41; 20.28
ταῦτα abs.	25/15/55+37	19.28; 23.49
οὐχί	9/0/17+3	6.39Q; 12.51Q
* οὐχί. . .ἀλλά	0/0/5	12.51Q
ἀπὸ/ἐκ τοῦ ὄχλου	0/1/4+1	9.38; 19.39
* παρά compar.	0/0/4	
* ἡ-παραβολὴ-αὕτη	2/1/9	20.9, 19
* παραγίνεσθαι	3/1/8+20	7.4Q; 8.19
παρατηρεῖν, -ησις	0/1/4	20.20
* παραχρῆμα	2/0/10+6	4.39; 5.25
* παρέχειν	1/1/4+5	6.29Q; 7.4Q
πᾶς pleonastic	Common	4.37; 5.17
* πᾶς/ἅπας-ὁ-λαός	1/0/10+6	8.47; 9.13
* παθεῖν inf.	1/1/5+4	17.25Q; 22.15
* πάτερ abs.	0/0/7	22.42; 23.46
* οἱ-πατέρες-ἡμῶν/ὑμῶν	2/0/7+18	6.23Q; 11.47Q
παύεσθαι	0/0/3+6	8.24; 11.1Q
* πειρασμός	2/1/6+1	8.13; 4.13Q
* πέμπειν	4/1/10+11	20.11, 12
περί + gen.	20/13/40+64	4.37; 5.15
περίχωρος	2/1/5+1	3.3MA; 8.37
* πιμπλάναι (πλήθειν)	2/0/13+9	5.26; 6.11
πίπτειν ἐπί + acc.	5/1/8+3	5.12; 20.18
* πλῆθος	0/2/8+16	23.1, 27
* πᾶν/ἅπαν τὸ π.	0/0/4+3	8.37; 19.37
* πλήν	5/1/15+4	22.22, 42MA
* πλούσιος	3/2/10	18.23; 6.24Q
πνεῦμα ἅγιον	3/1/8+17	4.1Q; 11.13Q
ποιεῖν + adv.	2/3/9+2	9.15; 6.27Q
* τί-ποιήσω/-μεν/-σιν	1/1/8+2	19.48; 20.13
πόλις	26/8/39+42	4.31, 43
ἐν-τῇ-πόλει	0/0/3+2	23.19
πολύ (n.)	1/1/6+2	23.27
πορεύεσθαι	29/0/51+37	4.42; 5.24

ποῦ	4/3/7	8.25; 17.31Q
πούς	10/6/19+19	8.35, 41
* παρὰ-τοὺς-πόδας	1/0/5+6	8.35, 41
* πρός + vb. dicendi.	0/5/99+52	4.36, 43
* προσδέχεσθαι	0/1/5+2	12.36Q; 15.1Q
* προσδοκᾶν	2/0/6+5	3.15; 8.40
προσέχετε ἑαυτοῖς	0/0/3+2	21.34; 12.1Q
προσκαλεσάμενος ἕνα/δύο		
+ gen.	0/0/3+2	7.18Q
* προστιθέναι	2/1/7+6	3.20
* προσφωνεῖν	1/0/4+2	6.13; 23.20
* πρὸ/κατὰ/ἀπὸ/ἐπὶ		
-προσώπου/ον + gen.	1/1/6+6	21.35; 10.1Q
πάντες-οἱ-προφῆται	1/0/3+3	11.50Q; 13.28Q
πτωχός	5/5/10	
* ῥῆμα	5/2/19+14	3.2; 20.26
* τὸ.-ῥ-τοῦτο	0/0/4	9.45; 18.34
* τὰ-ῥ-ταῦτα	0/0/4+4	24.11
σάββατον (s.)	4/5/13+7	6.6; 23.54
* τῇ-ἡμέρᾳ-τοῦ/τῶν-σ.	0/0/4+2	4.16
σαλεύειν	2/1/4+4	6.38Q, 48Q
σήμερον	7/1/11+9	5.26; 23.43
σιγᾶν	0/0/3+3	9.36; 20.26
σκάπτειν	0/0/3	6.48Q
σοφία	3/1/6+4	21.15; 11.49Q
σπεύδειν/σπουδή	0/1/4+2	
σταθείς	0/0/3+6	18.40
στηρίζειν (cf. ἐπι-)	0/0/3+1	
* στραφείς (-πρός)	3/0/7	22.61; 23.28
σύ + impv.	2/0/5+4	9.60Q; 19.19Q
* following verb	0/0/4+2	19.42; 23.40
* συγγενεύς, -ής, -ις, -εία	0/1/6+3	21.16
* συγκαλεῖν	0/1/4+3	9.1; 23.13
συμπορεύεσθαι	0/1/3	7.11Q; 14.25Q
* σύν	4/6/23+52	5.19; 8.1
* οἱ-σὺν-αὐτῷ/-οῖς	0/1/4+3	9.32
* συνέχειν	0/1/6+3	4.38; 8.37
* σωτηρία (cf. -ήρ, -ήριον)	0/0/4+6	
*τε	3/0/9+140	21.11; 22.66
τέκνον (1st word, voc., cf.		
πάτερ)	1/1/3	
τελεῖσθαι, pass.	0/0/3	18.31; 12.50Q
τελώνης (approvingly)	6/2/10	3.12; 7.29

τις, τι	21/33/78+112	6.2; 8.46
* + nouns	1/2/38+62	8.27; 9.19
+ ἐξ	0/0/3+4	22.50; 11.15Q
* τίς + opt.	0/0/7+4	9.46; 18.36
* τὸ-τίς/τί	0/0/5	9.46; 19.48
+ part. gen.	1/1/5+1	22.24
τόπος	10/10/19+18	4.37; 6.17
τράπεζα	2/2/4+2	19.23Q; 22.30Q
τύπτειν	2/1/4+5	6.29Q
ὑγιαίνειν	0/0/3	5.31; 7.10Q
* ὑπάρχειν	3/0/15+25	8.41; 9.48
* τὰ-ὑπάρχοντα	3/0/8+1	8.3; 11.21Q
ὑποδεικνύειν-ὑμῖν	1/0/3+1	6.47Q; 12.5Q
* ὑποστρέφειν	0/0/21+11	8.37, 39
* -εἰς-τὸν-οἶκον	0/0/4	8.39; 11.24Q
* ὕψιστος	1/2/7+2	6.35Q
* Φαρισαῖος sing.	1/0/7+4	
* φίλος	1/0/15+3	21.16; 12.4Q
* φοβεῖσθαι, of God	1/0/6+5	
μὴ-φοβοῦ	0/1/5+2	5.10; 12.32Q
φόβος	3/1/7	5.26; 8.37
* φυλάσσειν	1/1/6+8	8.29; 11.21Q
φυτεύειν	2/1/4	17.6Q
* φωνεῖν = cry out	0/0/4+1	8.8, 54
φωνή	7/7/14+27	19.37; 23.23
* + γίνεσθαι	0/1/4+4	9.35, 36
* χαίρειν = rejoice	3/1/11+5	19.37; 22.5
* χάρις	0/0/8+17	4.22; 6.32Q
* χήρα	0/3/9+3	
χρόνος	3/2/7+17	20.9; 4.5Q
χώρα	3/4/9+8	3.1; 19.12Q
* (ἐν)-αὐτῇ-τῇ-ὥρᾳ	0/0/5+2	20.19; 10.21Q
* ὡς = when, while	0/1/19+29	20.37; 23.26
* ὡσεί	3/1/9+6	3.23; 9.28

General Bibliography

(For works pertinent to particular passages see Index, or *ad loc.*)

Abbott, E.A., 'Gospels', *Encyclopaedia Britannica* (9th edn; London, 1879)

Aland, K., *Synopsis Quattuor Evangeliorum* (4th edn; Würtemberg, 1967)

Aland, K., Black, M., Martini, C.M., Metzger, B.M., Wikgren, A., *Novum Testamentum Graece* (Nestle–Aland 26th edn; Stuttgart, 1979) = N–A[26]

Alexander, P.S., 'Midrash and the Gospels', in C.M. Tuckett, ed., *Synoptic Studies* (Sheffield, 1984)

Allison, D.C., 'The Pauline Epistles and the Synoptic Gospels', *NTS* 28 (1982), pp. 1-32

Astruc, J., Conjectures sur les mémoires originaux dont il paroît que Moyse se servit pour composer le livre de la Genèse (Brussels, 1753)

Bailey, J.A., *The Traditions Common to the Gospels of Luke and John* (Leiden, 1963)

Bailey, K.E., *Poet and Peasant* and *Through Peasant Eyes* (combined edn., Grand Rapids, 1983)

Balch, D.L., 'I Cor 7.32-35 and Stoic Debates about Marriage, Anxiety and Distraction', *JBL* 102/3 (1983), pp. 429-39

Bammel, E., ed., *The Trial of Jesus* (London, 1970)

Bammel, E., 'Das Ende von Q', in *Fs* Stählin (1970), pp. 39-50

Barrett, C.K., *The Gospel according to St John* (2nd edn; London, 1978)

Bauckham, R., 'The Liber Antiquitatum Biblicarum of Pseudo-Philo and the Gospels as "Midrash"', in R.T. France and D. Wenham, eds., *Gospel Perspectives*, III (Sheffield, 1983)

Bauer, W., translated, adapted and augmented by Arndt, W.F., and Gingrich, F.W., *A Greek-English Lexicon of the New Testament and Other Early Christian Literature* (4th edn; Chicago, 1952) = BAG

Baur, F.C., *Kritische Untersuchungen über die kanonischen Evangelien, ihr Verhältnis zueinander, ihren Character und Ursprung* (Tübingen, 1847)

Best, E., *A Commentary on The First and Second Epistles to the Thessalonians* (Black; London, 1972/1979)

Black, M., *An Aramaic Approach to the Gospels and Acts* (Oxford, 1967)

Blass, F., and Debrunner, A., translated by Funk, R.W., *A Greek Grammar of the New Testament* (Cambridge, 1961) = BDF

Boismard, M-E., and Benoit, P., *Synopse des quatre évangiles en francais*, Vol. II, *Commentaire* (Paris, 1972)

Bonnard, P., *L'Evangile selon Saint Matthieu* (Neuchâtel, 1963)

Bornkamm, G., *Fs*, D. Lührmann and G. Strecker, eds., *Kirche* (Tübingen, 1980)

Bovon, F., *Luc le théologien: Vingt-cinq ans de recherches (1950-1975)* (Neuchâtel/Paris, 1978)

Bowker, J.A., *The Targums and Rabbinic Literature* (Cambridge, 1969)

Braun, H., *Spätjüdisch-häretischer und frühchristlicher Radikalismus* (Tübingen, 1957)

Braun, H. *Fs*: H.-D. Betz et al., eds., *Neues Testament und christliches Existenz* (Tübingen, 1973)

Brown, R.E., *The Birth of the Messiah* (London, 1977)

Brown, S., *Apostasy and Perseverance in the Theology of Luke* (An. Bib. 36; Rome, 1969)

Bultmann, R., *The History of the Synoptic Tradition* (London, 1968, ET 2nd edn; *Die Geschichte der synoptischen Tradition* (Göttingen, 1931))

Bultmann, R., *Fs*: W. Eltester et al., eds., *Neutestamentliche Studien für Rudolf Bultmann* (Berlin, 1954)

Bultmann, R., *Fs*: E. Dinkler ed., *Zeit und Geschichte* (Tübingen, 1964)

Cadbury, H.J., *The Style and Literary Method of Luke*, I-II (Cambridge Mass., 1920)

Campbell, T.H., 'Paul's "Missionary Journeys" as reflected in his Letters', *JBL* 74 (1955), pp. 80-87

Carrington, P., *The Primitive Christian Calendar* (Cambridge, 1952)

Carrington, P., *According to Mark* (Cambridge, 1960).

Cavallin, H.C.C., *Life after Death*, I (Conjectanea biblica NT 7, Lund, 1974).

Cerfaux, L., *Fs*: F. Neirynck, ed., *L'Evangile de Luc* (BETL 32, Gembloux, 1973)

Charles, R.H., ed., *The Apocrypha and Pseudepigrapha of the Old Testament in English* I-II (Oxford, 1913)

Charlesworth, J.H., *The Old Testament Pseudepigrapha*, I-II (London, 1983/5)

Conzelmann, H., *The Theology of St Luke* (London, 1960; ET *Die Mitte der Zeit*, 2nd edn)

Conzelmann, H., *Fs*: G. Strecker, ed., *Jesus Christus in Historie und Theologie* (Tübingen, 1975)

Credner, K., *Einleitung in das Neue Testament*, I (Halle, 1836)

Creed, J.M., *The Gospel according to St. Luke* (Macmillan; London, 1930)

Cullmann, O., 'Das Thomasevangelium und die Frage nach dem Alter der in ihm enthaltenen Tradition', *TLZ* 85 (1960), pp. 321-34

Dahl, N.A., 'Die Passionsgeschichte bei Matthäus', *NTS* 2 (1955), pp. 17-32

Dalman, G., *Arbeit und Sitte in Palästina*, I-VII (Gütersloh, 1928-1942)

Dalman, G., *Die Worte Jesu* (2nd edn; Leipzig 1930)

Danker, F.W., *Jesus and the New Age* (St. Louis, 1972)

Daube, D., *Fs* E. Bammel et al., eds., *Donum Gentilicium* (Oxford, 1978)

Davies, W.D., *The Setting of the Sermon on the Mount* (Cambridge, 1964)

Degenhardt, H., *Lukas—Evangelist der Armen* (Stuttgart, 1966)

Delobel, J., 'L'Onction par la pécheresse', *ETL* 42 (1966), pp. 415-75

Derrett, J.D.M., *Law in the New Testament* (London, 1970)

Devisch, 'Le Document Q, Source de Matthieu', in M. Didier, ed., *L'Evangile de Matthieu* (BETL 29; Gembloux, 1970)

Dibelius, M., *Die Formgeschichte der Evangelien* (6th edn; Tübingen, 1971)

Dietrich, W., *Das Petrusbild der lukanischen Schriften* (BWANT 94; Stuttgart, 1972)

Dodd, C.H., *The Founder of Christianity* (New York, 1970)

Dodd, C.H., *Historical Tradition in the Fourth Gospel* (Cambridge, 1963)

Dodd, C.H., *The Parables of the Kingdom* (London, 1936)

Drury, J., *The Parables in the Gospels* (London, 1985)

Drury, J., *Tradition and Design in Luke's Gospel* (London, 1976)

Dupont, J., *Les béatitudes*, I-III (Paris, 1958-1973)

Dupont, J., *Fs: A Cause de l'évangile* (LD 123; Paris, 1985)

Eichhorn, J.G., *Einleitung in das Neue Testament*, I-II (Leipzig, 1804)

Elbogen, I., *Der jüdische Gottesdienst in seiner geschichtlichen Entwicklung* (3rd edn; Frankfurt, 1931)

Ellis, E.E., *The Gospel of Luke* (New Century; 2nd edn; London, 1974)

Farmer, W.R., *The Synoptic Problem* (2nd edn; Dillsboro, 1976)

Festinger, L., Riecken, H.W., and Schachter S. *When Prophecy Fails* (Minneapolis, 1956)

Finegan, J., *Die Überlieferung der Leidens- und Auferstehungsgeschichte Jesu* (BZNW 15; Giessen, 1934)

Fitzmyer, J.A., *The Gospel according to Luke*, I-II (AB 28, 28A; New York, 1981/5)

Fjärstedt, B., *Synoptic Tradition and I Corinthians* (Uppsala, 1974)

France, R.T., and Wenham, D., eds., *Gospel Perspectives* I-IV (Sheffield, 1980-83)

Fuchs, A., *Sprachliche Untersuchungen zu Matthäus und Lukas* (Ana. Bib. 49; Rome, 1971)

Fuchs, A., 'Die Behandlung der Mt/Lk Übereinstimmungen gegen Mk durch S. McLoughlin und ihre Bedeutung für die Synoptische Frage', in *Probleme der Forschung* (SNTU A3; Vienna/Munich, 1978)

Fuchs, E., *Fs*: G. Ebeling et al., eds., *Festschrift für Ernst Fuchs* (Tübingen, 1973)

Gaston, L., *No Stone on Another* (NT Supp. 23; Leiden, 1970)

Geiger, R., *Die lukanischen Endzeitsreden* (Bern/Frankfurt, 1973)

Gingrich, F.W., *Fs*: E.H. Barth et al., eds., *Festschrift to Honor F. Wilbur Gingrich* (Leiden, 1972)

Goodspeed, E.J., *New Chapters in New Testament Study* (New York, 1937)

Goulder, M.D., 'Characteristics of the Parables in the Several Gospels', *JTS* ns. 19 (1968), pp. 51-69

Goulder, M.D., *The Evangelists' Calendar* (London, 1978) = *EC*

Goulder, M.D., 'A House Built on Sand', in A.E. Harvey, ed., *Alternative Approaches to New Testament Study* (London, 1985)

Goulder, M.D., *Midrash and Lection in Matthew* (London, 1974) = *MLM*

Goulder, M.D., 'On Putting Q to the Test', *NTS* 24 (1978), pp. 218-39

Goulder, M.D., 'The Order of a Crank', in C.M. Tuckett, ed., *Synoptic Studies* (Sheffield, 1984), pp. 111-30

Grässer, E., *Das Problem der Parusieverzögerung* (BZNW 22; 2nd edn; Berlin, 1966)

Green, H.B., *The Gospel according to Matthew* (New Clarendon; Oxford, 1975)

Greeven, H.: A. Huck, *Synopse der drei ersten Evangelien/Synopsis of the First Three Gospels* (13th edn; fundamentally revised, Tübingen, 1981)

Griesbach, J.J., J.P. Gabler, ed., *Opuscula Academica* II (Jena, 1825)

Grundmann, W., *Das Evangelium nach Lukas* (3rd edn; Berlin, 1966)

Gundry, R.H., *Matthew* (Grand Rapids, 1982)

Gunkel, H., *Die Psalmen* (Göttinger Handkommentar zum AT, 4th edn; Göttingen, 1929)

Haenchen, E., *The Acts of the Apostles* (= 14th edn; *Die Apostelgeschichte*, ET Oxford, 1971)

Haenchen, E., *Die Bibel und Wir*, I-II (Tübingen, 1968)

Haenchen, E., *Fs*: W. Eltester et al., eds., *Apophoreta* (Berlin, 1964)

Hahn, F., *Christologische Hoheitstitel* (2nd edn; Göttingen, 1964)

Harnack, A., *Die Briefsammlung des Apostels Paulus* (Leipzig, 1926)

Harnack, A., *Luke the Physician* (= *Lukas der Arzt*, ET London, 1907)

Harnack, A., *The Sayings of Jesus* (= *Sprüche und Reden Jesu*, ET London, 1908)

Hennecke, E., and Schneemelcher, W., eds., *New Testament Apocrypha*, I-II (ET London, 1963-65)

Hengel, M., *Nachfolge und Charisma* (Berlin, 1968)

Hengel, M., *Acts and the History of Earliest Christianity* (= *Zur urchristlichen Geschichtsschreibung*, 1979; ET London, 1979)

Hill, D., *The Gospel of Matthew* (London, 1972)

Hoffman, P., *Studien zur Theologie der Logienquelle* (Neutestamentliche Abhandlungen nf 8; 2nd edn; Münster, 1972)

Holtz, T., *Untersuchungen über die alttestamentlichen Zitate bei Lukas* (Berlin, 1968)

Holtzmann, H.J., *Die synoptischen Evangelien, Ihr Ursprung und geschichtlicher Character* (Leipzig, 1863)

Hull, J.M., *Hellenistic Magic and the Synoptic Tradition* (SBT 2.28; London, 1974)

Jeremias, J., *The Eucharistic Words of Jesus* (= 3rd edn; *Die Abendmahlsworte Jesu*, ET London, 1966)

Jeremias, J., *Jerusalem in the Time of Jesus* (= 3rd edn; *Jerusalem zur Zeit Jesu*, ET London, 1969)

Jeremias, J., *The Parables of Jesus* (= 6th edn; *Die Gleichnisse Jesu*, ET revised, London, 1963)

Jeremias, J., *Die Sprache des Lukasevangeliums* (KEK, Göttingen, 1980)

Jeremias, J., *New Testament Theology* I (London, 1971)

Jülicher, A., *Die Gleichnisreden Jesu*, I-II (Tübingen, 1910)

Kilpatrick, G.D., ed., H KAINH ΔIAΘHKH (British and Foreign Bible Society, London, 1958)

Kilpatrick, G.D., *Luke: A Greek-English Diglot for the Use of Translators* (London, 1962; based on 3rd edn; of the preceding)

Klostermann, E., *Das Lukasevangelium* (Handkommentar zum NT; 2nd edn; Tübingen, 1929)

Kopp, C., *The Holy Places of the Gospels* (Freiburg, 1959/Edinburgh, 1963)

Kraus, H.-J., *Worship in Israel* (ET Oxford, 1966)

Kuhn, K.G., *Fs*: G. Jeremias et al., eds., *Tradition und Glaube* (Göttingen, 1971)

Kümmel, W.G., (P. Feine-J. Behm-), *Introduction to the New Testament* (= 14th German edn; London, 1966)

Kümmel, W.G., *Das Neue Testament, Geschichte der Forschung seiner Probleme* (Freiburg, 1958)

Kümmel, W.G., *Fs*: E.E. Ellis et al., eds., *Jesus und Paulus* (Göttingen, 1975)

Lagrange, M.-J., *L'Evangile selon S. Matthieu* (3rd edn; Paris, 1927)

Lagrange, M.-J., *L'Evangile selon S. Luc* (5th edn; Paris, 1941)

Lake, K., *The Earlier Epistles of St. Paul* (2nd edn; London, 1919)

Lambrecht, J., *Once More Astonished* (New York, 1981)

Laufen, R., *Die Doppelüberlieferungen der Logienquelle und des Markusevangeliums* (BBB 54; Bonn, 1980)

Leaney, A.R.C. *The Gospel according to St Luke* (Black; London, 1958)

Lightfoot, R.H., *The Gospel Message of St Mark* (Oxford, 1950)

Linnemann, E., *Parables of Jesus* (London, 1966)

Linnemann, E., *Studien zur Passionsgeschichte* (Göttingen, 1970)

Lohmeyer, E., and Smauch, W., *Das Evangelium des Matthäus* (3rd edn; Göttingen, 1962)

Loisy, A., *L'évangile selon Luc* (Paris, 1924)

Lührmann, D., *Die Redaktion der Logienquelle* (WMANT 3; Neukirchen, 1969)

Luz, U., *Das Evangelium nach Matthäus*, I (EKK 1/1; Zürich/Neukirchen, 1985)

McNeile, A.H., *The Gospel according to St Matthew* (London, 1915)

Maddox, R., *The Purpose of Luke-Acts* (FRLANT, Edinburgh, 1982)

Manson, T.W. *The Sayings of Jesus* (London, 1949) = Manson

Manson, W., *The Gospel of Luke* (Moffatt; London, 1930)

Marshall, I.H., *The Gospel of Luke* (New International; Exeter, 1978)

Ménard, J.-E., *L'Evangile selon Thomas* (NHS 5; Leiden, 1975)

Metzger, B.M., *A Textual Commentary on the Greek New Testament* (1971)

Metzger, B.M., *Fs*: E.J. Epp et al., eds., *New Testament Textual Criticism* (Oxford, 1981)

Michel, O., *Fs*: O. Betz et al., eds., *Abraham unser Vater* (Leiden, 1963)

Mitton, C.L., *The Formation of the Pauline Corpus of Letters* (London, 1955)

Miyoshi, M., *Der Anfang des Reiseberichts Lk 9.51-10.24* (Ana. Bib. 60; Rome, 1974)

Moore, G.F., *Judaism*, I-III (Cambridge, Mass., 1927-30)

Morgenthaler, R., *Die lukanische Geschichtsschreibung als Zeugnis* (ATANT 15; Zürich, 1948)

Morgenthaler, R., *Statistik des neutestamentlichen Wortschatzes* (Zürich/Frankfurt 1958)

Morgenthaler, R., *Statistische Synopse* (Zürich/Stuttgart, 1971)

Neirynck, F., *Evangelica* (BETL 60; Leuven, 1982)

Neirynck, F., *The Minor Agreements of Matthew and Luke against Mark* (BETL 37; Leuven, 1974)

Ott, W., *Gebet und Heil* (SANT 12; Munich, 1965)

Palmer, H., *The Logic of Gospel Criticism* (London, 1968)

Patsch, H., *Abendmahl und historischer Jesus* (Stuttgart, 1972)

Pesch, R., *Jesus ureigene Taten?* (Freiburg, 1970)

Philips, G., *Fs*: *Ecclesia a Spiritu Sancto edocta* (BETL 27; Gembloux, 1970)

Polag, A., *Fragmenta Q* (Neukirchen, 1979)

Potin, J., *La Fête juive de la Pentecôte*, I-II (LD 65; Paris, 1971)

Rehkopf, F., *Die lukanische Sonderquelle* (WUNT 5; Tübingen, 1959)

Rengstorf, K.H., *Das Evangelium nach Lukas* (NTD; Göttingen, 1937)

Rese, M., *Alttestamentliche Motive in der Christologie des Lukas* (SNT 1; Gütersloh, 1969)

Rigaux, B., *Fs*: A.Descamps et al., eds., *Mélanges bibliques en hommage au R.P. Béda Rigaux* (Gembloux, 1970)

Robinson, J.A.T., *Redating the New Testament* (London, 1976)

Rogerson, J., *Old Testament Criticism in the Nineteenth Century* (London, 1984)

Roloff, J., *Das Kerygma und der irdische Jesus* (Göttingen, 1970)

Rutherford, W.G., *The New Phrynichus* (London, 1881)

Sabbe, M., ed., *L'Evangile selon Marc* (BETL 34; Gembloux, 1974)

Sanday, W., *Studies in the Synoptic Problem* (Oxford, 1911)

Schenk, W., *Der Passionsbericht nach Markus* (Gütersloh, 1974)

Schlatter, A., *Der Evangelist Matthäus* (5th edn; Stuttgart, 1959)

Schmid, J., *Matthäus und Lukas* (Freiburg, 1930)

Schmid, J., *Fs*: J. Blinzler et al., eds., *Neutestamentliche Aufsätze* (Regensburg, 1963)

Schmid, J., *Fs*: P. Hoffmann et al., eds., *Orientierung an Jesus* (Freiburg, 1973)

Schmidt, K.L., *Der Rahmen der Geschichte Jesu* (Berlin, 1919)

Schmithals, W., *Das Evangelium nach Markus* (OTK 2. 1/2, Gütersloh/Würzburg, 1979)

Schnackenburg, R., *Fs*: J. Gnilka, ed., *Neues Testament und Kirche* (Freiburg, 1974)

Schneider, G., *Das Evangelium nach Lukas* (OTK 3. 1/2; Gütersloh/Würzburg, 1977)

Schniewind, J., *Das Evangelium nach Matthäus* (NTD, 11th edn; Göttingen, 1964)

Schrage, W., *Das Verhältnis des Thomasevangeliums zur synoptischen Tradition und zu den koptischen Evangelienübersetzungen* (BZNW 29; Berlin, 1964)

Schramm, T., *Der Markus-Stoff bei Lukas* (SNTSMS 14; Cambridge, 1971)

Schubert, P., *Fs*: L.E. Keck et al., eds., *Studies in Luke-Acts* (London, 1968)

Schulz, S., *Q: Die Spruchquelle der Evangelisten* (Zürich, 1972)

Schürer, E., G. Vermes and F. Millar rev. and eds., *The History of the Jewish People in the Age of Jesus Christ (175 B.C.—A.D. 135)*. I-III.1 (Edinburgh, 1973-1986)

Schürmann, H., *Das Lukasevangelium*, I (Herder 3.1; Freiburg, 1969) = Schürmann

Schürmann, H., *Quellenkritische Untersuchung des lukanischen Abendmahlsberichtes*: 1. *Der Paschamahlbericht* (Münster, 1953) = *Pmb*, 2. *Der Einsetzungsbericht* (Münster, 1955) = *Esb*, 3. *Jesu Abschiedsrede* (Münster, 1957) = *JAr* (NTA 19/5, 20/4-5)

Schürmann, H., *Traditionsgeschichtliche Untersuchungen zu den synoptischen Evangelien* (Düsseldorf, 1968) = *TU*

Schürmann, H., *Ursprung und Gestalt* (Düsseldorf, 1970) = *UG*

Schürmann, H., *Fs*: R. Schnackenburg et al., eds., *Die Kirche des Anfangs* (Leipzig, 1977)

Schweizer, E., *Das Evangelium nach Lukas* (NTD3 18th edn; Göttingen, 1982)

Schweizer, E., *The Good News According to Matthew* (= NTD 1973; ET London, 1976)

Scrivener, F.H.A., *A Plain Introduction to the Criticism of the New Testament* (4th edn; London, 1894)

Sherwin-White, A.N., *Roman Society and Roman Law in the New Testament* (Oxford, 1963)

Smith, G.A., *The Historical Geography of the Holy Land* (25th edn; London, 1931)

Stanton, V.H., *The Gospels as Historical Documents*, II (Cambridge, 1909)

Stählin, G., *Fs*: O. Böcher et al., eds., *Verborum Veritas* (Wuppertal, 1970)

Steck, O.H. *Israel und das gewaltsame Geschick der Propheten* (WMANT 23; Neukirchen, 1967)

Stendahl, K., *The School of St Matthew* (Uppsala, 1954)

Strack, H.L., and Billerbeck, P., *Kommentar zum Neuen Testament aus Talmud und Midrasch* (3rd edn; Munich, 1956) = SB

Strecker, G., *Der Weg der Gerechtigkeit* (FRLANT 82; 2nd edn; Göttingen, 1966)

Streeter, B.H., *The Four Gospels* (London, 1924)

Suggs, M.J., *Wisdom, Christology and Law in Matthew's Gospel* (Cambridge, Mass., 1970)

Talbert, C.H., *Literary Patterns, Theological Themes and the Genre of Luke-Acts* (Missoula, 1974)

Taylor, V., *Behind the Third Gospel* (Oxford, 1926)

Taylor, V., *The Passion Narrative of St Luke* (SNTSMS 19, ed. O.E. Evans; Cambridge, 1972)

Trilling, W., *Das wahre Israel* (3rd edn; Munich, 1964)

Trocmé, E., *The Passion as Liturgy* (London, 1983)

Tuckett, C.M., 'On the Relation between Matthew and Luke', *NTS* 30 (1984), pp. 130-42

Tuckett, C.M. *The Revival of the Griesbach Hypothesis* (SNTSMS 44; Cambridge 1983)

Tuckett, C.M., ed., *Synoptic Studies* (JSNTS 7; Sheffield, 1984)

van Unnik, W.C., *Tarsus and Jerusalem* (ET London 1962)

Vermes, G., *Jesus the Jew* (London, 1973)

Vermes, G., *The Dead Sea Scrolls in English* (London, 1968)

Vielhauer, P., *Aufsätze zum Neuen Testament* (Munich, 1965)

Vögtle, A., *Das Evangelium und die Evangelien* (Düsseldorf, 1971)

Weiser, A., *Die Knechtsgleichnisse der synoptischen Evangelien* (SANT 29; Munich, 1971)

Weisse, C.H., *Die evangelische Geschichte kritisch und philosophisch bearbeitet* (Leipzig, 1838)

Wellhausen, J., *Das Evangelium Lucae* (Berlin, 1904)

Wernle, P., *Die synoptische Frage* (Freiburg, 1899)

Wilkinson, J., *Egeria's Travels* (London, 1971)

Wilson, R.McL., *Gnosis and the New Testament* (Oxford, 1968)

Wilson, S.G., *Luke and the Law* (SNTSMS 50, Cambridge 1983)

Wink, W., *John the Baptist in the Gospel Tradition* (SNTSMS 7; Cambridge, 1968)

Wrege, H.-J., *Die Überlieferungsgeschichte der Bergpredigt* (WUNT 9; Tübingen, 1968)

Zahn, T., *Das Evangelium des Lucas* (2nd edn; Leipzig, 1913)

Zmijewski, J., *Die Eschatologiereden des Lukas-Evangeliums* (BBB 40; Bonn, 1972)

INDEX AUCTORUM

JOURNAL FOR THE STUDY OF THE NEW TESTAMENT
Supplement Series